Principles of Environmental and Resource Economics

NEW HORIZONS IN ENVIRONMENTAL ECONOMICS

General Editors: Wallace E. Oates, *Professor of Economics, University of Maryland, USA* and Henk Folmer, *Professor of General Economics, Wageningen University, The Netherlands and Professor of Environmental Economics, Tilburg University, The Netherlands*

This important series is designed to make a significant contribution to the development of the principles and practices of environmental economics. It includes both theoretical and empirical work. International in scope, it addresses issues of current and future concern in both East and West and in developed and developing countries.

The main purpose of the series is to create a forum for the publication of high quality work and to show how economic analysis can make a contribution to understanding and resolving the environmental problems confronting the world in the twenty-first century.

Recent titles in the series include:

The Political Economy of Environmental Taxes
Nicolas Wallart

Trade and the Environment
Selected Essays of Alistair M. Ulph
Alistair M. Ulph

Water Management in the 21st Century
The Allocation Imperative
Terence Richard Lee

Institutions, Transaction Costs and Environmental Policy
Institutional Reform for Water Resources
Ray Challen

Valuing Nature with Travel Cost Models
A Manual
Frank Ward and Diana Beal

The Political Economy of Environmental Protectionism
Achim Körber

Trade Liberalisation, Economic Growth and the Environment
Matthew A. Cole

The International Yearbook of Environmental and Resource Economics
2000/2001
A Survey of Current Issues
Edited by Tom Tietenberg and Henk Folmer

Economic Growth and Environmental Policy
A Theoretical Approach
Frank Hettich

Principles of Environmental and Resource Economics
A Guide for Students and Decision-Makers
Second Edition
Edited by Henk Folmer and H. Landis Gabel

Principles of Environmental and Resource Economics

A Guide for Students and Decision-Makers
Second Edition

Edited by

Henk Folmer

Professor of General Economics, Wageningen University and Professor of Environmental Economics, Tilburg University, The Netherlands

H. Landis Gabel

Professor of Economics and Management, INSEAD, France

NEW HORIZONS IN ENVIRONMENTAL ECONOMICS

Edward Elgar

Cheltenham, UK • Northampton, MA, USA

Published by
Edward Elgar Publishing Limited
Glensanda House
Montpellier Parade
Cheltenham
Glos GL50 1UA
UK

Edward Elgar Publishing, Inc.
136 West Street
Suite 202
Northampton
Massachusetts 01060
USA

A catalogue record for this book is available from the British Library

Library of Congress Cataloguing in Publication Data

Principles of environmental and resource economics : a guide for students and decision-makers / edited by Henk Folmer, H. Landis Gabel—2nd ed.
    (New horizons in environmental economics)
    Includes bibliographical references and index.
    1. Environmental economics. 2. Natural resources—Management. I. Folmer, Henk, 1945– II. Gabel, H. Landis. III. Series.

HC79.E5 P6944 2000
333.7—dc21

                                                                99–086198

ISBN 1 85898 944 2 (cased)
Printed and bound in Great Britain by MPG Books Ltd, Bodmin, Cornwall

Contents

PART I   GENERAL ENVIRONMENTAL ECONOMICS

PART II   BUSINESS ENVIRONMENTAL ECONOMICS

Boxes

Figures

Tables

Contributors

Thomas Aronsson is Professor of Economics at Umeå University, Sweden. He is currently doing research on welfare economics, environmental economics and public economics. He is also a co-author of *Welfare Measurement, Sustainability and Green National Accounting.*

Jean-Philippe Barde holds a PhD in economics from Paris University and is Principal Administrator in the OECD Environment Directorate, in charge of OECD programmes on the integration of economic and environmental policies. He is a member of several scientific committees on the environment and has been a teacher of environmental economics at Paris University. He is the author, co-author and editor of many articles and several French and English-language books on the environment. His latest book is *Economie et Politique de l'Environnement* (Presses Universitaires de France, Paris, 1992).

Charles Corbett is Assistant Professor of Operations and Technology Management at The Anderson School at UCLA. He holds a Drs in operations research from Erasmus University Rotterdam (the Netherlands) and a PhD in operations management from INSEAD in Fontainebleau, France. His research focuses on supply-chain management and environmental management and has been published in a range of leading academic and practitioner journals. His environmental research revolves around the impact of standards and contracts for environmental improvement.

Samuel Fankhauser is an economist at the European Bank for Reconstruction and Development in London. Prior to joining EBRD he worked for several years at the World Bank and the Global Environment Facility and was a research associate at the Centre for Social and Economic Research on the Global Environment at University College London. His professional interests include energy and environment issues and the economic impacts of climate change. He served as a lead author for the second and third assessment reports of the Intergovernmental Panel on Climate Change. A Swiss national, he holds MSc and PhD degrees from the London School of Economics and University College London, respectively.

Henk Folmer is Professor of General Economics at Wageningen University and Professor of Environmental Economics, Tilburg University, The Netherlands. He served as first President of the European Association of Environmental and Resource Economics from 1987 to 1993 and on the EC Task Force on the Single Market and the Environment. He has published widely in a large variety of international outlets in the fields of environmental and resource economics, econometrics, labour economics and regional economics. He is co-editor of *The International Yearbook of Environmental and Resource Economics: A Survey of Current Issues*, which is published annually by Edward Elgar.

Jürgen Freimann is Professor of Management Science and Environmental Management at the University of Kassel, Germany. He is the author of various publications in the fields of management science, environmental management and methodology.

H. Landis Gabel is Professor of Economics and Management and Associate Dean for the MBA Programme at INSEAD. He holds a BSc, MBA and PhD (economics) from the University of Pennsylvania and an MSc (economics) from the London School of Economics. Professor Gabel's research focuses on microeconomics and public policy, and he has published papers in economics, legal, environmental and business journals. Professor Gabel founded INSEAD's Centre for the Management of Environmental Resources in 1989 and co-directed it until 1995.

Nick Hanley is Professor of Environmental Economics at the University of Glasgow, Scotland. His main areas of research interest are environmental valuation, cost–benefit analysis and the economics of sustainable development. With Clive Spash, he is author of the popular book *Cost–Benefit Analysis and the Environment* (Edward Elgar), and with Jay Shogren and Ben White, he is author of the graduate text *Environmental Economics in Theory and Practice* (Macmillan). He is on the editorial board of the *Journal of Environmental Economics and Management* and is currently combining work and pleasure in a study on the economics of mountaineering.

Per-Olov Johansson is Professor of Economics at the Stockholm School of Economics. His current research interests include environmental economics – in particular valuation issues, 'green' net national product measurement and cost–benefit analysis – health economics – in particular valuation of health risks and properties of health insurance schemes – and industrial organization. He has also undertaken research in macroeconomics and public economics.

Helmut Karl is Professor of Economic Policy at the University of Jena, Germany. His research interests include the economics of environmental policy and regional economics. He is a member of several economic associations. He is the author of numerous publications in the field of regional economic policy as well as environmental and resource economics and policy. Recently his main research interests have focused on the field of European environmental policy.

Jari Kuuluvainen is Professor of Social Economics of Forestry at the University of Helsinki, Department of Forest Economics. He has published studies on timber markets, forest products export markets, non-industrial private timber supply and on economic growth and renewable natural resources.

François Lévêque is Professor of Economics at the Ecole des Mines in Paris where he also heads CERNA, a research centre in industrial economics. Over the past ten years his academic interests have been centred on the economics of regulation. His works in this area have mainly concerned the economic analysis of environmental policy instruments (especially voluntary approaches) and the economic analysis of the deregulation of public utilities, particularly in the industrial sectors of transportation and energy. He has edited, authored and contributed to many books on these topics in French and in English. His most recent publications are a textbook in the economics of regulation (*Economie de la réglementation*, Coll. Repères, édition La Découverte, 1998) and a co-edited contributed work (*Voluntary Approaches in Environmental Policy*, Kluwer Academic, 1999). François Lévêque is a member of several academic societies and has organized a number of international conferences.

Karl-Gustaf Löfgren has been Professor of Economics at the University of Umeå since 1988, having been appointed there as an Assistant Professor in 1972. In 1979 he became Professor of Resource Economics at the Swedish University of Agricultural Sciences. He was Visiting Professor at the University of Wisconsin in 1980 and 1996 and at the University of California, Berkeley, in 1987. He is a member of the editorial board of *Environmental and Resource Economics* and the *German Economic Review*. He is Associate Editor of *Natural Resource Modelling* and *Ambio*. He has conducted research in the fields of resource and environmental economics, labour economics and macroeconomics and is currently working on 'green' net national product measurement.

Daniel McCoy is an economist at the Economic and Social Research Institute in Dublin. He is also a lecturer in environmental economics at Trinity College, Dublin. Prior to joining the ESRI, he was a lecturer in the Economics Department and research associate at the Centre for Social and Economic Research on the Global Environment at University College London and an economist at the Central Bank of Ireland. He is editor of the Journal of the

Statistical and Social Inquiry Society of Ireland. His research interests include macroeconomic forecasting, public finance and environmental economics.

Alain Nadaï is economist at the Center for the Study of Improvement and Regulation, Carnegie-Mellon University, Pittsburgh. His main research activity has been focused on the economics of environmental regulation. It has been applied to the EU greenhouse abatement policy, the EU and US pesticide registrations and the EU products eco-labelling regulation.

Carsten Orwat is at the Department of Economics of the University of Jena, Germany. His main fields of research are environmental policy and corporate environmental management. He has authored and co-authored several titles on environmental policy.

Eirik Romstad is Head of Research in the Department of Economics and Social Sciences at the Agricultural University of Norway. He holds an MSc in natural resource management from the Agricultural University of Norway, and a PhD in resource economics from Oregon State University. Main areas of research include environmental policy instruments, monitoring and enforcement, and pollution and public goods from agriculture. He is a member of the editorial board of the *Journal of Forest Economics*, and has been a visiting scholar at the Ohio State University, the Swedish University of Agricultural Sciences and Wageningen University, The Netherlands.

Kathleen Segerson is Professor of Economics at the University of Connecticut. She also holds a joint appointment in the Department of Agricultural and Resource Economics. Professor Segerson's research is primarily in the area of the economics of pollution control, with particular emphasis on the incentive effects of alternative policies. She specializes in the application of legal rules and principles to environmental problems. Professor Segerson has been actively involved in professional organizations, particularly the American Agricultural Economics Association (AAEA) and the Association of Environmental and Resource Economists (AERE). She was recently an editor of the *American Journal of Agricultural Economics* (*AJAE*), and has served as an associate editor for the *AJAE* and the *Journal of Environmental Economics and Management*. She has also served as Vice-President and as a Member of the Board of Directors of AERE.

Mordechai Shechter is Professor of Economics at the Department of Economics and Department of Natural Resources and Environmental Management at the University of Haifa, Israel, and Director of the Natural Resources and Environmental Research Centre, also at the University of Haifa. He serves as Review Editor of the Third Assessment Report of the Intergovernmental Panel on

Climate Change (IPCC); member of the International Advisory Committee of the Rosenberg International Forum On Water Resources; Chairperson of the Committee on Regional Research & Development Centers of the Ministry of Science; member of the Editorial Board of the *Journal of Environmental and Resource Economics*; member of the Steering Committee of RICAMARE, an EU Concerted Action on Global Change in the Mediterranean; and on the Board of Directors of Israel's Society for the Protection of Nature.

Bernard Sinclair-Desgagné is Professor of technology economics and management at the École polytechnique de Montréal, where he is associated with the Jarislowsky Chair on technology and international competition and with the NSERC industrial chair on site remediation and management. He is also a Senior Research Fellow at CIRANO – the interuniversity research center on the analysis of organizations, where he acts as director of the 'organisational design and incentives area' and leads the research project on the management of major technological risks. Much of his current research work focuses on environmental economics and risk management, particularly from the perspective of the business firm.

Jim Skea is the Director of the Policy Studies Institute, London and a professor at the University of Westminster. Until 1998, he was Director of the UK Economic and Social Research Council's Global Environmental Change Programme. His main research interests are energy and sustainable development and the interactions between environmental regulation and technical change more generally. Much of his current work focuses on policies for mitigating or adapting to climate change. He is a lead author and review editor for the third assessment report of the Intergovernmental Panel on Climate Change.

Sjak Smulders is a Research Fellow of the Royal Netherlands Academy on Arts and Sciences. He is affiliated with the Department of Economics and the Centre for Economic Research at Tilburg University. His main research interests are in growth theory, trade theory, and the interconnections between these fields and environmental economics. He holds a PhD degree from Tilburg University where he has been teaching since 1994 and was Visiting Assistant Professor at Stanford University.

Olli Tahvonen is currently a professor of environmental economics at the Finnish Forest Research Institute, Helsinki. Previously he was Professor of Economics at the University of Helsinki, Department of Economics. He has published studies in the fields of economics of fisheries, transboundary pollution problems, economic growth and natural resource scarcity, economics of climate change, stock externalities, nonrenewable resource markets, forest economics and environmental ethics.

R. Kerry Turner is Director of CSERGE and Professor of Environmental Sciences at the University of East Anglia. He has published widely on a range of environmental economics and management topics. He serves on a number of regulatory and advisory boards and committees in the UK. He is chief editor of the journal *Environmental and Resource Economics* and a joint editor of the journal *Regional Environmental Change*.

Alistair Ulph is Professor of Economics at the University of Southampton and from January 2000–December 2001, President of the European Association of Environmental and Resource Economists. He has published widely on a range of economic topics, but with an emphasis on resource and environmental economics and labour economics. He served as economic assessor for a public enquiry into the Hinkley Point 'C' Nuclear Power Station, and has been a consultant on a range of projects for UK government departments, the European Commission and the ILO. His current research interests are trade and the environment and the impact of environmental liabilities on financial markets.

Carel Vachon currently works in the area of strategic planning for the Quebec Ministry of Research, Science and Technology. From 1997 to Autumn 1999, she was co-director of the research project on major technological risks at CIRANO. A member of the Québec Bar, she holds a bachelor-of-law degree from McGill University and a master's degree in economics from the University of Montréal.

Luk Van Wassenhove is Professor of Operations Management and Operations Research and Associate Dean for Research and Development at INSEAD. He holds degrees in mechanical and industrial engineering, and a PhD in operations research. Before joining INSEAD in 1990, he held faculty positions at the engineering school of the Catholic University of Leuven, Belgium, and at the Econometric Institute of Erasmus University Rotterdam, The Netherlands, where he was the Head of the Operations Research Department. He has held visiting appointments at Harvard Business School, the University of Rochester and Southampton University. His research interests are in modelling complex operational, tactical and strategic problems in manufacturing, distribution and services, in particular process design for quality and responsiveness. Besides theoretical work (reflected by some 70 papers in major journals), he is also involved in case development, executive education and consulting activities.

Aart de Zeeuw is Professor of Environmental Economics at Tilburg University and director of graduate studies at the Center for Economic Research (centER) in The Netherlands. He is past-president of the European Association of Environmental and Research Economists and a member of the editorial boards of *Environmental & Resource Economics*, *Resource and Energy Economics* and *International Game Theory Review*. His major fields are environmental and resource economics and economic theory.

Tomasz Żylicz, Microeconomics Chair, directs the Warsaw Ecological Economics Centre established at Warsaw University in 1993. From 1989 to 1991 he served full time in the Polish Ministry of Environment, where he was responsible for the design of a major policy reform as well as for managing the state-budget environmental protection expenditures. Since 1997 he has been a member of the European Consultative Forum on the Environment and Sustainable Development. He has taught and written widely on environmental economics and policy.

Introduction

H. Landis Gabel and Henk Folmer

Nearly thirty years ago, Barry Commoner and Paul Erlich, early writers in environmental science, were reputed to have coined the expression:

$$I = PCB$$

To explain, the total human environmental impact (I) is determined by the product of three terms. One is population (P). The second is per capita consumption (C). The third is the environmental burden (B) created by a unit of consumption.

During the lifetime of the reader of these lines, the world's population will triple. More children will be born than in all of human history up to this generation. The change from a rising rate of population growth to a declining rate passed in the last decade, yet population will continue to grow through the new century before stabilizing at a level perhaps twice today's. Nearly all the net growth will be in what are now poor countries.

Per capita consumption has followed a trend as dramatic as the population 'explosion'; per capita consumption has been rising rapidly throughout most of the world over the same timespan as the period of rapid population growth. But whereas there is theoretical and empirical reason to hope that population will stabilize, there is no such hope for consumption rates. Rich countries seek continually higher consumption standards, and poor countries have legitimate aspirations to consume at the level of the rich.

The combination of very rapid rates of increase in P and C has resulted in an unprecedented human impact on the natural environment in the last century. Recent concern for environmental protection, a concern appearing within the reader's lifetime, is not due to a morality unique to this generation. Rather, resources that were previously economically free – they were not scarce relative to demand – suddenly became extremely scarce, economically valuable, and thus worth protecting.

With sudden scarcity and economic value has emerged a new problem, dormant heretofore. Environmental resources often do not trade in markets and so are often unpriced or underpriced. In a market economy, they are therefore overconsumed. This was irrelevant when the resources were economically free or at least cheap, but now the natural problem of rising scarcity is exacerbated by the unnatural problem of economic waste.

Given the ratio of poor to rich of about 4:1, the forecasted net growth of the poor noted above, and their expectation of higher consumption standards, the twenty-first century will see the denouement of this unprecedented story of environmental impact. How the story ends will depend on the final term in the expression above – B. Will it prove possible to reduce the environmental burden of each unit of consumption to offset the inevitable rise in total world consumption? Although it is difficult to forecast the worldwide per capita consumption level fifty years hence, if it continues to grow as it has in the last half-century, it will rise by a multiple of five. Since global population will likely double, B must be cut by 90 per cent to stabilize our collective environmental impact. That the second report to the Club of Rome, *Factor Four: Doubling Wealth, Halving Resource Use*, by Von Weizsäker, Lovins and Lovins, goes less than half-way to the goal warns how great a challenge it is.

In fact, even cutting B by 90 per cent may not suffice. That only stabilizes our collective environmental impact at its current level; it does not guarantee that that level is sustainable. By many measures, we are running unsustainably even now. Virtually all of Sub-Saharan Africa is harvesting wood at unsustainable rates; natural habitats are rapidly being converted to agriculture there, in South America, and in South East Asia; tropical forests are being depleted; world fish stocks are being harvested at unsustainable rates; and the carbon content of the atmosphere rises with unknown but worrisome long-term consequences.

To reduce the environmental impact of a unit of consumption will require a significant change in traditional patterns of human economic behaviour. That, in turn, will require a significant change in the determinants of the individual economic decisions of billions of producers and consumers: information on the environmental effects of resource use; consumption tastes; production technology; the discount rate; property rights that define endowments; relative prices; regulatory constraints on the freedom to make decisions; cultural and religious norms that prescribe the range of admissible actions, and many others. All of these must be changed so that the individually rational albeit constrained choices of producers and consumers aggregate into a much more environmentally benevolent world society.

Of course, many of these changes will come about one way or another. As environmental resources become harder to find, fewer will be used and substitutes will appear. This will occur irrespective of laws or regulations or markets. Yet if we are to endure the era of rising natural resource scarcity with minimum social distress, we must seek wise policies to ensure that we do not waste these precious resources now, and that we allocate what in some cases are fixed reserves suitably between generations.

Work has already started towards doing more with less or at least achieving less malignant consumption. Households separate their wastes, CFCs (chlorofluorocarbons) have been phased out, automobile fuel efficiency has improved enormously and the emissions coming out of tailpipes are so much cleaner that despite the increased automobile use in the developed world, NO_x emissions have stabilized and SO_x emissions have declined in recent years. Lead has effectively disappeared from the emissions stream. Rivers that were dead 25 years ago now have fish, and forests and grasslands are expanding in Europe. The list of accomplishments is long even though much must still be done and the difficulty of doing it will constantly increase.

Households and firms face new or rising taxes on energy consumption and emissions into water. National governments struggle with choices between jobs, investment, trade and the environment. The choices are complicated by uncertainty about the physical nature of the environment and natural resources, the preferences of future generations, and the dynamic interactions between economic and ecological systems. Choices must be made, too, about the specific instruments of policy: taxes, direct regulation, property rights, liability rules, education.

Environmental and natural resource problems have become increasingly international in the sense that their consequences are not confined to the countries where the problems originate. Examples include overfishing of oceans, pollution of transboundary rivers, acid rain and global warming. In the case of international environmental problems, there exists no institution with jurisdiction to enforce compliance with whatever environmental policy might be fashioned in the international arena. Incentives must be created to induce the voluntary compliance of sovereign states.

The need to address environmental problems at the international level has been clear ever since *Limits to Growth*, the first report to the Club of Rome, was published in 1971. It was further emphasized at the Conference on Environment and Development in Stockholm in 1972 and in the First Environmental Action Programme of the (then) European Community in 1973. New international dimensions of environmental protection were developed by the World Commission on Environment and Development (the 'Brundtland Commission') in the report, *Our Common Future*, published in 1987, and at the second UN Conference on Environment and Development (UNCED) in 1992. The Brundtland Commission was the first official commission to adopt and promote to the international agenda the notion of sustainable development as a prerequisite for continued societal existence.

The architects of UNCED recognized that the patterns of production and consumption in the industrialized market economies were major contributors to environmental degradation. Those economies did not have the right to deprive developing countries and economies in transition of fair access to the planet's limited 'environmental space'. Furthermore, action had to be taken in anticipation of the development of today's poorer countries. Without such action, their population and economic growth could condemn to irrelevance the hoped-for achievements of the developed nations. Other major themes of UNCED were the polluter pays principle (PPP) and the user pays principle, the need to internalize environmental costs, the precautionary approach to environmental change and the use of economic instruments as tools of public policy ('Declaration of Rio' and 'Agenda 21').

Effective international environmental policy requires coordination between countries because environmental regulations can become a source of trade distortion if some countries use environmental policy as a hidden trade barrier while others do not. This applies in particular to unions of states like the European Union. At the European level, the focus of much environmental legislation has shifted towards the European Commission in Brussels, through the medium of environmental directives. Piecemeal moves to protect the environment prior to the Single European Act of 1987 were consolidated under the Act, and environmental protection was given an explicit place in the treaty. The establishment of the Internal Market in January 1993 required harmonizing different national laws, including environmental measures.

The growing importance of environmental and resource problems and the increasing infiltration of environmental policy into virtually every sector of the social order require widespread understanding of the basics of environmental and resource economics and policy. This applies to those who make policy at the local, regional, national and international levels, as well as to decision-makers in firms and other non-governmental organizations. It also applies to students who will be confronted with environmental and resource problems in a wide variety of disciplines.

The present volume provides an introduction to the basics of the economic aspects of environmental and resource problems and policy. It is made up of three parts.

Part I, 'General Environmental Economics', focuses on the economic causes of environmental and resource misallocation in a market economy, the economic policy instruments available to combat them, and the ways to analyse the economic implications of environmental policy initiatives. Considerable attention is paid in Part I to the problem of valuation since it underlies virtually all applied work in the field. Part II, 'Business Environmental Economics', shifts the focus from the public policy-makers to the business policy-makers, arguing that more attention should be paid in environmental economics to processes taking place within the firm. Part III, 'Selected Topics', ranges widely over issues such as international trade and environmental policy, natural resource management, social accounting, and growth and environmental protection. Each section is reviewed in more detail below.

GENERAL ENVIRONMENTAL ECONOMICS

There is widespread opinion that markets are the most effective and efficient institutions to allocate scarce resources. On the other hand, ample evidence exists that the environmental problems consequent to rising population and consumption levels are exacerbated by the malfunctioning of markets. One purpose of Part I is to analyse what markets can and cannot do and to discuss how malfunctioning markets can be fixed.

Another objective is to show how economic analysis of environmental problems can help formulate practical environmental policies. This implies that we should look in detail at what environmental policy aims to accomplish and in what circumstances it operates. What is the economic rationale for embarking on a particular policy venture? How will environmental policies and instruments affect economic processes? How should the costs and benefits of environmental policies be analysed and evaluated?

Chapter 1, 'Markets and externalities' by Karl-Gustaf Löfgren, starts by discussing the working of markets. Special attention is paid to market failure caused by externalities and to mechanisms to correct for externalities. An externality exists if one consumer or producer cares directly about another's production or consumption, as in the case of pollution by a neighbouring firm. If externalities are present, the market will not necessarily result in an efficient provision of natural resources and environmental quality. This means that social institutions other than the market, such as the legal system or government intervention, are required to obtain efficiency. Cases with and without the need for intervention are identified. Moreover, some basic forms of government intervention are dealt with. Hence, Chapter 1 lays the foundations for discussion of the instruments of environmental policy later in the volume.

In Chapter 2, 'Microeconomics of valuation', Per-Olov Johansson examines the economic theory that underlies, or should underlie, the valuation of environmental assets which plays an important role in environmental management. Valuation is inherently an applied empirical process, but as the author of the chapter points out, published studies have too often been flawed by insufficient regard for the theory on which they should be based. The chapter surveys the theoretical properties that monetary measures of environmental asset values should possess. The author considers the extent to which monetary measures can be used to estimate the value of changes in environmental quality, and specific sections of the chapter look at how risk is best handled and at the problems that arise in aggregating individuals' valuations to get social preferences.

Valuing environmental assets is not simple, nor is it cheap in practice. Yet wise environmental policy-making requires some sense of the benefit of environmental protection both to compare to its cost and to set priorities. This motivates Chapter 3, 'Valuing the environment', which elaborates directly on Chapter 2. Mordechai Shechter starts by asking the rhetorical question: Can we use a monetary yardstick to value the environment? Concluding that the answer is 'yes', he goes on to survey various practical techniques to do so, including direct valuation, the travel cost method, hedonic pricing, wage differentials, cost of illness, the collective choice approach, and the contingent valuation method. Although each of these methods has strengths and weaknesses, the author notes with chagrin that policy-makers use few of them, sometimes for understandable reasons, but often at the cost of poor decision-making.

Cost–benefit analysis has been a mandatory element of environmental regulation in the United States since the early 1970s, and it is seen with growing frequency in Britain and on the Continent. In Chapter 4, 'Cost–benefit analysis', Nick Hanley carries the reader through the actual stages of a cost–benefit study, with special attention to the problems that commonly appear with the methodology in practice. The author examines also the ethical issues that surround the use of cost–benefit analysis. Finally, he considers some alternatives to cost–benefit analysis.

Chapter 5, 'Goals, principles and constraints in environmental policies' by Tomasz Żylicz, focuses on criteria such as effectiveness, efficiency, equity and sustainability, and on policy principles such as 'polluters pay', 'users pay' and 'victims pay' which allocate the costs of policy initiatives. Attention is paid to typical policy failures. The notion of an optimal level of pollution is discussed, as is the problem of perverse incentives that the market mechanism may create for economic agents. The conclusion of the chapter is that economic analysis can assist policy-makers in assessing the costs and benefits of alternative market interventions and in developing the right tools and instruments for environmental policy.

Chapter 6, 'Environmental policy and policy instruments' by Jean-Philippe Barde, discusses and compares several categories of tools: regulations and standards, environmental taxes and charges, tradable permits, deposit refund systems, damage liability and compensation. All are seen in actual operation, although not in all countries. The focus here is on the experiences of the OECD countries. It appears that different groups of countries employ different sets of instruments to address basically the same problems because of different conditions, for example, sociopolitical settings. Nevertheless, countries can learn from each other's experiences, and environmental economics can provide useful insights.

Previous chapters implicitly assume that the consequences of policy implementation are reasonably predictable. In Chapter 7, 'Impact analysis of environmental policy', Samuel Fankhauser and Daniel McCoy argue that this is often not the case. As they say, 'There is a multitude of feedbacks between the economy and the environment, as well as within the economy itself, and without an appropriate model it is often difficult fully to work out the repercussions of a policy change.' In the chapter, the authors cover several classes of models including input–output, macroeconomic, general equilibrium, and integrated assessment models, to show via the practical example of climate change how they can be used and the strength and weakness of each in forecasting the impact of environmental policy. It turns out that these models may be useful for different purposes and time horizons, they have different data requirements, and they make different assumptions about economic processes.

BUSINESS ENVIRONMENTAL ECONOMICS

Part II, 'Business Environmental Economics', shifts the focus of the volume from the public policy-maker in Part I to the business policy-maker. It is important to pay explicit attention to the firm for several reasons. First, firms are rarely passive in the public policy-making process. They are usually active participants – and sometimes even the protagonists – in virtually every story of policy formulation and implementation. So it is important that we examine the role firms play to see to what extent (and why) they are supportive or injurious to the implementation of the policy ideas discussed in this book. The first chapter of Part II deals with these questions directly. Second, in market economies, managers of private sector firms make most of the actual allocation decisions for environmental resources. If public policy measures aimed at reducing emissions from production are to succeed in mitigating the problem of market failure, they will do so only indirectly by inducing an improvement in the quality of the decisions made by these managers. So we must trace the path of environmental policy through the firm to its ultimate consequences for the efficient allocation of environmental resources. Chapters 9 to 15 cover the most important of these managerial issues.

Chapter 8, 'A firm's involvement in the policy-making process' by François Lévêque and Alain Nadaï, investigates the circumstances in which a firm's involvement in the regulatory process takes place and the payoff provided by this involvement. After presenting both empirical and theoretical arguments to sustain the claim for the involvement of the firm, the authors look explicitly at four forms of such involvement. These forms include support for public policy, its obstruction, voluntary action under regulatory threat, and cooperation with the government to design environmental policy.

It is customary for both environmental economists and policy-makers to assume that the firm is a 'black box', within which perfectly rational managers make profit-maximizing decisions that can be modelled without any need to 'pierce the corporate veil'. Such an assumption ignores many issues that are intrinsically interesting and relevant to the actual success of public policy. The reader will see in Chapter 9, 'Corporate responses to environmental concerns' by Landis Gabel and Bernard Sinclair-Desgagné, that firms are not perfectly efficient black boxes, and that they suffer from organizational failures which are analogous in many ways to the market failures covered in other parts of this book. Managers must try to correct organizational failures just as public policy-makers must try to correct market failures, and neither will ever succeed perfectly. Systems design in both areas must take this reality into account.

Chapter 10, 'Environmental issues and operations strategy' by Charles Corbett and Luk Van Wassenhove, considers a firm's structure and decision areas and examines how they are influenced by environmental issues. The term 'operations' traditionally refers to all aspects of product and process design, production and distribution logistics. More and more, it includes reuse, recycling, re-manufacturing and reverse logistics (reverse materials flows). Using a well-known framework for operations strategy, the authors look at many operations variables including cost, quality, reliability, flexibility, capacity planning, facility location, inventory control and capital allocation. They conclude that implementing environmental programmes in the operations function requires no radical overhaul of operations strategy because of the analogies the authors find with existing management concepts used there.

One cause of organizational failure is imperfect information. Chapter 11, 'Environmental management and information systems' by Jürgen Freimann, explicitly addresses the management and the public policy challenge of improving the quality of this information and its use. As the author says, what is needed – in the hands of managers and stakeholders with the power to influence the image and welfare of a company – are comprehensive environmental information systems giving a reliable picture of the firm's relations to society and nature. The author goes on to discuss the basic principles of eco-accounting and eco-auditing and to describe several systems employed by firms in different countries.

One objective of any environmental policy is to encourage innovation. Indeed, the impact of regulation on innovation may in the long run be of greater importance than its impact on static resource allocation efficiency. Chapter 12, 'Environmental technology', by Jim Skea, considers the incentives for, and the means by which, environmental technology is developed and adopted by industry. It starts with an exploration of the environmental technology concept and then identifies relevant insights from the economics of technical change. The author examines the evolution of the market for environmental goods and services, and the role that government activities have played in it. The chapter ends by drawing together key conclusions regarding the factors influencing the development of environmental technology.

The reader is undoubtedly aware of the claims many companies make for their 'green' products. Is this just routine marketing using a particular slogan or are there substantive differences between marketing environmental product attributes and marketing other product features? Helmut Karl and Carsten Orwat pick up this question in Chapter 13, 'Environmental marketing and public policy'. In fact, there is a variety of economic phenomena that are to some extent peculiar to environmental marketing: the external benefits of green products, the public goods attribute of some types of environmental knowledge, asymmetric information, and opportunistic behaviour of economic agents. These causes of market failure may justify public policy involvement in product marketing.

Chapter 14, 'Dealing with major technological risks', is concerned with the assessment, allocation and control of risks of catastrophic 'man-made' accidents. The authors, Bernard Sinclair-Desgagné and Carel Vachon, survey the main problems and policy issues involved for both the private firm and the public policy-maker. The chapter has sections on risk assessment, risk sharing and risk control. Risk control is separated into two logically different policy matters: prevention and mitigation. The chapter deals explicitly with both private and public policy.

Environmental economics textbooks invariably cover market-based environmental policy instruments with chapters or sections devoted to environmental taxes and marketable rights. Surprisingly, rules of legal liability are commonly neglected. Chapter 15, 'Liability for environmental damages', corrects the deficit with an introduction to both the theoretical and the empirical literature. In this chapter, Kathleen Segerson examines how incentives are affected *ex ante* by the likelihood of penalties imposed *ex post*. This chapter and the previous one are paired in that they both deal with large and infrequent accidents whose probability and severity are subject to human control. As the author argues, taxes and property rights trading are more readily applicable to conscious decisions to emit continuous flows of effluents than to issues of catastrophic risk.

SELECTED TOPICS

Is the analysis up to this point in the volume sufficient to address environmental problems in an international context? When going from problems within a country to problems involving multiple countries, is the only difference one of scale? Henk Folmer and Aart de Zeeuw address these questions in Chapter 16,

'International environmental problems and policy'. The answer they give is that there are major differences. Most turn on the fact that there is no analogy with a national environmental policy body with the jurisdiction to define universal policy and then enforce it universally. The result is that there is a degree of voluntary cooperation necessary among countries in the international arena that is unnecessary when dealing within national domains. But how is cooperation facilitated? The authors look at several methods like side payments, interconnection of different national concerns, and retaliation, all in a game-theoretic setting. Finally, they take up some new international instruments like Joint Implementation and Clean Development Mechanism which have currency in the context of greenhouse gas abatement.

Chapter 16 used environmental protection and trade liberalization as an example of 'interconnection'. In Chapter 17, 'Environment and trade', the interconnection between environmental policy and trade policy reappears, but the focus is different. Alistair Ulph examines the reciprocal relation between the two policies. How does environmental policy affect trade and trade policy affect the environment? Do 'pollution havens' exist? Will trade liberalization cause a 'race to the bottom' as countries competitively weaken their domestic policies? With a taxonomy of small versus large country, perfect versus imperfect competition, and free versus inhibited foreign relocation, Alistair Ulph carries the reader through the analysis, the empirical evidence and the policy implications.

'Green taxation', the title and topic of Eirik Romstad and Henk Folmer's Chapter 18, deals with the problems of implementing environmental taxes. It considers substitutes for direct emission taxes when monitoring and implementation costs are excessively high. It also pays attention to green tax swaps and argues that green taxes are subject to erosion (similar to labour taxes), instability and inconsistency which limit the substitution of environmental taxes for other distortionary taxes. It also addresses various other issues that are in the limelight in the context of the greening of taxes. Might capital flight be a problem? By contrast, might first-movers actually reap a competitive advantage over competitors without such a tax (the 'Porter Hypothesis')? Is the 'double dividend' real? The authors pick up these and other policy issues to conclude that taxation is an important instrument but that free lunches are unlikely to be common.

Students of macroeconomics are typically taught in one of their first classes that net national product is a measure of output and not welfare. Yet the concept has a natural appeal as a measure of well-being. In Chapter 19, 'Social accounting and national welfare measures', Thomas Aronsson reviews the literature concerning how the national accounts can best be modified to serve the objective of measuring social welfare. But even if one knew how to do the modifications, there are still important valuation problems in imperfect market economies which the author discusses. And can a measure of social welfare be used as an indicator of sustainability? Alas, it cannot, for reasons explained in the chapter.

'Can economic growth go on without a deteriorating quality of the environment? Is economic growth still desirable if we take its adverse consequences for the environment into account? What are the effects of environmental policy on economic growth?' These three questions start Chapter 20, 'Economic growth and environmental quality'. Sjak Smulders presents a unifying framework to show how environmental economics and the modern theory of economic growth can be combined to provide a theoretical perspective on the questions.

Chapter 21, 'The economics of natural resource utilization' by Olli Tahvonen and Jari Kuuluvainen, deals with a topic that is highly important in itself, as optimal resource utilization is a basic aspect of sustainable development. The chapter starts with a classification of natural resources and a discussion of one of their basic features: property rights. Next, attention is paid to non-renewable resource utilization. The basic utilization model developed by Hotelling is discussed, as well as extensions of this model and taxation of resource extraction. The question of whether non-renewable resources have become scarce is also dealt with. Next, attention is paid to renewable resources. Last, two examples of renewable resource utilization, fisheries and forestry, are presented. With respect to the former, the debate between maximum sustainable yield and economic optimality is taken up. Next, attention is paid to overfishing in open-access fisheries and to various solutions to this problem. In the context of the economics of forestry, the optimal rotation period and forest management planning at the stand level are dealt with.

Chapter 22, 'Waste management' by Kerry Turner, is about the particular and important problem of solid waste and the industrial system that must be designed to deal with it. Developed economies generate quantities of waste that exceed the environment's absorptive capacity, requiring decisions regarding policy emphasis on source reduction, recycling, or alternative means of final disposal of many different kinds of waste. The reader will find in this chapter references to many of the issues raised earlier in the book – market distortions, policy principles and problems of organizational failure – as the author argues his point that economies require, but currently lack, an integrated, effective and efficient waste management system.

CONCLUSIONS

Economic activities are principal sources of environmental pressure in the form of pollution, resource demands and spatial claims. Yet clearly there is much more than economics to the solution. As we noted at the start of this Introduction, the proximate causes of the 'environmental crisis' are found at other doors: population growth and rising standards of living. Debate on whether the former is to be desired arouses intense passion. The latter is clearly needed in most of the world and equally clearly sought in the rest, whether actually needed or not. The pressure on the environment will be unrelenting.

Thus, by default we must look for greater efficiency in using the environment. To what degree can this book contribute to the objective of reducing the environmental burden of our daily activities by 90 per cent or so? Will it help achieve sustainable development? We believe that a thorough understanding of economics will prove invaluable. It gives us the basic means of understanding why free markets waste environmental assets. It helps us fashion the institutions and policy measures to remedy this failing. It is still not everything. Much of the work will have to be done with new technological discoveries about which economics can say little specific. Yet even here, economics, with its focus on incentives, can help fashion the policies that make research and technological development more likely. It can help us understand the role of risk, including environmental risk, inherent in new technology. We understand better now than before how important the clear definition of property rights is; the same is true regarding legal liability for the use of those rights. Economics can help us estimate the costs and the benefits of alternatives. It can provide us with some ability to anticipate the often unanticipated consequences of alternative policies. By understanding the role that firms play in the policy-making process, we may be better able to build coalitions supporting policy, just as by understanding international trade and commercial interests, we may be better able to ensure voluntary cooperation with international environmental agreements. We all must hope that with knowledge will follow a more easily sustainable future.

PART I

General Environmental Economics

1. Markets and externalities

Karl-Gustaf Löfgren

1. INTRODUCTION

There is conventional wisdom that markets and market economies mostly lead to socially desirable outcomes. Yet it is also a well-known fact that economic activity frequently has socially undesirable environmental consequences. Experience tells us that things are not always what they seem, or as Chesterton (1961) puts it: 'a paradox is a truth that stands on its head to attract attention'. The purpose of this chapter is to discuss, intuitively, what markets can do – and what they cannot do – in terms of allocating resources in a socially desirable manner. In this way, we can reconcile the seemingly conflicting outcomes of economic interaction. We will also consider possible remedies for what economists call market failures. We will concentrate exclusively on failures that are caused by what we refer to as externalities. This concept will be defined more fully below, but for the moment the reader may consider it the unwanted environmental consequences of economic activities.

In a market economy where externalities are present, there are, theoretically, many apparently similar ways in which environmental policy can improve the allocation of resources. However, in practice, it is not clear which policy measures are the most successful. Therefore this chapter also contains a discussion of the pros and cons of different practical policy applications.

2. THE BLESSING OF THE MARKET

Generally, you do not buy goods that do not improve your personal situation. At the same time, you would not be able to buy if the seller felt that he would be the loser in the exchange. Hence, given any initial allocation of goods among traders, the opening up of trade cannot be but an improvement of the initial allocation. A trader would always block any disadvantageous trade offer. Moreover, if a group of individuals wants to trade, it is not inconceivable that they will find all the mutually advantageous trades, sooner or later. If the number of individuals is large, this will be difficult, or at least take a long time, when there are no coordinating (market) arrangements. The human brain would soon, however, create tools to simplify the discovery of advantageous trades. Say, for example, that a market administrator is chosen who starts the trading process by announcing an arbitrarily given set of prices. Agents specify what they are willing to buy and sell at the prices quoted. If the buying and selling decisions are inconsistent, the market administrator adjusts the set of prices according to the following rule: if, in a particular market, the aggregate quantity demanded exceeds the aggregate quantity supplied, he will raise the price in that particular market; if the opposite holds, he will lower the price. The agents are allowed to renew their bids, and the process described above, called the *tâtonnement* process, continues until a simultaneous consistency is achieved of buying and selling decisions in all markets. Then actual trading is taking place.

What are the conditions under which trading takes place? Obviously, since everybody pays (gets) the same price and buys (sells) all that he wants at that price, the utility of all individuals cannot be improved by a reallocation of goods from one individual to another. If we give any demander one more unit this will improve his position, but the position of the supplier will deteriorate, since he already trades all that he is willing to trade under the ruling trade conditions. To see this more clearly consider Figure 1.1.

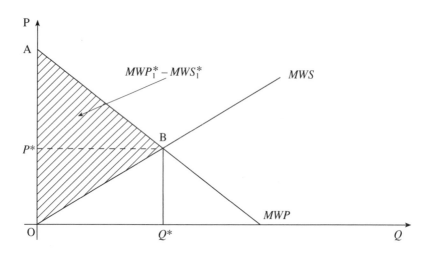

Figure 1.1   The totem of the market or the maximization of the surplus

The 'marginal willingness to pay' curve, *MWP*, denotes the aggregate net demand of good Q at any given common price (measured along the vertical axis). The word 'marginal' is used to highlight the fact that the *MWP* curve tells us what the market is willing to pay for the last unit bought. It is evident that the higher the price, the lower the aggregate demand. Similarly, the 'marginal willingness to sell' curve, *MWS*, represents the aggregate net supply of good Q at any common price. It gives us the price which the market accepts to sell the last unit. The price P^*, at which the *MWP* curve cuts the *MWS* curve, is particularly interesting. At this point the aggregate volume sold coincides with the aggregate volume supplied, and all desirable transactions can be carried out. This is an equilibrium and the situation where the market administrator has done his job and trading can take place.

What are the gains from trading? For the first unit, the aggregate marginal willingness to pay exceeds the aggregate compensation the sellers need to supply it on the market by the distance $MWP_1 - MWS_1$. By moving unit by unit towards the equilibrium volume and summing the net willingness to pay for each unit up to Q^*, where the net willingness to pay is zero since the curves cross, we end up with the area OAB. This area can be subdivided into two sub-areas. The triangle OBP* represents the surplus which accrues to the sellers. Price exceeds the marginal willingness to sell for all units except the last unit sold. The triangle P*AB represents the surplus which accrues to the buyers. The marginal willingness to pay exceeds the price for all units except the last. The sum of the two triangles – the area OAB – measures the total gain from trade, which consists of the surpluses of buyers and sellers. Note that if we sell one additional unit the aggregate *MWP* is lower than the aggregate *MWS*, and in the aggregate there is a loss from trading an additional unit. The *MWP* curve is what is called the demand curve in economic terms, and the *MWS* curve is the supply curve. The point where demand and supply are equal is called the market equilibrium.

It is, of course, true that few real markets have a market administrator or an auctioneer, but economic theory assumes, as a first approximation, that a market where many traders are present functions as if there were a market administrator (that is, as in a perfect market). The bottom line is, therefore, that the existence of perfect markets guarantees that all mutually advantageous trades are realized and that the outcome is socially desirable in the sense that one cannot improve the situation for one individual without worsening it for someone else. This is essentially Adam Smith's famous 'invisible hand' theorem. A selfish price-taker competing with others intends only his own gain, and he is in this, as in many other cases, led by an invisible hand to promote an end which was no part of his intention,[1] namely an efficient exchange.

3. MARKET FAILURES CAUSED BY EXTERNALITIES

We have already mentioned that environmental problems cannot normally be handled in a socially desirable manner without policy interactions in the market system. Given that we espouse a belief in the blessings of the market, we would blame environmental problems on a failure of markets. We will leave this conjecture open for the moment, and turn to a definition of externalities. This will enable us to embed environmental problems in a broader class of phenomena which cause market failures.

Baumol and Oates (1988) state that an externality is present whenever some individual's (say A's) utility or production relationships include real (that is, non-monetary) variables, whose values are chosen by others (persons, corporations, governments) without particular attention to the effects on A's welfare.

The consumption of antibiotics, for example, causes bacteria to become resistant, which will complicate future recovery from bacterial attack. The production of knowledge in society probably affects the production technology of individual firms; the emissions from smoke stacks have a deteriorating effect on the 'living conditions' of both firms and individuals. These phenomena belong to the class of externalities. The examples show that externalities can be both good and bad. The externality created by the production of knowledge is a public good, since it improves the production technology of firms and also the utility of consumers. The consumption of antibiotics contains an element of a negative externality (a bad), since it reduces the utility of other individuals' future use of the drug. It is, however, obvious that the fact that antibiotics cause externalities does not mean that they should not be used; the trick is to balance the harm done against the obvious beneficial effects of the drug in such a way that a socially desirable consumption level is generated. There are few reasons to believe that the demand and supply of antibiotics in a free market would generate the optimal consumption level. This is also recognized by governments: therefore the prescription of antibiotics is regulated (in most countries).

However, there is no externality involved if an increase in the demand for tankers raises the price of steel and hence affects the welfare of the purchasers of cars. The reason is that there is no direct link between the technology of car production and the demand for steel; that is, the number of tankers sold does not directly affect the technology used in car production. The rise in the price of steel is a correct reflection of the fact that steel has become a scarcer resource, which has pecuniary repercussions for all users – direct or indirect – of steel.

3.1 Public versus Private Externalities

Many of the externalities above have the character of public goods; that is, they are consumed by all, and the consumption by one individual does not affect what is left for consumption by other individuals. Broadly speaking, a public goods externality is consumed by all people in equal amounts; for example, air pollution, in terms of sulphur dioxide or carbon dioxide, has an equally deteriorating effect on the environment for every resident in the area. An increase in the population of the area will not reduce the level of sulphur dioxide.

An amenity is another typical example of a public goods externality, but this time a positive one. For example, beautiful views can be enjoyed by all people passing by, providing benefits for all viewers. After you have seen the Grand Canyon it is still there to be enjoyed by later visitors. It is not difficult to understand why it is inefficient to charge for the consumption of positive public goods externalities. It is because the consumption of amenities by one individual does not, in general, influence the level of satisfaction of another individual. Hence a charge would inhibit one person's consumption and satisfaction without increasing that of others. Accordingly, public goods externalities are sometimes referred to as 'undepletable externalities'.

An example of a positive private externality, albeit rather unusual, is the slaughter of cattle in Argentina around the turn of the nineteenth century. This was done because of interest in the hides. The meat was left at the place of slaughter to be enjoyed by the poor. This externality no longer exists as the meat is more valuable (nowadays) than the hide. It is obvious that this is a depletable or private externality, since a piece of meat taken away by one person will not be available to others. Since it is possible exclusively to charge the person who is enjoying the externality, the externality is depletable. The generator of the externality may find it profitable to produce the good 'with particular attention to the effects on A's welfare'. This means, by definition, that the externality is eliminated.

Another example of a private externality, this time a bad, is a firm that dumps its solid waste outside your summer cottage. The externality is obviously depletable since it cannot destroy the environment surrounding, say, your cousin's cottage in another country.

There are cases where it is not clear whether we are dealing with a typical public or private externality. However, the policy problem tends to be the same for any form of externality: how do we design the incentive structure facing the parties to an externality so as to induce socially desirable behaviour? As it turns out, policy measures for correcting the inefficiencies created by any kind of externality, public or private, are essentially the same. The difference is, perhaps, that the more private the externality, the more likely it is that it can be (will be) regulated by markets and market transactions.

4. CORRECTING FOR EXTERNALITIES

We will deal with the problem of correcting for externalities in the simplest possible setting.[2] First, we will discuss a case where there are two firms, and where the production of firm 1 causes firm 2 an externality, which is in relation to the production of firm 1. One unit of production in firm 1 creates an externality (a cost) for firm 2 which in total amounts to kq, where k is a constant and q is the number of units produced in firm 1. More particularly, every q units of output in firm 1 creates a loss of kq dollars for firm 2. To keep the analysis as simple as possible, we will not deal explicitly with the production decision of firm 2. Suffice it to say that its profit is:

$$\pi_2 = -kq, \tag{1.1}$$

which also shows that every extra (marginal) unit produced in firm 1 inflicts a loss on firm 2 of k dollars.

Firm 1 produces and sells its output in a competitive market, where there are many sellers and buyers. The participants in the market consider, therefore, the market price p as a given constant. The cost of production increases with q. We can write the profit of firm 1 as:

$$\pi_1 = pq - TC(q). \tag{1.2}$$

The first term is the total revenue, which is the price times the volume sold or the marginal valuation of the good times the volume. The second term is the total cost, and note that the cost firm 1 inflicts on firm 2 is not in the cost function $TC(q)$ of firm 1.

Both firms are assumed to maximize their own profits, although we are not dealing with the maximization decision of firm 2 explicitly. How would the production of firm 1 be determined under profit maximization? For each unit it sells, it gets p dollars, and each extra unit costs, say $MC(q)$. Clearly, it would be willing to supply an extra unit as long as the price exceeds the extra (marginal) cost $MC(q)$.[3] In Figure 1.2 the revenue relevant for profit maximization and the cost structure of firm 1 are depicted. We have also portrayed the marginal cost inflicted on firm 2 by each extra unit of production in firm 1.

It is obvious that firm 1 makes a profit on all units up to q^*. The profit it has earned up to q^* is marked by the shaded area A. This is also the maximum profit, since if the firm chooses to sell units beyond q^*, it will lose on each extra unit, since the marginal cost, $MC(q)$, is larger than the price, p, for all units to the right of q^*. The value of the externality it causes for firm 2 is the shaded area below the q axis, which is denoted B. It is obvious from Figure 1.2 that it is impossible to avoid the external effect without shutting down firm 1. This is, however, not necessarily the socially desirable outcome. What society would like to do is to maximize the social surplus from the production of firm 1. Here this corresponds to choosing q in such a manner that the sum of its own profits, minus the costs it inflicts on firm 2, is maximized.

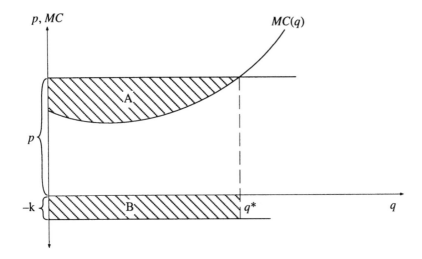

Figure 1.2 The profit maximization of firm 1 and the marginal external effects it causes firm 2

4.1 Internalizing the Externality

This example leads us to the first method of correcting for the externality. If firm 1 owned firm 2, it would have reason to care about the detrimental effects the production of firm 1 had on firm 2. The decision problem of the owner of both firms would be to maximize:

$$\pi_1^T = pq - TC(q) - kq \tag{1.3}$$

The revenue function is the same, but the total cost function and the marginal cost function have extra components, kq and k, respectively. We say that the externality kq has been internalized by introducing a single owner of both firms. The determination of the socially desirable production level is illustrated in Figure 1.3. The relevant marginal cost function is now $MC(q) + k$, and the firm makes a profit as long as the price exceeds the augmented marginal cost function $MC(q) + k$.

The socially desirable level of production is given by, where society's marginal valuation of the good, p, coincides with its social marginal cost, $MC + k$. We can also see from Figure 1.3 that the social surplus (the profit at the socially desirable level of production) is given by the magnitude of the shaded area A^s and that $0 < q^s < q^*$, that is, the socially desirable production level is

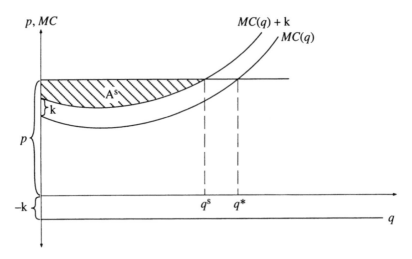

Figure 1.3 Profit maximization when the externality is internalized

positive, but less than the original decentralized solution q^*. It would have been zero if k had been large enough to neutralize all surplus A^s.

If firm 1 owned firm 2 the externality would disappear, since private and social marginal costs would, under such conditions, disappear. It is therefore relevant to ask whether there is any incentive for a single owner to materialize. Clearly, the profit (value) of firm 2 increases when production is reduced from q^* to q^s, while the profit value of firm 1 decreases. The aggregate profit, however, would increase after merging of the firms and consequently the production of the socially desirable production level [from A – B to A^s]. This means that there is an incentive for one owner (here firm 2) to buy out the other, given that the value of the two firms corresponds to their profits in the free market solution. Hence, given 'perfect asset markets', the arbitrage possibilities (possibilities of making a safe profit) of a merger would, in theory, sooner or later be taken care of by some party, and the social inefficiency arising from the externality would disappear. In other words, more markets and complete information could automatically correct for the externality.

4.2 Pigouvian Taxes

Now we understand how the externality can be internalized, the next step is to come up with an alternative policy proposal to correct the externality.

If we tax firm 1 with a tax *t* per unit equal to the value of the marginal external effect k, the firm will be induced, via the profit motive, to choose the socially desirable level of production. It will stop the expansion of production, where:

$$p = MC(q^s) + t = MC(q^s) + k, \qquad (1.4)$$

which, from the last equality, results in the socially desirable production level q^s, depicted in Figure 1.3. Here the marginal damage is assumed to be independent of the production level of firm 1 (equal to k). In general, the marginal damage will vary with the production level. The emission tax is under such circumstances set equal to the marginal externality at the socially desirable production level. The tax t is called a Pigouvian tax after Arthur C. Pigou, who in 1920 suggested the technique of using taxes (subsidies) to correct for socially undesirable (desirable) outcomes caused by externalities.

This method has long been, and still is, the most widely suggested cure for externalities, at least in textbooks on environmental economics. However, alternatives such as tradable emission permits (see section 4.4) are growing in popularity.

From the example above it seems as if a direct regulation, given perfect foresight, would do equally well. That is, suppose we told the firm in Figure 1.3 that the maximum allowable output was q^s, would we then not achieve the same allocation as under a Pigouvian tax equal to $t = k$? In the example above the answer is yes, but in a more realistic setting where there are many firms (industry) and in which everyone produces public 'bads', we would like to obtain a given level of cleaning up at the lowest cost in the aggregate. This is very difficult if we do not have exact knowledge of the production technologies at the firm level. It may easily happen that a regulation requiring, say, a 20 per cent cut in emissions from each firm results in an excessive social cost for achieving a 20 per cent cut in the aggregate emission level. The same Pigouvian tax on each unit emitted, the level being determined by the value of the marginal externality at the social optimum, means that each firm will abate its emissions (essentially 'eliminate' k in the example above) as long as the tax ($t = k$) exceeds the marginal abatement costs. If the abatement costs exceed the tax, it pays to pay the tax and, if the opposite is true, it pays to abate.[4]

Each firm would then, in equilibrium, have an abatement level determined by the equality between the Pigouvian tax and the abatement cost of the marginal unit (the marginal abatement costs). Since the tax is equal for all firms, they would all have the same marginal abatement costs. This is indeed a necessary condition for a cost-effective abatement policy. To see this, say that the marginal abatement cost differs between firms. It would then be cost-saving to reduce abatement in firms where marginal abatement costs are high and increase abatement where costs are low. Such reallocations are not profitable if marginal abatement costs are equal at all emission sources. Clearly, if abatement were determined by a direct regulation, it would only be by sheer luck that regulations were allocated in such a manner that marginal abatement costs were equal for each firm in the industry.

There is at least one more advantage to a tax, as opposed to direct controls, in that the emission tax provides a continuing incentive for the polluter to abate emissions. When a tax is imposed, firms are encouraged to seek new low-cost ways of abating emissions, regardless of how much they are already abating, since such a technology would exempt the firm from taxation.

A potential disadvantage of a Pigouvian tax is that extensive monitoring of emissions is required to make sure that the desired level of pollution is obtained. This is, of course, also true for individually designed regulations. However, it can be argued that if all polluters are required to use the same cleaning technology, such as a catalytic converter for cars, the administrative costs of the regulation can be kept to a minimum. Hence, if cost-effectiveness and the administrative costs of monitoring are taken together, it is conceivable that there are cases in which a mandated technology will represent the lowest-cost alternative.

There are other obvious situations where direct controls are preferable to a tax. For example, a simple ban is more effective than a Pigouvian tax when dealing with a highly toxic substance. Another situation is where quick alterations in the level of emissions are required to meet, for example, changing weather conditions. Naturally, a tax could be altered to meet varying emission targets, but it is clearly impractical and expensive to do so frequently.

Economists tend to claim that, with a few obvious exceptions, a tax to regulate emissions is generally superior to direct controls. The principle that 'the polluter pays' has, however, been challenged by economists claiming that a subsidy will work just as well; that is, the polluter is paid to reduce pollution. Our intuition clearly tells us that whether the polluter is paid for the emissions he abates or is taxed for those he does not, the outcome would be the same. This intuition is, however, not quite correct. A subsidy, contrary to a tax, improves the profit conditions for the firms within the industry and, although emissions from individual firms would decline, this is not necessarily true at the level of the industry as a whole. This is because firms enter the market as long as profits are higher than normal, and a subsidy means that profits remain higher than normal for a greater number of firms in the industry than under a tax regime. Hence, too many firms would, in a dynamic perspective, be attracted to the industry, and the allocative effects of a subsidy would not be the same as those of a Pigouvian tax.

In practice, there is an additional difficulty with a subsidy. The level of the subsidy has to be based on some benchmark emission level, which would give the incumbents an incentive to misallocate resources, emitting more than necessary to establish a favourable benchmark – too favourable from society's point of view.

The conclusion is that whereas our intuition tells us that a subsidy would also be cost-effective, further reflection tells us that a subsidy is not sufficient for a socially desirable outcome.

Another somewhat counter-intuitive proposition is that competitive polluting outputs are not necessarily excessive. To be more precise, if there were an externality-producing branch of industry, say the transport sector, our intuition and Figures 1.2 and 1.3 would tell us that an unregulated competitive market solution would generate too many transport services. Broadly speaking, since all activities within the transport sector – transportation by car, train, boat and air – all generate externalities in terms of unwanted emissions, a socially desirable outcome will involve a reduction in all these activities. Again, this intuition is not correct. The picture given by Figures 1.2 and 1.3 is a partial equilibrium view. When all repercussions of appropriate Pigouvian taxes on transport services are taken into account, the final outcome could very well mean less car and air transportation, but more boat and railway transportation. The reason is fairly obvious. The emission caused by the train per ton/mile is less than that caused by the car. It is clear, then, that a socially desirable outcome may call for a decrease in the use of automobiles (compared with the unregulated market solution) and some offsetting increase in the use of railways, in spite of the fact that trains produce undesirable emissions. Total emissions would certainly decrease as a result of the suggested substitution.

Another much-debated issue among economists is whether the victims of externalities should be compensated. If the number of victims is large, efficient treatment of them prohibits compensation, and this is true for both depletable (private) and non-depletable (public) externalities.

The reason is related to the fact that taxes are preferable to subsidies as a means of controlling emissions. If all the neighbours of a factory were fully compensated for, say, the effects of smoke, no one would have any incentive to move away from the factory. It is then certainly conceivable that too many people would choose to live under smoky conditions and be fully compensated – without benefit to anyone. Broadly speaking, too many people would engage in 'victim activity'.

This point can be enlarged upon (see, for example, Coase, 1960). It could be argued that the victims should be taxed for the cost their decision to locate near the polluting factory imposes on the factory owners. Coase's idea is that when residents select a home near the factory, they impose an external cost on the generator of the externality. This cost takes the form of a higher Pigouvian tax for the owners of the factory, reflecting greater social damage from the pollution due to the rise in the number of victims. However, if the number of victims is large, the Pigouvian tax will essentially be independent of the number of victims and one can neglect this social cost from locating close to the factory. The conclusion is that correct incentives should be provided to victims so that they take defensive actions, such as investing in air-cleaning devices or moving to new locations further away from the source of pollution; that is, they should neither be compensated nor taxed.

4.3   Markets and Property Rights – the Coase Theorem

Ronald Coase has also presented an interesting view on how direct market transactions between polluter and victim can, without any interventions from policy-makers, produce socially desirable outcomes. The setting is an economy where property rights are well defined and where there are few polluters and victims. We will illustrate Coase's idea with an example from a conflict over land use.

In the northern part of Scandinavia there is a conflict over land use between the industries of reindeer husbandry and forestry. Both industries use common land. On the one hand, the Laplanders (the reindeer-owners) claim that modern forestry destroys, among other things, the pastures for reindeer. On the other, there are the claims of the forestry industry that the reindeer destroy the plants during the regeneration period. The conflict over land use is a clear example of external diseconomies. The production function of forestry depends on the intensity of reindeer husbandry, and the production function of reindeer husbandry depends on the intensity of forestry. To simplify the analysis, we assume that the intensity of forestry affects reindeer husbandry negatively, while the effects of reindeer husbandry on forestry are negligible.

Let $B^F(x)$ be the net revenue from forestry, when forestry is conducted at intensity x. Moreover, let $B^R(x)$ be the net revenue that falls on reindeer husbandry when forestry is conducted at intensity x. The socially optimal scale of forestry is the solution to:

$$\max_{x} S(x) = B^F(x) + B^R(x), \tag{1.5}$$

that is, to choose x, the intensity of forestry, such that the sum of the net revenues from forestry and reindeer husbandry is maximized.

The same intuition that helped us derive the conditions for cost-effectiveness now tells us that x must be chosen such that the net revenue of the last unit (the marginal net benefit from forestry) equals the marginal net cost it imposes on reindeer husbandry: the marginal net benefits of forestry should be equal to the marginal net cost forestry imposes on reindeer husbandry.

The solution is illustrated in Figure 1.4. At the optimum x^* the net revenue from the last unit produced in forestry,

$$\frac{dB^F_*}{dx},$$

equals the marginal net cost which falls on reindeer husbandry,

$$-\frac{dB^R_*}{dx}.$$

If forestry were allowed to choose its own harvest rate, it would harvest until marginal net revenue is zero, that is, x^F was produced. Thus we see that the private optimum results in a level of forestry activity that is too large. On the other hand, if reindeer husbandry were allowed to decide the rate of forestry production, forestry production would not be allowed at all, that is, point x^R would be chosen.

This conflict over land use may be solved by internalizing the externality by allowing forestry to merge with reindeer husbandry. The goal functions of society and forestry in such circumstances would coincide. Other possible ways of solving the conflict are direct regulation or the use of taxes as discussed in section 4.2.

But why should the reindeer husbandry industry allow a level of forestry production which is too high? Both forestry and reindeer husbandry would

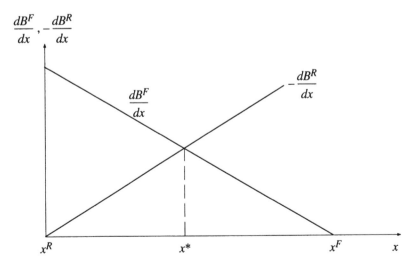

Figure 1.4 Illustration of Coase's theorem

gain if forestry were compensated for reducing its harvest rate by a sum of money ε, where

$$0 < \frac{dB^F}{dx} < \varepsilon < -\frac{dB^R}{dx}$$

as long as the intensity of forestry is greater than x^*. Thus forestry can be 'bribed' to produce at the socially optimal rate. Moreover, if reindeer husbandry has property rights to the land, forestry can buy the right to use the land by paying a sum of money

$$\varepsilon' - \frac{dB^R}{dx}$$

such that

$$0 < \varepsilon' - \frac{dB^F}{dx} < \frac{dB^F}{dx}$$

as long as x is smaller than x^*. Hence the allocation of property rights does not have any bearing on whether or not the optimal scale of production is attained. However, it does have a bearing on income distribution. These facts are made clear by Coase's (1960) theory, referred to as the Coase theorem:

If costless negotiation is possible, rights are well specified and redistribution does not affect marginal values, then:

1. The allocation of resources will be identical, whatever the allocation of legal rights.
2. The allocation will be efficient, eliminating the problem of externality.

The theorem assumes that transaction costs are zero and that property rights are well defined. Property rights do not necessarily mean the ownership of the land. It could, for example, be sufficient for the Laplanders to own a well-defined right to use the land for reindeer husbandry, while the forest industry had the right via, say, a lease contract, to conduct forestry. The land could be owned by the state. Much of the conflict has been concerned with the exact content of the property rights of the Laplanders which might have contributed (together with positive transaction costs) to the fact that most people perceive the conflict as being unresolved. Another important complication in the forestry–reindeer example is the implicit assumption that only two parties are involved. Assume that negotiations are conducted between one landowner and many reindeer owners. Now there is an incentive for a reindeer owner to conceal his true willingness to pay in the hope that others are harmed by forestry to such an extent that the 'contract' goes through. In other words, it pays for the individual to be a free rider. In economic theory this is often referred to as the 'free-rider problem'. If the number of reindeer owners increases, it is conceivable that the free-rider problem becomes increasingly serious, and the actual scale of forestry will approach the private optimum x^F.

4.4 Marketable Emission Permits

The idea behind Coase's theorem is that a small number of agents are able to exhaust all mutually advantageous trades, even if the institutional arrangements, apart from the well-defined property rights necessary for a market solution, are absent. However, since markets have socially desirable consequences, it may in certain circumstances be a good idea to create artificially markets which are not likely to materialize on their own. Say, for example, that we know the level of the socially desirable sulphur dioxide emissions in the Amsterdam area. How can we efficiently allocate the permissible level of emissions to firms emitting sulphur dioxide? Since the number of victims is large, and since property rights are not easy to define, the Coase theorem is not applicable. Pigouvian tax is possible, but an interesting alternative is to create a market for emission permits. This was first suggested by Thomas Crocker (1965).

The profitable firms with high abatement costs have a high willingness to pay for sulphur dioxide emission permits, and rightly so since society's opportunity costs of getting rid of these emissions, the (marginal) profits, are high. Relatively unprofitable firms and firms with low cleaning costs have, for opposite reasons, a low willingness to pay for the right to emit sulphur dioxide, because the opportunity costs of getting rid of their emissions are low. Would not a free market for emission permits in these circumstances allocate emissions in a socially desirable manner?

To be more precise, assume that there are n firms that emit sulphur dioxide, and that the ith firm emits E_i tons of sulphur dioxide at full capacity utilization. To simplify the formal analysis, we assume that each firm's average variable cost, AVC_i, is constant up to full capacity utilization, and that the cleaning cost per unit of emissions is constant and equal to r_i. Moreover, assume that each unit of output corresponds to one unit of emissions. Firm i's cost and revenue structure is given in Figure 1.5.

The firm faces a price per unit of output equal to p, and makes a unit profit equal to $p - AVC_i$. In the absence of efficient charges, the firm will produce at full capacity utilization $\bar{q}_i$ and emit $\bar{E}_i = \bar{q}_i$ units of sulphur dioxide.

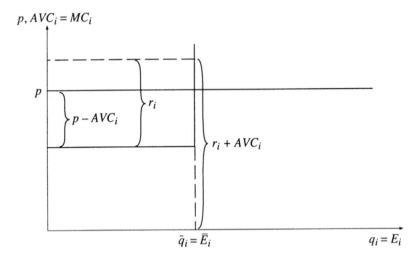

Figure 1.5   The cost, revenue and emission conditions in firm i

The firm's maximum willingness to pay for a permit to emit a unit of sulphur dioxide, SO_i, is $p - AVC_i$. If it pays this amount it will break even. If the abatement cost/unit is less than $p - AVC_i$, the best alternative for the firm and for society is to clean each unit produced (we assume that the externality is completely eliminated, that is, cleaning is perfect). However, in Figure 1.5 $r_i > p - AVC_i$ and the firm would have to go out of business if it were forced to clean its production. In other words, the firm's willingness to pay for a permit for emitting one unit of sulphur dioxide, p_{E_i} equals:

$$p_{E_i} = \text{Min} \,[p - AVC_i \,, r_i] \; i = 1, 2, \ldots, n. \tag{1.6}$$

Clearly, if $r_i > p - AVC_i$ it will only be willing to pay $p - AVC_i$, since cleaning costs would in these circumstances undo all profits. If the opposite holds $(p - AVC_i > r_i)$, it will not buy an emission permit if it costs more than cleaning (more than r_i), even if it can afford it in the sense that the profit per unit remains positive.

In Figure 1.6 we have ranked the firms' (marginal) willingness to pay for emissions, which also equals society's opportunity cost (the net value of production lost) to get rid of the sulphur dioxide, from the highest to the lowest.

Firm 1 is willing to pay p_{E_1} dollars/ton to emit E_1 tons of sulphur dioxide, while the lowest willingness to pay is p_{E_n} for E_n units. Clearly, since the diagram also represents society's opportunity cost for getting rid of the emissions, we would like to minimize this cost. Hence we would want the firm with the lowest

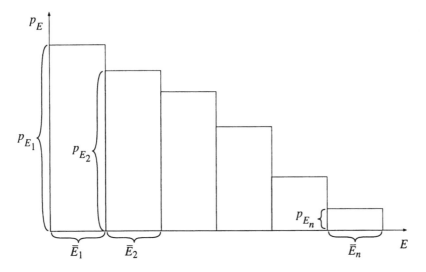

Figure 1.6   The willingness to pay for emissions (society's opportunity cost)

willingness to pay (the lowest opportunity cost) to abate its emissions, while those with the highest opportunity costs should continue to emit. This is exactly what the establishing of a market for tradable permits would achieve. The step function in Figure 1.6 is the aggregate demand curve for emission permits. If the socially desirable level of emissions is E_0, and society chooses to sell emission permits to the same extent, there will be an equilibrium price, p_E^0, where the vertical supply curve crosses the demand curve for emission permits (see Figure 1.7, where the step function has been smoothed out).

It is clear that emission permits will be bought by firms with high opportunity costs for cleaning. These firms will neither cut back on production nor abate emissions. Firms that have a willingness to pay which is lower than the market price will shut down if $p - AVC_i < r_i$, or clean output if $p - AVC_i > r_i$. Mixed solutions, where the firm both abates emissions and buys emission permits, are possible in a more realistic setting where the willingness to pay for emissions depends on the volume of emissions and the cleaning cost depends on the degree of abatement.

The socially desirable volume of emission permits, E_0, is determined by the equality between the demand curve for emission permits (the opportunity cost to eliminate the permission), and the curve which measures society's marginal willingness to pay for (marginal benefit of) getting rid of the emissions (the ME^- curve in Figure 1.7). The reader should note that a low emission level comes with a high marginal abatement cost (opportunity cost to eliminate the emission). As in the tax case, it requires a great deal of information about

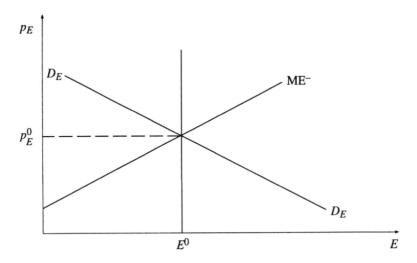

Figure 1.7   The market for emission permits

valuations and technology in society to determine this level correctly. The best
we can hope for is probably a cost-effective solution, which means that we
obtain a given level (not necessarily the socially desirable level) of abatement
at minimum cost. Marketable emission permits also provide incentives to
improve abatement technology, since the cleaning of emissions results in compensation in terms of revenues from the sales of permits in excess of the new
lower emission level.

That permits are marketable is a special advantage from a dynamic
perspective. The establishment of new firms, shutdowns, and technological
progress all change the demand for emission permits, and trade in permits is
a flexible way of adapting to new conditions. In a growing economy, it is
conceivable that Pigouvian taxes will have to be frequently adjusted. When
there is a market for permits the price of an emission permit will rise automatically, reflecting the fact that the right to pollute has become a scarcer
resource.

In an inflationary economy, a permit is also more flexible than a tax. Without
frequent adjustments of the Pigouvian tax, environmental quality will be eroded
under a tax regime. The price of a permit will simply follow the general price
level, and will therefore be preferable to a Pigouvian tax.

Compared with direct controls at the firm level (see section 4.2), a market
for emission permits has the obvious advantage of being a regulation that is
cost-effective.

5. SPECIAL PROBLEMS

What we have done so far is to design environmental policy under certainty and under the implicit assumption that the sources of pollution stem from firms active in competitive markets. The latter means that both firms and buyers are many, and that no cartels are formed, either of firms or of buyers. The former means that we are neglecting all the uncertainties of real life. However, from an environmental point of view the most important uncertainties concern the positions of the demand curve for permits (or more generally the marginal abatement cost curve) and the marginal willingness to pay for cleaning the emissions. Both problems are important in practice, and we will explain them briefly.We will also deal with externalities in a monopoly (that is, in an industry consisting of one firm), and finally with an important technicality for policy called a non-convexity, which can severely hamper the possibility of reaching a socially desirable outcome as a market solution.

5.1 Uncertainty

We will start with a case where the regulator is uncertain about society's MWP curve, which is clearer than the case where the demand curve for emission permits is uncertain. Consider Figure 1.8, which is essentially the same as Figure 1.7.

In Figure 1.8, we have highlighted the fact that one can reach the same allocation under a Pigouvian tax and a market for emission permits. The tax will coincide with the equilibrium price for the permit, $t^0 = p_E^0$. Both the tax and the number of emission permits are based on the assumption that the relevant opportunity cost to clean is represented by the curve $D_E - D_E$, and that the marginal benefits from emissions are correctly represented by the ME^- curve. The policy means are, under these conditions, equivalent. Assume, however, that we have correct information on the demand curve (the opportunity cost to clean), but that the true benefit curve is ME_1^-, which means that we are underestimating the benefits of a cleaner environment. The number of permits should be E_1 instead of E_0 and the Pigouvian tax should be t^1 instead of t^0. The social loss from excessive emissions is, however, the same under both policy regimes. It corresponds to the shaded area L in Figure 1.8 and consists of the difference between the marginal willingness to pay for emissions, and the opportunity cost to clean the emission for the excessive number of emissions $E_0 - E_1$.

The equivalence between a tax and a market for emission permits, in a situation where there is uncertainty about the marginal willingness to pay, is also demonstrated for a case when the marginal benefits from reducing emissions are overestimated. The exercise is left to the reader. The intuition underlying the result, that uncertainty about the marginal benefit curve does not matter in

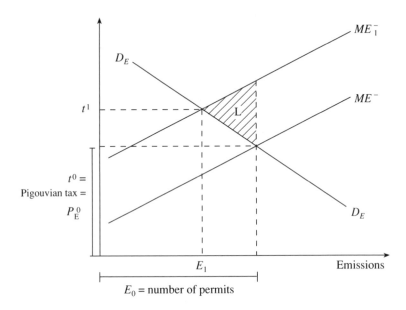

Figure 1.8   Pigouvian tax versus a market for permits when the ME⁻ *curve is uncertain*

a comparison between a tax or marketable permits, is that the policies are designed under perfect knowledge about the conditions of the acting parties in the market, that is, the firms which pay the tax or buy the emission permits. Hence we know exactly how the firms will react to the alternative policy measures, which depend on the same beliefs (right or wrong) about the marginal benefit curve.

A more complicated situation arises when the marginal benefit function is known with certainty, but the opportunity cost to clean is not known and wrongly estimated. This means that the policy-makers, in the case of marketable permits, are able to control volume (the number of permits) but that the price of the permits is uncertain. If a Pigouvian tax is chosen, the 'price of the emissions' (the tax rate) is certain, while the volume of emissions is uncertain. A possible case is depicted in Figure 1.9.

Here t^0 represents the Pigouvian tax which is based on the presumption that the marginal benefit function is ME^- and the demand function for permits is $D'_E - D'_E$. E_0 is the number of permits issued under the same assumption. If the true opportunity cost of cleaning is $D''_E - D''_E$, the market price for the original volume of permits becomes P''_0, and too much cleaning is carried out since the opportunity cost of cleaning is underestimated. The social loss from the mistake is the difference between the opportunity cost of cleaning and the

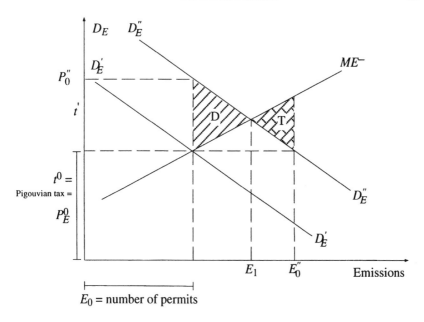

Figure 1.9   Comparison between tax and a market for emission permits when the opportunity cost of cleaning (the demand curve) is uncertain

marginal benefit function for the extra emissions needed to reach the socially desirable number, E_1. The loss is measured by the area labelled D.

Under a Pigouvian tax equal to t^0 there will be too little cleaning and emissions will be E_0''. The reason is that the Pigouvian tax underestimates the 'equilibrium price' for emissions, owing to an underestimation of the demand curve for permits. The social loss is the area T, which is the difference between the marginal benefits and the opportunity cost of cleaning for the units emitted in excess of the socially desirable level of emissions.

In this case the area T is less than D, and a Pigouvian tax is preferable to a market for permits. It is easy to construct a case where the opposite is true. What would happen, for example, if the marginal benefit curve were vertical? Clearly, since the desirable number of permits would be independent of the demand function, a market for permits would give the right answer whereas a tax would lead to excessive emissions. The opposite would be true if the marginal benefit curve were horizontal; that is, the willingness to pay for a reduction of emissions were independent of the volume of emissions. Now the tax would work perfectly, while the market for permits would allow too few emissions.

The essence is that the choice between marketable permits or taxes, from the point of view of our ignorance about the position of the relevant demand and cost functions, is an empirical matter. What can be said is that if the slope of the marginal benefit function were steep – this would be the case when one was dealing with hazardous waste – close control of quantity becomes important, and marketable permits are preferable to Pigouvian taxes. On the other hand, if the marginal willingness to pay for cleaning up the volume of emissions is constant, a tax is a better method than controlling emissions through a fixed amount of marketable permits.[5]

5.2   Imperfect Competition and Externalities

We will here deal with a special case of imperfect competition, which is known as monopoly, where a single seller faces many buyers. This means that the monopolist, when he decides how much to produce to maximize profits, takes into account what his production does to the market price. In perfect markets the firms are so numerous that they take the market price as parametrically given. Hence if a competitive solution is compared with a monopoly solution for the same market, we will find that the monopoly produces too little output and charges too high a price. If, in addition, it pollutes, this means that the social costs the pollution causes have to be internalized into the cost structure of the firm. The latter can, for instance, be done through a Pigouvian tax. Without going into detail, we can say that the monopoly solution to externalities contains two market failures: too little is produced and too much is emitted per unit of output. The policy problem can now be illustrated by the rather sterile Figure 1.10. Say that the original equilibrium is determined by the intersection of two curves (structural relations, related to the demand and cost conditions of the monopoly) P and E. The uncontrolled solution is point e_0, q_0, and the social optimum is given by point A with emissions e_A and production q_A. To move the economy to the social optimum it is not sufficient to move only one structural relation. We will have to shift both curves in Figure 1.10. Say that the E curve is shifted downwards to E' by a 'Pigouvian like' tax, and the P curve is shifted upwards to P' by a subsidy per unit of output which increases production. In this way we can make both curves intersect at point A, the socially desirable outcome.

The lesson is that, since externalities in a monopoly comprise two market failures, we will, in general, need at least two means to move the economy to the socially desirable outcome. There are, however, obvious practical problems connected with the subsidization of a monopoly, which is already making an extra (monopoly) profit from restraining production. A subsidy would mean that the profit were even larger. Therefore, in practice, a policy-maker would have to go for a second-best solution and choose a 'Pigouvian like' tax in such a way

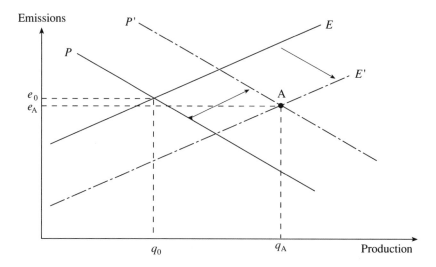

Figure 1.10   The policy problem under monopoly and externalities

that the social surplus is maximized, given the restriction that no other policy means are allowed. In terms of Figure 1.10, he would choose to move the E curve in such a way that the crossing with the P curve were as close as possible to the socially desirable outcome. The resulting tax would depend on the demand and cost functions in a rather complex way. However, since a monopolist is producing less than an industry in perfect competitive circumstances, we will not be surprised if the second-best Pigouvian tax on emissions is lower than the corresponding first-best tax. The lower output means, in itself, less environmental damage.

5.3   Non-convexities

So far we have essentially dealt with the externality problem at the level of the firm. However, to determine the Pigouvian tax structure in an economy with externalities we must, in practice, solve a complicated control problem, where the preferences of all consumers and the technologies of all firms are involved. The idea is to pick one socially desirable outcome to aim at. The next problem is how to get there. If we use Pigouvian taxes it must be true that the optimizing actions of firms and consumers within a market economy with Pigouvian taxes lead us to a market solution which corresponds to the socially desirable outcome we aimed at in the first place. This is certainly not self-evident, and it turns out that the existence of externalities, if they are serious enough, leads to a complication which economists (and mathematicians) call non-convexities.

Consider Figure 1.11, where the shaded area represents the production possibility set of an economy where two goods are produced as outputs. A production possibility set is, broadly speaking, the feasible production possibilities of goods, given existing resources of labour, capital and energy.

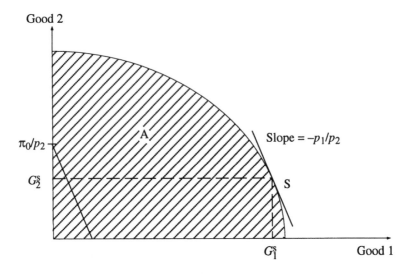

Figure 1.11   The convex production possibility set A

Any point within the set is feasible, but the efficient points (given that more is always better than less) consist of the boundary of the set and are all, potentially, socially desirable outcomes. The boundary is called the transformation curve. Set A has the property that if we choose any two points which belong to the set, all points on a straight line between the two points also belong to the set. Such a set is called a convex set.

Say that we would like the firms to produce at point S on the boundary, where much of good 1 and little of good 2 are produced. How can we achieve this? Since firms are maximizing profits, we should make it relatively more profitable to produce good 1 than good 2, and this can be done by imposing Pigouvian taxes to make the price the producer receives for good 1 higher than the price for good 2. Given that we can neglect costs, the total profit in the economy can be written as:

$$\pi = P_1 G_1 + P_2 G_2, \qquad (1.7)$$

where P_1 and P_2 are the prices the producer receives of the two goods, and G_1 and G_2 are the corresponding volumes. For a given level of profit, say π_0, equation (1.7) represents a straight line:

$$G_2 = -\frac{P_1}{P_2}G_1 + \frac{\pi_0}{P_2}. \qquad (1.8)$$

The slope of the line is

$$-\frac{P_1}{P_2},$$

and when $G_1 = 0$, we have

$$G_2 = \frac{\pi_0}{P_2}.$$

The line is depicted inside the production possibility set in Figure 1.11. If we increase the profit requirement at constant prices, the line will be moved in a north-easterly direction. Given the slope we have chosen, it will eventually be a tangent at point S on the transformation curve. A little reflection reveals that point S, the socially desirable outcome, maximizes total profit at the chosen prices. In other words, the socially desirable outcome can be reached by profit maximization within a market economy provided the price system is 'right' – which can be achieved by economic instruments such as Pigouvian taxes. Further reflection also reveals that any point on the transformation curve can be reached by profit maximization, provided that the price ratio P_1/P_2 is appropriately chosen: this can be done by, for example, taxes.

Consider now Figure 1.12, where we have drawn a production possibility set which is non-convex. The test is that if we choose any two points on the transformation curve, no points on the straight line between the two chosen points will belong to set B. As an example consider a steelworks and a laundry industry. The steelworks can produce 1 unit of output with 1 unit of labour: for example, 10 units of output with 10 units of labour, 20 units of output with 20 units of labour, and so on. Similarly, the laundry industry can produce 10 units of output with 1 unit of labour, for example, 100 units of output with 10 units of labour, 200 units of output with 20 units of labour and so on, if *no* steel is produced. If the steelworks does produce, the output of the laundry industry is halved. This means that, for example, the convex combination 20 units of labour, 10 units of steel and 100 units of laundry is not possible.

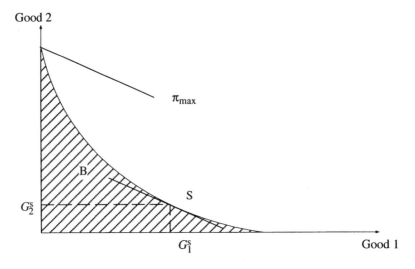

Note: The profit in the tangent point S is lower than the profit in the corner where only good 2 is produced.

Figure 1.12   The non-convex production possibility set B

Assume that, as in the preceding figure, point S is the socially desirable outcome. To reach it through profit maximization the idea is to introduce a price system where the price the producer receives for good 1 is higher than for good 2. However, this will no longer work. Profit maximization under such a price system will move us to a corner solution in which only good 2 is produced. Note that the profit in the tangent point S is lower than the profit in the corner where only good 2 is produced. In other words, the socially desirable outcome cannot be reached in a market economy where competitive firms maximize profits.

The shape of the transformation curve in Figure 1.12 means that the possibility of transferring resources, from the production of good 2 to the production of good 1, deteriorates as the production of good 1 increases from zero to the corner solution.[6] This is a consequence of the fact that the transformation curve is bent towards the origin, and this is exactly what one would expect an extremely negative externality to produce, that is, when the production of one good hampers the production of another.

The relevance of non-convexities for environmental policy is that they make it more difficult to reach a socially desirable outcome. Market solutions generated from profit and utility maximization do not necessarily produce socially desirable outcomes, even if we try to correct for the negative external effects that are not handled by markets.

6. VALUATION OF BENEFITS AND COSTS OF POLLUTION CONTROL

To use policy instruments such as emission permits and Pigouvian taxes appropriately, one has to measure, in terms of money, the damage done by pollution (the marginal benefits from abatement) as well as the opportunity cost of control. If a change for the better is considered we want to measure the net benefits of control.

Since environmental problems are, generally speaking, caused by the lack of appropriate markets, it is natural that valuing environmental goods concerns to a large extent the valuation of goods not priced in any market. For example, how do you measure the value of the damage done by water pollution, or to put it in benefit terms: what are the benefits to be realized by controlling discharges into water from sources such as pulp and paper mills?

Many environmental goods have 'public goods' properties in the sense that they are consumed by all people in almost the same quantities. The problem of valuing the benefits of, say, cleaner air is technically the same problem as valuing the willingness to pay for national defence. The theory of public goods provides both theoretical and practical answers.

Economists and econometricians have also, since the end of the 1940s, worked specifically on the environmental valuation problem. An early contribution was made when the famous American economist and statistician, Harold Hotelling, in a letter to the Director of the National Park Service in 1947, said that a recreational site could be indirectly valued via the travel costs of its visitors (the travel cost method).

Hotelling's idea was that the number of trips made by the nearest visitors constitutes the demand for the site at almost zero price (travel costs are almost zero) and that the number of trips made by the visitors at large distances constitutes the demand close to the 'choke-off price' (the price at which demand is zero). In this manner, by also considering the travel costs of visitors at intermediate distances, one is able to construct a demand curve (or an MWP curve) for recreation. The area below such a curve measures the total aggregate willingness to pay for the recreational site.

The damage done by air pollution in a certain area can be indirectly valued by comparing the cost of housing in the polluted area with the price of the same kind of housing in a non-polluted area. The difference between the house prices measures, in ideal circumstances (when the goods are really the same; statistical techniques can be used to control for differences), the damage done by air pollution or the value of cleaner air. This method is usually referred to as 'hedonic pricing'.

There are many environmental damages which cannot be valued by means of the travel cost method, and the hedonic pricing model cannot be used to evaluate people's willingness to pay for the preservation of rare flowers or animals. By asking people hypothetical questions about their willingness to pay for such things as the preservation of species, cleaner air or a cleaner river, one can hope to reveal part of the true value of these environmental goods. This method is usually referred to as the 'contingent valuation method'. It has recently become very popular, but is also much debated.

Sometimes it is wise to solve part of the valuation problem by creating new markets or by a more precise specification of property rights. By establishing a market for permits, firms' marginal willingness to pay for emissions is elicited. Unfortunately, without knowing the marginal benefits of getting rid of the emissions (the ME^- curve in Figure 1.7), we cannot determine the optimal number of permits. The property right idea introduced by Coase can, if one picks an appropriate situation to apply it to, solve the valuation problems on both sides of the market. In this manner, both the valuation and the environmental problems are solved simultaneously.

Thus the valuation of environmental goods is difficult, and all the methods above have – in spite of considerable scientific progress – their disadvantages. Many of the details are covered in Chapter 2 of this volume.

7.   CONCLUDING COMMENTS

We have made frequent use of the terminology 'a socially desirable outcome'. We have defined it as a situation where goods are allocated in such a manner that one cannot improve the situation of one individual without worsening it for someone else. It is obvious that a socially desirable outcome has attractive efficiency properties. If it were possible to improve the situation of one individual without worsening it for someone else, it would be wrong to say that the initial allocation was efficient.

Economists refer to socially desirable outcomes as Pareto-optima, named after the Italian economist and sociologist, Wilfred Pareto, who was the first to introduce the concept in economics. Technically it is a partial ordering, since we cannot, without using subjective values, rank two efficient situations. Assume that we have a 'two-person economy' with a given endowment of goods (no production) to be allocated to the two individuals. It would be efficient to give the whole bundle to either person (there are also other efficient allocations), but we cannot say, without introducing a value judgement, to whom we should give the goods. Essentially this comes down to saying that efficiency considerations are easier for economists to deal with than distributional issues.

The nice thing about a perfect market economy (an economy with many consumers and firms which compete with one another and which contains no externalities) is that it generates a socially desirable outcome or a Pareto-optimum. If externalities are present, we have to correct the incentives in the economy in order to produce a Pareto-optimum. The ways in which this can be accomplished have been the subject of this chapter.

It has also been implicit in the discussion here that externalities are a problem, since markets which can handle all the unwanted consequences of economic interaction do not exist. The reasons for the lack of markets can be many, but when we are faced with a public goods externality such as air pollution, it will be obvious that a spontaneous market to deal with the problem is very unlikely to materialize.

On the other hand, we would expect the seriousness of the externality problem, *ceteris paribus*, to decrease with the number of markets in the economy. This means that we would expect the environmental problems in a market economy to be less serious than in a command (planned) economy.

FURTHER READING

There are numerous books, elementary and more advanced, which deal with externalities and environmental problems. Any elementary textbook in economics contains a section dealing with markets and externalities.

Among the more specialized elementary textbooks on environmental economics, we would like to recommend the following:

Dasgupta, P.S. (1982), *The Control of Resources*, London: Basil Blackwell.
Fisher, A.C. (1981), *Resource and Environmental Economics*, London: Cambridge University Press.
Tietenberg, T. (1992), *Environmental and Natural Resource Economics*, New York: HarperCollins.

Among the more advanced textbooks are the following:

Baumol, W.J. and W.E. Oates (1988), *The Theory of Environmental Policy*, Cambridge: Cambridge University Press.
Dasgupta, P.S. and G.M. Heal (1992), *The Economic Theory of Exhaustible Resources*, Cambridge: Cambridge University Press.

A kind of bible on the theory of environmental economics is:

Mäler, K.G. (1974), *Environmental Economics: A Theoretical Inquiry*, Baltimore: Johns Hopkins University Press.

This book is recommended for advanced students. Mäler has also written a chapter relevant for students of externalities in:

Kneese, A.V. and J.L. Sweeney (eds) (1985), *Handbook of Natural Resource and Energy Economics*, Vol. I, Amsterdam: North-Holland.

Environmental policy problems are dealt with in more detail in Chapters 7 and 9 in this volume. A good elementary textbook which covers both modern welfare economics and environmental economics is:

Johansson, P.O. (1991), *An Introduction to Modern Welfare Economics*, Cambridge: Cambridge University Press.

ACKNOWLEDGEMENTS

The author wishes to thank the participants of the COPERNICUS Environment and Resource Economics workshop held in Wageningen, The Netherlands, 17–19 May 1993, for their comments, and Professor Henk Folmer of Wageningen University, who helped to make the final version comprehensible, at least to economists.

NOTES

1. Adam Smith, *The Wealth of Nations*, first published in 1776, Book IV, Chapter II, p. 477.
2. The example is borrowed from Varian (1987).
3. Technically, the marginal cost function is the first derivative of the total cost function

$$\frac{dTC(q)}{dq} = MC(q)$$

   which corresponds to the slope of the total cost curve.
4. The abatement option was assumed away in our one-firm example.
5. This was first shown by Weitzman (1974). It is possible to construct hybrid systems where taxes and subsidies, together with direct regulations, are used simultaneously. These are, disregarding the 'costs of complexity', better than both marketable permits and taxes.
6. Note that if the transformation curve is linear this rate of transformation will be constant and if it is curved, as in Figure 1.12, the rate of transformation will increase with such a move.

REFERENCES

Baumol, W.J. and W.E. Oates (1988), *The Theory of Environmental Policy*, Cambridge: Cambridge University Press.

Chesterton, G.K. (1961), *Mr Pond's Paradoxer* (*The Paradoxes of Mr Pond*), Stockholm: Biblioteksförlaget.

Coase, R.H. (1960), 'The problem of social cost', *Journal of Law and Economics*, **3**, 1–44.

Crocker, T.D. (1965), 'The structuring of atmospheric pollution control systems', in H. Wolozin (ed.), *The Economics of Pollution*, New York: Norton.

Pigou, A.C. (1920), *The Economics of Welfare*, London: Macmillan.

Varian, H.R. (1987), *Intermediate Microeconomics: A Modern Approach*, New York: Norton.

Weitzman, M.L. (1974), 'Prices versus quantities', *Review of Economic Studies*, **41**, 477–91.

2. Microeconomics of valuation

Per-Olov Johansson

1. INTRODUCTION

There is a huge literature on the practical methodologies that can be used to
assess the value of environmental assets. It might seem quite natural to simply
concentrate on these practical approaches. After all, one is ultimately interested
in estimating, say, the willingness to pay for a particular environmental project.
However, such a view overlooks the fact that the money measures used in
empirical studies are, or at least should be, derived from economic theory. That
is, they should be defined in such a way that they are consistent with, and have
the properties suggested by, economic theory. There are many examples in the
empirical literature of studies that are flawed because the authors lack sufficient
knowledge about the theoretical foundations of the measures they define and
estimate. It is therefore important for practitioners also to have a good understanding of the microeconomics of valuation.

   The purpose of this chapter is to provide a survey of the theoretical properties
of the money measures most often used in empirical studies within the environmental field. The chapter is structured as follows. As a background, section
2 briefly presents different demand and consumer surplus concepts for a priced
private commodity. This is the standard case found in any textbook on microeconomics. Section 3 introduces public goods and the decision problem facing
an individual who values not only his consumption of private goods but also
the environment. A simple graphical toolkit for such analysis is developed.
Section 4 defines consumer surplus measures for an environmental asset. The
properties of these consumer surplus measures are examined and discussed in
section 5. Section 6 discusses the possibility of using market prices to assess
the value of changes in environmental quality. It is often claimed that an
individual not only values his or her own consumption of goods and services
generated by the environment. In addition there might be altruistic values and
existence values. These considerations and their implications for valuation are
discussed in section 7. The question of how to handle risk is addressed in section
8, while section 9 presents a useful interpretation of money measures. Section
10 is devoted to the aggregation issue, that is, the question of whether we can

obtain any useful information from the sum across individuals of their monetary valuation of an environmental asset. The chapter ends with a few concluding remarks. An appendix provides some technical details and a brief discussion of producer surplus measures, since environmental projects often affect firms' profits. Individuals are affected by (value) such changes in their capacity as owners of firms.

2. CONSUMER SURPLUS MEASURES FOR A PRICED PRIVATE COMMODITY

The focus of this chapter is the theory for valuation of environmental assets. Nevertheless, as a point of reference, it is useful first to consider the standard case found in any textbook on microeconomics. That is, an individual's demand for and valuation of a private commodity such as bread or wine or petrol. In Figure 2.1, x denotes the quantity of the commodity purchased by the considered individual, while p denotes the unit price of the commodity. The demand curve depicted in the figure is assumed to have a negative slope. The lower the price of the commodity, the more of the commodity is purchased. There is a substitution effect; that is, a change in demand in response to the price decrease, holding the individual's utility constant. This effect is positive in the case of a decrease in the price. There is also an income effect. This states the rate at which the individual's demand changes as a response to an increase in income, prices remaining constant.[1] The considered good is assumed to be normal, implying that the income effect is positive; if the good instead were inferior, the income effect would be negative. The sum of the substitution and the income effects yields the total response of demand to a small change in the price. This relationship holds, all other things being equal. That is, other parameters that might affect demand, such as prices of other commodities and the individual's income, are kept constant. Changing the price of another commodity and/or income would shift the demand curve outwards or inwards in the figure. The kind of demand function considered here is referred to as an ordinary or a Marshallian demand function. The ordinary or Marshallian demand is the demand relationship that we can observe in a market.

The area to the left of the ordinary demand curve above the ruling price, say p^0 in Figure 2.1, of the commodity is referred to as a consumer surplus. This surplus is often interpreted as a measure of what an individual is willing to pay over and above what he actually spends on the commodity. However, this is a questionable interpretation. In order to see why, let us introduce a compensated or Hicksian demand curve. Then the individual is kept at a pre-specified level of utility. If we consider a *ceteris paribus* decrease in the price of the

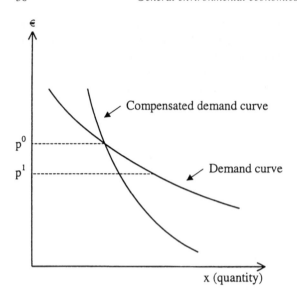

Figure 2.1   Marshallian and Hicksian demand curves

commodity, the individual's utility will obviously increase. Therefore, in order to preserve the pre-specified level of utility, the individual's income must be adjusted (reduced) as the price is changed (reduced). In terms of Figure 2.1, let us assume that we want to keep the individual at the utility level corresponding to price level p^0. If the price is decreased we must reduce the individual's income in order to keep him at his initial level of utility. If the price is increased above p^0 his income must instead be increased in order for him to be able to attain the initial level of utility.

Changing the commodity price and simultaneously adjusting income so that the individual remains at the pre-specified level of utility traces out an income-compensated or Hicksian demand curve of the kind illustrated in Figure 2.1. If the commodity is normal in the sense that demand increases with income, the compensated demand curve is steeper than the Marshallian demand curve. This is so because the Hicksian demand curve presumes that income is reduced when the price of the commodity is reduced. This obviously counteracts the increase in the demand for a commodity associated with a decrease in its price (provided demand is increasing in income). Similarly, if the price is increased, then something must be added to income in order to preserve the initial level of utility. This counteracts the reduction in demand following a price increase. Also note that the Marshallian and Hicksian demand curves intersect (coincide) when the price is equal to p^0. This is so because the Hicksian demand curve is drawn under the assumption that the individual's utility level is throughout preserved at the level corresponding to price p^0. At this price the two demand curves correspond to the same level of utility (income). Hence they must coincide.

The area to the left of a Hicksian demand curve can be given an interpretation in terms of income. Let us consider the Hicksian demand curve depicted in Figure 2.1. Assume that the price is reduced from p^0 to p^1. The area to the left of the Hicksian demand curve between the two prices corresponds to the maximum income the individual is willing to give up in exchange for the considered decrease in price. Recall that we reduce income as the price is reduced so as to keep the individual at the level of utility attained when price is equal to p^0. If the price instead is increased from p^1 to p^0, the area corresponds to the income compensation the individual must obtain in order to be as well off with the increase in price as without it. Thus, in the case of a Hicksian demand curve, the consumer surplus can be given a straightforward interpretation in terms of income. The area to the left of the Marshallian demand curve between p^0 and p^1 in Figure 2.1 cannot be given the same interpretation (since the area differs from the corresponding area to the left of the Hicksian demand curve). In fact, and as hinted at above, there is no simple interpretation of the Marshallian consumer surplus measure.[2] This is also an important reason why economists prefer to use compensated demand functions rather than ordinary ones in welfare evaluations.

We have thus far considered a Hicksian demand curve that is drawn under the assumption that the individual throughout remains at the level of utility corresponding to price p^0. However, we could let the individual stay at another level of utility, say the one obtained if price equals p^1. This would generate another compensated or Hicksian demand curve, intersecting (coinciding with) the Marshallian one, not at p^0 but at p^1. This concludes our brief review of demand concepts for private commodities. For further discussion of Marshallian and Hicksian demand concepts for priced commodities and their properties, the reader is referred to any textbook on microeconomics.

Finally, the reader should note the following. Our money measures are not related to actual payments or compensations. The measures are used to find out how much an individual would be willing to pay for a change or the compensation he would need to accept a change voluntarily. We simply transform changes from unobservable units of utility to observable monetary units. In terms of Figure 2.1, since we don't know what his utility function looks like, we cannot figure out whether he would gain 10 or 50 or 500 units of utility if the price fell from p^0 to p^1. In contrast, we can estimate/observe how much income he is willing to give up in exchange for the price decrease.

3. INTRODUCING ENVIRONMENTAL COMMODITIES

The commodity considered in the previous section is called a private good. A pure private good (say, an apple) is characterized by rivalry and exclusivity. For rival goods, extra or additional consumption involves extra or marginal costs of production. Exclusivity means that one person's consumption of a unit of a commodity excludes others from consuming that unit of the good. Some goods and services generated by the environment can be labelled private goods. The fish a fisherman catches and the berries a bilberry-picker gathers provide examples.

However, for many goods and services generated by the environment one or both of these properties do not apply. The opposite of a private good is called a public good. A public good is characterized by the fact that it is non-rival. This means that one person's consumption of the good does not affect others' consumption of the good. For example, if you switch on your television set to watch a news programme, this will not affect other news watchers. Thus the marginal cost of having an extra watcher is virtually equal to zero. Similarly, if an additional bird-watcher arrives at a site, this will not reduce the possibility for those who are already there to watch birds. Thus, in this case also, the marginal cost of having an additional watcher is virtually equal to zero. However, it might be the case that the marginal cost becomes positive if the number of consumers passes some critical level. In the case of bird-watchers, if so many people visit the site that there is crowding, then an additional visitor will adversely affect those already there. Then the marginal visitor inflicts a cost on others.

Sometimes, it is also argued that a (pure) public good is non-exclusive. That is, it should not be possible to exclude a person from consuming the good. This might be true for some public goods. For example, if somebody installs a filter in a smokestack in order to improve the air quality in the local surroundings, it is hardly possible to exclude visitors from (free of charge) breathing the air in the area. In other cases, it is possible to exclude individuals from consuming the good. An example is provided by cable television, where only paying viewers are allowed to consume.

It is thus important to realize that there is a whole range of goods, ranging from purely private ones to purely public ones. In addition, often a 'package' of goods and services is consumed. This is true for a charter trip to the Bahamas, where the traveller purchases a particular combination of goods, including the flight, a hotel room of a particular standard and with a particular distance to the nearest beach, and so on. In order to be able to watch birds, one must typically travel by car or bus to the site in question. In a sense the bird-watcher can be viewed as producing a recreational service using petrol, time and other factors as inputs (although, of course, he also consumes the service he is producing).

Let us consider an individual who values both his consumption of private goods and services (food, housing, cinemas, and so on) and his consumption of environmental goods and services (water quality, air quality, bird-watching, and so on). In order to simplify the exposition and to be able to make a simple graphical illustration, we assume that there is just one commodity of each type. This assumption can be interpreted as follows. The consumption of different private goods and services is aggregated into a single private commodity. This is similar to the aggregation procedure often employed in macroeconomics, where we typically use an aggregate measure of private consumption. Similarly, we assume that we can somehow aggregate 'consumption' of different environmental goods and services into a single environmental commodity. We will label this commodity (an index of) environmental quality. In what follows, environmental quality will be considered as a pure public good that is supplied free of charge. (It is assumed that any costs for an improved environmental quality are covered by lump-sum taxes.)

From the point of view of an individual there need not be any fundamental difference between the private good and the good we label environmental quality. More is reasonably preferred to less of both goods. Thus letting him consume more of one good without reducing his consumption of the other good would increase his level of utility. It is not unreasonable to assume that there is a trade-off between the two goods. Let us assume that this assumption holds. Then if the individual's consumption of one good is reduced, it is possible to keep his utility unchanged by allowing him to consume more of the other good. The indifference curves are then downward sloping in the usual way, familiar from microeconomics. This case is illustrated in Figure 2.2, where the private good is denoted x and environmental quality is denoted z. If the individual's tastes exhibit a diminishing marginal rate of substitution, then the slope of indifference curves gets flatter as we move to the right in Figure 2.2. The more that is already consumed of a good, the less the individual is willing to give up of the other good in exchange for an additional unit of the first good.

Thus, although one of the goods considered here is environmental quality, we can employ the tools familiar from any textbook on microeconomics. This is not to say that there might not be cases where we must deviate from the standard assumptions. To illustrate, if environmental quality means quality of the air to breathe, it does not make sense to let this quality approach zero, since the individual will die. There will simply be no trade-off between the private good and air quality if we consider sufficiently low levels of air quality. On the other hand, if environmental quality is taken to mean the quality of a particular natural park, most of us can certainly survive without the park. In any case, the standard assumptions about individual choice found in any textbook on microeconomics will be used as the benchmark or basic case.

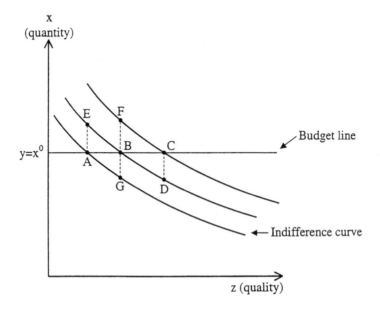

Figure 2.2   Compensating and equivalent variations associated with changes in environmental quality

Let us next assume that the individual under consideration has a fixed income. This income is spent on the single (aggregated) private good, since we have assumed that environmental quality is supplied free of charge. The individual's budget line is therefore horizontal in Figure 2.2. Let us assume that the individual's budget constraint is $y = px^0$, where y is the fixed income, p (in what follows set equal to unity) is the price of a unit of the private good, and x^0 is the number of units of the private good purchased when income is y. Given these assumptions, the budget line will be situated x^0 $(= y)$ units above the origin. Where on this budget line the individual ends up depends on the quality of the environment. It is assumed that the individual is unable to affect this quality. The better the quality of the environment, the further to the right on the budget line the individual will end up. Thus the higher the quality of the environment, the higher the utility of the individual.

4.   CONSUMER SURPLUS MEASURES FOR AN ENVIRONMENTAL COMMODITY

Equipped with the tools presented in the previous section, let us now consider the following experiment. Assume that the individual is at point B in Figure 2.2, and that environmental quality is improved so that the individual is moved to point C. There is no way to observe directly how much this improvement is valued by the individual, at least not in terms of utility. However, assume that the individual's income is reduced in such a way that the individual is moved to point D. Then he remains at his initial level of utility following the considered improvement in environmental quality (since both points B and D are on the initial indifference curve). Thus we can let the individual express his valuation of the improvement in environmental quality in terms of something observable, namely income. The considered individual's willingness to pay for a shift from point B to point C in Figure 2.2 is measured by the vertical distance C–D.

Consider next a deterioration in environmental quality such that the individual is moved from point B to point A in Figure 2.2. This shift reduces the individual's level of utility. The individual's willingness to pay for this shift must be negative; that is, he would need a compensation in order to be at least indifferent to the shift. A monetary compensation corresponding to the vertical distance A–E would keep the individual at his initial level of utility (that is, on the indifference curve passing through point B).

The money measure just defined is referred to as the compensating variation. This is a payment (compensation) such that the individual remains at his initial level of utility following an improvement (deterioration) in, say, environmental quality.

Alternatively, we might let the individual remain at the final (rather than at the initial) level of utility. Consider once again an improvement in environmental quality moving the individual from point B to point C. Consider the monetary compensation the individual would need in order voluntarily to accept that there is no improvement in environmental quality. The vertical distance B–F in Figure 2.2 measures this compensation. This is so because points F and C are situated on the same (the 'final') indifference curve. If we consider a move in the opposite direction, say from B to A, the individual would be willing to pay an amount corresponding to B–G in the figure in order to 'prevent' environmental quality from deteriorating. Then he would end up on the same indifference curve as if the environment deteriorated from B to A.

This monetary measure is known as the equivalent variation. It is a compensation (payment) such that the individual attains the same level of welfare as if environmental quality were improved (deteriorated). Thus the equivalent variation is a compensation for an improvement in environmental quality that fails to occur while it is a willingness to pay for preventing deterioration in environmental quality.

The reader should note that we need both these measures in order to be able to define willingness to pay measures (or compensation measures) for shifts of environmental quality in both directions (that is, from B to C and from B to A in Figure 2.2). The reason is that for shifts in one direction a measure will reflect the willingness to pay while it will correspond to a compensation for shifts in the opposite direction. In what follows, willingness to pay will often be abbreviated WTP, while WTA will refer to willingness to accept compensation. The compensation variation is often abbreviated to CV, while EV refers to the equivalent variation.

The reader should note the following. The money measures of a non-priced commodity whose quantity/quality is exogenously changed (from the point of view of the individual), as is the case in Figure 2.2, is somewhat easier to define than the corresponding measures for a priced commodity that can be purchased in any quantity. In the latter case we have a substitution as well as an income effect; see section 2 or any textbook on microeconomics. In the case of exogenous changes in quantity/quality of a non-priced commodity there is no possibility for the individual to adjust (substitute) his consumption following a change in a parameter.

However, in both cases one can use indifference curves and budget lines to derive compensated demand (or WTP) curves. In the case of environmental quality, we can use Figure 2.2 to calculate the WTP for a shift from B to C, the WTP for a shift from C to a point to the right of C, and so on. Depict these 'points' in a figure with euros on the vertical axis and environmental quality on the horizontal axis. Connecting the points yields (a rough estimate of) a compensated demand curve for environmental quality; it is a rough estimate since we here define WTP for non-marginal changes. Two such compensated demand (or rather marginal WTP) curves are depicted in Figure 2.3. Note that in drawing these compensated demand curves the individual is held at a particular level of utility. Assume that point B in Figure 2.2 is taken to be the initial level of utility (and that point B in Figure 2.2 corresponds to environmental quality z^0 in Figure 2.3). Then the compensated demand or marginal WTP curve based on the CV measure holds the individual at the utility level (indifference curve) corresponding to point B. If point C in Figure 2.2 is taken to be the final level of utility, then the marginal WTP curve based on the EV measure holds the individual at the indifference curve passing through point C. Since environmental quality, by assumption, is non-priced, the change in consumer surplus caused by a change in environmental quality is measured as an area under a compensated demand curve. We can speak of a (change in) consumer surplus since the vertical distance between a point on the horizontal axis in Figure 2.3 and the marginal WTP curve measures what the individual is willing to pay for a small increase in z over and above the price of z (which is equal to zero). In Figure 2.3, the change in consumer surplus associated with a change in environmental quality from z^0 to z^1 is equal to area 1 or area 1 + 2, depending on whether we base our evaluation on the compensating variation measure or the equivalent variation measure. This is in contrast to a priced private good, where we measure the change in consumer surplus due to a price

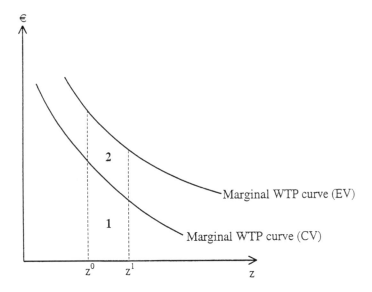

Figure 2.3   Ordinary and compensated WTP curves for environmental quality

change as an area to the left of a (compensated) demand curve between the initial and the final price; recall Figure 2.1.

In this chapter we will not discuss the details of how to estimate a (compensated) demand curve for environmental quality. However, let us consider a simple illustration. Assume that we are considering air quality in a region. The present level of air quality is somehow known by everyone to be equal to 50 on a scale running from 0 (worst possible quality level) to 100 (best). We make the current level of air quality correspond to environmental quality z^0 in Figure 2.3. A random sample of people, drawn from the population of those living in the region, is asked for their willingness to pay for a small improvement in air quality from 50 to, say, 52. Suppose that the average WTP for this sample is €20. Another random sample of people is asked for their willingness to pay for a shift in air quality from 50 to 54. Let us say that the average WTP in this sample is €30. Then by looking at the difference between the two WTP estimates we can infer that the average WTP for a shift in air quality from 52 to 54 is €10 (holding the level of utility at the level corresponding to the one achieved when air quality is 50). Thus in terms of Figure 2.3 we have estimated two 'points' on the compensated demand curve near and to the right of z^0 holding the individual at his initial level of utility. As is expected, the WTP for the first change, that is, from 50 to 52, exceeds the WTP for the change from 52 to 54. This indicates a downward-sloping demand curve.

Asking people about their WTP for changes in air quality from 50 to, say, 56 and from 50 to 58, respectively, would provide us with further 'points' on a compensated demand curve. The survey method used in this simple illustration is called the contingent valuation method. The reader is referred to Chapter 3 for details on this and other empirical methods used in assessing the WTP for environmental quality.

Finally, the reader should note the following. When the quantity purchased of a commodity is fixed from the point of view of the individual, some authors prefer to speak of compensating surplus and equivalent surplus, respectively, instead of compensating and equivalent variation, respectively. In any case, in what follows we will throughout call them the compensating variation and the equivalent variation, respectively.

5.   PROPERTIES OF MONEY MEASURES

Our two money measures defined in the previous section have a nice theoretical property. Whenever a project increases an individual's utility, the compensating variation will be a payment, while the equivalent variation will be a compensation. This result holds for much more general cases than the one considered in Figure 2.2. The reader might consider a project which increases the price of the private good but improves the quality of the environment. Such a project might increase, leave unchanged or reduce the individual's level of utility. However, if the CV (EV) for the project is a payment (compensation), we know that the project has increased the individual's utility; see also the appendix. If the CV turns out to be a compensation while the EV is a payment, we know that the project reduces the individual's level of utility. If it holds that CV = EV = 0, then we know that the project in question leaves utility unchanged. In this sense our money measures truly indicate how a project affects utility. Using Figure 2.2, the reader can easily verify this property. Hint: start from point B and let the project cause a simultaneous increase in the price of the private good and in environmental quality. The price increase will shift the budget line downwards. The improvement in environmental quality will move the individual to the right along the new budget line. Whether the project causes utility to increase or decrease depends on how much you increase the price relative to how much you improve environmental quality. Finally, define the CV and the EV associated with the project. You will find that they have the sign property established above.

This property of our money measures also holds in the case where we have many private goods and a multidimensional indicator of environmental quality. A project might cause a change in many or even all relative prices in the economy as well as affecting many of our different indicators of environmental quality. Some prices might go up while others go down. Similarly, the project might have a positive impact on some environmental indicators (say, reduce sulphur emissions) and a negative impact on others (say, adversely affect a natural park). Still, our money measures will truly indicate how the individual's unobservable utility is affected by the considered and very complex project. In practice this means that although we don't know what an individual's utility function looks like, simply by collecting information on the CV and/or EV associated with a project we can infer whether or not the project increases the individual's level of utility. For the practical methodologies one can use to collect information on our money measures, the reader is referred to Chapter 3.

The question arises whether our money measures can be infinitely large. Obviously, the WTP for a change is bounded by the individual's income (if we disregard the possibility that he has a fortune or is able to borrow money). However, a compensation is of course not related to income; that is, the WTA might be infinitely large. In order to be able to say more, it is important to make a distinction between essential and non-essential commodities. A commodity is said to be essential if there is no combination of other goods that can entirely compensate you for the loss of the essential commodity. However much you get of other commodities, your utility without the essential commodity is lower than the lowest possible utility you would achieve with the essential commodity. An example is provided by life. There is no compensation for the certain loss of life. If an environmental commodity is essential, the indifference curves will not intersect the vertical axis. This case is illustrated in Figure 2.4(a). Since the indifference curves do not 'reach' the vertical axis it does not make sense to define money measures for changes that would cause environmental quality to fall to zero. A simple illustration is provided by air quality. If this quality approaches zero, death will follow. Hence, it does not make sense to define money measures for cases involving a shift to a zero air quality (since we cannot meaningfully define the level of utility associated with death).

If the considered environmental commodity is non-essential, then the indifference curves will intersect the vertical axis. This case is illustrated in Figure 2.4(b). In this case, we can also define money measures in the case where environmental quality goes to zero. In fact, it can be shown that our two money measures will be finite for a non-essential commodity. An example of a non-essential commodity is a forest used for recreation. If the forest is cleared, there will be a loss of utility for those using it for recreation. However, these people would either find other forests to visit or turn to other leisure activities; that is, the loss of utility will be finite.

Another property of our money measures is that the EV for an environmental project exceeds the CV for the same project, at least if environmental quality is a normal good. A private good is said to be normal if the demand for the good increases with income. In terms of Figure 2.1, the demand curve will shift

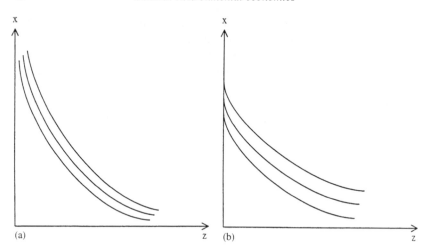

Figure 2.4   An essential (a) and a non-essential (b) environmental commodity

outwards if the individual's income is increased. In the case of a non-priced public good (environmental quality) we can make the following interpretation. The public good is normal if the marginal WTP for the good increases with income. In terms of Figure 2.3, an increase in the individual's income (or level of utility) will shift the marginal WTP curves outwards. The reason why the WTP curve corresponding to the EV measure in Figure 2.3 is situated above the curve based on the CV measure is the fact that the final utility level is assumed to exceed the initial one. Recall that the EV measure keeps the individual at the final level of utility, while the CV measure holds him at the initial level of utility. Thus the commodity we label environmental quality in Figure 2.3 is normal since the EV for an increase in the quality of the commodity exceeds the CV. (In fact, the same holds if we consider deterioration in environmental quality. Both money measures will have a negative sign but the EV (say, −100) will be closer to zero than the CV (say, −150) and hence larger. See the appendix, where the sign convention used in this chapter is established.)

This result has an important implication for applied research in the field. Let us assume that we have collected preference information by asking individuals how they value some change in environmental quality. If the money measure is interpreted as an equivalent variation and the good is normal, we know that the resulting amount of money would be larger than if individuals had been questioned about their compensating variation.

Even though theory, as indicated above, tells us that CV and EV of the same change should differ in magnitude in general, empirical comparisons reveal unexpectedly large differences between willingness to pay and willingness to accept compensation; see, for example, Rowe et al. (1980), Hammack and Brown (1974), Bishop and Heberlein (1979), Brookshire et al. (1982), Coursey et al. (1987) and Knetsch and Sinden (1984). No simple and completely convincing explanation of these large differences is available. However, an interesting idea put forward by Hanemann (1991) for environmental goods is that the substitution possibilities between environmental goods and other goods (money) play a crucial role. The more difficult it is to replace a loss of environmental goods with other goods; that is, the steeper the indifference curves are to the left of the initial combination of private and environmental goods, the higher the compensation needed in order for the individual to accept the loss. In turn, this tends to create a large difference between the compensation or loss measure (WTA) and the willingness to pay (WTP) for more environmental goods. On the other hand, if there is a high degree of substitutability between environmental goods and ordinary market goods, then the compensation measure and willingness to pay should be close in value.

The same reasoning may be applied to health. An experiment with real payments/compensations by Shogren et al. (1994) reveals a convergence of WTP and WTA for a market good. However, for a non-market good (reduced health risk) with imperfect substitutes, they record a persistent difference between the WTP and the WTA. See Morrison (1997) and Shogren and Hayes (1997) for further discussion of these results. Several other possible explanations for the frequently observed large differences between the WTP and WTA measures have also been suggested. In particular, the conventional utility theory has been questioned. For example, in terms of prospect theory, the value function is assumed to be steeper for losses than for gains, so that an unpleasant change in status will elicit a more extreme response than will a seemingly equivalent desirable change. See Gregory (1986) and Harless (1989) for a detailed discussion of these explanations.

Sometimes we are interested in ranking several different proposed projects. For example, one project might improve air quality in an area, another project might improve water quality in the area, and a third project might reduce the cost (that is, price) of a private good. Which of these projects would an individual prefer? In order to check whether our money measures provide the same ranking as the underlying utility function, let us perform the following experiment. In terms of Figure 2.5, let project 1 cause an increase in income moving the individual from point A to point B. Thus this project moves the individual from the solid budget line in the figure to the dotted one (with environmental quality unchanged). Project 2 causes an improvement in environmental quality such that the individual is moved from point A to point C. Since both projects move the individual to the same indifference curve, we can conclude that the individual is indifferent between the projects.

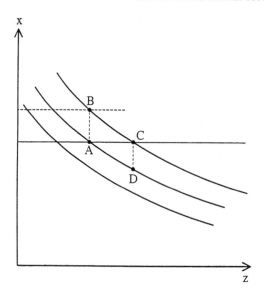

Figure 2.5   The ranking problem

Let us first check if our EV measure provides us with correct information on the two projects' impact on utility. The EV corresponding to the first project is obviously the income change itself; that is, the distance A–B in Figure 2.5. The EV associated with the second project is also the distance A–B. Thus our EV measure tells us that the considered individual is indifferent between the two projects. Let us next check the CV measure. The distance A–B gives the CV associated with the first project. The distance C–D gives the CV associated with the second project (since points D and A are both situated on the initial indifference curve). Unless the utility function happens to be such that the vertical distance between the indifference curves is the same for all z levels (that is, as we move to the right or left) in the figure, our two CV measures will differ. In general the CV measure will wrongly indicate that one project is preferred to the other, although the individual is indifferent between them.

These results hold for much more complex projects than the simple ones illustrated in Figure 2.5. The EV measure can be used to rank any number of projects which change relative prices, incomes, and/or environmental quality variables. It will rank the projects in the same order as the individual's utility function. In general, this is not true for the CV measure. Thus the CV measure must be used with great care if the object is to compare different projects.

It should be stressed that both money measures are suitable for binary comparisons, for example for a comparison of a particular improvement in water quality with no improvement at all. The ranking problem appears if we want to compare, that is, rank, several different measures, say, one that improves water quality, and the other that improves air quality. For the sake of completeness the following should also be noted. Let us assume that we want to evaluate moves from either of two or more initial commodity bundles (say points A and B in Figure 2.5) to one and the same final bundle (point C). Then the reader can proceed as above to show that the moves/bundles are ranked in the same order by both the CV measure and the individual's utility function. This is not necessarily true for the EV measure. For an empirical study facing this problem in using the EV measure see Johansson et al. (1988). In sum, the EV measure will provide us with correct information if we have one initial point of reference (say point A in Figure 2.5), while the CV measure works if there are several initial points (say A and B) but only one final point (say C).[3] This is mentioned here in order to underscore that all money measures of utility change have their limitations. It is important to be aware of such theoretical limitations when using the measures in applied research.

6. USING A MARKET PRICE TO VALUE AN ENVIRONMENTAL RESOURCE

We can obviously use market data to assess the value of a priced good. But can we use market data to value changes in the quality of an environmental asset? Possibly, since the demand for a private good depends on its own price, the prices of other goods, income, and sometimes also on environmental quality. Thus if environmental quality changes, the demand curve for some private commodity might shift. This shift might provide us with information on how the change in environmental quality is valued. However, there are several problems in using market data to estimate the value of an environmental asset. As explained earlier, an uncompensated consumer surplus measure does not express the consumer's WTP, in general. Although this problem can be overcome by estimating a compensated demand function, severe problems remain.

In order to illustrate both the approach and the kind of problem encountered, let us assume that we want to assess the value of a natural park using travel cost data. The compensated demand curve for the number of trips to the park is taken to be the one denoted x^A in Figure 2.6. Thus the higher the travel cost to the park, the fewer visits are undertaken.[4] We start by calculating the compensating variation, that is, the area to the left of the compensated demand curve in Figure 2.6 above the market price, the current travel cost per trip, which is taken to be p^0, treating all other prices and income as fixed.[5] The compensating variation is given by the area to the left of the compensated demand curve above the ruling travel cost. By assumption, there is a choke price such

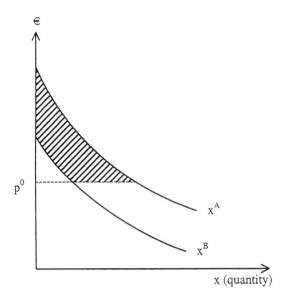

*Figure 2.6   Using compensated demand curves for a private commodity to
value changes in environmental quality*

that no trip is undertaken if the travel cost exceeds this amount of money. In
practice this means that we assume that trips to the park constitute a non-
essential commodity.

Let us repeat this procedure but at a lower quality of the natural park. For
example, the park might have been affected by pollution. This shifts the
compensated demand curve for trips to the left in the figure. The new curve is
denoted x^B in Figure 2.6. Calculate the area to the left of this compensated
demand curve above the ruling travel cost. The difference in the two compensating variations, that is, the shaded area, can be interpreted as a monetary
evaluation of the park's quality deterioration. If the quality goes to zero, that
is, if the park is entirely destroyed, the shaded area would have to be extended
so as to cover the entire area to the left of curve x^A above the ruling travel cost.
(The travel cost itself is not included in the loss. This is so because the amount
of money previously spent on trips is now spent on other valued things.)

Seemingly we have a way of using market data to assess the value of a non-
priced environmental asset. However, this conclusion holds only if the private
commodity (trips) and the environmental resource are what is known as weak
complements. The meaning of weak complementarity is that the individual
attributes no value to quality shifts in the environmental resource if the price

of the non-essential private good (trips) is so high that he does not use the resource (he does not visit the park). This is a reasonable assumption if the private good is shirts. Why bother about changes in the quality of a shirt if its price is so high that you don't buy it? However, even an individual who does not visit the park might value a natural resource like a park. Such values can be due to altruistic concerns or concern for an endangered species living in the park; see Section 7 for further discussion of altruistic and existence values. Thus the shaded area in Figure 2.6 captures the monetary valuation of a quality deterioration if the park only provides use values to individuals. Other values are not captured by this valuation technique. For further details on the theoretical foundations of this technique, see Smith (1991).

Another possibility occurs if we can find a perfect private substitute for a non-priced environmental asset. A possibly poor example is provided by mineral water as a substitute for tap water. Under certain circumstances, it is possible to use the market price of mineral water to evaluate quality shifts in the tap water. However, once again we are unable to recover any WTP due to altruistic or existence values. See Chapter 3 for details on the use of market prices to assess the value of environmental resources.

7.   USE VALUES, ALTRUISM AND EXISTENCE VALUES

A typical feature of many environmental resources is that they provide values of many different types. Following Boyle and Bishop (1985) and Randall (1991), we may distinguish between three more or less distinct use values. First, there are consumptive use values such as fishing and hunting. Second, some resources provide non-consumptive use values. For example, some people enjoy bird-watching, while others gain satisfaction from viewing wildlife. Third, a resource may also provide services indirectly through books, films, television programmes and so on. These values are related to an individual's own use of natural resources. Even a pure egoist might value the environment for one or more of these reasons.

It is often claimed that people are concerned not only about their own welfare but also about the welfare of others. Even if a person is unaffected by a particular project, he may be concerned about the project's impact on others, that is, express altruistic concerns. Such altruistic concerns are usually not valued on the market and are hence difficult to capture using market data: it is difficult to estimate from market data the total monetary value which people place on changes in environmental variables. As is evident from Chapter 3, the contingent valuation method, CVM for short, has therefore become an important tool for evaluating environmental projects.

A pure altruist is a person who values the welfare of others but respects their preferences. In other words, the pure altruist is concerned with the level of utility attained by others. He does not care about how others attain their utility; that is, he does not impute his own preferences with respect to what others should do or should not do. Thus he respects others' valuation of the environment, for example.

Milgrom (1993), drawing on results derived by Bergstrom (1982), has argued forcefully that one can completely forget any purely altruistic components in a social cost–benefit analysis. Milgrom thus implicitly claims that one should ask people about their willingness to pay for changes in their own use of a natural resource. If altruism is pure, one can simply forget about a WTP for improvements in the environmental quality of others; that is, concentrate on use values.

In order to explain Milgrom's result let us assume that there are just two individuals. Individual 1 is a pure altruist, and we want to define his total WTP for an improvement in environmental quality. If individual 2 is assumed to pay for the project according to his willingness to pay, he will remain at his initial level of utility. Thus his utility level is unaffected by the considered project. Therefore, our pure altruist will only pay for his own valuation of the quality improvement. Recall that individual 2's level of utility is unaffected by the project since he pays so as to stay at his initial level of utility. This is the explanation for the fact that a pure altruist's total WTP is equal to his WTP for use values. However, if the project affects the utility of individual 2, for example because he does not have to pay for the project, then our pure altruist's total WTP will exceed (fall short of) his WTP for use values if the project increases (reduces) the utility of individual 2. Thus the case considered by Milgrom (1993) is just a special case.

There might be other kinds of altruists than pure ones. A paternalistic (with respect to the environment) altruist is concerned with others' possibility to enjoy or consume the environment. This kind of altruist ignores how a project affects the utility of others. Therefore, the paternalistic altruist is willing to pay something extra for a project that improves the possibility of others to enjoy the environment. Thus his total WTP is the sum of his WTP for use values plus his WTP for his altruistic concerns.

It should be pointed out, however, that environment-focused altruism is just one (rather extreme) form of paternalistic altruism. For example, another (equally extreme) form is wealth-focused altruism, in which one cares only about the other person's income or wealth and is indifferent to variations in his possibility to enjoy the environment. However, in both cases the person's total WTP is the relevant benefit measure to be used in a social cost–benefit analysis; see Chapter 4 for details about the meaning of such an analysis.

There are also other forms of altruism, such as impure altruism, where a person derives satisfaction from the pure act of giving, and intergenerational altruism. The latter can, however, be viewed as covered by our analysis since individual 1's utility function can be thought of as covering all generations he cares about (that is, individual 2 can be interpreted as a short cut for all generations). For more on the concept of impure altruism, see Andreoni (1989, 1990).

An individual may also take the view that every habitat or species has a right to exist. Therefore, and for this reason alone, he may derive satisfaction from, and be willing to pay for, measures taken to preserve endangered species. This can be labelled a pure existence value. Thus, at one extreme we have pure egoists who (possibly) derive use values from environmental resources. At the other extreme we have individuals who are some kind of altruists, and care for endangered species.

8. VALUATION IN A RISKY WORLD

Thus far we have considered money measures in a certain world. The individual has been assumed to know with certainty all consequences of a project. This is a restrictive assumption, to say the least. Often we must make decisions even if they involve the risk of death. For example, a flight trip involves a risk of a serious accident. Still people continue to fly. Sometimes, in order to save money, people fly with a low-fare airline although its safety reputation is not the best. Some continue to smoke although smoking reduces their survival probability. There are many such examples where there seems to be a trade-off between risks to life and other valued things. There are many other types of risks faced and somehow handled by individuals. Thus people seem able to make rational (?) decisions even in the case of risks.

In this section, we briefly discuss the definition of money measures in a risky world. For simplicity, we concentrate on the case of risk, that is, the case where the probabilities that different states of the world will occur are known. To illustrate, the individual knows that there is a 50–50 chance that a project will cause the extinction of an endangered species. We do not here treat the case where the probabilities are unknown (pure uncertainty).

Let us start by considering a very simple example.[6] Initially there is a 50–50 chance that a species living in a forest area will become extinct due to severe pollution. Thus there are only two (future) states of the world, extinction or survival. Let us now consider an individual who cares about the endangered species in question. He derives a higher level of utility if the species survives than if it becomes extinct. His expected level of utility is a weighted average of the utility levels he will attain with and without the species, using the probabilities of survival and extinction as weights. Thus we can write

$U^E = 0.5U^s + 0.5U^e$, where U^E refers to expected utility, U^s refers to the utility level (say 10 units) achieved if the species survives, U^e refers to the utility (say 5 units) achieved if the species becomes extinct, and 0.5 is the probability that the species survives[7] (which is also the probability that it becomes extinct since the probabilities must sum to unity).

A project reducing pollution in the area is under consideration. If undertaken, this project will increase the survival probability of the endangered species from 0.5 to 0.8. This would increase the expected utility of an individual who cares about the species, since the chance of the good state occurring is increased. In turn, this means that he would be willing to contribute to the considered project. The individual is asked about his WTP for the project. Thus he is asked to pay for the shift in the probability of survival of the considered species. The most obvious payment scheme or contract is a non-contingent or state-independent payment. Then the individual pays one and the same amount of money regardless of what state of the world actually happens to occur, that is, regardless of whether the project turns out to be successful or not in saving the species. The reader can interpret this as meaning that the individual is asked for his WTP before the project is undertaken, that is, before he knows the actual outcome of the project. (However, from a strictly theoretical point of view such an *ex ante* payment interpretation is not self-evident or necessary.)

The money measure we just have defined keeps the individual at his initial expected level of utility. Thus this money measure can be labelled a non-contingent compensating variation. Such a non-contingent payment is sometimes called the (compensating variation) option price in the literature on environmental economics. We could, however, conceive of variations. For example, starting from the non-contingent contract, let the individual pay €1 less if the bad state occurs, but so much more if the good state occurs that he remains at his initial level of expected utility. Proceeding in this way, a willingness-to-pay locus of the kind illustrated in Figure 2.7 is obtained. In the figure, the non-contingent compensating variation falls on the 45-degree line. This is so because along the line the individual pays the same amount of money in both states of the world. Thus the individual is willing to pay at most an amount corresponding to the distance O–A in the figure. This amount is 'paid' regardless of what state of the world happens to occur. The WTP locus illustrates the fact that there might be an infinite number of contracts, that is, types of compensating variations, such that the individual remains at his initial level of utility. This is in sharp contrast to a certain world, where there is just a single compensating variation measure. The reason for this difference is the fact that when two states of the world are possible, we can reallocate payments across states in such a way that expected utility is kept constant. If there is only one state of the world, as is the case under certainty, such reallocations are obviously not possible.

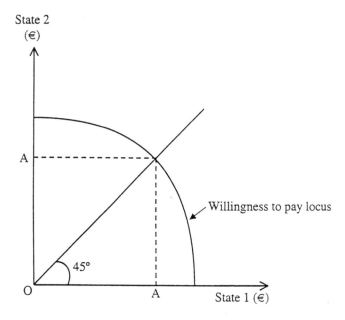

Figure 2.7   A willingness-to-pay locus when there are two states of the world

Although there are many money measures or contracts to choose among, virtually every empirical study of risky projects uses a non-contingent money measure (either the non-contingent compensating variation or the non-contingent equivalent variation).[8] One important reason for this is probably the fact that such a payment is easier to understand than more complex payment schemes where the payment varies across states. Another reason is the fact that a non-contingent contract has all the nice properties discussed in Section 5. This is not generally true for other contracts along the WTP locus in Figure 2.7. It would take us too far to derive this result here. The intuitive reason, however, is the fact that there will be a correlation between the payment made provided a particular state occurs and the marginal utility of income in that state. This covariance might be such that the expected payment is negative although the project causes expected utility to increase.[9] This is the problem one faces in using the expected compensating variation. This measure yields the sum across states of the WTP for a change in environmental quality in a particular state of the world multiplied by the probability that the state occurs. To illustrate, assume that a risky project either is successful and improves environmental quality or fails and causes a deterioration in such quality. Assume that a particular individual is willing to pay €10 if state 1 occurs (good environmental quality), while he needs a compensation equal to, say, €10 in order to voluntarily accept state 2 (bad environmental quality). If there is a 50–50 chance that state 1 occurs, his expected compensating variation is zero (0.5(10 –0.5(10). Still, the risky project might increase or reduce the considered individual's expected utility. It will increase his expected utility if the marginal utility of a euro is higher in state 1 than in state 2, and vice versa. Recall that in order to go from euros to units of utility we multiply euros by the marginal utility of income, and that the marginal utility of income need not be the same in the two states.[10]

Finally, it might be appropriate to mention the concept of option value. In a seminal paper Weisbrod (1964) argued that an individual who was unsure of whether he would visit, say, a national park would be willing to pay a sum in excess of the expected consumer surplus (in our case the expected CV) to ensure that the park would be available:

> To see why, the reader need recognise the existence of people who anticipate purchasing the commodity (visiting the park) at some time in the future, but who, in fact, never will purchase (visit) it. Nevertheless, if these consumers behave as 'economic men' they will be willing to pay something for the option to consume the commodity in the future. This 'option value' should influence the decision of whether or not to close the park and turn it to an alternative use. (Weisbrod, 1964, p. 472)

One would thus expect the difference between the non-contingent willingness to pay (option price) and expected consumer surplus, called 'option value', to be positive. Furthermore, if the option value were positive, one would know that the expected consumer surplus was an underestimate of the gains from preserving a national park, for example. This would simplify cost–benefit analysis in cases where an expected consumer surplus measure, but not the non-contingent money measure or option value, is available. This is so at least if we have a project whose costs fall short of its expected benefits. Provided option value is positive, we then know for sure that we have underestimated the benefits and hence the (social) profitability of the project. However, due to the problem, hinted at above, with the sign property of expected consumer surplus measures, option value might be positive or negative.[11] In other words, we cannot be sure that option value is positive in the above park example by Weisbrod. It might be negative; we simply don't know. Therefore, option value is not a particularly useful tool (unless in very special cases; see, for example, Johansson (1993) for details).

9.   AGGREGATE WTP IN TERMS OF A DEMAND CURVE

This section, which is much inspired by Suen (1990) and Mäler (1974), presents an interpretation of willingness-to-pay measures for 'discrete' projects in terms of a market demand curve. By discrete we here mean that a project of fixed size is either undertaken or not. It is hoped that this interpretation, which is valid for projects in a certain as well as in a risky world, is useful as a complement to the interpretations supplied in most other textbooks.

Thus far we have considered a single individual's valuation of a project. Suppose now that there are H individuals with different valuations of the proposed project. We can then plot the different individuals' WTP for the project in a kind of demand figure. This is illustrated in Figure 2.8(a). We simply calculate the number of individuals who are willing to pay at least a particular amount of money for the project. This yields one point on the curve. Then we take another and lower amount of money and calculate the (reasonably larger) number of individuals who are willing to pay at least that amount. This yields another point on the curve. Proceeding in this way traces out the demand curve in Figure 2.8(a).

More formally, the valuation of the project is described by a distribution function $F(p) = \text{prob}\{CV(p)\}$, where p is a proposed average price or cost ('market price'). Thus $F(p)$ yields the relative number of individuals who are willing to pay no more than €p for the project. Since an individual either 'purchases' the project or does not, aggregate or total market demand for the project is $D(p) = H(1 - F(p))$, where H is the total number of individuals, and $D(p)$ is the demand curve; that is, it yields the number of individuals who are willing to pay at least €p for the project. The total (compensated) consumer surplus can be interpreted as the area to the left of a demand curve above p^0, as is illustrated in Figure 2.8(a), where p^0 can be interpreted as the price or the average cost of the project. The area under the demand curve can be interpreted as aggregate willingness to pay for the proposed project. The fat horizontal part of the demand curve in Figure 2.8(a) illustrates the case in which a fraction of individuals report a zero willingness to pay for a project, because they derive no net benefits from the project (say, do not plan to visit a proposed park).

It need not be the case that everyone is willing to pay a non-negative sum of money for the project, as is illustrated in Figure 2.8(b). If the project provides a pure and unpriced public good which everyone has to consume, the total willingness to pay is given by area CV' less area CV" in Figure 2.8(b). In this case, some individuals need a compensation to voluntarily accept the project. For example, not everyone is willing to pay for military defence. Similarly, a project might increase both the price of a private commodity and environmental quality. Such a project might increase or reduce utility depending on individual preferences. Therefore, some individuals might report a positive WTP for such a project while others report a negative WTP. On the other hand, if the project provides a priced private service, the consumer surplus is equal to the area to the left of the demand curve above the market price for the service, that is, CV in Figure 2.8(a). This is so because those not willing to pay at least €p^0 would refrain from purchasing the service.

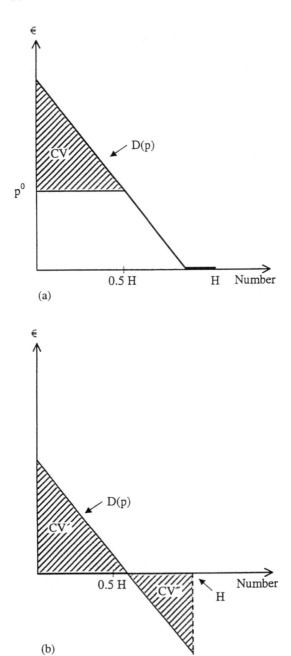

Figure 2.8   Aggregate demand curves for a discrete project

Using Figure 2.8(a) or 2.8(b), one can also locate the median voter, that is, the person/voter who accepts to pay an amount of money such that 50 per cent of the voters would accept a higher payment and 50 per cent would be prepared to accept only a lower payment in exchange for the considered project. In other words, there is a 50–50 chance that this amount would be accepted in a majority-voting referendum. The reader can figure out the WTP of the median voter by moving vertically from the point corresponding to $0.5H$ in Figure 2.8(a) or Figure 2.8(b); recall that there are H individuals in the population.

10.   AGGREGATION

Thus far we have mostly been concerned with the definition and measurement of money measures at the individual level. If there are many individuals, we might simply add together the CVs or EVs of each individual to obtain an aggregate CV or EV as we did in the previous section. There is of course nothing wrong with such aggregates *per se*, but the central question is what, if any, useful information can the decision-maker extract from the total willingness to pay for a proposed measure. After all, behind an aggregate, there are typically both those who gain and those who lose. It is sometimes claimed that a positive aggregate CV, which is equivalent to a positive average willingness to pay, means that those who gain from a project can, at least hypothetically, compensate those who lose from it.[12] If true, this claim would mean that a distributional analysis of a project's consequences would be simplified. A positive aggregate CV or EV would indicate that those gaining from a project could compensate those losing from it. Thus everyone could ultimately gain from a project that generates a positive aggregate CV or EV. However, more than 25 years ago, Boadway (1974) proved this claim to be false (as will be further discussed below). Thus the aggregation issue is still of central importance in project evaluations.

A simple way of illustrating the aggregation issue is by introducing a social welfare function. This is much like the individual's utility function. The social welfare function is simply a function of the utility levels of all individuals such that a higher value of the function is preferred to a lower one. Such a function is often called a Bergsonian welfare function, after Abram Bergson, who first used it. Alternatively it is called a Bergson–Samuelson social welfare function.

Figure 2.9 illustrates three different and commonly employed social welfare functions for a society consisting of two individuals (assuming here sufficient degrees of measurability and comparability of individual utilities; see Boadway and Bruce (1984, ch. 5) for details). Along the horizontal axis we measure utility (denoted U^1) of individual 1 and along the vertical axis utility (denoted U^2) of individual 2. The indifference curves yield combinations of the two individuals' utility levels such that society, according to the chosen social welfare function, attains a particular level of social welfare. It is sometimes argued that society's welfare is equal to the sum of the utilities of different individuals. This view is called utilitarianism, and was first introduced by Jeremy Bentham in the eighteenth century. In a utilitarian society, the social welfare indifference curves are negatively sloped straight lines, as is illustrated in Figure 2.9(a). That is, society is willing to give up one unit of individual 1's utility for a gain of one unit of individual 2's utility. This holds regardless of the degree of inequality in society; society is completely indifferent to the degree of inequality between individuals. Note that W^i for $i =1,2$ in the figure denotes social welfare level i and W^2 represents a higher social welfare than W^1.

Another view of inequality is expressed by the indifference curves in Figure 2.9(b). Society should be willing to accept a decrease in the utility of the poor only if there is a much larger increase in the utility of the rich. Accordingly, society's indifference curves are strictly convex, that is, become flatter as we move to the right.

A more extreme position, associated with John Rawls (1972), is to argue that the welfare of society depends only on the utility of the poorest or worst-off individual. In this case, society's indifference curves can be viewed as L-shaped. As is illustrated by the dotted vertical line in Figure 2.9(c), society is better off if the welfare of the poorest individual, individual 2 in the figure, is improved. Starting from the dotted line and moving horizontally to the right, it can be seen that society gains nothing from improving the welfare of the richer individual 1.

We have given a short presentation of the concept of the social welfare function, and illustrated some of its properties. The function can be used to assess the social profitability of any project in a certain world. In principle, one checks if the project moves society to a higher or a lower social welfare indifference curve. However, one cannot directly observe a social welfare function. In an attempt at least partially to handle this problem, one might use money measures. Then, in the case of a society consisting of two individuals, the change in social welfare due to an environmental project can be expressed as follows:

$$\Delta W = w^1 \cdot CV^1 + w^2 \cdot CV^2 \qquad (2.1)$$

where ΔW denotes the change in social welfare, w^h denotes the marginal social utility of income attributed to individual h ($h = 1,2$), and CV^h is the compensating variation for individual h. Thus each individual is attributed a weight by society. Typically, a low-income earner is attributed a higher weight than a high-income earner. This is true even for a utilitarian society (where w is a measure of the marginal utility of income, and since the marginal utility of income is typically assumed to be higher for a low-income earner than for a high-income earner). In a Rawlsian society w is set equal to unity for the poor individual and equal to zero for the rich one. Thus such a society attributes weight only to the (sign of the) *CV* of the poor individual. If the social indifference curves are strictly convex, as in Figure 2.9(b), the weights will depend on how unequally utility is distributed between the individuals.

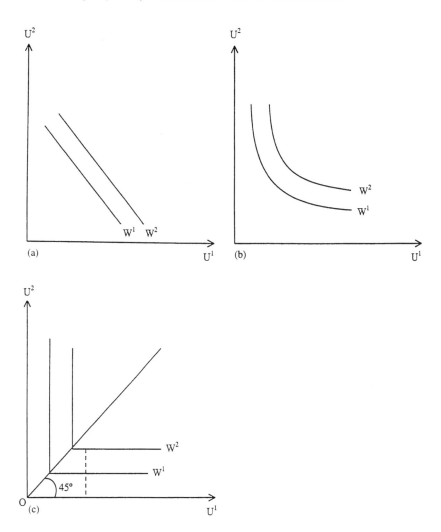

Figure 2.9   Utilitarian (a), strictly convex (b) and Rawlsian (c) social indifference curves

Equation (2.1) illustrates the danger in adding unweighted CVs. To provide a simple numerical example, let us assume that individual 1 is the low-income earner. Set w^1 equal to 2 and w^2 equal to 1; that is, society attributes a higher weight to the low-income earner than to the high-income earner. Moreover, assume that the project under consideration is such that $CV^1 = -100$ while $CV^2 = +110$. Aggregate CV is positive, indicating that the project is worthwhile. However, the project will reduce social welfare, ($W = -90$), since it is so unfavourable to the poor. This provides a simple illustration of the danger of using the aggregate CV as an indicator of a project's social desirability.

We would face exactly the same problem if the analysis were instead based on the equivalent variation measure. In this case, the change in social welfare is:

$$\Delta W = \omega^1 \cdot EV^1 + \omega^2 \cdot EV^2 \qquad (2.2)$$

where the marginal social utility of income is now denoted ω. The reason is the fact that the EV measure holds individuals at their final levels of utility (rather than at their initial levels). Therefore the weights w and ω need not coincide. (In turn, this means that it is theoretically possible to have a project such that the sum of CVs is positive while the sum of EVs is negative, or vice versa.)

If the distribution in society is optimal, or society has at its disposal means for unlimited and costless redistributions, then monetary gains and losses can be summed across individuals (since we then can set $w^1 = w^2 = \omega^1 = \omega^2$). In all other cases a weighting procedure is required. Since the weights are not directly observable, one faces a formidable problem in assessing the social profitability of a project from which some gain while others lose.

In some cases it may be possible to estimate a social welfare function for a particular country. In fact, such attempts have been undertaken. Dantzig et al. (1989) and Yunker (1989), for example, have estimated social welfare functions for the US economy. Alternatively, one may choose a particular social welfare function in order to show how different distributional considerations affect the outcome of a social cost–benefit analysis.

Mäler (1985) has suggested that the choice of compensated money measures should in some cases be influenced by distributional considerations. Suppose that initially, that is, before a reasonably small project is undertaken, society is indifferent to small changes in income distribution. Then the equivalent variation measure, which is based on initial incomes and so on, is the relevant measure. On the other hand, if we believe that income distribution with the project is such that small changes in income distribution will not affect social welfare, then the cost–benefit analysis of the project should be based on the compensating variation measure; this measure is defined in terms of final levels of incomes and so on. See Mäler (1985) for details.

Yet another possibility is simply to calculate the unweighted sum of gains and losses and supplement this figure with a distributional analysis where gains and losses are allocated to different groups, for example high-income earners, low-income earners, young people, elderly people, people suffering from severe illness, and the like.

The final approach suggested here is to discuss the outcome of a valuation experiment in terms of compensation criteria. In a certain world, it is sometimes claimed that if the sum of CV^h is positive, then gainers from the project can, at least hypothetically, compensate those who lose from the project. If the sum of EV^h is positive, the losers are claimed to be unable to 'bribe' those who would gain from it not to undertake the project. The two compensation criteria referred to here are known as the Kaldor criterion and the Hicks criterion, respectively; see Kaldor (1939) and Hicks (1939). Unfortunately, it has been shown that one cannot, in general, interpret a positive sum of CVs or EVs as meaning that a compensation test is passed. This so-called Boadway paradox, see Boadway (1974), is basically due to the fact that the vector of prices and the compensated incomes used in defining CV and EV measures does not correspond to a general equilibrium. In order to illustrate, let us consider an economy consisting of two individuals. Moreover, consider a project such that $CV^1 = 100$ and $CV^2 = -90$. Thus individual 1 is willing to pay €100 for the project while individual 2 would need a compensation equal to €90 to be indifferent to the project. Consider a (hypothetical) redistribution of €95 from individual 1 to individual 2. Seemingly both individuals would then be better off with the project than without it. However, the act of redistribution might affect (general equilibrium) prices in such a way that one individual's real income (purchasing power) turns out to be lower than without the project.[13] Then he will attain a lower level of utility with the project and redistribution than without the project. In other words, we cannot be sure that a positive aggregate CV (or EV) allows us hypothetically to redistribute income in such a way that everyone gains from the project. See Boadway and Bruce (1984) for a detailed examination of this issue. Also note that compensation is hypothetical, implying that some will actually gain while others will lose from the typical project. Thus compensation tests do not provide a way of avoiding the distributional issue.

11. CONCLUDING REMARKS

This chapter has been devoted to a brief summary of many of the properties of the most common money measures used in valuation experiments. By necessity, the derivation of the different properties has been sketchy. It is hoped, however, that the chapter has given the reader an idea of the basic results of valuation theory. In particular, we have established that both the compensating variation and the equivalent variation correctly indicate whether an environmental project increases or reduces an individual's level of utility. We have also shown, or at least indicated, that this holds also in a risky world (if we use the non-contingent CV or EV measure). Even though our money measures have nice properties at the individual level, they must be used with great care at the aggregate level. The sum across individuals of their CVs (or EVs) cannot be used as an indicator of a project's desirability, in general. The 'problem' is the fact that society is not indifferent to a project's distributional impact. Therefore, in general, some kind of weighting procedure is required in order to provide the decision-maker with correct information about a project's social desirability.

Nevertheless, if we collect information on people's monetary valuation of a change in environmental quality it is important that our money measures have a sound foundation in economic theory. It does not make much sense to spend a great deal of money on collecting information about and analysing a flawed measure. After all, the money measures typically used assume (rightly or wrongly) that individuals behave in the way assumed in conventional micro-economic theory. That is, individuals are assumed to behave as if they solved a well-behaved utility maximization problem. If they do not behave in this way, our money measures will lack meaning. Then one must model behaviour in another way, and check what money measures such behaviour generates and what properties these new measures will have. That is, however, another story. In the usual way, when the author (teacher) is unable to solve a problem, it is left to the reader (student) as an exercise.

APPENDIX

A.1 The Sign Convention Used in This Chapter

In order to establish the sign convention used in this chapter, let us define our money measures in the following way:

$$V(y - CV, z^1) = V(y, z^0)$$

$$V(y + EV, z^0) = V(y, z^1) \tag{2A.1}$$

where $V(y,z)$ is the (indirect) utility function, y is income, z denotes environmental quality, and a superscript 1 (0) denotes the final (initial) level of environmental quality. The better the environmental quality, the higher is the individual's utility. Thus if z^1 exceeds z^0, CV must be positive in order to preserve the equality between the left-hand-side and the right-hand-side utility levels in the first line of equation (2A.1). Similarly, *EV* must be positive in the second line of (2A.1) if z^1 exceeds z^0. Thus both *CV* and *EV* will be positive (negative) in the case of an improvement (a deterioration) in environmental quality. In other words, they will have the same sign as the change in the individual's utility.

A.2 The Path-dependency Problem

In section 2 (see note 2), we hinted at a path-dependency problem when several prices (or several parameters) are changed. This path-dependency problem, which occurs in the case of Marshallian demand curves, can be explained as follows. Consider two different commodities. Let us first reduce the price (p^1) of commodity 1 and calculate the associated change in consumer surplus in the 'market' for commodity 1. The reduction in p^1 will shift the position of the demand curve for commodity 2 (to the right or to the left depending on whether the two commodities are complements or substitutes). Draw the demand curve for commodity 2 given the new lower price of commodity 1. Next, reduce the price (p^2) of the second commodity, and calculate the associated change in consumer surplus in the market for commodity 2. Let us denote the sum of these two consumer surpluses A.

Next, let us repeat the experiment but changing the two prices in reverse order. Thus we start by drawing the demand curve for commodity 2, given that p^1 is held at its initial (or pre-change) level. Reduce p^2 and calculate the associated change in consumer surplus for commodity 2. Then, given the new lower p^2, draw the demand curve for commodity 1 and calculate the consumer surplus change associated with a decrease in p^1. Denote the sum of these two consumer surplus changes B.

The problem is the fact that A is different from B, in general, although we consider the same price changes. In other words, the magnitude (and sometimes even the sign) of the total consumer surplus depends on the order in which we change prices, and not only on the size of the price changes. The reason is the fact that we calculate two different consumer surpluses in market 1 (and in market 2). The first is calculated under a demand curve for commodity 1 drawn given that p^2 is held at its initial level. The second consumer surplus is calculated under a demand curve drawn given that p^2 is held at its final level. In exactly the same way we have two different consumer surplus measures for commodity 2 (corresponding to p^1 being held at its initial and final levels respectively). The problem is the fact that the shift in the demand curve for commodity 1 as we lower p^2 need not be equal to the shift in the demand curve for commodity 2 as we lower p^1. This 'asymmetry' is due to 'asymmetric' income effects. Therefore the two aggregate consumer surpluses, denoted A and B above, need not coincide. In the case of Hicksian demand curves, there are no income effects. Thus there is no path-dependency problem in the case of Hicksian demand curves. See, for example, Johansson (1993) for further details.

A.3 Producer Surplus Measures

This chapter is primarily concerned with individuals' valuation of (environmental projects). However, they might also be affected through changes in profits.[14] Let us consider a firm that produces a single output using some variable input(s), for example labour. Its stock of real capital (buildings and machinery) is considered to be fixed in the short run. The firm is assumed to be a quantity adjuster; that is, it is so small that it takes all prices as given. Figure 2A.1 depicts the firm's supply curve. This curve can be interpreted as the firm's marginal cost curve. Thus it yields the increase in the firm's total costs as its output is increased by a small amount. Typically, it is assumed that the marginal cost curve has a positive slope. Thus the extra cost incurred if the output level is increased from, say, 10 units to 11 units is smaller than the extra cost incurred if output is increased from 100 to 101 units. The reason is that we here assume that the firm's stock of real capital is fixed. Therefore we expect that adding more and more variable inputs, say labour, will add less and less

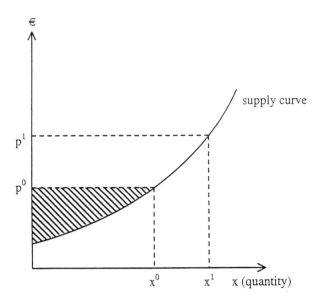

Figure 2A.1   A producer surplus measure

to output. The first labourer adds more to output than the tenth labourer; that is, labour has a decreasing marginal productivity.

If the firm is a profit-maximizer, it will choose a level of production such that the marginal cost of production is equal to the unit price of its output. If it increases production beyond that level, the cost of producing another unit of output will exceed the price the firm gets for that unit. This would reduce profits. If the firm produces fewer units of output than the level yielding equality between price and marginal cost, the cost of producing an additional unit of output falls short of the price the firm will get for that additional unit. Thus increasing output will increase profits. This shows that a profit-maximizing firm will select a level of production such that marginal cost is equal to price. In Figure 2A.1, the profit-maximizing level of output is x^0, given that the firm faces a fixed price equal to p^0 per unit of output.

By definition, fixed costs, such as the costs of buildings and machinery, are independent of the level of production the firm chooses in the short run. In general, therefore, interest is focused not on profits, but on quasi-rent or producer surplus. This is the difference between the firm's revenues and variable production costs. In Figure 2A.1 the current price, denoted p^0, times the level of production yields the firm's revenues. Since the firm is assumed to maximize profits, it will produce x^0 units and receive revenues equal to $p^0 x^0$. The area under the supply curve in Figure 2A.1 adds up to the firm's variable costs. The sum of the extra cost incurred by producing the first unit plus the extra cost incurred in producing the second unit of output, and so on, must add up to the total variable cost. The shaded area in Figure 2A.1 captures the difference between revenues and total variable costs when the firm supplies x^0 units of output. Thus the shaded area is a measure of producer surplus.

If the price of the firm's output increases to p^1, say due to the implementation of a large environmental project that uses the firm's product as input, the firm will supply x^1 units of output. The increase in producer surplus is equal to the area to the left of the supply curve between p^1 and p^0. Note that this area can be interpreted both as a compensating variation and as an equivalent variation. The area yields the firm's maximal WTP for a price increase from p^0 to p^1. Similarly, the area corresponds to the minimal compensation (WTA) the firm needs in order to willingly accept that the price is not increased from p^0 to p^1. Since there are no income effects involved, the two money measures coincide for the firm.

For the individual considered in the main text, an increase in producer surplus for a firm that he is an owner of (possibly together with many others) can be interpreted as a shift upwards in his budget constraint. In terms of Figure 2.5, his income increases so that the budget line shifts from the solid one to the dotted one.

FURTHER READING

Virtually all introductory textbooks on environmental economics and natural resource economics cover the valuation issue. There seems no reason to try to discriminate between such books. At a more advanced and hence more technical level, the book by Freeman (1993) provides a full coverage of the theoretical aspects of the problem as well as a thorough presentation of the different empirical methods that are available. An early and classical but advanced treatment is found in Mäler (1974). Other advanced treatments include Braden and Kolstad (1991) and Johansson (1987, 1993, 1995). The classical book by Mitchell and Carson (1989) on the contingent valuation method, see Chapter 3, contains a non-technical overview of the theoretical aspects of the valuation problem.

NOTES

1. In the present context, where we consider a decrease in a price, the income effect can be interpreted as due to an increase in real income or purchasing power.
2. If several prices are changed, one faces a path-dependency problem. The magnitude of the Marshallian consumer surplus measure depends, in general, on the order in which prices are changed, i.e. it is path-dependent. In sharp contrast, the Hicksian measure is path-independent since there are no income effects in the case of Hicksian demand curves. See the appendix for details.
3. See also equation (2A.1) in the appendix. This equation illustrates that the magnitude of CV is directly related to the magnitude of z^0 (the initial level of environmental quality) while EV is directly related to the magnitude of z^1 (the final level). The relationship between CV and the final level (z^1) is more complex since they both appear on the left-hand side of the first line in equation (2A.1). Similarly, there is a complex relationship between EV and the initial level (z^0). Thus inspection of (2A.1) gives a clue to the ranking problem discussed here.
4. In practice, we might interview visitors about their travel costs, number of visits per year, travel distance to the park, and socioeconomic variables such as income, age and household size. These variables can be used to estimate a (compensated) demand function for trips to the park.
5. Alternatively, the evaluation could be based on the EV measure.
6. Throughout we restrict attention to the case where only two different states of the world are possible. This means no real loss of generality.
7. This approach can also be used in the case of fatal risks (say, due to pollution of the air or water). Then 0.5 is interpreted as the survival probability, U^s is the utility of being alive, and U^e is interpreted as (either the 'utility' of being dead or more typically) a bequest function representing the considered individual's care for his heirs. Even if this interpretation might seem distasteful, life is risky, and individuals do engage in risky activities such as flying, mountain-climbing, smoking, and so on. Thus they are prepared to take (fatal) risks in order to obtain valued things.
8. The analysis performed in this section draws on the CV interpretation. However, the analysis would be identical if the individual instead remained at his final expected level of utility; that is, if we used an EV interpretation.
9. An exception is the case with individually insurable risks (say insuring one's house against fire), that is, the case where a known fraction of individuals will end up in one state of the world and the remaining fraction will end up in the other state. Under certain assumptions, it is then

possible to design the contract in such a way that an individual's marginal utility of income is evened out across the two states (that is, the covariance will vanish since there is no variation in the marginal utility of income). If risk is insurable, this contract will yield a larger expected payment than a non-contingent contract. See, for example, Graham (1981) or Johansson (1995) for details.

10. The marginal utility of income typically depends on both the size of income and environmental quality. Thus, more formally, we have $\Delta U^E = \lambda^1 \cdot 0.5 \cdot 10 - \lambda^2 \cdot 0.5 \cdot 10$, where ΔU^E is the change in expected utility, and λ^i is the positive marginal utility of income in state i ($i = 1,2$). Thus, ΔU^E is positive, equal to zero, or negative, depending on whether λ^1 exceeds, is equal to, or falls short of λ^2. In turn, λ^1 may differ from λ^2 due to differences in income and/or environmental quality between the two states. Also, note that if we consider a non-contingent (i.e. state-independent) CV, it holds that $\Delta U^E = (\lambda^1 \cdot 0.5 + \lambda^2 \cdot 0.5) \cdot CV$. Thus, ΔU^E and CV must have the same sign, since by assumption $\lambda^i > 0$.

11. Recall that option value is defined as the difference between option price and expected consumer surplus.

12. A similar claim is often made with respect to the aggregate EV measure.

13. For example, individual 1 might prefer Pepsi while individual 2 prefers Coca-Cola. Redistributing income will shift the demand curves for Pepsi and Coca-Cola and hence shift their equilibrium prices, in general. These price shifts might be such that an individual is worse off with the project and redistribution than without the project.

14. Setting aside here the possibility of foreign ownership, both private and public sector firms are ultimately owned by domestic individuals. Their disposable incomes are affected by changes in profits.

REFERENCES

Andreoni, J. (1989), 'Giving with impure altruism: applications to charity and Ricardian equivalence', *Journal of Political Economy*, **97**, 1447–58.

Andreoni, J. (1990), 'Impure altruism and donation to public goods: a theory of warm glow giving', *Economic Journal*, **100**, 464–77.

Bentham, J. (1791), *Principles of Morals and Legislation*, London: Doubleday.

Bergson, A. (1938), 'A reformulation of certain aspects of welfare economics', *Quarterly Journal of Economics*, **52**, 310–34.

Bergstrom, T.C. (1982), 'When is a man's life worth more than his human capital?', in M.W. Jones-Lee (ed.), *The Value of Life and Safety*, Amsterdam: North Holland.

Bishop, R.C. and T.A. Heberlein (1979), 'Measuring values of extra-market goods: are indirect measures biased?', *American Journal of Agricultural Economics*, **61**, 926–30.

Bishop, R.C. and T.A. Heberlein (1984), 'Contingent valuation methods and ecosystem damages from acid rain', University of Wisconsin-Madison, Dept. of Agricultural Economics, Staff Paper no. 217.

Blackorby, C. and D. Donaldson (1990), 'The case against the use of the sum of compensating variations in cost–benefit analysis', *Canadian Journal of Economics*, **13**, 471–9.

Boadway, R.W. (1974), 'The welfare foundations of cost–benefit analysis', *Economic Journal*, **84**, 926–39.

Boadway, R.W. and N. Bruce (1984), *Welfare Economics*, Oxford: Basil Blackwell.

Boyle, K.J. and R.C. Bishop (1985), 'The total value of wildlife resources: conceptual and empirical issues', invited paper, Association of Environmental and Natural Resource Economists Workshop on Recreational Demand Modelling, Boulder, CO, 17–18 May.

Braden, J.B. and C.D. Kolstad (eds) (1991), *Measuring the Demand for Environmental Quality*, Amsterdam: North-Holland.

Brookshire, D.S., M.A. Thayer, W.D. Schulze and R.C. d'Arge (1982), 'Valuing public goods: a comparison of survey and hedonic approaches', *American Economic Review*, **72**, 165–77.

Coursey, D.L., J.L. Hovis and D.W. Schulze (1987), 'The disparity between willingness to accept and willingness to pay measures of value', *Quarterly Journal of Economics*, **102**, 679–90.

Dantzig, G.B., P.H. McAllister and J.C. Stone (1989), 'Deriving a utility function for the U.S. economy', *Journal of Policy Modelling*, **11**, 391–424.

Freeman, A.M. III (1993), *The Measurement of Environmental and Resource Values. Theory and Methods*, Washington, DC: Resources for the Future.

Graham, D.S. (1981), 'Cost–benefit analysis under uncertainty', *American Economic Review*, **71**, 715–25.

Gregory, R. (1986), 'Interpreting measures of economic loss: evidence from contingent valuation and experimental studies', *Journal of Environmental Economics and Management*, **13**, 325–37.

Hammack, B. and G.M. Brown Jr (1974), *Waterfowl and Wetlands: Toward Bioeconomic Analysis*, Baltimore: Johns Hopkins University Press for Resources for the Future.

Hanemann, M.W. (1991), 'Willingness-to-pay and willingness-to-accept: how much can they differ?', *American Economic Review*, **81**, 635–47.

Harless, D.W. (1989), 'More laboratory evidence on the disparity between willingness to pay and compensation demanded', *Journal of Economic Behavior and Organization*, **11**, 359–79.

Hicks, J.R. (1939), 'The foundation of welfare economics', *Economic Journal*, **49**, 696–712.

Johansson, P.-O. (1987), *The Economic Theory and Measurement of Environmental Benefits*, Cambridge: Cambridge University Press.

Johansson, P.-O. (1993), *Cost–benefit Analysis of Environmental Change*, Cambridge: Cambridge University Press.

Johansson, P.-O. (1995), *Evaluating Health Risks. An Economic Approach*, Cambridge: Cambridge University Press.

Johansson, P.-O., B. Kriström, and L. Mattsson (1988), 'How is the willingness to pay for moose hunting affected by the stock of moose?', *Journal of Environmental Management*, **26**, 163–71.

Kaldor, N. (1939), 'Welfare propositions of economics and inter-personal comparisons of utility', *Economic Journal*, **49**, 549–52.

Knetsch, J.L. and J.A. Sinden (1984), 'Willingness to pay and compensation demanded: experimental evidence of an unexpected disparity in measures of value', *Quarterly Journal of Economics*, **98**, 507–21.

Mäler, K.G. (1974), *Environmental Economics. A Theoretical Inquiry*, Baltimore: Johns Hopkins University Press.

Mäler, K.G. (1985), 'Welfare economics and the environment', in A.V. Kneese and J.L. Sweeney (eds), *Handbook of Natural Resource and Energy Economics*, vol. I, Amsterdam: Elsevier.

Marshall, A. (1920), *Principles of Economics*, 8th edn, London: Macmillan.

Milgrom, P. (1993), 'Is sympathy an economic value? Philosophy, economics, and the contingent valuation method', in J.A. Hausman (ed.), *Contingent Valuation: A Critical Assessment*, Amsterdam: North-Holland.

Mitchell, R.C. and R.T. Carson (1989), *Using Surveys to Value Public Goods. The Contingent Valuation Method*, Washington, DC: Resources for the Future.

Morrison, G.C. (1997), 'Resolving differences in willingness to pay and willingness to accept: comment', *American Economic Review*, **87**, 236–40.

Randall, A. (1991), 'Nonuse benefits', in J.B. Braden and C.D. Kolstad (eds), *Measuring the Demand for Environmental Quality*, Amsterdam: North-Holland.

Rawls, J. (1972), *A Theory of Justice*, Oxford: Clarendon Press.

Rowe, R.D., R.C. d'Arge and D.S. Brookshire (1980), 'An experiment on the economic value of visibility', *Journal of Environmental Economics and Management*, 7, 1–19.

Shogren, J.F. and D.J. Hayes (1997), 'Resolving differences in willingness to pay and willingness to accept: reply', *American Economic Review*, **87**, 241–4.

Shogren , J.F., S.Y. Shin, D.J. Hayes and J.B. Kliebenstein (1994), 'Resolving differences in willingness to pay and willingness to accept', *American Economic Review*, **84**, 255–70.

Smith, V.K. (1991), 'Household production function and environmental benefit estimation', in J.B. Braden and C.D. Kolstad (eds), *Measuring the Demand for Environmental Quality*, Amsterdam: North-Holland.

Suen, W. (1990), 'Statistical models of consumer behavior with heterogeneous values and constraints', *Economic Inquiry*, **28**, 79–98.

Weisbrod, B.A. (1964), 'Collective-consumption services of individual-consumption goods', *Quarterly Journal of Economics*, **78**, 471–7.

Yunker, J.A. (1989), 'Some empirical evidence on the social welfare maximization hypothesis', *Public Finance*, **44**, 110–33.

3. Valuing the environment

Mordechai Shechter

---

1. INTRODUCTION

One of the central themes in the field of environmental economics has been the valuation of environmental resources. These resources or 'assets' include air, surface- and groundwater, woodlands, unique natural landscapes, wetlands, and so on. They provide three functions: first, they provide ecological system support, second, they are 'negative' inputs (sometimes referred to as waste 'sinks') in the production process, for example, groundwater contaminated by industrial waste; third, they are amenities which are 'consumed' directly by individuals in the form of clean air, water for household uses, recreational services in natural areas.[1] Along with other economic goods and services, all three environmental functions contribute, directly or indirectly, positively or negatively, to people's well-being.[2] The environmental functions, and therefore the assets which provide them, are in fact also economic goods or services because in modern society they are not free; their provision, maintenance and conservation entails the sacrifice of *other* goods or services. They are distinguished, however, from conventional economic goods and services in that their use does not always involve market transactions. Consequently, explicit market-determined valuation, that is prices, usually does not exist for them. That is why they are often referred to as 'non-market' goods.

The discussion above implies that if people prefer, say, clean air to polluted air, their welfare would increase if more clean air were provided. However, there does not exist a social institution in which these economic desires can be realized. In the case of other assets, economic desires are expressed through a market, where the forces of demand and supply interact. Unfortunately, market transactions for environmental 'commodities' are not possible. The reason for this can be found in the nature of many environmental amenities. They are called public goods in economic theory. A public good is an economic good (or service) which, once provided to an individual, cannot practically be withheld from any other individual who wishes to consume it (non-excludability; see Chapter 1). Moreover, for certain types of consumption, consumption by one individual does not affect the quantity available to others (non-rivalry). Thus, once cleaner air is made available for a neighbourhood, anybody living in that neighbourhood can enjoy it. Even if one individual were to pay for it, no one else could be prevented from enjoying it. Economists call these non-paying consumers of clean air or any such commodity 'free riders'. There are no market incentives provided by buyers paying a price to cover the supply costs of the good to induce firms to provide these commodities, as in the case of conventional goods. The supplier would never be able to recoup the cost of providing it because everybody would have an incentive to 'free-ride'. There is, however an opposite incentive to over-use the freely provided asset. In the case of clean air, pollution that essentially uses up clean air and replaces it with dirty air arises because there is no mechanism by which firms can be made to pay for their polluting activities. A market for clean air does not exist because in the absence of government intervention, firms derive no benefit from not polluting, or conversely providing the public good, clean air. Clean air and other environmental assets are nevertheless economic goods because, as research has shown, people are willing to pay for them.

If markets fail to provide goods for which there is demand, they may be provided by other mechanisms. In the case of environmental assets – as with many other public goods – governments generally assume the role of provider. Few other institutions, if any, would have the political power and infrastructure needed to ensure that users pay for their consumption of public goods (for example, through the general tax system, or through special taxes imposed on polluters). The task of the government is to help implement the social desires of the community for the environmental good. In order to accomplish this, it must know the value to consumers of these assets.[3]

The purpose of this chapter is to provide a brief, 'bird's-eye-view' of the main approaches to 'measuring', that is, assigning a monetary value to the benefits (or *avoided* damages) from improving, protecting or preserving environmental resources. We begin, first, by arguing that there is a need for such measures and that money can, and even should, be employed as a yardstick in valuation of environmental assets. We proceed to describe a number of measurement techniques, based on either observed market behaviour or on stated preferences, which economists have used to this end. A not-terribly-cheerful note on the role of valuation studies in real-life decision-making follows. Finally, for the benefit of readers wishing to go more deeply into the subject, references to more detailed treatments of these approaches are provided throughout the chapter.

2. CAN WE USE A MONEY YARDSTICK TO VALUE ENVIRONMENTAL ASSETS?[4]

People pay for environmental assets, either directly or indirectly. They pay directly when they spend money and time to travel to unique natural sites; by contributing to organizations that promote nature conservation and environmental causes. They pay indirectly when they pay higher prices or rents for a house in a less polluted or quieter neighbourhood, or when they purchase bottled spring water on the supposition that it is safer to drink than tap water. Economists consider the maximum sum individuals are willing to pay for an increase in the provision of some environmental amenity (given income level and other relevant attributes) to be a reasonable expression of its value to its consumers. It is considered to represent the 'price' the good or asset would have fetched had markets existed. And, as we well know, in perfectly competitive markets, equilibrium prices reflect the change at the margin in consumers' utility from the consumption of the good or service, that is, the (marginal) improvement in the level of well-being.

Nevertheless, as an attempt to monetize welfare changes, valuation involves an important implicit assumption, namely, that the individual possess all the relevant information regarding the effect of environmental amenities, either negative (for example, pollution on health) or positive (for example, outdoor recreation on level of enjoyment) on their welfare. In reality, people often do have misconceptions about the true effects, and act upon mistaken perceptions rather than on the basis of accurate knowledge. For example, in dealing with air quality, it is doubtful that individuals are completely aware of the full consequences of polluted air on their health, and hence, on their well-being. This qualification, however, is not characteristic of environmental assets only. Is a potential car-buyer always, or even most of the time, completely familiar with the various technical qualities of different cars? Or of a stereo set? How often is the decision merely based on hearsay, external appearance or friends' recommendations, that is, on very imperfect knowledge?

So, we claim that the answer to the question posed in this section's heading is 'Yes': money can be used to value environmental benefits. But *should* money be employed as a yardstick in valuing environmental improvement or degradation? There are those who would argue that there exist intrinsic qualities associated with environmental assets which go beyond any attempt to capture them in a single economic index. True, one cannot deny that there are services of the environmental assets that probably defy quantitative measurement; but to what extent, if any, would they differ from, for example, the spiritual manifestations associated with the purchase of a religious object that can be purchased at a store? Or the aesthetic satisfaction derived from the purchase of a work of art? All this is not nullified by the fact that the religious or artistic object in question does carry an economic price tag, which captures the value placed upon it by the pious or art-loving buyer.

Still, even the most fervent advocates of a money yardstick would probably agree that there are a number of weighty measurement issues unique to environmental amenities that cannot easily be resolved, if at all. One obvious measurement issue involves the threat to the very survival of the human race and life on this planet. Could any finite value be consistent with the welfare associated with the survival of humankind in the long run? Are there any finite monetary values consistent with long-run sustainability of life on planet earth? Some go further to argue that valuation suffers from being a strictly anthropocentric approach: it measures changes in human welfare, where the individuals involved in the valuation exercise may ignore altogether intrinsic value associated with the very existence of the living creatures and non-living constituents of nature.

Most valuations, however, deal with relatively small, non-catastrophic changes in the state of environmental assets, where the advantages of using monetary measures are notable. First, money measures provide an explicit and clear expression of the degree of public concern with an environmental issue, via the willingness of members of society to pay for the environmental good; in a sense, it measures the intensity of the public's preferences and concerns. Furthermore, in many policy contexts *implicit* monetary valuations are made anyway by decision-makers. Take, for instance, the case of health care. Life expectancy of the entire population or of a certain group of patients is at stake. But when investments are in one programme and not in another, implicit monetary values of the number of lives saved, or number of injuries avoided, as a result of undertaking programme X and not Y, are implicitly made. The same is true in the case of investments in alternative highway safety programmes to reduce traffic fatalities. A second argument supporting monetizing environmental quality is that the use of monetary measures makes comparisons possible with other monetary benefits and costs arising from alternative uses of public funds.

If the principle of monetary valuation is accepted, how do we actually measure people's valuations of environmental assets and their associated service flows in money units? Over the past forty years or so,[5] economists have devised, adapted, or modified a growing number of methods and approaches to valuation. Broadly speaking, a widely accepted classification of benefit valuation methods distinguishes between *indirect* and *direct* methods. The former group infers an implicit value for a non-market good from observable prices of market goods and services, which are related in some way – as complements to or substitutes for the environmental good or service of interest. They are therefore based on observable market behaviour of individuals as consumers of these goods and services. The latter aims at revealing valuations of and demand for an environmental good through consumer surveys where, through appropriately constructed questionnaires, individuals are asked to state their preferences for, or valuations of, the environmental good or service. In general, economists tend to have more faith in market-determined valuations, namely prices which result from the interaction of the decentralized forces of supply and demand.

In the absence of government intervention, such market-determined prices are considered 'objective' and 'real' in the sense that they reflect the 'true' preferences of individuals. In any case, they are not elicited under hypothetical and artificial market conditions, as is the case with the direct approaches.

3.   USING MARKETS TO VALUE ENVIRONMENTAL ASSETS AND SERVICES: THE INDIRECT APPROACH

The indirect approach postulates an explicit relationship between the demand for a market good and the quantity (or level) of environmental goods, known as *weak complementarity* (see Chapter 2). It posits that the consumption of the market good is affected by level of the environmental good or asset associated with it; for example, improved water quality in a lake would attract more visitors. Using this form of demand interdependence as the point of departure allows the investigator to infer how the demand for the market good shifts in response to changes in the availability (or the quality) of the environmental good. From these shifts in the *observable* demand function for the market good, a money-metric value for the *non-market* goods can be derived. Thus, air quality (the environmental good) may influence housing (the market good) prices: better air quality is expected to coincide with higher property values in the cleaner neighbourhoods. In fact, the line of causation and interdependence can be very circuitous: air pollution also affects health and therefore the demand for medical services. These added costs, incurred in the more polluted neighbourhood, reduce the demand, and therefore the value, of housing in these neighbourhoods. The extent and direction of observable shifts in demand enables economists, through an assortment of econometric techniques, to impute willingness to pay (WTP) values for environmental goods.

The essentials of the indirect approaches may be depicted with the aid of Figure 3.1. The curve denoted D_0–D_0 represents a demand schedule for some market good (that is, the amount demanded by consumers at different prices). Other things being equal, the lower the price, the greater the quantity demanded of that good. The demand interdependence assumption postulates that, given a change in the level of some environmental asset or amenity, the demand for the market good will shift, as shown by the curve D_1–D_1. Now, at each and every price, more will be demanded since better quality induces additional demand for the good. However, as the curves are drawn in a price (vertical axis) times quantity (horizontal axis) space, the shaded area between the two curves[6] measures in money units the benefits gained, that is, the value of the environmental asset or amenity.

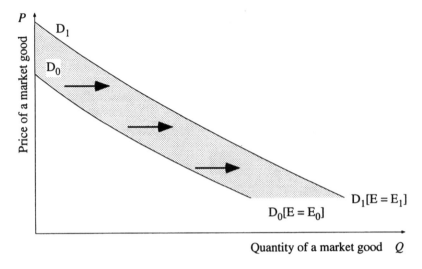

Figure 3.1 Measuring environmental benefits from shifts in the demand for a market good

3.1 Valuing *in situ* Environmental Assets: the Travel Cost Method

The travel cost method (TCM) was the earliest valuation method employed by environmental economists.[7] It has been employed chiefly in studying the demand for, and value of, natural resources (national parks, nature reserves, open space), which serve as input services in 'producing' outdoor recreation activities and related amenities: hiking, camping, fishing, boating, swimming, wildlife-watching, and the like. Characteristically, these services are consumed *in situ*: individuals must travel to the site in order to experience and enjoy them. This activity typically involves both money outlays related to travel and on-site expenditures, as well as the implicit cost of travel time. TCM exploits this observed consumption pattern, where consumers indirectly reveal their implicit valuation of the natural resource services through observable travel behaviour. In this case, the computation of the value of time spent in recreation activities (for example, wages forgone), the cost of travel (for example, money spent on petrol), and entrance and other site fees constitute a basis for computing the demand price, or value, of the resource. Basically, TCM assumes that the benefits that individuals derive from their pursuits within a recreation area are directly related to the distance that they are prepared to travel in order to visit it and, hence, to their (money and time) cost of travel and other related expenditures. Since this value arises only if people have access to the natural resource for recreational use, it can be considered to be the value of the site, or the implicit 'price' the public would have been willing to pay to secure this form of land use at that natural site.

Basically, in applying the TCM, the investigator collects data on the volume of visits (V_i) to a given recreational site from n different residential areas $(i = 1, ..., n)$, or zones, classified according to distance from the site or, alternatively, travel time. Per capita visit *rates*, $V_i/P_i = v_i$, where P_i is the total population in zone i, are then expressed as a function of travel cost variables (money and time), c_i, and socioeconomic and demographic characteristics, z_i:

$$v_i = f(c_i, z_i)$$

This relationship actually traces a demand function for the recreation site, where c serves as the equivalent of a market price 'signal': the visit rate declines as distance and, hence, costs, increase. For example, in what may be considered a typical TCM study, Duffield (1984) specified the following functional form:

$$\ln v_i = \beta_0 + \beta_1 d_i + \beta_2 s_i + \beta_3 Y_i$$

where d_i is distance, s_i measures the availability of substitute recreation sites to the population in zone i, and Y_i is mean income of the population in zone i. In this study it was necessary to convert physical distance units into money values by using external estimates of the value of travel time and other travel expenditures per unit of distance. When we have estimated the function, we can proceed to calculate consumer surplus measures of value (see Chapter 2 for details).

TCM was originally employed to attach a value to a natural recreation site whose recreational services, for historical, institutional or cultural reasons, have been provided free or at nominal prices (entrance fees). TCM then was used to value a limited range of services provided by an environmental resource; that is, those associated strictly with recreation, excluding a range of other environmental services. The impetus for using TCM to value what was at the time considered a 'non-tangible' output was born out of the need to attach a value to recreational services for a cost–benefit analysis (CBA) of water resource projects. The more comprehensive CBAs involved comparing the benefits from outdoor recreation services with other potential, and conflicting, uses of the water resource (for example, damming a river for flood control as against leaving it to flow through its natural course). The objective was explicitly to compare the economic benefits of recreational activities with those of more traditional uses of water resource projects.

During the forty-odd years since its appearance in the professional literature, TCM has naturally been refined and expanded to deal with more complex situations than in its initial applications. It has often been used to derive values for improvements in the natural resources base, for example, the water quality of water bodies within recreational areas. This is done by using the information gathered for estimating the value of a site's recreational services to value changes in the environmental assets and the level of amenities provided by them. Figure 3.1 above can be used to illustrate the idea. The D_0–D_0 curve would now denote the demand for recreation at a given park, with the vertical axis representing travel costs, that is, the 'price' of reaching the recreation site. When the quality of a water body in the park is improved, the demand curve shifts to D_1–D_1, as either people who never visited the park are now willing to incur the costs of visiting, or people who do visit it would tend to visit it more often. The area between the two curves can therefore be interpreted as representing the money value of the benefits gained.

To summarize: TCM affords a basis for deriving use values of environmental amenities in certain cases, specifically when these amenities are provided by *in-situ* natural resources used for outdoor recreation.

3.2 Valuing Urban Environmental Amenities: the Hedonic Price Model

In most cases, the value of an environmental amenity cannot be revealed via market behaviour connected with travelling expenses to the place of consumption of the service. Other approaches are needed. One of the earliest approaches has been the hedonic price model (HPM) which has been employed to value environmental amenities, such as pollution and noise level, through the impact that these amenities have on property values. The most common application of HPM in the environmental literature has dealt with the impact of polluted air on residential housing values (Ridker and Henning, 1967; Anderson and Crocker, 1971). To the extent that property values partly or fully capitalize pollution-induced damages, HPM may be used to unravel the value of clean air or of quietness embodied in housing prices.[8]

The basic notion underlying hedonic prices is that every market good is composed of a 'bundle of attributes'. The price of, say, a house, p_h, is a function of the 'prices' of the individual attributes. In the case of a house, structural attributes, such as size, age and number of rooms, would be denoted by the vector **S**. Neighbourhood attributes, such as the quality of the school system, open spaces and access to shopping areas, would be denoted by the vector **N**. The environmental amenity of interest, for example, air quality, noise level, or proximity to a waste disposal site, would be denoted by E. The composite price function would then be denoted by:

$$p_h = f(\mathbf{S}, \mathbf{N}, E)$$

Under the assumption that the housing market is in equilibrium, and that the supply of housing is fixed (at least in the short run), it can be shown (Freeman, 1993) that in any given city neighbourhood, for a household which maximizes a utility function of the form

$$u = u(x, \mathbf{S}, \mathbf{N}, E)$$

where x is the composite good, and the maximization is subject to a budget constraint which incorporates the cost of the housing unit, the following first-order condition holds:

$$MRS_{Ex} \equiv (\delta u/\delta E) / (\delta u/\delta x) = dp_h / dE$$

The expression says that the marginal rate of substitution between the market good and the public good, or, in other words, the willingness to pay for an additional unit of E, is equal to the *observable* schedule of the marginal *implicit price function* for the environmental attribute $E - dp_h / dE$. In the normal case, one would expect the latter to be a decreasing function in p_h. Price will decline with additional quantities of the environmental good. It can therefore be viewed as a locus of all the individual marginal WTP in any given location, that is, a demand schedule for the environmental attribute in the given location.[9]

Using econometric techniques, the researcher can therefore estimate the hedonic price function. The implicit price function for air quality would reveal how much more households would be willing to pay for a house in a neighbourhood with better air quality, compared with an identical house in a polluted neighbourhood. This is then the value attached by consumers to improvements in urban air quality in the context of the housing market. Thus, as in the case of TCM, HPM exploits the fact that consumers reveal their valuation of the environmental amenity through their actual consumption behaviour in a market.

The HPM has been extended to value environmental amenities using wage differentials in the labour market which arise because of variation in urban amenities across cities. Here, the underlying assumption is that, given mobility and time, households migrate between cities in search of, for example, better air quality. Households that value better air quality would be willing to accept lower wages for better air quality. In this case, the researcher would estimate a hedonic wage function in addition to the hedonic property function. The value of the amenity would be the sum of the value component of the attribute in each function. Here, the value of the urban environmental amenity is based on consumer behaviour in two interrelated market goods.

3.3 Valuing Environmental Risks to Human Life: Wage Differentials in the Labour Market

In many of the applications of HPM, valuation of environmental amenities has been tied particularly (although by no means solely) to the health impacts of air pollution and to their influence on housing prices. There are, however, extreme instances where environmental pollution poses increased death risks. In such cases, policy-makers may wish to focus directly on the benefits from programmes designed to reduce these risks. Here, the pertinent issue is the value of a human life saved. It is crucial to note that the issue centres on the value of life in a statistical sense of reducing mortality risks, that is, the value of a 'statistical life' and not the life of any one recognizable individual. A more appropriate way to phrase the question is 'What are the benefits of reducing mortality risks from, say, two deaths to one for each 100 000 individuals?' The ethical debate concerning the appropriateness of valuing human life will not be covered here.[10] It should be noted that a range of values of human life based on empirical studies has been employed by the US Environmental Protection Agency in assessing environmental programmes.

Much of the literature on human-life valuation is based on hedonic market price studies. Basically, these studies have derived statistical life values on the basis of data from labour markets on wage differentials among groups of workers exposed to different levels of fatal or non-fatal occupational risks (see Box 3.1). The theory behind the hedonic price approach stipulates that, as in the case of housing, the price of a job (that is, the wage) can be decomposed into the prices of the relevant attributes that define the job, one of which is the degree of risk involved. Workers in riskier jobs must be compensated with higher wages for bearing additional risks. For example, let job A be riskier than job B and have the higher wage of the two, with an annual average differential of $100. The 'riskiness' of job A is given by $r_A = 2/1000 = 0.002$ (that is, 2 fatalities per year) and the riskiness of B is given by $r_B = 0.001$. Taking the wage and risk differentials together, the implied value of one statistical life is $100/(0.002 - 0.001) = \$100\ 000$.

Although the idea behind this approach appears simple enough, there are a number of serious methodological issues that lessen its universal applicability in the environmental arena. The first problem is the issue of transferability. Can inferences based on valuation derived from the labour market, where risks are by and large voluntarily accepted (given sufficient monetary compensation) be used to assess situations where risks are borne involuntarily, as is the case with exposure to environmental pollutants? A second major problem is identical to the one encountered in the housing hedonic model. Wage compensations are a true representation of workers' valuation of mortality risks only if they are fully informed about these risks, a doubtful proposition in many

---

BOX 3.1   WAGE–RISK STUDIES AND
STATISTICAL LIFE VALUES

A number of studies reported in the literature have estimated the value of a statistical life from wage–risk differentials, most of them in the United States and Great Britain. Fisher et al. (1989) summarized a number of studies and, after adjustments to render the results as commensurable as possible, came up with a range of estimates for the mean value of a statistical life of between $1.6 million to $9 million (in 1986 US dollars). With the exception of a couple of high values, most of the studies yield mean estimates within the US$1.6 to $4 million range. Comparable figures for a statistical case of *morbidity* are few. A value of US$883 000 has been reported for the value of a statistical case of chronic bronchitis, and $200 000 per case of chronic lung disease (Cropper and Oates, 1992).

---

instances. Finally, in countries where wages are set nationwide and do not reflect local amenities (such as air quality), or where wage compensations for job safety have been institutionalized through union negotiations and are based more on relative bargaining power in the labour market than on relative job risk, it would probably be difficult, if not impossible, econometrically to extract amenity values or life values, respectively, from wage differential analyses.

3.4   Valuing Health Damages from Market Behaviour: the Cost of Illness Method

The Cost of Illness method (COI) has often been employed to estimate economic gains from improved health. COI estimates the changes in private and public expenditures on health care and the value of lost production, on the basis of the relationship between excess morbidity or mortality and ambient pollution levels (usually referred to as 'dose–response functions') (see Box 3.2). But these expenditures (for example, working days lost in Box 3.2) do not necessarily measure everything that households spend, or are willing to pay to avoid poor health.

Typically, reductions in pollution-induced health effects result in savings in four cost categories:

1. Out-of-pocket expenses associated with illness or injury.
2. Forgone earnings, or the imputed value of restricted activity days.

BOX 3.2 DOSE–RESPONSE FUNCTIONS

A dose–response function relates the incidence of cases of ill-health or death to the (in the present context) level of pollution, as well as other intervening variables likely to affect ill-health, such as smoking, age and so on. These functions are typically estimated from relatively large databases, where, unlike the case of clinical studies, it is difficult to control for these intervening variables. The estimation therefore requires rather sophisticated statistical techniques in order to delineate the impact of pollution. Although estimating dose–response functions is usually carried out by epidemiologists and public health researchers, the pioneering study relating air pollution to mortality (incidence of deaths in the population) was carried out by two economists, Lave and Seskin (1977). They found that a 1 per cent reduction in air pollution (measured as the ambient concentration of sulphate and total suspended particulate matter, TSP) with all other variables held constant, would give rise to a 0.12 per cent reduction in mortality. They proceeded to use these relationships in order to derive a monetary value to health damages, using the COI approach.

In a related study, Ostro (1983) used a large database from the US to carry out a regression analysis relating morbidity (incidence of disease in the population) and variables such as race, marriage, income, social status, sex, cigarette consumption, work status, temperature, rainfall and population density. His analysis showed that, *ceteris paribus*, a 1 per cent reduction in TSP leads to a 0.45 per cent reduction in 'working days lost' (a common measure of overall morbidity), and to a 0.39 per cent reduction in 'restricted activity days' (another common measure of overall morbidity, which also captures the impact on the non-working segment of the population).

---

3. Avertive or defensive expenditures owing to pollution, for example, the cost of installing and operating air-conditioners, time allocated to increased physical exercise or the cost of moving to a cleaner neighbourhood.
4. Disutility associated with pollution-induced illnesses, for example, pain, stress and anxiety (sometimes referred to as psychological costs of pollution).

By its very nature, COI overlooks the last two: preventive expenditures and the psychic disutility associated with health damages. This leads to an underestimation of the full burden of pollution imposed on individuals, because COI estimates tend to reflect only part of individual experience.

The reason for this serious shortcoming is that COI rests on the premise that improvement in well-being is synonymous with maximizing society's output of goods and services, as commonly measured in national income accounts by net national product (that is, gross national product (GNP) – depreciation), or its equivalent – net national income. But this is not necessarily synonymous with society's welfare or well-being. Goods and services certainly contribute to our well-being, but so do environmental assets, even if they do not enter these output measures. In the same vein, COI overlooks sick-day losses owing to the impact of pollution on retirees, housewives and children, because they are not part of the workforce and as such their bed-days do not reduce society's measured output. Clearly, their welfare is nevertheless affected by pollution. Thus COI is not considered to be a satisfactory method for estimating WTP. On the positive side, however, COI is intuitively appealing and data on earnings and medical expenditures are relatively easy to obtain. This has led to its popularity among researchers, economists and non-economists alike.[11]

Another problem with the COI approach is that households do not usually bear the full economic consequences of work-loss days due to morbidity unless it permanently incapacitates future productivity and leads to a permanent reduction in earning. This is because – in many countries – sick-leave coverage (often by the employer) is rather commonplace; medical expenditures are covered or reimbursed by national health insurance or by health-maintenance organizations, which in turn are often heavily subsidized by government. Moreover, people do not normally possess the information which would enable them fully to assess the economic impact of exposure and disease and hence incorporate that information in determining the level of medical expenditures. The pollution-induced outlays are largely borne by society, and would be poorly reflected in the WTP of the individual household. In these situation, COI – if it incorporates government, in addition to private, outlays on health – could yield higher values than the indirect methods which aggregate market-revealed valuations of *individual* households.

3.5   Valuing Environmental Amenities as Inputs in the Production of Human Health

The household production function method (HPF) analyses the behaviour and decisions of households when they engage in self-production (and, subsequently, consumption) of services using other goods and services, and often also time, as inputs in the production process. In the environmental economics field HPF often focuses on the enhancement of health or the prevention of health damages due to pollution. Improved health contributes to well-being on four counts:

1. It reduces expenditures on health-care services, thus increasing the amount of income left for production and consumption of utility-enhancing goods and services.
2. It reduces the amount of time spent on averting potential damages.
3. It further diminishes the negative impact on welfare by limiting income loss due to sick-days taken, or by increasing income due to health-related productivity gains.
4. It reduces the disutility associated with being ill.

To this end, the household consumes an array of market goods and services, including health care. For example, households attempt to rectify or prevent health damages associated with air pollution by installing air-conditioners or air-filters, by refraining from outdoor activities during high-pollution periods, or by buying medicines for the treatment of pollution-induced respiratory ailments.

Better air quality, however, reduces the need for or use of these commodities; that is, clean air may be considered a 'substitute' commodity. HPF treats the environmental amenity, market goods and services (including health-care goods and services) as 'inputs' in a process of 'producing' health. Improved environmental quality thereby reduces the reliance on preventive and curative 'inputs'; that is, it reduces the demand for the other market inputs. In applying the method, the investigator uses data on household behaviour to estimate the household health production function. From this function the researcher derives the implied trade-off between an increase in the level of the relevant environmental amenity and expenditures on the other health-related inputs. For example, other things being equal, better water quality may reduce the occurrence of digestive tract illnesses, and thereby the consumption of health-care services, which entail both private and social monetary outlays. Thus HPF enables the investigator to calculate the implicit value of changes in the provision of non-market environmental assets through the indirect effect on the consumption of market-priced health inputs.

To illustrate, consider the following case[12] where a person's utility is a function of a composite market good, x, and his health status, H:

$$U = f(x, H)$$

To maintain or promote his health, the individual combines some private good, q (say, the purchase of an air-filtering system) and a non-market environmental good, E (say, air quality), through a health production function,

$$H = \phi(q, E)$$

Under the assumption that our individual maximizes utility subject to a budget constraint and the health production function, it can be shown (for example, Smith, 1991) that his valuation, W, of an additional unit of E is given by

$$W = p_q(\phi_E / \phi_q)$$

where p_q is the price of q and ϕ_i are the partial derivatives with respect to E and q. Indeed, W expresses the amount of money this person will save in expenditures on q, for a given utility level and prices of the two private goods, as a result of a unit increase in E. The idea here is that if there exist data which would make it possible statistically to estimate the health production function, one could obtain an estimate of the monetary value of the environmental good without knowing the utility function.

Although seemingly similar, HPF and COI are methodologically distinct. It is not possible to go into detail here; an example should suffice. While taken into account by HPF, COI overlooks preventive expenditures, money spent by a household to ward off the effects of a deteriorated environment. For example, an asthmatic person may install an air-conditioner as a means of protecting herself against the bad effects of air pollution. This expenditure would be excluded from COI.

Values of a statistical life have also been obtained by a method which belongs to the HPF genre. It has often been referred to in the literature as the averting behaviour approach. The method focuses on market behaviour with respect to the purchase of goods and services that may reduce the risk of death, for example, seat belts or smoke detectors. Here, other things being equal (that is, the consumption of all other goods and services, income, and so on), the value of a small reduction in mortality risk provided by the device is measured by the value of the device. The preventive devices, or risk-reducing services, can also be viewed as inputs in the process of producing more 'longevity' in the statistical sense.

Finally, as an aside, a little reflection will show that the travel cost method can also be viewed as a type of an HPF, a recreation production function model, where travelling expenses, equipment and environmental amenities are combined by the household in 'producing' recreational services at natural sites.

3.6 Valuing Local Environmental Goods: the Collective Choice Approach

In a recent paper, Wallace Oates (1996) proposed yet another indirect approach for the estimation of demand for environmental assets (and valuation using the consumers' surplus measure), namely, the collective choice (CC) approach. This approach is well known in the literature on local public finance, and has been employed for the past 25 years to estimate the demand for municipal services, some of which can be classified as *local* public goods. Interestingly, the very first application of this approach involved the estimation of the demand for an environmental resource – municipal parks (and police services).[13] Oates suggests that economists explore the prospects for extending it to other locally based environmental resources, such as air quality, water quality and noise, whose levels are often influenced, if not outright determined, by the members of the community through the political process. The attractiveness of this approach stems from its being grounded in observed behaviour, albeit in the political arena rather than the market.

The CC approach attempts to derive the demand function on the basis of the observed levels of the municipal services across communities, under the assumption that the realization of the level was decided upon by citizens through collective choice institutions, such as the legislative process or direct referenda.[14] Specifically, the observed outcome is associated with the demand of some decisive voter, usually the 'median voter'. This implies that there is a majority voting system in which the quantity selected is such that half the population wants more and half the population wants less than that quantity, and the median voter is the one who 'tips' the scale in favour of the level to be provided. It is further assumed that the representative household has an income level equal to the median income for the community, so that the quantity of municipal commodities chosen by any community is the amount which is desired by the consumer with the median income for that community. This allows the investigator to associate the observed municipal budget allocation for any community with a point on the demand curve of the median voter of that community.

The standard model is based on a sample of jurisdictions for which there are observed fiscal outcomes. The basic demand function for the median voter is usually of the form:

$$G = g(t, Y)$$

where G is the quantity demanded of the local service, t is the median voter's tax share (eventually converted to a variable expressing the 'price' of the local good), and Y is his income (the median family income in the jurisdiction). On multiplying both sides of the equation by the (unobservable!) price of a unit of the public good, P, which, to simplify the estimation procedure, is assumed to be uniform across communities, one gets on the left-hand side the expression $E = GP$, which is the level of expenditure in the community on the public service, data for which are usually readily available. Similarly, on the right-hand side of the equation, we get an implicit expression for the 'tax price', T, since $t = T/P$. T is the median voter's 'tax price' for a unit of the service, and the tax share, t, is calculated as the ratio of the median house value in the community to the total value of taxable property in the community.[15] This is based on the assumption that most local public services are financed by property taxation. After further simplifications, the standard model ends up with an expression for the demand equation, consisting of empirically measurable variables, of the form:

$$\ln E = c + \alpha \ln t + \sigma \ln N + \beta \ln Y + v$$

where N stands for the population of the community, α is an estimate of the price elasticity of demand, and β is income elasticity. Finally, as in the case of standard demand analysis, a monetary value for the public good can then be obtained through the associated (Marshallian) consumer's surplus.

It should be noted, however, that the CC approach cannot be used when the outputs of environmental goods are determined *externally*; that is, by the central government authorities, as in the case of national standards for ambient air quality which must be met in all jurisdictions.[16]

4.   STATED PREFERENCES: USING HYPOTHETICAL MARKETS TO EXTRACT VALUATIONS DIRECTLY

There may be situations in which the data necessary to apply any of the indirect methods discussed in the previous section are either lacking or difficult to obtain. More importantly, there is the case of non-use benefits, which are not associated with the actual use of an environmental asset or consumption of environmental services, and therefore cannot be easily coupled with the consumption of a market good. It is widely thought that these benefits cannot be valued through any indirect method.

In the absence of appropriate data or interdependent market goods, the alternative is to ask people directly what their willingness to pay for a change in environmental quality is. The valuation technique known as the contingent valuation method (often referred to as 'CVM') accomplishes this. CVM invokes a framework of a contingent (that is, hypothetical, sometimes also referred to as 'constructed') market, used to elicit valuations from individuals.

In recent years the term 'stated preference experiments' (SP) has been broadened to cover any direct valuation method; that is, any method which aims to elicit explicit or implicit valuations of an environmental asset through an appropriately constructed set of queries. There are no actual behavioural changes involved; respondents merely *state* that they would behave in a certain fashion. Under CVM, hitherto, the most widely used SP approach, individuals are prompted to state their WTP for the changes in the (quantity or quality) of the environmental good in question, either through an open question format or a dichotomous choice procedure (DC).[17] More recently, a group of methods, often referred to as 'conjoint analysis' (CA) (Louviere, 1994, 1998),[18] has been attracting the attention of valuation practitioners, and applied in the field of environmental valuation, specifically as an alternative to CVM. CA encompasses a variety of multi-attribute preference elicitation techniques, extensively employed by market researchers to evaluate potential new products and new markets for existing products. One of the principal attractions of this approach is that it allows for a direct valuation of the *attribute components* of the environmental good, for example, attributes associated with components of a stream, such as biochemical oxygen demand (BOD) and dissolved oxygen, instead of a single, general term, 'water quality'.

4.1 Valuing through Constructed Markets: the Contingent Valuation Method[19]

Assume an individual has a utility function of the form $u(x; z)$, where x is a market goods and z is a an environmental good.[20] Our individual is a rational person, and strives to maximize utility by choosing the number of units of x. The level of the provision of the environmental good, however, is determined by a relevant authority for example, the Environment Ministry or the Environmental Protection Authority. The individual therefore maximizes utility through varying the quantity of x, subject to a budget constraint, $px = y$, where p is the (market) price of x and y is income. The solution of this optimization yields the individual's demand functions for x, the market good:

$$x = h(p; z, y)$$

We can now define the indirect utility function, $v(p, z, y) \equiv u[h(p, z, y), z]$, that values utility at the optimal x. Next, suppose an environmental improvement takes place, and z is increased by the authority from z^0 to z^1, with no change in market prices and income. It must follow that utility (welfare) in the new state, u^1, is higher that utility in the initial state, u^0, namely,

$$u^1 = v(p, z^1, y) > u^0 = v(p, z^0, y)$$

The highest sum our individual would be willing to pay (*WTP*) for this change[21] is the amount of money that equates the two terms above. In terms of the indirect utility function,

General environmental economics

$$v(p, z^1, y - WTP) = v(p, z^0, y)$$

WTP is the amount of money that, if extracted from the individual after the change in z, will leave him – in terms of his level of well-being – as well off as he was before the change. It is that sum of money which, when subtracted from income, keeps well-being constant at its original level before the increase in the environmental good from z^0 to z^1, *the money equivalent of the improvement*. Likewise, one can analyse the reverse situation: what is the minimum sum of money the individual is willing to accept, as a kind of a 'bribe' in order to consent to a decrease in z? This sum is called willingness to accept (*WTA*).[22] Given the public-good nature of most environmental assets, summing up these valuations over all households in the relevant community yields a monetary value for a change in the level of z.[23]

Davis (1963) was the first to employ a crude form of CVM to estimate the benefits of a recreation area in Maine. Since then CVM studies have queried people about their valuation of a wide spectrum of benefits from environmental improvements. These include, among many others, water-quality enhancement for recreation; reduction in air-pollution-induced respiratory ailments; reductions in mortality risks from hazardous wastes; improved visibility in national parks; reducing acid-rain damages to fish and wildlife; preserving endangered species and biodiversity.

There are two primary assumptions of the direct valuation methodology. The first is that the consumer is the best judge of his best interests, and the second that the consumer's ability to rank preferences is both rational and knowledgeable. Therefore, special attention must be paid to the design of any CVM study because the hypothetical nature of the CVM methodology could result in uncertainty, doubt and even irrationality in the average consumer when confronted with an imaginary commodity. Attention must also be paid to the constructed market. The 'market' is composed of the commodity to be valued, the institutional context of its provision (for example, national or local government), and the means of financing it, or the so-called 'payment vehicle' (for example, general taxes, local taxes, one-time versus annual payments, a charge on utility bills, entry fees). Using questionnaires and surveys, individuals are induced to volunteer information regarding the maximum sum of money they would be willing to pay for the non-market good, as if they were going to 'purchase' it in the hypothetical market.

Although CVM has made substantial inroads during the past 25 years into mainstream environmental economic research, doubts remain with respect to the reliability of direct valuation, mainly because of the presence of strong hypothetical underpinnings. None the less, research by environmental economists, as well as sociologists and psychologists, into the validity and reliability of CVM has so far indicated quite encouraging results *vis-à-vis* other methods of preference measurements. There have not been many studies so far that compared hypothetical and actual willingness to pay (see Box 3.3). The overall impression from those that did is, however, that in general they did not report on significant or unexplainable gaps between WTP values yielded in these two cases.[24]

BOX 3.3   VALUATIONS COMPARED: DIRECT VERSUS INDIRECT APPROACHES

In theory, at least, CVM should produce the same valuations as any other method purporting to measure WTP. Given the hypothetical nature of the CVM, it is understandable that a number of researchers attempted to assess its reliability and accuracy against behaviour-based approaches. Comparisons have most often been made between the CVM and TCM, HPM or HPF (Cropper and Freeman, 1991; Graves, 1991; OECD, 1989; Shechter, 1992). Although the figures tend to diverge widely in the case of WTA, results for WTP, on the whole, are quite encouraging, and bestow a measure of credibility on CVM (NOAA, 1993). Naturally, the degree of correspondence hinges on several crucial parameters, such as the elicitation technique used in the CVM and the nature of the commodity being valued.

A number of interesting attempts were made to compare hypothetical and actual WTP in an *experimental* setting. A couple of studies, which dealt with private goods – strawberries and hunting permits (reported in Cropper and Oates, 1992) – did not detect any statistically significant differences between the mean values of WTP under the two experimental settings.

Yet the hypothetical nature of CVM, and the fact that it depends on sample survey data, could weaken the assumption of rational and knowledgeable consumers, and give rise to a number of biases. Biases occur in CVM studies for several reasons. For example, the scenario might contain incentives for respondents to misrepresent their true WTP in order to influence the final outcome (strategic bias). It might also inadvertently contain cues (reflecting the researchers' own biases, for example) that might subconsciously affect the WTP responses. In order to enhance the reliability of a CVM study, environmental economists have been working on developing guidelines and protocols for bias reduction and detection. Thus researchers have stressed that the key scenario elements must be understandable, meaningful and plausible. The WTP questions must be clear and unambiguous. Respondents should be familiar with the commodity to be valued. Ideally, of course, respondents should also have had prior valuation and choice experience with respect to consumption levels of the commodity so that they will have reasonably well-formed values. The likelihood that this condition will be met is rather small. All in all, the investigator must do his utmost to prevent potential response biases (see Box 3.4).

BOX 3.4   POTENTIAL BIASES IN CVM

Mitchell and Carson (1989) have catalogued and analysed a large number of potential biases that may affect respondents' valuation elicited through a CVM survey. A bias would occur whenever responses overstate or understate true value in some systematic rather than random fashion.

The most worrisome bias is the *strategic bias*, which occurs when respondents deliberately state a sum which is different from their true WTP. They may do so either because they want to influence the final outcome in favour of what they would like to see as the desired level of provision of the public good, or if they believe the stated amount would affect the eventual sum they would be charged. That is, they would try to free-ride. To date, however, most empirical studies designed to test for the existence of this bias indicate that it is a relatively minor problem (for example, Milon, 1989), especially when respondents are queried about their WTP rather than WTA.

A different set of biases is associated with the design of the CVM experiment, the most troubling one being the *starting-point bias*. Here, the elicitation method introduces a 'clue' that may influence the WTP response, through a tendency of respondents to anchor the final, maximum WTP response at or near the sum used as a starting-point in the bidding process. A similar problem arises when the payment vehicle (entrance fee, a municipal tax) is resented by the respondents, say, on ethical grounds, and influences the stated WTP amount. Yet another set of biases involves *mis-specifying* the CVM scenario. In this case the respondent simply does not respond to the scenario intended by the investigator, because he or she either does not understand the scenario, or interprets it in a different way, and provides an inappropriate answer. CVM practitioners are of course aware of these shortcomings, and are continuously engaged in efforts to devise elicitation mechanisms which would minimize these types of biases.

Finally, CVM has played a major role in the debate on non-use benefits. In using CVM in this context, people are almost invariably queried in a direct way to state their WTP for non-use benefits, sometimes for complex issues such as ecological balance, biodiversity, the preservation of tropical forests or protection of endangered species. All the methodological problems raised in connection with the use of CVM might turn out with extra force in this case, because of the difficulty of accurate commodity description, lack of familiarity with the commodity being assessed, and the lack of experience with anything remotely approaching such commodities in actual markets. Nevertheless, very recently CVM has been favourably reviewed by a panel of highly respected economists, co-chaired by two Nobel laureates, Arrow and Solow (NOAA, 1993; see also Carson et al., 1996).

4.2 Valuing Attributes of Environmental Assets: Conjoint Analysis

The basic idea underlying all CA methods is that commodities possess value because of their attributes.[25] In CA all possible attributes of the good in question are first identified and are associated with a cardinal or ordinal measurement scale. Focus groups are often used to identify the important attributes of the environmental good under study. From the set of all permutations of attributes and possible values that these attributes could take, a smaller, more manageable subset of combinations is chosen. A dominant feature in the environmental economics literature dealing with the applications of these marketing research tools is that, in addition to the various attributes of the environmental good, the choices include at least one monetary attribute, such as price, the cost of provision or access cost. Respondents are then asked to rank or rate the various combination options (or select a most preferred one from the set) in a series of carefully conducted experiments. This process yields marginal rates of substitution (MRS) for specified changes in the different attributes of the good under study.

SP techniques are designed to measure the rates at which people are willing to accept such trade-offs. By including a monetary cost, we can express these trade-offs in dollar terms, or marginal WTP valuation of attributes. Indeed, it has been argued that CVM is the most simplified stated preferences technique: there are only two attributes (cost and the quantity or quality of the non-market good), and two choices: paying the cost and getting the good, or not. Advocates of conjoint analysis techniques would argue that CV produces poor approximations to the true value of the good, because people never engage in explicit trade-offs between the environment and money. However, ranking or comparing among attributes of the environmental commodity, and thereby *implicitly* making trade-offs between the environmental commodity and money, is a more common experience.

It should also be pointed out that having attribute-specific valuations can greatly facilitate the carrying out of *benefit transfer* studies, in which, due to the high costs of carrying out a separate study, benefit values derived for one site are applied – after proper transformation – to the valuation of another site. If the components of total valuations are available, as in the case in conjoint analysis, an improved estimate of total value for the new site will be obtained by combining the actual level of the relevant attributes at the new site with the attribute-specific benefits of the studied site.

In Box 3.5 we briefly describe two specific conjoint analysis methods: rated pair format (RPF) and contingent ranking (CR).[26] The rated pair format method focuses on choosing in a systematic fashion between pairs of choices, and measures respondents' valuation of slight variations in attributes by requiring them to evaluate trade-offs among various attributes. Contingent ranking ranks a set of attribute bundles where each bundle, or combination of attributes, represents a hypothetical 'good'.

BOX 3.5   TWO EXAMPLES OF CONJOINT ANALYSIS

In a series of RPF experiments, focusing specifically on valuing air-pollution-related health damages[27] (Desvousges et al., 1997; Johnson and Desvousges, 1997), respondents were sequentially presented with a series of pairs of health-related conditions, or 'commodity bundles'. A bundle defined the health condition in terms of (1) pollution-induced disease attributes such as type of the health episode (for example, coughing, coughing with wheezing), (2) the duration of the episode, restrictions on daily activities, and (3) the disease-related costs to the household (health maintenance expenditures that are not covered by government or health insurance packages). Differentiation across bundles was achieved through varying attribute levels. Household were asked to compare sequentially between pairs and, further, to rate the intensity of their preference for the preferred pair. The goal of the analysis was to estimate a function that maps attributes into a utility index that is consistent with the observed individuals' rating data, on the assumption that one can specify (indirect) utility as a function of commodity attributes, personal characteristics *and* the cost variable. Using ordered logit or probit regression techniques and some additional assumptions, the authors were able to derive estimates of the parameters of the utility function, that is, the coefficients

---

associated with the health attributes, with individual characteristics and with cost. If the function is specified as being linear in these parameters, then these coefficients estimate the respective marginal effects on utility. Specifically, the cost parameter represents the marginal utility of money, since any decrease in health expenditures (associated with improved health) corresponds to a marginal increase in income which can be spent on other goods and services. It is then possible to convert marginal utilities of the health attribute to marginal WTP valuations by dividing them by the marginal utility of money.

A typical application of CR was carried out by Foster and Mourato (1997), who investigated the possibility of imposing restrictions on pesticide use in cereal production.[28] These pesticides have been shown to cause illness in humans as a result of field exposure, as well as a decline in farmland bird species. Accordingly, the selected attributes were: number of bird species, cases of illness and the price of a loaf of bread, which presumably would be affected if these farming practices were halted, and alternative, more costly methods, but less injurious to people and the environment were adopted instead. Three levels were specified for each attribute. For the environmental attribute: 9, 5 and 2 bird species in decline; 100, 60 and 40 cases of ill-health per year for the health attribute; and 60, 85 and 115 pence per loaf for the affected farm output, yielding a total of $3^3 = 27$ distinct commodity bundles. Respondents were then confronted with these options, and asked to rank them, thereby enabling the investigator to obtain information about their preference structures. One can show that the above specific values imply a range of implicit values of 0.42–2.75 pence per case of illness avoided *per loaf* of bread, and 3.57–18.33 pence per species conserved *per loaf* of bread. By stating their ranking of the various bundles, respondents reveal their implied valuations, their WTP for the various attributes.

Some words of caution are in order, however. There are many design issues yet to be resolved in the application of CA methods to valuing environmental assets, notwithstanding widespread interest and a measure of enthusiasm among valuation practitioners, in light of the inherent weaknesses of CVM. Efficacious ways must yet be devised to avoid some of its inherent drawbacks such as session length, lack of validation tests, and the impact of learning and fatigue which could influence results. Smith (1997) has recently cautioned that it is too early to compare the performance of conjoint strategies with CVM, and that more experience is needed before an evaluation of this questioning mode for environmental resources can be developed. This is an especially salient argument, because some practitioners have been concluding that CA avoids the problems of CVM. Finally, it is important to remember that rating and trade-off models provide estimates of *marginal* WTP, or MRS, based on commodity to commodity comparisons, and these are definitely not *total* WTP for a change in the environmental good.

5.   FROM NUMBERS TO POLICY: WHAT IS THE VALUE OF MONETARY VALUES?

Preceding sections have been devoted to explaining how to measure changes in environmental quality in monetary units. Since policies involving environmental improvements and environmental regulation entail costs, much debate has understandably focused on the expected benefits as the rationale for spending on such policies (see Box 3.6). Although all the benefit valuation methods presented use a common yardstick, namely, money, there is no unique correct method; rather, each has its advantages and disadvantages. The refinement of existing techniques and the development of new ones to accommodate a wider range of values is a major challenge to economists.

However, despite advances in valuation made over the past 40 years, a serious gap remains. The methods have not been routinely incorporated into the decision-making process.[29] This raises the question: if the product is so useful, why isn't it fully utilized? After all, it is often argued that what politicians understand and grasp best is numbers, particularly when it comes to dollars and cents. While it is not possible to provide complete answers, one could nevertheless offer a few explanations for the gap between academic studies and practice. This may help to convince decision-makers that in spite of the still many 'holes', there is a substantial amount of cheese mass from which it is worth taking a bite.[30]

There is a strong resistance to attaching money values to intangible environmental benefits arising from aesthetics, preservation of wildlife, human health, and the like. It is often asserted that, first, these are and cannot be valued, and second, that on moral grounds no such tag *should* ever be attached to them. The implication of the first objection, in economic terms, is that their value is infinite; that is, no expense should be spared in saving them from impending damage, or for rehabilitating them. This is erroneous. In a world of limited resources relative to human wants, there is indeed a limit to what society can spend on these uses, important and valued as they may be. Environmental benefits do carry a finite price tag.

BOX 3.6   ECONOMY-WIDE BENEFIT ASSESSMENTS

This chapter has focused on the *micro* aspects (those concerned with individual decision units, such as individuals, households or firms) of the economic theory which underlies valuation methodologies. However, it is the *aggregate*, or economy-wide benefits and damages which are most relevant in environmental decision-making.

In recent years several attempts to derive such aggregate, national benefit estimates have been made in a number of countries, especially the US and Western Europe. For example, air pollution control policies in the United States, over the decade of 1970s, has yielded benefits (by avoiding damages) in the range of $9 to $92 billion (1984 US dollars), with the most reasonable point estimate being $37 billion (Portney, 1990). These benefits resulted from improvement in both stationary and mobile emissions, associated with reductions in health, materials, agricultural and aesthetic damages (Cropper and Oates, 1992). For 1978 alone, the benefits from both air and water pollution control amounted to 1.25 per cent of GNP (Freeman, 1982). Furthermore, cost–benefit analysis has received a substantial boost from the 1981 Executive Order 12291; it has been performed in the rule-making process by the Environmental Protection Agency (EPA) for all major environmental regulations.

Estimates of national damages from environmental degradation have also been carried out in number of European countries (reported in OECD, 1989; Navrud, 1992). In the Netherlands, for example, air, water and noise pollution damages in 1986 represented 0.5–0.9 per cent of GNP. This is probably an underestimate, since in reaching this figure the researchers did not attempt to monetize all known damages. A parallel study in Germany yielded a rather high estimate of 6 per cent of GNP for 1985.

It should be noted that economy-wide studies (as reported, for example, in Kuik et al., 1992) are also concerned with the impact of regulatory programme outlays on macroeconomic variables, for example, GNP, price level and inflation, unemployment, and so on. This topic is discussed at greater length in Chapter 7.

It is an altogether different argument to say that there are some things in life which should not be valued in money terms, for moral, philosophical or other reasons. That is to say, people simply refuse to associate them with 'any monetary yardstick', period! Although this is a perfectly defensible stand, one should be fully aware of its implications in the present context. Decisions on allocating scarce public or private funds to these purposes must be made using some criterion, whether explicitly or implicitly, for ordering the 'worthiness' of competing uses for these funds. Any decision which allocates funds to the preservation, rehabilitation or improvement of environmental assets and services necessarily takes them away from other presumably no less deserving uses. Many supposedly 'money-value-free' prioritizations in the policy decision-making process tacitly attach price tags to the selected choices (for example, the cost of injury and property damage due to accidents which could have been avoided by building an overpass at a busy intersection).

Policy-makers and the public at large have often been preoccupied with the question of who stands to benefit from and who should bear the costs of a change in environmental quality. Economists have been slow to incorporate distributive concerns into benefit studies. For example, in interpreting the results of a typical valuation study, say, of an air pollution abatement programme which results in positive net benefit to a community, the numbers only say the following: regardless of who bears the cost of abatement (for example, consumers through higher prices, producers through reduced profits, or workers through lower wages, or unemployment), or who stands to reap the benefit (for example, the people who live in the polluted neighbourhoods), a significant reduction in pollution levels would be a rational policy imperative. Unfortunately, many empirical valuation studies have neglected to address distributional issues and, though understandable on purely methodological grounds, this tends to reduce their effectiveness in terms of policy-making. It is essential in many cases explicitly to address the thorny problem of the distribution, or incidence, of benefits and costs among different groups or sectors; that is, who stands to benefit from, and who would bear the costs of pollution abatement.

There may be other reasons for the lukewarm response to valuation studies which have nothing to do with the studies *per se* (OECD, 1992). Political considerations and the bureaucratic framework will surely influence the prospects of implementing the policy prescriptions of valuation studies.[31] It seems that from the point of view of successful impact on policy, what counts most is the relevance of a valuation study to an issue which is high on the political agenda at the time of the study's appearance (as well, of course, as the quality of the product!). These circumstances are conducive to another essential element: gaining access to the media as an effective means of reaching the public and policy-makers. Media exposure (let us hope, undistorted) sometimes seems to be a crucial factor in this respect.

Finally, as is the case with similar analyses which cause the decision process to become 'transparent', a well-conducted study of environmental benefit valuation involves explicit presentation of all the assumptions, parameters and the manner in which decisions have been arrived at. This may be anathema to those who would prefer a degree of fuzziness, feeling more secure with an 'opaque' process. Some simply dislike results which run counter to what they believe *a priori* should be the preferred alternative. In ancient times they might kill the messenger that brought undesired news; today they shelve the study.

NOTES

1. Most of this chapter focuses on the last two functions: resource inputs and amenities. The term 'resources' will be used to denote the former and 'services' to denote the latter.
2. The terms 'well-being', 'welfare' and 'utility' will be used interchangeably. Economists in formal analyses use the last term. The second term is more often used in normative economic analyses, specifically when dealing with society's level of well-being.
3. The next chapter dwells extensively on the decision-support technique economists recommend for this task, namely, cost–benefit analysis.
4. The reader is referred to Chapter 2 which touches on some of the issues addressed here.
5. Many economists, however, would probably trace the beginnings of *measurement* efforts in this area to the now celebrated 1947 letter from the economist Harold Hotelling (whose name is associated with another important contribution to the depletable resource literature, the Hotelling Rule for optimal extraction) to the Director of the US National Park Service. In the letter Hotelling suggested a method for quantifying recreation benefits, which later became known as the travel cost method (see below). The method was not scientifically introduced into the economic literature until ten years later, in a paper published in 1958 by Trice and Wood.
6. Note that any area in Figure 3.1 is given by P (price, or dollars per unit of the good), multiplied by Q (quantity, or the number of units), yielding the total dollar amount spent on that quantity.
7. Trice and Wood (1958), and especially Clawson (1959) and Knetsch (1963), McConnell (1985) provide an advanced review of the subject.
8. For an excellent review of the method see Freeman (1993).
9. These will not necessarily be identical for all locations in a city since N differs across neighbourhoods.
10. The interested reader is referred to a volume by Jones-Lee (1982) that deals extensively with this issue. It is interesting to note that the Jewish Talmud, going back to the second century AD, took a somewhat similar approach. The slave market served in this case as the basis for assessing health damages (due to injury). The price mechanism of the slave market placed a value on a slave according to his expected lifetime contribution to his master's revenues; that is, the maximum that the buyer would be willing to pay for the slave. Compensation for bodily injuries of slaves and free people alike was determined by the differential price of a slave, with and without an injury.
11. This approach, too, pre-dates modern economic science. Writing in the late seventeenth century, Sir William Petty employed a simpler version to compute the loss 'sustained by the Plague, by the Slaughter of Men in War, and by the sending them abroad into the Service of Foreign Princes' (quoted in Fein, 1976).
12. For a comprehensive review of the HPF method, see Smith (1991).
13. Bergstrom and Goodman (1973).
14. Diamond and Housman (1993), two long-time critics of the contingent valuation method, argue that collective choice mechanisms, based on observed choices, are a much better

reflection of citizen preferences for environmental public goods than contingent valuation surveys, which are based on hypothetical markets.

15. That is, the value of real estate as assessed by the municipality for tax purposes.

16. But, as Oates points out, *over*-attainment, say, above the prescribed standard of minimum level of environmental quality, can still be associated with jurisdictional choice. In this case the CC approach could probably be usefully applied.

17. In the DC (also referred to as 'binary type question') format respondents are presented with a money value (drawn from an appropriate predetermined set of values) and are asked whether they would or would not agree to pay the indicated sum. Presumably this format is better suited to the task of eliciting WTP valuations than the 'open-question' format (which simply asks for the maximum WTP sum) because it mimics actual purchase decisions. (Sometimes, however, researchers have combined the two formats, by following up the DC question with the open format; see, for example, Shechter, et al., 1998). Using this format, however, results in some loss of information on the distribution of WTP responses, since it does not yield the respondent's maximum WTP. Hanemann (1984), drawing on McFadden's (1973) random utility model, formulated the theoretical foundations for the analysis of DC data and the calculation of welfare measure. Cameron (1988) provided an alternative, and presumably more straightforward approach to analysing these data.

18. Conjoint analysis has also been referred to as stated preference experiments, but the latter term has in recent years been widened to include *all* direct valuation methods. We shall also adhere to the wider coverage definition.

19. The standard reference for CVM is Mitchell and Carson (1989). See also Bjornstad and Kahn (1996).

20. Our exposition follows the standard WTP formulation; see, for example, Fisher (1996), or Chapter 2.

21. Also termed the 'compensating surplus' measure of utility change; see Chapter 2.

22. A lively debate in recent environmental economics literature has centred on the appropriateness of using WTP compared with WTA. Some, notably Knetsch and others (for example, Knetsch and Sinden, 1984) have argued that WTA is the only valid measure. In the case of WTA, individuals are asked to value a good which they supposedly 'own' (for example, clean air), while in the case of WTP they are asked to 'purchase' the improvement in air quality, thus implying that they do not yet possess it. Interestingly, this issue was discussed within the framework of ancient Jewish Oral Law. In assessing damages for suffering associated with pain, it was argued by Maimonides (the great twelfth-century scholar and biblical commentator) that the proper compensation should be based on how much an individual *would be willing to pay to avoid* such suffering (that is, WTP). But another contemporary scholar argued that compensation should rather reflect the person's *willingness to accept* such an injury (that is, WTA).

23. We refer the reader to Chapter 2 where various critical remarks about aggregation have been made.

24. It should be noted that this was not the case when, instead of WTP, WTA measures were used.

25. This premise, incidentally, is not unique to conjoint analysis; we have seen earlier that it also underlies the hedonic price model approach. However, conjoint analysis is a *direct* approach, while hedonic price is an *indirect* one.

26. Mackenzie (1993) provides a useful comparative survey of SP models.

27. There are also an increasing number of applications of SP in the natural resource economics literature. For example, Adamowicz et al. (1994) use SP to explain recreational site choice, and Adamowicz et al. (1998) to assess passive use values.

28. Lareau, and Rae (1989) is another interesting application, involving the valuing of an environmental nuisance – odour. See also Smith and Desvousges (1986).

29. The OECD recently carried out a survey on case studies in six countries – Germany, Italy, The Netherlands, Norway, UK and the US to analyse why valuation studies had been rarely used in practice (OECD, 1992). See also Barde and Pearce (1991) where the six case studies are reported in fuller detail.

30. The US has been more ready to do this than Europe, at least until recently. Under President Reagan's 1981 Executive Order 12291, many proposed environmental measures have been

put to a cost–benefit test (although this was not the sole, or even the overriding decision criterion). Later legislative acts, dealing with the setting of regulation for toxic substances and pesticides, also called for weighting benefits against costs in setting environmental standards.
31. This is referred to as 'concordance with the institutional framework' (Opschoor and Vos, 1989).

REFERENCES

Adamowicz, W., J. Louvier and M. Williams (1994), 'Combining revealed and stated preference methods for valuing environmental amenities', *Environmental Economics and Management*, **26**, 271–92.

Adamowicz, W., P. Boxall, M. Williams and J. Louvier (1998), 'Stated preference approaches for measuring passive use values: choice experiments and contingent valuation', *American Journal of Agricultural Economics*, **80** (February), 64–75.

Anderson, R.J. and T.D. Crocker (1971), 'Air pollution and residential property values', *Urban Studies*, **8**, 171–80.

Barde, J.P. and D.W. Pearce (eds) (1991), *Valuing the Environment: Six Case Studies*, London: Earthscan.

Bergstrom, T.C. and R.P. Goodman (1973), 'Private demands for public goods', *American Economic Review*, **63** (3), 280–96.

Bjornstad, David J. and James R. Kahn (eds) (1996), *The Contingent Valuation of Environmental Resources*, Cheltenham, UK: Edward Elgar.

Cameron, T.A. (1988), 'A new paradigm for valuing non-market goods using referendum data: maximum likelihood estimation of censored logistic regression', *Journal of Environmental Economics and Management*, **15**, 355–79.

Carson, R.T. et al. (1996), 'Was the NOAA panel correct about contingent valuation?', RFF Discussion Paper 96–20. Washington, DC: Resources for the Future.

Clawson, M. (1959), 'Methods of measuring the demand for and value of outdoor recreation', Reprint no. 10, Washington, DC: Resources for the Future.

Cropper, M.L. and A.M. Freeman (1991), 'Environmental health effects', in J.B. Braden and C.D. Kolstad (eds), *Measuring the Demand for Environmental Quality*, Amsterdam: North-Holland.

Cropper, M.L. and W.E. Oates (1992), 'Environmental economics: a survey', *Journal of Economic Literature*, **30** (2), 675–740.

Davis, R.K. (1963), 'Recreational planning as an economic problem', *Natural Resource Journal*, **3**, 238–49.

Desvousges, W.H. et al. (1997), 'Valuing stated preferences for health benefits of improved air quality: results of a pilot study', TER Technical Working Paper no. T-9702. Durham, NC: Triangle Economic Research.

Diamond, P.A. and J.A. Hausman (1993), 'On Contingent Valuation Measurement of nonuse values', in J.A. Hausman (ed.), *Contingent Valuation: A Critical Assessment*, Amsterdam: North Holland.

Duffield, J. (1984), 'Travel cost and contingent valuation', in K.V. Smith (ed.), *Advances in Applied Microeconomics*, Greenwich, CT: JAI Press.

Fein, R. (1976), 'On measuring economic benefits of health programs', in R.M. Veatch and R. Branson (eds), *Ethics and Health Policy*, Cambridge, MA: Ballinger.

Fisher, A.C. (1996), 'The conceptual underpinnings of the Contingent Valuation Method', in D.J. Bjornstad and J.R. Kahn (eds), *The Contingent Valuation of Environmental Resources*, Cheltenham, UK and Brookfield, USA: Edward Elgar.

Fisher, A., D. Violette and L. Chestnut (1989), 'The value of reducing risks of death: a note on new evidence', *Journal of Policy Analysis and Management*, **8** (1), 88–100.

Foster, V. and S. Mourato (1997), 'Are consumers rational? Evidence from a contingent ranking experiment', paper presented at the 8th Annual Meeting of the European Association of Environmental and Resource Economists, Tilburg, The Netherlands.

Freeman, M.A. (1982), *Air and Water Pollution Control: A Benefit–Cost Assessment*, New York: Wiley.

Freeman, M.A. (1993). *The Measurement of Environmental and Resource Values*, Washington, DC: Resources For the Future.

Graves, P.E. (1991), 'Aesthetics', in J.B. Braden and C.D. Kolstad (eds), *Measuring the Demand for Environmental Quality*, Amsterdam: North-Holland.

Hanemann, W. Michael (1984), 'Welfare evaluations in contingent valuation experiments with discrete responses', *American Journal of Agricultural Economics*, **66** (August), 332–41.

Johnson, F.R. and W.H. Desvousges (1997), 'Estimating state preferences with rated-pair data: environmental, health and employment effects of energy programs', TER Technical Working Paper no. T-9701. Durham, NC: Triangle Economic Research.

Jones-Lee, M.W. (1982), *The Value of Life and Safety*, Amsterdam: North-Holland.

Knetsch, J.L. (1963), 'Outdoor recreation demands and benefits', *Land Economics*, **39** (4), 387–96.

Knetsch, J.L. and J.A. Sinden (1984), 'Willingness to pay and compensation demanded: experimental evidence of an unexpected disparity in measures of value', *Quarterly Journal of Economics*, **94**, 507–21.

Kuik, O.J., F.H. Oosterhuis, H.M.A. Jansen, K. Holm and H.J. Ewers (1992), *Assessment of Benefits of Environmental Measures*, London: Graham and Trotman.

Lareau, Thomas J. and Douglas A. Rae (1989), 'Valuing WTP for diesel odor reductions: an application of contingent ranking technique', *Southern Economic Journal*, **55** (3), 728–42.

Lave, L.B. and E.P. Seskin (1977), *Air Pollution and Human Health*, Baltimore: Johns Hopkins University Press for Resources for the Future.

Louviere, Jordan J. (1988), 'Conjoint analysis modelling of stated preferences', *Journal of Transport Economics and Policy*, **10**, 93–119.

Louviere, Jordan J. (1994), 'Conjoint analysis', in Richard P. Bagozzi (ed.), *Advanced Methods of Marketing Research*. Cambridge, MA: Basil Blackwell.

Mackenzie, John (1993), 'A comparison of contingent preference models', *American Journal of Agricultural Economics*, **75** (August), 593–603.

McConnell, K. (1985), 'The economics of outdoor recreation', in A.V. Kneese and J. Sweeney (eds), *Handbook of Natural Resource Economics*, Amsterdam: Elsevier.

McFadden, D. (1974), 'Conditional logit analysis of qualitative choice behavior', in P. Zarembka, *Frontiers in Econometrics*, New York: Academic Press.

Milon, J. (1989), 'Contingent valuation experiments for strategic behavior', *Journal of Environmental Economics and Management*, **17**, 293–308.

Mitchell, R.C. and R.T. Carson (1989), *Using Surveys to Value Public Goods: The Contingent Valuation Method*, Washington, DC: Resources For the Future.

NOAA (National Oceanic & Atmospheric Administration) (1993), 'Natural resource damage assessments under the Oil Pollution Act of 1990', *Federal Register*, **58** (10), 4601–14.

Navrud, S. (ed.) (1992), *Pricing the European Environment*, London: Scandinavian Universities Press.

Oates, W.E. (1996), 'Estimating the demand for public goods: the collective choice and contingent valuation approaches', in D.J. Bjornstad and J.R. Kahn (eds), *The Contingent Valuation of Environmental Resources*, Cheltenham, UK and Brookfield, USA: Edward Elgar.

Opschoor, J.B. and H.B. Vos (1989), *Economic Instruments for Environmental Protection*, Paris: Organization for Economic Cooperation and Development (OECD).

OECD (Organization for Economic Cooperation and Development) (1989), *Environmental Policy Benefits: Monetary Valuation*, Paris: OECD.

OECD (Organization for Economic Cooperation and Development) (1992), *Benefits Estimates and Environmental Decision-Making*, Paris: OECD.

Ostro, B. (1983), 'The effects of air pollution on work loss and morbidity', *Journal of Environmental Economics and Management*, **10**, 371–82.

Portney, P. (ed.) (1990), *Public Policies for Environmental Protection*, Washington, DC: Resources for the Future.

Ridker, R.G. and J.A. Henning (1967), 'The determination of residential property values with special reference to air pollution', *Review of Economics and Statistics*, **49**, 246–57.

Shechter, M. (1992), 'Israel – an early starter in environmental pricing', in S. Navrud (ed.), *Pricing the European Environment*, London: Scandinavian Universities Press.

Shechter, M., B. Reiser and N. Zaitsev (1998), 'Measuring passive use value: pledges, donations and CV responses in connection with an important natural resource', *Environmental and Resource Economics*, **12**, 457–78.

Smith, K.V. (1991), 'Household production functions and environmental benefit estimation', in J.B. Braden and C.D. Kolstad (eds), *Measuring the Demand for Environmental Quality*, Amsterdam: North-Holland.

Smith, K.V. (1997), 'Pricing what is priceless: a status report on non-market valuation of environmental resources', in H. Folmer and T. Tietenberg (eds), *The International Yearbook of Environmental and Resource Economics 1997/1998: A Survey of Current Issues*, Cheltenham, UK and Lyme, USA: Edward Elgar.

Smith, K.V. and W. Desvousges (1986), *Measuring Water Quality Benefits*, Boston, MA: Kluwer Nijhoff.

Trice, A.H. and S.E. Wood (1958), 'Measurement of recreation benefits', *Land Economics*, **34** (3), 195–207.

4. Cost–benefit analysis

Nick Hanley

1. THE ORIGINS OF CBA

Cost–benefit analysis (CBA) is used as a tool for policy and project analysis throughout the world. Attempts have been made to incorporate the *environmental* impacts of project/policies within CBA, in order to improve the quality of government and agency decision-making. Many technical problems persist, however, in applying CBA to environmental issues. Some think that CBA is rather limiting in terms of the kinds of impacts it can consider, how it incorporates these impacts and whether it describes well enough the way in which ordinary people would like decisions to be taken over environmental issues (in other words, whether it is a democratic methodology). Alternative decision-aiding methodologies, such as weighting and scoring schemes, environmental impact assessment, multi-criteria analysis and cost-effectiveness analysis have been put forward as preferable in some sense to CBA. However, economists continue to maintain an energetic defence of CBA since (i) ignoring CBA implies taking no account of economic efficiency, defined in terms of a comparison of social costs and benefits, and since (ii) CBA is backed up by a welfare-theoretic underpinning.

The development of CBA (or benefit–cost analysis, as it is known in North America) has recently been set out by Hanley and Spash (1994) and Pearce (1998a). In the United States, federal water agencies, principally the Bureau of Land Reclamation and the US Army Corps of Engineers, were among the first to make use of cost–benefit analysis. As early as 1808 Albert Gallatin, US Secretary to the Treasury, was recommending the comparison of costs and benefits for water-related projects. The Flood Control Act (1936) required the Corps of Engineers to evaluate the benefits and costs of all water resource projects, 'to whomsoever they accrue', thus invoking a comparison of social costs and benefits. Early analytic efforts in the water resources area, while unsophisticated, served to stimulate research into the use of economics to aid budget allocation decisions in other areas. Under the auspices of the Federal Interagency River Basin Committee, a practical guide to CBA was produced in 1950, nicknamed the Green Book, before being replaced by Budget Circular

A-47. Besides providing practical guidance, these publications encouraged academic interest.

Otto Eckstein (1958) was among the first to relate the CBA techniques being employed to welfare economic foundations (see also McKean, 1958). His book *Water Resource Development* critically investigates the techniques for benefit estimation using market information. Systems analysis was soon being applied to water resource management with the aim of exposing the interdependencies of river systems, for example by Krutilla and Eckstein (1958) and by Arthur Maass and associates (1962). During this era water quantity was the primary concern, but as the rate of dam construction slowed, attention began to turn to other issues. The 1960s saw growing concern over the quality of the environment; this was evident in the work of the Water Quality Program at Resources for the Future. Researchers began to focus upon the benefits of both water quantity and quality, which since it involved recreation benefits which were essentially non-market, raised interesting new problems for CBA. Notable among this early benefits research is Clawson and Knetsch (1966), which includes development of the travel cost method (see Chapter 3).

Interest expanded from water-based recreation into public goods such as wildlife, air quality, human health and aesthetics, which required a faster development of non-market valuation methods such as contingent valuation (see Chapter 3). Another new aspect of the research of the 1970s and 1980s was the recognition of the importance of non-use values (Chapter 2). For the first time, increasing attention was paid to CBA in relation to environmental aspects of US government policy-making (for a comprehensive survey see Froehlich et al., 1991). Formal CBA techniques have been required to support environmental regulations in the USA since the early 1970s. A process of development occurred with the move from the National Environmental Policy Act of 1969 requiring Environmental Impact Assessments, to Presidential Executive Order 12291 of 1981 explicitly requiring the application of CBA to new regulations (see Smith, 1984, for an assessment of this Executive Order). In the case of environmental legislation, the Executive Order made mandatory the assessment of the environmental benefits of new legislation. CBA would also be required for particular environmental problems, for example the disposal of mine wastes and discharge of hazardous substances into public water systems. In addition, legislation such as the Comprehensive Environmental Response, Compensation and Liability Act (CERCLA) 1980 and the Oil Pollution Act (1989) brought the issue of environmental damage assessment (and therefore environmental valuation) before US courts, culminating in the infamous *Exxon Valdez* incident. For a summary of the use of CBA in recent US environmental, health and safety legislation, see Arrow et al. (1998).

In the UK, as in the rest of Europe, the development of both research and practice in CBA was slow by comparison. CBA applications were initially largely transportation-based, starting in 1960 with the M1 motorway project. This was followed by the use of CBA on the London Victoria underground line in 1963, the 1970s Channel Tunnel proposals, and, infamously, in an enquiry into the siting of a third London airport in 1971. This last was notable on three counts: first, the very large amount of resources devoted to the CBA process itself; second, the inclusion in monetary terms of some environmental impacts (for example noise); and third, the poor effect which the process had on the use of CBA in government. This may be traced partly to the fact that the site selected as most preferred on CBA grounds was generally regarded as the least desirable location, whilst the site least preferred on CBA grounds was the only site with any local authority support (Dasgupta and Pearce, 1972; Pearce, 1998a).

The Department of Transport developed a routine for CBA of new roads, known as the COBA procedure, which included monetized values for time and accident savings, but this procedure was heavily criticized for its failure to include environmental impacts (Nash, 1990). Such impacts were included separately, latterly through a Manual of Environmental Appraisal with the Department refusing to monetize environmental impacts, thus preventing their inclusion in the CBA itself (see Hanley and Spash, ch. 12). Recent moves within transport appraisal have been towards multi-criteria analysis (DETR, 1998).

The UK government began revising its cost–benefit analysis procedures with regard to the environment in 1990. This process can be traced at least partly to the publication of the Pearce Report, commissioned by the Secretary of State for the Environment (Pearce et al., 1989). Government and public reaction combined to produce a new White Paper in response, *This Common Inheritance* (HMSO, 1990). This recommended that environmental impacts be brought into formal appraisal procedures wherever possible. The means to do this were pushed forward on two separate fronts, namely policy appraisal and project appraisal. Guidelines on incorporating environmental impacts in policy appraisal were issued in September 1991. As the guidelines state (DOE, 1991, p.1):

> A government's policies can affect the environment from street corner to stratosphere. Yet environmental costs and benefits have not always been well integrated into government policy assessments, and sometimes they have been forgotten entirely. Proper consideration of these effects will improve the quality of policy making.

It seems as though this document did not have the desired effect, in that a review in 1997 found few examples of formal CBA appraisal of new policies by government departments. However, the document had publicized the availability of 'new' CBA techniques, especially in the context of environmental valuation, and has perhaps succeeded more in establishing the *principle* of an assessment of policy which took both benefits and costs into account. It is certainly the case that examples of environmental policy guidance from CBA can be found in the UK in the 1990s, including the development of a landfill tax, the setting of national air quality standards, in assessments of different elements of agri-environmental policy, and in the development of a tax on quarrying (see Hanley, 2000). Moves to reduce regulatory burdens, and a desire to internalize external costs, were also important in producing this impetus.

CBA was also being increasingly used in the UK for the appraisal of projects with environmental impacts. The Environment Agency, charged with an official duty to take account of benefits and costs, developed a Manual of Benefits Assessment, which gives guidance on benefits transfer procedures for water quality improvements. The Ministry of Agriculture, Fisheries and Food (MAFF) uses CBA techniques which include environmental effects to assess proposed investments in coastal defences. The Forestry Commission has for some time regularly included estimates of recreation and biodiversity values in its rate-of-return calculations for forests. Finally, HM Treasury has issued a series of guidance documents on how CBA is best carried out at the governmental level (HM Treasury, 1997).

Within the European Union, it is again possible to find many examples of the use of CBA in the policy process, for example in The Netherlands, Austria and Sweden, although the governments of Germany, Italy and Ireland do not appear to ever use CBA in this way (RPA, 1998). The European Commission avoided the use of CBA in its formulation of new directives up until the early 1990s, with many significant environmental directives being issued without any formal consideration of costs and benefits (Pearce, 1998b). For example, the Bathing Waters Directive (1976), the Packaging and Packaging Waste Directive (1994) and the Drinking Water Directive (1978) may all have imposed on member states costs greatly in excess of benefits. Pearce argues that, since the Maastricht Treaty, attitudes towards CBA within the Commission have changed, with draft directives affecting the environment being increasingly subject to some form of cost–benefit comparison. Examples include revisions to a directive on air pollution from municipal waste incinerators, and the planned EU Acidification Strategy.

In what follows, we first of all consider the welfare economics background of CBA. This is important, for it roots this decision-making method in theory. Next, the various stages which comprise an actual CBA are set out in brief. Section 4 then outlines some of the important problems faced in applying CBA to environmental issues, and section 5 takes up another problem in detail: that of the ethical issues which underlie the use of CBA. In section 6, we give a brief consideration to uncertainty and how CBA copes with this pervasive feature of environmental decision-making. Finally, we outline some alternatives to CBA (section 7), before drawing some conclusions in section 8.

2. THE WELFARE ECONOMICS BACKGROUND

In Chapter 2, we learnt about the principal economic theories concerned with the measurement of 'welfare'. CBA is firmly based in this theory in a number of ways. First, in terms of how gains and losses are measured. For consumers, welfare effects are evaluated as changes in consumers' surplus, ideally measured using the exact welfare measures of compensating and equivalent variation (when quantities are allowed to vary) or compensating and equivalent surplus (when quantities are fixed to the consumer). For example, if an energy tax increases the price of electricity, we can estimate the welfare effect of this on the representative consumer by the fall in their consumers' surplus. This would be a measure of one cost of the policy in a CBA. In environmental applications of CBA, we are often concerned with studying changes in the quantities of public goods, such as air quality or landscape quality. Environmental resources possess the qualities of non-rivalness and non-excludability in varying degrees. For changes in a public good which are determined exogenously, we can use willingness to pay, or willingness to accept compensation, as money measures of these welfare amounts. For changes in producer welfare, CBA utilizes estimated changes in producer surplus (or quasi-rents) when prices change. Welfare impacts on production can, alternatively, be traced back to impacts on the owners of the factors of production (for example, change in land rents). We can also make use of the concept of opportunity costs to assess the costs of using scarce resources for one purpose, in terms of the foregone benefits from allocating these resources to their (next-best) alternative use.

The second way in which CBA is based on welfare economics relates to what counts as a benefit or cost. Since welfare economics evaluates alternative resource allocations in terms of relative effects on utility, so CBA includes as 'relevant' any impact on utility, bad or good, irrespective of whether it is reflected in market prices. Thus, reductions in air quality which reduce the utility of people living and working in a city are relevant costs, even though not all of this cost may be reflected in changes in market values.

Finally, CBA is tied into welfare economic theory in terms of the aggregation and comparison of benefits. Clearly, there will be very few policies or projects which affect one individual only. Thus we need to be able to compare welfare changes across individuals. Also, it is somewhat obvious that all projects/policies will involve a mixture of gains and losses, and thus that we need to be able to add up positive and negative impacts across individuals and compare them in order to say something about the net impact on social welfare. As Chapter 2 makes clear, interpersonal utility comparisons from the point of view of social welfare are problematic, since we cannot assume that gains and losses of utility are equally socially valuable at the margin. Adding up compensating or equivalent variations for a policy may give us a net figure for gain or loss, but unless we know something about the social welfare function (SWF), it is hard to say anything about the overall effect on social well-being. The Bergson–Samuelson SWF is most commonly 'used' (in a thought-experiment kind of way) in CBA. Note, however, that the SWF is defined in terms of utility amounts, whereas empirically we work with money measures of these (such as willingness to pay). The weights used in an SWF based on money measures represent the relative marginal utilities of income of different groups or individuals in society. However, typically we do not know the empirical magnitudes of these parameters.

The somewhat pragmatic solution adopted by CBA has been to fall back on the sum of surplus changes and opportunity costs for a project, which may then be weighted to take account of distributional effects, for example by putting a higher weight on benefits accruing to poor groups. This weighting is especially likely to be done in applications on CBA in developing countries (see, for example, Brent, 1990), but is much less likely to be done in developed countries. The use of the sum of money benefits and costs as a measure of the change in social welfare is based on the Kaldor–Hicks criterion, which asks: 'could the gainers compensate the losers and still be better off?' This criterion, proposed independently by Nicholas Kaldor and John Hicks in 1939, involves a comparison of benefits and costs as a measure of the net welfare effects of a policy/project. It effectively separates the issue of economic efficiency from that of the distribution of gains and losses. Practically, it implies comparing the sum of benefits across all those who gain with the sum of costs across all those who lose, and seeing if this number is positive (in which case the proposal passes the CBA test) or negative (in which case it fails). Where benefits and costs accrue over time (the usual case), then discounting is typically used to add up impacts over different time periods. As Johansson notes in Chapter 2, there are many problems with the Kaldor–Hicks criterion from a theoretical viewpoint. However, it remains as the principal underlying theoretical support of why governments *should* undertake CBA analysis of potential policies/projects, since it is the only way in which we can talk about the CBA test as a measure of a project's potential contribution to welfare.

In conclusion, CBA has strong links with welfare economics, but a somewhat shaky foundation in terms of interpersonal welfare impacts. The CBA process can be said to be a test of economic efficiency/inefficiency, but no strong conclusion can be then drawn about the net impact on social welfare. Distributional issues are usually kept separate. Acceptance of the Kaldor–Hicks criterion as a way of social decision-making also implies acceptance of a number of beliefs: these include comparability of gains and losses, that compensation is possible for all losses; and that ends are prioritized over means. We defer discussion of these until section 5 below.

3.   STAGES OF A CBA

In any CBA, several stages must be conducted. Whilst many will disagree on how these stages are identified, the following structure provides a guide to some essential steps. We now briefly discuss each of these in turn: for more details, see Hanley and Spash (1994).

Stage 1   Definition of Project/Policy

This definition will include (i) the reallocation of resources being proposed (for example the development of a wilderness area); and (ii) the population of gainers and losers to be considered. The motive for (ii) is to determine the population over which costs and benefits are to be aggregated. Sometimes, this population will be determined by law or by institutional procedure. In other cases, discretion is permitted. In the example mentioned above, do we count only those people in the immediate vicinity of the area (say, at the district level), only those people paying for the development (which may be all UK taxpayers) or affected persons at the regional, national or supranational level? This last category of potential beneficiaries and losers may seem unlikely, but the wilderness might well be valued in its undeveloped state by people living far distant from it. Further integration of environmental policies in the European Union is another example where supranational interests may be the relevant ones, in terms for example of counting transboundary pollution impacts in national CBAs.

Stage 2   Identification of Project Impacts

Once the project is defined, the next step is to identify all those impacts resulting from its implementation. Consider a project to build a new motorway. Stage 2 would include a listing of all resources used in constructing the road (concrete, steel, labour hours); effects on local unemployment levels; impacts on traffic movements; effects on local property prices; effects on time savings and accidents; effects on wildlife populations and impacts on the quality of landscape in the area not picked up by changes in property values. Two important concepts here are *additionality* and *displacement*. Additionality refers to the net impacts of the project. If a government were appraising the introduction of lower speed limits to reduce road fatalities, this benefit should be measured net of any reduction in fatalities that would have occurred without this policy change (due, for instance, to improvements in car design). Displacement is often important when CBA is applied by development authorities at the regional level of government, when two possibilities arise. Consider a plan to subsidize the building of new car factory in Tayside in Scotland. Will this displace output from some existing plant in any other region of Scotland? If so, the extent of such crowding out needs consideration, as does whether the outputs of the two plants are truly homogeneous. This is unlikely, so that perfect (that is one-for-one) displacement is rarely encountered. Secondly, the Tayside plant may displace no Scottish output, but may displace output elsewhere in the UK; if the Scottish development agency is responsible to the UK national treasury, then this could be considered as another case of displacement.

Stage 3   Which Impacts are Economically Relevant?

From the discussion in section 2 above, we know that from a welfare economics perspective, society is interested in maximizing the weighted sum of utilities across its members. These utilities depend, amongst other variables, on consumption levels of marketed and non-marketed goods. The former include a range of items from food to theatre visits, while the latter include fine views and clean air. The aim of CBA is to select projects which add to the total of social utility by increasing the value of consumables and nice views by more than their opportunity costs. Thus, what are counted as positive impacts, which from now on will be referred to as *benefits*, will either be increases in the quantity or quality of goods that generate positive utility or a reduction in the price at which they are supplied. What we count as *costs* (that is negative impacts) will include any decreases in the quality or quantity of such goods, or increases in their price. These negative effects also include the using up of resources (inputs to production) in a project, since if an hour of labour or a bag of cement is used up in constructing a bridge, it cannot be used simultaneously in constructing a dam. This is the concept of opportunity cost referred to above.

The crucial point here, raised previously above, is that the environmental impacts of projects/policies are relevant for CBA so long as they either (i) cause at least one person in the relevant population to become more or less happy; and/or (ii) change the level or quality of output of some positively valued commodity. For example, the environmental impacts of a new bridge from the Scottish mainland to the Isle of Arran could consist of a deterioration of landscape quality and of adverse effects on fish spawning grounds. The former is relevant to the CBA if at least one person dislikes the landscape change; the latter is relevant if at least one fisherman finds he catches fewer fish per hour at sea (or alternatively must expend more resources to catch the same number of fish). The absence of a market for landscape quality is irrelevant; similarly, the absence of a market for air quality is irrelevant when we consider the impacts of a new coal-fired power station on acid rain.

One class of impacts that should be excluded from a CBA is transfer payments. Good examples are reductions of indirect tax revenue due to a project going ahead, or additional unemployment benefits becoming payable. Neither of these flows constitutes a using up of real resources (such as labour hours), but are merely redistributions of money through the government. Less indirect taxes received (a loss) are cancelled out by less taxes paid (a gain) (Sugden and Williams, 1978). For this reason, most government guidelines on CBA (for example HM Treasury, 1997) recommend the exclusion of such transfer payment effects. There are, however, two exceptions. The first is where a tax is designed to correct a market imperfection (for example, a pollution tax attempting to make polluters pay the social cost of their actions). Here, taxes can be interpreted as shadow prices, as discussed below. However, where environmental taxes are present, they are unlikely to be set at a rate which is equal to marginal external costs. The second exception is where the government decides to place unequal weight on gains and losses attached to different groups within society in any year. Here, gains and losses will not cancel out.

Stage 4   Physical Quantification of Relevant Impacts

This stage involves determining the physical amounts of cost and benefit flows for a project, and identifying when in time they will occur. In the bridge example, this would include: the number of vehicles per year crossing the bridge; the time savings accruing to those using the bridge instead of the existing ferry service; the number of years the bridge will last before major repairs are necessary; and the extent to which fish populations will be disrupted. For environmental impacts such as the last of these, the use of environmental impact analysis is clearly important. All calculations made at this stage will be performed under varying levels of uncertainty. For example, the effect on fish populations may be very difficult to predict, whereas the amounts of concrete and steel needed to construct the bridge are relatively easy to predict. In some cases, it may be possible to attach probabilities to uncertain events and calculate an 'expected value' for costs and/or benefits (see Chapter 2).

Stage 5   Monetary Valuation of Relevant Effects

In order for physical measures of impacts to be comparable, they must be valued in common units. The common unit in CBA is money, whether dollars, pounds or yen. This use of money as the unit of account is merely a device of convenience, rather than an implicit statement that money is all that matters. Markets generate the relative values of all traded goods and services as relative prices: prices are therefore very useful in comparing tonnes of steel used in constructing the bridge with working hours saved in using it, since not only are both made co-measurable, but some indication of their current relative scarcity is provided. Prices, in other words, carry valuable information. The remaining tasks for the CBA analyst are then to:

(a) predict prices for value flows extending into the future;
(b) correct market prices where necessary; and
(c) calculate prices (relative values in common units) where none exist.

When part of the output of a soil conservation project, for example, is an increase in crop outputs over a 30-year time period, knowledge of the prices of these crops over this time-span is central to the estimation of project benefits. There is an important point here, since future prices may change in both real and nominal terms. If the former is occurring, then we need to know, for example, how the price of wheat will change relative to the price of corn (that is, the rate of exchange between them). However, inflation can push up the prices of both without their relative values changing. The CBA should typically be carried out in real prices, with discounting (see below) being done at the real discount rate.

Tasks (b) and (c) consist of adjusting market prices. In a perfectly competitive market, under certain assumptions, the equilibrium price indicates both the marginal social cost (MSC) and marginal social benefit (MSB) of the production of one more (or one less) unit of that good. This is because opportunity costs of production are given by the supply curve (given perfectly competitive input markets), whilst the demand curve is a schedule of marginal willingness to pay (as Chapter 1 made clear). Clearly there will be many cases, however, when the market price is a bad indicator of both MSC and MSB. If this is the case, *shadow* prices can be used to reflect true resource scarcity. Three cases can be distinguished: imperfect competition; government intervention in the market; and the absence of a market.

If there is imperfect competition in a market, microeconomic theory shows that market price will not equal marginal cost in most cases. If outputs for a project are being supplied by an imperfectly competitive firm, then it may be necessary to estimate shadow prices for these based on marginal costs.[1] Government intervention in markets can also create a need for shadow pricing. Suppose the project in question will lead to an increase in agricultural output (say as a result of land drainage). How should one more unit of such output be valued? If more milk is to be produced by keeping more dairy cows, then surely the market price of milk indicates the marginal social benefit? This will *not* be so if the government artificially holds up the price of dairy products above world market levels. Most Western governments do indeed support their agricultural sectors, and most do it partially by holding up prices. This may be achieved by a mixture of import levies, intervention buying and deficiency payments. In this case, then, the net social value of output needs to be computed: this is often done using 'producer subsidy equivalents', which express the percentage of farm-gate price which is accountable as net social benefit. For an example of the effects such adjustments make on cost–benefit calculations, see Whitby et al. (1998).

Commonly in environmental applications of CBA, the analyst is faced with the difficulty of placing a value on a good not traded in markets and for which no obvious price exists. In this case, there are a number of techniques available that seek to estimate the economic value of such goods, as set out in detail in Chapter 3. For example, if a CBA is being conducted on a new nuclear power station, one benefit is that less electricity is needed from alternative, fossil-fuel-powered generating stations. Fossil-fuel stations emit sulphur dioxide (SO_2) and nitrous oxides (NO_x), both contributors to acid rain. So one benefit of the nuclear station is lower acid-rain-causing emissions, and thus (on this measure) cleaner air. Estimates for such avoided external costs are clearly part of the CBA process in this case. When society chooses between alternative uses of scarce resources which affect human life as well, then this creates a need for shadow prices to be placed on avoided deaths, illnesses and non-fatal accidents. For a recent survey of such estimates, see Cookson (1998).

Stage 6 Discounting of Cost and Benefit Flows

Once all relevant cost and benefit flows that can be expressed in monetary amounts have been so expressed, it is necessary to convert them all into 'present value' (PV) terms by discounting. This subject will be intensively discussed in Chapter 5, so here we give a very brief treatment. Due to the existence of a market interest rate, to impatience, and to risk, future cost and benefits flows need to be converted into 'present values' to make them comparable with each other. This is achieved through the process of discounting. The present value now of a cost or benefit (X) received in time t with a discount rate of i is calculated as follows:

$$PV = X_t [(1 + i)^{-t}] \qquad (4.1)$$

The expression in square brackets in equation (4.1) is known as a discount factor. Discount factors have the property that they always lie between 0 and +1. The further away in time a cost or benefit occurs (the higher the value of t), the lower the discount factor. The higher the discount rate i for a given t, the lower the discount factor since a higher discount rate means a greater preference for things now rather than later. Discounting often has a profound impact on the outcome of a CBA analysis.

Stage 7 Applying the Net Present Value Test

The main purpose of CBA is to help select projects and policies which are efficient in terms of their use of resources. The criterion applied is the net present value (NPV) test. This simply asks whether the sum of discounted gains exceeds the sum of discounted losses. If so, the project can be said to represent an efficient shift in resource allocation, given the data used in the CBA. In other words, the NPV of a project is as follows:

$$NPV = \sum_{t=0}^{T} B_t(1+i)^{-t} - \sum_{t=0}^{T} C_t(1+i)^{-t} \qquad (4.2)$$

Note that no costs or benefits before year 0 are counted. The criterion for project acceptance is: accept if and only if $NPV > 0$. Based on the Kaldor–Hicks criterion, any project passing the NPV test is deemed to be an improvement in social welfare.

There are a number of alternatives to the NPV criterion. The two most commonly employed are the internal rate of return (IRR) and the benefit–cost ratio. The IRR is a measure frequently employed in financial investment appraisal. It is the rate of interest which, if used as the discount rate for a project, would yield an NPV of zero, and is interpreted as the rate of return on the resources (investment funds) used up in the project. This can be compared with the opportunity cost of these investment funds, which might be the market rate of interest. However, the IRR is flawed as a measure of resource allocation for two principal reasons. First, many projects can generate multiple IRRs from the same data set, so the analyst does not know which to select as the decision-making criterion. This 'multiple roots' problem arises when a project's net benefit flow over time changes sign more than once: for example, when three years of net cost are followed by two years of net benefit, and then three years of net cost. In general, such net benefit flow patterns have as many IRRs as they have changes of sign.[2] Second, the IRR is unreliable when comparing performance across many projects in a portfolio. This is because the IRR only compares the return on one project relative to the opportunity cost of funds: ranking projects on the basis of their IRRs is less reliable than ranking them in terms of NPVs, and may result in 'wrong' decisions being made, especially when choosing between alternative projects (for a worked example, see Lumby and Jones, 1999). The benefit–cost ratio is simply the ratio of discounted benefits to discounted costs. The decisions rule becomes: proceed iff the benefit–cost ratio exceeds unity.

An optional part of the seventh stage involves changing the weights in the NPV function. As Chapter 2 pointed out, the NPV measure only works as a welfare change measure if we assume that the existing distribution of income is, in some sense, optimal. This is because we do not know the correct marginal utilities of income with which to weight benefits and costs, whilst benefits and costs are also at least partly expressed in terms of willingness to pay, which depends not just on preferences but also on *ability* to pay. For these reasons, an optional stage which follows the NPV calculation is to examine the effects of different weighting schemes on NPV values. Suppose that the impacts of a motorway project can be divided up according to which group in society they affect, groups being defined on income grounds alone. This might give the results shown in Table 4.1.

Table 4.1   Road impacts by income group

Group affected	Impact discounted (£) (− a loss, + a gain)
G1 Low income	−2.4 million
G2 Middle income	+1.1 million
G3 High income	+2.3 million

The conventional NPV calculation implicitly puts an equal weight (equal to unity) on all these impacts, giving a NPV of +£1 million, so the project would be accepted. However, society might place more importance on each £1 of impact on poor groups than on rich groups. This could be reflected in a different weighting scheme. One possible set of weights would be $w_i = (Y^*/Y_i)$, where w_i is the weight to be attached to impacts on group i, Y^* is mean household income across all groups, and Y_i is mean income within group i. This gives a higher weight to poorer groups than to richer groups, and the NPV formula becomes:

$$NPV = w_1 B_1 + w_2 B_2 + ... w_n B_n \qquad (4.3)$$

where B_n are discounted net benefits to group n. This is a Bergson–Samuelson social welfare function, as discussed in Chapter 2.

This may seem like an attractive option, but there are severe problems here. First, what weights should be used in a practical context? Marginal utility of income weights is typically not known, and relative income is only one ground on which to differentiate between groups. How should these groups be defined, and how easy is it to work out how much each group will be affected? For these reasons, this unequal weighting procedure (sometimes known as 'revisionism') is rarely practised at the public agency level, with the exception of projects in developing-country contexts.

Stage 8   Sensitivity Analysis

The NPV test described above tells us about the relative efficiency of a given project, given the data input to the calculations. If these data change, then clearly the results of the NPV test will change too. But why should data change?

The main reason concerns uncertainty. In all *ex ante* cases of CBA, the analyst must make predictions concerning future physical flows (for example, traffic movements) and future relative values (for example, the price of fuel). None of these predictions is made with perfect foresight. When environmental impacts are involved, then uncertainty may be even more widespread; for example, if a policy to reduce global greenhouse gas emissions is planned, then the impacts of this in terms of avoided damage may be subject to a very wide range of predictions (Bolin, 1998).

An essential final stage of any CBA is therefore to conduct sensitivity analysis. This means recalculating NPV when the values of certain key parameters are changed. These parameters will include:

(a) the discount rate,
(b) physical quantities and qualities of inputs,
(c) shadow prices of these inputs,
(d) physical quantities and qualities of outputs,
(e) shadow prices of these outputs, and
(f) project life-span.

One intention is to discover to which parameters the NPV outcome is most sensitive. For example, in appraising a new coal mine where the NPV has been calculated as positive, by how much in percentage terms does the world coal price have to fall before the NPV becomes negative? By how much do labour costs need to rise before NPV becomes negative? By how much does our forecast of the lifetime of the pit need to fall before NPV becomes negative? What is the impact of changing the discount rate? Once the most sensitive parameters have been identified, then (a) forecasting effort can be directed at these parameters to try to improve our best guess; and (b) where possible, more effort can be made once the project is under way to manage these parameters carefully, although most will be outside the control of the decision-maker. The NPV decision will often depend crucially on the choice of discount rate: this will certainly be so for projects with long-term effects, such as woodland planting, toxic waste disposal and research and development of alternative energy sources.

4. APPLYING CBA TO THE ENVIRONMENT: WHAT ARE THE PROBLEMS?

The application of CBA to environmental management is fraught with problems. In this section, we briefly comment on some of these (for more detailed discussion, see Hanley and Spash, 1994). To begin with, though, consider four examples.

First, suppose we are conducting an appraisal of a policy to introduce a tax on nitrogen fertilizers to reduce nitrate pollution in sensitive lakes and rivers. Here we must be able to predict (a) the response of farmers to the tax, (b) where these farmers are located and (c) the likely consequent change in water quality. Point (b) is important since the impact of a kilo of nitrogen fertilizer on water quality depends crucially on when and where that fertilizer is put on the land; whilst predicting (c) will depend on a whole host of environmental factors. We must also be aware of other influences on water quality: will these change over the time period we are considering? Once these difficulties have been resolved, we then need to be able to value the increase in water quality in money terms. This will include both market and non-market values, for example, changes in commercial fishing and changes in bird numbers and species.

Second, consider a project to flood a valley in order to generate hydroelectricity. The analyst knows that amongst the project costs will be labour and materials for construction. But wildlife will be destroyed as the valley is flooded; as we argued above, this is an economic cost which cannot be ignored. Yet some of the benefits of preserving the valley's biodiversity might currently be unknown. The dam might, for example, destroy a potential cure for cancer. Project benefits include cost savings by generating electricity from the dam rather than by the next cheapest source. But will these cost savings vary over the lifetime of the project? What will be the effect on the storage capacity of the dam as deforestation takes place further up the watershed? The dam will irreversibly change the valley it floods: are there special considerations in such cases? The NPV of the project will vary according to the discount rate, but which rate should be used?

As a more extreme example of CBA under uncertainty, consider the question as to what level of global response is appropriate to counter climate change. Under the Kyoto agreement, signatory countries are obliged to reduce emissions of greenhouse gases by a variety of target levels (for example, by 12.5 per cent for EU countries). But is this enough or too much? One way of answering this question is by comparing the costs and benefits of reducing greenhouse gases by more or by less. Benefits include avoided damages due to climate change, plus avoided damages due to other impacts of reducing greenhouse gases. For example, in the case of CO_2, lower fossil fuel use also implies lower emissions of pollutants such as SO_2 and NO_x, with consequent savings in local air pollution problems. Costs comprise abatement costs for greenhouse gases, that is the costs associated with reducing them or with locking up more of the existing stock by creating new sinks (such as new forests). However, great uncertainty exists over the magnitude of both the costs and the benefits of further control. This uncertainty is greatest on the benefits (avoided damages) side. As Bolin (1998) has pointed out, there are still huge scientific uncertainties about the physical impacts of climate change, whilst there are also many uncertainties about how economies will adapt to these climatic changes (Sedjo, 1998). Given this, how can economists produce reliable estimates of the money value of avoided damages?

As a last example, suppose a development authority plans to build a barrage across an estuary to increase property values and generate opportunities for marina developments. The barrage will harm waterfowl populations by flooding feeding grounds. The development authority is compelled to carry out a CBA of the project, but who will check that the benefit figures it uses are not over-optimistic, or that it has not excluded certain costs since they fall outside its jurisdiction? By bending the rules of the CBA procedure, the agency can maximize the likelihood that the project will go ahead. CBA can thus be used as a means for economic agents to maximize their utility (or rents): this is sometimes referred to as 'institutional capture'.

Summarizing, the main problem areas in applying CBA to environmental issues include the following.

1. *The valuation of non-market goods, such as wildlife and landscape.* How should this be done, and how much reliance should society place on estimates so generated? Are we acting immorally by placing money values on such things? Chapter 3 discusses the different valuation tools available to economists; we briefly outline some ethical issues below.
2. *Ecosystem complexity.* How can society accurately predict the effects of changes in economic activity on complex ecosystems? For example, how well can we predict the effects on an aquatic ecosystem of effluent inputs? Non-linearities and surprises may be expected in such systems, but CBA copes with such phenomena rather badly. Ecosystem complexity can be seen as one example of uncertainty in CBA, and CBA does not cope very well with this, as we explain below.
3. *Discounting and the discount rate.* This raises several important questions. First, should society discount future costs and benefits? If so, what rate should be used, and should this be the same for environmental impacts as for those involving market goods? Empirical evidence suggests that people have different discount rates for different goods (see, for example, Luckert and Adamowicz, 1993), with environmental costs being subject to lower rates. Does discounting violate the rights of future generations? Harrod, many years ago, described discounting as a polite expression for rapacity. It is certainly true that operating a 'maximize net present value' rule lays potentially heavy costs on future generations. It may not be feasible to potentially compensate for these losses, due to the difficulty of signing binding intergenerational contracts, thus violating the Kaldor–Hicks

criterion. Chichilnisky (1997) has recently pointed out that discounting is not even a necessity from the viewpoint of intertemporal efficiency. However, this view would not be shared by all (see, for example, Pearce et al., 1990). For a recent summary of the literature on the environmental discount rate, see Scheraga and Sussman (1998).

4. *Institutional capture.* Is CBA a truly objective way of making decisions, or can institutions capture it for their own ends? There are many examples of agencies which are forced to undertake CBA doing so in a way which maximizes the chance of a favourable outcome to them (see Hanley and Spash, 1994). This possibility makes it desirable that CBA processes be open to external inspection, although the technical nature of the analysis means it is difficult for non-experts to assess how well it has been conducted.

5. *Sustainability and CBA.* CBA is concerned with the efficiency of resource allocation, whilst sustainability is an intra- and intergenerational fairness issue. This means that subjecting projects and policies to a CBA test is not a test of their sustainability. CBA explicitly allows trade-offs between natural and man-made capital, and thus can lead to violations of the so-called 'strong sustainability' criterion.[3] Some authors (for example Pearce et al., 1990) have suggested imposing sustainability constraints on CBA. For example, this could include the need to undertake shadow projects to offset depletions in the natural capital stock, across some portfolio of projects/policies.

5.   ETHICS AND CBA

A common starting-point in many models of non-market valuation is the assumption of a utility function where 'the environment' appears as an argument essentially no different from any other good or service which provides utility. An important question, however, is whether the environment should always be treated as just one more consumption good, in terms of how we characterize people's value systems. Recent empirical evidence suggests that a substantial portion of the population think of certain features of the environment in a different way to that assumed by standard economics (for a summary, see Hanley and Milne, 1996). This makes the valuation process (a) more difficult, and (b) possibly irrelevant. The existence of such views (which are often characterized as lexicographic[4] or rights-based) also has implications for cost–benefit analysis itself, as they challenge the Kaldor and Hicks compensation tests on which CBA is founded.

The standard representation of how an individual values environmental quality changes rests on an assumption about the ethical beliefs of the representative agent; namely, that they are utilitarian (Spash and Hanley, 1995).

Utilitarians place ultimate importance on the consequences of actions (a teleological perspective); utility is the ultimate consequence, so that all such individuals are interested in is comparing alternative states in terms of the amount of utility they generate, irrespective of how this occurs. The ability to compare alternative resource allocations solely in terms of their effect on (a) individual utility and (b) aggregated money-equivalent measures of utility is, of course, a fundamental working assumption of welfare economics. Within this framework, a natural extension which has occurred is to treat direct environmental benefits similarly to other benefits, by assuming that they can be traded off against other benefits (other goods).

However, some recent evidence suggests a refusal to trade off losses in environmental quality against increases in income for certain individuals (Stevens et al., 1991; Spash and Hanley, 1995; Hanley and Milne, 1996). Such individuals might be characterized as holding a rights-based ethic regarding environmental quality, which is at odds with the utilitarian ethic, and therefore with conventional economic values (Mazotta and Kline, 1995). Persons holding a rights-based ethic will refuse such a trade-off if they believe that it is our moral duty to preserve rainforests, for example. No increase in their income would compensate them (hold them on the same utility level) for a reduction in the level of an environmental good, W, (so that their minimum willingness to accept compensation (WTAC) is infinite). Such individuals might be willing to pay some positive amount for an increase in W; it might thus be argued that WTP rather than WTAC measures should be sought, since this would minimize the extent of 'ethical protests'. However, what is easiest to measure is not the same as what should be measured, and if environmental losses are in prospect, then assuming individuals have some claim to the current level of environmental quality, WTAC is the correct measure to specify. Alternatively, people holding rights-based beliefs may be unwilling to pay for protection of the current level of W, believing that it *should* be protected (that is, they refuse a choice over protection). Such people would be counted as 'protest bidders' in contingent valuation, and thus their preferences would be ignored. This results in the side-lining of a section of the public within the CBA context.

If individuals with rights-based beliefs indeed exist, then this may invalidate the principal foundation of cost–benefit analysis as a means of making judgements over whether a resource reallocation improves or reduces social welfare. This foundation, as we have already seen, is the Kaldor–Hicks principle, which states that a resource reallocation is welfare-improving if the gainers *could* compensate the losers and still be better off. But if the losers suffer environmental costs for which, due to their beliefs, they would reject *any* amount of money compensation, then the possibility of compensation is violated and the principle can no longer be applied (Griffin, 1995; Spash and Hanley, 1995). However, the economist might well point out that society is *forced* to make trade-offs. For example, in deciding to conserve a wilderness area we forgo development benefits; in allocating more money to wildlife protection, we may have less to spend on schools and hospitals. Given that choices have to be made, we could thus argue that rights-based preferences are an unaffordable luxury.

However, it would be wrong to jump from this to say that neoclassical environmental economics, and the cost–benefit analysis paradigm which is central to it, describes environmental values in a way which resonates with everyone. For those persons who hold such beliefs, CBA will never provide a good way of describing how they see the world. Indeed, as Holland (1995) has observed, if moral or ethical motives dominate how we think of the environment, then in a way it makes no sense to ask people what they are willing to pay to protect the environment, since this is the wrong framing of the decision. Plato's criticism of 'the view of the human psyche as a bundle of preferences', all in equal need of satisfaction, was that this would lead to undesirable outcomes unless moderated by reason and spirit. The modern equivalent may well be the use of cost–benefit analysis constrained by ecological and ethical limits in deciding how best to manage the natural environment. As Holland says (p. 32), 'we probably could learn to see ourselves in the way that CBA requires ... The question is whether that is what we want.' Yet the economist would respond: if wants are unlimited and resources are scarce, then choices have to be made, and these choices imply the relative values we place on things. CBA, in a sense, is just a method for weighing up our options in this very real context.

6.   UNCERTAINTY

Consider the example of a CBA which addresses the environmental costs of a new pollutant entering a river. Three situations regarding our knowledge of these environmental costs are possible. First, scientists may be unsure about what physical impacts the pollutant will have; this implies that not all 'states of the world', $\{s_1 ... s_n\}$, are known. Second, scientists may be able to identify all possible impacts $\{s_1 ... s_n\}$ but not be able to identify the probability distribution of these states of the world. Third, all possible states of the world and their probability distribution may be known. Most treatments of *risk* in economics are concerned with the circumstances of the third case, but not of the first two. If we know all possible states of the world and their probabilities, then expected values can be estimated along with their certainty equivalents. These can then form part of a CBA. However, if either not all states of the world are known, or if their probabilities are unknown, then we face a situation of true, or hard, uncertainty. In this case, which is likely to describe many environmental management situations, then CBA must fall back on sensitivity analysis, which estimates net benefits under different, known states of the world. We could then base decision-making, if desired, on tools from decision science, such as the minimax regret criterion (although see Grout, 1981, for an economist's critique of this rule).

One policy area that is characterized by extreme uncertainty is climate change, since we do not know with certainty the likely damages this will cause under a range of emission scenarios. Economists are divided on the best response to such uncertainty. Tietenberg (1998) points out that we do not even know the shape of the damages curve, which may be highly non-linear. Costs of control vary according to how greenhouse gas (GHG) emissions are reduced, and in terms of who undertakes the reductions (which countries, which agents). Given the huge uncertainties involved, Tietenberg argues, it is wrong to set targets for climate change policy using CBA. Pearce (1998c), however, argues that by not using CBA to set targets, we risk making a very expensive mistake: the fact that uncertainty is high is a reason for doing CBA, rather than following either of two alternative decision rules: (a) act now because of the precautionary principle or (b) do nothing now until we learn more. Pearce notes that estimates do exist of control costs and avoided damages,[5] and that the desired direction of change in emissions can be determined from an examination of these relative values. Pearce calls for a CBA which 'embodies these uncertainties' (yet gives point estimates for marginal benefits!). Pearce also argues that CBA should be done because it identifies who gains and who loses from climate change and by how much: for example, developed countries lose 1.3–1.6 per cent of GDP per year, whilst developing countries lose 1.6–2.7 per cent of GDP in his analysis. This shows, according to Pearce, that developing countries should not be exempt from taking partial responsibility for reducing GHG emissions. In contrast, Tietenberg states that deciding not to reduce GHG emissions on CBA grounds would be unwise even if currently estimated marginal costs of control are less than currently estimated marginal benefits, since future damages are *potentially* enormous and are also irreversible.

7. ALTERNATIVES TO CBA

Alternative decision-aiding methodologies, such as environmental impact assessment, cost-effectiveness analysis and multi-criteria decision-making have been put forward by some authors as preferable in some sense to CBA. Such alternatives are sometimes suggested as being preferable specifically because they avoid placing monetary values on environmental effects, which is seen as undesirable on ethical, scientific or strategic grounds. Alternatives are also put forward because many dislike the focus of CBA on economic efficiency as the sole criterion on which policy is judged. Finally, CBA has also been accused of being a technocentric 'black box' technique, which is not inclusive enough within a democratic society.

Environmental impact analysis has been widely used for project appraisal in the UK and elsewhere, and is in fact mandatory for certain types of projects under EU Directive 85/337. It has also been used at the policy level, for example in terms of strategic environmental assessment (NHMRC, 1994). Needless to say, though, environmental impact analysis presents only very limited information about the implications of policy choice for society, since it ignores all non-environmental impacts.

Cost-effectiveness analysis (CEA), where the most economically efficient means of achieving some predetermined target is sought, is also used worldwide: for example, for health policy assessment and nuclear decommissioning in The Netherlands, and for judgements on contaminated land remediation in Canada (RPA, 1998). In the UK, its use in a policy-making context has been largely confined to health-care issues, although compliance cost assessments, undertaken through the Cabinet Office of all proposed regulations since 1995, contain elements of a CEA. Its use has also been promoted in land-use policy analysis (MacMillan et al., 1998). However, CEAs pay no attention to whether the prospective benefits of the 'best' policy design are greater or less than the costs. Society could therefore expend large amounts of resources pursuing inefficient standards and targets if CEA were the only means of analysis used. CEA is also useful in permitting the reallocation of spending across policies with outcomes measured in equivalent units, in order to achieve greater benefits for the same cost. This is an alternative approach to CEA than the usual one of cost-minimizing over a given target. For example, recent work in the US has shown that the expected cost per life saved across a wide range of health, safety and environmental regulations varies from $200 000 to $6.3 trillion (Hahn, 1998). This is an indication of highly inefficient policy design which could be improved by reallocating spending across this suite of policies. Notice here that a standard outcome measure is available to compare policies, in terms of expected lives saved.

Multi-criteria decision-making (MCDM) covers a wide variety of techniques, all of which seek to evaluate project/policy impacts on a number of different indicators, subject to system constraints. Such indicators may be monetary (for example, incomes to rural farmers or the costs of establishing forest plantations) or non-monetary (for example, physical measures of environmental stress or jobs created). Policy success may be judged in terms of weighted scores across impacts, or in terms of a distance function which compares realized levels for indicators with target levels specified by the analyst. The ability to include both monetary and non-monetary measures of objectives, and to include a wider range of objectives, is clearly an advantage relative to CBA. However, MCDM techniques may be criticized on a number of levels. First, unlike CBA, MCDM is not supported by a coherent theory of social welfare. Second, the weights used in MCDM to compare impacts are unlikely to represent consumer preferences, thus decisions made using MCDM may well fail on grounds on representativeness and democracy. Scaling systems used for impact categories (where impacts are not monetized) may be essentially arbitrary. Finally, MCDM is potentially just as liable to institutional capture, and is just as technocentric and non-inclusive, as CBA. For an application of MCDM to environmental policy, which includes the use of 'fuzzy set' theory to compare monetary and non-monetary impacts, see Liu et al. (1998).

Other alternatives include the cost–utility approach used in health economics, whereby benefits are measured in units of quality-adjusted life years (QUALYs), and costs are measured in money (Drummond et al., 1987). This might best be seen as a form of cost-effectiveness analysis. For an application which applies this technique to risky outcomes (where benefits are in terms of expected QUALYs), see Kirigia (1998). Finally, risk–benefit approaches can be used, whereby monetary costs per unit reduction in risk can be compared across policy/project alternatives.

Another way about thinking of alternatives to CBA is to propose decision rules which might replace CBA in some, but not all, settings. One such rule is the safe minimum standard (Farmer and Randall, 1998), which states that no depletion of natural capital is allowed below some crucial minimum level, so long as the costs of preventing this diminution are not unreasonably high. For a proposal of how 'unreasonably high' might be defined, see Berrens et al. (1998). For an investigation of the relationship between CBA and the safe minimum standards approach, see Farmer and Randall (1998).

8. CONCLUSIONS

CBA is now a well-established part of applied welfare economics, and of public policy and project analysis. It is quite apparent that, if a CBA approach has already been adopted, then including environmental impacts within this (a) makes for more efficient decision-making and (b) explicitly recognizes the impacts of the economy on the environment, and the contribution that the environment makes to the economic process and to utility. It can be argued, however, that including environmental impacts within CBA is not the best way of protecting the environment, since CBA explicitly permits trade-offs: this *might* mean that consistently applying the CBA rule can lead to declining natural capital stocks over time, unless shadow project rules are also imposed. The environment might thus be better served under alternative decision rules, such as the safe minimum standard; yet this involves a degree of environmental absolutism, and is a less precise decision rule than CBA.

It is also hard on equity grounds to ensure that the CBA process is necessarily compatible with sustainable development, both with regard to inter- and intra-generational fairness. As we have already seen, CBA is mainly concerned with efficiency: incorporating distributional considerations in a satisfactory way is problematic (though not impossible, some would argue). For CBA to be automatically consistent with sustainable development, it would therefore probably be necessary to impose a variety of sustainability constraints on the process, especially if a non-declining natural capital stock view of sustainability is adopted. How best to do this is an important issue for future research, since we would not like to restrict trade-offs unduly as welfare (and increases in welfare over time) itself depends partly on efficient trade-offs being allowed. It is also apparent that *environmental* applications of CBA run into awkward methodological problems such as the treatment of uncertainty, discounting and moral considerations. All of these are problems which require further attention from researchers.

However, most economists would still argue that CBA has a useful role to play in the decision-making process. As Pearce (1998b) has pointed out, ignoring costs and benefits can lead to very inefficient and wasteful legislation. The CBA process itself has useful attributes, in terms of identifying costs and benefits (and who they fall on), and by structuring thinking about an issue in a way that establishes the important parameters for discussion. It is also a means of introducing public preferences into environmental policy-making, which would seem a valuable end in itself.

FURTHER READING

Aside from the references mentioned in the text, the reader might also like to consult the following books on cost–benefit analysis. They are listed in order of (increasing) difficulty:

Gramlich, E.M. (1990), *A Guide to Benefit Cost Analysis*, Englewood Cliffs, NJ: Prentice-Hall.

Zerbe, R.O. and D.D. Dively (1994), *Benefit–Cost Analysis in Theory and Practice*, HarperCollins College Publishers.

Pearce, D.W. (1983), *Cost–Benefit Analysis*, London: Macmillan.

Brent, R.J. (1996), *Applied Cost–Benefit Analysis*, Aldershot, UK and Brookfield, USA: Edward Elgar.

Johansson, P.-O. (1993), *Cost–Benefit Analysis of Environmental Change*, Cambridge: Cambridge University Press.

NOTES

1. Although see Sugden and Williams (1978).
2. As Lumby and Jones (1999) point out, this is due to the fact that the IRR is the root of a polynomial equation, and as Descartes showed 500 years ago, there are many roots to such equations.
3. Strong sustainability is usually interpreted as requiring a non-declining stock of natural capital over time.
4. Lexicographic preferences imply that one good is always prioritized over any other good: in other words, the marginal rate of substitution between the first-ranked good and all other goods is zero.
5. Pearce cites estimates of $50 per ton of carbon for marginal benefits of control and $5–$20 per ton of carbon for marginal costs.

REFERENCES

Arrow, K., M. Cropper, G. Eads, R. Hahn, L. Lave, R. Noll, P. Portney, M. Russell, R. Schmalensee, V.K. Smith and R. Stavins (1998), 'Is there a role for benefit–cost analysis in environmental, health and safety regulation?', *Environment and Development Economics*, **2**, 196–201.

Berrens, R., D. Brookshire, M. McKee and C. Schmidt (1998), 'Implementing the Safe Minimum Standard approach', *Land Economics*, **74** (2), 147–61.

Bolin, B. (1998), 'Key features of the global climate system', *Environment and Development Economics*, **3** (3), 348–65.

Brent, R.J. (1990), *Project Appraisal for Developing Countries*, New York: New York University Press.

Chichilnisky, G. (1997) 'The costs and benefits of benefit–cost analysis', *Environment and Development Economics*, **2** (2), 202–5.

Clawson, M. and J.L. Knetsch (1966), *Economics of Outdoor Recreation*, Baltimore, MD: Johns Hopkins University Press.

Cookson, R. (1998), 'An alternative approach to valuing non-market goods', in M. Acutt and P. Mason (eds), *Environmental Valuation, Economic Policy and Sustainability*, Cheltenham, UK and Northampton, USA: Edward Elgar.

Dasgupta, P. and D.W. Pearce (1972), *Cost–Benefit Analysis: Theory and Practice*, Basingstoke: Macmillan.

Department of the Environment (1991), *Policy Appraisal and the Environment*, London: HMSO.

DETR (Department of the Environment, Transport and the Regions) (1998), *A New Deal for Trunk Roads in England: Guidance on the New Approach to Appraisal*, London: DETR.

Drummond, M., G. Stoddart and G. Torrance (1987), *Methods for the Economic Evaluation of Health Care Programmes*, Oxford: Oxford University Press.

Eckstein, O. (1958), *Water Resource Development: The Economics of Project Evaluation*, Cambridge, MA: Harvard University Press.

Farmer, M. and A. Randall (1998), 'The rationality of a safe minimum standard', *Land Economics*, **74** (3).

Froehlich, M., D. Hufford and N. Hammett (1991), 'The United States', in J.-P. Barde and D. Pearce (eds), *Valuing the Environment: Six Case Studies'*, London: Earthscan.

Griffin, R. (1995) 'On the meaning of economic efficiency in policy analysis', *Land Economics*, **71** (1), 1–15.

Grout, P. (1981) 'Social welfare and exhaustible resources', in J.A. Butlin (ed.), *Economics of the Environment and Natural Resource Policy*, Boulder, CO: Westview Press.

Hahn, R. (1998) *Risks, Costs and Lives Saved: Getting Better Results from Regulation*, Oxford: Oxford University Press.

Hanley, N. (2000) 'Cost–benefit analysis and environmental policy-making', *Environment and Planning C*, forthcoming.

Hanley, N. and J. Milne (1996), 'Ethical beliefs and behaviour in contingent valuation', *Journal of Environmental Planning and Management*, **39**, 255–72.

Hanley, N. and C. Spash (1994), *Cost–Benefit Analysis and the Environment*, Aldershot, UK and Brookfield, USA: Edward Elgar.

Hicks, J.R. (1939), 'The foundations of welfare economics', *Economic Journal*, **49**, 696–712.

HM Treasury (1997), *Appraisal and Evaluation in Central Government*, London: HMSO.

HMSO (1990), *This Common Inheritance: Britain's Environmental Strategy*, London: HMSO.

Holland, A. (1995), 'The assumptions of cost–benefit analysis: a philosopher's view', in K.G. Willis and J.T. Corkindale (eds), *Environmental Valuation: New Perspectives*, Oxford: CAB International.

Kaldor, N. (1939), 'Welfare propositions of economics and inter-personal comparisons of utility', *Economic Journal*, **49**, 549–52.

Kirigia, J. (1998), 'Cost–utility analysis of schistosomiasis intervention strategies in Kenya', *Environment and Development Economics*, **3** (3), 319–46.

Krutilla, J.V. and O. Eckstein (1958), *Multiple Purpose River Development: Studies in Applied Economic Analysis*, Baltimore, MD: Johns Hopkins University Press.

Liu, A., A. Collins and S. Yao (1998), 'A multi-objective and multi-design evaluation procedure for environmental protection forestry', *Environmental and Resource Economics*, **12** (2), 225–40.

Luckert, M. and W. Adamowicz (1993), 'Empirical measures of factors affecting the social rate of discount', *Environmental and Resource Economics*, **3** (1), 1–22.

Lumby, S. and C. Jones (1999), *Investment Appraisal and Financial Decisions*, London: International Thompson Business Press.

Maass, A. and associates (1962), *Design of Water-Resource Systems*, Cambridge, MA: Harvard University Press.

MacMillan, D., D. Harley and R. Morrison (1998), 'Cost-effectiveness analysis of woodland ecosystem restoration', in M. O'Connor and C. Spash (eds) *Valuation and Environment: Principles and Practices*, Cheltenham, UK and Northampton, USA: Edward Elgar.

Mazotta, M. and J. Kline (1995), 'Environmental philosophy and the concept of non-use value', *Land Economics*, **71** (2), 244–9.

McKean, R. (1958), *Efficiency in Government Through Systems Analysis*, New York: Wiley.

Nash, C.A. (ed.) (1990), 'Appraising the environmental effects of road schemes: a response to the SACTRA Committee', University of Leeds: Institute for Transportation Studies, Working Paper 293.

National Health and Medical Research Council (1994), *National Framework for Environmental and Health Impact Assessment*, Canberra: Australian Government Publishing Service.

Pearce, D.W. (1998a), 'Cost–benefit analysis and environmental policy', *Oxford Review of Environmental Policy*, **14** (4), 17–25.

Pearce, D. (1998b), 'Environmental appraisal and environmental policy in the European Union', *Environmental and Resource Economics*, 489–501.

Pearce, D. (1998c), 'Economic development and climate change', *Environmental and Development Economics*, **3** (3), 389–91.

Pearce, D., A. Markandya and E. Barbier (1989), *Blueprint for a Green Economy*, London: Earthscan.

Pearce, D., E. Barbier and A. Markandya (1990), *Sustainable Development: Economics and Environment in the Third World*, Aldershot, UK and Brookfield, US: Edward Elgar.

RPA (1998), 'Economic evaluation of environmental policies and legislation', Report to DGIII, European Commission, Risk and Policy Analysts, Loddon, Norfolk.

Sedjo, R. (1998), 'How serious are the damages associated with global warming?', *Environmental and Development Economics*, **3** (3), 398–401.

Scheraga, J. and F. Sussman (1998), 'Discounting and environmental management', in T. Tietenberg and H. Folmer (eds), *The International Yearbook of Environmental and Resource Economics 1998/1999: A Survey of Current Issues*, Cheltenham, UK and Northampton, US: Edward Elgar.

Smith, V.K. (1984), *Environmental Policy under Reagan's Executive Order*, Chapel Hill, NC: University of North Carolina Press.

Spash, C.L. and N. Hanley (1995), 'Preferences, information and biodiversity preservation', *Ecological Economics*, **12**, 191–208.

Stevens, T.H., J. Echeverria, R.J. Glass, T. Hager and T.A. More (1991), 'Measuring the existence value of wildlife: what do CVM estimates really show?', *Land Economics*, **67** (4) 390–400.

Sugden, R. and A. Williams (1978), *A Practical Guide to Cost–Benefit Analysis*, Oxford: Oxford University Press.

Tietenberg, T. (1998), 'Economic analysis and climate change', *Environment and Development Economics*, **3** (3), 402–404.

Whitby, M., C. Saunders and C. Ray (1998), 'The full cost of stewardship policies', in S. Dabbert, A. Dubgaard, L. Slangen and M. Whitby (eds), *The Economics of Landscape and Wildlife Conservation*, Oxford: CAB International.

5. Goals, principles and constraints in environmental policies

Tomasz Żylicz

1. INTRODUCTION

This chapter explains how economists approach environmental policy questions and why their advice has not been translated into many applications. For many years there seemed to be a wide gap between what economists recommended and what policy-makers were willing to accept and implement. While the former emphasized the need to arrive at decisions by carefully balancing costs and benefits, the latter paid more attention to social and political consequences. Only in the 1990s did environmental economic analysts start to address typical policy-makers' concerns in a more systematic way, resulting in a better understanding of economic considerations on the policy side.

The chapter consists of eight sections. Section 2 starts with definitions of three key economic concepts – effectiveness, equity, and efficiency – the last of which has been the traditional focus of economic analyses. It also defines the sustainability concept and relates it to the previous concepts. In the third section the notion of an economically optimal environmental policy is introduced. In the fourth section, attention is turned to uncertainty and various social constraints that policy-makers have to take into consideration. Several practical principles, including the well-known polluter pays principle, which serve as useful rules of thumb are discussed next. Some additional questions on what and how environmental policies actually protect are raised in the sixth section. Section 7 identifies typical policy failures encountered in real-world situations. The chapter ends with a brief assessment of the role played by economists in environmental policy debates.

2. CONFLICTING APPROACHES TO ENVIRONMENTAL POLICY

Like any other policy, an environmental policy has to compromise between different demands and expectations, many of them often conflicting with one another. Conservationists would like to protect natural habitats from economic development. Industrialists demand that protection measures do not hamper growth, and do not impose excessive burdens on firms. Social critics are concerned with fairness of the distribution of environmental protection costs among various groups and strata. In this regard three notions are crucial: effectiveness, efficiency and equity.

A policy is called *effective* if it solves the problem it was supposed to. Thus the notion of effectiveness is closest to what would be the most likely focus of environmental activists and environmentally concerned citizens. Effective policies are those that clean the air, restore the lakes and save species from extinction. The question of effectiveness does not refer to the costs such policies may imply, nor does it take into account any other social problems which may arise as a result of their implementation.

In contrast, economists are concerned with the idea of efficiency attempting to take into account both costs and effects of a given policy or action. This implies that effects are made commensurate with costs by evaluating the former in the same terms as the latter. Monetary evaluation is the most obvious method to employ, but other – less typical – measurement units are possible too, for example, energy units. A policy is said to be *efficient* if its costs are justified in terms of its effects or, to put it more precisely, if it maximizes the positive difference between benefits and costs. As in the case of effectiveness, the idea of efficiency leaves aside the question of fairness, that is, who will pay the costs, and who will benefit from the effects. Unlike effectiveness, however, efficiency addresses the question of whether a policy is worthwhile. Thus an efficient air quality policy pushes emission abatement requirements up as long as incremental benefits resulting from the cleaner air exceed the costs of the cheapest alternative to meet such requirements.

Efficiency is a difficult concept to apply, as environmental benefits are often difficult to evaluate in economic terms (see Johansson, Chapter 2 and Shechter, Chapter 3 in this volume). This is why a somewhat less stringent concept of cost-effectiveness has been in common use. A *cost-effective* policy achieves any given effect at the least possible cost. Thus, if the objective is to clean up a lake, of all effective policies the cost-effective one will be the one which restores the lake to life at minimum cost. It should be stressed here that neither effectiveness nor cost-effectiveness *per se* provides a criterion to judge whether a policy is worthwhile to pursue, that is, in the example above, whether the lake should be restored or the economy's scarce resources spent on something else. Efficiency provides a theoretical criterion, but of course there are additional aspects that environmental policy has to take into account.

Fairness has been another important issue raised in connection with environmental policies ever since such policies were formulated and implemented. There is no universally accepted definition of fairness, and economists prefer to talk about *equity* whenever they discuss the distribution of costs and benefits among parties concerned. Making a policy equitable means balancing costs and benefits across all parties concerned by appropriately distributing benefits and/or letting beneficiaries pay an adequate share of costs.[1] For instance, a policy aimed at preservation of biodiversity will be judged inequitable if the costs affect the local population in areas adjacent to protected habitats, for example by constraining development opportunities without offering them a fair share in benefits from conservation.

As shown in the brief overview above, environmental policies can be viewed from several different perspectives. Traditional environmental activists would perhaps assess policies from the point of view of their effectiveness. More sophisticated activists would ask whether they are cost-effective, as the same effect can be achieved at various costs.

Economists, in turn, tend to raise efficiency questions. Although difficult to answer, these questions are extremely important, for two reasons. First, it is not sufficient to design a set of cost-effective policies to address environmental problems such as specific levels of acid-rain abatement, eutrophication control, solid waste disposal and so on. Even though each of these problems can be individually solved in the cheapest way, there is no reason to believe that the collective outcome will be what people would prefer to have, if you consider the costs to be borne. It might turn out, for instance, that the eutrophication control has become too strict *vis-à-vis* the waste disposal measures. It might have been better to relax the eutrophication controls a bit, and switch the resources saved in this way to substantially improving the waste disposal situation. Second, the resources spent on the environment altogether as a result of a series of cost-effective sectoral policies might turn out to be too few or too many in comparison with what was spent on meeting other needs.

In the 1980s long debates over alternative approaches to environmental policies led to the emergence of the sustainable development concept. Although there is no universal understanding of sustainability,[2] most definitions embrace the idea as expressed in the Brundtland Report (WCED, 1987), that is, to meet the needs of the present without compromising the ability of future generations to meet their own needs. Sustainability thus implies not only short-term equity (meeting the needs of the present), but also a much deeper concept of inter-generational equity.[3] A *sustainable* policy has to address environmental problems in a way that maintains both the physical and social bases for further development. The idea of sustainability goes far beyond the scope of conventional environmental economics. It is difficult to operationalize, because much uncertainty exists whether the present use of natural and man-made resources is compatible with their future use. Regarded by many as cloudy, the idea of sustainability nevertheless serves as a guide for policy-makers to balance their quest for economic efficiency with equity considerations, and to adopt a long-term perspective. It also helps to assess what is certainly *not* sustainable. In particular, with respect to the environment and natural use of resources, the sustainability concept directs attention to the physical volume of inputs and outputs flowing through the world economy. This flow, conveniently called 'throughput', has been largely ignored by economic analyses, which focus on the monetary value of the selected components rather than on the physical scale.[4] However, because many important components are not captured by commercial transactions, monetary analyses often fail to recognize the important information derived from studies of the global throughput which, for obvious reasons, cannot grow indefinitely.

Despite theoretical and practical problems, there have been attempts to operationalize sustainable development by proposing rules on how to use the environment and natural resources in a sustainable way. The following three principles were suggested by Daly (1990, p. 41):

(1) With respect to the physical volume of inputs into the economy and its outputs: by consciously limiting the overall scale of resource use, shift technological progress from the current pattern of maximizing throughput to maximizing efficiency understood as the ratio of economic effects achievable from a given throughput.

(2) With respect to renewable resources: by exploiting these on a profit maximizing sustained yield basis,[5] prevent them from driving to extinction. More specifically this means that:

    (a)   with respect to resources serving as inputs such as plants and animals, harvesting rates should not exceed regeneration rates;

    (b)   with respect to resources serving as 'sinks' such as the atmosphere of Earth, waste emissions should not exceed the renewable assimilative capacity.

(3) With respect to exhaustible resources: maintain the total stock of natural capital by depleting non-renewable natural components (such as mineral deposits) at a rate corresponding to the creation of renewable substitutes.

Principle (3) reflects what has been referred to as 'strong' sustainability, that is, maintaining the total stock of natural capital rather than compensating for its depletion by investing in man-made capital. In contrast, 'weak' sustainability allows for substitution between the two types of capital, as long as the so-called Hartwick (1977) rule is satisfied: the revenues from depletion of exhaustible resources are invested rather than consumed. Here the natural capital can decline if man-made capital is increased by the same amount. Economists debate whether the two types of capital are substitutes or complements. While to some extent both types can certainly substitute for each other, it is obvious that the former provides necessary inputs to virtually all production processes. This suggests that 'strong' rather than 'weak' sustainability provides a more relevant reference for policy-making.

Various sustainability principles such as those mentioned above are very general, and do not give many practical clues on how to design environmental policies. Increasingly, however, more specific recommendations are being formulated, and their language becomes closer to that used by politicians and businessmen.[6] What is even more important, the principles help us to realize that environmental issues need to be seen in a much broader perspective than before. They are not just a matter of 'protection', but a matter of a long-term economic strategy.

3.   AN ECONOMICALLY OPTIMAL ENVIRONMENTAL POLICY

If economists were to advise on designing environmental policies, the most likely suggestion would be to achieve efficiency by maximizing aggregate net benefits, that is, the difference between total benefits and total costs (Baumol and Oates, 1988). In principle this approach need not contradict equity considerations. For if a policy is efficient there is always a possibility of distributing its net benefits in such a way as to make everybody better off than in a non-efficient scenario. Moreover, by endowing property rights to individuals, it is theoretically possible to transfer costs and benefits across society according to almost any pattern. This makes a strong case for separating efficiency from equity concerns, and concentrate on efficiency.

However, studying real-life policy cases proves that the distribution of costs and benefits is most often ignored, and a situation of property rights from the pre-policy period is implicitly assumed. Not only may this imply that the benefits do not match the costs borne by various individuals, but also that some individuals are even made worse off. This is a typical outcome of many policies aimed at increased efficiency, especially in countries without adequate social security services. Thus the rationale of efficiency, that is, the possibility of enjoying the maximized sum of net benefits, turns out to be a privilege distributed in a not necessarily fair way. Nevertheless many economists have viewed efficiency as an ideal reference point for designing sound environmental policies.

It is a tradition in economics to consider many important variables, including costs and benefits, as functions of a single variable under the control of a decision-maker (see Hanley, Chapter 4 in this volume). In the case of environmental policy the level of pollution or the level of exploitation of a natural resource can serve as examples of such variables. It is then assumed that this variable can be flexibly determined by the policy-maker so as to meet any criterion s/he may wish to choose. If the objective is to maximize the sum of net benefits, then one can apply the following argument. Choose any initial level of the control variable, and ask whether increasing its value by a small amount would imply more benefits or more costs. These incremental benefits are called marginal benefits (MB). Likewise, incremental costs are called marginal costs (MC). As long as MB > MC, it is worthwhile increasing the level of the control variable. If one finds that MB < MC, then it pays to reduce the level, since what one loses in terms of forgone benefits (MB) one more than compensates for in terms of avoided costs (MC). Thus, unless one hits a boundary of the control variable's domain earlier, the only point where the net benefits are maximized is when MB = MC. The important corollary is that an efficient policy should aim at equating marginal costs with marginal benefits of environmental protection.

The MB = MC criterion has largely remained a theoretical reference point for various policy instruments (see Löfgren, Chapter 1 and Barde, Chapter 6 in this volume).

Time dimension can be added to this analysis by introducing a rate of discount. To many people, discounting future values is unfair and arbitrary. Yet without discounting, intertemporal choices would be difficult to make. The rationale for discounting results from a so-called time preference. Let us assume that there is no inflation (which does not change the idea but makes the calculations less complex). Most people are not indifferent to getting either $1000 today or $1000 a year from now; they would prefer to have it sooner rather than later. But how about having $1000 now or $1500 a year from now? Most of us would probably prefer the latter option. Perhaps there is some amount of money $1000(1 + δ) between $1000 and $1500 that makes us indifferent to having either $1000 now or $1000(1 + δ) a year from now. The number δ which renders the two options equivalent is called the rate of time preference. It is a fundamental component of any discount rate used in order to compare costs and benefits accruing at different points in time. If $δ = 0.025$ (2.5 per cent) then we would consider $1025 a year from now as equivalent to $1000 now and $1000 a year from now is equivalent to $1000/(1 + δ)$, that is, approximately $976 today.

It is easy to extend this concept to time intervals of any length. The present value of $1000 two years from now is $1000/(1 + δ)^2$ and so on. If a project requires costs of 1000, 100 and 200 now, a year from now and three years from now, respectively, then its discounted sum of costs is $1000 + $100/(1 + δ) + $200/(1 + δ)^3$. If it provides the investor with benefits of $300, $400, $400 and $300 after the first, second, third and fourth year, respectively, its discounted sum of benefits is $300/(1 + δ) + $400/(1 + δ)^2 + $400/(1 + δ)^3 + $300/(1 + δ)^4$. The net present value, NPV – a key concept used in cost–benefit analysis – is the difference between the discounted sums of benefits and costs. As before, the

MB = MC criterion (with discounting used to account for the time dimension of benefits and costs) helps to identify maximum NPV.

Substituting 2.5 per cent for δ in the example above would yield NPV equal $33.35. Mere subtraction of (undiscounted) costs from (undiscounted) benefits would give the difference of $100. This can be interpreted as NPV with zero discount rate. Thus discounting with positive rates reduces the value of projects whose costs come earlier than benefits. The same example recalculated with 5 per cent discount rate will render a negative NPV.

Most projects require costs to be borne before benefits can be enjoyed. Environmental projects are often characterized by high costs and by benefits extending over a long period of time. Or the time lapse between launching a project and reaping its fruits can be long.

The conclusion some people draw from these facts is that discounting is anti-environmental and anti-sustainable. Indeed, high discount rates may imply negative NPV for projects with benefits that are modest but sustainable over a long period of time. Applying a zero discount rate, however, is not a good solution. First, it is incorrect since people do reveal time preference. Second, it is also counterproductive from the environmental point of view: zero or low discount rates favour excessive investment, leading to an increased throughput, with all its risk of resource exhaustion and environmental degradation and the waste of capital. Most economists agree on the need for applying realistic discount rates. At the same time, they indicate that it is more appropriate to address sustainability concerns directly rather than by ignoring or underestimating the time preference of people.[7]

In some analyses economists apply an abstract measure of benefits net of costs, called *utility*. It can then be assumed that welfare is improved if aggregate utility is increased. However, in order to make intertemporal comparisons, future utilities need to be discounted. Thus a welfare maximization criterion reads:

$$\sum_{t=0}^{\infty} u_t / (1 + \delta)^t, \qquad (5.1)$$

where u_t is the utility in the year t and, as before, δ is a discount rate.

Formula (5.1) attaches declining weights to the welfare of future generations. Thus a development scenario transferring wealth from the future to the present would yield a higher NPV than one keeping u_t constant (or rising). Hence maximizing a flow of discounted welfare may contradict the definition of sustainability introduced in the previous section. On the other hand, this definition is sometimes seen as too rigid to reflect all scenarios which are discussed in actual policy debates and meet some long-term fairness criteria at the same time. It was proved that, under reasonable assumptions (Chichilnisky, 1996), any notion of long-term 'optimality' is equivalent to maximizing the following formula, often referred to as the Chichilnisky criterion:

$$\alpha \sum_{t=0}^{\infty} u_t /(1+\delta)^t + (1-\alpha) \lim_{t\to\infty} u_t, \text{ for some } \alpha \in [0,1] \qquad (5.2)$$

The second component in this sum represents the undiscounted welfare of a single generation in a distant future. Of course, for $\alpha = 1$ the Chichilnisky criterion boils down to formula (5.1). On the contrary, for $\alpha = 0$, the intergenerational distribution of utility does not count, as long as welfare is maximized for generations that are far ahead. Intermediate αs correspond to combinations of NPV and the future welfare condition.

In order to derive further implications of formula (5.2), one needs to make additional assumptions. First, let us define u as a function of consumption c and the state of the environment s, $u_t = u(c_t, s_t)$. Second, let the relationship between c and s be given by the following equation:

$$s_{t+1} = s_t + r(s_t) - c_t, \text{ and } s_0 \text{ is given}, \qquad (5.3)$$

where r is the natural regeneration rate. If $r \equiv 0$, then s should be interpreted as an exhaustible resource whose stock can only decline over time. If $r > 0$, then s corresponds to the stock of a renewable resource which can be kept constant if $c_t = r(s_t)$ for all $t \geq 0$ (that is, when the consumption equals the regeneration rate).

Two rather unexpected theorems can be proved.[8] First, for any $\alpha \in (0,1)$, and any constant a > 0 the problem:

$$\text{Max}_c \, \alpha \sum_{t=0}^{\infty} u(c_t, s_t)/(1+\delta)^t + (1-\alpha) \lim_{t\to\infty} u(c_t, s_t), \qquad (5.4)$$

subject to: $s_{t+1} = s_t + r(s_t) - c_t$, with s_0 given

does not have a solution. Second, if the discount rate goes to zero with time, that is, $\lim_{t\to\infty} \delta_t = 0$, then the problem above has a solution; the solution is exactly the same as for the NPV maximization (with a declining rate of discount):

$$\text{Max}_c \sum_{t=0}^{\infty} u(c_t, s_t)/(1+\delta_t)^t, \qquad (5.5)$$

subject to: $s_{t+1} = s_t + r(s_t) - c_t$, with s_0 given.

The intuition behind the first theorem is that increasing consumption temporarily – resulting in its temporary decline later on – may increase the first operand of the addition in formula (5.4) without affecting the asymptotic behaviour, that is, the second operand in (5.4). What it says in plain language is that discounting with a constant positive rate cannot be reconciled with keeping future generations at least as well off as the present generation. Then the second theorem says that the reconciliation can be reached by applying a variable discount rate which tends to zero over time. But does such a discount rate make economic sense at all?

It was observed earlier that people do apply positive discount rates when making decisions about the future. However, there is empirical evidence that the discount rates applied to future projects tend to decline with the futurity of these projects. In addition, there is also some theoretical justification for this phenomenon (Beltratti et al., 1998, pp. 63–4). Thus testing for sustainability of a policy may apply standard cost–benefit analysis tools provided that implications of a very long-run perspective – such as declining discount rates – are taken care of.

4.   INFORMATION AND UNCERTAINTY

One reason why policy-makers have not so far followed economists' prescriptions is that any estimates of marginal costs and marginal benefits are affected by a wide margin of uncertainty, although, for different reasons, neither benefits nor costs are usually known with accuracy, so that often the MB = MC rule cannot be adopted as a practical guide even in the short run. In the long run additional problems result from ambiguities affecting discount rates.

Environmental standards and other regulations are most often justified in non-economic terms. This should not be a surprise, as it is impossible to attach a price tag to everything. How could one put a price on human life and health constantly threatened by various man-made environmental dangers? How could one convincingly price the Acropolis of Athens now dissolved by acid rain? What is the value of saving a species from extinction? Even though economists are prepared to give answers to all of these questions, they must admit that both their methodologies and the accuracy of their measurements are disputable (see Johansson, Chapter 2 and Shechter, Chapter 3 in this volume). In such circumstances it is more practical to check policy measures against non-economic criteria too.

In addition, there are instances where uncertainty does not come from economics, but rather from natural sciences. Chains of cause–effect relationships leading from anthropogenic impacts to environmental changes, and finally to human health and welfare consequences, are often not known in detail. Thus, reliance on too sophisticated models may more easily lead to blunders than basing the policy on common sense and on some simple rules of thumb. Engineers in designing bridges apply margins for uncertainty; perhaps environmental planners should do the same in certain cases. This is called 'safe minimum standards' or 'prudent estimates of critical loads'.

Quite different sorts of uncertainty affect the cost side. There are few, if any, pricing controversies. The main problem arises in connection with assessing what costs should be viewed as expenditures inevitable in meeting environmental requirements. It is easy to point at large amounts of money allegedly needed to comply with a regulation; industrial lobbies raise this argument continuously. Of course the argument is based on the extra cost of an 'end-of-pipe' treatment on top of an existing technological process. Indeed, control technologies may be costly, but there are often cheaper alternatives available.

First of all, process-integrated refinements aimed at better utilization of inputs lead to fewer waste products, and improve the environmental performance of a firm almost for free. It turns out that such changes may even lower production costs in some cases, and environmental requirements thus help to stimulate purely commercial innovation (see Corbett and Van Wassenhove, Chapter 10 in this volume). For instance, the global programme for phasing out CFCs revealed that their substitutes in certain applications are not only less harmful, but also cheaper (see Gabel and Sinclair-Desgagné, Chapter 9 in this volume). Sometimes it is possible to reduce emissions by switching to another input mix or by changing product design. Lastly, there is always an option to scale down production, relocate production facilities, or simply shut down a plant. The last option may prove to be a viable solution if the plant was barely making a profit even in the absence of strict environmental regulations. All in all, before costly 'end-of-pipe' equipment is installed, a number of more intelligent alternatives ought to be screened. Further, public interest in a region can be served best if the decision on who should abate how much is arrived at after determining who offers the cheapest options.

No firm will share information on the true costs of doing business. Such a disclosure would affect its strategic position *vis-à-vis* its competitors. Information on abatement costs would additionally affect its position *vis-à-vis* a regulatory agency by constraining its bargaining opportunities over environmental requirements. It is quite natural that industries – in their own interest – overstate future compliance costs. No government nor any other external body can unravel all the options that are open to a firm. After all, it was ultimately lack of entrepreneurship that caused the centrally planned systems in Europe, attempting to substitute administrative coordination for free enterprise, to collapse. The lesson learnt from their failure is relevant for environmental policy too.

The pursuit of self-interest can be used as a guide to lowering environmental protection costs, and the market is the best mechanism to reveal what expenditures are really inevitable to meet environmental requirements. Markets can reveal what is the cost society really has to bear to meet these requirements. Then, in turn, economic instruments can 'harness' market forces to work for the environment's sake. Economic instruments perform a number of useful functions. But their most important task is to minimize overall costs of environmental protection through a cost-effective differentiation of control requirements. To be precise, those agents with the lowest abatement costs should be given the most stringent requirements. As argued above, for obvious reasons no agent, whether a firm or a consumer, would provide the regulatory agency with the information needed to take such decisions. Arriving at least-cost solutions thus requires that market forces are set to work, and take advantage of the cost-saving potential of economic instruments.

Environmentalists know, however, that markets have been a mixed blessing. Indeed, much harm is done within the framework of thriving market forces both in the developed and the less developed world. It is therefore necessary to assess as objectively as possible what can be expected from markets, what information they can successfully provide, and where they will not be helpful at all. The distinction between scale and allocation decisions has proved to be a useful methodological starting-point.

To regulate the environment means to decide first to what extent a given resource, say the carrying capacity of the atmosphere or an aquifer, could be used; this is called the 'environmental utilization space' (Opschoor, 1992) or 'scale' (Daly, 1992); and, second, what portion of the resource should be allocated to any of its potential users. The first decision addresses the *scale* aspect, the second the *allocation* aspect. To quote a specific example: millions of polluters contribute to the eutrophication of the Baltic Sea. If the sea is to be restored, the influx of nutrients (phosphorus and nitrogen) has to be reduced. It has been estimated that bringing the total influx down to the level observed in the 1950s would do the job (Wulff and Niemi, 1992). This can be done in a number of ways. One way would be to require that every polluter reduce the nutrient discharges by a uniform rate to meet the overall objective. But certainly there are many other ways to allocate requirements between various regions, economic sectors and individual sources (Gren et al., 1997). The first (hypothetical) decision to reduce the overall influx of nutrients is an example of a scale decision. It provides a framework for another decision, that of allocation, that is, on how to distribute tasks among all the parties concerned.

These two aspects can be addressed separately. But they can also be treated jointly by starting with the allocation of tasks, thus arriving at the overall scale as a result of individual contributions. Also market forces can be utilized to determine either of the aspects. However, the role markets can play in either case may vary.

A competitive market is a superior mechanism for calculating equilibrium prices by revealing people's preferences and unravelling what entails the least cost in providing goods or services. In this capacity it has never been surpassed by any other institution. However, markets cannot do the impossible. For instance, they cannot process information that does not exist. In particular they cannot estimate the value of an environmental resource if the resource is not freely exchanged and/or if its contribution to human welfare, both direct and indirect through its role in a wider ecological–economic system, is not fully known. Likewise they cannot convincingly evaluate benefits which are future benefits, especially those to people who do not yet exist. Hence, while it is quite legitimate and rewarding to employ the market as an allocation mechanism, it would be unreasonable to rely on it in determining scale decisions.

This separation principle is well illustrated by marketable permits (see Barde, Chapter 6 in this volume). The volume of all permits issued determines the scale aspect of a policy. But the allocation is left to market forces either by auctioning the permits or by making permits transferable after distributing them in an administrative way. Marketable permits utilize market forces exactly in the domain where these can play an outstanding role, and keep them out from where they may sometimes do more harm than good. Note that the choice between marketable permits and other economic instruments, such as charges or taxes, is a choice between assigning priority to economy or to environment. In an uncertain world, with taxes the financial outcome of environmental policy is less likely to cause surprise, whereas with marketable permits the scale of protection is less likely to cause surprise (see Löfgren, Chapter 1 and Barde, Chapter 6 in this volume).

Dealing with uncertainty has led policy analysts and politicians to borrow some concepts from the theory of games. To play a game means to take the chance of losing while expecting to win. Game theorists have developed an elaborate conceptual framework to assess and prioritize strategies given their adequacy under alternative scenarios. As a rule, strategies that are promising from one point of view are inappropriate from another. For instance, if one pursues a development policy aimed at short-term financial profits, then one may be surprised by its adverse health or environmental effects. And vice versa, an environmentally effective policy may turn out to be an unexpected burden, especially if judged from a short-term perspective. Are there strategies which do not sacrifice one goal for another in an uncertain world? In many applications there are, and they are called 'win–win' or 'no-regret' strategies. An example of such a strategy would be to invest in projects which result in economic development and environmental improvements simultaneously.

The no-regret approach to environmental policy is another recent contribution to empirically assessing alternative policy measures. It calls for adopting not necessarily those that are superior with respect to the theoretical criterion of efficiency, but those that are likely to prove robust when tested against a mix of other criteria as well. The World Bank, for instance, has identified a number of no-regret policies which serve both economic development and a better environment. They include poverty reduction through a redistribution of wealth, elimination of subsidies for the use of fossil fuels and water, improved sanitation, endowing farmers with property rights on the land they farm and so on (World Bank, 1992). This does not mean that there is no trade-off between environmental quality and the level of material production, or between short-term increase in production and the ability to sustain this level over a longer period of time. It simply means that it is sometimes possible to eliminate false dichotomies by screening options carefully and selecting measures which address several concerns at the same time.

5.   POPULAR PRINCIPLES IN ENVIRONMENTAL POLICY

As pure theoretical criteria, such as efficiency or cost-effectiveness, are difficult to apply in real-world situations, environmental policies have often referred to several simple practical principles. These include such well-known maxims as 'polluter pays', 'polluters pay', 'user pays', 'victim pays', the 'precautionary principle', and the 'subsidiarity principle'. Although frequently quoted, these principles nevertheless are far from obvious to everyone, and there are controversies about their exact meaning.

The polluter pays principle (PPP) is probably the best-known guideline for environmental policy (OECD, 1992). There are, however, two definitions in use. PPP in the broadest sense means that the polluter is financially responsible for whatever harm its activities may cause, no matter whether they stay within the limits set by the law or not. Even though such a broad range of responsibilities has been theoretically possible under jurisdictions adopted in many countries and encouraged by the OECD since 1991, most policies try to enforce a narrower version. PPP in a strict sense means that the polluter is financially responsible for complying with whatever environmental requirements are set by relevant authorities.

As it turns out, even this more restricted form of PPP, officially endorsed by the OECD since 1972, has been difficult to apply in practice. An alternative wording of PPP would be 'no-subsidy principle'. But important exceptions to this principle are acknowledged and tolerated by the OECD. Subsidies for polluters to meet environmental requirements are approved if the following three conditions are met: (1) the subsidy does not introduce significant distortions in international trade and investment;[9] (2) without the subsidy, affected industries would suffer severe difficulties; and (3) the subsidy is limited to a well-defined transition period adapted to the specific socioeconomic problems associated with the implementation of a country's environmental policy (OECD, 1992).[10]

Some governments have developed a very peculiar understanding of the PPP (Opschoor and Vos, 1989, pp. 28–30). The Federal Government of Germany, for instance, considers certain investment subsidies compatible with the PPP as long as polluters are responsible for the rest of abatement efforts, including, most importantly, operation costs. On the other hand, the Swedish government extends the PPP to justify introducing 'control charges': raising funds to more effectively regulate the polluters and monitor their compliance. Some governments admit that they violate the PPP for equity reasons if the polluter is a municipal body, as in the case of the United States Construction Grant Program to subsidize sewage treatment in urban agglomerations.

As the PPP has been frequently misinterpreted and misunderstood, it is important to define what this concept actually encompasses and what it does not.[11] First of all it was established 'to avoid distortions in international trade and investment' (OECD, 1992), which may occur when polluters are subsidized. Seen from such a perspective, the PPP offers a reasonable and appealing common cost allocation principle. The choice of this particular principle was motivated by economic considerations. These suggest that once prices of goods and services reflect their full social costs, including environmental ones, market forces start to work for a good purpose, and less intervention is necessary to achieve the desired environmental effects.

There are three features which are often associated with the PPP, even though they should not be. First, PPP is not an equity-motivated principle. One may judge it equitable that the polluter pays, but who eventually bears the burden of protective measures is a different question.[12] As a matter of fact, most deliberate violations of the PPP, such as subsidizing the construction of municipal sewage treatment plants, have been motivated by equity concerns. Second, PPP is not a liability principle. It is not a matter of designating who is responsible for pollution: whether the supplier of an environmentally unfriendly product (for example the producer of a pesticide) or the user (for example the farmer). It is merely a matter of determining at what level it is most appropriate to account for environmental costs and/or to step in with regulations. Third, PPP is not synonymous with environmental taxation. It can be implemented in many different ways, ranging from pollution charges to direct regulations, as long as polluters are forced to take protective measures (see also Barde, Chapter 6 in this volume).

When strict financial responsibility of a polluter is difficult or impractical to enforce, governments sometimes apply the polluters pay principle (note the plural form!), charging polluters the overall environmental protection costs. This principle assumes that polluters are charged more or less in proportion to the environmental stress they cause, in order to raise funds to support protection activities needed to comply with regulations. The French pollution charges recirculated, that is, paid back to the polluters to subsidize their abatement activities, are a well-analysed example of that sort. Also in The Netherlands similar programmes have been in operation, although the Dutch authorities prefer to point to the so-called 'causation principle' as a justification for their charging polluters as a whole, and recirculating money for environmental control purposes. In Poland, the funds originating from pollution charges contribute more than a third of the overall investment expenditures, and they have become an important component of the country's recovery programme (Żylicz, 1998).

Both 'polluter pays' and 'polluters pay' should be distinguished from a simple 'user pays principle'. Here, environmental protection is achieved through the operation of a facility, for example sewage treatment plant or landfill, serving a group of users. If the facility is financially self-sufficient, then it can be said that the user pays principle applies; that is, the users pay for its operation. Even though the concept seems to be clear at first glance, ambiguity may arise when the costs of a facility are not or cannot be divided among the users proportionally, because of the heterogeneity of services required. This happens if, for instance, there is no obvious way to assign the overhead costs of the facility to what various users discharge. Cross-subsidies, that is, subsidies of one category of users to another, may happen as a result. Sometimes the cross-subsidy is deliberate, for example, charging industrial users for water supply more than municipal ones, and serves an equity purpose. In such cases, it would be more appropriate to talk about a 'users pay principle', but this term is not used.

Like the 'Polluter Pays', the 'User Pays' is basically a 'no-subsidy principle'. But in many countries and in many instances these principles have been violated due to equity considerations. This is somewhat paradoxical, since the principles were often primarily warranted not so much on efficiency as on equity grounds. It has been known since the 1960s that in a two-party setting efficiency does not require the polluter to be charged for the harm done to the victim. What is important is that the property rights to the environment are assigned unambiguously and can be enforced, such that the polluter and victim are prepared to negotiate, and that the transaction costs of any potential protection agreements are negligible.[13] Thus sometimes the efficiency question can be disconnected from the allocation of protection costs: these can either be borne by the polluting or by the polluted party. If for equity reasons (or for any other reason) the polluter is not expected to pay, then efficiency can be achieved by letting the 'pollutee' subsidize ('bribe') the other party not to pollute. This is referred to as the 'victim pays principle'. It has been widely debated,[14] and occasionally applied in agreements to curb transboundary pollution (Żylicz, 1991).

Even though short-term efficiency may often be achieved irrespective of who shall bear the responsibility to pay protection costs, it is rather obvious that in the long run it is the polluter, or the user, who should bear the burden. Otherwise they are in fact subsidized, which will direct economic activities to the domain where they cannot be sustained, and will remove an incentive for environment-saving technological innovations. For these reasons, the 'polluter pays', and 'user pays' principles should be seen as useful policy guidelines.

Apart from the cost-related principles discussed above, there are others inspired by non-financial considerations.

As for the 'no-regret' approach, the motivation for the 'precautionary principle' can be derived from game-theory concepts and corresponds to the so-called minimax strategy, that is, a strategy to minimize the worst possible outcome. This principle is nothing more than a general recommendation to expect an unfavourable course of events, and to choose policy measures accordingly. However, it has several useful consequences. One is to establish 'safe minimum standards' (see Section 3 above) when dealing with materials or technologies whose environmental and health effects have not yet been fully researched. Such standards, based on whatever fragmentary evidence is available, should prevent major surprises even if the worst is going to happen.

An example of another corollary derived from the precautionary principle is the use of financial guarantees for the worst possible outcome. These can be gradually lowered subject to further evidence reducing the likelihood of a worst-case scenario. This is the rationale behind 'environmental performance bonds', suggested mandatory for agents entering potentially hazardous activities. An environmental performance bond is an insurance, to be bought by an economic agent willing to enter an activity which may lead to serious adverse environmental effects, whose price depends on the scientific assessment of risks involved (Perrings, 1989). Insurance provides funds for remediation if necessary. But an even more interesting feature of this instrument is the prospect of linking the price of the bond to the ongoing evaluation of the agent's performance, including the ability to convince the authorities (or the general public) of the safety of its operations. Thus this can also contribute to the technological and scientific progress aimed at reducing uncertainty.

The 'subsidiarity principle' is a postulate originating from political and social considerations. It states that policy measures should be determined by the lowest level of authority suited for a given problem. In other words, it can be seen as a 'decentralization principle'. In the European Union it has been applied to let the member states adapt their policies to the Union's directives in a creative way, and make them compatible with local preferences.[15] From a sociological point of view this principle is much more than a simple safety-valve against the omnipotence of centralized bureaucracies. It is a recognition of the fact that people not only have different preferences but also aspirations to monitor the resources they are responsible for. The 'subsidiarity principle' can be linked to the deeper concept of *regionalism*, that is, an 'approach to the study of society as based on the recognition of distinct differences in both cultural and natural attributes of different areas that, nevertheless, are interdependent' (Odum, 1983, p. 512). The consequences of adopting a regional outlook are twofold. First, because of the uniqueness of their natural attributes, different regions may require different 'customized' measures, standards and policies.[16] Second, these policies should treat the region as a whole, and serve both environmental and human needs.

The regional approach can be viewed as yet another manifestation of the sustainable development philosophy. It would be difficult, and also not sustainable, to promote policies which do not take into account local aspirations. Such policies would be either poorly enforced or, if effectively enforced against the will of the local people, would be a force disrupting the stability of the political structure which implemented them. Non-sustainability would then result from impairing either the natural or social base of the region's development. On the other hand, however, as observed by Odum above, regions are interdependent and the decisions taken by one region may affect any other region. If there is a possibility for a region to 'free-ride' on others, or to dispose of a problem through creating an 'externality' (see Löfgren, Chapter 1 and Folmer and de Zeeuw, Chapter 16 in this volume), it is in the interest of all regions concerned to exert a mutual coercion jointly agreed upon. The 'subsidiarity principle' always has to be judged against specific considerations that may require a supraregional authority for the common good.

Similar qualifications apply to any of the principles discussed above. They were developed as useful rules of thumb to point to options that are adequate most of the time, or in nearly all typical circumstances. It was made clear in this chapter, however, that there is no underlying theory implying that these principles are generally valid rules of successful environmental policy-making.

6. WHAT TO PROTECT AND HOW?

Two important technical questions have to be answered before an environmental policy can be drafted. These are: (1) Who or what shall we protect? Should we protect the environment for ourselves, or rather should we protect ourselves against possible hazards scattered throughout the environment? In the latter case, do we want to protect an average individual or the most susceptible sub-population? (2) How far should we intervene in spontaneous economic development processes? In particular, should we regulate industries by imposing requirements derived from the best-known abatement technologies, or by imposing requirements derived from an assessment of the environmental 'carrying capacity' or utilization space? The most likely answer of economists to both questions would be to estimate costs and benefits of each alternative and to select the most efficient one. As indicated in section 3 above, this is not the approach that has been followed in practice. Environmental policy-makers cannot escape making hard social choices and explicit political decisions by simply referring to the outcome of a cost–benefit analysis.

There are two broad orientations with respect to the first question mentioned above: the environmental and the health approach. Within the former, priority is given to environmental considerations. These may turn out to be more restrictive than the health aspects. For instance, coniferous forests are more vulnerable to acid rain than humans are.[17] Thus an environment-oriented ambient standard for sulphur dioxide will be stricter than a health-oriented one. Also, within the realm of natural ecosystems there are some that are more vulnerable than others. Looking at the most fragile one would probably require the total elimination of a pollutant or the reduction of it to the natural background concentrations, if it is a naturally occurring substance, like sulphur dioxide.

It is very unlikely, though, that environmental policy would adopt the general rule to protect the most fragile ecosystem. Likewise, for practical reasons, it is unlikely that within the framework of the health orientation, it would follow the rule to protect the most vulnerable sub-population. Rather, one can observe that a more pragmatic approach is adopted of setting ambient requirements so as to protect a typical ecosystem considered to be the most important one, and/or an average individual. With respect to the most vulnerable ones (both ecosystems and humans), the best a policy-maker can do is to protect them from the environment. This strategy is practised by establishing rescue programmes for threatened species, creating gene banks and so on. Advising asthmatics to stay indoors during smog alerts, or excluding certain sites from being visited by pregnant women and children, as well as by other high-risk groups, serves a similar purpose. This is far from a recommended solution, but in some instances, at least in the short run, there are no other politically viable methods of proceeding.

The second important question is whether to do what is technologically possible, or what is environmentally desirable. It would be optimal to have an easy technological solution to every environmental problem. Unfortunately this is not the case, and environmental or health requirements imply constraints on economic development. What is environmentally desirable may not be tech-nologically possible.

The problem can be best explained in the context of the distribution of emission permits among polluters affecting air quality in a given area. Each of these polluters has a certain production plan leading to certain pollution loads unless abatement measures are enforced. Which measures should be imposed?

One approach is to require everyone to apply the very best abatement technology. This is how such mysterious acronyms as BACT, RACT or BATNEEC were invented and used in some countries. They stand for best available control technology, reasonably available control technology and best applicable technology not entailing excessive costs, respectively. Thus some environmental policies have relied on the requirement that every source is equipped with state-of-the-art technology. This is the 'source- or technology-based approach'. Standards based on this are called emission- or source-oriented standards. This philosophy has a few advantages, the most important of which are simplicity and appeal to common sense: everybody does what can, and thus ought to, be done.

It has several drawbacks. First, requiring that everybody does what is technologically possible, even in the more liberal BATNEEC version, may not be cost-effective, since different polluters will probably end up with different marginal costs of abatement. Second, if the area of concern is filled with a large number of polluters, the overall impact on the air quality can be intolerable, even if every plant is equipped with a BACT device. The technology-based approach may thus violate not only the cost-effectiveness, but also the effectiveness, criterion. The same argument certainly applies to consumer behaviour. If, for instance, the number of cars becomes too large, then even if each of them were equipped with frontier technology, the total emissions would be excessive.

Despite such objections, in 1996, the European Union adopted the Integrated Pollution Prevention and Control (IPPC) Directive mandating emission sources to apply 'best available technique' (BAT). Even though the Directive does not prescribe a specific technology, it requires emission to be regulated – source by source – up to the level that corresponds to an existing technical option. There is no mechanism to achieve cost-effectiveness under the IPPC Directive.

An alternative approach is to ignore the existing polluters, and to define the desired air-quality target level. This represents the 'ambient-quality approach', standards based on which are called ambient standards. Thus an environmental policy may start with an ambient standard which is translated into total emissions allowed in the region in order to meet this standard. It may turn out that production plans of industries together with consumers' plans are incompatible with the standard even if each were using its respective state-of-the-art abatement technology (like BAT). The only way to meet the standard would then be to reduce the number of pollution sources. This obviously imposes a constraint on economic development. Policy-makers can then apply economic instruments, such as taxes or marketable permits, which help to comply with the constraint at minimum cost. Otherwise, determining which of the pollution sources are to be eliminated may be arbitrary and may lead to excessive costs.

Real-world environmental policies usually apply a mixture of technology-based and ambient-quality approaches. One way to operate is to start with the former to obtain an initial assessment of the total pollution in a geographical area assuming that all polluters will follow good abatement practices. If the total pollution happens to stay within the tolerable limits, no steps, apart from enforcing technology-based emission ceilings, have to be taken. Only if it exceeds the limit must the policy-maker go beyond what is technologically available and directly constrain the number of sources.[18] Another way is to start with an ambient-quality target, translate it into the total pollution load which can originate from an area, and distribute emission permits so as to not exceed the total. Perhaps, with respect to polluters whose presence in the area is seen as crucial, for example, for employment reasons, the permits will take into account available abatement technologies.

7. TYPICAL POLICY FAILURES

Much progress has been made ever since conscious environmental policies were first implemented. For most of the developed market economies, this era started in the 1960s. At the same time, many abatement measures adopted were undoubtedly far from efficient. Many failed to comply with simple cost-effectiveness criteria. Some policy measures even worsened rather than improved environmental conditions. While the lack of a good theory or expertise available occasionally played a role, an important reason for these policy failures was the 'political economy' of the decision-making process.

Environmental policy blunders may be caused by inadequate technical expertise, for instance, wrong toxic levels accepted as a base for setting standards. These then simply reflect the inaccuracy of our scientific knowledge. Perhaps someone had a vested interest in miscalculating environmental risks, or in preventing the academic world from determining a more precise dose–response relationship, but this does not create a systematic bias in assessing what constitutes a good reference point for regulatory decisions. There are illustrations of both under- and overestimated risks from emitting certain chemicals into the environment. Considering freons as perfectly safe gases until as recently as the early 1980s provides the best example of the former. On the contrary, setting the maximum PCB (polychlorinated biphenyl) concentration in fish meat in the USA in the 1970s at the level of 2 ppm (parts per million) was probably too stringent when confronted with the toxicological evidence that became available later. It should be noted that the polluters may have vested interests both in underestimating environmental risks, for obvious reasons, and in overestimating them; for example, if they expect they can adapt to stricter standards sooner than their less alert competitors (see Lévêque and Nadaï, Chapter 8 and Gabel and Sinclair-Desgagné, Chapter 9 in this volume).

An often-quoted example of a policy failing to conform with any cost-effectiveness criteria is the US Clean Air Act as amended in 1977. The amendments required all new electricity plants to install costly desulphurization equipment. This regulation substituted an older one which allowed the plants to meet sulphur pollution targets by any abatement measures, such as switching to cleaner coal from Western states. As a result of their heavy political lobbying, coalminers from the Appalachia – who supply the market with heavy sulphur coal – succeeded in eliminating all cheaper options and made electricity buyers pay $4.2 billion per year for the higher abatement costs (Howe, 1993). Similar failures can be found in many European Union regulations.

A policy failure which was very typical in the former centrally planned economies, although in a less transparent form found in other countries as well, is the imposition of requirements too strict to be taken seriously. The result is not only lack of compliance, but also a much more devastating long-term effect in the form of undermined authority of environmental administrators and disrespect for the law. With its 32 $\mu g/m^3$ ambient standard for SO_2 (mean annual concentration), Poland exceeds the EU (where the 80–120 $\mu g/m^3$ standards apply), Switzerland, and the USA. Poland is not an exception among the central and eastern European countries, and its SO_2 standard, adopted in the 1980s, is not an isolated case. The Estonian maximum daily concentration of 50 $\mu g/m^3$ is even stricter, as it does not allow for compensating 'dirty' days of, for example, 80 $\mu g/m^3$ with 'clean' ones of, for example, 20 $\mu g/m^3$; whereas in fact even larger variations in ambient conditions are quite common because of weather variability and other factors. Imposing unrealistic standards is an example of setting policy goals based on what is environmentally desirable without taking into account compliance costs. Of course this may be the result of poor judgement. More likely, though, it is a sort of green rhetoric of politicians: an excuse for not adopting any sincere measures to solve the problem.

Some of the best-known policy failures have been those caused by perverse incentives inherent in ill-defined property right systems or related to the process of establishing such rights. For decades, for instance, in a number of Latin American countries, burning or otherwise clearing the forest has been the easiest way to acquire ownership entitlement to the land thus 'developed'.[19] The mechanism is an important cause of tropical deforestation. Even though some countries, for example Costa Rica, have recently progressed in basing the land acquisition process on more rational criteria, the poverty of small settlers and the vested interests of large corporate holders contribute to the inertia of the old policies.

The case of water rights provides a somewhat less drastic example of how a similar mechanism may lead to the excessive use of a renewable resource. In the western United States, but also in some other regions throughout the world, water users need to 'justify' the validity of their permits by keeping water abstractions at a certain level. If their demand for water either permanently or temporarily drops, they have an incentive to keep using the water just as before in order not to lose the permit. This is the so-called 'use it or lose it' principle, a maxim which has been kept stubbornly alive and is utilized by legislators despite repeated criticisms.[20] Not only does it encourage wasteful use, but it also prevents permits from becoming marketable, and hence creates a double restraint for environmental policies to achieve cost-effectiveness.

Much more subtle varieties of policy failure are those caused by introducing economic incentives without an exact regulatory or behavioural objective. In many countries road transport taxation generates revenues substantially higher than necessary to cover the direct cost of maintaining the road network.[21] This suggests that the taxes, to the extent that they reflect environmental costs, can play a role in stimulating a move towards a more environmentally responsible use of cars. A closer scrutiny, however, proves that this is not the case (Button, 1992, pp. 50–51). First, among the least-taxed vehicles one can find those which, such as heavy trucks, generate particularly intense environmental and road damages. Second, the taxation generally consists of a sizeable fixed component which does not increase with the amount of travel, and therefore incentives to travel less are too weak once the vehicle tax has been paid. As a result, transport taxes, however high, are very far from an efficient Pigouvian mechanism.

Even worse than that, in some countries massive government interventions in the transport sector have created perverse incentives to actually increase rather than reduce the amount of traffic. In Germany, for instance, those who travel to work by car receive an income tax allowance, which affects the choice between a private car and public transportation. Many cities throughout the world have experimented with direct subsidies for public transportation. The most common result of such experiments is a negligible transfer from private car to public transport and an immense net increase in demand for the latter, wiping out any environmental benefits of the modal switch (Button, 1992).

Thus an OECD case study of environmental impacts of the transport sector concludes that '(1) prevailing intervention failures lead to an oversupply of transport ... and (2) a number of these failures induce direct damage to the environment' (Barde and Button, 1990, p. 18). In some cases, for example the relative undertaxation of truck transport, the failure is caused by yielding too much to an identifiable interest group (truck companies) or by giving high priority to regional development (believed to be best served by keeping the costs of freight transport low). In many instances, however, detrimental effects of taxes and subsidies intended as 'environmental', or at least as environmentally harmless, do not emerge because of any targeted lobbying efforts but rather as an unpredictable result of entangled politics of taxation.

Environmental impacts of the transport sector illustrate challenges of so-called policy integration aimed at coordinating various aspects of government interventions. Much research has been done to analyse economic consequences of environmental policies (see Fankhauser and McCoy, Chapter 7 in this volume), but the other direction is crucially important too. Policies intended to regulate or support specific sectors, such as transport or agriculture, interfere or simply undermine environmental policies, thus imposing on these additional (sometimes unexpected) constraints.

Examples such as those referred to in this section make clear that environmental policies, whose important purpose is to correct market failures, themselves also fail quite often. Sometimes this failure is rooted in politics and could have been avoided had the government or environmental authorities found a feasible mechanism for compensating potential losers. Sometimes correcting the failure does not demand a political compromise but simply requires a better analysis and more insight into the system to be regulated. In any event, studying the economic aspects of alternative policies can assist in identifying and dealing with the constraints that these policies inevitably face.

8.   DO ECONOMISTS CONTRIBUTE TO ENVIRONMENTAL POLICY DEBATES?

The purpose of this chapter was to report on how economists approach environmental policy, and what constraints they are confronted with. There are three major concepts that economic analysis applies to assess policies and to recommend specific measures: effectiveness, efficiency and equity. The traditional focus was efficiency, or a somewhat weaker criterion of cost-effectiveness. Only in the late 1980s did economists notice that the real-world policy-makers largely ignored their recommendations. For instance, surveys show that the scope of use of economic instruments has been much smaller than theoretically envisaged. What makes the economists' advice of so little practical value?

First of all, one must admit that, despite the widespread disappointment among economists, there are a number of successful applications of economic approaches to environmental policy. In the United States marketable pollution permits lowered abatement costs by thousands of millions of dollars. In Europe, deposit–refund systems helped to deal with the plague of wasteful packaging, and environmental charges, even at relatively low levels, did provide incentives for improvement. Some charges, for example the Dutch water pollution charge, have had significant impacts on emissions and their abatement. In economies in transition, recovery programmes crucially depend on the operation of environmental funds originating from pollution charges. These are just a few examples of when economists' advice has been taken into consideration.

However, it should be observed that economists' early interests largely omitted what was the focus of environmental activists and policy-makers. While the former were preoccupied with effectiveness, the latter seemed to be overwhelmed with equity questions, as well as the administrative practicality of alternative solutions. Not many economists were ready to adopt a pragmatic approach, to study dilemmas confronting politicians, and to provide them with politically viable recommendations.

A distinction between the traditional economic approach and one that incorporates various concerns voiced by non-economists has often been compared with the division between 'environmental economics' and 'ecological economics'.[22] While past experience may justify linking the former with a single analytical method, that is, that of 'neoclassical economics' and game theory, and the latter with the sustainability concept, most recent developments indicate that both fields largely overlap now. One can observe 'neoclassical' and game-theoretic analyses of complex ecological–economic problems which previously seemed to be beyond the domain of economics.

What do economists contribute to environmental policy debates? First, they assist policy-makers in assessing costs and benefits of alternative measures or projects to determine whether these are recommendable on economic grounds. Second, they advise on the available instruments to carry out a given policy, and suggest those that are most likely to bridge the gap between common-sense expectations and economic efficiency. Third, they pay attention to indirect effects of alternative policies which are often overlooked by non-economists; for that reason economic models can be important and revealing.

Various objectives are articulated and promoted by various interest groups. However, there is no natural constituency for macroeconomic efficiency, since the effects are usually distributed among wide social strata, and no particular group directly gains from it. It is here where economists play a stimulating role as a surrogate interest group pushing for solutions that minimize overall costs to be borne by society.

NOTES

1. There is also a less technical and more political notion of equity which refers to providing citizens with services they 'deserve', and charging them what they 'can afford', but it will not be used in that sense in this chapter.
2. See Pezzey (1989) for a thorough review and analysis of many definitions introduced in professional literature and politics language.
3. See Buchholz (1997) for an elementary exposition of an intergenerational equity rationale and criteria.

4. The 'materials balance' approach, initiated by Kneese et al. (1970) and followed by very few economists, is exceptional in its emphasis on studying the physical volume of matter flowing through the economy. The approach keeps track of all the material inputs (including those raw materials which are not purchased, such as air), and outputs (including those which are not sold, such as waste products) of economic activities. It indicates that what commercial transactions capture and conventional economic analyses deal with is but a fraction of the flow which determines production and consumption, as well as the characteristics of the environment we live in. See Ayres (1998) for a recent exposition of the materials balance approach.

5. See Tahvonen (Chapter 21 in this volume) for an explanation of the 'profit-maximizing sustained yield' concept.

6. Young (1992) derives more than 30 practical 'prescriptions' from the sustainability concept, addressing more directly the issues public policy has to deal with.

7. Weitzman (2000) carried out a large survey of economists asking them what real (that is, net of inflation) interest rate would be most appropriate for calculating NPV of environmental projects with very long time horizon, such as measures to mitigate climate change. The rate most commonly argued for was 4 per cent.

8. Proofs of these theorems require standard microeconomic assumptions on $u(c,s)$, such as concavity, separability, that is, $u(c,s) = u_1(c) + u_2(s)$, and monotonicity of u_1 and u_2. We refer readers to Beltratti et al. (1998) for further technicalities and bibliographic details.

9. If it does, that is, if it creates an unfair advantage over competitors from other countries, ecological dumping takes place. See Rauscher (1992) for a deeper analysis of this problem; subsidies can be substituted by more liberal standards on what the polluter is responsible for.

10. The European Union was more specific in defining the terms of a 'transition'. Initially a six-year period was envisaged (1974–80) with maximum subsidy rates of 45 per cent, 30 per cent, and 15 per cent.

11. This paragraph and the next are based on unpublished material written by Jean-Philippe Barde.

12. Economists study the so-called 'tax incidence' to see how the burden of an imposed payment or regulation is divided among producers (through reduced profits) and consumers (through reduced real purchasing power). In general, the incidence depends on the shape of supply and demand curves rather than on intentions of taxing authorities. In particular, it does not depend on whether the seller or the buyer is technically made responsible for transferring the tax to the Treasury.

13. This is the idea widely known as the Coase theorem; see Löfgren (Chapter 1 in this volume). Readers should be aware that this theorem requires a number of formal assumptions that are quite restrictive.

14. It has been recognized, for instance, that in Europe, trying to achieve substantial CO_2 emission reductions at minimum cost would require that Western European countries compensate the rest of the continent for its abatement effort beyond what the East is prepared to undertake as part of its domestic policies (Bohm and Larsen, 1994).

15. In the United States the concept of 'federalism' has been studied; it is equivalent to the European subsidiarity principle.

16. See Barde (Chapter 6 in this volume) for an illustration of the welfare loss caused by setting standards that are computed as 'average' for several locations.

17. It has been established that long-term exposure to concentrations of sulphur dioxide as low as 20 $\mu g/m^3$ inhibits growth and can be harmful. In contrast, these concentrations can be twice as high before they lead to evident adverse health effects.

18. This can be done in a number of ways, such as total bans on development projects, establishing zones for specific activities, regulating the level of production or simply distributing pollution permits in a stricter way than suggested by technological considerations.

19. In Brazil a very complicated system of public land allocation and solving land disputes encourages clearings larger than those used for subsistence or commercial purposes. By clearing the land one not only claims the entitlement but also prevents squatters from invading the economically useful 'core' of one's estate (Binswanger, 1989).

20. The continuous use of a water-discharge or air-pollution permit is a prerequisite for keeping it under the Polish environmental law; however, after 1989 this law was reformed for greater

effectiveness and efficiency. It is amazing how persistently the law-makers insisted on including the 'use it or lose it' clauses in all the drafts of new legal acts.

21. In The Netherlands they cover 434 per cent of road expenditures, in the UK 335 per cent, in New Zealand 235 per cent, in Sweden 230 per cent, and in Denmark 214%. In some other countries they cover between 100 per cent and 200 per cent of such expenditures. See Button (1992, p. 49).

22. Both orientations have their academic societies: the Association of Environmental and Resource Economics (mostly in the USA) and the European Association of Environmental and Resource Economics, and the International Society for Ecological Economics, respectively. Both have their journals: *Journal of Environmental Economics and Management* (the publication of the US association), *Environmental and Resource Economics*, and *Ecological Economics*, respectively.

REFERENCES

Ayres, Robert U. (1998), 'Rationale for a physical account of economic activities', in Pier Vellinga et al. (eds), *Managing a Material World. Perspectives in Industrial Ecology*, Dordrecht: Kluwer, pp. 1–20.

Barde, Jean-Philippe and Kenneth Button (1990), 'Introduction', in J.-P. Barde and K. Button (eds), *Transport Policy and the Environment. Six Case Studies*, London: Earthscan, pp. 1–18.

Baumol, W.J. and W.E. Oates (1988), *The Theory of Environmental Policy*, 2nd edn, New York: Cambridge University Press.

Beltratti, Andrea, Graciela Chichilnisky and Geoffrey Heal (1998), 'Sustainable use of renewable resources', in G. Chichilnisky, G. Heal and A. Vercelli (eds), *Sustainability: Dynamics and Uncertainty*, Dordrecht: Kluwer, pp. 49–76.

Binswanger, Hans P. (1989), 'Brazilian policies that encourage deforestation in the Amazon', Environment Department Working Paper No. 16, Washington, DC: The World Bank.

Bohm, P. and B. Larsen (1994), 'Fairness in a tradeable-permit treaty for carbon emissions reductions in Europe and the former Soviet Union', *Environmental and Resource Economics*, **4** (3), pp. 219–39.

Buchholz, Wolfgang (1997), 'Intergenerational equity', in T. Żylicz (ed.), *Ecological Economics. Markets, Prices and Budgets in a Sustainable Society*, Uppsala: The Baltic University, pp. 19–22.

Button, Kenneth J. (1992), *Market and Government Failures in Environmental Management. The Case of Transport*, Paris: OECD.

Chichilnisky, Graciela (1996), 'Sustainable development: an axiomatic approach', *Social Choice and Welfare*, **13** (2), 219–48.

Daly, H.E. (1990), 'Sustainable development: from concept and theory to operational principles', in K. Davis and M.S. Bernatam (eds), *Resources, Environment and Population*, New York: Population Council and Oxford University Press, pp. 25–43.

Daly, H.E. (1992), 'Allocation, distribution, and scale: towards an economics that is efficient, just and sustainable', *Ecological Economics*, **6**, 185–93.

Gren, I.-M., K. Elofsson and P. Jannke (1997), 'Cost-effective nutrient reductions to the Baltic Sea', *Environmental and Resource Economics*, **10** (4), 341–62.

Hartwick, John M. (1977), 'Intergenerational equity and investing the rents from exhaustible resources', *American Economic Review*, **66**, 972–4.

Howe, Charles W. (1993), 'The U.S. environmental policy experience: a critique with suggestions for the European Community', *Environmental and Resource Economics*, **3** (4), 359–79.

Kneese, A.V., R.U. Ayres and R.C. d'Arge (1970), *Economics and the Environment. A Materials Balance Approach*, Baltimore: Johns Hopkins University Press.

Odum, E.P. (1983), *Basic Ecology*, Philadelphia: Saunders College Publishing.

OECD (Organization for Economic Co-operation and Development) (1992), *The Polluter-Pays Principle. OECD Analyses and Recommendations*, Paris: Environment Directorate, OECD (OCDE/GD(92)81).

Opschoor, J.B. (1992), 'Sustainable development, the economic process and economic analysis', in J.B. Opschoor (ed.), *Environment, Economy and Sustainable Development*, Groningen: Wolters-Noordhoff.

Opschoor, J.B. and H.B. Vos (1989), *Economic Instruments for Environmental Protection*, Paris: OECD.

Perrings, C. (1989), 'Environmental bonds and environmental research in innovative activities', *Ecological Economics*, **1**, 95–110.

Pezzey, J. (1989), 'Economic analysis of sustainable growth and sustainable development', Environment Department Working Paper No. 15, Washington, DC: The World Bank.

Rauscher, M. (1992), 'On ecological dumping', paper presented at the 2nd Conference of the International Society for Ecological Economics, Stockholm.

WCED (World Commission on Environment and Development) (1987), *Our Common Future*, Oxford: Oxford University Press

Weitzman, Martin (2000), 'Gamma discounting', *American Economic Review*, forthcoming.

World Bank (1992), *World Development Report 1992. Development and the Environment*, Oxford: Oxford University Press.

Wulff, F. and Å. Niemi (1992), 'Priorities for the restoration of the Baltic Sea – a scientific perspective', *Ambio*, **21**, 193–5.

Young, M.D. (1992), *Sustainable Investment and Resource Use. Equity, Environmental Integrity and Economic Efficiency*, Paris: UNESCO.

Żylicz, T. (1991), 'The role for economic incentives in international allocation of abatement effort', in R. Costanza (ed.), *Ecological Economics. The Science and Management of Sustainability*, New York: Columbia University Press, pp. 384–99.

Żylicz, T. (1998), 'Environmental policy in economies in transition', in T. Tietenberg and H. Folmer (eds), *The International Yearbook of Environmental and Resource Economics 1998/1999: A Survey of Current Issues*, Cheltenham, UK and Northampton, US: Edward Elgar, pp. 119–52.

6. Environmental policy and policy instruments

Jean-Philippe Barde[1]

1. INTRODUCTION

The evolution of environmental policies since the early 1970s has been characterized by two main features: first, the development of a number of 'principles' designed to base these policies on firm and internationally recognized grounds, the 'polluter pays principle' being the most important one (see Chapter 5); and second, the development and deployment of the so-called 'policy instruments' designed to implement and enforce environmental policies.

A wide array of policy instruments is deployed in many countries (see Box 6.1); a description of all of them would go beyond the scope of this chapter, whose objective is to provide an overview of the main policy instruments, that is: regulations and standards, voluntary agreements, taxes and charges, subsidies, tradable permits, deposit refund systems and damage compensation. Other instruments such as education and information will not be treated.

The selection of policy instruments by governments is based on the characteristics described below and on the application of criteria for selecting (mixes of) instruments. In general these criteria will relate to: (1) environmental aspects (environmental effectiveness); (2) economic aspects (efficiency); and (3) political and administrative aspects (such as distributional issues, acceptability and simplicity). Whenever possible, the 'performance' of the instruments will be discussed in terms of these criteria.

2. REGULATIONS AND STANDARDS

2.1 Background and Definition

When environmental policies were adopted in the late 1960s and early 1970s, the authorities in most industrialized countries turned largely to regulatory control, either by creating new regulations or by adapting existing ones. This approach was often opposed to the so-called 'economic approach' which

BOX 6.1   THE ARRAY OF ENVIRONMENTAL POLICY INSTRUMENTS

TYPE	EXAMPLES
Command and control	Licences/permits Ambient quality standards Emission standards Process standards Product standards
Economic instruments	Charges Taxes Tradable permits Subsidies Deposit-refund systems
Liability, damage compensation	Strict liability rules Compensation funds Compulsory pollution insurance
Education – information Voluntary approaches	Unilateral commitments Public voluntary schemes Negotiated agreements
Planning	Zoning Land use

advocated the use of 'economic instruments' such as taxes, charges and marketable permits (see below). The regulatory or 'command and control' (CAC) approach remains the most commonly used in environmental policy, even though the economic approach is becoming increasingly important.

The CAC approach consists of the promulgation and enforcement of laws and regulations prescribing objectives, standards and technologies that polluters must comply with; for instance, laws on water and air pollution, and waste disposal. Generally, within the framework of such laws, specific rules are usually prescribed in the form of standards. There are four categories of standards:

1. *Ambient quality standards* specify the characteristics of the receiving (ambient) environment, for example, the maximum concentration of nitrates

in drinking water, of sulphur dioxide in the atmosphere or the maximum noise level near houses; in fact, they constitute an environmental objective which can be achieved by different (or a mix of) policy instruments, including the types of standards listed below.

2. *Emission or discharge standards* are the maximum allowable discharges of pollutants into the environment, for example, maximum biochemical oxygen demand (BOD) discharge into water or maximum SO_x emission into the atmosphere by an industry. In its extreme form, an emission standard is a ban on the use or discharge of a substance, usually a toxic one.
3. *Process standards* specify the type of production process or emission reduction equipment that polluting plants must install (for example, a specific type of scrubber, pipe, water purification device and so on).
4. *Product standards* define the characteristics of potentially polluting products such as chemicals, detergents, fertilizers, automobiles and fuels.

Categories 2–4 are relevant in the context of direct regulation.

2.2 Criteria for Fixing Standards

Four types of criteria are, or should be, used for the determination of environmental standards: environmental, technological, economic and political. Note that these criteria can also apply to the setting and implementation of other policy instruments such as pollution charges and taxes.

Environmental criteria

Environmental considerations preside over the setting of environmental policy instruments, and in particular over the level of standards. This relates, for example, to the maximum acceptable concentrations of pollutants in air, water, food and so on to ensure health and safety, that is, threshold levels in nature to ensure welfare or protect economic activity from being impaired (for example, water resources, soil productivity, biological diversity and climate). This is a vast and complex domain where biologists, ecologists, climatologists, engineers, statisticians and so on come into play.

In this context, a number of key elements are needed to make an appraisal of standards possible. For instance, the evaluation of 'dose–effect relationships', such as the health effects caused by exposure to a given concentration of SO_x in the atmosphere, is needed to calculate damage functions in the form of morbidity or mortality elasticities. Uncertainties and irreversibilities must also be assessed: what level of risk can be deemed acceptable on ecological, health, economic or other grounds? What risk of cancer is society ready to accept *vis-à-vis* the numerous benefits provided by chemical substances? Such issues may become confused as there is often a gap between risk as perceived by the public and as evaluated by experts. Studies have indicated that a number of environmental risks, considered minor by experts, are perceived as dangerous and considered a priority for action by the public or vice versa. This is all the more complex because environmental risks, *stricto sensu*, are combined with hazards owing to social habits such as smoking and diet.

The issue of irreversible effects (for example, the extinction of species) is also a complex issue: what weight or what vote can be attributed to future generations? To what extent can artificial (man-made) assets replace natural assets (see Chapters 3 and 4)? One form of regulation can be the ban of an activity or product likely to cause such irreversible effects. In case of uncertainties one can apply the 'precautionary principle' whereby protection measures are taken before scientific certainty is obtained (see Chapter 5). So-called 'no-regret policies' can be implemented, that is, policies providing benefits in the presence of uncertainties; for example, even if the exact contribution of greenhouse gases to global warming is not known, reducing the emission of these gases would provide additional benefits in the form of energy savings and abatement of other pollutants such as SO_x and NO_x.

Technological criteria

Fixing environmental standards and regulations necessarily requires reference to technological feasibility. Standards will usually be enforceable to the extent that technical possibilities exist or are likely to be developed. This is why environmental regulations often refer to concepts such as 'best available technology' (BAT) or 'best practicable means' (BPM).

Five types of approaches to fixing standards can be identified (Barde, 1992):

1. Standards can be based on an existing technology already applied in a number of plants and easily transferable to others. This corresponds to the 'currently available' technology, and could be called the 'average standard approach'.
2. Standards and regulations often refer to BAT. This is an existing technology but applied by advanced and high performing industries. Adopting BAT implies a real effort. We can call this the 'model standard approach'.
3. Governments may decide to implement a technology which is still at the experimental level and has not yet reached the industrial development stage. The challenge for polluters is to achieve this technological development. This can be called the 'experimental standard approach'.
4. There may be cases where there is a need for stringent and urgent action but no available technology. Public authorities may nevertheless choose to impose standards leaving a predetermined time frame for industry to develop appropriate compliance technology. It is of utmost importance that, when fixing such standards, public authorities implement accompanying measures

such as research and development programmes, and pilot and demonstration projects jointly organized and financed by the public and private sectors, otherwise failure is most likely. A case in point was the so-called 'Muskie Law' (1970) in the US which required a 90 per cent reduction of carbon monoxide, hydrocarbons and NO_x automobile emissions within five to six years. No technology was available at the time and the automobile industry was unable and unwilling to comply. The compliance schedule was extended in 1973 and 1977, and finally the deadline was postponed until 1980. This failure obliged the government to set up an entirely new policy. At the same time in Japan, stringent automobile emission limits fixed in 1972 with a four-year deadline, postponed until 1978, were successfully met thanks to a research and development programme by industry and government.

5. Finally, an approach can be advocated which takes into consideration the cost of complying with regulations and standards: 'economically reasonable standards or technology'. This is a vague, albeit current concept: cost may be deemed reasonable for one single plant, an industry sector, a region and so on. This is usually negotiated and decided on a case-by-case basis with little, if any, global economic rationale.

This typology of approaches does not correspond strictly to reality, but it helps to clarify concepts and the possible (mix of) situations and policies. It also shows that technology-based standards are not without ambiguities and shortcomings. In particular, it is crucial to ensure that regulations and standards can and will evolve over time, whenever technological progress occurs. There is a need to strike a subtle balance between stability for industry (which must be able to plan its investments in a stable regulatory context), and the need to stimulate technological innovation. While BAT may not provide a strong stimulus to technical change, the fourth approach mentioned above is likely to trigger innovation, provided it is wisely implemented. Studies indicate that the implementation process of regulations is a key component of technological change.

We will now take an analytical look at innovation and pollution abatement costs. In Figure 6.1 we assume that technical progress enables industry to lower its marginal cost of pollution abatement (that is, the cost of removing one additional unit of pollutant) from A_1 to A_2. If the emission standard is S_1, the marginal abatement cost will decrease from C_1 to C_2 and industry will enjoy a cost reduction equal to the shaded area. One can also transfer the benefit of this technical progress to society by imposing a more stringent emission standard, S_2, thus keeping the marginal abatement cost at the same level as before.

This example shows two important facts. First, industry will be reluctant to reveal new technologies in order to avoid public authorities imposing ever more stringent measures based on new technologies. Second, it is not easy to ensure that the benefits of technical progress are effectively transferred to

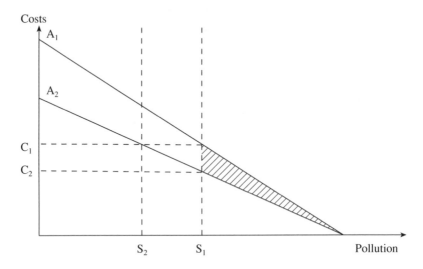

*Figure 6.1	Impacts of more stringent emission standards on the marginal cost
of pollution abatement*

society. We will see that imposing emission taxes and charges automatically
induces polluters to reduce their emissions in case of technological progress.

Economic criteria

Environmental and technological criteria are not sufficient to set environmental standards. As already mentioned, economic consideration also plays a key
role. An 'ideal' standard on scientific and technical grounds may well be
nonsense on economic grounds. Chapters 1 and 2 have shown that economic
analysis determines an optimum level of pollution (or environmental quality)
when abatement and damage costs are equal at the margin. Ideally, environmental standards should correspond to this optimum level of discharge.

This economic appraisal requires that both the costs and benefits of an environmental policy be evaluated. While cost functions should not be too difficult
to calculate (for example, the cost of pollution abatement), benefits are quite
difficult to evaluate in economic (monetary) terms. There is, however, an
increasing use of monetary estimates of environmental benefits and damages
in decision-making. For instance, the 'regulatory impact assessment' procedure
in the United States requires that any new major regulation be subject to a comprehensive economic assessment, including an economic evaluation of costs and
benefits. Finally, economic evaluation should also take into account irreversible
effects and future generations (see Chapter 3).

Political criteria

In setting policy instruments, decision-makers are confronted with a number of 'political' constraints:

1. *Equity*: will a regulation or tax affect different segments of society in an equitable manner? Who will bear the costs and who will benefit; what regions, income categories, economic sectors? Should compensation and mitigation measures be implemented?
2. *Precaution*: when uncertainty remains as to the effects of certain pollutants, should a margin of safety be defined? How large should it be? Should any measure be taken at all? Decision-makers may choose to apply the 'precautionary principle' defined earlier (Chapter 5).
3. *Acceptability*: this must be reached through appropriate consultation of the parties (public authorities, industry, trades unions, the general public and so on). There are 'cemeteries of regulations' full of unenforced regulations owing to lack of consultation and consensus.
4. *Simplicity*: complex regulations are difficult to implement and enforce because they are misunderstood or are simply too costly to apply. This also holds for economic instruments.

2.3   Strengths and Weaknesses of Regulations

The regulatory approach to environmental protection, compared with the 'economic approach' (see below) presents advantages and shortcomings.

One advantage of regulations is that there is a long-standing experience in other fields of public concern, such as health and safety, labour and so on. In some cases existing regulatory structures and institutions can be used. Another advantage is that regulations may provide an effective means of preventing hazards and irreversible effects. Finally, regulations provide a promise as to the achievement of environmental goals on emission flows: once an emission standard is fixed, one should be sure that emissions will not exceed this limit, provided there is effective enforcement.

On the other hand, regulations have a number of weaknesses:

1. Enforcement often proves to be difficult or weak, mainly owing to the great number of controls, administrative requirements, staff (inspectorate, corps of engineers, lawyers and so on), legal procedures in case of non-compliance and so on. The situation varies between countries, but it is generally acknowledged that lack of staff to carry out controls and enforcement makes the probability of being caught rather small; even so, non-compliance fines are usually too low to function as a real deterrent. A low non-compliance

fine multiplied by a low probability of being caught remains preferable to having to pay the marginal cost of pollution abatement.

2. Another drawback of regulations is that they may too easily be subject to bargaining and negotiations between public authorities and the private sector. It is, of course, natural that while a polluting plant is seeking a licence to operate, the terms and conditions of this licence should be subject to negotiations. However, one must strike a delicate balance, and negotiations can become easily influenced and challenged by lobbies and pressure groups. Industry often prefers to be subject to direct regulations rather than to taxes and charges, because it is much more difficult to negotiate and evade taxes. Obviously, industry is strongly in favour of voluntary approaches which open a wide scope for negotiations (see section 3).

3. A major limitation of regulation is that it is static and lacks incentives. Regulations and standards, laboriously negotiated, are not likely to evolve rapidly, especially when embodied in legislation. For instance, technical progress will become embodied in new regulations and standards only after a long time.

4. Finally, regulations are costly, not only at the enforcement level, but mainly because they are not efficient in economic terms. This is why economic instruments (in particular, taxes, charges and tradable permits) are being increasingly introduced in environmental policies (see below).

2.4   Regulatory Reform

Environmental policies have always been in constant evolution, in particular to devise more cost-effective policies. In order to minimize some of the pitfalls of regulations mentioned above, environmental 'regulatory reforms' have been, and still are, implemented in a number of countries, basically following two approaches: first, the implementation of new policy instruments such as taxes and voluntary approaches; these instruments are mostly used as complements to existing regulations, although they could replace them (see below). The second approach involves the improvement of existing regulatory systems, for example integrated permits, life-cyle analysis (a form of analysis that identifies and assesses the likely environmental consequences of a product throughout its life cycle, both upstream, starting with its resource use and its earlier stages of production, and downstream), extended producer responsibility (an application of the life-cycle approach), reduced administrative burden ('red tape'), better provision of information, involvement of stakeholders and so on. Box 6.2 provides an example of regulatory reform measures in the USA.

BOX 6.2   ENVIRONMENTAL REGULATORY REFORM IN THE USA – SOME EXAMPLES

President Clinton issued a report, *Reinventing Environmental Regulation*, in March 1995. The US Environmental Protection Agency's response, summarized in the slogan 'cleaner, cheaper, smarter', encompassed a number of initiatives:

- *Reducing paperwork and cutting red tape*: 1400 pages of obsolete environmental rules were to be eliminated. Ten million hours of paperwork for large and small businesses seeking to comply with environmental laws were eliminated; a further 10 million hours of paperwork were due to be eliminated by the end of 1996.
- *Making it easier for businesses to comply with environmental laws* through common-sense compliance incentives (Environmental Leadership Program) for small businesses, to enhance businesses' ability to meet environmental requirements through innovative approaches; funding of Small Business Compliance Centers for the metal-finishing, printing, automotive repair and farming industries.
- *Using innovation and flexibility to achieve better environmental results* by cutting red tape and finding the cheapest and most efficient ways to achieve higher environmental performance standards.
- Basing environmental regulations on *environmental performance goals*, while providing maximum flexibility in the means of achieving them.
- *Increasing community participation and partnerships* through expanding public access to EPA's information, establishing performance partnerships to combine federal funds to meet environmental needs and partnerships among EPA, industry and other groups to improve drinking-water safety.
- Enacting *simpler regulations,* understandable to those affected.
- Promoting *environmental justice*, that is, an equitable distribution of costs and benefits.
- Encouraging *self-policing* by companies and voluntary agreements.

> • Implementing 'place-based programs', that is, taking an *ecosystem* as the basis for designing a management strategy (rather than an approach based on administrative boundaries).
>
> *Source*:   US EPA (1996).

3.   VOLUNTARY APPROACHES

3.1   Definition and Current Practice

Early in the development of environmental policies, the rigidity of direct regulations both for the regulator and for regulated entities led to the search for alternative approaches. Therefore a number of 'voluntary approaches' were devised as early as the 1970s and are now developing rapidly in most industrialized countries. In general terms, voluntary approaches can be defined as commitments from polluting actors (for example industries) to improve their environmental performance. One important characteristic is that these commitments are not a response to a regulatory measure, but stem from some kind of private initiative or 'contract' with public authorities. Voluntary approaches have taken different forms, reflected by a diverse terminology: self-regulation, voluntary agreements, voluntary codes, covenants and so on, to quote just a few. However, the different types of voluntary approaches can be subsumed in three main categories (Börkey et al., 1999).

Unilateral commitments
These are unilateral commitments by the private sector to undertake a series of activities or to comply with guidelines or codes of conduct designed to protect the environment. The key characteristic is that these commitments are made at the initiative of the private sector, usually to prevent the emergence of a new regulation, to improve its environmental performance and public image. The objectives and means of implementation are also set up by the concerned firms, usually manufacturer associations.

One example of such a self-regulatory arrangement is the 'Responsible Care' initiative launched by the Canadian Chemical Producers' Association and now applied in many countries. Under this scheme, participating chemical industries adhere to a 'code of conduct' and guiding principles for an improved environmental performance of firms (see Box 6.3 for the US case).

BOX 6.3   MANAGEMENT PRACTICE CODE OF
THE AMERICAN CHEMICAL MANU-
FACTURERS' ASSOCIATION

- Community Awareness and Emergency Response (CAER): Ensure emergency preparedness and foster community right-to-know.
- Pollution Prevention: Promote efforts to protect the environment by generating less waste and reducing emissions.
- Process Safety: Prevent fires, explosions, and accidental releases.
- Distribution: Reduce the risk to public carriers, customers, contractors, employees, and environment posed by the transportation and storage of chemicals.
- Employee Health and Safety: Protect and promote the health and safety of employees or people visiting company sites.
- Product Stewardship: Promote the safe handling of chemicals from initial manufacture to distribution, sale, and ultimate disposal.

Source: Mazurek (1998a)

Unilateral commitments are widespread in the industrialized world, particularly in the USA where more than 2000 firms have joined nine different initiatives in different economic sectors. In Japan, this approach has been developing since 1995 (Responsible Care) and in 1997, the Federation of Japanese Industries (Keidanren) launched a comprehensive 'Voluntary Action Plan for the Environment' involving 137 industry organizations. In the European Union, unilateral commitments are less common: 27 commitments in 1997, most related to the Responsible Care initiative (UNEP, 1998) (see Figure 6.2).

Public voluntary schemes
Within public voluntary schemes, participating firms agree to comply with objectives, rules or guidelines developed by public bodies such as environmental agencies. For example, public authorities develop management principles and/or objectives with which firms are invited, but not *a priori* obliged, to comply.

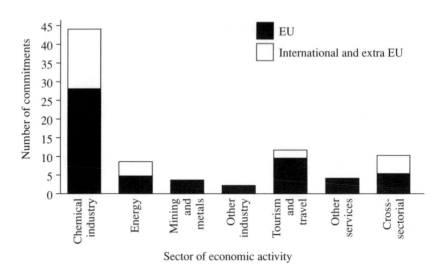

Source: UNEP (1998).

Figure 6.2 Unilateral commitments in the EU and in the rest of the world

This type of voluntary approach is mainly used in the USA, where more than 7000 corporations are participating in such programmes. An example of such a non-mandatory regulation is the US '33/50 initiative' launched by EPA, seeking voluntary cooperation from industrial firms to cut release of toxic chemicals, that is, a 33 per cent reduction in release and transfer of toxic chemicals in 1991–92, and a reduction by 50 per cent by 1995. In the EU, few public voluntary programmes are in force; one example is the Eco-Management and Auditing Scheme (EMAS), developed by the European Commission since 1993, which firms are invited to implement.

Voluntary programmes are basically complements to existing policy instruments, either to induce industry to do 'something more' or to pave the way for future regulations or other policy measures.

Negotiated agreements

Negotiated agreements (NAs) are real contracts between public authorities and industry. These contracts ('agreements') usually comprise objectives, a time schedule, compliance and control provisions, and possibly sanctions. If the objectives are achieved, the public authorities agree not to introduce new pieces of legislation, regulations, or other instruments such as taxes. In case of non-compliance, public authorities (at national, regional or local level) will introduce new legislation or regulation. Although considered by both the private sector

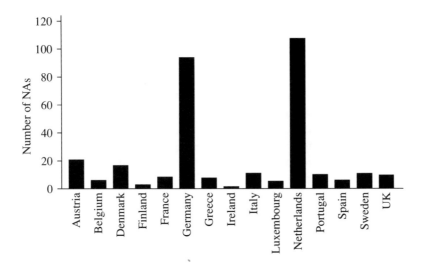

Source: European Commission (1996).

Figure 6.3   Number of negotiated agreements in the EU member states (1996)

and government as a more flexible approach than regulation, negotiated agreements can precede future regulatory measures. This approach is developing rapidly in industrialised countries with different modalities.

In the USA, only two NAs were in force in 1998: the 1994 'Common Sense Initiative' covering six industrial sectors, and the 1995 'XL' project directed to individual firms (Mazurek, 1998b).

In Japan, NAs play a key role. 'Pollution agreements' started in Japan in 1964 as local government initiatives. The purpose of these agreements was to compensate for the lack of environmental regulations in the early 1960s. Hence, these initiatives were rather a precursor of regulations and/or designed to fill regulatory gaps and resolve local difficulties. About 2000–2500 NAs are concluded every year. As of September 1996, 31 000 agreements are in force (Imura, 1998).

In the European Union, NAs are the most common form of voluntary approach. A survey indicates more than 300 NAs in force, covering most industrial and energy sectors (European Environment Agency, 1997). As shown in Figure 6.3, Germany and The Netherlands make the largest use of NAs; for instance, in The Netherlands, so-called 'covenants' are a key policy instrument in environmental policy.

3.2   Pros and Cons of Voluntary Approaches

As indicated above, there is a variety of voluntary approaches (VAs), and widely different practices according to countries. One interesting feature is the degree of integration with the regulatory system. In Japan, VAs are often designed to make up for the lack of regulation. On the contrary, in The Netherlands, 'covenants' are an integral part of the government environmental plan and are based on a two-tier system: first a general agreement between the government and an industry branch, fixing the overall objective; second a series of legally binding contracts between the government and each individual firm joining the agreement. The conditions of these individual contracts are integrated into the permits.

What are the advantages of VAs?
The main advantage of VAs is their flexibility when they replace complex and burdensome regulations: flexibility for the private sector to apply the most appropriate means to achieve the targets; flexibility for public authorities when heavy control and sanction procedures are avoided. When VAs are based on a quantified objective, they can be compared to a 'bubble' or an emission 'cap' approach, that is, an imaginary glass dome (a bubble), covering several different sources of pollution; polluting emissions must not exceed a certain level inside this 'bubble' and a global pollution reduction objective is fixed, leaving industry free to take the most cost-effective measures to achieve this objective, including some form of trading of emissions (see section 5 below). In this case, VAs can yield cost savings. However, VAs do not provide, *a priori*, a cost-minimizing solution by equalization of marginal abatement costs like taxes and tradable permits.

VAs also promote a more cooperative and proactive approach of private stakeholders (industry, environmental NGOs, trade unions) that are directly involved in the negotiation process and often take the initiative of the agreement. But firms will enter agreements if the avoided cost of a public regulation is larger than the cost of the agreement.

Are VAs environmentally effective? While some voluntary schemes have proved to be quite successful, available evidence is still scant and anecdotal; in particular, it is difficult to assess whether environmental achievements are really the outcome of the VA or would have occurred anyway ('business as usual' scenario).

There are, however, a number of problems associated with VAs.

1. *Weak control*: the control of the achievement of VAs is potentially weak, either because industry does not provide adequate control mechanisms , or

because of the lack of sanctions, on the side of the private sector as well as on the side of the public authorities.

2. *Free-riding* can occur, for example when firms benefit from a collective agreement (such as absence or regulation or tax), while not sharing the collective effort required by the agreement. The risk of free-riding is greater if the agreement does not contain monitoring and sanction provisions. This underlines the need for effective control and sanctions in voluntary approaches.

3. *Transaction costs*: if the number of stakeholders is high, the cost of negotiation and of setting the agreement may be high: for example cost associated with negotiations, the organization of parties (such as manufacturers' associations), monitoring, provision of information and so on. Therefore, the cost of achieving an agreement must not exceed the benefits. Such evaluations seem rarely made, so that the real net benefit of VAs is largely unknown.

4. *Administrative cost*: to make sure that VAs (in particular negotiated agreements) achieve their objectives, there is a tendency to add a series of safeguards in the form of legal or administrative requirements (monitoring, sanctions, regulatory threat and the like). In the end, NAs tend to become of a quasi-regulatory nature, with significant administrative costs and loss of the flexibility advantages of voluntary approaches.

5. *Regulatory capture*: there is a risk that powerful and well-organized industry organizations 'capture' the policy and regulatory process by avoiding or obstructing the introduction of a regulation and/or influencing the regulatory process to their own benefit, to the detriment of society. When negotiating an agreement, private companies will be induced to implement lax objectives, rather than ambitious ones. The 'business as usual' scenario, whereby targets set in the agreement are those which would have been reached in any case, is not uncommon.

4. ENVIRONMENTAL TAXES AND CHARGES

4.1 Background and Definition

Chapter 1 showed that environmental degradation can be defined, in economic terms, as external costs. One means to internalize these costs is to make polluters pay a tax or charge (see definitions in Box 6.4). An emission charge or tax can be defined as a payment for each unit of pollutant discharged into the environment or for each unit of environmental damage. Assuming polluting emissions can be measured with reasonable accuracy, such a payment is very easy to impose. For instance, a thermal power plant can be charged an amount

BOX 6.4   DEFINING ENVIRONMENTAL TAXES AND CHARGES

A distinction should be drawn between charges and taxes.

- **Taxes** (according to the classification in OECD's 'Revenue Statistics') are defined as 'compulsory *unrequited* payments to general government. Taxes are unrequited in the sense that the benefits provided by governments to taxpayers are not normally in proportion to their payments.'

  According to OECD, what defines an *environment-related tax* is not so much the formal description of the tax as 'environmental' as the real and potential effect of a tax on the environment, regardless of what it is called. From an environmental point of view, it is the effect of a tax on behaviour patterns that matters. In other words, any tax affecting the price or cost of an environmentally detrimental product or activity is considered to be an environment-related tax.
- **Charges** are compulsory *requited* payments, that is, a service is provided in proportion of the payment (for instance, sewerage charges). Charges can also be paid into specific 'funds' and earmarked for specific environmental purposes, without necessarily having a direct proportionality to the service rendered.
- **Emission charges or taxes** are direct payments based on the quantity and quality of pollutants discharged. For instance, water effluent charges are used to varying degrees in many countries. Air pollution charges and taxes are also used in a few OECD countries. Noise charges and taxes are levied on aircraft in a few countries, in systems ranging from crude to more elaborate.
- **Product taxes** are applied to, and thus increase the relative prices of, products which create pollution when they are manufactured, consumed or disposed of. This constitutes a major part of the taxes with an environmental impact in most OECD countries. Taxes on energy (for example carbon and sulphur taxes on fuels) form a large category. Other examples are taxes on fertilizers, pesticides and batteries.

Source: OECD

of 700 dollars per tonne of sulphur dioxide emitted into the atmosphere; a pulp mill or a manufacturer of dairy products can be charged 100 dollars per tonne of BOD discharged into a river. The pollution tax is in fact a payment (a price) for the use of environmental resources (the atmosphere, the water, soil and so on). Hence internalizing environmental costs implies paying a price for the use of environmental resources. Since such prices are not fixed 'spontaneously' in existing markets, administrative prices can be fixed through an intervention of public authorities, hence by imposing taxes.

Polluters will react automatically to the tax by reducing emissions to the level where the unit rate of the tax and the marginal pollution abatement cost (that is, the cost of removing one additional unit of pollutant) are equal. In Figure 6.4 the marginal abatement cost (*MAC*) curve increases from right to left because the more a pollutant is abated, the higher the unit (marginal) costs. If a tax with a rate t_1 is imposed, the polluter will abate pollution from C to P_1 because beyond this level (B on *MAC*) it is cheaper to pay the tax than to abate emissions further.

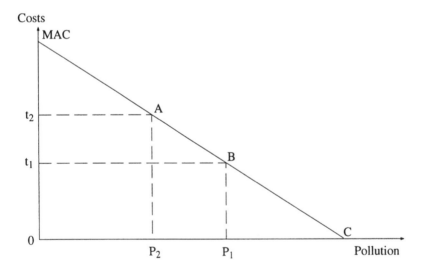

Figure 6.4   Pollution tax and the level of abatement

Obviously, the higher the level of the tax, the higher the level of abatement (for example, with a tax t_2 the level of abatement is $CP_2 > CP_1$). Assuming marginal abatement functions are reasonably well known, the desired level of pollution abatement will be automatically obtained with an appropriate level of tax.

The consequences of pollution taxes can be better understood when referring to what economists call the 'optimal' level of pollution. This optimum level corresponds to the point where *MAC* equals marginal damage cost (*MDC*). Any departure from this level (point A in Figure 6.5) implies a welfare loss, because either pollution damage exceeds abatement costs (moves to the right of A on *MDC*) or abatement costs are higher than damage costs (move to the left of A on *MAC*). None of these situations is satisfactory from an economic point of view.

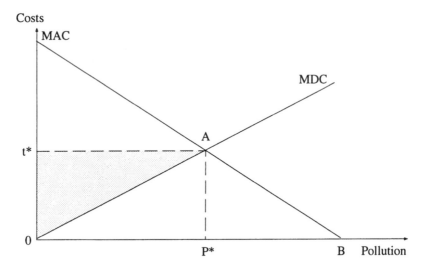

Figure 6.5   The optimal level of pollution

Ideally, the pollution tax should be fixed to obtain this optimal level: a tax fixed at level t^* would achieve the optimal pollution level P^* (Figure 6.5). This of course implies that the marginal damage costs can be estimated, a condition difficult to fulfil in reality (see Chapter 3). It is interesting to see that with a tax t^*, the payment of the polluter can be divided into three parts: surface P^*AB, which is the total pollution abatement cost (surface under *MAC*); surface $0AP^*$, which is the residual damage tax, corresponding to the residual damage $0P^*$ (surface under *MDC*); and surface $0t^*A$, that is, a 'residual tax' which can be interpreted as the payment of a tax for using scarce environmental resources. Note that surface $0AB$ reflects the total value of the internalized environmental costs (abatement costs plus damage costs).

We can see that the tax imposes an additional burden on the polluter who pays the abatement costs (P^*AB) plus the tax ($0t^*AP^*$). If an emission standard P^* were imposed, the polluter would only pay the pollution abatement costs.

This feature of pollution taxes has very important financial and distributive consequences. Although the tax can minimize the global abatement costs, that is, the sum of abatement costs of all polluters (see below), individual polluters will bear heavier costs owing to the payment of the tax on top of abatement costs. This is one reason why industry is often strongly opposed to environmental taxes and charges. Furthermore, taxes imply a financial transfer to the government which entails significant distributive consequences.

4.2 Advantages of Taxes

If the only virtue of taxes were automatically to achieve a given level of pollution abatement, this would not constitute a great advantage over standards and regulations. Pollution taxes have three major additional advantages (see also Chapter 18): they minimize total abatement costs; they constitute a permanent incentive to reduce pollution; and they provide a source of revenue. We shall briefly review these three features.

Taxes minimize total abatement costs
If the objective is to reduce total emissions by 80 per cent, it does not make economic sense to impose a uniform 80 per cent abatement on each polluter if the abatement costs of, say, polluter A are four times higher than those of polluter B. It is collectively more efficient to require more abatement at lower costs from polluter B and less from polluter A.

Assume (see Figure 6.6) four factories F_1, F_2, F_3 and F_4 with different marginal abatement costs: MAC1 < MAC2 < MAC3 < MAC4. With a uniform emission standard, S, the objective would be to achieve a total reduction of emissions equal to 4S (SA + SB + SC + SD). If a uniform tax, t, is applied, each factory will fix its abatement level where MAC equals t. Thus each factory will have different abatement levels ($P_1 > P_2 > P_3 > P_4$). For instance, factory 1 with low marginal abatement costs abates more pollution (but pays less tax) than factory 4 which pollutes more but pays more tax. The total cost saving obtained with the tax is represented by the sum of the shaded areas of factories 3 and 4 minus the shaded area of factory 1.

A number of empirical evaluations of the gains obtained with taxes or tradable permits (see below) have been made; they indicate that cost savings can be substantial (for example, Tietenberg, 1990, indicates a number of cases where least-cost policies can be up to 22 times cheaper than command and control).

Taxes provide a permanent incentive to pollution abatement
Emission standards do not provide an incentive to polluters to reduce pollution beyond the standard (except in the search for a good 'public image' or in

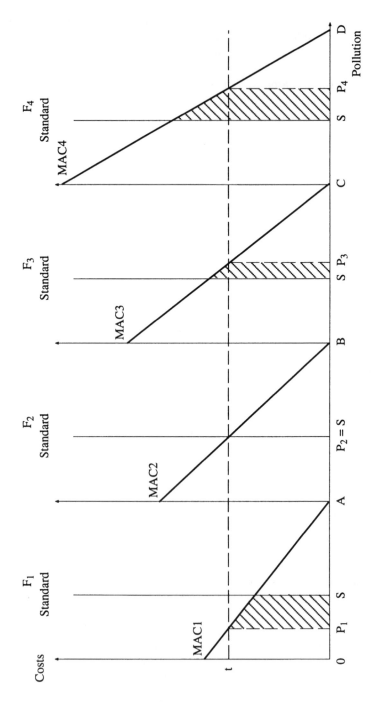

Figure 6.6   Different marginal abatement costs, uniform standards and uniform taxes

anticipation of further tightening of emission limits). However, a tax provides a double stimulus.

First, it is a stimulus to reduce pollution when abatement costs decrease. Assume that, owing to technical progress, the marginal abatement cost is reduced from MAC1 to MAC2 (Figure 6.7). In the case of an emission standard P_1, the level of emission will remain unchanged (see also Figure 6.1) and the polluter will save surface B. If, however, a tax, t, is imposed, emissions will be reduced to level P_2.

Second, a tax is a stronger stimulus to technical change (that is, to develop more efficient pollution abatement techniques). This is because technical change (shifting from MAC1 to MAC2) provides a double cost saving: abatement costs (surface D + B) and reduced tax (surface C).

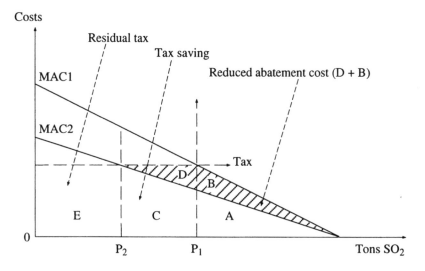

Figure 6.7   Standards, taxes and incentives to pollution abatement

Taxes provide revenue

Taxes provide government revenue which can be added to the general government budget or earmarked for specific environmental purposes (for instance, water pollution charges in France, Germany and the Netherlands are earmarked for financing water treatment facilities). The OECD, EUROSTAT and the International Energy Agency have developed a joint statistical framework for data on ecotaxes, defined as any tax likely to produce a beneficial impact on the environment, regardless of its initial objective. Thus energy taxes, which have a purely fiscal purpose, are considered to be 'environment-related taxes' because of their beneficial environmental impact; what matters most is the tax base and the *price signal*.

On that basis, results for 21 countries indicate that 'environment-related' taxes account for between 3.8 and 11.2 per cent of total tax revenue, depending on the countries concerned, or 7 per cent on average (OECD, 1999a). As a percentage of GDP, these taxes vary between 1 and 4.5 per cent. Practically all the revenues arise from taxes on petrol and diesel fuel (two-thirds of revenues), transport and electricity. Very few taxes are levied on heavy fuels used by heavy industry. Next come revenues from vehicle taxes. The proportion accounted for by other ecotaxes (such as pesticides, detergents and so on) is negligible. Another feature is that industry is relatively little affected, owing to various, sometimes numerous exemptions.[2]

A key issue is the *sustainability* of the revenue from environmental taxes. While the tax rate has to be sufficiently high to have an incentive effect,[3] the more the incentive works, the more pollution will diminish and therefore the less tax revenue will be collected. For instance, taxes on polluting fuel oils in Sweden have led to their virtual disappearance from the market. Again in Sweden, the revenue obtained from the sulphur tax has fallen rapidly owing to the environmental success of the tax: before the tax was introduced, annual revenue was estimated at 0.5 – 0.7 billion Swedish kronor. Between 1991, when the tax was introduced, and 1997, revenue fell from 0.3 to under 0.2 billion Swedish kronor. Similarly, leaded petrol has disappeared altogether in several countries. In other words, there is a contradiction between the environmental effectiveness of the tax and its fiscal effectiveness, leading to a potential conflict between the ministries of finance and the environment. In practice, however, the conflict between effectiveness and revenue is not so clear cut. In order to ensure that revenue is sustainable, there will be a tendency to tax products with low demand elasticity, such as energy products.

4.3 Implementing Environmental Taxes[4]

Implementing pollution taxes requires a number of practical issues to be solved. These concern mainly the rate of the tax, the 'linkage' with emissions, uncertainties, the distributive implications and political acceptability:

1. *The rate of the charge* must be fixed at a level that ensures that environmental objectives can be achieved. This implies that pollution abatement cost functions (MAC) can be calculated with sufficient accuracy. Although this can be done in a number of instances, numerous uncertainties and lack of data still remain (see Chapter 3). Also, such 'efficient' tax rates often turn out to be too high to be acceptable or implementable on economic (for example, the financial burden on industry or impact on competitiveness) or

political grounds. One solution is then to increase rates progressively according to a predetermined schedule, thus allowing industry to adapt and plan necessary investments. One must also ensure that the function of taxes is not eroded by inflation, for example, by means of indexation.

2. *The assessment basis of environmental taxes must reflect emissions as closely as possible.* This may be easy in some cases, for example, when taxes apply to easily measurable pollutants emitted by stationary sources (such as SO_x in electric utilities and solid wastes). However, emissions are not always easy to monitor (for instance, because of mobile and diffuse sources) or may comprise a complex combination of different substances. One solution is to use the so-called 'proxy variables', such as fuels or production inputs. For instance, it is easier to tax the carbon content of fuels than carbon dioxide emissions. Two remarks are in order: first, measurement difficulties occur equally with both standards and taxes; and second, the closer the 'linkage' between emissions and the tax, the greater the environmental effectiveness of emission taxes. If such 'linkage' cannot be established satisfactorily, the use of taxes should be reconsidered or even abandoned.

3. *Uncertainty*: there always remain uncertainties as to the effectiveness of taxes if rates are too low, emission abatement cost functions are not well known, if the tax can be avoided (for example, petrol is bought in a neighbouring country where there is no levy) or if linkages are inappropriate. Also, there may be time lags before emissions are effectively reduced after application of the tax. In such cases, taxes seem largely inappropriate for controlling toxic and hazardous substances; these are better controlled by means of direct regulations or bans (see Section 2).

4. *Distributive implications*: it is often asserted that taxes have regressive effects on income categories. For example, energy taxes are likely to have stronger income effects on poorer households (Pearson and Smith, 1991). The possible regressive impacts of carbon taxes are heavily debated. Distributive impacts also concern various industry sectors. Although such impacts also apply to regulatory instruments, they need careful consideration. One important policy rule is that distributive impacts should not be alleviated through tax concessions (which would 'kill' the tax purpose), but by means of separate compensation measures (for example lump-sum payments), in the context of income and social policies and not in the context of environmental policies.

5. *Political obstacles*: there are a number of political obstacles to using eco-taxes. When environmental policies started in the early 1970s, the 'command and control', that is, regulatory, approach was almost exclusively used (although economists were already making a strong plea for the economic approach, while other parties were almost unanimously

opposed to it). Such opposition, although less virulent, still remains. Industry is opposed mainly on competitiveness grounds, that is, that taxes entail additional constraints and financial burdens. Industrialists also fear that taxes will reduce their bargaining power *vis-à-vis* public authorities (there is more room for negotiating a permit than the payment of a tax). The general public is sometimes opposed because charging for pollution is considered as 'purchasing the right to pollute'. There is also, especially in 'green' circles, a general contention that since market mechanisms are the very cause of environmental degradation, they should not be used for environmental protection.

One can say, however, that to a large extent this debate has become obsolete. Industry begins to realize that economic instruments are global cost-minimizing devices, which can ensure a better cost sharing and leave maximum flexibility in adaptation. There is still, however, reluctance to pay charges and taxes and a fear that these will affect international competitiveness. Governments, faced with growing demand for better environmental quality and with increasingly complex issues, are seeking more efficient policy tools and additional financial means. Generally speaking, direct regulation of societal processes seems to have reached a level of decreasing efficiency, resulting in calls for 'deregulation', regulatory reforms, 'self-regulation' or voluntary approaches. In fact, the enforcement of regulations itself turns out to be difficult, costly and, in many cases, insufficient. Finally, public awareness of these concerns and successful experiences in a number of countries have to a large extent weakened the opposition to market-based instruments.

5. THE ISSUE OF SUBSIDIES AND TAX DISTORTIONS

Subsidies play an important, albeit ambiguous role in environmental policy. A distinction must be drawn between two types of subsidies: subsidies specifically designed to protect the environment and economic subsidies with unintended (often negative) effects on the environment.

5.1 Environmental Subsidies

Environmental subsidies in general are payments to induce economic agents to undertake certain environmentally benign measures, such as installing abatement equipment. Subsidies are regarded as inefficient instruments in the long run; they might be claimed by enterprises or individuals for abatement activities or measures that they would have (under)taken even without the subsidy. A more fundamental argument against subsidies is that they are incompatible with the polluter pays principle. It is fair to say, however, that in practice exceptions to the polluter pays principle have been accepted: for example, for subsidies for anti-pollution measures in transition periods for sectors that are faced with economic problems, and for the development of clean technologies. These arguments might be especially relevant for economies in transition to becoming market economies. Nevertheless, the fundamental and long-term arguments against subsidies are valid.[5]

Basically, short-term responses to a subsidy and a tax lead to the same result. But the long-term implications are different: the total supply curve for the industry will be pushed out so that new entry is induced, output expands and pollution may increase. Moreover, a subsidy scheme may make it profitable for the firm to start off by polluting more in order to qualify for larger subsidies. Finally, they provide less inducement for the development of permanent new abatement technology.

5.2 Distortionary Subsidies

A number of direct and indirect subsidies can produce adverse effects for the environment. One such measure is a series of *direct economic subsidies.* For example, *farming subsidies* (estimated at 297 billion dollars a year in OECD countries in 1996, or 1.3 per cent of GDP) are one of the causes of overfarming of land, excessive use of fertilizers and pesticides, dry soil conditions and other problems (OECD, 1996b). Similarly, irrigation water is often charged below its real price, which leads to wastage (in the USA, irrigation water is subsidized to the extent of 75 per cent). In the area of *energy,* subsidies on coal, the most polluting fuel, still came to 7 billion dollars in 1996 in six OECD countries, which admittedly was lower than the 16.5 billion dollars for 1989. It is estimated that subsidies to industry amounted to 49.3 billion dollars in 1993; when subsidies encourage the use of certain raw materials and greater energy consumption, there can be negative fall-out in terms of recycling and waste (OECD, 1998).

Indirect subsidies can arise from a series of tax measures (tax variations or exemptions). For instance, *coal,* the most polluting fuel, is also the least taxed; in OECD countries in 1995, the average coal tax per barrel of oil equivalent was 0.3 dollars in 1995, compared with 22 dollars for oil. The *transport* sector, a major source of pollution and other harmful effects, is affected by many distortions. The virtually systematic undertaxing of diesel oil in many countries has led to a constant increase in the number of diesel vehicles, which are more polluting and noisy, and to undue development of road transport of goods. In countries of the European Union, the proportion of diesel fuel comes to between 30 and 61 per cent (except for Finland, where it is only 16 per cent) (EUROSTAT, 1996). Other tax provisions such as income-deductible commuting expenses, tax-free parking space, tax-free aviation fuel, are obviously detrimental to the environment. Eliminating distortionary subsidies and tax provisions is a key aspect of environmental policy. Box 6.5 describe some 'green' tax reforms.

BOX 6.5   GREEN TAX REFORMS

Any 'green' tax reform entails many aspects, ranging from the in-depth reform of existing taxation to the introduction of new taxes. This means that the objective pursued by the reforms is not only environmental. Many other benefits may be obtained, in fiscal terms (a better return), in economic terms (greater efficiency by internalizing externalities and eliminating distortions), and in terms of employment (the 'double dividend' argument; see Chapter 18).

This approach is opposed to the dogma of 'fiscal neutrality', whereby the sole objective of taxation systems is to obtain maximum revenue with minimum distortion and minimum impact on behaviour patterns. Some tax experts view mixed objectives with suspicion and are often opposed to the use of taxation for other than strictly fiscal purposes. Yet there are very few taxes which either accidentally or deliberately do not exert some influence on behaviour or on economic structures. In some countries, many tax measures cover related objectives (for example in France the cost of heat insulation for housing is tax-deductible as a means of encouraging energy savings). Environment is a case in point, and many taxes are observed to produce negative effects in this respect. Similarly, a growing number of eco-taxes are deliberately aimed at altering behaviour patterns.

But while eco-taxes, by definition, are not fiscally neutral, green fiscal reforms are generally implemented in a context of a *constant tax burden*, in the sense that new eco-taxes tend to offset reductions in existing taxes. In fact, a constant tax burden is an essential condition of the *acceptability* of eco-taxes. Industry in particular is strongly opposed to eco-taxes on the grounds of a possible loss of competitiveness. Similarly, consumers may fear that eco-taxes might lead to price increases; it is then essential to show clearly that other taxes are being reduced to ensure the political acceptability of green tax reforms. This approach is now implemented in a growing number of countries.

Finland was the first country to introduce a carbon tax in 1990, followed by a progressive greening of the tax system. While the carbon tax started in 1990 at a fairly modest level of FIM 24.5 per ton of carbon, the rate has been steadily increased since, to reach FIM 374 in 1998. This evolution has been accompanied by a number of significant changes in the tax system. The greening of the tax system is being pursued by measures such as the exemption of rail transports from the electricity tax (1998) and the implementation of a new waste landfill tax (September 1996). This increase in green taxes is compensated by a reduction of the tax wedge on labour (reduced income tax and social insurance contributions) with the explicit objective to reduce unemployment.

In *Sweden*, the 1991 tax reform was based on a significant reduction in income tax, which was largely offset by a series of new eco-taxes, especially on carbon, sulphur and nitrogen oxides, by a restructuring of energy taxation and by a broadening of the VAT tax base. The net effect was a 6 per cent redistribution of GDP, including about 1 per cent related to eco-taxes.

Denmark has also been engaging in a general reform of its tax system over the period 1994–98 with a continuing evolution of energy-related taxes until 2002. The main objectives of the reform are the reduction of marginal tax rates in all income brackets; the elimination of a series of loopholes in the tax law; and a gradual transfer of tax revenue from income and labour to pollution and scarce environmental resources (Danish Ministry of Finance, 1995). Since 1996, the authorities have introduced new eco-taxes on industry's use of energy (on CO_2 and SO_2), rising gradually until 2000. The revenue produced by these taxes is reverted entirely to industry in the form of investment aids for energy saving and reduced employers' social security contributions.

In *The Netherlands,* between 1971 and 1998, the system of environmental taxes and charges gradually evolved from being essentially a means of financing environmental protection programmes to consisting of a series of unallocated eco-taxes. Until 1988, about seven specific environmental charges (on water, air, waste, noise, soil and chemical waste) were levied to finance specific environmental protection measures. These charges were yielding limited revenue, and were complex to implement. Therefore the 1988 General Environmental Provision Act replaced all these charges by one single 'general fuel charge'. Between 1988 and

1998 this earmarked charge was replaced by a series of taxes (on fuels, waste, groundwater, uranium and small energy users). The revenue of the 'energy-regulating tax' on small energy consumers (households, small businesses, office blocks, and the like), introduced in 1996, is paid back to households in the form of reduced income tax and to employers in the form of reduced social security contributions (Vermeend and Van der Vaart, 1998). An overall shift from direct to indirect taxation is to start in 2001.

Switzerland has introduced two new eco-taxes: from 1 July 1998, on extra light heating oils, and from 1 January 1999, on volatile organic compounds (VOCs). The revenue is to be fully returned to households in the form of reduced compulsory sickness insurance premiums. A general green tax reform is being considered for 2001.

France initiated a green tax reform in 1998, consisting mainly in streamlining existing environmental taxes and charges into a 'general tax on polluting activities' to be paid in the general government budget, with parts earmarked to specific purposes.

Italy and the *United Kingdom* initiated a green tax reform in 1999, mainly through increases of energy taxes.

6.   TRADABLE PERMITS[6]

6.1 Background

In 1968 the Canadian economist Dales proposed the creation of markets for 'pollution rights' (Dales, 1968). The basic idea is that instead of fixing emission standards, governments would distribute or sell 'pollution permits' corresponding to the total amount of tolerable or allowable pollution. These permits can then be sold and purchased on the market. As long as such transactions can benefit trading partners, the market will function and the cost of pollution abatement will be minimized, as in the case of taxes.

The rationale for using tradable permits can be developed by considering the situation facing two industrial plants that emit sulphur dioxide. For a given emission limit, the marginal cost of removing one tonne of sulphur dioxide is 1500 FF for plant 1 and 6000 FF for plant 2 (Figure 6.8). Cost savings can be achieved if plant 1 abates more than plant 2. For instance, if the emission limit is strengthened by one tonne of sulphur dioxide for plant 1 (that is, an additional abatement cost of 1500 FF) and lowered by one tonne for plant 2 (that is, a cost saving of 6000 FF), a total cost saving of $6000 - 1500 = 4500$ FF is obtained. It would be difficult to achieve this result under emission standards, because the

Marginal abatement
cost (Fr/t/SO$_2$)

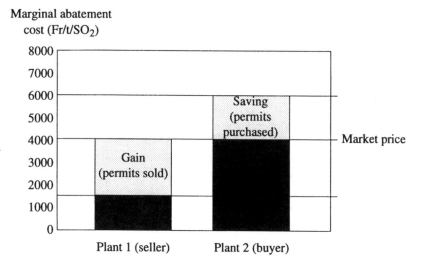

Figure 6.8   Tradable permits and cost-saving

government lacks the detailed cost information and, in any event, would be under pressure to set uniform emission standards.

This cost-minimizing result could be obtained under a tradable permits approach. If such pollution permits are tradable, both parties will be induced to trade for their mutual benefit. Assume that a market for permits exists and that the market price for a one-tonne permit is 4000 FF. It will be profitable for plant 1 to abate emissions beyond the initial emission limit, up to the point where its marginal cost is equal to the market price, and to sell permits corresponding to this additional abatement, thus making a gain of 4000 – 1500 = 2500 FF. Plant 2 will buy one tonne worth of permits for 4000 FF, thus economizing 6000 – 4000 = 2000 FF. Both plants gain from the trade and the total gain is 4500 FF. Plant 1 will sell permits until its marginal abatement cost reaches 4,000 FF and plant 2 will buy permits until its marginal cost decreases to 4000 FF.

6.2   Implementing Tradable Permits

Advantages of tradable permits
Tradable permits constitute a theoretically ideal system. The main advantages are:

1. Trading partners will all gain and the cost is nil for government so that substantial cost savings can be achieved for the economy (just as in the case of taxes).

2. The total quantity of pollution (that is, the number of permits on the market) is fixed *a priori* so that there is no uncertainty as to the achievement of environmental objectives (contrary to the case of taxes). If a new pollution source comes on the market (for example, a new plant), this additional demand for permits will increase the price, but hold constant the total pollution quantity.
3. New plants can settle in a controlled area by buying permits from existing plants, thus making economic growth and environmental protection in this area compatible.
4. Tradable permits automatically adjust to inflation (the price of permits increases), contrary to taxes, which need periodic adjustment or indexation.

Implementation issues
There are, however, a number of difficulties and issues with the application of tradable permits:

1. The main problem is the initial allocation of permits: they can be allocated free of charge ('grandfathering') or they can be sold (auctioned). Grandfathering implicitly assumes that initial rights to use the environment are granted to polluters. When permits are auctioned, polluters have to pay the price of the permit, on top of emissions abatement costs. This higher cost burden is similar in the case of an emission tax. One advantage of auctioned permits is that they absorb the scarcity rent on the environment, otherwise captured by polluters; also, permit sales provide revenue which can be used by government, for example to reduce distortionary taxes ('double dividend' approach). The major disadvantage of auctioning permits is that most emitters would face higher costs than under the emission standards approach (as in the case of taxes) and thus would not be likely to support the tradable permits approach.

   In practice, permits have mostly been grandfathered. The problem is then to fix a baseline for the attribution of the permits. One approach is to attribute permits according to past emissions of sources. For the US SO_2 allowance trading programme, permits were initially allocated to electric facilities largely on the basis of estimates of historical emissions. Obviously, the initial allocation of permits involves controversial decisions.
2. Another issue is the complexity and administrative cost of such systems which require a series of rules and sophisticated infrastructures to monitor transactions. When rules are too complex, transaction costs (bargaining, compliance with rules, monitoring) may become high. Experience shows that transaction costs are higher when a tradable permit system is added to an existing full set of regulations; on the contrary, when tradable permits are implemented at an early stage to a new environmental concern (for example

CO_2 or ozone-depleting substances), the system is less burdened by long-standing regulations and transaction cost are lower.

3. The distributive implications of tradable permits are increasingly of concern. First the initial allocation of permits raises obvious equity issues. Grandfathering may create rents: for instance the rising scarcity of ozone-depleting substances (ODS), created by the US allowance trading programme, windfall profits to ODS producers; these profits were taxed away through a special tax. Another concern is the unequal distribution of environmental benefits: groups of citizens fear that pollution will simply be transferred to another region, thus creating local 'hot spots'. While this can be true for pollutants subject to localized impacts (SO_2), this is not the case for 'global' pollutants such as CO_2. In the first case, specific regional requirements can be designed to prevent localized impacts.

4. Finally, there may be strong political opposition to allowing market forces to regulate the environment, although existing tradable permit systems operate under strict regulatory controls.

6.3   Tradable Permits in Practice

Tradable permit systems are implemented in a few instances only. In Europe very few applications exist. In Germany, the air pollution legislation allows the transfer of emission reduction obligations (offsets) but this possibility has been used in less than 2 per cent of cases. In The Netherlands, power plants 'bubbles' are allowed under a covenant signed between the 12 Provinces and the Association of Electricity Producers (SEP) in 1990; a 50 per cent cost saving for reaching new emission standards is expected. In the United Kingdom, provisions for intra-firm bubbles for power plants were introduced in 1996. In Switzerland, provisions for tradable permits for volatile organic compounds and nitrogen oxides exist in the canton of Basel; but the narrowness of the market and restrictive transaction rules have made the system largely ineffective. Australia and Canada have also introduced a few provisions for pollution trading.[7]

Tradable permits have been applied on a large scale only in the USA. The early efforts begun in the mid-1970s consisted of a set of programmes known as the 'Emissions Trading Program' (see Box 6.6). These programmes have not been a great success, however, in reducing the overall costs of air pollution control. A major change occurred when the new 1990 Clean Air Act mandated a tradable permit programme for suphur dioxide (SO_2). In 1995, EPA implemented phase 1 of the SO_2 Allowance Trading (or 'Acid Rain') Program aiming to achieve a 50 per cent reduction (below 1980 levels) of SO_2 emissions from electric utilities by the year 2010. This new programme is characterized by a 'cap and trade' approach: an annual cap on total emissions is fixed each year and allowances are allocated according to an estimate of emissions during the period 1985–87. New sources must purchase allowances from allowance holders or the EPA (the EPA is auctioning 2.8 per cent of annual allowances). The cost savings are expected to reach 20–50 per cent over the period 1995–2000. The price of permits, initially estimated at $750–1500 per ton of SO_2, fell to $250 as the first trades took place, and was at $70–150 in 1998. This indicates that the flexibility of the system triggered increased innovation and productivity. Other trading schemes have been successfully operated in the United States, in particular on lead in gasoline, ozone-depleting substances and in the Los Angeles air basin (for SO_2, nitrogen oxides and ozone precursors).

BOX 6.6   MAIN FEATURES OF THE US EMISSIONS TRADING PROGRAM

The Emissions Trading Program, which started in the mid-1970s, was not based on a total emission 'cap', but offered emission sources the option (not an obligation) to comply with existing regulations, by using the following flexibility mechanisms:

- *Offsets*: when a new installation (emission source) wants to settle in an area where total emissions must not increase, it must 'offset' its additional emissions by obtaining emission-reduction credits from another existing source that will reduce its emission by at least the same amount.
- *Netting*: when an existing source is implementing large modifications, it can be exempt from permitting/licensing procedures, provided total emissions are kept below the existing level.
- *Bubbles*: Within a given installation, any emission reduction measure can be taken at different emission sources (stacks, valves etc.), provided the total emission complies with the emission limit. The name evokes an imaginary 'bubble' over the entire installation.
- *Banking*: a firm reducing its emission below the required level, can 'bank' the corresponding emission reduction credits for future use or sale.

Although named 'Emission Trading Program', these flexibility mechanisms hardly involve the actual operation of a market. As a matter of fact, this programme was not very successful: between 1977 and 1986, the number of 'trades' was small and cost savings modest (Hahn and Hester, 1989).

Tradable permits are used successfully for fishing quotas in several countries (Australia, Canada, Iceland, The Netherlands, New Zealand and the USA). Table 6.1 gives an overview of the main tradable permit systems in operation in OECD countries.

It is interesting to note that various forms of international trading of carbon dioxide are to be implemented in the context of the Kyoto Protocol to the UN Framework Convention on Climate Change (UNFCCC). At least three different mechanisms are envisaged.

1. A system of international trading of CO_2 emission permits; this raises formidable practical and political difficulties to be discussed and, it is hoped solved through the post-Kyoto negotiating process (Conferences of Parties).
2. The 'joint implementation', enabling a country to reduce CO_2 emission in another country where abatement measures are less costly; the country having paid the investment abroad would be credited with the corresponding amount of CO_2 emission reduction. This system applies only to Annex 1 countries (that is, OECD countries and countries in transition).
3. A 'clean development mechanism', designed to assist developing countries to participate in the implementation of the UNFCCC. Following a transfer of 'clean' technologies from a developed to a developing country, the developed country would be credited with the amount of reduced CO_2 emissions achieved through the clean technology. This is in fact a form of joint implementation specially designed for developing countries.

6.4 Conditions for a Successful Application of Tradable Permits

Tradable permits are not applicable in all circumstances, and past and current experiences indicate that many conditions affect the performance of the programme. Some lessons from existing experience are mentioned below.

- Marginal abatement costs must vary between polluters; the greater the differential, the greater the cost savings and the propensity to trade.
- The market must be large enough, that is, there must be a sufficient number of actors.
- There must exist a potential for emitters to reduce abatement costs.
- Fixing a total emission 'cap' ('cap and trade') is preferable to emission reduction credits.
- The rules for initial permit allocations must be clear and fixed *a priori* (grandfathering or auction).
- The traded commodity (pollutant) must be clearly identified and measurable.
- The permits must be legally secure.

Table 6.1 Main tradable permits systems in force (1998)

Country/area/agents	Programme	Commodity	Effects	Savings
Air protection				
USA / Air Quality Control Region	EPA emission trading (1975–)	Emission reduction credits (ERC)	Mixed	$1–12 bn (until 1986)
USA / refineries	EPA lead in gasoline (1983–87)	Lead additives	Elimination of lead	$226 mn
USA / firms	EPA ozone-depleting substances (ODS) (1986–98)	ODS allowances	Compliance with Montreal Protocol	49%?
USA	SO_2 allowance (1990–)	SO_2 allowances	Early reductions	$225–375 mn (25%–34%)1995
USA / Los Angeles area	RECLAIM (Regional Clean Air Incentive Market, 1994–)	NO_x and SO_2 allowances	8.3% and 6.8% annual reductions planned for NO_x and SO_2	Over $40 mn
USA / engine producers	Averaging, banking, trading	Emission cap for each engine model produced for HC + NO_x	75% reduction planned for HC	?
USA / Northeast / stationary	Ozone transport commission, NO_x budget (1994–2003)	NO_x allowances	75% reduction planned	$80 mn/yr (30%)
Switzerland	Basel Canton (1993–)	Volatile organic compounds	Very few trades	?
Poland / Chorzów	Demonstration project (1991–92)	ERC	Speeding up abatement plans	?

Water resource management				
USA and Australia	Tradable water abstraction rights (since 19th century)	m^3/yr	Stability of use	?
Germany / Hamburg	Groundwater abstraction fee (1989–)	Retiring water rights	Transfer of water rights	?
Water protection				
USA / Wisconsin	Fox River (1980–)	BOD	Ambient quality	?
USA / Colorado / point-non-point	Dillon Reservoir (1984–)	Phosphorus	Reduced eutrophication	$1370/kgP (hypothetical)
USA / North Carolina / point-non-point	Tar-Pamlico River (1989–)	Phosphorus and nitrogen	Nutrient discharges reduced by 28%	?
Australia / states	Interstate salinity trading (1982–)	'Salt-credits'	Reduced salinity	?
Australia / New South Wales	Hunter River salinity trading (1992)	Salt allocations for coal mines	Reduced salinity	?
Fisheries				
Australia, Canada, Iceland, The Netherlands, New Zealand, USA	Selected fish species	Individual transferable quota (ITQ)	Conservation efficiency, rents	?

Source: based on OECD (1999b).

- Transaction costs must be low.
- Trading rules must be simple and transparent.
- Appropriate monitoring and control mechanisms must be implemented.
- Key stakeholders must be convinced that they will benefit from the system.
- Tradable permits systems are easier to implement when applied to new policies, rather than added to long-standing existing regulatory structures.

7.   DEPOSIT–REFUND SYSTEMS

Packaging is a major environmental problem in industrialized countries: in the early 1990s, it represented about one-third of the total volume of waste, that is, more than 50 million tonnes (154 kg per head) per year in the European Union. This is why deposit–refund systems (DRS) are widely used as a management tool in this field. However, the notion of DRS can be extended beyond packaging.

DRS can be defined as a refundable product charge: they are paid when buying a product and refunded when the product is returned to an appropriate dealer. DRS apply to a number of consumer products such as car hulks, car batteries and refrigerators, but they mainly apply to consumer product packaging, such as beverage containers, glass bottles, plastic containers, metal cans and so on.

Whereas a tax on products (for example, a tax on packaging) will exert a stronger direct influence on producers or consumers, a deposit produces a direct impact on consumers, although in both cases all economic agents are directly or indirectly influenced. The purpose of DRS is to induce buyers of the product to return the packaging for reuse, safe disposal or recycling.

DRS prove all the more effective when deposits are high. Returns of 90–95 per cent can be achieved. The benefits of DRS are reductions of the waste stream, reduced litter and reduced material use. On the other hand, operating costs (handling, storage, energy and transport) may turn out to be high and must be compared with the benefits.

8.   DAMAGE LIABILITY AND COMPENSATION

It would seem *a priori* logical to require polluters to pay for the damage they cause. In fact this would be economically efficient and equitable if victims received full compensation for the entire damage they suffer. Assume that the damage costs caused by a polluter are perfectly known (line MDC in Figure 6.7).

The polluter will compare the pollution abatement costs (MAC) and will reduce the emissions as long as it is cheaper to do so than to pay the damage costs (that is, when MDC = MAC, point A in Figure 6.9). We know that this level of pollution, P^*, is called the optimal pollution level because costs and benefits are equal at the margin (benefits are defined as the damage avoided). The fact that polluters pay abatement costs plus the cost of residual damage results in a 'full internalization' of environmental costs.

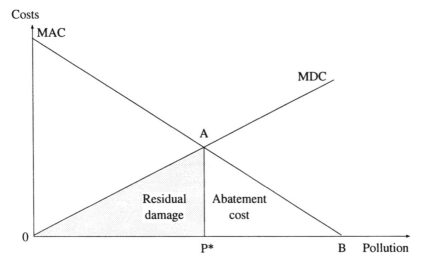

Figure 6.9   The optimal level of compensation

Hence damage compensation constitutes an efficient approach. But this requires a number of conditions to be met:

- that damage costs are correctly evaluated;
- that polluters and victims can be identified;
- that the causal relationship between pollution and damage can be established;
- that such a procedure can be enforced without excessive complexity and costs.

These conditions are obviously difficult, if not impossible, to fulfil in reality, so that environmental policies mainly rest upon direct regulations and various types of economic instrument as described above. There is, however, a tendency to exert a stronger pressure on polluters by reinforcing their liability.

On legal grounds, a number of countries have introduced the so-called 'strict' or 'no-fault' liability for environmental damage. Here, it suffices to prove that the damage was caused by a given polluter to make him liable to pay compensation, even in the absence of fault from the polluter. This particularly applies in cases of accidental pollution (for example, Seveso, Bhopal, Sandoz and oil spills) or when preventive measures cannot be taken. For chronic pollution, the 'residual damage' is sometimes 'legal' as it reflects a level of pollution considered socially 'acceptable' and embodied in an emission and/or ambient standard. In this case compensation is generally not paid.

However, considerable caution still needs to be exercised in employing the use of damage compensation as a general principle of environmental policy. While it is rather a matter of equity to ensure that victims are not spoiled in the case of accidental pollution, it is difficult to set up systems whereby any damage above a given threshold would call for systematic compensation of victims of pollution. The OECD polluter pays principle makes no reference to damage liability and compensation. There is, however, an evolution in this respect. On the one hand, the OECD recommendation on 'The Application of the Polluter Pays Principle to Accidental Pollution' does not apply to damage, but simply requires that the cost of measures to prevent and control accidental pollution be borne by the causers of this pollution, whether the measures are taken by them or by public authorities, for example, measures for containing the damage of an oil spill, cleaning beaches and so on. On the other hand, the 'Convention on Civil Liability for Damage Resulting from Activities Dangerous to the Environment', accepted by the Council of Europe in 1993, stipulates that any form of damage can be compensated for under the conditions set out in the convention.

9.   CONCLUSION: ECONOMIC INSTRUMENTS WITHIN POLICY MIXES

This overview on environmental policy instruments can be concluded by highlighting two key characteristics of current trends in environmental policies: first, a rapid increase in the use of economic instruments; second, the development and implementation of complex 'policy mixes'.

9.1   A Growing Role for Economic Instruments

The use of economic instruments to protect the environment (such as taxes, charges or tradable permits) has spread considerably in OECD countries. A first OECD survey (OECD, 1989) reflecting the situation in 1987 in 14 OECD countries identified 150 cases of economic instruments (including subsidies) out of which 80 were environmental charges and taxes. Since then, the situation has continued to evolve and a number of countries have implemented or are intending to introduce new economic instruments. In some countries the number of economic instruments has increased by 50 per cent between 1987 and 1993. Since then, the number of applications of economic instruments has continued to grow, in particular with a significant increase in the use of environmental taxes. The application of emission taxes and charges, in the 1970s and 1980s, constituted the first 'wave' of economic instruments. These related mainly to water effluent and solid waste charges.

It may be said that the emphasis placed by some countries on environmental taxes, especially as part of new 'green tax reforms', reflects the latest generation of economic instruments. This tendency is due to many factors (Barde, 1992, 1997; OECD, 1994), particularly the need to improve the efficiency of policies based to a great extent on rigid and cumbersome regulations (see section 2). It has also appeared that 'integrating' environmental policies effectively with sectoral policies (such as energy, transport or agriculture) is the best way of making such policies more effective (OECD, 1996a). In this context, fiscal instruments provide an ideal means of injecting appropriate signals into the market, of eliminating or reducing structural distortions (such as unsuitable energy and transport tariffs) and of internalizing externalities, while at the same time improving the efficiency of existing measures. The end result is a real structural readjustment of economies.

Other factors that account for the tendency include the need for more tax revenues to finance the general government budget, as well as specific environmental funds or programmes, and the search for 'alternatives' to traditional regulations, as part of the move towards 'regulatory reforms' or 'deregulation' which currently prevails in most industrialized countries (OECD, 1997).

Tradable permits have also developed, although to a smaller extent, but their use is likely to increase in the context of climate change policies. Figure 6.10 shows the evolution of economic instruments from 1970 to 2000.

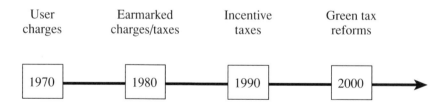

Figure 6.10   The evolution of economic instruments

9.2 Policy Mixes

Environmental policies can be implemented through a variety of policy instruments. None of them is a panacea. Some instruments will be better adapted to specific environmental problems and economic circumstances. It would be inappropriate, for instance, to impose taxes on hazardous substances, as a strict control or ban would be more effective. Fixed, mobile and diffuse sources cannot be treated in the same manner. In all cases one must strike a delicate balance to ensure the achievement of both environmental effectiveness and economic efficiency. Many other factors come into play, such as distributive and trade effects. The choice of instruments should be based on a number of economic, social and political criteria (see Box 6.7).

BOX 6.7   TWELVE CRITERIA CONCERNING
CHOICE OF ENVIRONMENTAL POLICY
INSTRUMENTS

There are many criteria concerning the choice of environmental policy instruments. As an example, 12 key criteria are presented here; but many others could be defined.

1. *Environmental effectiveness.* The most important criterion is to what extent policy instruments will achieve environmental objectives. Certain instruments may be better adapted to specific environmental purposes. For instance, it may be more effective to impose a ban on hazardous substances rather than a tax.
2. *Economic efficiency.* Policy instruments should achieve goals at minimum cost to society.
3. *Incentive.* There should be a continuous incentive to reduce pollution and to foster technical innovation. This 'dynamic efficiency' aspect is essential.
4. *Flexibility.* Polluters should have maximum flexibility in the ways and means to comply with environmental requirements, e.g., in the choice of abatement techniques and adaptation strategies. This flexibility is a key condition for achieving economic efficiency and environmental effectiveness.
5. *Simple mode of operation.* Complex regulations or economic instruments can result in poor compliance, fraud, and excessive administrative and compliance costs.

---

6. *Cost of implementation.* All components of implementation costs must be taken into account: monitoring, licensing, enforcement, etc.
7. *Integration in sectoral policies.* Environmental policies must be properly integrated with other sectoral policies having an environmental impact, e.g., transport, energy and agricultural policies. For instance, energy taxation must internalize environmental cost; appropriate control of pesticides and fertilizers implies removal of related agricultural subsidies.
8. *Minimization of regressive distributional effects.* Policy instruments may have socially regressive impacts, e.g., by increasing the price of certain commodities (basic necessities). These distributive impacts must be mitigated and/or compensated.
9. *Political acceptability* depends on many factors such as cost, simplicity, transparency, public participation, etc. Conformity with existing institutional framework is of particular relevance.
10. *Economic impact.* The wider economic effects of policy instruments must be carefully assessed and controlled, e.g., effects on prices, employment, competitiveness, economic growth.
11. *Trade and international competitiveness* are increasingly taken into account in the choice of policy instruments.
12. *Conformity with international agreements.* Environmental policies operate within the framework of many international conventions, protocols and agreed principles such as the polluter pays principle. Trade rules must also be complied with within the GATT/WTO context.

Source: Adapted from J.-Ph. Barde, 'Douze critères pour choisir un instrument de politique environnementale', *Ecodécision*, January 1994.

But most importantly, in most instances different instruments are used in combination in the context of 'policy mixes'. Past controversy principally focused on the issue of economic instruments versus regulations. The present situation is characterized by the prevalence of mixed systems, where regulations are used in combination with economic instruments and voluntary approaches. In such systems economic instruments complement regulation by providing additional incentives for pollution abatement (dynamic efficiency), more cost-effectiveness (static efficiency) and often a source of revenue, either for financing environmental measures such as treatment of effluents, waste collection and processing (charges and earmarked taxes), or for feeding the general government budget (taxes). In any case, tradable permits require a regulatory framework (fixing the emission cap).

The actual combinations of economic instruments and regulations vary considerably between countries and according to the type of pollution. In some cases, economic instruments constitute the cornerstone of the policy (for example, waste water charges in France, Germany and The Netherlands). In other instances, economic instruments only provide an additional financial incentive device (for example, some types of product taxes); in yet others they constitute an optional tool and opportunity for cost savings (tradable permits in the United States). Green taxes operate in addition to existing regulations. However, this situation may evolve in the future as in several countries a more prominent role is given to economic instruments, not only by introducing new ones but also by making them more effective through higher rates of taxes and charges capable of inducing actual changes in polluters' behaviour. Green tax reforms also offer an opportunity for structural adjustments in the economy.

New 'policy mixes' are likely to appear, for instance: combinations of voluntary approaches with tradable permits; an emission cap could be fixed through a negotiated agreement and implemented by trades between the participating parties (for example an industry branch). Mixes of taxes and tradable permits are also envisaged: for instance, reductions of CO_2 emissions could be achieved by trading permits between stationary sources, while mobile sources (transport sector) would be subject to taxes.

FURTHER READING

A volume about the political economy of the environment with detailed chapters on the polluter pays principle, regulatory instruments, taxes and tradable permits (in French) is:

Barde, Jean Philippe (1992), *Economie et Politique de l'Environnement*, Paris: Presses Universitaires de France.

A comprehensive and accessible handbook on environmental economics is:

Pearce, David and Kerry Turner (1990), *Economics of Natural Resources and the Environment*, London: Harvester Wheatsheaf.

On the practice of economic instruments, the following are comprehensive surveys and assessments of the use of economic instruments in industrialized countries (available in English and French):

Barde, J.-Ph. (1997), 'Economic instruments for environmental protection in OECD countries', in OECD, *Applying Market-Based Instruments to Environmental Policies in China and OECD Countries*, Paris: OECD.

Smith, St. and H.B. Vos (1997), *Evaluating Economic Instruments for Environmental Policy*, Paris: OECD.

OECD (1999), *Economic Instruments for Pollution Control and Natural Resources Management in OECD Countries: A Survey*, Paris: OECD.

The role of eco-taxes and their integration into fiscal systems (available in English and French) is discussed in:

OECD (1996), *Implementation Strategies for Environmental Taxes*, Paris: OECD.

OECD (1997), *Environmental Taxes and Green Tax Reform*, Paris: OECD.

O'Riordan, T. (ed.) (1997), *Ecotaxation*, London: Earthscan (English only).

On the current experience in the implementation of tradable permits, see:

OECD (1999), *Implementing Domestic Tradable Permits for Environmental Management*, Paris: OECD.

On voluntary approaches, see:

European Environment Agency (1997), *Environmental Agreements*, Copenhagen: EEA.

Börkey, P., M. Glachant and F. Lévêque (1999), *Voluntary Approaches for Environmental Policy in OECD Countries*, Paris: OECD (English and French).

On regulatory reform, see:

Lee, N. (1997), *Reforming Environmental Regulation in OECD Countries*, Paris: OECD.

NOTES

1. The opinions expressed in this chapter are the author's own, and do not necessarily reflect the views of the OECD.
2. For a detailed assessment, see OECD (1999a).
3. Considering that we are in a 'second-best' universe, below the ideal of a 'Pigouvian' tax.
4. See also Chapter 18.

5. For the theoretical aspects of subsidies, the interested reader is referred to Pearce and Turner (1990), ch. 7; and Baumol and Oates (1988), ch. 14.
6. I am grateful to David Harrison Jr for comments on this section.
7. In the context of the Kyoto Protocol to the UN Framework Convention on Climate Change, several countries (Denmark, Norway, the UK) are working on the design of possible domestic trading schemes for CO_2 (1999).

REFERENCES

Barde, J.-Ph. (1992), *Economie et Politique de l'Environnement*, Paris: Presses Universitaires de France.
Barde, J.-Ph. (1997), 'Economic instruments for environmental protection: experience in OECD countries', in OECD, *Applying Market-based Instruments to Environmental Policies in China and OECD Countries*, Paris: OECD.
Barde, J.-Ph. (1999), 'Environmental taxes in OECD countries: an overview', in OECD, *Environmental Taxes in China and OECD Countries*, Paris: OECD.
Baumol, William J. and Wallace E. Oates (1988), *The Theory of Environmental Policy*, Cambridge: Cambridge University Press.
Börkey, P., M. Glachant and F. Lévêque (1999), *Voluntary Approaches for Environmental Policy: An Assessment*, Paris: OECD.
Dales, John (1968), *Pollution, Property and Prices*, Toronto: Toronto University Press.
Danish Ministry of Finance (1995), *Energy Taxes on Industry in Denmark*, Copenhagen.
European Commission (1996), 'Study on voluntary agreements concluded between industry and public authorities in the field of environment', Enviroplan, Copenhagen.
European Environment Agency (1997), *Environmental Agreements: Environmental Effectiveness*, Environmental Issues Series, no. 3, vols 1 and 2, Copenhagen.
EUROSTAT (1996), 'Structures of the taxation systems in the European Union', Brussels: Office for Official Publications of the European Communities.
Hahn, R.W. and L.G. Hester (1989), 'Marketable permits: lessons for theory and practice', *Ecology Law Quarterly*, 16.
Imura, I. (1998), *The Use of Voluntary Approaches in Japan: an Initial Survey*, Paris: OECD.
Mazurek, J. (1998a), *The Use of Unilateral Agreements in the United States: The Responsible Care Initiative*, Paris: OECD.
Mazurek, J. (1998b), *The Use of Voluntary Approaches in the United States: an Initial Survey*, Paris: OECD.
OECD (1989), *Economic Instruments for Environmental Protection*, Paris: OECD.
OECD (1994), *Managing the Environment: The Role of Economic Instruments*, Paris: OECD.
OECD (1996a), *Integrating Environment and Economy: Progress in the 1990s*, Paris: OECD.
OECD (1996b), *Subsidies and Environment: Exploring the Linkages*, Paris: OECD.
OECD (1997), 'Reforming environmental regulation in OECD countries', report prepared by N. Lee, Paris: OECD.
OECD (1998), *Improving the Environment Through Reducing Subsidies*, Paris: OECD.
OECD (1999a), *Consumption Tax Trends*, Paris: OECD.
OECD (1999b), *Implementing Domestic Tradable Permits for Environmental Management*, Paris: OECD.

Pearce, David and Turner, Kerry (1990), *Economics of Natural Resources and the Environment*, London: Harvester Wheatsheaf.

Pearson, M and St. Smith (1991), 'The European carbon tax: an assessment of the European Commission Proposal', Institute for Fiscal Studies, London.

Tietenberg, T.H. (1990), 'Economic instruments for environmental regulation', *Oxford Review of Economic Policy*, **6**, (1).

UNEP (1998), 'Voluntary industry codes of conducts for the environment', Technical Report no. 40.

US EPA (1996), *Re-inventing Environmental Regulation*, Washington, DC.

Vermeend, Willem and Jacob Van der Vaart (1998), *Greening Taxes: The Dutch Model*, Deventer: Kluwer.

7. Impact analysis of environmental policy

Samuel Fankhauser and Daniel McCoy

1. INTRODUCTION

When considering environmental policies, one key concern of decision-makers is the economic impacts of the proposed measures. A policy will generally only be implemented if the burden it imposes is reasonable compared to the expected environmental gains (a notion often formalized in a costs–benefit analysis; see Chapter 4), and if there is no cheaper way to achieve the same results (cost-effectiveness analysis). Analysts use a wide range of tools to assess the economic consequences of environmental policy, including surveys, econometric analysis, sectoral models and economy-wide models. Some of these tools are relatively simple in structure; others are highly complex. None of them is *a priori* superior to the others. The choice of the appropriate approach depends on the problem at hand.

Nevertheless, there is a trend to rely increasingly on sophisticated, computer-based models to describe the complex pattern of intersectoral and intertemporal relationships observed in a modern economy. The analysis of environmental policy is no exception. There is a multitude of feedbacks between the economy and the environment, as well as within the economy itself, and without an appropriate model it is often difficult fully to work out the repercussions of a policy change.

This complexity led Nobel prize economist Paul Samuelson to describe economic modelling as 'mental gymnastics of a peculiarly depraved type'. The purpose of this chapter is to show how such modelling can be used to help in forecasting the economic impact of environmental policy. The focus will be on economy-wide models.

Empirical modelling, with the large-scale models concentrated on in this chapter, typically consists of a series of simulations carried out by making changes to the values of exogenous model parameters in order to analyse the impact on the endogenous variables of the model. Variables are called exogenous if their value is determined outsided the model. A variable is endogenous if its value is determined within the model. For example, a model may treat an environmental tax as exogenous, since its level depends on government decisions made independently of the model. However, the economic consequences of imposing this tax, such as the revenue raised, are considered endogenous, since their value depends on how activity in the model is altered by the tax. A model with this structure could be used to study the economic consequences of a new environmental tax. Typically, the 'with-tax' simulation scenarios would be compared to an initial forecast referred to as the business-as-usual or baseline scenario, with different assumptions on the use of the additional revenues (for example, a reduction in other forms of taxation, such as those on labour).

Several classes of economy-wide models exist. The chapter will introduce the main types and assess their relative strengths and weaknesses. It will stress that different approaches should be seen as complements, rather than substitutes. To underline this point the chapter is deliberately confined to practical examples from only one topic – climate change – thus illustrating how different approaches are able to shed light on different aspects of the same problem. This is for expository reasons only. Economic modelling can be and has been applied to a wide range of environmental policies. We start with an overview of the different approaches to modelling the economy-wide impacts of environmental policy.

2. DIFFERENT MODELLING APPROACHES

Economic analysis is typically based on what is called a partial equilibrium approach. Most of the theoretical underpinning introduced in Parts I and II of this volume, for example, reflects this view. Partial equilibrium analysis is characterized by a focus on only one particular economic sector or factor, neglecting feedbacks from and to other sectors of the economy. Such a simplification can often be reasonable for analytical convenience or in order to keep a model mathematically tractable. Sometimes, this simplification may be sufficient because the side-effects are too small to be relevant. The point is further illustrated in Figure 7.1.

Consider first the upper diagram in Figure 7.1, which shows a simple supply and demand analysis. Suppose a tax is then introduced, shifting the supply curve up and to the left, from S to S'. As an initial effect the price will rise from P_0 to P_1, and the equilibrium quantity produced and consumed reduces from Q_0 to Q_1. However, these need not be the only changes. Suppose the activity in question was road transport, and the tax was levied per person kilometre driven. The initial change in the quantity of car journeys consumed, Q_0–Q_1, may then also affect other goods. For example, we could expect that

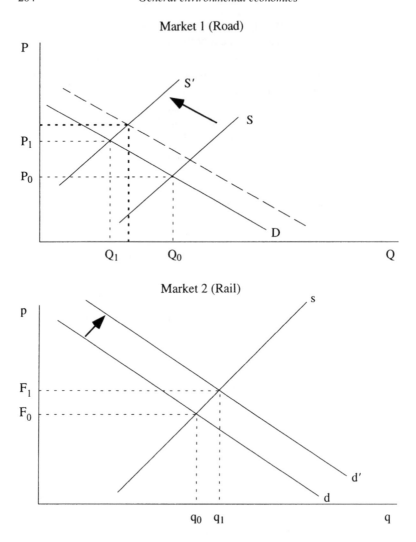

Figure 7.1   Interactions between markets

fewer cars will now be sold, and that the demand for a substitute, like rail
journeys, will increase.

The market for rail journeys is depicted in the lower diagram of Figure 7.1.
The demand schedule has shifted up and to the right, as a result of the tax-
induced price increase in road transport. With more people taking trains, rail
prices will eventually go up, from F_0 to F_1. Of course, this price rise will again
have repercussions on the market for private transport. Some people will shift

back to private transport, so the demand schedule in the upper diagram will shift slightly to the right, triggering further price and quantity changes in this market, as represented by the dashed lines. This in turn affects the second market again, and so on until a new equilibrium is reached.

A partial analysis will neglect the second market and simply register the initial changes in price and quantity of first market, P_1–P_0 and Q_0–Q_1. For many problems this will suffice, and they can be adequately studied with methods other than economy-wide models, such as surveys, econometric analysis or sectoral models. Surveys have, for example, been used to measure the impacts of environmental policy on firm location behaviour, often referred to as 'capital flight' whereby firms relocate to avoid strict environmental regulation; see Jeppesen and Folmer (2000) for an overview of this topic. Impacts of environmental regulation on specific industries have been assessed using econometric studies. These econometric studies model a specific cause, such as standards on ground-level ozone, and examine the effect, such as impact on industrial activity levels or firm location; see Henderson (1996) for a good example of the impact of this type of air quality regulation in the USA.

Unfortunately, not all environmental policies lend themselves to partial analysis. In fact, environmental interventions are prone to affect either several sectors simultaneously – for example, regulations on waste which will affect all waste-producing sectors alike – or they concern sectors of such overall importance that impacts will be felt over the whole economy. Energy is a prime example. In such cases, disregarding intersectoral linkages would seriously flaw the analysis. In order to incorporate second-order effects, environmental policy assessment has increasingly become a domain of more comprehensive modelling approaches.

Several such approaches exist. Classifying according to the underlying economic theory, Boero et al. (1991) distinguish between macroeconomic models on the one hand, and resource allocation models on the other. This latter category can again be divided into general equilibrium and input–output models. Macro models are the classic instrument of economic forecasting, notably used to predict macroeconomic performance indicators such as growth, inflation and unemployment rates; but they are also useful for policy analysis. General equilibrium and input–output models, on the other hand, are more concerned with microeconomic efficiency and the optimal use of resources, that is, with the question of how a given set of available resources should be used to guarantee the highest possible output. Input–output models, in particular, have a long tradition of being used as an instrument for economic planning in this way.

Input–output tables often form the backbone of both macroeconomic and general equilibrium models but they provide important insights in their own right, as the next section will demonstrate. Economic models of all types can be combined with models of natural systems and the environment. This is usually done in cases where the interlinkages between economic and natural systems are particularly complex or where they are at the core of the analysis. This type of analysis is known as integrated assessment. In the remainder of the chapter, the above-mentioned approaches – input–output analysis, macroeconomic modelling, general equilibrium analysis and integrated assessment – are examined in more detail.

3.   INPUT–OUTPUT ANALYSIS

3.1   Description

Like most of the economic instruments presented in this chapter, input–output (I/O) analysis had been in the economist's toolkit long before environmental issues became a widespread concern. The approach was pioneered by the American economist Wassily Leontief, who completed the first input–output table for the USA in 1936. Today I/O tables are calculated in most industrialized countries, often on a very disaggregated level with 50 or more different sectors.

The key purpose of an I/O table is to describe systematically the sectoral interdependences in an economy and to record the many transactions taking place between the different sectors of an economy. For example, the production of a commodity like a car requires a host of inputs from other industries, such as steel, electronics, glass, as well as other motor vehicles, which are needed to transport all inputs to the place of construction. In turn, the production of glass, electronics and steel will itself require a number of inputs, including motor vehicles as well as more glass, electronics and steel. The interrelationships in a modern, specializing economy can thus be rather complex, and listing them in a systematic way is one of the main virtues of an input–output table. An illustrative table with two sectors is shown in Table 7.1.

Table 7.1   An illustrative input–output table

	Agriculture	Industry	Final demand	Total output
Agriculture	25	20	55	100
Industry	15	5	30	50
Factors of production	60	25		
Total inputs	100	50		

Table 7.1 should be read as follows: inputs to a production process, that is the purchases of a sector, are depicted in the columns, while the output from a sector is seen in the corresponding row. Thus, in our example, producing an agricultural output worth 100 units requires 25 units of input from the agricultural sector itself (seeds, for instance), 15 units from the industrial sector (machinery and so on) and 60 units of other inputs, or factors of production, like labour and natural resources.

The corresponding row tells us that of a total output of 100, 25 units are taken over by the agricultural sector itself (the seeds again), while 20 units are used as inputs to the industry. The remaining 55 units are consumed, that is, they are not reused as inputs to another sector. This is called the final demand (which, in a more disaggregated table, may be further divided into household consumption, government consumption and exports). A similar pattern emerges for the industrial sector. Note that if the flows are measured in money terms (which we assume here), an economic equilibrium will require that the value of inputs be equal to the value of output in each sector.

So far the table has only been used descriptively, that is, to give a picture of the various flows in an economy. The main purpose of an I/O table, however, is the analysis of changes in the structure of an economy. As it is now, the table also tells us that in order to satisfy a demand of 55 in agricultural products and 30 in industrial goods, the economy is required to produce 100 and 50 units in the agricultural and industrial sector, respectively. In addition, production factors of $60 + 25 = 85$ are needed. We may then ask what the consequences are if, say, environmental regulations cause a drop in the final demand for industrial goods from 30 to 15. Obviously, fewer inputs would be required for the industrial sector. For example, industry's demand for agricultural inputs may initially fall from 20 to, say, 15. However, this will in turn induce a reduction in the input requirements of the agricultural sector, which will again spill over to the industrial sector, and so on. What would the overall effect be? Being concerned about the unemployment rate, governments may also want to know about the impact on labour requirements, or more generally, on production factors. Input–output analysis is able to answer both questions.

To tackle these questions, a series of simple, if somewhat tedious, mathematical operations is carried out, which leads to the formation of a new table called the Leontief inverse. The Leontief inverse explicitly accounts for indirect (second; third- and higher-round) effects and thus enables us to compile the overall effect of a certain change in final demand. There is an important assumption underlying this calculation; that of constant input coefficients, which requires that the ratio of used inputs to total output produced remains constant, independent of the number of units produced. For example, if 15 units of industrial inputs are needed to produce 100 units of agricultural output, we assume that this ratio of 0.15 will hold for all output levels. Constant input coefficients are a crucial characteristic of input–output analysis. Under which circumstances such an assumption can be justified is, however, debatable. We will come back to this issue later.

With constant input coefficients, we can rewrite the first two rows of Table 7.1 in a more general form as

$$0.25\ X^A + 0.4\ X^I + D^A = X^A$$
$$0.15\ X^A + 0.1\ X^I + D^I = X^I$$

where D^A and D^I denote the final demand for agricultural and industrial goods, respectively. X^A and X^I are the connected total output levels. That is, if we set $D^A = 55$, $D^I = 30$, $X^A = 100$ and $X^I = 50$, we recover Table 7.1. This equation system can be solved for X^A and X^I, the total output requirements, as a function of final demand. These can be represented as follows:

$$X^A = 1.46\ D^A + 0.65\ D^I$$
$$X^I = 0.24\ D^A + 1.22\ D^I$$

This is the alternative formulation we sought (see the appendix for a derivation of these results). It is now easily derived that a drop in the final demand for industrial goods (D^I) from 30 to 15 will reduce the required output of agricultural and industrial goods to $1.46 \times 55 + 0.65 \times 15 = 90$ and $0.24 \times 55 + 1.22 \times 15 = 32$ units, respectively. Factor requirements decrease proportionally, to $54 + 16 = 70$ units. An isolated change in one sector was able to affect the whole economy.

To introduce environmental considerations, Table 7.1 can be augmented in a variety of ways, the most ambitious being the construction of complete ecological economic models through the inclusion of an entire ecological sub-table – see, for example, Daly (1968). Attempts in this direction have usually not been very successful, partly because of data problems, partly because ecological processes are often too complex to fit into the rigid I/O framework. Less ambitious extensions have involved the addition of extra rows and columns for ecological inputs and outputs, or the incorporation of pollution abatement activities. Table 7.2 shows the possible structure of an environmentally augmented I/O table.

Such augmented I/O models have been used in a variety of applications, including environmental taxes, pollution abatement schemes and the study of the distributional impacts of policies, providing results which can often be surprising. In a study on Norway, for example, it emerged that a seemingly clean sector like schooling is actually responsible for a substantial amount of sulphur dioxide, dust and hydrocarbons, mainly because of its high purchases from the dirty pulp and paper sector (Førsund, 1985). In another study Common (1985) investigated the distributional impacts of energy taxes, testing whether poorer households, which spend a higher portion of their income on energy, would indeed be more heavily affected, as is often claimed. Although the study confirmed the overall regressive character of an energy tax, it showed that its regressiveness is considerably softened by the fact that rich households tend to consume a commodity bundle which is comparatively more energy-intensive to produce, and whose price will thus rise more strongly.

Table 7.2   An extended input–output table with environmental sectors

	Economic sectors	Final demand	Total output	Discharge to environment
Economic sectors				
Factors of production				
Total economic inputs				
Environmental inputs				

3.2   Example

A good example of how input–output analysis can be used to analyse environmental policy measures is Proops et al. (1993), who use I/O tables for Germany and the UK to evaluate available greenhouse abatement strategies in these two countries. Unlike the carbon emissions models introduced elsewhere in the chapter, the study does not attempt to measure the welfare consequences of a certain greenhouse policy. Instead, and in accordance with the relative strength of their chosen tool, the authors mainly aim at describing the relationship between the structure of an economy and the amount of carbon it emits. They first of all work out the contributions – direct and indirect – of each sector to total emissions. Based on this, they deduce the consequences of certain changes in the economic structure (for example a shift from private to public transport) on the carbon budget. Or, reversing the order, they can estimate the structural adjustments necessary to meet certain emission targets.

To proceed with this aim, the traditional I/O tables had to be complemented with a supplementary table showing the carbon emissions of each sector. In the

Proops et al. study there were 47 sectors. Most of them emit carbon only indirectly via the burning of fossil fuels. The carbon emissions table was therefore calculated by multiplying the fossil-fuel requirements of each sector with the carbon content of the corresponding fuel, and adding up over the set of utilized fuels. For the few sectors where carbon is also emitted directly, the figures were adjusted accordingly. In addition, carbon is also emitted by households, for example through their consumption of oil or coal for heating and gasoline for transport. These emissions were attributed to final demand. Using techniques similar to those introduced in section 3.1, the relative carbon contributions of each sector can then be calculated.

The advantage of an I/O model in this context is that by considering inter-sectoral linkages it is able to attribute not only the direct emissions from production but also indirect contributions stemming from the carbon already incorporated in the inputs used. The fact that this latter category is more important in most cases underlines the importance of using such an approach. Not surprisingly, the list of the most carbon-intensive sectors resulting from this exercise is headed by the sectors involved in the provision or processing of fossil fuels – coal extraction, electricity generation, mineral oil processing, gas, and electricity distribution. These are followed by energy-intensive industrial sectors like iron and steel, pulp and paper, stone and clay, glass, and chemical products. At the bottom of the list we find service sectors, like banking and finance or telecommunication.

This pattern points towards one of the main conclusions from the study. Recent years have seen a steady shift in the economic structure of developed countries away from industrial production to the service sector. Clearly, if services are less carbon-intensive than industry, a continuation of this trend should – everything else being equal – lead to a reduction in carbon emissions over time. To underline this point, Proops et al. recalculate the tables for a future economy in which the final demand for services has grown at 8 per cent per annum, while all other sectors have changed such that the overall growth remains at 2 per cent per annum. The consequences of such an accelerated expansion of the tertiary sector would be a reduction in carbon emissions of 3–10 per cent per annum. At the same time, employment would rise by over 3 per cent, thanks to additional jobs created in the more labour-intensive service sector. Further analysis of similar scenarios leads the authors to the conclusion that, owing to the ongoing trend towards the service sector, meeting CO_2 emission targets may not be as expensive as is often assumed.

3.3 Assessment

Of the techniques presented in this chapter, none is able to predict policy impacts with more sectoral detail than I/O analysis. The computational capabilities of modern calculators allow the processing of tables with several dozens of sectors without complication and within reasonable time. It is clearly this high level of disaggregation that is the main virtue of I/O models, and, consequently, they are most often used where it is important to analyse the detailed sectoral consequences of a policy measure.

However, high disaggregation comes at a price. To be able to cope with a large number of sectors, I/O analysis has to impose strong conditions on the structure of the production processes, the main one being the assumption of constant input–output coefficients. This assumption implies what economists call constant returns to scale, that is, a technology where a doubling of all input factors will also lead to a doubling of output. If output is more (less) than doubled, economists talk about increasing (decreasing) returns to scale. There are many examples of technologies with non-constant return to scale, and they cannot be captured in I/O models. Constant I/O coefficients also make it difficult to model the substitution of one input factor for another (for example capital for labour). Although there are ways to overcome these restrictions at least partially, the options available to input–output modellers are still rather limited, compared to the rich set of technologies provided by neoclassical economic theory.

At first sight, such restrictions may seem undesirable, and on theoretical economic grounds they are certainly unsatisfactory. However, for applied work the important question is only whether or not a given assumption is reasonable for the problem under consideration. In other words, we need to know in which cases a constant coefficient technology may be a realistic approximation for the real world, and, consequently, input–output analysis should only be used then.

In the case of input–output coefficients it seems intuitively apparent that they are more likely to change in the long run. A change in the input–output ratio is equivalent to a change in production technology, and we know that technological adjustments are easier to achieve the longer the time horizon. In the short run industries may be locked into a certain technology, while in the long run they will be able to replace inappropriate machinery and streamline the production process. As a consequence it emerges that I/O analysis may be preferable for short-run analysis, say over a time period of 10–15 years. This distinguishes input–output analysis from other resource allocation models, like general equilibrium models, which usually emphasize the long run. Unlike macroeconomic models, dicussed in the next section, which are even more short-run in character, I/O does not provide a comprehensive analysis of transitional adjustment costs – higher unemployment and inflation for example – although, changes in prices and production factor requirements may serve as an indicator.

4. MACROECONOMIC MODELS

4.1 Description

Macroeconomic models, or structural models as they are sometimes called, are used to explain and predict the overall level of activity in an economy over time. Macroeconomic model-building became popular in the late 1940s, largely as a result of the emergence of Keynesian economics as orthodox theory and the development of a system of national accounts in most countries to facilitate economic planning. The leading figure in early macro model-building was Lawerence Klein who, in addition to developing a large econometric model of the USA, pioneered the United Nations sponsored LINK project which links existing models of national economies.

Initially macroeconomic models were used as a pedagogical tool to describe the behaviour of the economy in a systematic manner based on the framework of the national accounts. These accounts were set up internationally in the 1940s, largely through the work of Richard Stone and Simon Kuznets, in order to allow for analysis of government economic interventions in line with the general macroeconomic theory postulated by John Maynard Keynes in 1936. The national accounts are compiled, in varying degrees of complexity, in nearly every country. Their main task is to account for a country's total economic activity over a given time period, usually a year. The standard measure of economic activity used in the national accounts is gross national product (GNP) or some variant of it. The components of activity in the economy that sum to GNP are usually presented in the accounts under three equivalent methods – the expenditure approach, the income approach and the output approach. These involve calculating total economic activity by either adding up, respectively, all the spending, all the incomes or all the output produced in the economy in a given year.

There are many macroeconomic models in existence and these are used for a variety of purposes, such as forecasting economic performance or for use in analysing the impact on the economy of various policy measures. By the late 1960s the application of macro models had changed focus towards their forecasting capabilities. The time-frame of macro models for this purpose is generally limited to forecasting between five and seven years into the future. This is a relatively short-time frame for consideration of the impact of many environmental policy initiatives, like measures to reduce the long-term consumption of fossil fuels. The main forecasts relate to macroeconomic variables like output growth, inflation, unemployment, balance of payments and so on. This forecasting use provides a baseline scenario for economic performance, that is, how the economy is likely to behave in the coming few years. This baseline forecast facilitates the other main use of macro models in analysing various policy measures, such as increased expenditure on pollution abatement technology. The predicted changes in the economic variables brought about by this policy change can be compared to the baseline forecasts in order to determine its impact. These features of macro models can make them a practical tool for analysing the interrelationship between economic performance and the environment. In the last decade many of the large-scale macro models in operation have been adapted to perform these tasks.

A macro model is made up of a system of interrelated equations, which describe the behaviour of the economy over some recent historical time-span, and sets of important economic variables, like prices and levels of consumption. In building a macroeconomic model, economic theory is drawn upon to specify a system of behavioural equations in the model, for instance to describe the likely relationship between after-tax wage rate and the supply of labour in the economy. In addition the model often includes identities, or definitions – such as national income equals consumption plus investment plus government expenditures – to ensure that its results are consistent with the set of national accounts discussed above.

The behavioural equations in the model are then estimated over a historical time period (often having to make use of limited or inadequate data). Given the relationship among economic factors, the model can only be solved when all the equations are considered simultaneously. Macro models tend to be based on Keynesian foundations. That is, unlike general equilibrium models they do not assume that all markets will have to be cleared, that is, demand and supply equated in all markets, for the model to be solved. Econometric or statistical tests are used to check the results of the estimation procedure on the equations. If they are deemed plausible by the modeller and pass some specified acceptance criteria they are included in the model.

As an example of a very simple macroeconomic model, consider the following three equations:

$$Y = C + I + G \tag{7.1}$$
$$C = a + b\,(Y - T) \tag{7.2}$$
$$T = c + d \cdot Y \tag{7.3}$$

where $a > 0, c > 0, 0 < b < 1$ and $0 < d < 1$.

In this example the capital letters denote variables, Y (national income), C (consumption expenditure by households), I (investment expenditure by firms), G (government expenditure) and T (taxation). The lower-case letters are parameters on which we impose restrictions in their sign and magnitude subject to economic theory. Equation (7.1) is the equilibrium condition that says that in the economy, aggregate supply, represented by Y, must equal aggregate demand, the sum of the three expenditures C, I, G. In this model I and G are exogenous variables; that is, their values are determined outside the model. However, we have three endogenous variables (Y, C and T) which are determined by the three equations (7.1) – (7.3).

Equations (7.2) and (7.3) are behavioural equations showing how C and T are determined. From (7.3) we see that taxation depends on Y by the parameter d, which is the marginal tax rate. This is restricted to be a fraction so as not to exceed 100 per cent, $0 < d < 1$. Even if $Y = 0$, there will be positive tax revenues from bases other than income, for example capital. Parameter c is therefore assumed positive. From (7.2) we see that C depends on Y and T. $Y - T$ is the disposable income net of taxes. Parameter b can be interpreted as the marginal propensity to consume out of disposable income. Again, consumption is assumed to be positive even if $Y - T$ is zero, $a > 0$, since some consumers may be running down their other wealth holdings. The parameters a, b, c and d are unknown and have to be estimated econometrically.

Even in this simple model the interdependences between variables are evident. One can thus appreciate the complexity in most operational macro models given that the number of equations involved can be hundreds, in some cases thousands, describing the economy in great detail. Welfare maximization is the overall objective of economic policy. However, macro models do not explicitly model welfare functions but rather use activity measures, like GNP, as a proxy. Measures such as GNP are often poor indicators of welfare (see Chapter 20), because they exclude many welfare-enhancing, non-market activities, like voluntary community work, and because they take no account of environmental bads, like pollution.

The usefulness of macro models for policy analysis came under strong academic attack in the mid-1970s, in what is commonly known as the Lucas critique. In essence, the critique is that in making forecasts macro models use fixed estimates of relationships that held in the past but now may be altered by the change in policy, and if this is so then the estimated effects of the change will necessarily be incorrect. An example of this phenomenon would be that estimates of energy elasticities based on past data might be taken as fixed estimates for forecasting the impacts of carbon taxes, yet as a consequence of the policy change the incentive to improve energy efficiencies will have altered. If these efficiencies do change during the forecasting period, then the model predictions will be wrong. This critique led to a major shift away from the use of large-scale macro models during the 1980s, but some are still being used, as we describe in the next section.

4.2 Example

The most prominent macroeconomic models used for forecasting and policy analysis are normally country-specific rather than global models. These tend to be rather large structural models with relatively high levels of sectoral disaggregation. A good example of an operational macro model used by the European Commission to analyse environmental issues is the HERMES model. The HERMES project was set up in the early 1980s in the aftermath of the OPEC-II oil price shocks. Each member country was initially expected to a develop a national model which could then be linked with the other country models. In the end only seven country models were developed. However, the level of disaggregation varies between the country models, as does the emphasis placed on particular sectors which reflect structural differences between economies. The modelling of the energy sector, for instance, will differ in emphasis depending on, for example, whether the country is a net exporter or importer of fuels. As a consequence of these differences in specification only the four largest countries (France, Germany, Italy and the UK) are linked by the HERMES model (see Standaert, 1992).

The treatment of energy within a macro model, such as the HERMES, has important implications for the usefulness of these models in examining environmental policy decisions on greenhouse gas abatement. Aggregate energy is primarily treated as an input in the production sectors of these models. In more sophisticated models, energy can be disaggregated in a separate sub-model into different energy products. This disaggregation can allow for substitution between the different fuels, where the optimal energy mix is determined by relative energy prices. These disaggregated fuel types can also be included into a model of consumer demand, which facilitates more accurate modelling of the impact of taxes on energy consumption and the choice of fuel mix. A further option modellers can consider is to include a sub-model containing a set of balances of environmental emissions. These environmental balances can be generated by a set of emission factors that result from the level of activity and the mix of energy forecasted by the model. Macroeconomic models of this type can be described as 'top–down' approach in contrast to 'bottom–up' analysis, that would focus primarily on the energy–environment aspects and then attempt to create links back to the economy (see, for example, Bradley and FitzGerald, 1992).

The main application of the HERMES models for environmental purposes has been the examination of the macroeconomic consequences of carbon/energy taxes in the EC. The impact of a carbon/energy tax of $10 per barrel of oil equivalent using linked HERMES models for the four largest member states of the EC is shown in Table 7.3. The results of simulations introducing such a tax suggest that the impact of this measure would be quite modest in terms of economic activity. In the first scenario none of the tax revenue is redistributed back into the economy, but is used to reduce the international portion of public debt. This results in inflation, as measured by changes in the price level, being 3.7 per cent higher and the level of activity in the economy, as measured by

Table 7.3 Impact of a carbon/energy tax of $10 per barrel of oil equivalent using HERMES on the four largest EU member states (Germany, France, Italy, UK)

	Scenarios		
Volumes	Without redistribution	Redistribution via employer's social security contributions	Redistribution via personal income tax
Consumption	1.8	−0.3	0.7
Investment	−1.6	−0.7	−0.8
Exports	n.a.	−0.4	−0.6
Imports	n.a.	−0.7	−0.6
GDP	−1.6	−0.2	0.3
Employment	−0.9	−0.3	0.0
Prices			
CPI	3.7	1.4	2.7

Note: All variables expressed as percentage change in the level after seven years compared to the reference case.

Source: European Commission (1992).

GDP, being 1.6 per cent lower than the baseline scenario seven years after the tax is first introduced.

In the other scenarios presented in Table 7.3, where the revenues from the tax are redistributed in order to reduce either social security contributions or personal income taxes, the impacts on inflation and activity in the economy are much reduced. Many economists discuss the scope of coupling the introduction of environmental taxes with a fiscal reform, and envisage the prospect of a 'double dividend', whereby the environment is improved and, at the same time, economic activity also benefits; see Chapter 18 by Romstadt and Folmer. This results from the tax revenues being used to reduce other, more distortionary taxes, such as income taxes. An application of the Irish HERMES model showed that such a double dividend exists for Ireland if the revenues are used to reduce the highly distortionary social security taxes on labour (FitzGerald and McCoy, 1992). This model indicated that Irish CO_2 emissions could be reduced by about 3.5 per cent below its 'business-as-usual' level due to the proposed EC carbon tax, while GNP would actually increase by nearly 0.5 per cent above its predicted level. As evidenced by results like these, the inclusion of environmental objections need not necessarily have adverse macroeconomic consequences. However, Goulder (1997), in an extensive review of the empirical studies, finds that the conditions under which the double dividend holds are quite rare in practice.

4.3 Assessment

Macro models can be informative in practice, even accepting the Lucas critique, when they are used with care and judgement. There is widespread experience with the use and understanding of these models, which is a considerable advantage for practical applications. The level of sectoral disaggregation allows macro models to analyse specific impacts of policy for sensitive sectors of the economy. Macro models have much better articulated dynamic properties, which facilitates estimation of adjustment costs of policy changes for the economy. Intertemporal decisions can be handled explicitly by specification of asset markets (such as those for company stocks and government bonds) to determine interest rates, which influence consumption and savings decisions in the economy. Given that their construction is determined using historical empirical data, these models are often more related to reality than the general equilibrium models to be discussed below.

The critics of macro models would argue that developments in economic theory over the last two decades have not been adopted in applied macroeconomics. Macroeconomic models thus may suffer from limitations such as assumptions on non-optimizing individual behaviour, the absence of explicit welfare functions and a focus on short-term dynamics. In deciding on the suitability of macro models for environmental policy analysis, their main weakness must be weighed up against their main strength. The weakness is the limited time horizon of five to seven years for forecasting the impact of policy change. Fundamental structural and relative price changes would be limited in such a time period, so diminishing the usefulness of the model. The main strength of macro models is that they are good at providing predictions of the big macroeconomic numbers like growth, inflation, unemployment, balance of payments and so on, which makes them a persuasive instrument in influencing decision-making.

5. GENERAL EQUILIBRIUM MODELS

5.1 Description

If macroeconomic models are driven by changes in the aggregated quantities of the national accounts, general equilibrium (GE) models emphasize changes in prices instead. GE analysis basically involves the interaction of demand and supply conditions in many markets to determine the prices of many goods. GE models are not usually estimated but are rather calibrated, as is explained below.

The study of general equilibrium theory has had a long tradition in economics stemming from the pioneering work of Léon Walras, a nineteenth-century French economist. Equilibrium in the economy is achieved at a set of prices that equates supply and demand in every market. This set of prices is described as market-clearing prices. GE analysis places emphasis on the interconnections of the different sectors in the economy and examines the impact of changes in relative prices, caused for example by the introduction of an environmental tax. A very simple general equilibrium model with two sectors is the road and rail example in Figure 7.1 above. Modelling all of these interconnections is a complex task requiring large amounts of data. The advent of computable general equilibrium (CGE) models in the last 15 years has helped to relax these data-handling restrictions.

Welfare is explicitly accounted for in GE models by modelling that individuals maximize their utility (or satisfaction), given their preferences and the available income. This feature of GE models makes them attractive to the economic academic community in that the outcomes are based on solid micro-economic foundations of optimal behaviour on the part of economic agents. GE models focus on examining the economy in different states of equilibrium and compare the welfare implications between these states. This technique is described as comparative static analysis. These models are not concerned with modelling the dynamic adjustment that occurs between the transition from one equilibrium position to another. Given that it can take considerable time for prices to adjust to bring supply and demand back into equilibrium, GE models are essentially long-run models. In most GE models price and quantity variables are endogenously determined, the only exogenous variables relate to preferences, technology and policy instruments. Many applied GE models are restricted by making certain non-critical parameters exogenously fixed; this is due to difficulties in solving the model but also a consequnce of lack of data.

The level of sectoral detail in these models tends to be limited in practice, particularly with global models, due to the multiplicity of variables needed to locate a general equilibrium solution. However, this need not necessarily be the case, particularly with CGE models, since, unlike macroeconomic models, parameter values do not need to be estimated from historical time series. GE models are not usually estimated empirically, but rather parameters are positioned, or 'calibrated', such that the model replicates the data of the base period. Values are attached to the key parameters using estimates from other studies or based on the modellers' own prior views; then the other parameters are adjusted to reproduce the baseline data. These models often bear little resemblance to reality but can be thought of 'as numerical implementations of theoretical models' (Boero et al., 1991).

5.2 Example

There are many single-country CGE applications, but general equilibrium models have also been particularly successful in analysing international trade. A global model of this type is needed to analyse the impacts of worldwide efforts to mitigate climate change. Several global CGE models have been developed over the last few years for analysing environmental policy impacts. A good example of an operational CGE model used for this purpose is the Emissions Prediction and Policy Analysis (EPPA) model, developed at the Massachusetts Institute of Technology. Based on the earlier OECD GREEN model (OECD, 1992), EPPA is a multi-sector, multi-region, dynamic CGE model used for evaluating the implications and economic costs of international agreements to reduce greenhouse gas emissions. The model uses a 115-year time horizon, from 1985 to the year 2100. It divides the world into 12 regions which are linked by bilateral trade. The economic structure in each region consists of eight production sectors and four consumption sectors, in addition to the

Table 7.4   The cost of the Kyoto Protocol with and without trade in emission reductions (in billion US$, for the year 2010)

Region	Cost of compliance		Capital flows with trade*
	No trade	Full trade*	
USA	37.6	10.9	−9.3
Japan	34.4	3.3	−3.2
European Union	30.3	6.3	−5.6
Other OECD	12.8	3.1	−2.7
Central and Eastern Europe	4.7	2.0	−1.6
Former Soviet Union	0.0	−4.2	5.0
Rest of the world	0.0	−10.2	17.2
World	119.8	11.2	−

Note: * Full trade entails the unrestricted exploitation of all Kyoto mechanisms (joint implementation, the clean development mechanism, and emission trading) and involves all parties to the Protocol.

Source: Ellerman et al. (1998).

government, an investment sector, and two 'backstop' sectors that will produce perfect substitutes for refined oil and electricity in the future (Yang et al., 1996). Note the long time horizon which is a characteristic of GE models compared to the other modelling approaches already discussed.

Models like EPPA can be used to analyse the economic consequences of international agreements such as the 1997 Kyoto Protocol to the UN Framework Convention on Climate Change. Based on regional estimates of the marginal cost of reducing greenhouse gas emissions, EPPA can calculate the economic costs for each region of meeting the Kyoto emission targets. It can also calculate differentials in marginal costs and simulate the market in emission reductions that might emerge as a result of the provisions in the Protocol on the transfer of emission reductions between countries (the so-called Kyoto mechanisms). Model simulations show that the Kyoto mechanisms could lead to significant cost savings (compared to a situation without trade in emission reductions), and to a substantial flow of capital from developed countries to developing countries or economies in transition. It also shows that many regions are likely to rely heavily on emission reductions bought abroad in order to meet their obligations. Table 7.4 shows some results for illustration.

5.3 Assessment

The use of GE models for environmental policy analysis would seem to have many positive features. The long-term focus of these models coincides with the time required for environmental policy measures, like a carbon tax, to percolate through the economy. The focus on the efficient allocation of resources between time periods is compatible with environmental concerns. GE models give specific attention to the optimization of welfare, which makes for more penetrating comparisons of policy outcomes. GE models are suitable tools for addressing policy-relevant topics such as determining the optimal level of environmental taxation in the presence of other distortionary taxes, see Bovenberg and Goulder (1996).

The direct modelling of preferences and technologies, which are exogenous to the simulations, allows GE models to overcome the Lucas critique of macro models. Based on solid microeconomic foundations, GE are more amenable to incorporation of state-of-the-art theoretical advances, such as forward-looking expectations. Even purely theoretical GE models have sometimes been used for policy evaluation purposes, such as the work by Bovenberg and de Mooij (1994) on the double dividend hypothesis.

But GE models do have a number of limitations for practical policy-making decisions. Most GE models assume perfectly competitive markets throughout the economy, which is not representative of the real world in which many cases of market failure exist, such as monopoly power or imperfect competition. GE models have problems dealing with market failure at the individual level too. For example, suppose a person uses a coal fire as his main source of heating even though he knows of a more economical and environmentally friendly alternative. The person may not adopt the alternative heating source because he may face a credit constraint. GE would take an individual's current behaviour as being optimal, although a policy that subsidized the purchase of the better technology could improve welfare. GE models need to force all parameters to arrive at equilibrium solutions, yet this may not reflect reality.

GE models are concerned with relative prices but say nothing about actual price levels, nor levels of economic activity, nor adjustment costs, like those arising from unemployment. The changes that GE models capture are those relative to the business-as-usual or baseline scenario. However, the baseline scenario may not adequately accord with actual levels of prices or activity in the economy given that GE models are calibrated to accord with reality only in the base year, as explained above. This absence of information on the adjustment path an economy might take in moving between equilibria can be a serious limitation on relying exclusively on GE models for practical policy-making purposes.

6.   INTEGRATED ASSESSMENT MODELS

6.1   Description

The terms 'integrated assessment' and 'integrated assessment modelling' are both relatively recent, but the idea of combining models from several disciplines into an integrated, multidisciplinary framework is not new. Efforts of this kind are probably as old as the discipline of environmental economics itself. Broader definitions of integrated assessment encompass any analysis involving multiple disciplines, and also include more informal ways of collaboration, such as expert panels (see, for example, Weyant et al., 1996). In the present context a more narrow definition seems appropriate, and we will use the term 'integrated assessment' to mean modelling work that combines economic analysis and the natural sciences.

One of the earliest and more prominent examples of integrated economy–environment modelling is the work by Meadows et al. (1972) on the scarcity of natural resources and the limits to growth. In the 1980s integrated models were used to study control policies for acid rain and simulate the pattern of acid depositions – the National Acid Precipitation Assessment Program in the USA, and the RAINS models for Europe and, more recently, Asia. In the1990s integrated assessment has gained prominence as a tool for the analysis of global climate change.

Unlike the models discussed in earlier sections, which all have clearly defined characteristics, the group of integrated assessment models is very heterogeneous – in terms of structure and modelling philosophy, as well as size. And they have a wide range of applications. Most environmental cost–benefit analyses (see Chapter 4) and natural resource utilization models (see Chapter 16) are essentially integrated assessment models. They combine a simple representation of the economy with an equally simple representation of natural systems. Integrated models also differ with respect to the degree of integration. Some models have a simple linear structure, where the outputs of one module, for example, particulate emissions from economic activity, are the inputs of another, such as a human health assessment. Other models include a multitude of economy–environment interlinkages and feedbacks. The following types of integrated assessment models have sometimes been distinguished (see for example Weyant et al., 1996 and Kolstad, 1998):

- *Policy evaluation models*. These comprehensive, process-based models seek to project the physical, ecological, social and economic consequences of different courses of action. Policy evaluation models tend to be complex and can often only be run on powerful supercomputers.
- *Policy optimization models*, which seek to optimize key policy control variables. Environmental cost–benefit analyses are examples of optimization models. Because of the need to keep the model solvable, these models tend to have a simpler structure.

Whatever the overall structure of an integrated model, the structure of its economic component will be one of the generic types discussed above; that is, it will either be an I/O, macro, general equilibrium or partial equilibrium (sectoral) model. The EPPA model, for example, has been designed as an integral part of an integrated assessment project. In this sense, integrated assessment is not a new type of model, but an extension of the traditional approaches of economic analysis.

6.2   Example

Economic models dealing with the costs of greenhouse gas abatement, such as those introduced in sections 4.2 and 5.2, have traditionally been concerned with the costs of an emission constraint. What would be the cost to the economy if greenhouse gas emissions were to be limited? This is the main question in the mind of policy-makers at the level of national government, and CGE and macro-economic models are well suited to answer it. But at a global level the main concern is not the emission (the flow) of greenhouse gases, but their atmospheric concentration (the stock). Solving the problem of climate change will ultimately require the stabilization of the atmospheric concentration of greenhouse gases. The analysis of policies that have a concentration, rather than an emission sta- bilization objective, requires a different type of model from the ones introduced in earlier sections. What is required is an integrated model that combines an economic component of greenhouse gas abatement with a representation of the global carbon cycle modelling the accumulation of gases in the atmosphere.

An example of such a model is MERGE (a Model for Evaluating the Regional and Global Effects of greenhouse gas reduction policies; see Manne and Richels, 1995). MERGE is a multiregional, intertemporal market equilibrium model with a detailed (bottom-up) description of the energy sector. The global economy is modelled in a general equilibrium fashion. But MERGE also has features of a macro model, in that individual regions maximize the discounted utility of consumption through adequate savings and investment decisions. The economic component of the model is coupled with a climatological component that allows the simulation of atmospheric concentration and temperature trends.

A key question that models such as MERGE can help to answer is that of the optimal timing of emission reductions. For any concentration goal that may be agreed on, people can choose from a variety of different emission paths that would all meet the target. Each of them would impose different costs. Models like MERGE can be used to identify the emission path that imposes the lowest costs. Examples for different levels of atmospheric concentration are shown in Figure 7.2.

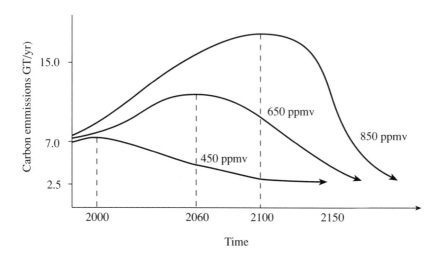

Figure 7.2   Optimal greenhouse gas emission paths under different concentration targets

A mix of economic and climatological factors are at work that determine the humped-shaped emission paths characteristic of most of these simulations. Limited restraint in the short term, followed by significant emission cuts in the medium and long term may be an attractive policy because:

- earlier emissions carry a lower weight in the stabilization budget, as they will have partially decayed at the target date for stabilization;
- the need for reductions coincides better with the availability of new and cheaper backstop technologies;
- polluting capital can be replaced at the end of its economic and technical life, without a need for premature scrapping;
- the return earned on productive investments in early periods can pay for additional greenhouse gas abatement in the future (the discounting effect).

Other factors, such as the stimulating effect of early abatement on the development of clean industries, somewhat counterbalance the above effects, and the exact shape of the optimal emission path is still under debate. Ultimately the question of the appropriate concentration level and associated emission path will be decided at the negotiating table. But integrated assessment models such as MERGE can play a useful role in informing this debate.

6.3 Assessment

Given the complexity of economy–environment interlinkages, the interdisciplinary approach of integrated assessment seems to be a natural extension of the economics toolkit for environmental applications. Indeed, much environmental economic research has traditionally been integrated without the research teams necessarily being aware of this moniker.

The main application of integrated assessment is the study of the environmental impacts of economic activity – measuring the environmental costs of transport, for example, or the impact of agricultural practices on soil quality and biological diversity. The instrument is less used for the analysis of the economic impacts of environmental policy, which is the focus of this chapter. There are applications, though. One important one is the assessment of environmental policies that take the form of an environmental standard, for example on air or water quality. To analyse such cases economic models have to be augmented with an environment module that translates quality standards back into constraints on emissions, which can in turn be imposed on the economic model. The discussion on acid rain in Europe, for example, is heavily influenced by the notion of critical loads – the idea that acid depositions in any one place should remain within the limits that the natural systems found there can tolerate. To analyse the economic impact of this policy, a dispersion and deposition model is needed to trace depositions back to their sources, and impose the appropriate emission constraints. The cost of these constraints can then be calculated in the economic component of the model. The RAINS model mentioned above was essentially developed to serve this purpose. An application to climate change is the MERGE model discussed above.

Experience with integrated assessment shows that the integration of models from different disciplines can be a difficult process. Researchers often find that different disciplines think in different dimensions and scale – both in terms of space and time – and the outputs produced by one model component are not necessarily those required by another. Economic models tend to require and produce time series of annual data, typically on a sectoral or country level. Ecologists, in contrast, tend to be concerned with systems of a much smaller scale. And global scientific models usually divide the world into grid cells that bear no resemblance to national borders. Disciplinary models need to be adjusted before they become compatible. Recognizing and resolving these differences can be a fruitful process, though. At least in the case of climate change, one of the main benefits of integrated assessment in the view of many has been the improved dialogue and mutual understanding between the various disciplines.

7. MODEL COMPARISON AND CONCLUSIONS

Estimating the economic consequences of environmental policies is a difficult endeavour. The high level of interdependences in a modern economy implies that measures originally planned for one sector will frequently spill over to other areas and ultimately affect the whole economy. To come to grips with interdependent problems, economists rely more and more on complex computer models: input–output analysis, macroeconomic modelling and general equilibrium analysis. To better capture the complex web of interactions between economic and natural systems, economic and environmental models are increasingly combined with integrated assessment models.

General equilibrium analysis is based on the notion that commodity prices adjust until supply equals demand in each sector. Policy impacts can be analysed by comparing the overall welfare and the set of equilibrium prices before and after an exogenously imposed shock, such as an environmental tax. By comparing the two equilibrium situations GE models mainly shed light on the long-run consequences of a measure, once the economy has had enough time to adjust to the new situation.

Of course the transition from the old equilibrium to the new one may not be smooth and the economy may suffer under a wide range of adjustment problems. Such effects can best be captured in a macroeconomic model. Macro models rely less on the equilibrating power of prices, but assume that prices and wages adjust gradually to a new situation, thus permitting a temporary dis-equilibrium in the markets. Together with an explicit implementation of intertemporal aspects, this allows a far more accurate modelling of transitional adjustment costs and an analysis of macroeconomic indicators like unemployment, inflation or economic growth. On the other hand, macro models do not incorporate welfare directly and often concentrate on only one measure of activity, usually GNP.

The analysis of detailed sectoral impacts is the main virtue of input–output analysis. Distinguishing between numerous sectors, input–output tables provide a rich source of data which, by superimposing a rigid analytical framework, can usefully be employed for in-depth examinations of structural impacts. Of course, a similar degree of disaggregation would in principle also be available from GE models. In fact, input–output tables form the basis of many GE models. But then the data requirements for GE analysis are generally so high that only medium-size models with aggregated tables are tractable. I/O analysis avoids this problem by imposing a set of strong restrictions on production technologies. This, however, comes at the expense of basically restricting its scope to the short run and painting a somewhat uniform picture of a multifaceted world.

All these approaches display a considerable degree of complexity and are correspondingly expensive and time-consuming to develop and implement. For minor policy measures, or those that are expected to concern only a few sectors, a case may be made for a partial equilibrium analysis, the traditional tool of economic analysis, in which everything outside the narrowly defined field of examination is artificially held constant.

In some situations it does not make sense to study economic systems in isolation, because the interlinkage with the environment is too strong or because they are too important. In these cases economic analysis needs to be integrated in an interdisciplinary framework. All modelling approaches discussed in this chapter are in principle suitable for integrated assessment. However, the constituent parts of an integrated assessment model need to be carfully selected. Experience shows that models from different disciplines are often difficult to combine, not least because they operate at different geographic or time-scales. And of course, an integrated assessment can only ever be as good as its underlying parts.

To summarize, there is no perfect model which offers everything. Each approach has its strengths, as well as its weaknesses, and the choice of the correct model should therefore be determined by the problem at hand. If we are mainly interested in long-run aspects, a general equilibrium model may be most appropriate. For an estimation of the transitional impacts on inflation and unemployment, we may want to use a macroeconomic model; to learn about the consequences on the economic structure, we may turn to an input–output model. Other problems may primarily affect one particular market without exposing significant spillovers, rendering high-power modelling unnecessary. In such cases a partial equilibrium analysis may provide the most lucid insights. If we are concerned about environment–economy interlinkages, an integrated model is called for.

Successful economic modelling is thus very much a question of choosing the correct analytical approach. There is also an inherent danger with big models that, because of their size and complexity, they tend to be treated as black boxes, whose output is accepted without sufficient scrutiny.

Nevertheless, on a whole the careful use of models can be and has been very fruitful for policy analysis, both environmental and non-environmental. To summarize the virtues and dangers of large-scale modelling for policy use one can do no better than quoting Shoven and Whalley (1984): 'The point to be emphasised is not that ... models are either right or wrong, but that policy decisions have to be made and that ... models are capable of providing fresh insights on policy options not available from other sources.' The advent of modern, computer-based tools notwithstanding, estimating the economic impact of environmental policy remains an art, as much as it is a science.

FURTHER READING

There is a variety of texts on input–output analysis. A good introduction is, for example, provided in the volume by Proops *et al.* (1993) cited in the References. A standard reference, also including several environmental economic applications, is

Miller, R.E. and P.D. Blair (1985), *Input–Output Analysis. Foundations and Extensions*, Englewood Cliffs, NJ: Prentice-Hall.

Macroeconomic models are based on the vast body of mainstream macroeconomic literature. A good introductory text is

Sachs, J.D. and F. Larrain (1993), *Macroeconomics in the Global Economy*, London: Harvester-Wheatsheaf.

A good survey article, touching on issues like the Lucas critique, is

N.G. Mankiw (1990), 'A quick refresher course in macroeconomics', *Journal of Economic Literature*, XXVIII (December), 1645–60.

The paper by Shoven and Whalley (1984) cited in the References provides a similar survey on general equilibrium modelling. Another, fairly tractable introduction into this rather technical subject is

Dinwiddy, C.L. and F.J. Teal (1988), *The Two-Sector General Equilibrium Model: A New Approach*, Deddington: Philip Allan.

Literature on integrated assessment is relatively scare, and predominantly deals with applications to climate change. There is no textbook as such, and one of the best source remains the book chapter by Weyant et al. (1996), cited in the References. Other good discussions of this topic are contained in:

Kelly, D.L. and C.D. Kolstad (1999), 'Integrated assessment models for climate change control', in H. Folmer and T. Tietenberg (eds), *International Yearbook of Environmental and Resource Economics 1999/2000: A Survey of Current Issues*, Cheltenham, UK and Northampton, USA: Edward Elgar.
Parson, E.A. and K. Fisher-Vanden (1997), 'Integrated assessment models of global climate change', *Annual Review of Energy and the Environment*, 22, 589–628.

APPENDIX   INPUT–OUTPUT NUMERICAL EXAMPLE

This appendix solves the input–output equations of section 3, and derives the results from a drop in final demand for industry output from 30 to 15. To do so, we will make use of the so-called Leontief inverse. In order to understand this inverse we need to make use of matrix algebra. A good introduction to matrix algebra for economists is contained in A.C. Chiang, *Fundamental Methods of Mathematical Economics*, New York: McGraw-Hill.

First, we will rewrite the first two rows of Table 7.1 in algebraic notation. Let X^j be the output of sector j. In our example A is Agriculture and I is Industry, such that $X^A = 100$ and $X^I = 50$. Similarly we denote final demand in each sector as D^J. The input coefficients we write as c_{ij}, where i = input and j = output. Thus, c_{AI} is the input coefficient of agricultural inputs used in the output of industry. That is, 20 units of agriculture are used in producing 50 units of industry output such that the coefficient is $c_{AI} = 20/50 = 0.40$. The full set of technical coefficients can be derived in this manner (the coefficent on primary inputs, or factors of production, can be denoted in a similar way):

$$c_{AA} = \frac{25}{100} = 0.25 \quad c_{AI} = \frac{20}{50} = 0.4$$

$$c_{IA} = \frac{15}{100} = 0.15 \quad c_{II} = \frac{5}{50} = 0.1$$

The first two rows of Table 7.1 can then be written as:

$$c_{AA} \cdot X^A + c_{AI} \cdot X^I + D^A = X^A$$
$$c_{IA} \cdot X^A + c_{II} \cdot X^I + D^I = X^I$$

This denotes the condition that total output X^j must equal the input requirements and the final demand in each sector. Gather the X^j terms to one side to get:

$$D^A = (1 - c_{AA}) \cdot X^A - c_{AI} X^I$$
$$D^I = (1 - c_{II}) \cdot X^I - c_{IA} X^A$$

Next we compact this notation for final demand in matrix form. We define the matrix of input coefficients as $\mathbf{C}$, such that:

$$\mathbf{C} = \begin{pmatrix} c_{AA} & c_{AI} \\ c_{IA} & c_{II} \end{pmatrix} = \begin{pmatrix} 0.25 & 0.4 \\ 0.15 & 0.1 \end{pmatrix}.$$

Using the identity matrix

$$\mathbf{I} = \begin{pmatrix} 1 & 0 \\ 0 & 1 \end{pmatrix},$$

we get the following matrix representation:

$$\begin{pmatrix} D^A \\ D^I \end{pmatrix} = (\mathbf{I} - \mathbf{C}) \begin{pmatrix} X^A \\ X^I \end{pmatrix} \tag{7A.1}$$

To solve for total outputs, rearrange such that

$$\begin{pmatrix} X^A \\ X^I \end{pmatrix} = (\mathbf{I} - \mathbf{C})^{-1} \begin{pmatrix} D^A \\ D^I \end{pmatrix} \tag{7A.2}$$

The matrix $(\mathbf{I} - \mathbf{C})^{-1}$ is an inverse matrix; in fact it is our Leontief inverse matrix. It is made up of the identity matrix subtracted from the technical coefficients matrix and the resulting matrix is inverted.

An inverted matrix is derived as follows. For instance if we had a matrix

$$\mathbf{G} = \begin{pmatrix} a & b \\ c & d \end{pmatrix}, \text{ then its inverse will be } \mathbf{G}^{-1} = \frac{1}{|\mathbf{G}|} \cdot \begin{pmatrix} d & -b \\ -c & a \end{pmatrix},$$

where $|\mathbf{G}| = a \cdot d - b \cdot c$ is called the determinant of $\mathbf{G}$, and the second matrix is called the adjunct of $\mathbf{G}$. For the inverse to exist, the determinant of $\mathbf{G}$ has to be non-zero (we cannot divide by zero). This is the case in our example.

Using the numbers in our example when $X^A = 100$ and $X^I = 50$, we can go about finding the final demands as in Table 7.1 using (7A.1) above

$$\begin{pmatrix} D^A \\ D^I \end{pmatrix} = \left(\begin{pmatrix} 1 & 0 \\ 0 & 1 \end{pmatrix} - \begin{pmatrix} 0.25 & 0.4 \\ 0.15 & 0.1 \end{pmatrix} \right) \cdot \begin{pmatrix} 100 \\ 50 \end{pmatrix} = \begin{pmatrix} 0.75 & -0.4 \\ -0.15 & 0.9 \end{pmatrix} \cdot \begin{pmatrix} 100 \\ 50 \end{pmatrix}$$

$$\begin{pmatrix} D^A \\ D^I \end{pmatrix} = \begin{pmatrix} 0.75(100) - 0.4(5) \\ -0.15(100) + 0.9(50) \end{pmatrix} = \begin{pmatrix} 55 \\ 30 \end{pmatrix}$$

Having descibed how Table 7.1 is determined, we can now address the question of how outputs will change when D^I is 15 rather than 30 by using (7A.2).

$$\begin{pmatrix} X^A \\ X^I \end{pmatrix} = \begin{pmatrix} 0.75 & -0.4 \\ -0.15 & 0.9 \end{pmatrix}^{-1} \cdot \begin{pmatrix} D^A \\ D^I \end{pmatrix} = \frac{1}{((0.75)(0.9) - (-0.15)(-0.4))} \begin{pmatrix} 0.9 & 0.4 \\ 0.15 & 0.75 \end{pmatrix} \begin{pmatrix} D^A \\ D^I \end{pmatrix}$$

$$\begin{pmatrix} X^A \\ X^I \end{pmatrix} = \frac{1}{0.615} \begin{pmatrix} 0.9 & 0.4 \\ 0.15 & 0.75 \end{pmatrix} \begin{pmatrix} D^A \\ D^I \end{pmatrix} = 1.626 \begin{pmatrix} 0.9 & 0.4 \\ 0.15 & 0.75 \end{pmatrix} \begin{pmatrix} D^A \\ D^I \end{pmatrix} = \begin{pmatrix} 1.46 & 0.65 \\ 0.24 & 1.22 \end{pmatrix} \begin{pmatrix} D^A \\ D^I \end{pmatrix}$$

We now have the equation system in the chapter for solving total output requirements in matrix form. Substituting in $D^A = 55$ and $D^I = 15$ we get

$$X^A = 1.46\, D^A + 0.65\, D^I = 1.46(55) + 0.65(15) = 90$$
$$X^I = 0.24\, D^A + 1.22\, D^I = 0.24(55) + 1.22(15) = 32$$

NOTE

Fankhauser is an economist at the European Bank for Reconstruction and Development in London and McCoy is an economist at the Economic and Social Research Institute in Dublin. The views expressed in this paper are the authors' own and do not necessarily reflect those of their respective organisations. The authors are grateful to Henk Folmer, Hans Opschoor, David Pearce and their former colleagues at CSERGE, University College London for comments on earlier drafts of this chapter.

REFERENCES

Boero, G., R. Clarke and L.A. Winters (1991), *The Macroeconomic Consequences of Controlling Greenhouse Gases: A Survey*, UK Department of the Environment, Environmental Economics Research Series, London: HMSO.

Bovenberg, A.L. and R.A. de Mooij (1994), 'Environmental levies and distortionary taxation', *American Economic Review*, **84**, 1085–89.

Bovenberg, A.L. and L.H. Goulder (1996), 'Optimal environmental taxation in the presence of other taxes: general equilibrium analysis', *American Economic Review*, **86**, 985–1000.

Bradley, J. and J. FitzGerald (1992), 'Modelling the economic effects of energy taxes: a survey', in F. Laroui and J.W. Velthuijsen (eds), *The Economic Consequences of an Energy Tax in Europe. An Application with HERMES*, Amsterdam: SEO.

Common, M. (1985), 'The distributional consequences of higher energy prices in the UK', *Applied Economics*, **17**, 421–36.

Daly, H. (1968), 'On economics as a life science', *Journal of Political Economy*, **76**, 392–406.

Ellerman, A.D., H.D. Jacoby and A. Decaux (1998), 'The effects on developing countries of the Kyoto Protocol and CO_2 emissions trading', MIT Joint Program on the Science and Policy of Global Change, Cambridge MA (http://web.mit.edu/globalchange/www/reports.html)

European Commission (1992), 'The climate challenge: economic aspects of the Community's strategy for limiting CO_2 emissions', *European Economy*, **51**, May.

FitzGerald, J. and D. McCoy (1992), 'The macroeconomic implications for Ireland', in J. FitzGerald and D. McCoy, (eds), *The Economic Effects of Carbon Taxes*, Dublin: Economic and Social Research Institute.

Førsund, F.R. (1985), 'Input–output models, national economic models and the environment', in A.V. Kneese and J.L. Sweeney (eds), *Handbook of Natural Resource Economics*, Vol. 1, Amsterdam: North-Holland.

Goulder, L. H. (1997), 'Environmental taxation in a second-best world', in H. Folmer and T. Tietenberg (eds), *The International Yearbook of Environmental and Resource Economics 1997/1998: A Survey of Current Issues*, Cheltenham, UK and Lyme, US: Edward Elgar.

Henderson, J.V. (1996), 'Effects of air quality regulation', *American Economic Review*, **86**, (4), 789–813.

Jeppesen, T. and H. Folmer (2000), 'The confusing relationship between environmental policy and location behaviour of firms: a methodological review of micro case studies', *Environment and Planning*, (forthcoming).

Kolstad, C.D (1998), 'Integrated assessment modeling of climate change', in W.D. Nordhaus (ed.), *Economics and Policy Issues in Climate Change*, Washington, DC: Resources for the Future.

Manne, A. and R. Richels (1995), 'The greenhouse debate. Economic efficiency, burden sharing and hedging strategies', *The Energy Journal*, **16** (4).

Meadows, D.H, D.L. Meadows, J. Randers and W.W. Behrens (1972), *Limits to Growth*, New York: Universe Books.

OECD (1992), 'The economic costs of reducing CO_2 emissions', *OECD Economic Studies*, Special Issue, no. 19/Winter, Paris: OECD.

Proops, J.L.R., M. Faber and G. Wagenhals (1993), *Reducing CO_2 Emissions. A Comparative Input–Output Study for Germany and the UK*, Berlin: Springer.

Shoven, J. and J. Whalley (1984), 'Applied general equilibrium models of taxation and international trade', *Journal of Economic Literature*, **XXII** (September), 1007–51.

Standaert, S. (1992), 'The macro-sectoral effects of an EC-wide energy tax: simulation experiments for 1993–2005', *European Economy*, special edition, no. 1.

Weyant, J., O.Davidson, H. Dowlatabadi, J. Edmonds, M. Grubb, E.A. Parson, R. Richels, J. Rotmans, P.R. Shukla, R.S.J. Tol, W. Cline and S. Fankhauser (1996), 'Integrated assessment of climate change: overview and comparison of approaches and results', in IPCC, *Climate Change 1995. Economic and Social Dimensions of Climate Change. Contributions of Working Group III to the Second Assessment Report of the Intergovernmental Panel on Climate Change*, Cambridge: Cambridge University Press.

Yang, Z., R. Eckaus, A.D. Ellerman and H.D. Jacoby (1996), 'The MIT emission prediction and policy analysis (EPPA) Model', MIT Joint Program on the Science and Policy of Global Change, Report no. 6, Cambridge, MA (see http://web.mit.edu/globalchange/www/reports.html)

PART II

Business Environmental Economics

8. A firm's involvement in the policy-making process

François Lévêque and Alain Nadaï

1. INTRODUCTION

Traditionally, relationships between industry and environmental policy have been examined in terms of impact. In such an approach, environmental policies are given and firms react to them. The firms comply with laws and decrees: they adopt technical standards and pay taxes; they invest in green technology; they close down plants and phase out hazardous products. But firms also adopt opportunistic behaviour: they localize new facilities in countries with less stringent environmental regulations; they do not comply with the law if control procedures are inefficient and the cost of penalties is too low. For both policy-makers and managers, concern for the impact of environmental policies on competitiveness and innovation is obviously a key issue. The focus of this chapter is different. Emphasis will be placed on how firms influence environmental policies, that is, how they contribute to shaping their regulatory environment.

Environmental standards, taxes and subsidies do not come out of the blue. They are the output of a series of consultations and negotiations between policy-makers and interested parties (industrial associations, consumers' associations, green groups). As pointed out by Spulber (1989), the actual adoption of a policy is preceded by a so-called regulatory process (or policy-devising process), the outcome of which determines how the regulations will be structured. In the field of the environment, this process starts when factors have triggered the idea of a regulation and an initial formulation has been made of the environmental problem the regulation is supposed to solve. The outcome is defined by considering the pollution reduction objective, the instruments to be used (for example, standards, taxes or subsidies), the time schedule and the enforcement with which the economic agents must comply.

According to economic theories, regulatory processes are fundamentally driven by the search for correcting market failures (Keeler, 1984), adjusting supply and demand of regulations (Stigler, 1971), reducing informational asymmetries (Laffont and Tirole, 1991) or learning and networking (Aggeri and Hatchuel, 1999). Our purpose is not to choose between these different theories, but to cast light on the circumstances in which a firm's involvement within the regulatory process takes place, and the pay-offs provided by this involvement.

A firm's involvement can take several forms. We examine four forms based on empirical evidence. These forms correspond to elementary strategic actions. They enable firms to shape their regulatory process instead of simply waiting for legislation and reacting to it. They are listed according to the relationship between a firm (or a coalition of firms) and the public authorities.

Firms can:

1. Support public authority intervention
2. Hinder public authority intervention by making use of their obstructive power
3. Take voluntary actions under the threat of governmental intervention
4. Cooperate with the government in defining environmental policies.

These forms are associated with specific circumstances in terms of information and incentives, and provide several advantages for firms, which are analysed in this chapter.

The chapter is divided into six sections. Section 2 provides empirical and theoretical evidence of a firm's influence on the regulatory process. The third section analyses the classical and well-known strategies of obstruction and support. The next two sections emphasize voluntary actions taken by firms and cooperation between industry and public authorities. Section 6 concludes.

2.   A FIRM'S INVOLVEMENT IN THE REGULATORY PROCESS: EMPIRICAL AND THEORETICAL EVIDENCE

2.1   Empirical Evidence

Currently there is a strong consensus within OECD countries to view the building up of close relations with industry as essential for the success of environmental policies. OECD countries endorse the use of industry consultation when designing new regulations. Dialogues with firms are considered to be key components of policy-making in the field of the environment. For instance, the establishment of national 'green plans' has involved extensive consultation with industrialists and firms' associations. In Australia, the Ecological Development Plan has prompted a number of comments and suggestions from the raw materials industry. Similarly, in Canada, consultation with the industrial sector was carried out before the launching of the Green Plan in December 1990.

In defining environmental policy, pride of place is currently given to consultation with industry for two reasons. First, most information concerning the amount of pollution, abatement costs and technology is private, that is, known only to firms. As a consequence, the regulator cannot fix the pollution reduction objective (for example, a threshold for an emission standard) before producing data or collecting them from industry. Producing data to assess the extent of pollution and safety of industrial processes and products may be very costly for policy-makers. Frequently it requires in-house expertise which regulators do not possess and cannot afford because regulatory agencies are subject to budgetary savings pressure from governments.

Second, environmental regulators are confronted with competitive issues. They are compelled not to induce trade distortions and negative competitive effects on industry. To prevent environmental issues from restricting trade liberalization, the designing of new national policies cannot be independent of what other countries are doing. This is reinforced by industrial globalization. One of the response options of a global firm to higher environmental standards is to relocate capacity and direct new investments towards other countries. In order not to reduce the competitiveness of the national industrial sector, potentially high compliance costs are offset by exemptions, rebates, subsidies and time deferrals. The current intensity of economic competition between nations is inducing national policy-makers to take into account the views of industrialists and consult them about the potential impact of their regulatory project on unemployment, industrial growth and competitiveness.

Moreover, it is commonly observed that companies undertake intense lobbying activities before any proposals are drafted by government. Is Brussels or Washington the prime forum in the world for industrial lobbyists and lobbying consultancy firms? The civil servants of DG-XI, the General Directorate of the European Commission in Charge of the Environment, are under daily pressure from industrial lobbies. The rule of thumb is that industrialists must intervene as early as possible in the European policy process. Once a directive is published, it is often too late for firms to defend their interests.

However, to influence the devising process of environmental regulations firms must allocate resources, mainly human ones (to say nothing of bribes when the administration is corrupt). This is why small and medium-sized enterprises generally tend to be excluded. These enterprises cannot appoint a regulatory affairs manager or contract a lobbying consultancy firm. Influencing the devising of environmental policies is the privilege of large and global firms. This is the reason that the examples provided in this chapter mainly concern large companies and consolidated industries.

2.2   Theoretical Insights

The standard economic theory of regulation, that is, the so-called public interest theory, views regulation as a means of correcting market failures where government is a benevolent maximizer of social welfare. It is assumed that policy-makers only pursue public interest goals and that information does not cost anything (that is, regulators are supposed to possess comprehensive information or to collect it free of charge). Within this framework, the influence of firms or other interested parties in devising public policy is excluded.

The influence of private interests on regulation can only be explained if the two hypotheses mentioned above are relaxed. The hypothesis that policy-makers aim solely at maximizing social welfare has been disputed by the so-called regulatory capture theory. This theory argues that regulations are captured by private interests represented in the policy-making process. The hypothesis of perfect information has been disputed by the so-called new economics of regulation (Laffont and Tirole, 1993). Within this theory, the cause of a firm's influence on regulation is rooted in informational asymmetries between industry and government.

According to the *regulatory capture theory*, the outcome of the policy-devising process depends on the intervention of interest groups. Regulations are provided in response to the demand of interested parties struggling among themselves to maximize the incomes of their members. The regulation is viewed as a commodity: regulatory pay-offs are exchanged between interest groups and policy-makers according to the rules of supply and demand. The determinant of success by firms in capturing the regulation is their ability to organize themselves into interest groups (Stigler, 1971). More specifically, the hypothesis is that an individual economic actor has no power over regulators and that collective action is the only means to obtain access to the market of regulations. Stigler (1971) argues that the cost of interest grouping depends on the size of the group and on the proximity of the interest to its members. As a consequence, small homogeneous groups will have lower organization costs and greater efficiency in their collective action. This is inspired by the Olson theory of collective action (Olson, 1965).

Whether the outcome of the regulatory process is largely or partially captured by private interests depends on whether the hypothesis regarding the public interest motives of policy-makers is deleted or not. Initial economic studies, which asserted that the regulations benefited regulated industry instead of maximizing social welfare, were carried out in the mid-1950s on the US regulation of the transport sector. They provided evidence that regulators only satisfy private interests. Once these findings began to be recognized, a significant wave of deregulation took place in the USA during the mid- and late

1970s. It concerned various sectors, such as railways, airlines, trucking, communication, banking, financial institutions and so on. This deregulation, it was argued by policy-makers, pursued public interest goals. Economists were obviously prompted to consider this new trend. This gave birth to a second set of theoretical and empirical investigations (Keeler, 1984; Peltzman, 1976) which includes a mix of public and private interest considerations in order to explain the history of regulation and deregulation. According to these new investigations, achieving public interest goals is not prevented by involvement of interest groups. Decisions of policy-makers are aimed at increasing social welfare and redistributing this increase among interest groups (via regulatory pay-offs) in order to obtain their political support. These models predict that those interest groups that are privileged by the policy-makers are the ones that enable welfare to be increased through regulation and to minimize the cost of political support. In short, the regulatory capture theory argues that the involvement of interest groups is triggered by their expectations of regulatory pay-offs, and that their success depends on the cost of their collective action and their economic and political power.

The *new economics of regulation* is based on the agency theory.[1] It focuses on the public policy hurdles caused by informational asymmetries and defines incentive systems to cope with them. The new economics of regulation provides original insights explaining why, how and when regulatory capture takes place.

According to this framework, regulatory capture is rooted in the process of public decision-making itself. Firms are *de facto* involved in public policy-making. They are invited by the regulatory agency to take part in the process because firms possess the information the agency needs. As pointed out above, collecting data from industry may be less costly for regulators than producing data. But firms have no reason whatsoever to tell regulators the truth. They know that the information required by regulators will be used to design a regulation which will affect their sales. Therefore it will be to their advantage to manipulate this information (that is, to lie) in order to obtain a less stringent policy. This leads firms to overestimate their abatement costs and underestimate their emissions. To limit this manipulation of information, policy-makers have to design an incentive system that aims at making firms adopt optimal behaviour (issuing true information). This addresses the typical problem of a so-called adverse selection within a principal–agent relationship:[2] the agent has access to an observation which is inaccessible to the principal; the agent uses this information to make his decisions but the principal cannot observe whether or not the agent has used the information in the way that best meets his interests (that is, the principal's interest).

According to the new economics of regulation, policy-making takes place within a complex set of agency relationships (Laffont and Tirole, 1991). The public authorities are divided into two entities: the government and the regulatory agency. The former acts as a principal, the latter as an agent. The government maximizes public welfare (including that of the regulatory agency, industry and consumers) but has no time to collect information and design the regulation. It relies for its decisions on information from the regulatory agency. The latter supervises the regulation process. To this end, as a principal, the regulatory agency engages in side contracts with agents, that is, the industry and other interest groups. The regulatory agency is self-interested. It colludes with interest groups by hiding information and sending false reports to the government in exchange for bribes from industry and promises with respect to careers for administrative executives and so on. This can be extended if we consider that the government acts as an agent for its constituents. This also holds for representatives of industrial associations for firms.

Within this model, industrial involvement depends on the cost of bribing the regulatory agency. In order to decide whether or not they will attempt to collude with the regulatory agency, firms compare their expected pay-offs (if the regulatory agency lies to the government and thus tries to direct the regulation according to the firms' advantage) with the cost of bribing. These costs are also evaluated by the government when designing the best incentive system for encouraging the regulatory agency to tell the truth, in order to avoid collusion with industrial interests.

In short, regulatory capture occurs when information asymmetries are not eliminated and depends on the self-interested motivations of the regulatory agency and on the costs of eliminating asymmetries. Collecting information from industry and designing an incentive system are not free of charge. Usually, the implementation of an efficient incentive system is based on very sophisticated institutions and mechanisms. Therefore their costs may be higher than the value of the information they provide to principals (Farell, 1987). Information asymmetries remain, which provides scope for regulatory capture.

In the following sections we will see that the regulatory capture theory and the new economics of regulation provide a sound background for understanding industrial involvement in devising environmental policies. However, both theories assume that a firm's involvement is based on perfect rationality. Finns choose between a complete set of alternative options and have complete knowledge of the consequences of their choices. In other words, they know *ex ante* abatement costs and technology, and interest grouping and lobbying costs, as well as the regulatory pay-offs – with which their involvement will provide them. We shall see that these circumstances are not always observed since radical uncertainties sometimes prevail, especially in the case of industry–government cooperation.

3.   SUPPORT AND OBSTRUCTION

The strategies of support and obstruction are classic and well known. They have been explained extensively by the regulatory capture theory presented above.

3.1   When Firms Support Governmental Intervention

In this case firms are involved in devising environmental policies in order to derive competitive advantages. Government intervention is used to realize competitive strategies. This type of strategy is widespread in the field of environmental issues (Barrett, 1992). A good example is the catalytic converter for cars. This concerned a process which involved European car manufacturers and its outcome has been interpreted as a success for German car manufacturers' involvement in the regulatory process.

In June 1985 a European Union (EU) directive was adopted which imposed different emission standards according to engine types. As a result, unleaded petrol had to be available throughout the EU and high-powered cars had to be equipped with three-way catalytic converters. This standard was later tightened in such a way that low-powered cars also had to be equipped with three-way catalytic converters from 1993 onwards.

At that time catalytic technology for cleaning exhaust fumes had already been developed by the German car industry, whereas other car manufacturers (such as the French) had almost no experience in it. Indeed, they had concentrated their efforts on another technological development, that of the clean engine.[3] The German technological orientation was based on two facts: (1) German industry was exporting cars to the USA and had to equip them with this technology in order to meet US standards;[4] and (2) the German authorities had regulated the lead content of petrol since 1976. As a result, almost all German large-engined cars were equipped with electronic injection, which is a technological prerequisite for installing the three-way catalytic converter. Moreover, Bosch had a monopoly on the mechanical parts of three-way converter technology (Hourcade et al., 1992).

German industry and the German regulatory authorities were very cohesive in their strategy of involvement in this European process, as we shall show below. The strategy consisted of proactively pressuring the EU regulators, even by implementing national regulations, in order to steer the EU process in a particular direction.

In 1982 the so-called 'acid rain' problem emerged as a major political issue. In 1984 the German government ratified a clean-car regulation. This regulation was approved by the various German partners, including the German car manufacturers. Given that such a decision was influencing trade in the EU, it was perceived as a barrier to free trade and became a European issue. From then on, regulatory decisions on car exhaust emissions were taken at a surprisingly quick pace in the EU. In 1984, NO_x emission standards were proposed by the EU Commission. However, the choice of the means to meet this requirement remained open. No specific technology had been suggested by the EU authorities, but this important issue created two opposing groups of countries: the first group was led by the Federal Republic of Germany and the second by France. Opposition focused on the question of whether an urgent decision should be made to implement the best available technology, as suggested and implemented by the first group and the German car industry; or whether this point should remain open until a more significant range of alternative technologies was available, as argued by the second group including the French car manufacturers. In July 1984, the German authorities overstepped the confines of the ongoing negotiations by approving, with the support of the German car manufacturers, a more stringent national regulation on car exhaust emissions. Clean-engine technology had not been developed enough to comply with this new German requirement, but the three-way catalytic converter was able to meet it. In other words, the new regulation was stringent enough to require use of the three-way converter technology and electronic injection. Two months later, the EU authorities decided to adopt emission standards on exhaust fumes that led to the adoption of catalytic technology in the EU.

An important point for understanding the strategy of firms is that, at that time, there was still significant uncertainty with regard to the capacity of clean-engine technology to reduce exhaust fumes and pollution. No arguments could be levelled at its potential, but the technology was not developed enough to prove it. In such a situation, time became a strategic variable.

On the one hand, time for research on this technology could have demonstrated its potential as an alternative to the catalytic converter. The strategy of the firms and national agencies in the first group resulted precisely in slowing down the research on the clean engine. Indeed, with the new regulation, resources previously allocated to clean-engine technology had to be redirected towards catalytic converter technology. Consequently, the private advantages associated with this regulation were varied for the German party. First, the producer of the technology, Bosch, gained an extension of its market. Second, the users of the technology, the German car manufacturers, derived advantages embodied in various kinds of cost. They benefited from a learning-by-doing advantage due to their experience of this technology: German cars had already been designed as such and improved over the years (Hourcade et al., 1992). They also benefited from the resulting competitive disadvantage for French car manufacturers. The latter had to face costs related to the reappraisal of their technological strategies: they lost, at least temporarily, the potential technological advantage they had anticipated through investing in research and development on the clean engine.

On the other hand, the regulatory authorities urgently needed a technological solution to tackle the political and environmental problem. Subsequently, the choice was obviously counterbalanced by a lack of flexibility regarding the technological directions which could still have been developed at that time. However, this loss in flexibility does not seem to have been irreversible, for French car manufacturers' research and development currently focuses on a new generation of engines combining both technologies.

The catalytic converter example casts light on three features of the supporting strategy which are shared by other famous examples such as CFCs (Gabel, 1995) and phosphate-free washing powder (Barrett, 1992). First, a firm's involvement in supporting regulation is based on the technological advantages a firm or a group of firms uses in order to orientate attention in such a way that competitors will be penalized. Second, when this is successful the involvement leads to the implementation of more stringent standards than initially considered by the regulator. For instance, the catalytic converter standard had been adopted in the EU for low-powered cars, although only large-engined cars were the target at the beginning of the process. Similarly, the proactive strategy *vis-à-vis* CFC regulation had led to a revision of the Montreal Protocol towards a shortening of the phase-out period of CFCs. Third, the question of whether a firm's involvement in supporting regulation distorts public interest is unclear. The answer requires assessing the impact of these strategies on social welfare. On the one hand, since the supporting strategy leads to higher pollution reduction, social welfare will be improved. On the other hand, it is not certain whether the selected technology supported by DuPont or Bosch is the best one. The question of the relative efficiency of the catalytic converter versus the clean engine has not yet been answered.[5] This reflects the pervasive difficulty of technology assessment. Some results of the economics of technological competition (Arthur, 1988) state that, in most cases, a particular technology can only be completely assessed after its full development. We have, then, the following paradox: the adoption decision which is supposed to be based on the assessment is a prerequisite for it. Therefore, in uncertain situations, the question of the impact of firms' supporting strategies on social welfare is unanswerable.

3.2 When Firms use their Obstructive Power to Hinder Governmental Intervention

Obstructive strategies of firms in policy-making can be very active. In the example described above, French car manufacturers tried actively to put pressure on the EU Commission in order to avoid the legal adoption of the catalytic converter. This illustrates that even when processes finally reach implementation of environmental measures, some firms may follow obstructive strategies.

We shall, however, illustrate the proactive nature of these strategies with an example of firms having been successful in blocking the regulatory process and, for the time being, the implementation of environmental measures.

Influenced by a growing consensus in favour of economic instruments and under the constraint of the international political agreement of the Toronto conference,[6] the EU Commission proposed to the European Council in June 1992 the adoption of a carbon/energy tax in order to stabilize greenhouse gas emissions. The proposed tax is part of the overall climate strategy of the EU Commission. It consists of taxing the primary energies according to their content of carbon and energy in order to trigger a cost-effective set of energy-saving actions in the economic system. The tax should be compensated by member states, in a way they would have to define by themselves, in order to achieve fiscal neutrality at national level. Industry has been the only non-governmental participant involved in this process. It has developed strong opposition to the Commission's project at both national and European level, the consequence of which has been to block the regulatory process, at least temporarily.

On average, direct energy costs represent approximately 2 per cent of industrial production costs. However, energy consumption is very high for some specific sectors. These sectors are mainly the energy industry and producers of raw materials (steel, aluminium, non-ferrous metals, glass and cement) and chemical intermediaries. These industries were the ones involved in the process. They became involved after the Commission's proposal had been well developed. Before this step, industrialists believed that the fiscal approach was above all a 'brainchild' of the Commission and had no future (Ikwue and Skea, 1994). Therefore, effective and concerted attempts to stop the process took place with the Commission's formal proposal to the Council in 1992.

Industrial strategies in this process differed between the energy sector and other sectors. The energy sector was involved in the process earlier and was divided according to obvious competitive issues. The coal industry, which should be severely affected by the project, was against the idea that a set of precautionary measures had to be taken in order to prevent the greenhouse effect. The nuclear industry could anticipate a significant competitive advantage and was in favour of the fiscal measure.

The European material and chemical industries[7] agreed, for their part, that, despite the remaining controversy on the greenhouse effect and its consequences, they had to participate in precautionary measures and reduce their greenhouse gas emissions. Therefore the environmental objective was not renegotiated by them. The negotiations focused rather on how to achieve the objective. It seemed obvious to all the firms in this industry that a tax would generate significant costs for them. Anticipation of a loss, generating a competitive disadvantage on the international market, was thus a perception shared by most EU energy-intensive firms. Moreover, even if competitive issues were at stake, such as those dealing with competition between the various materials, they were carefully avoided in the negotiation. Yet the impact of a carbon/energy tax on the competition is a critical point: research has shown that it may be significant but this is still subject to uncertainty (Nadaï and Ecobilan, 1993).

On this basis, industries' strategy in the process was characterized by their cohesion and their opposition to the proposed policy. Cohesion was partly brought about by the involvement of national and international federations of industries[8] whose main positions were as follows. They argued that, in order to be efficient, the greenhouse effect policy should take account of all greenhouse gases and all economic agents and should start by enforcing the less costly actions. These corresponded, according to the industrialists, to the reduction of the other greenhouse gas emissions, to energy-saving actions in industry in the former Eastern Europe and the developing countries, and to changes in the behaviour of the final consumers. They asserted that the efficiency of the specific EU tax proposal would therefore be poor, as it would trigger a very low reduction in energy consumption and would have tremendous negative economic effects. Among these effects, the threat of relocation of part of European industry towards the non-OECD area was a central argument. Finally, they attempted to direct the process towards the negotiation of a voluntary agreement of firms to reduce greenhouse gas emissions by the year 2000. But until now industrial representatives have not succeeded in quantifying an alternative proposal.

The outcome of industrial pressure in the process consisted of modifications in the EU tax proposal in the form of: (1) a condition regarding implementation of the tax in the EU: other OECD countries have to implement similar measures or measures having similar financial effects; (2) the possibility of graduated or full exemption from the tax for firms considered to be particularly sensitive in terms of international competition; (3) the possibility for the member states of allowing companies to claim tax exemption for investments in energy or carbon dioxide emission reduction; and (4) exemption from the tax for energies used as feedstocks or renewable energies. Eventually, the carbon/energy tax proposal was dropped by the Commission.

The success of industrial pressure in this obstructive strategy has been facilitated by the fact that no pro-tax groups have been involved in the process. As argued by Ikwue and Skea (1994), in the United Kingdom even green lobbies have withdrawn from the process because of the unpopularity of this project and the unpredictability of its impact on various sections of the population. At first sight, such a tax is indeed supposed to be costly for all agents concerned (industries and final consumers), as they all consume energy. However, such a tax is always 'recycled' in the economy, be it through public expenditure, compensations by means of reductions in other taxes, or other solutions. But the way in which this 'recycling' is carried out determines which agents will finally derive advantages from the process and which will bear negative pay-offs. In the particular case of the EU carbon/energy tax, the Commission has the power to require the member states to make this tax fiscally neutral at national level, but does not have the power to force the member states to change their tax system to achieve this goal. In other words: in view of its powers, the Commission could not adjust the allocative efficiency of the tax. This has certainly made it more difficult to identify the potential beneficiaries of this process. However, even if it had been possible for the Commission, uncertainties as to assessment of the impact of this tax would have remained, and uncertainty as to the impact on the dynamics of technological innovation in firms would remain.

It is interesting to compare this case with the examples described in section 3.1, where firms were divided into strategic groups according to the pay-offs they expected to derive from regulation. In this case, industries shared an anticipation of loss through this process and were uncertain as to the possibility of a competitive advantage for some of them in the new price context. As a result, no strategic group emerged in the process and all the industries were engaged in a collective action in order to block the process: industrialists preferred the *status quo* to a change with unknown effects.

4.   SELF-REGULATION: FIRMS TAKE VOLUNTARY ACTIONS UNDER THE THREAT OF GOVERNMENTAL INTERVENTION

Public intervention is not always required to force firms to reduce pollution. Market incentives (for example, consumers' willingness to pay more for ecologically sound products) may be sufficient to direct companies towards tackling environmental issues. It may seem surprising to deal with self-regulation in a chapter devoted to analysing the involvement of firms in policy-making. However, voluntary actions by industry may also be the outcome of subtle or open pressure from public authorities. Drawing on a variety of examples, this section emphasizes that voluntary actions by industry are in fact not always voluntary. They are taken under the threat of governmental intervention in connection with market incentives. Self-regulation is a means for firms to shape their regulatory framework: voluntary actions may nip a regulation in the bud or enable industry to direct the regulatory process to its own advantage.

4.1   Voluntary Actions in Connection with Public Policies: a Few Examples

The spectrum of 'voluntary' actions is extremely broad. The behaviour of firms should be seen against a background of different regulatory anticipations and perspectives. It is simple when administrative intervention is known in advance and its outcome is certain. A classic example relate to a firm's decision to drop a product or stop a process before a ban is imposed.

In July 1988, US TV journalists reported that a pesticide called Alar, used for protecting apple trees, was carcinogenic. It triggered a wave of panic among the public and led to an intense campaign against the agrochemicals industry by green groups. Due to legal regulations, the Environment Protection Agency (EPA) is not allowed to ban a pesticide through quick procedures. The legal ban requires at least two years to be put into operation. Alar's producers were certain that the EPA would launch the procedure and that it would lead to a ban. This expectation, combined with the negative effects on the firm's reputation when continuing to sell the pesticide until the legal ban, led to the voluntary withdrawal of Alar from the market. In other words, expected losses of reputation were assumed to be greater than the benefits related to two years of sales. Nowadays, it is very common for agrochemicals companies to drop old products with small market shares when they know that these products will not be reregistered by regulators (Nadaï, 1994).

Voluntary actions of industry may also be taken to prevent governmental intervention, which may be negative for firms. In the early 1990s, concern for contaminated areas emerged in France. Very toxic industrial waste had been discovered in a privately owned landfill in Montchanin. Most of the waste had been illegally dumped by companies which could not be identified or had ceased their activities. But chlorine compound emissions continued and some inhabitants had sustained injuries. In response to such a worry, large French companies involved in highly polluting sectors such as the chemicals, oil and raw materials industries set up a collective organization, 'l'Association Française des Entreprises pour l'Environnement', to cope with such old contaminated areas. The directors of Rhône-Poulenc, Elf, Lafarge Coppée, Total, Usinor-Sacilor and so on feared that the French government would make an inequitable decision in response to green and media pressure related to Montchanin. The risk for industry was a very significant increase in the tax on industrial waste. To nip this attempt in the bud large firms committed themselves to paying fees to the association they had created to resolve the contaminated area problem. In other words, they created a private fund, which was collectively monitored by industry itself rather than by the government.

Voluntary actions and public policy may not be so closely connected. The Responsible Care Programme (RCP) of the chemicals industry is an interesting example (Cunningham, 1998). Its implementation in European countries is not in the strict sense a response to a precise threat of governmental intervention. RCP is a chemicals industry action which calls on companies to demonstrate their commitment to improving all aspects of performance relating to the protection of health, safety and the environment. It was initiated in Canada in 1985. National industry associations in several countries (for example, the United States, Australia, France and Japan) have since established programmes. The setting up of the RCP is mainly aimed at developing an environmental communication platform. The main objective of firms is to regain consumers' confidence by providing them with information. An important component of this voluntary action concerns the development of environmental performance indicators and their dissemination outside the industry. These indicators are designed to measure the environmental progress achieved by chemical firms. This marked emphasis on environmental indicators is connected with a policy issue: the Eco-audit regulation. A European directive dealing with Eco-audit was adopted in March 1993. It prescribes the environmental information a firm has to collect according to a standardized form and stipulates that this information must be certified by third parties. However, the firms' participation in this eco-audit system is voluntary and most of the information is restricted. The initial aim of European regulators was to implement a compulsory system and to ensure information dissemination. The existence of self-regulatory actions such as the RCP has provided industry with a strong argument to persuade policy-makers not to implement the legislative project they had initially conceived. Today, European chemical companies may opt for the RCP, comply with the European directive or both.

This set of examples illustrates the wide variety of voluntary actions in connection with public policy. This form of self-regulation involves individual firms or industrial associations. Initiatives take different forms; they can range from anticipatory strategies when there is only a vague threat of legislation to strong reactions from industry towards a precise regulatory project.

4.2   A Step Ahead of the Sheriff

In the absence of market incentives, firms will commit themselves to self-regulation rather than wait for public decisions only when there is a real threat from the public authorities, when the outcome of the regulation is predictable and when it is less costly. Self-regulation may be less costly for firms if, first, the pollution reduction objective corresponding to such voluntary actions is lower than the objective planned by the authorities. But this is difficult to imagine since policy-makers have no reason to agree. The unique argument would be that voluntary actions make emission reductions possible without investment in regulatory resources. The less stringent objective offered by the self-regulation alternative may therefore be viewed as the counterpart to this administrative saving (Stranlund, 1995). Second, self-regulation provides flexibility, which allows companies to pursue the environmental objective in a more efficient manner. This is an alternative for firms to avoid bureaucratic red tape. Third, since the public authorities are not directly involved, the private information of firms is less published outside the industry. Despite these advantages, firms have to bear the organizational costs in taking voluntary action. Moreover, by making the first move, the industry will lose a few years of not paying the abatement costs while waiting for a public decision.

Thus it is clear that such a case requires very specific and low probability conditions. Public decision outcomes in the field of the environment are difficult to forecast. It is not certain that voluntary actions are less costly for firms and prove successful. Policy-makers may pursue their plans and ignore the progress achieved through self-regulation. Finally, voluntary actions involving several competing firms may fail because of free-riding.

Other arguments are required to explain voluntary actions connected with public policy. First, institutional aspects are worth considering. Voluntary actions reduce the pressure of government to overlegislate and increase the confidence of policy-makers in industry. When public authorities suspect industry of not being able to cope with environmental issues, voluntary actions are a means to regain the policy-makers' confidence in industry. Company initiatives may also counterbalance pressure on policy-makers of the green movement. More generally, voluntary actions contribute to changes in regulatory style or the policy-making regime. Through the reputation gains *vis-à-vis* policy-makers they provide, such actions facilitate evolution from authoritative policy-making to approaches with more consensus.

Second, voluntary actions provide advantages for the initiator *vis-à-vis* policy-makers and other interested parties. Self-regulation must not be looked upon only as an alternative to public legislation. In other words, voluntary actions are not only aimed at nipping a regulation in the bud and eliminating the prospect of legal measures. Voluntary actions may delay a regulation and may be accepted by public authorities as a temporary measure. They reduce pressure from media and green groups, which can lead to urgent but unsound public decisions. Self-regulation is therefore a first step. This is demonstrated by the case of contaminated areas in France (and also in the case of car recycling, see section 6). The voluntary action of major French firms has given birth to a contractual agreement between government and industry. The fund is now managed by companies in cooperation with a public agency and there is a financial contribution from the state. Generally speaking, by making the first move, industry can ensure its leadership in formulating the problem to be solved and defining the appropriate response. This directs the subject of discussions between all the interested parties and the agenda of the policy-setting process. Finally, as highlighted by the case of RCPs, voluntary actions put industry in a better position to bargain and negotiate with public authorities.

Third, voluntary actions not only respond to pressure from a public authority. Incentives from the market and the threat of regulation are closely related and will be examined in the next section.

4.3 Regulatory Pressure and Market Incentives

In our opinion, the threat of public intervention is not sufficient to force firms to self-regulation. The benefits for firms of making the first move are difficult to assess. This is because the precise content of the legal alternative is rarely known in advance and the advantages of being a step ahead of the sheriff are difficult to measure, while the costs of this are obvious, that is, the paying of abatement costs before a legal measure compels firms to do so.

Empirical evidence shows that voluntary actions that take place under the threat of governmental intervention are connected with market and reputation incentives. Public authority pressure is complementary to market incentives. When the latter are not sufficient to lead to voluntary reduction of pollution, a regulatory threat will push firms to self-regulation. This is an important means of reducing pollution when pure market incentives do not seem to be strong enough. Green product standards (that is, a standard set unilaterally by firms as opposed to eco-labels, which are set bilaterally by civil service and industry) are a good example. In the absence of any driving force other than market reputation, the adoption of these standards is limited to a few cases. Dolphin-friendly tuna, phosphate-free washing powders and non-tropical timber furniture have been adopted since everybody is currently supposed to be keen on dolphins, clean rivers and the Amazonian forest. The consumers' willingness to pay is apparent. When environmental concern is less sensitive, other incentives such as public authority pressure are required (Lévêque, 1995).

To conclude, the distinction between self-regulation originated by policy-makers or market forces is often blurred. In both cases, industry takes environmental measures in the absence of existing legislation. However, in one case public authorities play an indirect but significant role, while in the other they do not exert any influence. Despite this, it is relevant to emphasize voluntary actions since, as has been shown above, self-regulation is a means for firms to shape their regulatory framework: voluntary actions may nip a regulation in the bud or enable industry to direct the regulatory process to its own advantage.

5. WHEN FIRMS COOPERATE WITH THE GOVERNMENT IN DEVISING ENVIRONMENTAL POLICIES

If we assume that, in most cases, pollution reduction incurs costs for industry, it might seem strange that industry would cooperate with regulators. The aim of this section is to identify the circumstances and the reasons that account for such behaviour. Cooperation between industry and government can result in two policy instruments: regulation cum negotiation and voluntary agreements.

Regulation cum negotiation relates to the imposition of compulsory standards (including bans) by administrative bodies. It is close to the traditional command and control approach, except that the policy has been negotiated with all parties. Legislation is preceded by a bargaining phase relating to the pollution reduction objective and the measures by which it can be achieved.

A voluntary agreement is a contract between public authorities and industry. Generally speaking, the public authorities are the central government and the industrial parties are trade associations or industrial organizations. Within this bilateral setting, industry promises to meet a number of environmental objectives within a certain period of time. The government promises to refrain from imposing a regulation on the points dealt with in the contract before its expiry, but generally this promise is only an informal one. In general, voluntary agreements do not have legal sanctions in the case of non-compliance. This absence of any formal system of sanctions is compensated for to some extent by the existence of an informal sanction: if the contract is not respected, a regulatory arrangement, potentially more costly for the firms, will be introduced by the administration.

The main difference between the two instruments mentioned concerns their legal nature. Despite this difference, as pointed out by Glachant (1994), they are very similar since both are based on negotiations between industry and government.

5.1 Two Examples of Cooperation

Industry–government cooperation concerns the pollution reduction objective, the measures to achieve it, or both. It corresponds with a general pattern in policy-making in countries such as The Netherlands, or it takes place to cope with specific environmental concerns, in particular those related to waste recycling (for example, scrapped motor vehicles and discarded packaging).

The target group approach in The Netherlands
Setting and implementing environmental policy in partnership with industry is quite general in The Netherlands. In comparison with unilateral governmental

measures, those which are taken in cooperation with industry account for more than 80 per cent of the overall pollution reduction objective stated in the National Environmental Policy Plan. In accordance with this plan, published in 1989, a so-called target group strategy was implemented. This consists of setting up groups which bring together the relevant public authorities, business organizations and sectors in charge of making operational environmental targets put forward in the national plan. There is close cooperation between industry and government. Indeed, within these target groups, industry is involved in setting objectives and taking measures, as well as in control procedures.

For a given target (for example, reduction of volatile organic compounds (VOCs), see below), industry establishes a programme together with the authorities. This includes the pollution reduction objective and the conditions (with regard to technological, environmental and economical feasibility and to international agreements) which have to be met in order for it to be achieved. After this strategic discussion and negotiation, a project organization bringing together business representatives and public authorities is set up. It is entrusted with implementation of the programme. Within these project organizations, industry is therefore involved in formulating the implementation measures with respect to the relevant industrial sectors and individual firms. It is worth noting that industry also has a say in whether conditions for specific measures have been met and, accordingly, whether a further reduction in pollution can be implemented. Finally, industry is also associated with the authorities in controlling and assessing the progress achieved.

Within the target group approach, pollution reduction is not compulsory in a legal sense. Nevertheless, the Environment Directorate still has the possibility of using a general administrative order to make obligatory the implementation of measures decided upon by the target groups.

The KWS 2000 project provides a good illustration of this approach. It is aimed at the reduction of VOCs related to stationary sources. The pollution is mainly caused by all kinds of painting activities and the production and distribution of petrol and petroleum products.

With regard to paints, the KWS project focuses on product innovation, in which organic solvent-based paints are replaced by water-based paints. The paint target group gathers together all the participants of the chain, starting from the raw material producers (for example, the chemical industry) to users belonging to major industries (for example, car manufacturers) as well as to very small ones. Indeed, a change in the composition of paint concerns the industry, which has to develop different basic products, and the users, who have to accept changes in application, duration and appearance. Since the market trend has already been directed towards increasing the use of water-based paints, the issue has not been whether it is possible to use low-solvent paint but in which circumstances, at what pace and in what specific applications these alternative paints can be introduced. The consensus within the target group regarding objectives, conditions and implementation measures has been easily reached. Pilot and demonstration projects of various kinds of paint application have been launched with public financial support.

With respect to petroleum products, KWS 2000 is directed to reducing VOC emissions from the refining stage to the individual automobile. It focuses on the recovery of vapours that escape in various stages during the production and distribution process. The target group mainly includes large companies in the petroleum and automobile sector. Here, the abatement costs for firms are very high. In the absence of economic advantages to reduce pollution, consensus has been very difficult to achieve. The decision-making process related to the reduction of VOC emissions at the petrol station is noteworthy. There are two options. The first is to install a carbon canister on motor vehicles that absorbs vapour. The second is to install vapour balance systems in the petrol pump filling hoses. Obviously, oil companies support the canister system (that is, the first option) and car manufacturers the pump system (that is, the second option). Neither of the parties wants to bear the investment costs. In the absence of consensus, the target group has therefore postponed the decision. It has been explicitly stated that the choice between the two options will depend on international environmental policies, in particular the future regulation adopted in Germany. The Dutch government was in favour of the pump system but seems not to have been capable of imposing a decision on the oil companies. In 1991 the German government cut the knot in favour of the pump system and a general administrative order was established to adopt this technical standard.

Car recycling

In March 1993 a contractual agreement was signed by the French Ministry of the Environment and an industrial consortium of car manufacturers, motor vehicle suppliers, breakers and scrappers. The industry committed itself to reducing waste disposal to a maximum of 15 per cent per car as from 2002 (on a weight basis). This cooperative arrangement was the outcome of a process that lasted four years (Whiston and Glachant, 1996).

The disposal of cars attracted the attention of French policy-makers in 1989. This occurred within the framework of general environmental concern regarding the increase in waste production and the scarcity of landfilling facilities due to the NIMBY syndrome (not in my back yard). Motor vehicles were then looked upon as the prime waste problem to be solved (car disposals account for only 4 per cent of all waste but represent around 2.5 million tons per year). Initially, the positions of policy-makers and industry were strongly opposed. The former were envisaging a very stringent regulation whereas the latter were contesting the setting of any regulation.

Nevertheless, the threat of future legislation related to car waste disposal in connection with reputation incentives directed French car manufacturers towards taking voluntary action. For instance, Peugeot (including Citroën) has cooperated with CFF (the largest scrapping company in France) and Vicat (a cement works) in a pilot project for treating discarded automobiles. A pilot plant was built at Saint-Pierre de Chandieu, near Lyon, to handle three stages: the draining and dismantling of cars, scrapping of the wrecks and treatment of scrap residue (Den Hond and Groenewegen, 1993).

These company actions were accelerated in 1990 with the announcement of a strict German bill. The precedent of the catalytic converters, interpreted in France as a victory for German car manufacturers, was still very much in mind. The member state of the EU that introduces a policy first will have the advantage of influencing the contents of a future European directive. French companies and policy-makers were both upset by the German announcement, which speeded up convergence between the two parties. Moreover, the pilot projects undertaken by firms had demonstrated that reducing the amount of scrap waste was very costly and called for technological and organizational innovations. Several innovative solutions were envisaged, but they were difficult to assess and select *ex ante*. As pointed out by Aggeri and Hatchuel (1999), knowing which network of collecting scrapped vehicles should be established, the price of dismantling vehicles and to what point should they be dismantled, whether the recycling of polymers should be chemical or mechanical, whether profitable and sustainable markets for recycled parts exist and so forth, are all challenges which are still open and on which no one has a definitive position.

On this new basis, regulators and industry agreed on a flexible policy and the mutual contract of March 1993 was ratified.

Another classic example dealing with recycling is provided by the case of packaging waste. The implementation of the packaging waste consortium Eco-Emballage S.A. in France is the outcome of a regulatory process which was based on administrative and industrial partnership (Whiston and Glachant, 1996).

5.2   Cost-economizing, Network Economies and Learning Effects

The KWS 2000 and car recycling examples indicate the advantages firms have when they cooperate with policy-makers. First, in return for its cooperation, industry obtains a generous timescale and a reasonable certainty that government policy will not change in the decade to come because an intensification of government objectives is a low probability. Second, programme phasing gives firms the possibility of fitting abatement measures into their own investment schedule and of solving the remaining technical problems. Moreover, in relation to the KWS project, by participating in the decision-making process, firms are able to influence the kinds of measure that are to be taken and the conditions that have to be met before environmental measures have to be implemented. The conditions applicable to the implementation reduce the likelihood that the objectives will be achieved, but these conditions increase flexibility during the implementation period. Third, as the petrol station case adequately suggests, firms are not locked in cooperation; they can escape from the consensus approach and use their obstructive power. If gains from cooperation with the public authorities happen to be lower than expected, firms can refocus their regulatory strategy. Generally speaking, cooperation with public policy enables firms to negotiate and thus limit the pollution reduction objective and promote cost-cutting solutions to reach this objective.

One can also observe that to obtain these advantages collective action on the part of firms is necessary, and is required in the negotiation phase of the pollution reduction objective. Firms must exchange information on pollution emissions and abatement costs before giving a mandate to their representatives in charge of negotiations within committees. Cooperation increases the bargaining power of firms and results in economies of scale by lobbying.

Moreover, cost-economizing solutions may require inter-firm cooperation, since operational measures to achieve pollution reduction frequently involve various firms in different industries and thus lead to network economies. A good example is given by the case of packaging waste.

The cost of transporting waste is high and the packaging waste resource is atomized and heterogeneous. Many network economies are involved in collecting and sorting. As a consequence, an individual waste-producing firm has no interest in implementing its own specific post-consumption system. As pointed out by Lévêque (1995), the market would be inefficient in achieving a reasonable level of network economies. Letting firms organize themselves to cope with the negotiated objective would have led to the following scenario. Each homogeneous group of packaging firms sets up its specific waste system and competes to pre-empt the limited capacity of consumers in sorting. Thus the packaging waste recovery and recycling industry is divided into numerous branches and sub-branches specializing in different material/product combinations (recovery and recycling systems of glass bottles, plastic receptacles, ferrous soft drink cans, aluminium cans, composite beverage packaging, and so on). There are at least a dozen waste containers per household, apartment block or supermarket, and consumers waste a lot of time in sorting waste. The number of containers equals the number of specialized systems, which equals the high number of cooperative networks self-regulation provides.

This scenario is based on the idea that although a small number of large networks provide a higher collective gain for industry, free-riding impedes the setting up of such large cooperative organizations.[9] As a third party, public authorities may encourage or force the adoption of the inter-firm cooperative solution. The authorities can offer compensatory payments to firms, which have fewer interests in cooperation. They can also prevent free riding by using their coercive power or by introducing specific procedures and rules.[10]

It is also important to emphasize that voluntary agreements between industry and government presented in this section are the outcomes of a learning process. They reflect the state of initial uncertainty experienced by firms and public authorities.

As to car recycling, initial uncertainty is fourfold. First, the future state of legislation is not known in advance, particularly with respect to its stringency (that is, the quantitative objective of recycling), the liability principle and cost-sharing (that is, who will be responsible for paying – the owner of the vehicle, the last holder or the manufacturer?). Second, technology is embryonic. Several technological options are open, ranging from the very labour-intensive (which corresponds to a high degree of dismantling) to the use of melt reactors which separate the steel contents by means of energy emitted from organic components of cars. Third, a high level of economic uncertainty prevails as to recycling costs, the sensitivity of buyers to greener motor vehicles and the future extent of competition between manufacturers on recycling. Finally, there are organizational uncertainties. The future recovery and recycling system may be based on the current waste network (which includes breakers) or on a new system in which dismantling is controlled by car manufacturers and scrapping companies (Den Hond and Groenewegen, 1993). Moreover, within a company the setting up of a coherent internal organization is required which interlinks dismantling, design and supplying operations. In these conditions, 'there does not exist an asymmetry of information, but shared uncertainties between industrialists and between industrialists and the public authorities' (Agerri and Hatchuel, 1999). Thanks to pilot projects and practical experiments connected with the policy-making process, information is gradually collected and exchanged, and firms as well as regulators specify their preferences.

In the absence of a probability distribution of the future state of nature, decision-makers are unable to choose between different options. In such a context it is advisable not to make irreversible decisions, but rather to postpone them until a learning phase has provided sufficient knowledge for making the best choices. Industry–government cooperation is therefore a response to uncertainties to such an extent that it provides space for a learning process and can thus ensure dynamic flexibility.

As a conclusion, the circumstances and the company pay-offs related to cooperation with government can be stylized as follows. First, both parties (industry and public authorities) are confronted with informational uncertainties rather than informational asymmetries. As empirical evidence shows, the problem to be coped with is new for policy-makers and firms. Ready-to-use solutions are not available. Solving the problem calls for new technologies and organizations, which cannot be selected ex *ante* because information regarding their feasibility and performance is not available. Second, inter-firm cooperation takes place within cooperation between industry and the public authorities. Third, cooperation with government benefits firms because of the learning effects. Finally, public authorities facilitate harnessing of external economies of scale.

Not surprisingly, the advantages for firms due to the cooperative pattern are those between market and hierarchy. In a context of high uncertainties and network economies, this form of policy governance provides higher collective gains than the market form and higher flexibility than direct regulation through command and control.

6.   CONCLUSION

6.1   In what Circumstances does a Firm's Involvement Take Place?

Figure 8.1 summarizes the specific circumstances which characterize the different forms of a firm's involvement in devising environmental policies. The starting-point is prompted by the existence of a threat of government intervention. If the public authorities do not pose a threat (or if the threat is not credible), firms do not move. Indeed, as stated in section 4, pollution reduction prompted only by market incentives or by public opinion and green group pressure is beyond the scope of this chapter. When the threat of government intervention is credible (that is, government plans to regulate industry and impose legislation on polluting firms), two cases must be considered according to *ex ante* uncertainties.

In the first case, the policy-makers' willingness is perceived by firms but there is radical uncertainty as to the pollution reduction objective and implementation measures. Even policy-makers do not know which route to follow. They only know that environmental issues should be tackled (for example, because of the intensity of pressure from the media, green groups and public opinion). As a consequence, firms are unable to assess their losses or gains in respect of future legislation. It is in these circumstances that industry–government cooperation takes place.

In the second case, the content of environmental policies may be anticipated by firms. The pollution reduction objectives and the regulatory measures to achieve them may be forecast, at least in terms of a distribution of probability. Moreover, according to each policy scenario they anticipate, firms can evaluate their future abatement costs and competitive gains or losses. Depending on market and reputation incentives, particularly via final consumers, green groups and residents' associations, voluntary action or supporting (or obstructing) of regulation will come into play.

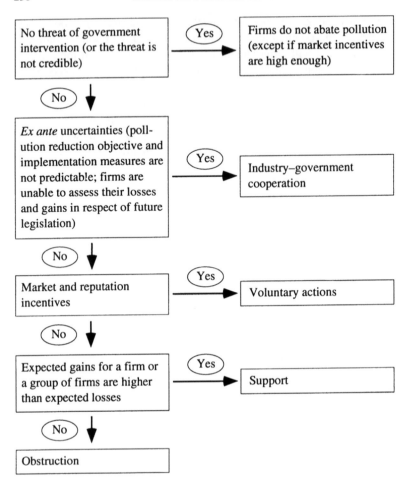

Figure 8.1   The circumstances and forms of a firm's involvement in policy-making

Firms should make a first move if the voluntary action they take to reduce pollution is less costly than the anticipated legal alternatives. We argued in section 4 that such a decision under the threat of public intervention cannot be envisaged in the absence of other incentives, since by taking the initiative they begin to pay abatement costs instead of postponing such expenditures until legislation comes into force.

Finally, if public authority intervention is the only stimulus for a firm to act, individual companies or industrial coalitions will support or obstruct the imposition of environmental policies according to their expected gains and losses, as put forward by the regulatory capture theory.

6.2 What are the Pay-offs of a Firm's Involvement?

The pay-offs for firms are fourfold. First, firms can limit the abatement costs. This applies in the cases of voluntary actions, obstruction and cooperation. With voluntary actions, this limitation is mainly obtained via the cost-cutting route to achieve the pollution reduction objective provided by self-regulation. Self-regulation provides flexibility, which allows companies to pursue environmental objectives in a more efficient manner (see section 3). Obstruction enables firms to limit the reduction pollution objective, which also holds for cooperation. Empirical evidence (see section 5) shows that negotiation with the authorities leads to the adoption of an environmental goal which is more limited than the objective initially supported by policy-makers. Moreover, cooperation also ensures flexibility as to implementation measures and the time horizon.

Second, a firm's involvement may provide a competitive advantage (see, Gabel, 1995). This happens when a firm or a group of firms supports government intervention. In this case, an increase in environmental expenditure for industry as a whole is observed, since regulators are encouraged to adopt more stringent standards by the leading firms in technological competition.

Third, government intervention may also provide a pay-off to industry, which is similar to a public good. For instance, in relation to packaging waste, the involvement of the authorities has created greater network economies than those that would have been provided by the market (see section 5). Government intervention was more efficient than the market and this benefited industry.[11]

Finally, besides these advantages related to each elementary strategy, the pay-offs of a firm's involvement must be assessed by considering the entire process, not just a particular step. In this chapter the different forms of a firm's involvement have been examined separately and from a static point of view. In the real world, firms' strategies change within the process of devising environmental policies. The forms of a firm's involvement are interconnected. For instance, as pointed out in section 4, voluntary actions may be followed by the setting up of environmental legislation. As we pointed out, in such a case one cannot say that a firm's strategy has failed. Indeed, the taking of voluntary action has facilitated subsequent strategic action, such as supporting a more stringent regulation to eliminate competitors (for example, DuPont's lobbying in CFC policies; see Gabel, 1995); or obstructing the setting up of an unwelcome measure (for example, RCP versus European Eco-Audit Programme; see also section 4). Another example is cooperation. Cooperation may be followed by obstruction. For instance, initially oil companies cooperated with the Dutch

Environment Directorate for the reduction of VOCs, but in the second stage they hampered the setting up of measures to be implemented (see section 5).

6.3   Does a Firm's Involvement Distort Public Interest?

A widely shared intuition is that a firm's involvement in the devising of public policies leads to a distortion of public interest. This explains why voluntary agreements between industry and government give rise to problems of accept-ability by public opinion (Carraro and Lévêque, 1999). For instance, the influence of business representatives on public decision-making is under discussion in The Netherlands. This is reinforced by the minor role the third party (such as environmental and consumers' associations) plays in the target group approach. According to economic theories of regulation, this issue has been the subject of controversy.

The regulatory capture model of Stigler (1971) assumes that the setting up of public policy is only governed by private interests. Among private interests, those of firms are best represented since collective action is easier for industry than for atomized and heterogeneous agents such as consumers or citizens. Other economists consider that policy-makers aim both at increasing social welfare and at satisfying private interests (Keeler, 1984) and point out that the maximization of social welfare can be ensured by rivalry among interest groups (Noll, 1989).

The new economics of regulation states that regulators are obliged to collect private information that firms possess on abatement costs and polluting emissions. Governments are therefore faced with adverse selection. Several sophisticated mechanisms have been devised to force firms to reveal true information. However, these mechanisms are rarely implemented because their costs are very high. As a consequence, the consultative and interactive process between industry and government provides only part of the information policy-makers need. This distorts social welfare since adverse selection is imperfectly overcome.

Empirical insights into a firm's strategic actions in devising environmental policies do not cut the knot between these different theories. However, they do cast light on three issues. A firm's involvement undoubtedly allows scope for regulatory capture, particularly when regulatory pay-offs can be anticipated. However, a firm's involvement may pursue other goals, as demonstrated in the case of cooperation. Firms themselves may need government intervention to tackle problems the market cannot always solve, in particular to reduce uncertainties and to limit free-riding. A firm's involvement in the devising of environmental policies and hence the risk of regulatory capture by industry cannot be avoided. The objective for policy-makers is to attempt to limit regulatory capture by establishing *ad hoc* rules and procedures, rather than to restrict a firm's involvement.

Traditionally, efficiency issues in relation to environmental policies have been addressed by policy-makers and scholars by comparing different policy instruments (for example, taxes, subsidies and standards) and examining how economic agents will react to them. This approach is not adequate. As emphasized here, the efficiency of public policy will also depend on the regulatory process, whatever the instruments adopted, since the degree of regulatory capture is determined within this process.

FURTHER READING

There are today a few elementary books that deal with a firm's involvement in the regulatory process. We especially recommend the following:

Owen, B.M. and R. Braeutigan (1978), *The Regulation Game*, Cambridge, MA: Ballinger Publishing Company.
Lévêque, F. (1996), *Environmental Policy in Europe: Industry, Competition and the Policy Process*, Cheltenham, UK and Brookfield, USA: Edward Elgar.

As to the literature related to interest groups, the seminal book (not recent but still very interesting) is:

Olson, M. (1965), *The Logic of Collective Action*, Cambridge, MA: Harvard University Press.

The reference book on the new economics of regulation is:

Laffont, J.J. and J. Tirole (1993), *A Theory of Incentives in Procurement and Regulation*, Cambridge, MA: MIT Press.

A recent book on voluntary actions of industry in pollution abatement is:

Carraro, C. and F. Lévêque (eds) (1999), *Voluntary Approaches in Environmental Policy*, The FEEM/KLUWER International Series on Economics, Energy and Environment, Netherlands: Kluwer Academic Publishers.

NOTES

1. The agency theory is presented in Chapter 15.
2. An agency relationship is when:
   - two individuals are involved, the so-called principal and the agent;

- the agent can choose an action from a given range of possibilities;
- the action affects the welfare of both the principal and the agent;
- the action of the agent is difficult for the principal to observe;
- the principal prescribes *ex ante* the pay-offs, depending on the result of the action observed by the principal.

Agency relationships are very pervasive in the economic realm, for example, a doctor and his patient, an insurance company and its client.

3. Clean engines consume petrol enriched with oxygen, so that their fuel consumption is reduced by up to 20 per cent.
4. The three-way catalytic converter was introduced and generalized in the United States in the mid-1970s in order to reduce NO_x emissions. Indeed, the increasing number of private cars triggered US regulatory authorities to regulate exhaust fume emissions very early (in the 1950s).
5. Nor has the question of HCFCs versus HFCs as substitutes for CFCs – see Gabel (1995).
6. The agreement stated the objective of reducing the amount of carbon dioxide emissions by 20 per cent by the year 2005.
7. These are concentrated and relatively homogeneous regarding their technologies in each industrial branch, and economically powerful in some European countries. France is one of them. Its energy-intensive industry accounts for 25 per cent of carbon dioxide emissions, 20 per cent of added value and 19.5 per cent of employment (Giraud et al., 1992).
8. Such as CEFIC (chemicals), UNICE (European Employers' Confederation), BDI (Confederation of German Industry) and the CBI (Confederation of British Industry).
9. Without government intervention, the equity allocation in a single company and the setting of differentiated prices according to materials and products would have been difficult to achieve. Informational asymmetries between firms and uncertainties related to the future price of materials impede such a collective agreement. Moreover, some producers have already implemented networks for collecting discarded packaging (for example, glass and paper packaging). There are no private incentives for them to join the new organization.
10. For instance, within packaging waste consortia such as Eco-Emballage in France and DSD in Germany, the ownership and use of the compatible standard is separated (that is, the standard is owned by the waste consortium) which avoids free-riding problems (Gabel, 1987). A green dot makes it easy to identify products belonging to firms that participate in the network, and thus provides a means for excluding recovery of discarded packaging generated by outsiders.
11. Another example is provided by the case of eco-labels. As pointed out by Lévêque (1995), public authority intervention ensures a gain in credibility *vis-à-vis* green products (the label is guaranteed by a public institution, not only by firms) and secures reputation trade-offs (when an agreement is reached on the features of the eco-label, *ex post* controversies, and hence the destruction of reputation by competitors, are more unlikely).

REFERENCES

Aggeri, F. and A. Hatchuel (1999), 'A dynamic model of environmental policies. The case of innovation oriented voluntary agreements', in C. Carraro and F. Lévêque (eds), *Voluntary Approaches in Environmental Policy*, The FEEM/KLUWER International Series on Economics, Energy and Environment, Netherlands: Kluwer Academic Publishers, 151–85.

Arthur, W.B. (1988), 'Competing technologies: an overview', in G. Dosi et al. (eds), *Technical Change and Economic Theory*, London: Pinter.

Barrett, S. (1992), 'Strategy and the environment', *Columbia Journal of World Business*, Fall and Winter.

Carraro, C. and F. Lévêque (1999), 'The rational and potential of voluntary approaches', in C. Carraro and F. Lévêque (eds), *Voluntary Approaches in Environmental Policy*, Kluwer Academic Publishers, pp. 1–15.

Cunningham, N. (1998), 'The chemical industry', in N. Cunningham and P. Grabosky (eds), *Smart Regulation – Designing Environmental Policy*, Oxford: Clarendon Press, pp. 135–265.

Farell, J. (1987), 'Information and the Coase Theorem', *Economic Perspectives*, **1** (2), Fall, 113–29.

Gabel, H.L. (1995), 'Environmental management as a competitive strategy: the case of CFCs', in H. Folmer, H.L. Gabel and H. Opschoor (eds), *Principles of Environmental and Resource Economics*, Aldershot, UK and Brookfield, USA: Edward Elgar.

Giraud, P.N., A. Nadaï and C. Charbit (1992), *Taxation des émissions de CO_2 et compétitivité de l'industrie en France*, Paris: Cerna, ADEME, Ministère de l'environnement.

Glachant, M. (1994), 'The setting of voluntary agreements between the industry and the government: bargaining and efficiency', *Business Strategy and the Environment*, **3** (2), Summer.

Hond, F. den and P. Groenewegen (1993), 'Solving the automobile shredder waste problem: cooperation among firms in the automotive industry', in K. Fischer and J. Schot (eds), *Environmental Strategies for Industry*, Washington, DC: Island Press, pp. 43–62.

Hourcade, J.C., J.M. Salles and D. Thery (1992), 'Ecological economics and scientific controversies: lessons from some recent policy making in the EEC', *Ecological Economics*, **6**, 211–23.

Ikwue, T. and J. Skea (1994), 'Business and the genesis of the European Community carbon tax proposal', *Business Strategy and the Environment*, **3** (2), Summer.

Keeler, T.E. (1984), 'Theories of regulation and the deregulation movement', *Public Choice*, **44**, 103–45.

Laffont, J.J. and J. Tirole (1991), 'The politics of government decision-making: a theory of regulatory capture', *Quarterly Journal of Economics*, **LVI**(4), 1089–127.

Laffont, J.J. and J. Tirole (1993), *A Theory of Incentives in Procurement and Regulation*, Cambridge, MA: MIT Press.

Lévêque, F. (1995), 'Standards and standards-setting processes in the field of environment', in R. Hawkins, R. Mansell and J. Skea (eds), *Standards, Innovation and Competitiveness*, Aldershot: Edward Elgar.

Nadaï, A. (1994), 'The greening of the EC agrochemical market: regulation and competition', *Business Strategy and the Environment*, **3** (2), Summer.

Noll, R.G. (1989), 'Economic perspectives on the politics of regulation', in Richard Schmalensee and Robert D. Willig (eds), *Handbook of Industrial Organization*, Vol. II, Amsterdam: North-Holland, pp. 1254–87.

Olson, M. (1965), *The Logic of Collective Action: Public Goods and the Theory of Groups*, Harvard Economic Studies, Vol. CXXIV, Cambridge, MA: Harvard University Press.

Peltzman, S. (1976), 'Toward a more general theory of regulation', *Journal of Law and Economics*, **19**, 211–40.

Spulber, D.F. (1989), *Regulation and Markets*, Cambridge, MA: MIT Press.

Stigler, G.J. (1971), 'The theory of economic regulation', *Bell Journal of Economic and Management Science*, **2** (1), Spring, 3–21.

Stranlund, J. K. (1995), 'Public mechanisms to support compliance to an environmental norm', *Journal of Environmental Economics and Management*, **28**, 205–22.

Whiston, T. and M. Glachant (1996), 'Voluntary agreements between industry and government: the case of recycling regulation', in F Lévêque (ed.), *Environmental Policy in Europe: Industry Competition and the Policy Process*, Cheltenham, UK and Northampton, MA: Edward Elgar. pp. 142–73.

9. Corporate responses to environmental concerns

H. Landis Gabel and
Bernard Sinclair-Desgagné

1. INTRODUCTION

Most environmental resources are allocated by managers within firms. According to some recent studies by the United Nations, the world's 500 largest companies are responsible for 70 per cent of world trade, 60 per cent of foreign investment and 30 per cent of world gross domestic product.[1] Hence, as customers, communities, private organizations and governments are becoming more sensitive to environmental issues, there is increasing pressure on firms to be environmentally careful. Firms are especially vulnerable nowadays to stringent public policies, severe lawsuits, or widespread customer boycotts which are likely to hit the environmentally complacent: the opening, integration and globalization of markets have greatly intensified competition. Concerned with securing their long-term viability, several companies have thus determined to make proactive investments, that is, anticipatory as opposed to reactive or mandated investments, in appropriate technologies and management systems. In the latter sphere, however, although a wealth of individual experience and specific solutions is available, there is a lack of overall environmental and economic concepts covering all functions of a company and yielding concrete recommendations for action.

This chapter discusses several systems of incentives and controls that firms may use in order to improve their management of environmental resources and to facilitate compliance with environmental regulations.

The traditional literature in environmental economics adopts a 'black box' view of the firm. According to this view, a firm is fully described by its production technology (or its cost function) and its competitive position in markets for inputs and outputs. The manager's only task is to use these data to compute an activity level that maximizes profit. All the information necessary to perform such a calculation is assumed to be available. Once the appropriate activity level is found, it is automatically implemented. In other words, what many see as the main challenges faced by a manager are assumed away.

In this traditional view, violations of environmental laws or standards only take place because the firm purposely chooses to violate them, that is, because the violations are expected to be profitable. Yet although it would be naïve to think that no violations are ever committed on purpose, it is equally unrealistic to believe that they are all the result of criminal will. A different view of the firm might grant that complex organizations occasionally make mistakes. That is, there are differences between the objectives of a firm's senior management and the actions of its employees. Furthermore, organizational failure might be causally linked to the firm's management systems.

One approach along these lines sees the firm as a collection of assets (see Hart, 1996 and the references therein). From this viewpoint, the manager and the firm put at each other's disposal some assets (for example the manager's skills and knowledge, the firm's office space and computers) that they own. It matters to a manager's actions who owns which asset. For example, a manager who is given some discretion on the use of a valuable resource will tend to drain that resource ('milk the cow') if its owner is the firm or someone else. With the creation and diffusion of tradable permits and markets for pollution rights, the environment is *de facto* becoming an asset. A 'property-right' view of the firm may then lead to some concrete suggestions concerning the design of contracts and the appropriate dispersion of environmental ownership between firm members. We will come back to this issue later in the chapter. This approach, however, has little to say about coordination, hierarchy and delegation.

It has also been argued (DeCanio, 1993, Gabel and Sinclair-Desgagné, 1993) that when the environment matters, one can fruitfully see the firm as a network of agency relationships. The division of labour within the firm implies the presence, explicitly or implicitly, of lines of authority and communication linking firm members. Those who have authority over others for the achievement of a given set of tasks are called principals; their subordinates are called agents. A key postulate is that a principal can only monitor the agents' performance imperfectly and indirectly. This informational problem characterizes agency relationships. One can see that in a multi-divisional firm, line managers are simultaneously principals for a group of workers and agents for some senior executives. Most firms are then truly fabrics of intertwined agencies. In the next section we will consider several managerial systems from this viewpoint.

The reader should be aware that we do not pretend to obtain new results or to present another survey of the now abundant literature on the economic theory of the firm.[2] Our intention is rather to emphasize some existing propositions that we deem useful for the implementation of corporate environmental strategies, and to make some plausible conjectures that are likely to be the focus of further research in this area.

The chapter outline is as follows. Section 2 is devoted to assessing various incentive and control systems of firms. Section 3 looks briefly at the issue of allocating property rights for environmental resources. Section 4 contains our final remarks and conclusions.

2. SYSTEMS OF CORPORATE INCENTIVES AND CONTROLS

Assume that, for whatever reason, a firm's principal wants to improve the firm's environmental performance. This could include reduced emissions into air or water, reduced environmental damage by the firm's products when used by customers, or reduced risk of an environmental accident. Characteristic of all these goals is that they are expensive in either money or time. Furthermore, the expenses are easily identified and they are in the present. Against them is set a benefit that is difficult to observe and quantify, perhaps probabilistic, and often realized in the future. The firm's principal wants improved performance, but the decisions that determine performance are made by employees (agents) who are motivated by self-interest. The principal, of course, controls the firm's rules of compensation and punishment and its technology of monitoring the agents' actions. But monitoring is imperfect and costly. How can the principal fashion the firm's systems of incentives and controls to optimize its financial and environmental performance?

Below, we consider several well-known managerial systems that are often mentioned by top executives and public policy-makers eager to slow down environmental depletion and to reduce the risks of environmental accidents. These systems include the compensation system, monitoring and auditing of non-financial objectives, internal pricing, horizontal task restructuring, centralization versus decentralization of decision-making, corporate sanctions, corporate culture and human resource management. This list is certainly not exhaustive. It includes those managerial systems about which the current knowledge of the economics of firms allows one to make overall and concrete, yet preliminary, recommendations.

2.1 The Compensation System

In Gabel and Sinclair-Desgagné (1993), we explored the extent to which an incentive-based compensation system could be used to deal with the multi-task principal–agent problem. The setting is one in which an agent allocates limited effort between two tasks. One task earns profit for the firm (and income for the agent), and the other task reduces the risk of an environmental accident. The principal wants to control the agent's effort allocation, but that allocation is not directly observable. All the principal can do is infer the agent's effort from some imperfect measure of performance. Should the principal link the agent's compensation to the measure of performance on environmental risk reduction?

We found that when the agent does not exert maximum effort, then it is optimal for the principal to use an incentive wage to reward performance on risk reduction. Furthermore, the optimal wage should be more sensitive to measured performance on a given task as the relative accuracy of this measurement improves.[3]

If the agent does expend maximum effort, on the other hand, then it may not be efficient for the principal to pay an incentive wage based on measured performance on environmental risk reduction. A fixed wage may be preferable. This rather surprising result has an intuitive rationale. If the agent's effort were already at its maximum, interaction between the principal and the agent would amount only to sharing the risk involved in having the firm's income depend on noisy performance assessments. Assuming that the agent is more averse to risk affecting his income than the principal, which seems realistic, the latter would have to bear most of that risk (or the agent would leave the firm). This implies that the agent's income level should be the same across all uncertain contingencies, which could only be achieved if the wage were constant.

In a recent paper, Tirole (1999) also addresses the general issue of whether managerial incentives should be directed towards either enhancing shareholder value or promoting the (possibly conflicting) objectives of various stakehold-ers. It is argued that the former is more compatible with stronger incentives and should therefore yield higher performance (wealth), but at the cost of generating biased decision-making. Tirole also makes the methodological point that the economic theory of the firm now offers the intellectual tools for making a lucid analysis of the benefits and costs of linking executive compensation directly to financial as well as non-financial results.

2.2　Monitoring and Auditing of Non-financial Objectives

In the analysis above, monitoring was costless, and its accuracy was given. In reality, every monitoring system is costly, and if the principal were to spend more money, he or she could usually improve the system's accuracy. Of interest is how the principal should make the optimal joint decision on the level of monitoring the effort on the non-financial environmental objective and the com-pensation for both tasks. (Monitoring of financial performance is also important, but one can assume that it is done irrespective of environmental concerns.)

The main benefit to the principal of a greater expenditure on monitoring is that it would improve the accuracy of the inference of the agent's effort on environmental risk reduction. As we said in section 2.1, the principal should increase the sensitivity of the wage to the performance measure. This would shift more of the risk of an environmental accident to the agent, and the agent would adjust by dedicating more effort to that activity, *ceteris paribus*. A further benefit of greater expenditure on monitoring is that it would also improve the principal's assessment of whether the agent was exerting maximal effort. As explained above, the choice of a salary system depends on this assessment.

The most obvious manifestation of this corporate policy approach is environmental auditing. Environmental audits are becoming common in large companies in exposed industries such as chemicals. One aspect of audits is invariably the quantification of the environmental effects of a firm's operations – a necessary condition for an objective incentive wage. And whereas surveys of management practice[4] do not suggest that many companies formally link compensation to the results of environmental audits, there is reason to believe that *de facto* links exist, none the less. As it was expressed in *The Economist* (1990), 'Audits allow chief executives to set goals for subsidiaries: get your reported emissions down to such-and-such level, or lose a bit of your bonus.'

Recent findings in Sinclair-Desgagné and Gabel (1997) and Sinclair-Desgagné (1999) suggest, furthermore, that basing compensation partly on environmental audits could create synergies between regular business tasks and environmental tasks. The proposed compensation scheme is intriguing and runs as follows. Let regular tasks be routinely monitored, and suppose that environmental tasks are audited only when monitoring shows performance on regular tasks to be high. Furthermore, let expected rewards be greater under an audit than without one, but let the agent be penalized if an audit finds that environmental performance is below standard. Clearly, a manager subject to this scheme should want to be audited. He would then work harder on regular tasks in order to raise performance on those tasks and trigger an audit. But since there is little benefit in being audited when the environment has been neglected, he would work hard on environmental tasks as well! Hence, under such a compensation scheme based on selective environmental audits, managers might stop seeing an unavoidable conflict between regular and environmental tasks and begin to perceive them instead as complementary.

2.3 Internal Pricing

An alternative approach to assigning a single agent multiple tasks, including a non-financial one, is for the principal to try to correct the firm's system of accounting prices to reflect their implicit values to the firm. With a logic analogous to that of Pigouvian taxes (Pigou, 1920) and decentralized decision-making in a market, if the firm were to internalize all externalities to the agent that are borne by the principal, then decentralized decision-making within the firm would again be optimal to the principal. How could this be done?

Note that this problem is similar to, but not precisely the same as, the familiar transfer pricing problem. The transfer pricing problem is commonly portrayed as one of finding the price for inter-division trade that comes closest to inducing an efficient level of that trade. Presuming no objectively available reference price, the challenge is to design an incentive mechanism to tease the correct price out of those firm members who know it.

The problem we consider here is again one of getting correct intra-firm prices, but there is no *prima facie* argument that individuals know the correct price and have an incentive to conceal it. Rather, the principal must construct truly unknown prices (or their expected values) from data that are costly to collect. This is often an explicit objective of environmental audits.

There are many cases in which companies have attempted to improve their environmental performance in this way. Three examples will be mentioned here. A European chemical producer has attempted to identify all environmental costs allocated to its overhead accounts and then to shift those costs to the products or processes that truly generate them. For example, legal fees incurred or expected and insurance premia are charged to specific profit and loss production centres or products. With altered product margins caused by additional charges against environmentally malevolent products, sales managers' incentives to sell environmentally benign substitutes increase.

Another example appeared some years ago in the US steel industry. When a policy to allow intra-firm emissions trading replaced command and control policies (as an experiment in the early 1980s), Armco Steel calculated the opportunity cost of its particulate effluents and charged its many facilities with the use-value of emission rights. Reoptimization earned the company a saving of $50 million (Bodily and Gabel, 1982).

A final example in the spirit of this corporate policy is the effort several European automobile producers, including Mercedes and Volvo, have undertaken to design models with an assumption that their makers will be responsible for reprocessing the cars at the end of their lifetimes. With the design teams responsible for the costs of recovery, remanufacturing, recycling or ultimate disposal, the cars should emerge less environmentally harmful.

Although this is a simple look at internal pricing, at a more subtle level, problems of impacted information and perverse incentives may assert themselves. For example, if intra-firm prices are adjusted for costs incurred by the principal but external to the agent, should the agent have the option to subcontract work with other firms? One can assume that there are external costs there, too, and that some of them may be borne by the principal. Under these (reasonable) assumptions, it is clear that questions of transfer pricing are not independent of questions of organizational form. Those questions could range from centralization versus decentralization of decision-making all the way to integration versus specialization of the firm's activities. This suggests the relevance of work such as that of Holmström and Tirole (1991), which attempts to integrate transfer pricing and organizational form. These authors admit that their work is exploratory and cannot offer specific predictions, but the questions it poses are relevant to environmental resource management. How much flexibility should units in the firm have? Is the opportunity cost of trading outside the firm high or low? Is monitoring of outside trading relations feasible, and if so, how?

This is not an artificial problem, and an example of it has appeared in the oil industry. A diversified oil company could burden its shipping division with the insurable and non-insurable costs of many kinds that the corporation would expect to incur should there be an oil spill. The intent would be to ensure a correct incentive for the division to undertake risk-minimizing actions like operating vessels with double-bottomed hulls. But once those costs were allocated, the division might decide to subcontract some of its shipping (for example, shipping in US waters where the legal liability for a spill is especially great) to small independent firms protected by their limited liability. Should this be permitted?

Precisely this question arose after the *Exxon Valdez* accident. Seeing the enormity of Exxon's legal liability and loss of reputation, top executives at Shell Oil's transport division decided to cease commercial tanker operations in US waters and contracted it to small shippers instead. Other oil companies refrained from following Shell's lead, and presumably employed other control systems instead.

2.4 Horizontal Task Restructuring

Assigning different responsibilities to one agent with a reward system designed to govern the allocation of his effort is an organizational option discussed above. Another option is to assign the different tasks to different agents and thus obviate the problem of designing a reward system for allocating effort. In essence, the amount of effort dedicated to the different tasks is centralized with the principal who decides on the number of agents assigned to each. But there is still the problem of how to define the tasks and how to structure the incentives for them.

Holmström and Milgrom (1991) explored the problem of task assignment on the basis of a monitoring criterion. They concluded that tasks which are easier to monitor and those which are harder to monitor should be assigned to different agents with strong and weak incentive compensation schemes respectively. The intuition goes as follows. As we said before, greater financial incentives should only be associated with activities that are more accurately monitored. Now if a single agent were made responsible for two tasks, one of them carrying strong pay incentives and the other not, he would allocate too much attention to the former task at the expense of the latter one. It is then better to assign each task to a different agent.

Since a reasonable assumption in the present context is that monitoring non-financial environmental tasks is inherently relatively difficult, it would follow that profit and loss objectives should be the domain of a specific agent with strong incentives, while caring about environmental risks should be the responsibility of another agent with a fixed salary. This seems consistent with commonly observed business practice. Firms often have line managers with profit and loss responsibility working under strong incentive salary plans based on financial measures, while staff with responsibility for environmental affairs have salaries independent of operating profit.

2.5   Centralization versus Decentralization of Decision-making

The example above suggests that centralization of decision-making can be and is often used to control agents' behaviour. In a paper that focused on antitrust compliance but which is also relevant to compliance with environmental regulations, Beckenstein and Gabel (1986) analysed a situation where agents' decisions were made with uncertainty as to their legality and probability of prosecution. In their analysis, the principal has two alternative ways of influencing the quality of those decisions. He may provide better information to agents and monitor their decisions. Alternatively, he may centralize decision-making, either by making decisions personally or by imposing standard operating procedures (defined by the principal) that would constrain the agents. Both of these solutions reduce the probability of unwittingly violating the law, but their costs are quite different. Information and monitoring entail explicit costs, while centralization of decision-making or standardization of procedures entails no explicit costs but raises the probability that legitimate and profitable actions would not be taken. That is, information and monitoring reduce the probability that agents make either error – violating the law and overlooking good prospects – while centralized decision-making or standardized procedures reduce the probability of making the first mistake while raising the probability of making the second.

As an example of this, a European firm in the agrochemical business recently set the following standardized operating procedure. It established a policy that some specified pesticides would not be sold to explicitly named markets and buyers when the company could not be assured that they would be used safely.

Beckenstein and Gabel (1986) showed that the choice between the two alternatives (and consequently the probability of violations and the cost of any level of compliance) depends, among other things, on the policy approach of the enforcement agency (or the actions of civil litigants). The enforcement agency's policy variables include the size of fines and (with civil litigants) the enforcement vigour. More vigorous enforcement results in more convictions but more acquittals as well. The analysis demonstrated that an increase in fines or in the likelihood that a violation would be prosecuted should prompt the principal to reduce monitoring and further centralize decision-making.[5] The intuition is that higher fines and more frequent prosecution increase the relative cost of violating the law, and centralization is more effective than monitoring to prevent this from happening.

2.6 Corporate Sanctions of Agents for Non-performance

Segerson and Tietenberg (1992) used a principal–agent model to analyse the issue of corporate versus individual legal sanctions for violations of environmental laws. A related issue which we address here is that of corporate-imposed sanctions for agents guilty of violating company environmental policy (presumably, whether or not the violation caused environmental damage).

It is common for companies that are exposed to the risk of environmental liability to attempt to shift some of it to the employees whose negligent actions may incur that liability. This can be done by threatening dismissal, for example, or by stating in the employment contract that legal aid and the indemnification of fines will be denied to any employee found personally liable for an environmental accident.

2.7 Corporate Culture

Corporate culture can be seen as a frame that allows employees to interpret their company's policy statements.[6] Those statements are necessarily broad ones and do not explicitly recognize all possible contingencies. What an autonomous employee should do in particular circumstances is therefore often dictated by the firm's history and current atmosphere rather than by explicit rules or contract clauses. Thus, having a strong internal culture in line with its objectives allows a firm to economize on communication with the employees and on persuasion of the public. This is why, we submit, companies (especially those preoccupied with the environment) place great emphasis on corporate culture.

2.8 Human Resource Management

In addition to making their technology and their physical capital less burdensome to the environment, companies may also invest in 'greening' their human capital. Winter (1988) describes several means used by firms to enhance their employees' ability to cope with growing environmental pressure. These means, which altogether became known as the 'Winter Model', include staff motivation and in-house training, selective promotions and recruitment, appropriate working conditions, and even environmental counselling for employees' households.

Employees will be interested in their firm's environmental performance if they are themselves environmentally concerned or if they have a stake in the company's future. The former is enhanced through environmental in-house training, the latter through in-house training in general.

Clearly, focused discussions with peers, case studies, business simulations, and speeches by respected executives or academics can contribute to increase an employee's environmental awareness.

General in-house training, on the other hand, contributes to developing firm-specific human capital, that is, skills and knowledge that are valuable only in the context of the given firm, as opposed to general-purpose human capital which involves skills and knowledge that are relevant for other potential employers. Employees with firm-specific human capital are more reluctant to leave the firm, because outside of it this capital is useless. They are therefore more prone to establish a long-term relationship with their current employer.

In a long-term agency relationship, salary and status-enhancing promotions are a standard way to align the incentives of agents properly. As Milgrom and Roberts (1992, pp. 383–4) argue:

> Promotions from within have the advantage that they resemble *tournaments*, which have three important advantages for providing incentives. First, tournaments require only comparative, *ordinal* information about who did better rather than the much costlier *cardinal* information about how much better a party has performed than some absolute standard. Second, even when the quality of each performance is separately and objectively measurable, *relative performance evaluation* may be a better basis for compensation if common factors affect the performance of all the participants. Third, because the bonus pool in a tournament is set in advance, the employer has no incentive to disparage or misrepresent the workers' performance in order to save having to pay performance bonuses

Ordinal information may be the only sort of knowledge available when it comes to assessing the performance of two plant managers with respect to long-term environmental risks and the prevention of environmental accidents. One manager might be obviously more careful than the other, but there is no way of assigning an objective measurement to their respective contributions. Concerning the development or the implementation of 'green' innovations, on the other hand, some numerical scales may exist (for example, number of patents obtained, amount of decrease in air or water emissions), but similar, unobserved market and organizational factors also affect the plant managers' performance on these dimensions. Comparative performance evaluation can be useful in this case for sorting out those who do best. Finally, promotion decisions that take into account a manager's environmental record allow the firm to make its commitment towards 'green' management explicit and credible.

Promotions from within, however, imply that recruitment occurs only at the bottom. This rigidity is the price to pay for maintaining the managers' motivation: their morale would probably suffer if their career paths within the firm were constantly crossed over by outsiders. Compared with the benefit for a firm of having more of its managers endorse its vital long-term interests, a reduction of the pool of applicants for some higher-level position might be innocuous. This is especially true if most of the habits, skills and knowledge which have been acquired in a given position are relevant higher in the hierarchy. It is then the company's task to offer career paths where the acquisition and usage of skills are cumulative.

Another way to augment a manager's long-term ties with the firm is to increase the value of the fringe benefits that the manager would lose if he were to leave. Pleasant and healthy working conditions, and access to family counselling are among those firm-specific benefits, which may also directly enhance an employee's environmental awareness and his receptiveness to the increasingly numerous policy statements about the environment.

3.   PROPERTY RIGHTS AND THE FIRM

Tradable pollution permits have been allowed by US environmental laws since 1978. But it is only with the Clean Air Act of 1990 that the idea of a market for pollution allowances has really taken off. In May 1992, three US utility companies – the Wisconsin Power & Light Company, the Tennessee Valley Authority, and the Duquesne Light Company in Pittsburgh – exchanged up to 35 000 allowances among one another.[7]

Theoretically at least, the creation of environmental markets should lead to an efficient use of environmental resources. The argument is that if property rights for pollution (or clean air) are clearly defined and enforced, then these rights, like those attached to any standard good, will be traded between the economic actors and will end up in the hands of the people – ecologists or polluters – who value them most.

The fact that ownership of pollution allowances has incentive properties for the agents within the owning firm is much less understood, however. A recent general proposition by Hart and Moore (1990) stipulates that highly complementary assets should be owned together. Let us illustrate this assertion with the following example.

Imagine that there are three parties – a principal, an agent, and the public – with potential access to two assets – a machine and a pollution permit. Those assets are *complementary* in the sense that one cannot be used without the other. Let the principal be the owner of the machine. The permit, on the other hand, can be owned by the principal or by the public.[8] A technical innovation would improve the cleanliness of the machine and yield the principal a rent B. The agent who operates the machine is, however, key to this innovation, and he incurs a personal cost C while seeking to innovate. Suppose first that the pollution permit is owned by the public. In order to produce, the principal then needs to purchase the permit from the public and this decreases the rent to a net level, say $\frac{1}{2}B$. If the contract linking the agent and the principal stipulates that the former gets a fraction s of the principal's rent, then the agent expends effort to innovate provided his reward, $s \frac{1}{2}B$, is greater that the cost C. Now, suppose instead that the principal owns both the machine and the pollution permit. The agent's contracted pay-off when innovation takes place is then raised to sB. Hence the agent's incentive to innovate is stronger when the principal owns the pollution permit than when the public owns it.

This naive example illustrates the important link between market solutions to environmental problems and corporate practices. Large environmental markets are now just spreading, generating much enthusiasm and controversy. Their design is still imperfect. It will improve as we understand better the incentives created by the ownership of environmental assets.

4.   CONCLUSION

Since the seminal work of Pigou (1920), environmental economists have been preoccupied with the problem of market failure. Similar concern has emerged more recently for the problem of regulatory failure (see Baumol and Oates, 1988, Tietenberg, 1990). It is our contention, and the message of this chapter, that there is a third institution subject to systematic failure with environmental implications. That institution is the business firm. To this institution relatively little attention has been given by environmental economists.

Most environmental resources, however, are allocated by managers in firms. Even if market prices of environmental resources were corrected for all externalities, which is the ultimate objective of market-based environmental policies, business policy-makers – the top executives of business firms – would still have to fashion what might be special systems to govern decisions of employees within their firms when the environment is at issue. This chapter discussed several systems of incentives and control to correct or at least attenuate organizational failures within business firms.

By organizational failures we mean systematic differences between the objectives of the firm's principals and the actions of their subordinates. This phenomenon has received renewed attention lately, as recent studies reveal that resistance from middle managers, and now indeed from top managers, is considered by senior executives and board members to be the biggest obstacle to the type of organizational and culture changes that companies need to implement.[9] Companies are now increasingly looking for better ways to cope with growing environmental liability and accelerating demand for environmentally responsible operations, strategies and products.

An important feature of organizational analysis, which is often implicit in this chapter, is that managerial systems are often complementary, that is, they fit together and may enhance or jeopardize each other. For example, sections 2.1 and 2.2 above explain that it may be optimal to accompany relatively more accurate audits of a manager's environmental performance with stronger incentive compensation schemes. Section 2.3 outlines Holmström and Tirole's attempt to integrate transfer pricing and organizational structure. Section 2.9 links promotion and recruitment policies. As Milgrom and Roberts (1992, p. 17) rightly emphasize, evaluating complementarities – how the pieces of a successful organization fit together and how they fit with a company's strategy – is one of the most challenging and rewarding parts of organizational analysis.

Some managerial systems, such as incentive compensation, internal pricing, task delegation and design, corporate culture, and organizational structure must be implemented voluntarily by the firms themselves. Others, such as environmental audits, corporate sanctions, and policies concerning human resources can be mandated by law. It is our view that effective and efficient public policy in this regard must be predicated upon a more subtle understanding of firms' compliance processes than the simplistic but traditional 'black box' view of neoclassical microeconomics. Research is beginning to appear (for example, Beckenstein and Gabel, 1986; Segerson and Tietenberg, 1992; Sinclair-Desgagné, 1994), that looks behind the corporate veil to examine how environmental policy directed at firms and individuals prompts adaptive behaviour.

FURTHER READING

Excellent reference works on principal–agent models are Milgrom and Roberts (1992) and Lazear (1995). Several key papers on organizations and economics appear in the Spring 1991 and Fall 1998 issues of the *Journal of Economic Perspectives*, in the November 1991 issue of the *Quarterly Journal of Economics*, in the March 1999 issue of the *Journal of Law, Economics and Organizations*, and in the January 1999 issue of the *Review of Economic Studies*.

The reader interested in practical questions concerning the implementation and operation of environmental management systems should also find the recent book by Epstein (1996) quite useful.

NOTES

1. *International Herald Tribune* (1992), 'Business sets guidelines for sustainable growth', 1 June.
2. The interested reader may consult the existing surveys by Hart and Holmström (1987), and Sappington (1991). For a stimulating assessment, from a Coasean perspective, of the economic theory of the firm, see Williamson (1985). Milgrom and Roberts (1992) also provide a lucid and extensive overview of the field.
3. Here, monitoring accuracy is *a priori* given, but it may be possible to make it an outcome of the analysis.
4. See Flaherty and Rappaport (1991), *The Economist* (1990), the United Nations Environmental Programme (1990), McKinsey and Company (1991), Kneese and Schulze (1975), and Business International Ltd (1990).
5. On this matter, see also Sinclair-Desgagné (1994). It is shown that if the regulator ignores the incentive system of the firm, then the resulting set of penalties forces the firm to be centralized.
6. This is roughly the definition proposed by Kreps (1990).
7. *Financial Times* (1992a), 'A market made out of muck', 10 June.
8. For example, the permit could be allocated freely to firms on the basis of their historical emissions, as is commonly done, or it could be auctioned.
9. *Financial Times* (1992b), 'Top bosses find change is as good as a pest', 10 June.

REFERENCES

Baumol, W. and W. Oates (1988), *The Theory of Environmental Policy*, 2nd edn, Cambridge: Cambridge University Press.

Beckenstein, A. and L. Gabel (1986), 'The economics of antitrust compliance', *Southern Economic Journal*, **52** (3), 673–92.

Bodily, S. and L. Gabel (1982), 'A new job for businessmen: managing the company's environmental resources', *Sloan Management Review*, **23** (4), 3–18.

Brookings Institution (1975), 'Pollution, prices, and public policy', Washington, DC.

Business International Ltd (1990), 'Managing the environment: the greening of European business', London.

DeCanio, S. (1993), 'Barriers within firms to energy-efficient investments', *Energy Policy*, **21** (9), 906–14.

The Economist (1990), 'A survey of industry and the environment', 8 September.

Epstein, M.J. (1996), *Measuring Corporate Environmental Performance. Best Practices for Costing and Managing an Effective Environmental Strategy*, Chicago: Irwin.

Financial Times (1992a), 'A market made out of muck', 10 June.

Financial Times (1992b), 'Top bosses find change is as good as a pest', 10 June.

Flaherty, M. and A. Rappaport (1991), 'Multinational corporations and the environment: a survey of global practices', The Center for Environmental Management, Tufts University.

Gabel, H.L. and B. Sinclair-Desgagné (1993), 'Managerial incentives and environmental compliance', *Journal of Environmental Economics and Management*, **24** (3), 229–40.

Hart, O. (1996), *Firms, Contracts and Financial Structure*, Oxford: Clarendon Press.

Hart, O. and B. Holmström (1987), 'The theory of contracts', in T. Bewley (ed.), *Advances in Economic Theory, Fifth World Congress*, Cambridge: Cambridge University Press.

Hart, O. and J. Moore (1990), 'Property rights and the nature of the firm', *Journal of Political Economy*, **98** (6), 1119–58.

Holmström, B. and P. Milgrom (1991), 'Multi-task principal–agent analysis: incentive contract, asset ownership, and job design', *Journal of Law, Economics, and Organization*, **7** (2).

Holmström, B. and J. Tirole (1991), 'Transfer pricing and organizational form', *Journal of Law, Economics, and Organization*, **7** (2), 201–28.

International Chamber of Commerce (1991), 'Environmental auditing', Technical Report Series no. 2.

International Herald Tribune (1992), 'Business sets guidelines for sustainable growth', 1 June.

Kneese, A. and C. Schulze (1975), *Pollution, Prices, and Public Policy*, Washington: The Brookings Institution.

Kreps, D. (1990), 'Corporate culture and economic theory', in J.E. Alt and K.A. Shepsle (eds), *Perspectives on Positive Political Economy*, Cambridge: Cambridge University Press.

Lazear, E.P. (1995), *Personnel Economics*, Cambridge, MA: MIT Press.

McKinsey and Company (1991), 'Corporate response to the environmental challenge'.

Milgrom, P. and J. Roberts (1992), *Economics, Organization and Management*, Englewood Cliffs, NJ: Prentice-Hall International.

Moore, J. (1992), 'The firm as a collection of assets', *European Economic Review*, **36** (2/3), 493–507.

Pigou, A. (1920), *The Economics of Welfare*, London: Macmillan.

Sappington, D. (1991), 'Incentives in principal–agent relationships', *Journal of Economic Perspectives*, **5** (2), 45–66.

Segerson, K. and T. Tietenberg (1992), 'The structure of penalties in environmental enforcement', *Journal of Environmental Economics and Management*, **23** (2), 179–200.

Sinclair-Desgagné, B. (1994), 'La mise en vigueur des politiques environnementales et l'organisation de la firme', *L'Actualité Économique*, **70** (2), 211–24.

Sinclair-Desgagné, B. (1999), 'How to restore high-powered incentives in multitask agencies', *Journal of Law, Economics and Organizations*, **15** (2) 418–33.

Sinclair-Desgagné, B. and H.L. Gabel (1997), 'Environmental audits in management systems and public policy', *Journal of Environmental Economics and Management*, 33, 331–46

Tietenberg, T. (1990), 'Economic instruments for environmental regulation', *Oxford Review of Economic Policy*, **6** (1), 17–33.

Tirole, J. (1999), 'Corporate governance', 1998 Presidential Address to the Econometric Society.

United Nations Environmental Programme (1990), 'Companies, organization and public information to deal with environmental issues'.

Williamson, O.E. (1985), *The Economic Institutions of Capitalism*, New York: The Free Press.

Winter, G. (1988), *Business and the Environment*, Hamburg: McGraw-Hill.

10. Environmental issues and operations strategy

Charles Corbett* and Luk Van Wassenhove

1. INTRODUCTION

All firms have, to some extent, a functional organization. A functional area which has attracted a lot of attention in recent years is the operations function, which deals with all aspects of production and distribution logistics and, in a broader sense, also with product and process design. The dramatic progress made in production and information technology since Ford introduced mass production early in the twentieth century, combined with some fundamentally new perspectives (often implemented initially by Japanese firms) on how to manage production processes, has led practitioners and academics to realize that careful management of operations is essential for competitive success and even survival. And, just as is the case for finance, marketing and personnel management, 'careful management of operations' requires not only doing things right on a daily basis but also having an appropriate operations strategy in place.

Consider the following example: in the near future, automobile manufacturers will be legally required to take back used cars and recycle them or dispose of them in an environmentally acceptable way. One response would be to await legislation, and then to simply take back each car and decide on a car-by-car basis how to deal with it. The costs involved would be prohibitive. A different response, which requires a much more long-term or strategic perspective, would involve redesigning cars to make them easier to dismantle, using materials easier to recycle, and forming joint ventures to set up the required logistics structures to transport and process the used cars and distribute the recycled materials. This way costs may be kept under control but, to make this possible, drastic changes will be needed in the manufacturers' design and production processes and distribution systems.

The aim of this chapter is to show how environmental issues can have an impact on just about every possible aspect of the operations function. In particular, we illustrate the impact of the factor 'environment' on operations strategy. In order to do so, we use the well-known framework for operations strategy developed by Skinner (1969), Hayes and Wheelwright (1984), Hayes, et al. (1988) and others. An overview of the framework is provided in Figure 10.1, the terms of which are explained below.

Figure 10.1   A framework for an operations strategy

A firm's operations strategy (captured in the right of the figure) should be formulated in coordination with the overall business strategy (captured in the left of the figure), defining how the firm intends to compete and in which markets. For example, following Porter's (1980) framework, a firm would have to decide whether to follow an industry-wide or a focused strategy, and whether to compete on the basis of low cost or to differentiate its products from the competition. According to Porter (1980), 'mixed' strategies cannot be successful. A business strategy formulated in these terms can be translated into requirements for the operations function, defined in terms of the following competitive priorities:

- cost;
- quality;
- dependability;
- flexibility;
- innovation.

While each of these competitive priorities is important for the long-term survival and growth of a firm, it is not considered possible to excel in all five dimensions simultaneously. Some car manufacturers offer cars with an acceptable design quality for a very low price, whereas others offer exceptionally well-designed cars but at a high price. In general, firms will choose to focus on a specific market segment by assigning different weights to each of the competitive priorities. These weights then represent the firm's 'operations mission', defining the task on which operations must focus. The operations function must then develop an operations strategy which is consistent with the given ranking of the competitive priorities. In the car manufacturer example above, the firm with the low-cost/average quality business strategy will need a very different operations strategy than the high-cost/high-quality firm. The former will generally need a highly automated and therefore highly capital-intensive assembly line, while the latter, through lack of production volume, will often have to rely more on highly trained manual workers and craftsmen.

In the operations strategy literature (see, for instance, Hayes et al., 1988), ten key decision areas have been distinguished; they are grouped into the 'structural' and 'infrastructural' decision areas, and refer to a firm's 'hardware' and 'software', respectively. They are discussed in more detail below. The structural decision areas are:

- aggregate capacity strategy (total capacity, utilization, follow or lead demand);
- facilities strategy (number of plants, size of plants, location of plants, focus of plants);
- technology strategy (degree of automation, flexibility, product design);
- vertical integration strategy (make-or-buy decisions, supplier control, buyer control, relation between vertically linked stages).

The infrastructural decision areas are:

- human resource management (management selection policies, management training policies, training of workers, reward systems);
- quality assurance and control systems (choosing quality levels, process design and control to ensure quality);
- production planning and inventory control systems (demand forecasting, assigning production to facilities/processes, production scheduling, order policies, size and location of inventories);
- information management;
- performance measurement and capital allocation systems (what to measure, setting standards and goals, investment policies);
- organizational structure and design.

How environmental issues can affect both competitive priorities and operations strategy is the subject of the remainder of this chapter. In section 2, we discuss each of the competitive priorities in the light of environmental issues. Sections 3 and 4 review the structural and infrastructural decision areas, respectively, again providing examples of how these are affected by environmental issues. Finally, section 5 concludes that, in our view, there are a number of analogies between environmental issues and other concerns in operations management, such as just in time (JIT) and total quality management (TQM). We propose that by exploiting such analogies, firms can improve their environmental performance without having to design and implement the appropriate programmes from scratch. An overview of these analogies is given in Table 10.1, and they are discussed in more detail in Corbett and Van Wassenhove (1993).

Table 10.1   Environmental programmes and existing concepts: some analogies

Environmental programme	Existing concept	Section
Reduction of hazardous inventories	Just In Time	4.3
Cooperating with customers and suppliers to reduce packaging and waste	Strategic logistics alliances for time-based competition	3.4
Zero waste	Zero defects, Total Quality Management	2.2
ISO 14000 environmental management systems standards	ISO 9000 quality management systems standards	4.2
Keeping pollution under control	Statistical process control	3.3
Design for environment, design for disposability	Design for manufacturability	2.2
Waste accounting	Managerial accounting	4.5
Environmental auditing	Financial auditing	4.5

2.   ENVIRONMENTAL ISSUES AND COMPETITIVE PRIORITIES

2.1   Cost

The costs of reducing pollution are often huge. Vogan (1996) estimated that pollution abatement and control spending in the United States totalled approximately US$121.8 billion.[1] Monsanto's investment in environmental protection doubled between 1988 and 1990, to US$85 million (*The Economist*, 1991a). At Bayer, 20 per cent of manufacturing costs are spent on environment, the same figure as for energy or labour (*The Economist*, 1990a). As a less obvious example: in Germany, the public sector projected spending of US$2.84 billion on noise abatement between 1991 and 2000 (Kipp, 1998). Airports and airlines, such as Amsterdam Schiphol and KLM, are increasingly hampered by combinations of pollution- and noise-related restrictions.

In some cases the benefits of pollution reduction are large and easy to quantify. The necessary investments to reduce pollution are then easy to justify economically in their own right, under the prevailing duties and prices for resources and raw materials. A well-known example of this is provided by 3M. By 1976, 3M had realized that the sharply rising cost of pollution control was threatening profitability, and this is why it introduced its '3P' programme: 'Pollution Prevention Pays'. To date, 3M has undertaken more than 4600 3P projects, which have eliminated 246 000 tons of air pollutants, 31 000 tons of water pollutants, nearly 4 billion gallons of waste water and almost 500 000 tons of sludge and solid waste. These projects also have produced total savings in excess of US$810 million (Zosel, 1998). Another example: Dow Corning realized a 33 per cent annual return on investment by recovering two substances previously considered waste. These examples, and others, are discussed in Royston (1980). We see that environmentally conscious manufacturing (ECM) can provide economic benefits (see also Weissman and Sekutowski, 1992). Another example of this phenomenon is how the Royal Caribbean International and Celebrity Cruise Ships will be the first ever powered by General Electric's gas turbines. In addition to reducing engine-room noise and vibration and cutting emissions, hence enhancing passenger comfort, this propulsion system will make it possible for ships to set sail with a reduced maintenance crew and smaller parts inventory (Valenti, 1998). For such cases, the key to inducing firms to improve environmental performance is to ensure that managers are aware of the opportunities available, so they can follow the same investment criteria as they would otherwise. Graphically, this corresponds to the far right portion, region 1, of the graph in Figure 10.2, where the curve representing the marginal costs of reducing pollution lies (significantly) below the horizontal axis.

In other cases, the economic benefits of improving environmental performance are significant but less obvious, corresponding to region 2 in Figure 10.2. For instance, increased pollution liability has sometimes led to firms paying huge sums of money: the Bhopal disaster cost Union Carbide at least US$470 million in punitive expenses (*The Hindu*, 1999). Exxon spent about US$300 million in direct compensation to fishermen and other residents for economic losses, and an additional US$1 billion in a civil settlement as a result of the Alaskan oil spill, which has led many American shipowners to dramatically increase their liability insurance (Martin, 1999). The current discounted value of the insurance industry's environmental liability exposure

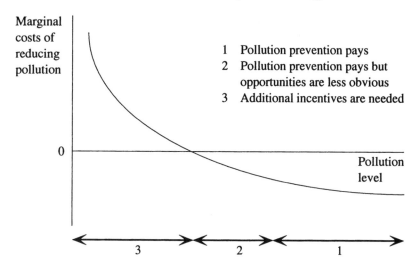

Figure 10.2   Marginal costs of reducing pollution

is estimated at US$40 billion to US$50 billion (Jernberg, 1999). As a result, insuring against the cost of pollution is becoming increasingly expensive. In Germany, though, such 'green' insurance became compulsory in some sectors in 1993 (*The Economist*, 1992d). Besides the insurance issue, the financial risks implicit in lending money to highly polluting firms may lead banks to charge them higher interest rates. DiCanio (1993b) discusses various reasons, related to informational and incentive issues, why firms often fail to invest in economically justifiable energy conservation projects. In DiCanio (1993a), he suggests, among other things, setting up an internal energy management profit centre as one possible way of overcoming the apparent investment barrier.

Finally, there are ecological investments that cannot be economically justified under the prevailing prices and tax structures, as in region 3 of Figure 10.2. Sometimes a firm may nevertheless adopt such investments, for example, for reputation or public relations reasons, but in general external measures will need to be taken if firms are to make the necessary improvements. Various types of measure are possible: prescribing particular technologies, providing (additional) economic incentives such as taxes on scarce resources or duties on emissions, and defining pollution limits or distribution of rights to pollute. It should be clear, however, that such measures have serious international trade implications. There is the issue of cost competitiveness: countries prepared to accept more pollution (whether this is the result of the ability to absorb more pollution or of a willingness to accept more environmental damage) may exploit this fact at the expense of more ecologically constrained countries. Governments that consider this a source of unfair advantage can impose higher duties on the imports involved, measures which can be hard to distinguish from protectionist ones (see, among others, Dean, 1992 and Chapter 17 of this volume). The same is true of a government setting particular product standards. America's ban on Venezuelan petrol is an example of an allegedly 'green' regulation whose importance for protecting public health or the environment is hotly disputed, and which can be interpreted as protectionist. The EU's refusal to accept beef treated with hormones is another such case (*The Economist*, 1998a). Another well-known example is that of the Danish government introducing legislation requiring all soft drinks to be sold in a particular type of returnable container, a requirement which domestic producers could meet more easily than foreign producers, as the latter could not use the same packaging for Denmark as for other countries. The legislation was approved by the European Union (EU), indicating that the environmental aspects outweighed those of free trade; it is easy to imagine cases where ecological considerations are abused to camouflage protectionist intentions.

To conclude, we see that ecological factors can seriously affect a firm's competitiveness. In some cases, this obstacle can be overcome by introducing cleaner and adequately cost-efficient technology; in others, though, firms may find there is no way of maintaining their current activities at a profitable level.

2.2   Quality

Quality plays an important role in determining a firm's competitiveness. Wal-Mart and several British supermarket chains encourage their suppliers to improve their environmental performance. BT (formerly British Telecom) buys 250 000 products from 20 000 to 30 000 regular suppliers. BT requires these suppliers to give assurances concerning their performance on a wide range of environmental issues; highly polluting firms will not even be considered (*ENDS Report*, 1992).

In the customer market, environmentally better products are sometimes perceived as having higher quality. Varta's share of the US$120 million British supermarket business rose from 5 per cent to 15 per cent on introducing cleaner batteries (*Fortune*, 1989), and Rubbermaid, Moore Business Forms and International Paper have dramatically increased their market share by offering greener products (see Biddle, 1993). In the US, 27 per cent of consumers have boycotted a product because of the poor environmental image of the manufacturer (Levin, 1990). Studies show that cause-related marketing is increasingly popular with the American people (Cone/Roper, 1999). In the UK, 70 per cent of adults are willing to pay extra for greener products (Stuller, 1990); in the US 82 per cent of those surveyed would pay 5 per cent or more extra (Levin, 1990). This means that even when an ecologically better version of a product is more costly to produce, it may yet be attractive for a firm to offer such a product. Market research groups such as the Roper group and Environics conduct regular international surveys of consumers' environmental attitudes and willingness to pay. But consumer willingness to pay a premium for a greener product can be expected to decrease when that product accounts for a larger proportion of the consumer's total budget, for example, in the case of petrol. Governments can then use economic incentives to persuade consumers to choose the greener product, for example, by imposing lower taxes on unleaded petrol. However, the precise conditions under which better environmental performance is perceived by customers as enhanced quality and is thus able to command a price premium are unclear. Consumers are then asked to pay for a public good, a cleaner environment, which of course creates a free-rider problem. This becomes less of an obstacle when consumers believe that the product is directly beneficial to them, as is true of, among other things, health foods or natural cosmetics. The positive externality exerted on the environment is internalized by such consumers. Chapter 13 contains a more extensive discussion of environmental marketing.

Allegedly superior environmental performance is frequently used as a marketing argument nowadays. To remedy the confusion caused among consumers by such green marketing, governments are increasingly introducing 'eco-labelling' schemes. The West German scheme has been the prototype; and various other European governments have implemented similar schemes. The European Union launched its official ecological label policy in March 1992. The policy is based on the 'cradle-to-grave' approach: its objectives are to promote products that have a reduced environmental impact during their entire life cycle and to provide consumers with better information on products' environmental impact, but without significantly affecting those products' fitness for use (Burdett, 1996). As of March 1999, nine national eco-labels were operating in seven EU member states including Germany's 'Blue Angel', Scandinavia's 'Nordic White Swan' the 'EKO' label in The Netherlands, and the EU Flower eco-label. To emphasize the desirability of reuse and the importance of the design phase, Huisingh (1990) prefers the expression 'from preconception to reincarnation' to 'from cradle to grave'. This more all-encompassing approach is entirely consistent with much of the recent literature on quality, especially TQM.

There is extensive literature on how to improve product and process quality by improving the design process, using tools such as quality function deployment, described in, for example, Hauser and Clausing (1988). There is no reason why much of this could not be applied to environmental considerations as well. With recyclability or disposability considered part of environmental quality, this quality, too, needs to be reflected in the design process. In 1998 Philips Electronics launched a company-wide initiative, Eco

Vision, which calls for an increasing percentage of products to be 'eco-designed' by 2001, with all business lines required to produce flagship green products in 1999 (Jusko, 1998). At 3M's Video Tape duplicating business, an innovative reusable plastic multi-transport system saved the company US$4 million per year in packaging waste and labour and inspired 3M 'intrapreneurs' to commercialize the product for the rest of the world (Business Wire, 1997a). Laws are even being introduced requiring manufacturers to take their products back when they are no longer used; this includes cars, computers and so on. Obviously, if product design does not anticipate this, recycling or disposal can be a costly business. For example, many parts of an automobile are in themselves not difficult to recycle, but the fact that they all require a different approach complicates matters, particularly when they are all heaped together without any labels indicating what's what. 'Design for environment' is a way of ensuring that products are easy to recycle or dispose of (Weissman and Sekutowski, 1992). It means, among other things, 'design for recyclability' or 'design for disposability': assembling all parts in such a way that they can easily be snapped apart, sorted and recycled, and labelling all parts to make them clearly recognizable. Composites, glues and screws are to be avoided, and the number of different kinds of materials (especially plastics) should be minimized. Kodak's recycling of 100 million one-time-use cameras (which are designed to be more than 86 per cent recyclable by weight), has helped with the elimination of more than 14 million pounds of waste from landfills (Business Wire, 1997b). By applying 'design-for-environment' principles, Kodak has created a product that allows photo-finishers to remove the film for processing and then return the cameras to Kodak for recycling and reuse. In 1996, Kodak recycled 74 per cent of one-time-use cameras in the USA. Toshiba Corporation has begun recycling tests on five home appliance and electrical products in preparation for a product recycling law set to take effect in Japan in 2001, according to published reports (Capital Cities–ABC Inc., 1998). BMW and Volkswagen have set up research projects devoted to making cars entirely recyclable (Kleiner, 1991), and Chrysler, Ford and General Motors have formed the 'Vehicle Recycling Partnership' (VRP) (*Machine Design*, 1993, p. 48). European automakers are developing recycling technologies in organizations similar to the VRP, in an effort to demonstrate their environmental responsibility and pre-empt legislative mandates (Eller, 1996). They are also setting voluntary targets for how much of the auto shredder residue (ASR) will be landfilled. The French automakers' proposal (known as CADRE) and the UK agreement (known as ACORD), for example, target a 40 per cent reduction of ASR by 2002 and 80 per cent reduction by 2015 (Eller, 1996). Japanese manufacturers are currently required by law to label the recyclable parts of their products (*Machine Design*, 1993, p. 50), while General Motors and Ford now require plastics companies to label their products with standard symbols (Berry, 1992).

A similar concept, 'design for manufacturability', originated when firms began to realize that the traditional approach, where research and development (R&D) simply designed the product and then threw it over the wall for manufacturing to figure out how to make it, was not very efficient. By letting teams from production and from R&D cooperate during the design phase, time to market could be shortened considerably and production made easier. 'Design for environment' represents a further extension of the horizons for which design departments are responsible.

2.3 Dependability

Dependability is the ability to deliver the right product to the right place at the agreed time. This dependability can be endangered by the environmental circumstances. A concentration of heavy industries is often found in strategically attractive locations. Air pollution in such areas sometimes reaches such worrying levels that local authorities order a temporary closedown of local heavy industries. In Mexico City, a 30 per cent cut in activity has been threatened for more than 200 of the biggest and dirtiest factories (*The Economist*, 1992a). Many other examples exist, from Mexico to Taiwan, of firms having been shut down as authorities step up enforcement. Increasing public awareness and fear of the potential dangers of toxic substances (Erikson, 1990) may well cause shutdowns to be ordered much more frequently by authorities if a firm does not permanently improve its safety management and reputation. Unless the affected firms have large and costly (and sometimes hazardous) inventories, such partial or complete closing down of plants may seriously affect dependability. Firms using a JIT system will particularly suffer in this case.

Another way in which dependability can be endangered is due to varying quality of environmental inputs. Some firms rely on water from the local river for use in their process, but if that water itself is occasionally polluted, they will find themselves confronted with a hard-to-control source of variability. The same problem can arise from using recycled products as inputs: the availability and quality of these may not be equal to that of virgin products.

As will be clear from the examples throughout this chapter, the environmental considerations can be endogenous or exogenous. In the former case, firms have to rethink their operations in order to reduce the environmental externality they impose on others: here, the key issue is more one of changing and adapting to new incentive structures. In the latter case, they have to find a way of dealing with the environmental externalities caused by others: the key issue here is to know which environmental threats may be expected and how to prepare for these. In contrast to the examples earlier in this chapter, the dependability examples given here display exogenous environmental considerations. There is also, however, an endogenous component: increase of delivery dependability in a JIT context often entails much smaller and more frequent deliveries, rendering distribution optimization more difficult. Particularly in the case of consumer goods, where retailers in some countries demand guaranteed overnight delivery throughout the country, the daily flows from supplier A to retail outlet B are frequently too small for direct full-truckload shipments. Hence a choice must be made between two evils: less-than-truckload shipments or combining flows by routing them through regional warehouses, which significantly increases the distance travelled. Neither, obviously, is an energy-efficient approach.

2.4   Flexibility

Flexibility, also, has two sides to it: the ability to respond quickly to customers' wishes and the ability to absorb changes in the (business) environment. To start with the former aspect, let us consider product mix flexibility. In many markets, customers are demanding an increasingly wide variety of products. The time when Henry Ford would offer customers 'any colour they want, as long as it's black' are over; nowadays, modern automobile assembly plants produce cars of all possible colours in arbitrary sequences. In many sectors, large batch production is out. Machines need to be changed from one product type to another much more frequently. Particularly when such changeovers include cleaning of machines, for instance in the case of a painting installation, this can easily lead to much more waste of materials and detergents. In short, market trends towards more flexibility are sometimes in conflict with ecological considerations.

Let us turn briefly to internal aspects of flexibility, those that the customer does not see. Being able to cope with rapid changes in environmental regulation and market pressures poses significant challenges to a firm's flexibility. With different countries introducing different legislation on packaging requirements, plants producing for an international market have to be flexible enough to be able to meet each of these different packaging requirements. Additionally, when environmental restrictions become tighter, for example, when effluent limits are tightened, plant managers have to ensure that they can respond without having to redesign the process entirely each time. This flexibility is particularly important in view of the unpredictable and fast-changing nature of environmental legislation. It may not always be possible to meet these challenges and stay competitive, in which case a firm obviously needs seriously to consider withdrawing from that particular market altogether.

2.5   Innovation

The fifth competitive priority is innovation. Strict environmental legislation and a high degree of environmental awareness in Sweden and Germany have forced innovation, so that their industries lead the world in environmental products and services (see Porter, 1990). The market in Western Europe for environmental goods and services was worth some US$94 billion in 1992, US$40 billion less than the market in the USA (quoted from *Environmental Business Journal, The Economist*, 1993). Japanese carmakers had an advantage over their European counterparts when the EU introduced a directive requiring catalytic converters in all new small cars, as similar standards had already existed for some time in their other main markets, the USA and Japan (Barrett, 1991).

Growing environmental consciousness has also led to innovative firms creating a range of new environmental products and services. Du Pont, having made safety a key point in all its operations, has formed a special division to sell its expertise to industrial customers; projected revenues are US$1 billion by the year 2000 (Kirkpatrick, 1990). Firms can offer to take back customers' waste as part of customer service, as ICI does (*The Economist*, 1990b). A number of firms have profited from the huge increase in complexity of waste disposal by offering a range of waste disposal services. Agrochemical companies might shift their focus from selling pesticides by the pound to selling integrated pest management (Kleiner, 1991, p. 40). Simultaneously, researchers are working on genetic engineering, with the intention of changing the characteristics of crops and making them more resistant to all kinds of disease, thereby reducing the need for pesticides. This is a good example of not merely introducing slight alterations to make a product less environmentally harmful, such as attaching catalytic converters to cars, but of eliminating the need for the product altogether. In the chemical industry, where some products are inherently environmentally damaging, innovation into environmentally safe products is recognized as essential for long-term survival, thereby justifying the often huge costs of developing such products.

According to Stalk (1988), rapidly introducing new products or replacing old ones is becoming a new source of competitive advantage: product life cycles are continuously shrinking. Consumers replace products long before their economic life is over; refrigerators, washing machines, hi-fi equipment and so on are often replaced not because they no longer function properly but because a newly introduced product has some additional features. Market pressures forcing firms to introduce new products more frequently may entail a global cost to society if products are not used for their full economic life. As product life cycles become shorter, reusability of (parts of) these products becomes more essential. Interface, a US$51 million multinational carpet and flooring company, has developed the 'Evergreen Lease' to transform its commercial product, carpet tiles, into a service (Hawken, 1997). Normally, flooring companies just sell carpet tiles, but Interface leases carpet services to building owners. As carpet tiles wear out and are replaced, the old ones are recycled and made into new tiles as part of the lease fee. Over time, the amount of material used will drop, saving the customer money and providing a superior product. Other examples of such innovative, service-based contracts replacing quantity-based procurement in the chemicals industry are given by Bierma and Waterstraat (1996); the effects of such contracts on customers' and suppliers' efforts to reduce consumption are analysed in Corbett and DeCroix (1999). Issues related to product and component recycling and reuse are discussed in more detail in section 4.3.

3.   ENVIRONMENTAL ISSUES AND STRUCTURAL OPERATIONS STRATEGY DECISIONS

3.1   Aggregate Capacity Strategy

In many cases, it is the capacity of a facility rather than how heavily it is being used that determines the amount of energy it will consume or pollution it will cause. This is true of transport services, but also of warehouses for frozen foods. If, in addition, demand for the service or product concerned is highly variable, for instance due to seasonal effects, holding overcapacity would be a natural solution. However, a trade-off needs to be made between the environmental costs of holding such overcapacity and the costs of deterioration in customer service that can result from having less capacity.

Another decision to be made is whether to let aggregate capacity lead or chase demand during a product's life cycle. Chasing or following demand entails increasing or reducing capacity in reaction to realized demand, whereas leading demand refers to adapting capacity in anticipation of changes in demand. Leading demand holds the attraction of being able to respond adequately if demand grows faster than predicted, and not having to disappoint many customers with excessive delivery times. However, having invested in capacity some time before it is fully utilized can turn into an embarrassment if changes in ecological legislation render it outdated by the time it is actually needed. Traditionally, this decision would involve a trade-off between costs of not being able to meet demand and costs of excess capacity; the environmental issue introduces an additional level of uncertainty.

3.2   Facility Location and Size

Increasingly tight environmental standards in highly developed countries can be a reason for firms to establish their operations abroad, possibly in developing countries. California's tough laws are given by manufacturers leaving for Arizona, Nevada or Mexico as a major reason for doing so (*The Economist*,

1991b), and the environmental performance of plants on the Mexican side of the border is not always on a par with that of their counterparts in the USA. A survey in The Netherlands (*NRC Handelsblad*, 1990) reveals that tighter environmental legislation would cause some 30 per cent of the affected firms seriously to consider moving their manufacturing operations abroad. Other studies conclude that, although the data are not inconsistent with the hypothesis of migration of dirty industries to pollution havens, several alternative explanations cannot be ruled out (see Lucas et al., 1992; Low and Yeats, 1992). A more recent and more comprehensive study of environmental capital flight is found in Jeppesen and Folmer (1999). In any case, migration is clearly not the intention of environmental legislation, and penal import duties on firms operating in less green countries are one possible countermeasure against such escapism. The opposite also occurs: Winter and Sohn rejected an otherwise perfectly acceptable location for a subsidiary in the USA on the grounds that the area was already too heavily polluted (Winter, 1988, p. 33).

Transport of (hazardous) waste is being increasingly strictly regulated, and the EU is promoting treatment of waste near to, or on the site of, its production to reduce the dangers involved in transport (*EIU European Trends*, 1991). The list of chemicals compiled by the United Nations as too hazardous to be transported is constantly growing. Waste consisting of such chemicals must be disposed of at the production site itself. However, increasingly strict demands placed on the treatment processes will often call for large, centralized waste treatment facilities to achieve economies of scale. The combined result of these two effects is that it is becoming more attractive to concentrate production in a small number of huge plants: a major European chemical firm told us that these trends could lead to plant closures and concentration of all production and associated waste treatment in only three plants worldwide, with just one plant replacing the current four plants in Europe.

It is not only disposal that is becoming an important factor in determining size and location of facilities: the various options available in product recovery management (PRM), varying from repair of used products to recycling of used materials, complicate this issue further (see section 4.3 for more on PRM). With new and used products and components moving both ways through the production and distribution network, the trade-offs between transport costs, production costs, economies of scale and other factors are sure to shift. For instance, the economies of scale in an assembly process may be totally different from those inherent in the process for disassembling the same product.

3.3   Technology Strategy

A crucial distinction in ecological technology is that between end-of-pipe measures, integrated controls and process design changes upstream. In the first case, the process is unchanged but any pollution or waste is treated as it is emitted by the process. In the second case, the process is more tightly controlled to reduce the amount of pollution or waste caused. In the third case, pollution or waste is eliminated altogether by redesigning the process. There seems to be a trend from no pollution treatment to end-of-pipe measures to integrated controls to process redesign. One reason for this is the increasingly tight standards for, and high costs of, pollution abatement and waste disposal. The more expensive it becomes to clean up afterwards, the more sense it makes to prevent having to clean up at all. Consider, for instance, the costs of disposing of hazardous waste. In the USA in 1978, hazardous waste could be dumped in a landfill for US$2.50 per ton; in 1987, costs were US$200 or more per ton. Burning it cost US$50 per ton in 1978, against US$200 per ton in 1987 or even US$2000 for particularly hazardous waste. In the early 1980s, garbage companies charged US$3 per ton to remove consumer or garden rubbish, but ten years later this already cost US$130 per ton. In fact, disposal of a product can be more costly than its actual value: a gallon of methanol costs US$0.85, but throwing it away unused costs US$1.20 (Buchholz et al., 1992, pp. 179–80, 198). By recycling cathode ray tubes from used computers, Digital saved more than US $1 million in hazardous waste landfill fees within a year (Rosenberg, 1992). Waste management is further discussed in Chapter 22.

It is interesting to compare this trend from end-of-pipe measures and integrated controls to process redesign with what has happened in quality control (see Wadsworth et al., 1986). When quality became an issue, statistical quality control (SQC) techniques, such as acceptance sampling, were used; batches found to be defective upon inspection would be scrapped or reworked. Later, statistical process control (SPC) was introduced; here the idea is to monitor key process characteristics and to adjust the process whenever it threatens to go out of control. This greatly reduces the proportion of defective units produced and the amount of scrap or rework. Even more recent is the trend towards off-line quality control, an approach involving redesigning the product and the process in such a way that the quality of the final product is robust to changes in process parameters (Taguchi and Clausing, 1990). To illustrate the analogy with ecological protection, consider a chemical process which causes a toxic gas to escape whenever the reaction temperature exceeds a certain critical level. The first step towards pollution reduction is to capture the gas whenever it is created and to treat it rather than letting it escape into the air or river; a camera allowing operators in the control room to visually monitor smoke emissions already helps to observe and react to problems more quickly. Step two is to control the reaction more tightly, so that the toxic gas is created less frequently. Some chemical plants have a computerized ecological monitoring system, with, for instance, a flashing green light warning that a maximum allowable pollution level is about to be reached. Step three, finally, could be to find a catalyst which will allow the reaction to take place at a much lower temperature, eliminating the toxic gas problem altogether. This development can be represented using the graph introduced in Figure 10.2. Without radical changes in process technology, it seems reasonable to expect marginal costs of pollution reduction to increase as pollution levels are reduced. However, as illustrated in Figure 10.3, introducing new process can shift the cost curves downward. The important point is that process improvement, as opposed to end-of-pipe measures, can be a way of escaping the pessimistic picture painted by Figure 10.2: even when improving ecological performance no longer seems economically justifiable, as in Figure 10.2, process improvement can ameliorate this situation by favourably affecting the costs of further pollution control.

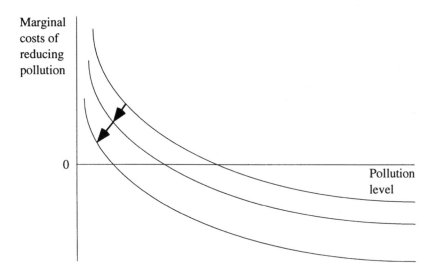

Figure 10.3   Process improvement reduces pollution reduction costs

Another significant trend is taking place in public policy. Rather than dictating specific controls on each individual emission source in a plant (such as BAT or BATNEEC; see Chapter 5 for further details), total emission limits are set, leaving operations managers more discretion to decide exactly how to keep pollution within those limits. This creates an important incentive to shift from end-of-pipe measures towards process design changes, as described above. Later on, in section 4.3, we shall see an example of a different way of using the additional freedom left to firms as a result of this shift in public policy.

Finally, the often rapid changes in environmental regulations make the technology issue a very tough one for firms to deal with. For example, what might have been considered an investment in ecological protection 15 years ago will nowadays be considered a standard part of a plant. Installing scrubbers in a smokestack is now frequently a mandatory ecological investment, but the smokestack itself used to be one too. Even with the best of intentions, complying with ecological standards when designing a new plant can be problematic. A European chemical firm submitted a proposal for a waste incinerator, incorporating state-of-the-art technology, in 1985. After a long administrative process, the permit for that particular design was finally granted in 1990, by which time the design was five years old, leading to public complaints that the firm was using outdated technology. However, getting a permit for the updated design would take another five years, and so on and so forth.

3.4   Vertical Integration Strategy

Just as transfrontier environmental problems often require cooperation between nations, production emissions require close cooperation between firms throughout the production and distribution chain if they are to be dealt with effectively. Full vertical integration may be one way of achieving closer cooperation, but other alternatives are also emerging, such as strategic R&D alliances and strategic logistics alliances.

Coca-Cola and Hoechst Celanese have formed a strategic R&D alliance. Coca-Cola invested in developing a soda bottle with 25 per cent recycled plastic, and Hoechst Celanese developed the new technology for Coca-Cola in order to remain their main supplier of plastic bottles. In return, Coca-Cola paid much of the R&D costs and allowed Hoechst to keep the rights of the technology (see Biddle, 1993).

The increasing importance attached to time-based competition (see, for example, Blackburn, 1991; Stalk, 1988) has led to the formation of strategic logistics alliances, aimed at reducing the amount of time wasted in supply chains. By cooperating closely with all other partners in the distribution chain, waste of time can be eliminated and the chain as a whole can become more flexible and competitive. One source of waste of time is frequent packaging and repackaging. During their journey from manufacturer to wholesaler to retailer to customer (and, soon, back to the manufacturer), products are often packaged and repackaged several times, going from bulk transport to large crates to cardboard boxes to individual consumer-size packaging. Disposing of surplus packaging is becoming more and more expensive, and the new German packaging laws (described below) mean a huge amount of work moving all that packaging back and forth through the distribution chain. If manufacturers already package their products in sizes and formats adapted to the needs of the final customer, repackaging can be minimized, yielding double benefits. Recent advances in supply chain management have led to dramatic reductions in inventories and improvements in customer service, and they show great promise to do the same for environmental improvement. This is also the premise of *industrial ecology*, a field which studies how systems of production and consumption can be designed in order to have a minimal impact on the environment (see, for example, Richards and Pearson, 1998).

In Germany, as of 1 January 1993, sales packaging must be taken back by retailers and manufacturers (and packaging manufacturers), and turned to new use or recycled packaging (Barrett, 1991). Setting up the appropriate two-way distribution network (DSD, for Duales System Deutschland) will cost US$10 billion and another US$1 billion per year to operate. Manufacturers in Germany now pay a licensing fee to carry a green dot on their products; the green dot guarantees that that product's packaging will be recycled. This green dot programme funds DSD (Biddle, 1993).

A key question in organizing for recycling is whether to perform product disassembly or recycling in house or whether to subcontract it to the growing number of independent disassembly and recycling facilities. One advantage of keeping it in house is the ability to show engineers where the problems are (see Baker, 1992). Companies such as DuPont and Dow Chemical have formed alliances with municipal waste collectors and recycling companies such as Waste Management Inc. to upgrade their recycling efforts (Basta, 1990).

Decisions concerning vertical integration are nowadays viewed in an entirely different light, due to the introduction of environmental legislation and the huge potential liability in case of accidents. The 'Superfund' legislation in the USA is a good example of this; in response to growing concern over health and environmental risks posed by hazardous waste sites, the US Congress established the Superfund Program in 1980 to clean up these sites. According to Bloom and Scott Morton (1991), Superfund may be the most costly regulatory measure ever enforced in the USA. It has been estimated that the EPA has coerced businesses to pay US$13.4 billion for clean-ups since the law was passed in 1980 (Gunther, 1995). It has collected another US$900 million through enforcement actions. The agency is now raising US$2 billion a year in clean-up agreements. Under this Act, liability for the costs of cleaning up toxic waste sites may be borne by almost anybody, sometimes even the bankers of the firm that deposited the waste. Moreover, this liability is 'strict', that is, regardless of fault or negligence on the part of the firm. It is also 'joint and several', which means that the government can pick on any single firm and require it to pay all clean-up costs, regardless of the amount of waste that particular firm actually dumped; that firm then has the right to sue other firms involved to achieve a 'fair' division of the costs. In addition, the law is retroactive, so that companies can be held liable for dumping that was perfectly legal at the time when it occurred (*The Economist*, 1990b). In its current form, the Superfund Act is said to cost too much and to achieve too little: RAND has estimated that no less than 88 per cent of insurers' costs due to Superfund go towards legal fees (*The*

Economist, 1992b). Many examples exist of innocent companies being forced to pay for clean-up of damage caused by others; for instance, in the early 1980s, the H.B. Reese Candy Co. of Hershey, Pennsylvania, shipped electrical equipment that contained toxic PCB-laden oil to a recycling facility near Jacksonville, where the equipment was to be salvaged and the PCBs incinerated. In the end, the PCBs were never burned. Instead, they leaked into the ground, contaminating nearby water wells. Even though the site operator clearly caused the problem, the candy maker had to pay. An estimated 26 000 businesses have been snared in the Superfund web by either the EPA or by companies seeking others to share clean-up costs (Gunther, 1995).

4.   ENVIRONMENTAL ISSUES AND INFRASTRUC-
TURAL OPERATIONS STRATEGY DECISIONS

4.1   Human Resource Management

A critical part of introducing an environmentalist approach in business is human resource management. At present, many plant managers are discouraged from taking any environmental action such as introducing cleaner technology, because of the reward systems in use. The plant manager is often evaluated solely in terms of the short-term profit made by the plant, while delaying introduction of environmentally sound technology may prove to be harmful to the firm in the long run. It can therefore happen that although top management is convinced of the need for an environmental approach to business, this need is not properly communicated to middle and lower management. Chapter 9 addresses these issues in more detail. Environmental actions taken by the plant manager, such as requesting an environmental audit on his own initiative, should be incorporated into the reward system. Many managers do not stay in the post long enough for the results of environmental action or negligence to show up before they move to the next job, but despite this they should be motivated not to skirt the issue. An example of an employee-centred initiative aimed at reducing pollution and rewarding and recognizing employees through a contest format was initiated by Dow Chemical Company through their WRAP programme, an abbreviation for Waste Reduction Always Pays. The WRAP programme, initiated at Dow in 1981, continued successfully into the 1990s and has been credited with annual savings of US$10 million (Baker, 1994).

4.2   Quality Assurance and Control Systems

One important internal measure of quality at all stages in a production process is the proportion of defective units produced. Obviously, the higher this proportion, the more scrap or rework is needed, both of which are a waste of resources. Appearance of waste and pollution in a production process can be interpreted as a sign that the process is not as efficient as it could be; it is not fully understood or properly controlled. Because it costs money to generate waste, and again to dispose of it, it is only natural to aim for 'zero waste' or 'zero discharge' (Kleiner, 1991). There is a clear analogy with the target of 'zero defects', one aspect of TQM. Despite being unachievable, aiming for zero defects has proved useful as a target, imposing a high degree of discipline on production through its philosophy of continuous improvement. TQM means, among other things, continually removing underlying causes of defects, thereby enabling increasingly tight control over a process. This leads to higher flexibility and reliability, with obvious competitive benefits. This is often cited as one of the main reasons for the success of Japanese manufacturers.

Worker involvement is essential, and can be achieved through, among other things, quality circles; similarly it is easy to imagine the setting up of 'green groups' as a step towards zero waste or energy-saving. The large amount of attention devoted to quality in recent years means that many firms have all sorts of (often successful) quality improvement programmes in place. By considering waste and pollution as quality problems, environmental performance can be improved without the need to develop an entirely new infrastructure.

In fact, the ISO 9000 quality standards, defined by the International Organization for Standardization (www.iso.ch), are rapidly becoming necessary conditions to compete in some industries, rather than a source of competitive advantage (Tattum, 1992). To receive ISO 9000 certification, a firm must have a quality management system in place to ensure consistent product quality. As of January 2000, over 300 000 firms worldwide had received ISO 9000 certification. Building on this success, and to avoid differences in environmental legislation distorting the global competitive marketplace, ISO introduced the ISO 14000 series of environmental management system standards in 1996. Renlon, one of the companies experimenting with the British Standard 7750 (the predecessor of ISO 14000), found that its relationship with its insurers has improved as a result, as there is now less danger from legal action over the effects of toxic chemicals; for the same reason they also believe it will be easier to raise funds (Carty, 1993). Over 12 000 firms have already been ISO 14000 certified to date (April 2000), and this number is growing rapidly. ISO 9000 has attracted a fair amount of criticism, especially for its emphasis on procedures and documentation; firms often report that up to 80 per cent of procedures and documentation required for ISO 14000 had already been implemented during ISO 9000 certification, making ISO 14000 a less painful experience than its predecessor. More extensive discussions of diffusion and implementation of ISO 9000 and ISO 14000 are given in Corbett and Kirsch (2000a,b).

In section 3.3 on technology strategy we examined the analogy between quality control and pollution reduction. Quality assurance can require going beyond the boundaries of the firm. Rubbermaid, for instance, reuses stretch foil. By closely cooperating with the processor carrying out the recovery of the stretch foil, and with Giant Foods, its customer, it ensures that the plastics recovered for reuse are of high quality and virtually free from contamination. This quality management is important, as it allows Rubbermaid to offer containers in a number of attractive colours rather than the usual black or grey that would result from using recycled plastics of lower quality (Biddle, 1993).

4.3   Production Planning and Inventory Control

Although a natural response to tightening pollution limits may be to install technological countermeasures, a more appropriate response may be to adapt production plans. An example of this is given in Bodily and Gabel (1982), who describe the situation of a steel mill in the USA (Armco's Middletown plant) in 1980. The Environmental Protection Agency (EPA) had proposed that Armco install hoods and baghouses to control particulates in its blast furnaces, open-hearth furnaces and basic oxygen furnaces. This would cost US$14 million to install, and also significantly raise annual operating costs. Armco was required either to install this equipment or to achieve an equivalent reduction of particulate emissions in some other way, for example, by limiting production. Armco already used a linear programming model to find the best combination of products and processes under the constraints of a fixed production capacity so as to maximize net revenue. It now faced an additional constraint, this time on the amount of pollution it was allowed to cause. Using the linear programming model with extra constraint on pollution revealed that installing the EPA equipment was only slightly less expensive than simply limiting production. In fact, had the 'bubble policy' already been introduced at that time, Armco could have saved a lot more. The bubble policy treats entire firms as being enclosed in a bubble and allocates each firm (each bubble) a specific total pollution limit. This allows firms to decide for themselves how to cut back pollution. Armco could have decided to clean the roads on the site, treat the road surfaces and limit traffic – this would have led to a reduction in particulates four times as high as with EPA's hoods and baghouses at a cost of only 6 per cent of EPA's proposals. This reflects, as we saw in section 3.3, the public policy trend away from dictating specific emission controls towards giving firms more leeway to decide for themselves how to reduce emissions.

Production planning and inventory management can become considerably more complex as a result of product recovery management (PRM). In PRM, various degrees of reuse of products can be distinguished (see Thierry et al., 1995):

1. *Repair*: used products are returned to 'working order', but generally at lesser quality than new products. This involves fixing and/or replacing broken parts; other parts are not affected.
2. *Refurbishing*: used products are brought up to a specified quality, and after inspection, approved modules are reassembled into refurbished products.
3. *Remanufacturing*: the quality standards here are as rigorous as for new products. After disassembly, all modules and parts are extensively inspected and replaced or repaired and tested. This can be combined with technological upgrading.
4. *Cannibalization*: here, a limited set of reusable parts is recovered and brought up to quality standards depending on how they will be reused. Only a small proportion of used products is reused in this option.
5. *Recycling*: the purpose here is to reuse materials from used products and components, rather than the products and components themselves. Identity and functionality of used products and components is lost in recycling.

Each of these options creates a material flow in the downstream to upstream direction. Production planning and inventory management now need to take into account the supply and quality variability of used products, flows of components in various states of (dis)repair in various directions, information systems to track how frequently a component has been reused and so on. This will generally involve closer cooperation between the members of a production and distribution chain, and may also require collaboration between competitors, for example to set up joint PRM programmes or to establish coding standards for reusable materials.

Inventory management can become a highly sensitive issue when the materials concerned are hazardous. Small pollution incidents are frequent and perhaps inevitable. However, if not managed properly a small incident can develop into a serious accident, potentially causing huge damage to the environment and the local community, and thereby to the firm. One of the main factors contributing to the Bhopal disaster was the presence of a large inventory of the extremely hazardous intermediate product methyl isocyanate (MIC). Stocks, even of hazardous materials, are in themselves not necessarily dangerous, but can drastically magnify an otherwise minor incident. After Bhopal, firms such as CIBA-GEIGY have reduced stocks of hazardous materials, and sometimes keep only as much as is strictly needed at any given moment. This corresponds closely to the widely acclaimed JIT philosophy: getting rid of work-in-process inventories and only producing the amount needed when it really is needed, in the smallest batches possible. This frequently involves rethinking and redesigning the process, but can lead to, among other things, much lower costs and higher flexibility. In many cases, 'lean is green' can be more than just a catchphrase.

4.4   Information Management

All the issues discussed in this chapter involve information being collected, given to the right person and being processed and acted upon, generating new information in the process. For example, in process control it is important that machine operators are given the correct amount of information at the correct time. The question then is, when should the control system issue a warning? If a wide tolerance interval is chosen, the system will be too late in issuing a warning, but when the tolerance interval is too narrow, it will issue too many false warnings and not be taken seriously by the operators.

This was one of the causes of the Bhopal disaster (Case Research Association, 1985): around midnight several workers noticed that their eyes had begun to water and sting, a signal that indicated an MIC leak. The leak, a small but continuous drip, was soon found. As minor leaks were a common occurrence, the operators were still not concerned and resolved to see to the problem after the tea-break. By then, it was too late. The leak could not be stopped, and a cloud of the highly toxic MIC was already drifting towards the town of Bhopal. For more on crisis management, see, for example, Shrivastava (1987), who argues that industrial crises are not really accidents as they can be prevented; or Mitroff et al. (1988), who discuss a general theory of crisis management. All but one of the serious accidents considered by Mahon and Kelley (1987) displayed early warnings and could have been prevented. Their study shows the importance of managing internal information flows appropriately.

External information flows are also important. The Bhopal disaster could have been considerably less serious if the local community had been aware of the plant's activities, and had known that lying on the ground with a wet towel against the face was a better thing to do than to run for it. Medical personnel would also have been more effective had they known what they were up against. A system of corporate risk disclosure is itself an effective risk management tool (Baram and Partan, 1990), as repeated reports of near accidents will increase public concern enough to (legally) enforce appropriate measures.

An open information policy sets an example for other firms and leads to more credibility with authorities and pressure groups. This can be important during negotiations over future legislation. Norsk Hydro and the South African energy company, ESKOM, publish extensive reports on their environmental performance. Public commitments are a way for firms to gain goodwill and to increase self-imposed pressure to fulfil their promises.

4.5   Performance Measurement and Capital Allocation

How disastrous the effects of an incorrect performance measurement system can be is illustrated by the extremely poor environmental state of Eastern Europe.

Apparently, Eastern European governments had found, using 'advanced econometric techniques', a fixed relationship between the input and output of plants. The input used by a plant was taken as the measure of a plant's performance, as it was easier to measure than output. This provided plant managers with a very strong incentive to maximize input per unit of output, contributing to the highly inefficient manufacturing practices encountered in Eastern Europe. (The amount of energy and other inputs required by an Eastern European plant per unit value of output is two to three times higher than that in the West, according to Żylicz, 1990).

Because a firm's viability can depend as much on its environmental as on its financial performance, stakeholders should not only be given access to financial reports, but also to adequate environmental reports. And, just as the financial data are audited by independent parties, firms should also regularly arrange environmental audits on all their operations to ensure than environmental technology and environmental management programmes are performing properly (see, for example, Harrison, 1984; International Chamber of Commerce, 1988; UNEP/IEO, 1990).[2]

It is felt that disclosure of the results of an audit, which are currently strictly internal, would reduce the cooperation of the people whose operations are being audited. This cooperation is essential for an environmental audit to succeed. On 23 March 1993, a voluntary EU environmental management and audit scheme (EMAS) regulation was adopted. In contrast to the ISO 14000 standard (see section 4.2), EMAS requires audit results to be published (Carty, 1993).

No pollution reduction programme can be introduced effectively if the firm does not know how much pollution it is causing; indeed only after being forced to disclose major emissions did Dow start measuring them at all, and the company found that it was emitting much more than it previously thought (Kleiner, 1991). As a result of the forced measurements, it spent a lot of effort cleaning up. A good understanding of where pollution is caused within a firm is necessary to be able efficiently to allocate costs. Often, duties on emissions are allocated to the various processes within a plant as part of overhead costs, thereby disguising the true cost of each process and product. Introducing a 'polluter pays principle' (see also Chapters 5 and 9) throughout the firm, as, for example, CIBA-GEIGY (see Eigenmann, 1985) has done, helps to provide the right incentives to managers and to customers to combat the sources rather than the symptoms of pollution.

Chapter 11 discusses environmental accounting in more depth. An advanced waste accounting system helps to give management insight into its processes, to prevent nasty surprises and to show how much progress is being made. The latter is essential for internal and external publicity: if the benefits of 3M's PPP or Dow's Waste Reduction Always Pays (WRAP) had not been measured, these programmes would not have been anywhere nearly as widely publicized and therefore probably less successful. Standard management accounting is often accused of hampering investment in new, uncertain, technology; it also makes ecological investments more difficult to justify (see Kaplan, 1984). A proper waste accounting system helps to show the real costs associated with a process, and therefore it enables a more appropriate evaluation of waste reduction investment proposals. For an additional advantage of comprehensive hazardous waste accounting and tracking, consider that unidentified waste can cost 20 times more to dispose of than identified waste (Buchholz et al., 1992, p. 149), presumably because of the extra care needed.

4.6   Organizational Structure

Finally, the organizational structure must be designed in such a way that environmental issues are dealt with appropriately by the firm. This requires instilling environmental awareness in all employees, but this alone is not enough. The following (real) example illustrates the case of a firm which had commissioned an environmental audit. The firm had a number of tanks containing some hazardous chemical, which should have been inspected on a regular basis. This was recognized by top management, who considered it the responsibility of the department using the chemical. That department realized that inspections were necessary, but it held the opinion that the site engineering department was responsible. That department, in turn, held the purchasing department which had bought the tanks responsible for their upkeep. Purchasing also realized the need for inspections, but thought that the suppliers would carry them out. During the environmental audit, the contracts concerning the purchase of the tanks were studied, and the suppliers were found not to be responsible for the tanks. After this, the tanks were inspected and indeed found to be leaking. This illustrates that awareness alone is not sufficient; environmental responsibility must be taken into account in the firm's organizational structure.

Another firm got itself into a mess by changing its organizational structure. The firm produced several kinds of beverage containers for all Western European countries: aluminium, glass, tin, plastic, PVC and others. The divisions had traditionally been organized per country, so that country managers would promote whatever was in the firm's best interests, rather than defend any particular type of container. Just as various European countries started introducing different laws on disposability of beverage containers and return systems, the firm reorganized into divisions by container material, creating separate divisions for glass containers, for aluminium containers and so on. As each country was contemplating a different kind of legislation, the 'glass manager' found himself fighting the 'plastic manager' as each now had highly conflicting interests. While 'glass' was advocating a compulsory return system, 'plastic' was pointing out the immense logistical problems involved with such a system, while yet another division was telling everybody how much better it would be to use an environmentally friendly one-way container.

5. CONCLUSION

Turning whatever ecologically minded intentions exist within firms into operational environmental programmes remains a major challenge. The literature on management of environmental issues provides very little guidance on how to forge this link between the normative and the practical. For an exception, see, for example, the book by Winter (1988), which contains a large collection of detailed and practical checklists, intended to aid managers in improving their firms' environmental performance. Without in any way meaning to downplay the problems involved, we do believe that in some cases implementing environmental programmes does not require the radical overhaul sometimes thought to be necessary. This is because there are a number of analogies between newly arising environmental programmes and existing successful management concepts which have been outlined above. By exploring such analogies, and finding out to what extent they hold in any particular case, it is possible to avoid having to implement environmental programmes from scratch by using the synergy available through the programmes already in place. Obviously, the relevance of any analogy and the extent to which it can be exploited is fully situation-dependent. With these analogies, we do no more than scratch the surface. In an given case, some of the examples above will be irrelevant, and many others are waiting to be recognized and exploited.

This chapter has reviewed operations strategy from various angles and provided examples of how environmental issues can affect a firm's operations. We have looked at competitive priorities and seen that environmental legislation can hurt some firms' competitiveness, but that environmental problems and corresponding legislation can also offer opportunities rather than threats. We have also seen that the effects of environmental issues on operations are much more wide-ranging than may be thought at first sight. Perhaps the most important message in this chapter is that the challenges in dealing with environmental issues are by no means always in conflict with modern views of how to manage the operations function in a competitive way. Concepts such as JIT, TQM and others display important (though not perfect) analogies with various ecological considerations. Finding ways that allow firms to improve their environmental performance further with less effort represents a very important area for further research, by academics and managers alike, from a wide range of disciplines.

FURTHER READING

There is a large collection of business books on environmental issues. Generally these are broader in scope than operations alone, and are often oriented more towards managers than academics. Two books containing a chapter on the link between TQM and environmental management are:

Bennett, S.J., R. Freierman and S. George (1993), *Corporate Realities and Environmental Truths: Strategies for Leading your Business in the Environmental Era*, New York: Wiley.
Spedding, L.S., D.M. Jones and C.J. Dering (eds) (1993), *Eco-management and Eco-auditing: Environmental Issues in Business*, Chichester: Wiley.

A good reference for ISO 14000 is:

Marcus, P.A. and J.T. Willig (eds) (1997), *Moving Ahead with ISO 14000: Improving Environmental Management and Advancing Sustainable Development*, New York: John Wiley & Sons.

Packaging and recycling of used packaging are the subjects of:

Stilwell, E.J. et al. (1991), *Packaging for the Environment: A Partnership for Progress*, New York: AMACOM.

An interesting book, with a separate part on inter-firm relations, is:

Fischer, K. and J. Schot (eds) (1993), *Environmental Strategies for Industry (International Perspectives on Research Needs and Policy Implications)*, Washington, DC: Island Press.

ACKNOWLEDGEMENTS

The authors would like to acknowledge warmly the excellent assistance provided by Theresa Jones in revising this chapter for the second edition.

NOTES

* This chapter was originally written when the first author was at INSEAD.
1. Throughout this chapter, measures are expressed in American units. One billion here means one thousand million, one ton is 907 kilograms, and one gallon is 3.785 litres.

2. A definition of environmental auditing is given by the International Chamber of Commerce (1988):

> Environmental auditing is a management tool comprising a systematic, documented, periodic and objective evaluation of how well environmental organization, management and equipment are performing with the aim of helping to safeguard the environment by:

- Facilitating management control of environmental practices;
- Assessing compliance with company policies, which would include meeting regulatory requirements.

REFERENCES

Baker, K. (1994), 'Dow Chemical Company (A): The WRAP Program', case study, Washington, DC: Management Institute for Environment and Business.

Baker, N.C. (1992), 'Return to sender: product disassembly burgeons', *Environment Today*, **3** (11), 1, 23–7.

Baram, M.S. and D.G. Partan (eds) (1990), *Corporate Disclosure of Environmental Risks: US and European Law*, Butterworth Legal Publishers, Reed Publishing.

Barrett, S. (1991), 'Environmental regulation for competitive advantage', *Business Strategy Review*, Spring, 1–15.

Basta, N. (1990), 'Plastics recycling gains momentum', *Chemical Engineering*, **97** (11), 37–43.

Berry, B. (1992), 'Automakers want to recycle all of the car', *Iron Age*, **8** (2), 28–9.

Biddle, D. (1993), 'Recycling for profit: the new green business frontier', *Harvard Business Review*, November–December, 145–56.

Bierma, T.J. and F.L. Waterstraat (1996), 'P2 assistance from your supplier', *Pollution Prevention Review*, Autumn, 13–24.

Blackburn, J.D. (1991), *Time-Based Competition: The Next Battleground in American Manufacturing*, Homewood, IL: Irwin.

Bloom, G.F. and M.S. Scott Morton (1991), 'Hazardous waste is every manager's problem', *Sloan Management Review*, Summer, 75–84.

Bodily, S.E. and L.H. Gabel (1982), 'A new job for businessmen: managing the company's environmental resources', *Sloan Management Review*, Summer, 3–18.

Buchholz, R.A., A.A. Marcus and J.E. Post (1992), *Managing Environmental Issues*, Englewood Cliffs, NJ: Prentice-Hall.

Burdett, B. (1996), 'Environmental labelling in the textile industries', *Chemistry and Industry*, Society of Chemical Industry, 18 November 1996, 882.

Business Wire (1997a), 'Reusable packaging solution creates new product at 3M', *Business Editors*, 4 November.

Business Wire (1997b), 'Kodak recycles its 100-millionth one-time-use camera', *Business Editors*, 13 February.

Capital Cities–ABC Inc. (1998), 'Toshiba set for recycling laws; tests recycling of five home appliances', *American Metal Market*, 15 July.

Carty, P. (1993), 'Standard sets environmental goals', *Accountancy*, May, 40–41.

Case Research Association (1985), 'Union Carbide of India, Ltd: the Bhopal tragedy', case developed by A. Sharplin, Waltham, MA: Bentley College.

Cone/Roper (1999), 'Data finds 8 in 10 Americans have more positive image of companies with causes, two-thirds will switch brands', *The 1999 Cone/Roper Cause Related Trends Report*, 8 March.

Corbett, C.J. and G.A. DeCroix (1999), 'Shared savings contracts in supply chains', manuscript, The Anderson School at UCLA.

Corbett, C.J. and D.A. Kirsch (2000a), 'International diffusion of ISO 14000 certification', manuscript, The Anderson School at UCLA.

Corbett, C.J. and D.A. Kirsch (2000b), 'ISO 14000: an agnostic's report from the frontline', *ISO 9000 + ISO 14000 News*, **9** (2), March/April, 4–17.

Corbett, C.J. and L.N. Van Wassenhove (1993), 'The green fee: internalizing and operationalizing environmental issues', *California Management Review*, **36** (1), 116–35.

Dean, J.M. (1992), 'Trade and the environment: a survey of the literature', in Patrick Low (ed.), *International Trade and the Environment*, World Bank Discussion Papers, 159.

DiCanio, S. (1993a), 'Agency and control problems in US corporations: the case of energy-efficient investment projects', mimeo, Santa Barbara: University of California.

DiCanio, S. (1993b), 'Barriers within firms to energy-efficient investments', *Energy Policy*, **21** (9), 906–14.

The Economist (1990a), 8 September, p. 12.

The Economist (1990b), 8 September, p. 22.

The Economist (1991a), 2 November, p. 71.

The Economist (1991b), 16 November, p. 71.

The Economist (1992a), 7 April, p. 61.

The Economist (1992b), 8 August, p. 11.

The Economist (1992c), 19 September, pp. 88–9.

The Economist (1992d), 19 September, p. 92.

The Economist (1993), 20 November, pp. 81–2.

The Economist (1998a), 3 October, p. S22.

Eigenmann, G. (1985), 'Environmental protection: a management task', paper presented at the 2nd World Congress of Engineering and Environment, 7–9 November, New Delhi, India.

EIU European Trends (1991), 'Environment report', no. 2, p. 52.

Eller, R. (1996), 'Regulatory concerns and new technology ... The view from Europe', *Ward's Auto World*, **32** (1), 19.

ENDS Report (1992), no. 208, May, pp. 22–4.

Erikson, K. (1990), 'Toxic reckoning: business faces a new kind of fear', *Harvard Business Review*, January–February, 118–26.

Fortune (1989), 23 October, p. 50.

Gunther, B. (1995), 'True polluters often escape while innocents pay', *The Tampa Tribune*, 24 July, p. 1.

Harrison, L.L. (ed.) (1984), *The McGraw-Hill Environmental Auditing Handbook*, New York: McGraw-Hill.

Hauser, J.R. and D. Clausing (1988), 'The house of quality', *Harvard Business Review*, May–June, 63–73.

Hawken, P. (1997), 'Magic carpet: how to make a profit by reusing waste; natural capitalism', *Foundation for National Progress*, **22** (2), 51.

Hayes, R.H. and S.C. Wheelwright (1984), *Restoring our Competitive Edge: Competing through Manufacturing*, New York: John Wiley & Sons.

Hayes, R.H., S.C. Wheelwright and K.B. Clark (1988), *Dynamic Manufacturing*, New York: The Free Press.

The Hindu (1999), 'Environmental manager and changing business perspectives', FT Asia Intelligence Wire, 14 April.

Huisingh, Donald (1990), Erasmus University Rotterdam (Netherlands), private communication.

International Chamber of Commerce (1988), 'ICC position paper on environmental auditing', *Industry and Environment*, October–December, 14–17.

Jeppesen, T. and H. Folmer (1999), 'The confusing relationship between environmental policy and location behavior of firms: a methodological review of selected case studies', *Environment and Planning*, forthcoming.

Jernberg, D.J. (1999) 'Superfund fallout', *Best's Review – Property–Casualty Insurance Edition*, **99** (10), 51.

Jusko, J. (1998) 'The competitive edge', *Industry Weekly*, Features, 6 July.

Kaplan, R.S. (1984), 'Yesterday's accounting undermines production', *Harvard Business Review*, July–August, 95–101.

Kipp, R. (1998), 'The German environmental market', *International Market Insight (IMI)*, 2 April, US & Foreign Commercial Service and US Department of State.

Kirkpatrick, D. (1990), 'Environmentalism: the new crusade', *Fortune*, 12 February, 44–55.

Kleiner, A. (1991), 'What does it mean to be green?', *Harvard Business Review*, July–August, 38–47.

Levin, G. (1990), 'Consumers turning green: JWT survey', *Advertising Age*, 12 November.

Low, P. and A. Yeats (1992), 'Do "dirty industries" migrate?', in Patrick Low (ed.), *International Trade and the Environment*, World Bank Discussion Papers, 159.

Lucas, R.E.B., D. Wheeler and H. Hettige (1992), 'Economic development, environmental regulation and the international migration of toxic industrial pollution: 1960–88', in Patrick Low (ed.), *International Trade and the Environment*, World Bank Discussion Papers, 159.

Machine Design (1993), 12 February, 46–52.

Mahon, J.F. and P.C. Kelley (1987), 'Managing toxic wastes: after Bhopal and Sandoz', *Long Range Planning*, **20** (4), 50–59.

Martin, G (1999), 'Valdez spill leaves bitter residue; oil is gone after 10 years, but ecological, economic fallout continues', *The San Francisco Chronicle*, 24 March.

Mitroff, I.I., T.C. Pauchant and P. Shrivastava (1988), 'The structure of man-made organizational crises', *Technological Forecasting and Social Change*, **33**, 83–107.

NRC Handelsblad (1990), 9 September.

Porter, M.E. (1980) *Competitive Strategy*, New York: The Free Press.

Porter, M.E. (1990), *The Competitive Advantage of Nations*, London: Macmillan.

Richards, D.J. and G. Pearson (1998), *The Ecology of Industry: Sectors and Linkages*, National Academy of Engineering, National Academy Press, Washington DC.

Rosenberg D. (1992), 'Designing for disassembly', *Technology Review*, November–December, 17–18.

Royston, M.G. (1980), 'Making pollution prevention pay', *Harvard Business Review*, November–December, 2–22.

Shrivastava, P. (1987), *Bhopal (Anatomy of a Crisis)*, Cambridge, MA: Ballinger Publishing Company.

Skinner, W. (1969), 'Manufacturing: missing link in corporate strategy', *Harvard Business Review*, May–June, 136–45.

Stalk Jr, G. (1988), 'Time: the next source of competitive advantage', *Harvard Business Review*, July–August, 41–51.

Stuller, J. (1990), 'The politics of packaging', *Across the Board*, January–February, 41–8.

Taguchi, G. and D. Clausing (1990), 'Robust quality', *Harvard Business Review*, January–February, 65–75.

Tattum, L. (1992), 'ISO 9000 in Europe: the competitive edge is dulled', *Chemical Week*, 11 November, 37–8.

Thierry, M.C., M. Salomon, J. van Nunen and L.N. Van Wassenhove (1995), 'Strategic issues in product recovery management', *California Management Review*, **37** (2), 114–35.

UNEP/IEO (1990), 'Environmental auditing', Technical Report Series no. 2.

Valenti, M. (1998), 'Luxury liners go green; Royal Caribbean Cruises' use of aeroderivative gas turbines', *American Society of Mechanical Engineering*, **120** (7), 72.

Vogan, C.R. (1996), 'Pollution abatement and control expenditures', *Survey of Current Business*, **76** (9), 48–67.

Wadsworth, H.M., K.S. Stephens and A.B. Godfrey (1986), *Modern Methods for Quality Control and Improvement*, New York: John Wiley and Sons.

Weissman, S.H. and J.C. Sekutowski (1992), 'Environmentally conscious manufacturing: a technology for the nineties', *Total Quality Environmental Management*, **1** (4), 369–78.

Winter, G. (1988), *Business and the Environment*, Hamburg: McGraw-Hill.

Zosel, T.W. (1998), Address at 3M Environmental Technology and Services, delivered to the US EPA Region 5 Waste Minimization /P2 Conference, 14 December.

Żylicz, T. (1990), Lecture given at INSEAD, 19 November.

11. Environmental management and information systems

Jürgen Freimann

1. INTRODUCTION: INCENTIVES OF CORPORATE ENVIRONMENTAL CARE

The activities of firms have many different consequences: some of these are obvious; some more hidden. Some coincide with the basic aims and objectives of an enterprise; some are just tolerated. Not all are equally important for the different 'stakeholders' of a firm (Freeman, 1984).

Some of the impacts can be expressed in monetary terms; for example, most materials used in production, sales, taxes, subsidies and so on. Management scientists and managers usually focus on these impacts. Others can at first often only be measured in physical units (for example, quantities and qualities of waste water running into a river; air pollution and noise at the workplace or in the vicinity of a plant), or be described in general terms (for example, the various risks involved in production; or the effects of production processes or products on the health of human beings, animals and plants). Economic theory tends to describe the latter as 'social costs' or 'externalities' of private enterprise, following the basic studies of William Kapp (1950).

These external impacts could be regarded as unimportant by a manager who is responsible for the financial success of a company. Yet more and more company leaders, as well as capital owners and management scientists, have begun to perceive this point of view as shortsighted and irrational: 'What a company really is, cannot be expressed purely in terms of marks and dollars. What we do and what we neglect has consequences for many people.'[1]

To take care of the social and ecological consequences of corporate activities, even if they promise no immediate financial gains, has turned out to be an element of a modern far-sighted management strategy for several reasons (see also the other chapters in Part II):

1. An increasing number of customers and investors prefer products of and investments in companies that show environmental responsibility.

2. Social acceptance by company workers, local residents, as well as by politicians, environmentalists and the general public, depends not only on a company's economic success but more and more on its social and ecological responsibility.
3. The European Union (EU) and the International Standards Organization (ISO) have established standards for corporate environmental management systems. The implementation of these standards is certified by independent verifiers and should result in various benefits for a company.
4 In cost terms, for example as a result of savings of energy and resource inputs or waste reductions, the new strategy may lead directly to economic benefits. (See also Chapter 12.)
5. In respect of different laws in various countries (for example, Japan and Germany), people who are affected by a company's activities can complain about damages and have a good chance of success, even if the firm's guilt has not been proven.

From an external point of view, we might assume that firms that have introduced basic policy principles including environmental aims and that use

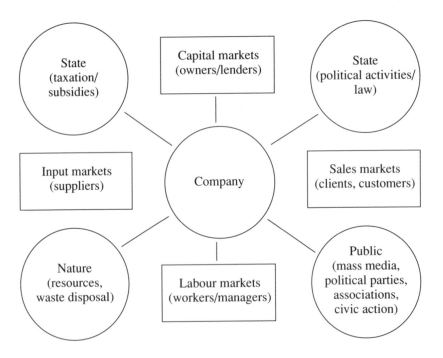

Figure 11.1   Social and ecological stakeholders of a company

their advertisements to demonstrate their increasing sense of responsibility (about 80 per cent of all corporations acting worldwide have introduced policy principles (McKinsey, 1991) have a greater sense of responsibility for the hidden environmental effects of their actions.

In order to keep the policy principles in touch with reality, companies have to check all the relevant consequences of their economic activities with respect to nature. Not only external observers, but also the management that honestly tries to follow environmental aims, need more sophisticated and valid information.

Therefore, managers as well as stakeholders (who have the power to influence the public image of a company and its economic welfare; see Figure 11.1) need:

- *Management systems* – systematic organizational measures, including periodical *audits* to check their operativeness, that guarantee that all the necessary steps will be implemented to prevent pollution and to improve corporate environmental performance.
- comprehensive environmental *information systems* – information tools presenting all the relevant ecological information requested by different stakeholders that present a reliable picture of the firm's relations with society and nature.

This chapter describes the structure and effects of corporate environmental management systems. The focus is on the Eco-Management and Audit Scheme (EMAS), which was brought into force by the European Union in 1993/95, and on the ISO 14001 which has been valid since 1996. Later, various instruments that have been developed to examine the environmental consequences of companies' activities in general or in connection with production processes or products will be analysed and discussed.

First, I will describe the environmental management system standards and describe what we know about the results of their implementation in companies. Second, the chapter gives a short review of the basic concepts of today's environmental information systems, mainly the concepts of ecological accounting and product line analysis. Third, two new instruments will be described: the concepts of eco-controlling and company testing. Finally, I will discuss the main problems and the political and economic future of ecological information systems.

The chapter is focused on experiences in German-speaking countries, because their systems are at a further stage than those in other countries (Van Buren, 1992). For example, the majority of companies and sites that participate in the EU's EMAS are located in Germany and Austria.[2] Regulations that require firms to provide information on their emissions or other environmental externalities to government authorities, such as the EU Environmental Information Directive and the Toxic Release Inventory in the US (Baram et al., 1990) are not included in this discussion. Although these regulations have important effects on corporate policies, they do not imply comprehensive information for the public, nor do they include special norms for a complete evaluation of different emissions and a firm's efforts to reduce them.

2.   ENVIRONMENTAL MANAGEMENT SYSTEMS

2.1   EU Eco-auditing/ EMAS

Auditing comes from financial management and originally included the accounting control of the actions of single departments or of the company's capital account. There was, and still is, the concept of the internal audit (revision), where the auditors are hired by the management itself, and the external audit, where the capital-owners hire the auditors from outside the company. As with the internal audit, the auditing concept was used in the 1960s in the area of production and quality control, and it has been used in the environmental area since the end of the 1970s, mainly in big US companies (Hedstrom, 1992).

Circulated by the International Chamber of Commerce (ICC) in Europe in 1989 (ICC, 1989), the concept of eco-auditing was removed from internal management control and extended to external accounting. In the EU variant, it now represents an EU regulation which became valid for all member states in 1993.[3]

At the centre of the EU EMAS are:

1. The implementation of an environmental policy, including overall principles and aims of action.
2. The implementation of a sophisticated environmental management system, including special objectives, an environmental programme and an effective management system for the company sites that participate in the audit scheme.
3. The repetitive testing of its suitability and workability by an internal auditor on behalf of the company's management.
4. The drafting of an environmental statement, assessed and validated by an independent accredited environmental verifier, in which the instruments installed, as well as the environmental success, are described.
5. The periodic publication of the validated environmental statement.
6. The company's right to use a statement to the effect that it participates in eco-auditing, combined with the right to use the EU eco-label in corporate advertising (but not in product advertising).

Participation in the EMAS is voluntary for the companies respecting company-sites, and it does not necessarily relate to all company branches or sites. The regulation includes the idea that the pressure of competition will encourage a large number of companies to participate in the audit scheme even if their previous voluntary environmental activity was rather limited.

In contrast to the former ICC audit, the EMAS includes external contacts with authorities and the public. An environmental review and an ecological evaluation of the results of environmental measures are elements of the implementation of an extensive environmental management system. This, again, implies the formulation of general environmental objectives and their organizational implementation and, moreover, their consolidation in personnel policy to ensure the social acceptance of the implemented environmental management system.

Figure 11.2 shows the management system and the auditing process and their contents.

The contents of both the environmental management system installed and the environmental statement are spelt out in detail in the EU regulation. The former contains the technical and organizational preparations for avoiding and minimizing the environmental impacts of production and emissions, as well as the related education and information policies. The latter must present information about productive activities and their main ecological problems. It also has to evaluate all quantitative environmental facts and mention the corporate policy, programme and goals. Furthermore, it has to assess environmental performance and set a date for the next statement. A special participation rule for workers and the works council, as was included in the Commission draft, is not included in the final regulation.

The environmental management system installed is governed by a two-step audit: first, by (internal or external) auditors of the company itself, whose work leads to the environmental statement; second, by accredited environmental verifiers who validate both the instruments installed and the statement to be published under conditions specified in the regulation. The verifier must be independent of the company's auditor. The accreditation and supervision of the verifiers has been regulated by national authorities of the member states.

2.2   ISO Standard 14001

The EMAS standard is defined by an EU regulation, which means that it is of direct legal validity in all EU member countries. It is part of the EU's environment policy that has been turning away from the former 'command and control' concept with its limited effects in comprehensive environmental measures. The EMAS participation is voluntary and rewarded with an official

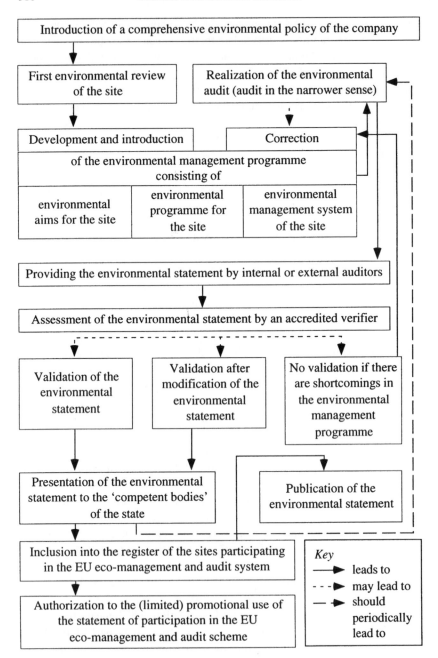

Figure 11.2   EU EMAS procedure

eco-label for the site. European companies as well as European sites of non-EU companies can participate in the scheme.

However, many companies do not restrict their activities to Europe. Therefore, a European system has a limited attraction for most of them. Moreover, the voluntary implementation of any kind of 'hand-made' internal environmental management system fails to have external effects such as image improvement and might fail to have the ecological effects intended as well. Even so, the International Standards Organization (ISO) installed another international standard for environmental management systems, called ISO 14001.[4]

The ISO 14001 standard is quite similar to the EMAS; therefore I will not describe it in as much detail as EMAS, but I will point out the main common features and differences (see, for example, Peglau and Clark, 1995).

1. EMAS is a legal system that is valid for the EU and companies operating in its member countries only; ISO 14001 was established by a private organization and can be applied by any company all over the world.
2. Both systems include specific organizational measures to avoid pollution and damages towards the environment and intend to improve the environmental performance of a company. Thereby, ISO 14001 is part of the 'ISO management standard family' and continues the tradition of the ISO 9000 quality management standards whereas EMAS has its own specific structure and terms.
3. Both systems force participating companies not only to install particular measures but also to carry out periodical internal checks and external audits by independent auditors. The main focus is on the working of the management system installed and not the environmental results of the companies' activities.
4. EMAS relates to single sites of participating companies whereas ISO 14001 is connected with the whole organization, sometimes including more than one local site.
5. Companies participating in the EMAS have to publish an environmental statement to inform the public. ISO 14001 does not include this duty.

2.3 Experiences[5]

One of the most important questions related to the effectiveness and acceptance of environmental management systems is the degree of participation within the economy. In relation to EMAS, the most significant fact, which even experts cannot explain, is that the great majority of participants are either sites of German companies or international companies situated in Germany. More than 74 per cent of the 2700 registered sites all over Europe are located in Germany. In relation to the different sizes of the EU member states, Austria proportionately has the largest share of participants, followed by Germany and the Scandinavian countries.[6] Compared with the total number of possible participating companies, the share of EMAS sites is far less than 1 per cent even in the German-speaking countries.

Figure 11.3 shows a comparison between the figures of EMAS and ISO 14001 participants. Although the ISO 14001 standard has existed for less than two years, whereas EMAS participation has been possible since 1995, there are more than twice as many ISO participants than EMAS sites worldwide. Even in the European Union, apart from Germany, there are more ISO than EMAS participants. Taking into account that some of them might have installed an EMAS as well as an ISO environmental management system, it can be expected that EMAS will have difficulties competing with ISO 14001, depending on the results of the recent amendment process of the EMAS regulation in Brussels.

Significantly higher than the number of EMAS participants is the number of companies that admitted in questionnaires that they did not know about EMAS and/or ISO 14001. The UNI/ASU research found that 28 per cent of the

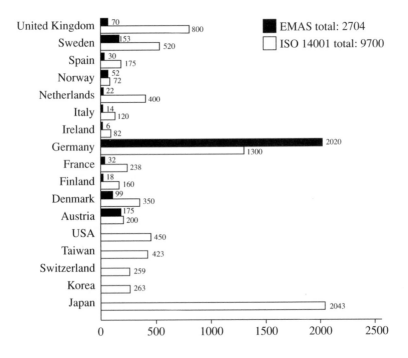

Figure 11.3   EMAS and ISO 14001 participants in different countries (as at April 1999)

executive managers did not know about the EMAS regulation (UNI/ASU, 1997, p. 54). The questionnaire of the Institute for Research on Social Chances Cologne, found that 33 per cent did not know the regulation as a whole and 36 per cent claimed to know it partly (Jaeger et al., 1998, p. 60). Even fewer managers knew the ISO 14001 standard. Fifty-four per cent of the respondents conceded not knowing it (ibid., p. 64).

The implementation of an environmental management system implies considerable costs for the realization of the EMAS project from the decision to participate up to the validation of the whole process and the registration of the site or organization. In relation to the results of the UNI/ASU questionnaire, these costs differ a great deal, from below €5000 to more than €1.000.000 (UNI/ASU, 1997, p. 24). The average costs of an EMAS project amount to €80.000, with the biggest part (more than €45 000) being internal costs. On average, nearly €17 500 has to be paid for external consultation, €7500 for each validation by the accredited verifier and the environmental statements and approximately €700 for the registration.

These costs are mainly influenced by the size of the sites. Another influencing factor is industry sector, but it is not as important as size. Because small and medium-sized enterprises tend to need external consultation more than larger companies, they have significantly higher shares of external expenditures.

Since EMAS and ISO 14001 participation is voluntary, companies will join the systems if the costs are offset by significant corporate benefits. These could be found in direct cost savings by reducing the input of resources and the output of waste by means of environmental management systems. Additionally, they could be found in benefits that can hardly be valued in monetary terms, such as image improvements.

In various questionnaires, managers reported some considerable cost savings in connection with measures of corporate environmental protection. About 30 per cent of the respondents in the UNI/ASU study claimed cost savings between €5000 and €50 000 per year and another 30 per cent claimed savings of between €50 000 and €250 000 per year. A total of 15 per cent obtained even more than €250 000 per year. Related to the EMAS costs as mentioned above, the average repayment time was less than a year and a half.[7]

The environmental organization structures established in management systems do not differ significantly from those structures required by regulatory law. The majority of the companies (83 per cent) have appointed environmentally responsible managers in senior positions as well as environmental specialists (57 per cent), as demanded by various environmental laws. Environmental committees exist in 46 per cent of the companies. By bringing together members of various departments, the environmental responsibility could be disseminated through all of the different departments and functions. The committees do not generally include the 'normal' employees but only a wider circle of experts. Thirty-seven per cent of the members of the works councils interviewed stated that 'normal' employees are members of environmental circles or committees. Oral (65 per cent) and/or written (67 per cent) instruction by superiors still seems to be the normal employee 'participation' in EMAS-formed corporate environmental management systems.

Many questionnaires try to establish whether the process of continuous improvement, which the environmental management systems intend, has already been initiated. Early studies (see, for example, Freimann and Schwaderlapp, 1996) found that the established structures – formal responsibilities, working and procedural instructions, periodical audits and detailed environmental manuals – result in strict formalism and clear documentation rather than in adaptable and innovative organizational structures and processes. This finding was not only gained from empirical studies. It seems to be an inevitable symptom of formal environmental management systems such as EMAS and ISO 14001 which are primarily installed to be externally audited and certified (see Freimann, 1997).

Recent empirical studies, and the conclusions drawn from their results, tend to confirm the early judgements. In the first place, EMAS environmental management systems are expert systems. The participation of the employees is said by most of the respondents to be very important, but in practice it is an exception. The participation of the works council is only found in a small minority of companies. The established structures mostly show no difference from those demanded by legal regulations. Therefore they do not improve corporate environmental care more than the obligatory ones did.

It is the formal structure of the systems themselves, and not only the special German method of implementation, that causes this phenomenon. The implementation requires systematic checks of all relevant corporate activities and complete documentation of all formal measures installed, at least in relation to the accredited verifier and – because it must publish an environmental statement – even partly in respect of the public. At the same time a process of continuous improvement of corporate environmental care should be established. According to the findings of modern organizational theory, this can only be realized by loosening strict regulations and structures and enforcing organizational learning and development.

Nevertheless, the implementation of an environmental management system is still a process with an open end, which raises the importance of corporate environmental care and of the actors dealing with this task. Following the basic theoretical analysis of Giddens (1986), even strict formal regulations include possibilities of change and development, creating scope for actors who manage to make use of it. EMAS constitutes 'recursive regulation', the results of which could only appear if actors 'live' the established structures. This also means, however, that this phenomenon cannot be ascertained through the current questionnaires because the management systems have only been in existence for a very short period.

3. BASIC CONCEPTS OF ENVIRONMENTAL INFORMATION SYSTEMS

Environmental information systems for products, production processes, factories and companies have been developed since the end of the 1970s. Although their number and methods have risen immensely, there are basically two streams of concepts to consider. These may provide some insight into the basic method-ological problems of qualitative environmental information systems that more recent approaches and variations also face.

3.1 Ecological Accounting

Ecological accounting (Mueller-Wenk, 1978) uses a closed, non-monetary information and evaluation system relating to the effects of business activities, and does not try to assess externalities in monetary terms.

The structure of ecological accounting is like that of the financial accounting system. For the different kinds of physical environmental impacts (especially consumption of resources, air pollution, waste and so on) a chart of accounts has to be established with one class of accounts for each form of pollution. Within this class there are other detailed accounts. The consumed quantity of substances is estimated in physical units (kg, ton, m^3). Subsequent material deliveries are added to special absorption accounts, thereby reducing the firm's environmental consumption. At the end of the period, all accounts have to be closed and integrated into a firm's eco-balance sheet, a list of the company's total consumption of different materials and energy.

After this, each item of the company's physical environmental consumption has to be valued by 'coefficients of equivalence'. The coefficients are regarded as a standard for ecological shortage (for example, depletion of resources or environmental stress of emissions) and contain the dimension of 'ecological unit per scale of physical consumption of substance' (for example, ecological units per MWh). The values of the equivalence coefficients depend on the ecological scarcity of the different materials or on the capability of the environment to absorb the different emissions. The closer the actual consumption or emission rate is to the socially acceptable rate (which has to be found subject to different social and natural conditions in a certain region), the lower the value of the coefficient.

These coefficients of equivalence, determined in a complex social evaluation process by an interdisciplinary team of experts and – in the case of common use of the concept – by the government, are used to value the firm's pressure on the environment. They serve as multipliers of volume consumption, eliminating different physical dimensions and permitting the evaluation of the total consumption of 'ecological units of account' in a given period. Table 11.1 shows an example of the system and its structure with some representative materials or emissions.

Table 11.1   Basic structure of ecological accounting

Substance or emission	Quantity	Equivalence coefficient	Ecological accounting units (EU)
(1)	(2)	(3)	(4) = (2) × (3)
Energy consumption (electricity)	7 700 000 kWh	15.75 EU/MWh	121 275
Material consumption			
iron	3 600 000 kg	0.0388 EU/t	141
tin	23 700 kg	72.7 EU/kg	1 730 000
Solid waste, non-toxic	2284 m^3	0.0114 EU/m^3	26
Gaseous waste (hydrocarbon)	29 771 kg	1401 EU/t	41 084
Total effect (sum of all ecological accounting units)			3 124 000

Source: Mueller-Wenk (1978), p. 68.

The values of the examples shown in Table 11.1 present the derivation of different units of account from the diversified coefficients of equivalence. They relate to the ecological risk of the respective substances and stress the eco-balance accordingly. As a whole, the system allows sophisticated analysis of a company's different pressures on the environment, as well as presenting one aggregated index number for the complete ecological pressure in a given period of time.

This concept was discussed in the literature and led to a number of practical projects (Simonis, 1980; Held, 1986; Braunschweig, 1988; Schulz, 1989). Comprehensive ecological assessment of materials consumption and waste emissions is an advantage, but also poses a significant problem. In fact, the firm's different impacts on the environment are extremely complex and not homogeneous. A comparative and comprehensive valuation neglects these differences; it even balances them. So it becomes possible to offset extreme air pollution by low use of resources.

The quantitative determination of the coefficients of equivalence, as well as the comprehensive report of the quantity of environmental consumption, is problematic. How long is the period for complete depletion of resources? How are the rights to use distributed worldwide? Which substances are included in detail in waste emissions and in purchased intermediate goods? How toxic are they? These questions pose a great many almost unsolvable problems.

Nevertheless, ecological accounting was an important step in the development of a reliable non-monetary environmental information system. It tried to evaluate and compare companies' impacts on the environment. Many of the questions considered above are relevant for any approach aiming at an ecological estimation of consequences, regardless of the method used, for example in product life cycle assessments.

Finally, there is one essential characteristic of the ecological accounting approach. It provides a single figure of measurement: the sum of all consumed accounting units. In a public statement one can use this figure as a reference number for political communication and discussion, even if its informative value sheds only a spotlight on the real dimension of the problem.

3.2 Product Line Analysis[8]

In sharp methodological contrast to ecological accounting, another environmental information system, called Produktlinienanalyse (product line analysis, PLA), will now be explained. Whereas ecological accounting reduces complexity and information by equally defined evaluation and by summing up various different material consumptions and emissions, PLA aims to compile all relevant detailed information and thereby extends complexity.

PLA was developed by a research task force of the Freiburg Oeko-Institut. First published in 1987, it relates to products and tries to investigate the ecological, social and economic consequences of their production, consumption and disposal. This is meant to increase knowledge for further decisions on product development.

The method's basis is the product line matrix as shown in Table 11.2. Here, the stages of the product's life cycle are defined within three relevant dimensions: nature, society and economy. These dimensions are split into a large number of operational sub-units. The stages in the product's life cycle – including the necessary transport – are placed in columns. Each field within the matrix documents the expected consequences.

The elements in the matrix have different degrees of precision depending on the stage of the planning and analysis process. They might only identify relevant spheres (for example, marking them with an asterisk), show the kinds of possible relations (positive, negative, high or low importance) or even specify quantities (consumption of resources, emissions, transportation expenditure, and so on).

Table 11.2   Product line matrix for the concept of product line analysis

	Nature (various criteria)	Society (various criteria)	Economy (various criteria)
1. Raw material production and treatment			
2. Transportation			
3. Production			
4. Transportation			
5. Trade/distribution			
6. Consumption			
7. Transportation			
8. Disposal			

Source: Projektgruppe (1987), p. 19.

3.3   Comparison of Basic Concepts and Further Methodological Developments

Comparing the ecological accounting approach with the PLA technique shows important differences. On the one hand, PLA refers to a smaller unit, namely a product, whereas ecological accounting explores a whole enterprise. On the other hand, ecological accounting is limited to the ecological dimension, whereas PLA also takes into account social and economic issues. Moreover, it documents all stages from production through consumption to disposal, no matter whether one or several economic units are involved.

As far as their methodology is concerned, both procedures aim at completeness and verification. Nevertheless, there are differences. Ecological accounting aims to assess a company's different environmental consumptions with equally defined values, measured on a cardinal scale, whereas PLA leaves it up to the user to decide to use either unvalued physical indicators of different dimensions (for example, quantities of waste, international work distribution and ethical problems of a product) or an equally defined (for example, monetary) valuation of the different qualitative attributes of a product.

PLA offers a complex set of several indicators concerning the environmental, social and economic quality of a product. It allows assessment of the whole range of effects a certain product might have, so that it can be improved in detail within multiple targets. Unlike ecological accounting, it does not rate product A over product B as a whole. An unequivocal assessment of this kind would only be possible if product A were favoured within all examined dimensions, which does not seem very realistic.

Due to its refinement, PLA seems to be appropriate in *ex ante* studies of product variations while the planning process is still in progress. Fundamental development alternatives can be compared and optimized by reducing the ecological disadvantages or risks of single attributes of a product. PLA might broaden the horizons of decision-makers and lead to the consideration of aspects within the marketing planning process that otherwise would not be taken into account.

For a summary of ecological assessment of products, processes and enterprises, it seems necessary to work on the complexity of the problem by summing up indicators, aggregating information and reducing the number of indices. With regard to this aspect, ecological accounting seems to be more promising, even if some information is lost in the process.

Several further developments within economic literature and practice therefore try to find a middle way between the concepts.

As far as ecological product balances are concerned (Rubik and Baumgartner, 1992; Umweltbundesamt, 1992; Bundesministerium, 1993), there are a large number of applied projects that are methodologically close to the concept developed by the Federal Environmental Bureau of Switzerland, which is based on the concept of ecological accounting (Bundesamt, 1984; Ahbe et al., 1990). Here, all relevant life-cycle stages are observed and the ecological valuation is summed up in multi-valued eco-profiles that refer to utilization of material and energy or the amount of air, soil and water by one index each.

The necessary standardization has led to the ISO 14040 standard for ecological product balances, which was published in summer 1997. This standard does not give detailed methodological directions but basic principles of eco-balancing. It is – as are other ISO standards for environmental management – the result of the work of different international teams such as the ISO Technical Committee Environmental Management and the Society for Environmental Toxicology and Chemistry (SETAC) and will be followed up by further standards for eco-balancing. One of these, the ISO 14041, was published in 1998 and two others will probably follow in 1999/2000. Some of the problems mentioned above will then be solved by way of standardization. Several companies all over the world use product eco-balancing and life-cycle assessment to optimize their recent products and to develop new products (Frankl and Rubik, 2000).

Another approach – the Eco-rational Path Method (EPM), developed by the Centre for Economic Studies at the University of Basle (Schaltegger and Sturm, 1991, 1992) – works on a project to determine the ecological as well as the monetary costs and benefits of corporate activities. This method leaves it to the user as to which set of indicators is observed and analysed. This makes the method particularly useful for companies' internal purposes. The analysis is always divided into two stages. First, an account of toxic agent flows is set up. Subsequently, these flows are weighted according to social–environmental goals. This estimation and valuation of ecological consequences is contrasted with an economic view which has to record all accountable costs and benefits so that in the end an evaluation of both the ecological and the economic effects is within reach. Although EPM is called 'accounting', so that one might expect a system of external accounting, it is especially useful for internal planning processes.

In practice, several companies' eco-balance sheets or environmental reports have been published all over Europe. The eco-report given by the German Kunert AG, for example, has been available since 1991. It is based upon the method of material and energy balancing, which documents all material and energy inputs and outputs for a given period. There is no aggregate ecological valuation. The second eco-report, published in 1992, for the first time offered the possibility of making comparisons between 1989, 1990 and 1991. Ecological deficits can be detected so that actions to correct them can be worked out. On the whole, this report shows the achievements and limits of the ecological optimization processes in the company.

Various companies in Germany and other countries followed suit (Fichter and Loew, 1997). More than 3000 environmental reports were published in Europe up to this time, most of them in Germany (because of EMAS participation), The Netherlands and Denmark. These last two countries are forcing large companies by law to publish 'green balances'.

The EU's EMAS also gave an immense impulse to voluntary corporate environmental disclosure, because all sites of companies that take part in EMAS have to publish an environmental statement. This is meant to inform the public about all aspects of environmental problems and activities of the company/site. The EMAS regulation, however, does not prescribe any method of environmental accounting or disclosure. Therefore the practice differs widely (Freimann, 1997). Most of the companies show more caution and reserve than needed to reduce negative images regarding their willingness to practise environmental care. The missing of clear targets of environmental reporting in the EMAS regulation is responsible for this, although some companies make use of the opportunity for reliable environmental disclosure.

The list of different methods of environmental accounting is far from complete. Nevertheless, the possible methods seem to be limited to the ecological accounting approach, aggregating available information to a single or to some valued figures, or the PLA, a method that selects some disaggregated social and ecological indicators. The questions to be answered are whether or not ecological indicators should be homogeneously valued (as is done in the ecological accounting approach), whether criteria other than ecologically related ones should be included, how the scope of the balance should be defined, and whether an *ex post* or *ex ante* perspective should be preferred.

It is unlikely that one answer is correct for all these questions. The decision must take into account the purpose of the information (for example, if it addresses external users or internal decision-makers) and the practicability of solving the problem. Further development, especially for external information purposes, must lead to standardization. The given practice of publishing individually designed eco-balances, as known from the German social accounting approach, merely aims to put one's product or company into a favourable light. This is not only harmful to ecological concerns, but also to the palliative eco-balanced company or product itself. It will be neccessary to find a consensus between political and economic interests that makes preparation and publication of eco-balance sheets compulsory. Only in this way can ecological progress be reliably assessed, and companies' legitimate interest to ensure social acceptance be achieved.

4. FURTHER DEVELOPMENTS: ECO-CONTROLLING AND COMPANY TESTING

Both in the area of companies internal considerations and introduction of ecological activities, and in the area of their external ecological accounting, new concepts have recently been developed and tested. One of these is the concept of eco-controlling (as proposed by the Institut für Ökologische Wirtschaftsforschung (IOEW), Berlin (Hallay and Pfriem, 1992)). Another concept of external information assessment of social and ecological effects of company activities, called 'company testing', has been developed by the Institut für Markt, Umwelt, Gesellschaft, Hannover, and is an extended US model (Tepper Marlin et al., 1994). Companies are assessed by an independent institute with respect to different features such as their sensitivity to ecological and social responsibility (Hansen et al., 1992). These concepts will now be described.

4.1 Eco-controlling[9]

This concept has two essential underlying assumptions that distinguish it from other concepts or from pure environmental information systems.

1. It is believed that the ecological challenge requires an early qualitative-oriented assessment of environmental activities and risks. Traditional monetary-oriented information systems are not considered appropriate.

2. This challenge has to be met by all functional executives of the corporate policy and can only be managed by a participating organization development process.

Accordingly, eco-controlling is drawn up as a social decision-making and implementation process, in which phases of cooperative policy formulation, information assessment and valuation, along with the strategic and operative conversion of activities, are related to each other by giving feedback (see Figure 11.4).

The process starts and ends with a goal-determination workshop in which all people with responsibility are involved and have to work on the formulation of operational ecological goals. Thereby, the process is actively supported by each person. The eco-controlling information system is based upon an assessment of all the relevant material and energy flows relating to all products, production processes and plant, as well as the company as a whole, including the building substance and area.

The ecological valuation (to find out potential environmental bottlenecks) follows the methodology of ABC evaluation analysis: category A contains all exceptionally relevant ecological problems requiring urgent action; category B includes ecological problems with medium-term need for action; and category

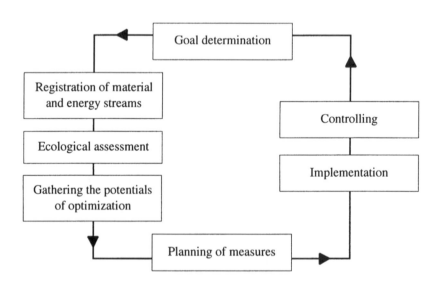

Source: Hallay and Pfriem (1992), p. 48.

Figure 11.4   Phases of the IOEW eco-controlling process

C covers non-problematic aspects of the analysed problems. This valuation is set up cooperatively and should be based on careful valuations.

After the analysis of potential bottlenecks follows the planning and implementation of arrangements within the scope of the company's ability and priorities. The performance review leads to the next eco-controlling cycle.

The eco-controlling concept was developed and tested in several practice research projects of medium-sized companies. It has proved useful, but needs the participation of external experts as change agents to widen the perspective and to take initiatives.

The concept shows pragmatic characteristics. Its aim is to give all corporate managers wide ecological sensitivity, so that after one run ecological awareness is irreversibly determined. Ecological optimization is not guaranteed because of the quite crude ecological valuation, which could lead to the result that the elimination of one bottleneck may give rise to a new one. This can only be prevented by the participation of experts from different departments and echelons of authority, who should not only be able to assess the consequences of the agreed environmental activities concerning their area of responsibility, but also have the motivation and power to enforce them consistently.

4.2 Company Testing

Company testing approaches the problem in a different way in relation to the information search as well as the provision of related activities (Hansen et al., 1992). It comprises an analysis of companies by independent institutions and is totally free from involvement of the company itself. Therefore the company must give information about features that indicate its concern for its social and ecological responsibility. Consumers in particular are the addressees of the information provided, so they are able to base their behaviour on the company test criteria and results. The information can also be used effectively in the capital and labour markets, so that the assessed companies can count on a remuneration from their market partners if they follow social and ecological aims.

The company tests performed up to now relate to the following aspects:
- willingness to cooperate with the testing institution and to provide information;
- women's emancipation;
- foreigner and minority issues;
- social engagement/sponsoring;
- political engagement;
- environmental performance;
- internal labour and social policy.

These issues are included in different social indicators and are investigated by making direct inquiries of companies or by studying secondary literature. The scope and industry membership of the assessed companies varies. Companies are not assessed by means of one single or a few key measures. In contrast to eco-controlling and eco-auditing, in which the internal or external information systems are part of a well-defined organizational process, the company testing approach does not include any organizational elements such as participation and utilization rules for different stakeholders. The user of the information provided has to evaluate the importance of the features with respect to his own attitudes.

The problems of company testing concern the justification of criteria and their transfer to quantifiable indicators allowing at least an ordinal judgement. This includes the question of the legitimacy, independence and neutrality of the institution conducting the company test, and its acceptance by companies and test addressees. These problems might have different importance according to different areas of the test. Particularly in the range of ecological results, problems will be fewer than in the political, social and ethical fields.

The users of company testing may have difficulty in making an overall judgement of the companies' social and ecological performance because of widely varying corporate profiles. Since only a few and quite different tests have been conducted, one cannot judge their effects and acceptance yet. Strong market responses as a result of ecological and social conflicts between companies and pressure groups, however (Dyllick, 1989), may indicate that company testing could promote socially and ecologically oriented consumer behaviour and, through this, environmentally conscious corporate policy.

Meanwhile three company tests were published, two dealing with the food industry (Unternehmenstester, 1995 and 1999) and one with the cosmetics and washing powder industry (Unternehmenstester, 1997). The fourth on household appliances is in preparation. They gained broad acceptance by the public, the mass media and the consumers' agencies. Empirical results about the importance of the criteria evaluated and published on the consumers' behaviour have not yet been finalized.

In the context of different environmental information systems, company testing includes characteristics in the field of external accounting that offer advantages over self-provided eco-balance sheets or environmental statements. The benefits are (institutionally guaranteed) neutrality and credibility of information, which cannot even be warranted by neutral eco-balancing auditors or verifiers. On the contrary, companies will be reluctant to publish negative results. This leads to negative test results for 'information-providing/cooperation' and prevents a differentiated judgement on the fulfilment of other criteria.

5. PROBLEMS AND PERSPECTIVES

5.1 Development of the Methods

Concepts for corporate- and product-oriented environmental information systems have been known for quite some time. Methodologically similar concepts for a qualitative evaluation of work systems, social characteristics of companies, and so on have been known for an even longer time and have been tested empirically (Freimann, 1989). A stage of development has been reached that allows their widespread use. The first impression given by the methodological diversity might suggest that much methodological work remains to be done. But most of the open questions concerning the methodological design have already been solved or can be solved by social conventions alone. The present diversity results from the lack of obligatory norms, at least in the field of external ecological accounting.

The first problem area with environmental information systems is the question of information availability. For example, if one wants to document the material items of a production process or product, including raw materials and intermediate products, the material ingredients must be known. Implementation projects have shown that this is not always the case. Not even suppliers can always provide this information. Sometimes they are not willing to pass it on for competitive motives. Further methodological developments will not solve these problems. Only proper physical and chemical analyses, or the market power of companies or consumers, will be helpful.

A more significant methodological problem concerns product eco-balances. Should an average social production technology be taken into account, or should different balances with regard to the technology used by every single producer be drawn up for competitive products? The latter is methodologically advisable but not useful for public diffusion and use of balances, because each single product might need to be balanced separately to get reliable results. Probably the decision to be reached has to be for a product balance on the basis of an average technology completed by a location-related process balance for the company concerned.

Even more difficult problems have to be faced in relation to the ecological evaluation of qualitative material characteristics of products and processes at the different levels of production, consumption and disposal. How scarce is a certain fossil fuel, how harmful is the burning or final disposal of certain kinds of waste, joint products or remains? There will be no 'objective' measure to compare and assess, as money provides for financial inputs and outputs. Moreover, sometimes the foundation for such an assessment is lacking within natural sciences.

Only convention may help, but there is still some controversy about its form. It is possible to set up an extensive catalogue of evaluation criteria (as with coefficients of equivalence within the ecological accounting approach or the eco-points of the product eco-balance). The other solution could be to forgo formal ecological assessment and to settle for selected social impact indicators (compare with material and energy balancing and the company testing concept).

Related to the problem of evaluation is that of aggregation. Aggregation is only possible in cases of standardized dimensions of valuation. The annual net profit of a company can only be found because all relevant activities and their results are valued along the same dimension, namely money. An aggregation reaching as far as this is not advisable for ecological valuations. So in this case one has to do without the clarity of one value (see, for example, the PLA and the eco-balancing of products).

The problem of aggregation is well known within all – including monetary – information systems, though it seems possible to solve it for the monetary ones. Aggregation always leads to a loss of information. Apparently unequivocal values are always gained by arbitrary valuation, but this stops no one from drawing up capital balances. Moreover, their publication is considered useful. So we should be cautious in using this argument with respect to ecological valuation only.

Several problems of the environmental information systems practised today are based on the interests that go with their implementation and use. Eco-balancing of beverage packaging leads to different results depending on whether it has been prepared by the glass industry or the metal container industry. This is not due to different methods, but to different assumptions regarding the number of use cycles of returnable bottles. To ensure neutrality and reliability means guaranteeing transparency concerning full information as well as the social utilization of the methods. One might favour a neutral authority (such as with the concept of company testing which is designed analogously to the German Stiftung Warentest) or allow those who are concerned and competent to submit their comments (for example, environmental pressure groups or workers' councils).

All these problems, however, need special solutions depending on the special purposes to be served by the environmental information system. External reporting calls for solutions or systems other than internal decision-making or controlling. Information about products needs another point of view in addition to reporting on a production process or the whole enterprise. This is why a system such as ecological accounting, that emphasizes the comprehensive ecological valuation of a whole firm accepting the loss of detailed information, is more suitable for external communication than for detailed internal planning.

Nevertheless, in principle, there are suitable systems available for all purposes. It seems that environmental information systems do not need much further investigation and development. What is needed is the promotion of social acceptance for those systems among producers and consumers, built into the concepts of eco-controlling and eco-auditing. The top priority is to ensure that companies and their pressure groups, as well as unions and employees, understand the benefit of environmental management and information systems and the necessity of their standardization so that they support the political enforcement process.

The difficult negotiations about the enforcement of the EU's EMAS show that conviction is not gained easily. Here, the EU Commission followed the industrial pressure groups and changed the obligatory draft into a voluntary one. Thereby, the dissemination of EMAS and its ecological effectiveness were probably drastically reduced. The amendment process of the 1993 regulation, which should lead to a new regulation in 2000, shows the same characteristics and is even more difficult because of the competition between EMAS and ISO 14001.

5.2 Social Implementation of Environmental Management and Information Systems

All experience with external corporate information systems shows that they are useful only when their content is standardized and when they have to be published. This is valid not only for the external addressees of the information, but also for those who have to provide it. Experience also shows that standardization is no obstacle to company information policy but that the obligations will not be met if they are not accepted by those involved.

Attempts in both directions have been made in respect of social accounting and eco-balancing. But both implementation concepts must fail, if not during the political process then in economic practice. Concerning the contents of the environmental statements, the EU regulation at least contains an external verifying procedure to increase the reliability of the declaration. But as long as companies do not accept that environmental information systems are only useful if they are reliable and revisable, they will only partially obey administrative rules. If it is left to companies to test their products and document their environmental friendliness, there will probably only be extremely eco-friendly companies and products, at least on paper. The prejudice of the public that industry is to blame for a considerable part of environmental problems will be promoted, rather than corrected, by such publications. Extensive and ecologically successful actions will hardly be improved.

There are reasons for internal problems during implementation as well. This applies not only to information systems, but to environmental management systems as a whole. Public statements by corporate management and a formal installation of a standardized environmental management system are insufficient. The environmental orientation of corporate actions must succeed at all levels of the organization. It is necessary to carry the environmental orientation into the organization from the outside as well. Employees, customers and active environmentalists play an important role in this process. They all need valid information to ensure serious long-term participation. Only if their importance is accepted within the company is it possible to implement internal and external environmental information systems.

Ambitious achievements (especially the eco-controlling concept developed by IOEW) ensure the participation of all involved during the process. This guarantees that those who have to contribute to drawing up the process can bring in their expectations at an early stage. Environmental management systems need to be 'lived' by all those internal and external stakeholders who are affected by the activities of a company. The continuous improvement of corporate environmental performance, which could be companies' contribution to sustainable development depends on information, dialogue and participation.

Generally, state-run environmental policy has to standardize and prescribe environmental information systems if it is to secure reliable ecological assessment of the environmental consequences of economic activities and production processes, as well as products and their use. Additionally, the establishment of neutral institutions (for product eco-balances or company testing) can ensure effectiveness and credibility. Environmental management systems should not be established as formal bureaucratic systems built up mainly for the purpose of external documentation and verification. Their main purpose is to gain benefits for both the companies and the environment. They must be implemented in the heads and hearts of the corporate managers and employees, and this requires a long-run social development process. But only these means will allow ecological aspects to become important in economic decisions – in the companies and in the markets as the central economic regulation systems of industrialized societies.

NOTES

1. Advertisement of German Shell Corporation (1982).
2. More than 90 per cent of the sites participating in EMAS are located in these two countries.
3. As the national authorities had to install special institutions for the national implementation of the EU regulation, the participation of companies in the scheme was possible 20 months after its effective date (see Europe Environment, 1993).
4. There are various other standards in the 14000 series, such as standards for product-eco-balancing (14040) and environmental performance evaluation, which cannot be discussed in detail in this chapter.
5. The data given in this section come from different German questionnaires and are not necessarily representative of the whole economy because companies taking part in questioning on environmental management are usually more environmentally conscious and active than others (see Freimann and Schwedes, 1999).

6. Up-to-date figures on participating sites in different countries can be downloaded from the Internet sites: http://www.ecology.or.jp/isoworld/english/analy14k.htm
7. But this method of direct benefit–cost allocation is questionable. The results of questionnaires cannot exactly make clear if and to what extent the cost savings the interviewees report are causally connected with the implementation of environmental management systems. Additionally, the interviewees mostly do not distinguish between direct EMAS costs and those costs that have to be paid for technical measures of environmental care. At least one cannot clearly judge the reliability of the cost savings statements because of the limited reliability of the cost accounting figures, especially in the field of internal costs and overheads.
8. The following is based on the concept of Produktlinienanalyse (PLA) as developed by the Freiburg Oeko-Institut. It differs from the concept of 'Product life-cycle assessment' (LCA) mainly by including social and economic consequences in its assessment (Umweltbundesamt, 1992). The usual LCA observes product life from the cradle to the grave only from the environmental point of view (for example, Steen and Ryding, 1992).
9. Also discussed under the heading of eco-controlling are concepts of monetary performance evaluation of environmentally motivated activities of companies (for example, Wagner and Janzen, 1991; Roth, 1992). These concepts cannot be described here.

REFERENCES

Ahbe, St., A. Braunschweig and R. Mueller-Wenk (1990), *Methodik fuer Oeko-Bilanzen auf der Basis oekologischer Optimierung*, Bern: Schriftenreihe Umwelt no. 133 des BUWAL, Bern: Bundesanstalt fuer Umwelt, Wald und Landwirtschaft.

Baram, M. et al. (1990), 'Managing chemical risks, corporate response to SARA', Title 111, Tufts University.

Braunschweig, A. (1988), *Die oekologische Buchhaltung als Instrument der staedtischen Umweltpolitik*, St Gallen: Ruegger.

BSI (British Standards Institution) (1992), *Specification for Environmental Management Systems*, BS 7750, London: British Standards Institution.

Bundesamt für Umweltschutz der Schweiz (1984), *Oeko-Bilanzen von Packstoffen*, Bern.

Bundesministerium fuer Umwelt, Jugend und Familie der Republik Oesterreich (1993), *Oekobilanzen von Packstoffen in Theorie und Praxis – eine Iststandserhebung*, Vienna.

Crane, Ed et al. (eds) (1992), *Corporate Environmental Responsibility, Proceedings of the Tutzing Conference*, 7–9 October 1991, Tutzing: Evangelische Akademie.

Dyllick, Th. (1989), *Management der Umweltbeziehungen. Offentliche Auseinandersetzungen als Herausforderung*, Wiesbaden: Gabler.

Europe Environment (Europe Information Service) (1993), *EC Council: Regulation Setting up an EC Eco-Management and Audit scheme*, no. 408; Brussels: European Union.

Fichter, K. and T. Loew (1997), *Wettbewerbsvorteile durch Umweltberichterstattung*, Schriftenreihe 119/97, Berlin: IOEW.

Frankl, P. and F. Rubik (2000), *Life Cycle Assessment in Industry and Business – Adoption Patterns, Applications and Implications*, Berlin: Springer.

Freeman, R.E. (1984), *Strategic Management – A Stakeholder Approach*, Boston: Pitman.

Freimann, J. (1989), *Instrumente Sozial-oekologischer Folgenabschaetzung im Betrieb*, Wiesbaden: Gabler.

Freimann, J. (1997), 'Environmental statements: valid instruments for measuring the environmental management success of a company?', *Environmental Management and Auditing*, **4** 109–15.

Freimann, J. and R. Schwaderlapp (1996), 'Implementation of the EU's EMAS Regulation in German Companies', *Eco-Management and Auditing*, **3** 109–12.

Freimann, J. and R. Schwedes (1999), 'EMAS-experiences in German companies: a survey on recent empirical studies', paper for the fifth Eco-Management and Auditing Conference at the University of Leeds, 1 and 2 July (to be published in the journal *Eco-Management and Auditing*).

Giddens, A. (1986), *Sociology: A Brief but Critical Introduction,* 2nd edn, London: Macmillan Press.

Hallay, H. and R. Pfriem (1992), *Oeko-Controlling – Umweltschutz in mittelstaendischen Unternehmen,* Frankfurt/New York: Campus.

Hansen, U., V. Luebke and I. Schoenheit (1992), 'Der Unternehmenstest als Instrument für ein sozial-ökologisch verantwortliches Wirtschaften', Arbeitspapier no. 1, Hannover: Institut für Marketing und Gesellschaft.

Hedstrom, G.S. (1992), 'Effective environmental auditing', in Ed Crane et al. (eds), *Corporate Environmental Responsibility, Proceedings of the Tutzing Conference*, 7–9 October 1991, Tutzing: Evangelische Akademie.

Held, M. (ed.) (1986), *Oekologisch Rechnen im Betrieb – Umweltbilanzierung als Grundlage umweltfreundlichen Wirtschaftens im Dienstleistungbetrieb*, Tutzinger Materialie No. 33, Tutzing.

ICC (International Chamber of Commerce) (1989), *Umweltschutz-Audits*, Cologne: ICC.

Jaeger, Th., Wellhausen, A., Birke, M. and M. Schwarz (1998), *Umweltschutz, Umweltmanagement und Umweltberatung – Ergebnisse einer Befragung in kleinen und mittleren Unternehmen*, Cologne: ISO.

Kapp, W.K. (1950), *The Social Costs of Private Enterprise*, Cambridge, MA: Harvard University Press.

McKinsey & Company (1991), *The Corporate Response to the Environmental Challenge – Summary Report*, Amsterdam: McKinsey.

Mueller-Wenk, R. (1978), *Die oekologische Buchhaltung*, Frankfurt: Campus.

Peglau, R. and B. Clark (1995), 'The European Eco-Management and Audit Scheme Regulation (EMAS) and the International Environmental Management Standard ISO 14001', *UTA International*, **1** (95), 66–73.

Projektgruppe Oekologische Wirtschaft (1987), *Produktlinienanalyse – Bederfnisse, Produkte und ihre Folgen*, Cologne: Kölner Volksblatt.

Roth, U. (1992), *Umweltkostenrechnung,* Wiesbaden: Deutscher Universitäts-Verlag.

Rubik, F. and T. Baumgartner (1992), *Technological Innovation in the Plastics Industry and its Influence on the Environmental Problems of Plastic Waste – Evaluation of Eco-Balances*, SAST Project no. 7, Brussels: EU.

Schaltegger, St. and A. Sturm (1991), 'Methodik der oekologischen Rechnungslegung in Unternehmen', WWZ-Studien no. 33, Basel: Wirtschaftswissenschaftliches Zentrum der Universität.

Schaltegger, St. and A. Sturm (1992), *Okologieorientierte Entscheidungen im Unternehmen*, Bern/Stuttgart/Vienna: Haupt.

Schulz, W. (1989), 'Betriebliche Umweltinformationssysteme', *Umwelt und Energie*, H. Gruppe, **12**, S.33–98.

Simonis, U.E. (ed.) (1980), *Oekonomie und Oekologie – Auswege aus einem Konflikt*, Karlsruhe: C.F. Mueller.

Steen, B. and S.O. Ryding (1992), 'The EPS enviro-accounting method', ILV-Report B 1080, Goteborg: University.

Tepper Marlin, A. et al. (1994), *Shopping for a Better World: The Quick and Easy Guide to all your Socially Responsible Shopping*, San Francisco: Sierra Club Books.

Umweltbundesamt der Bundesrepublik Deutschland (Projektgruppe Oekobilanzen) (1992), *Okobilanzen fuer Produkte, Bedeutung-Sachstand-Perspektiven*, UBA-Texte 38/92, Berlin: Umweltbundesamt.

Unternehmenstester (1995 and 1999), *Die Lebensmittelbranche*, Reinbek: Rowohlt (2nd edition 1999).

Unternehmenstester (1997), *Kosmetik, Körperpflege und Waschmittel*, Reinbek: Rowohlt.

Unternehmerinstitut e.V./Arbeitsgemeinschaft selbstaendiger Unternehmer (UNI/ ASU) (1997), *Öko-Audit in der mittelständischen Praxis – Evaluierung und Ansätze für eine Effizienzsteigerung von Umweltmanagementsystemen in der Praxis*, Bonn: ASU.

Van Buren, A. (1992), 'Corporate environmental accounting and disclosure', in Ed Crane et al. (eds), *Corporate Environmental Responsibility, Proceedings of the Tutzing Conference*, 7–9 October 1991, Tutzing: Evangelische Akademie.

Wagner, G.R. and H. Janzen (1991), 'Oekologisches Controlling – mehr als ein Schlagwort?', *Controlling*, 120 pp.

12. Environmental technology

Jim Skea

1. INTRODUCTION

Twenty years of modern environmental policy in developed countries have resulted in major improvements in the costs and effectiveness of techniques which lower levels of pollution and waste from industrial processes. Understanding the processes by which firms develop and adopt these improved techniques, and the nature of the incentives for them to do so, is of key importance from the point of view of both corporate strategy and public policy formation. This chapter links observed trends in the development and adoption of environmental technology (Ausubel and Sladovich, 1989) with broader insights derived from the economics of technical change.

The concept of *environmental technology* is elusive, and a plethora of terms has evolved to describe technology associated with improved environmental performance. A basic distinction is often made between *end-of-pipe technology* and *clean technology* (OECD, 1985). End-of-pipe refers to equipment which can be attached to existing industrial processes in order to mitigate the environmental consequences of their operation. The add-on nature of end-of-pipe technology inevitably pushes costs upwards. End-of-pipe technologies may operate by concentrating pollution or waste so that it can be contained in a specific location (waste disposal), by dispersing emissions to minimize the severity of their impacts (tall chimneys) or through transforming pollutants so that they are in a more environmentally acceptable form (throw-away flue gas scrubber systems). End-of-pipe technologies frequently give rise to cross-media effects, where the pollution is not avoided but is simply transferred from one environmental medium to another, for example, from air to water and waste in the case of throw-away flue gas scrubber systems.

Clean technologies, on the other hand, are process technologies which, by the nature of their technical characteristics, give rise to intrinsically lower levels of pollution and waste. Acknowledging that 'clean' is a highly ambiguous concept, the terms 'cleaner technology' or 'cleaner production' are often used instead (ACOST, 1992). Clean technologies can reduce costs as well as raise environmental performance. Defined in these simple terms, clean technologies are, in a generic sense, superior to end-of-pipe technologies. They represent a preventive approach to environmental management as opposed to the reactive approach symbolized by end-of-pipe techniques. As many firms now seek to adopt an anticipatory approach to environmental challenges, interest in both the concept and the practice of clean technology has grown. There is a resonance between the clean technology concept and the preventive flavour of recent corporate strategies and policies.

Some argue that the clean technology/end-of-pipe dichotomy is too simple (Irwin and Hooper, 1992). Table 12.1 provides a much more specific breakdown of various classes of environmental technology. Technology used for recycling, for example, whether inside or outside industrial plants, does not readily fit into the simple end-of-pipe/clean technology framework. Technology used for measuring and monitoring environmental performance, whether for management or regulatory purposes, is of economic importance (W.S. Atkins, 1991). Technology associated with products as opposed to processes is of great significance, not least because most waste occurrences in industrial economies are now associated with discarded consumer products rather than with unwanted industrial byproducts. It is also worthwhile maintaining a broad distinction between technologies which reduce waste and those which reduce pollution. This latter distinction relates to incentives for the adoption of environmental technology which are discussed in section 2.2.

Table 12.1   Categories of environmental technology

Class of technology	Definition
Pollution control	Air pollution control; effluent removal; noise abatement (classic end-of-pipe techniques)
Waste management	Handling, treatment and disposal of waste (end-of-pipe techniques)
Recycling	Waste minimization through the reuse of materials recovered from waste streams
Waste minimization	Production processes and techniques which minimize waste streams
Clean technology	Production processes which, by their nature, give rise to low levels of environmental impact
Measurement and monitoring	Sampling, measurement, data analysis
Clean products	Products which give rise to low levels of environmental impact through the entire life cycle of design, production, use and disposal

Source: based on ACOST (1992).

Especially in the field of waste management and disposal, the conceptual-ization of environmental technology has been based on systems approaches rather than on economic principles. This is exemplified by the concept of the *waste ladder*, a hierarchy of approaches to waste management which works from landfilling (least desirable), through incineration/thermal recovery, recycling, reuse and waste minimization to the most desirable option, waste avoidance. In practice, landfilling is the dominant mode of waste management, though it is becoming less so as landfill charges rise. It is not obvious in advance that it is economically ideal to move as high up the waste ladder as possible: it depends on the relative costs of the different options. Equally, the contention that clean technology is superior to end-of-pipe technology must be tested against the evidence in specific circumstances.

There are important differences between the incentives for and the means by which environmental technology is adopted by firms and those which apply to the adoption of technology more generally. Nevertheless, the relatively limited literature focusing specifically on the economics of technical change has some relevance (Dosi, 1988).

Early work addressed the relative importance of the *technology-push* (the availability of technical solutions) versus the *demand-pull* (market-related and other factors external to the firm) in influencing innovative activity (Mowery and Rosenberg, 1979). In general, the technology-push appears to be more important where innovation is tied to basic research, for example in the biotech-nology field. The demand-pull tends to dominate where market needs are urgent and specific (Freeman, 1982, p. 103). The nature and urgency of the pressures on firms to improve their environmental performance suggest that the demand-pull has been a dominant factor in the development of environmental technology. At the same time, environmental technologies typically rely on well-established physical and chemical techniques, suggesting that the technology-push has been a less significant factor.

More recent work on technical change has developed the concepts of tech-nological paradigms and technological trajectories to characterize innovation processes. A technological paradigm is defined as a pattern for solution of selected techno-economic problems based on highly selected principles (Dosi, 1988). A paradigm defines the technological opportunities for further innovations and some basic procedures for how to exploit them, thus channelling innovative activity in certain directions. Examples might be electricity generation based on steam cycles or the use of landfill as a solution to waste problems. Technical change within a paradigm relies heavily on learning-by-doing and is best viewed as a cumulative process. The cumulative nature of technical change can lead both firms and entire industrial sectors to become 'locked in' to specific technological approaches.

A technological trajectory represents progress made through economic and technological trade-offs within a given technological paradigm. The rate of progress along a trajectory and the intensity of the search for improved techniques will be influenced by demand conditions, for example, market parameters or government regulation. Changed demand conditions can also influence the viability of the current technological paradigm. Sufficiently large changes in the 'environment' in which a firm or an industry operates, including environmental pressures, can induce a paradigm shift in the techniques used.

The trajectory/paradigm framework can be used to illuminate the environmental technology concepts described above. The development of end-of-pipe technologies has typically been induced by specific and urgent demand-pull pressures, usually taking the form of environmental regulation. Often based on well-established techniques, end-of-pipe technologies allow firms to operate within the existing technological paradigm, though costs are inevitably pushed upwards. They are particularly attractive to firms and sectors which have become locked into specific technological solutions. Clean technologies, on the other hand, may be associated with paradigm shifts within the sector concerned. The time-scales over which paradigm shifts take place are inevitably longer than those associated with the introduction of end-of-pipe technologies. Also, new cleaner technological paradigms may emerge in the absence of a demand-pull created by environmental regulation. From the environmental point of view, this represents an autonomous improvement in performance. The replacement of coal-fired power stations by cleaner combined-cycle gas turbines in the UK exemplifies this phenomenon.

The literature on the economics of technical change also relies on the concept of 'appropriability', that is, the degree to which firms can realize economic returns from innovation. Clearly, if appropriability conditions are not right, innovation will not take place. In the past, regulation often forced environmental innovation in a simple fashion by creating potential losses (for example, plant closure) for firms which failed to innovate. However, firms which can anticipate changes in environmental controls may be in a position to appropriate the economic returns from new technology which complies with the anticipated standards. The returns may be realized by licensing the new technology to firms which have been less effective in anticipating developments.

The first section of this chapter explores the concept of environmental technology and identifies relevant concepts from the economics of technical change. The second section moves on to consider the demand side of the market for environmental technology, considering the role which regulation and market forces have to play. Section 3 addresses the supply of environmental technology, analysing the structure and the degree of maturity of the environmental services market. The fourth section goes beyond the simple supply side/demand side characterization in order to describe, by using examples, inter-firm activity in the environmental technology field as well as collaboration between firms and public authorities. Section 5 illustrates the various trends described in the previous sections with a specific case study of air pollution control in the power generation sector. In the final section the broader conclusions are drawn together.

2. INCENTIVES FOR ADOPTING CLEANER TECHNOLOGY

2.1 Regulatory Stimuli

The main stimulus for improved environmental performance at the firm level has been environmental regulation. The principles underlying various forms of environmental policy and regulation are discussed in more detail in Chapter 6. This section explores more specifically the interactions between regulatory style and incentives for technical change.

Since the late 1960s there have been at least three phases of environmental regulation. During the first phase regulators tended to be proactive and were driven by high levels of public concern about environmental damage. Following the 1973 oil crisis, a regulatory backlash followed, driven partly by the state of the world economy, and partly by a wide perception that 'excessive' environmental regulation was inhibiting commercial (as distinct from compliance) innovation which could act as a stimulus to economic growth (Rothwell, 1992). More recently, higher economic growth, coupled with a new wave of concern about problems such as acid rain and climate change, has provoked a reawakening of interest in environmental regulation. This new wave is characterized by a more sophisticated understanding of regulatory processes and their technological implications, as well as an interest in a wider range of regulatory instruments (Commission of the European Communities, 1993).

The key lesson to be learned from the earlier phase of environmental regulation is that it is not environmental regulation *per se* which inhibits commercial innovation, but poor formulation and implementation. Among the specific conclusions reached regarding this earlier phase (Ashford and Heaton, 1979; OECD, 1985; Rothwell, 1992) are that:

1. Very rapid compliance schedules associated with technology-forcing regulation provided inadequate time for learning-by-doing. Installing large quantities of new technology very quickly allows no time to develop and refine novel techniques.

2. Short compliance schedules steer industry towards quick-fix, end-of-pipe solutions as these are more likely to be available 'off the shelf'.

3. Inadequate consultation between poorly informed regulators and industry may lead to unrealistically or ambiguously formulated standards which do not provide clear signals regarding appropriate technological responses. This adds considerably to the perceived risks associated with developing innovative solutions.

4. As referred to in Chapter 6, the regulatory instruments used in the past, notably inflexible standards established in a 'command and control' mode, do not provide dynamic incentives to improve technology.

5. The uneven application of environmental standards, within countries and between countries, confers disadvantages on specific firms and operators in a way that has no economic or environmental rationale. Lack of harmonization also leads to a fragmentation of research and development (R&D) effort, as specific programmes become focused on specific regulatory regimes. With a more coordinated approach to environmental technology, R&D within and between firms could lead to more innovative solutions.

Most of these lessons have been absorbed to some degree in the more recent wave of environmental regulation. However, a fundamental tension remains between the demands of the public and pressure groups for high standards and rapid fixes, and the desire of industry for more measured approaches which may yield longer-term technological, economic and environmental benefits.

The tendency for regulatory regimes to become more harmonized across international boundaries is illustrated by the significant expansion of European Union (EU) environmental policy and the incorporation of environmental issues into the North American Free Trade Agreement (NAFTA). The European Community's new action programme on the environment (Commission of the European Communities, 1992) and the parallel effort to introduce a common system of Integrated Pollution Prevention and Control (IPPC throughout the EU (Commission of the European Communities, 1993) illustrate the newer approaches:

1. Within the IPPC system, it is proposed that rolling ten-year programmes will be established for tightening standards for specific classes of industrial plants. The performance to be achieved by the best available technology (BAT) at any time will be defined through consultations between public authorities, industry and other interested parties. New plants will be required to meet the standards defined by BAT, though operators will have flexibility to decide which technical means they use. Existing plants will be required to upgrade to the new standards (or close) within a ten-year time horizon. In principle, this should avoid one of the perverse effects of applying strict

standards to new plants only – that of operators retaining an older, more polluting plant in operation longer than would otherwise have been the case.
2. There is a desire for a more open dialogue between regulators, industry and other groups ('shared responsibility') in order to introduce more clarity and satisfy industry's demands for a stable and predictable regulatory regime.
3. R&D programmes are intended to stimulate more innovative technological solutions which should be applicable within the framework of the ten-year rolling programmes.
4. There is to be a move away from 'command and control' approaches and a greater emphasis on regulatory instruments which leave more discretion to industry in deciding which technical measures to adopt. There is a desire to make greater use of market-based instruments, such as taxes and tradable emission permits which, as discussed in Chapter 6, provide dynamic incentives for technological innovation. However, the notorious example of the EU's carbon tax proposal illustrates the political difficulties that may be associated with this approach (Karadeloglou et al., 1995).

As practical experience with market-based instruments for environmental protection is limited, there is little empirical evidence to support the hypothesis that their use provides incentives to improve technology. However, initial evidence from the USA, which has introduced a comprehensive emissions trading programme for sulphur dioxide, is promising. The cost of flue gas desulphurization (FGD) technology has dropped significantly since the programme was introduced. Emissions trading has established a benchmark 'price for pollution' against which equipment manufacturers are able to gauge the performance of their products. The intensification of competition which has resulted is apparently leading to improvements in cost and performance (Sorrell, 1994).

2.2 Linking Economic and Environmental Performance

The traditional view of firms is that the environment is a potential economic burden in that investment to comply with regulation diverts funds away from more productive activities (Irwin and Vergragt, 1989). Among small to medium-sized firms, this perception is still dominant. However, recent years have seen the development of more proactive attitudes, conditioned by the growing perception that some technical measures (cleaner technologies) offer both economic and environmental advantages. Regulatory pressures may be the factor that triggers awareness of such opportunities, but once these have been identified the search for cost reductions becomes an important motive.

The nature of the relationship between production processes and environmental pressures is the key factor. There is a useful distinction to be drawn between 'waste' on the one hand and 'emissions' on the other. The wastage of energy and raw materials gives rise to costs, both through higher purchasing requirements and, in the case of raw materials, through waste disposal. On the other hand, 'emissions' to the atmosphere or to water generally consist of smaller quantities of trace materials which create problems because of their toxicity or polluting nature rather than their volume. Recovery of these trace materials is seldom useful, practicable or economic from the point of view of the firm. In the absence of tangible external pressures, controlling them offers no benefit in cost terms.

In general, proactive environmental strategies, which have been described at length in the literature (Dorfman et al., 1992, 1993; Groenewegen and Vergragt, 1991; Jackson, 1993; Schmidheiny, 1992), have focused on cutting down on waste. The scope for reducing costs in this way depends on the abundance of 'low-hanging fruit', that is, technical options, sometimes rather simple ones, which yield high rates of return but which have not previously been taken up. There is strong evidence that many such measures are available to firms. Opportunities may have arisen because of a change in external circumstances, that is, demand conditions. For example, the substantial rises in energy prices which took place in the 1970s created many cost-effective opportunities to reduce fuel consumption. Similarly, rising landfill costs and the ever-expanding definition of hazardous waste provide economic incentives to make more efficient use of materials. However, many potential waste-reducing measures are not taken up simply because they escape the attention of management or because a lower priority is given to cost-saving as opposed to mainstream production investment. In most companies, cost-cutting investment is subject to demanding payback criteria. Wider social concerns about environmental issues can be the factor that triggers the search for cost-effective measures.

Although economic incentives steer firms towards the reduction of waste, such measures can also help to reduce emissions of pollutants. The amount of pollution emitted from a plant is closely linked to the amount of material or energy processed. Cutting down on waste and energy use has a gearing effect which will also serve to reduce pollution. In foundries, for example, melting metals prior to casting entails a significant amount of energy use and gives rise to atmospheric emissions. Reducing the amount of material wasted in the casting process reduces the amount of metal which must be melted and has consequent environmental benefits. In general, measures which reduce materials flows can also reduce the cost of pollution control required to meet emission standards (Dorfman et al., 1993).

The most celebrated corporate effort to reduce waste and pollution cost effectively has been 3M's Pollution Prevention Pays programme. Between 1975 and 1990, 3M identified 3000 different projects that saved $537 million while achieving substantial reductions in solid waste, waste water and air pollution (Schmidheiny, 1992, p. 100). There has been an accumulation of similar examples elsewhere. A study of 29 chemical plants in New Jersey, California and Ohio identified a mixture of process modifications, operational changes, equipment changes, chemical substitutions and product changes which typically reduced hazardous waste streams by 71 per cent and yielded an average payback of 13 months (Dorfman et al., 1992). In the titanium oxide industry, a move to continuous processing led to a 99.6 per cent reduction in sulphur dioxide emissions, a 40 per cent reduction in acid waste and a 25 per cent reduction in energy use (Groenewegen and Vergragt, 1991).

Achievements such as these come from a variety of sources: from substantial process changes as well as from picking the 'low-hanging fruit'. In some cases environmental benefits spring from fundamental process changes which would have been instituted even in the absence of environmental pressure. In other cases, environmental pressure may have been a contributory factor to process change, operating alongside other incentives such as reduced labour costs. This makes it clear that there is a wide range of incentives for improved environmental performance by firms. Regulatory pressures have been, and are likely to remain, an important factor. But wider social pressures coupled with the search for cost reductions will also play a role. Broadly speaking, the natural incentives to reduce waste will drive firms gradually towards higher standards of environmental performance. This natural rate of improvement is unlikely to satisfy wider social demands for reduced risks and lower ecological burdens, however. Ashford (1993) provides a more complete discussion of corporate motivations for pollution prevention programmes and the relationship with regulatory activity.

2.3 First-mover Advantage

A further feature of the more proactive approach to environmental management is the growing view that environmental challenges may provide commercial opportunities as well as either threats or simple cost-saving opportunities. This change in perception, particularly notable in large firms, is beginning to condition approaches towards technology development (Schmidheiny, 1992; Hirschhorn el al., 1993). The proactive approach is underpinned by several perceptions:

1. That public demands for higher standards of environmental protection will grow, and that consequently regulatory controls will inevitably continue to be tightened.
2. That environmental pressures will impinge on firms' activities through a more diverse set of channels than previously. Apart from regulation, consumer pressure is growing while investors are becoming more conscious

of the environmental performance of firms, through concern about potential environmental liabilities (for contaminated land, for example) as well as through ethical considerations (Williams, 1992).

3. That firms which correctly anticipate these trends will be in a better position to operate in the marketplace. Developing and adopting better technologies is a component of this proactive response.

This bundle of ideas has been neatly summed up in the concept of *first-mover advantage*. This concept has notably been applied at the level of countries as well as of firms (Porter, 1990). At the firm level, fast-mover advantage may operate in a number of ways:

1. Firms which move first, in advance of regulatory requirements, can define their own timetables for investment in new technology and do not have to move with the same degree of haste as reactive firms. The longer timetables may allow the development of more innovative, 'clean technology' solutions which confer both environmental and economic advantages.
2. When regulators do define BAT, the firm's own technologies and procedures may constitute the state-of-the-art which is adopted.
3. Firms may find themselves in the position of being able to support regulatory initiatives rather than opposing them, thus enhancing their wider public reputation.
4. Firms are able to appropriate potential economic advantages because their compliance costs are lower than firms which have not been proactive. Even more direct economic advantages may accrue if firms are in a position to license technology to others. However, there is also a risk that second-movers may appropriate compliance technology without incurring all of the development costs.

At country level, first-mover advantage can operate if strict regulatory regimes promote the development of compliance technology. If stricter standards are then picked up in other countries, the first-mover is in a position to take advantage of export opportunities. The comparative Japanese advantage in air pollution control technology following its introduction of strict controls in the 1970s is often cited. German pressure to spread strict environmental controls to other EU member states has been identified as a possible attempt to cash in on first-mover advantage (Boehmer-Christiansen and Skea, 1991). However, the very rapid application of air pollution controls in Germany in the 1980s meant that Japanese companies were able to exploit their first-mover advantage.

There is clear evidence that fast-mover advantage has operated in specific markets and specific circumstances. However, as in the case of Japanese success in German power plant emission control markets in the 1980s (described in section 5), this has often resulted from a fortuitous set of circumstances rather than from a set of deliberate strategic decisions. The concept of first-mover advantage has been used as a general rationale for putting in place more ambitious environmental policies at both the national and corporate level (Porter, 1990). However, there are almost certainly circumstances in which firms (or countries) which find themselves lagging behind first-movers will find it to their advantage to try to delay environmental regulation in order to give themselves time to catch up in technological terms. This is a rational response to 'second-mover disadvantage', which may be the corollary of first-mover advantage. Other possibilities exist, however. Gabel (1995) describes how, in the case of HCFCs and HFCs, a second-mover was able to leapfrog a first-mover in terms of technology.

3.   THE SUPPLY OF ENVIRONMENTAL TECHNOLOGY

Firms generating waste or pollution are not the only actors in the process of environmental innovation. While it is impossible to align environmental protection activity with headings of the standard industrial classification, the concept of an environmental services industry has proved useful. There is no precise definition of such a sector, but broadly it covers all enterprises that supply goods and services which help to measure, prevent, limit or correct environmental damage. There have been a range of estimates of the size of this market. These are very hard to compare because of differences in methodology and estimation procedures. The size of the market in the EU was estimated to be about 40 billion ecus (thousand million)/year in 1987 (Recherche Développement International, 1990), while ECOTEC has estimated the size of the UK market to be 0.7–1.0 per cent of GDP (ECOTEC, 1992). There is a general consensus that the market is growing.

Part of the difficulty associated with estimating the size of the market for environmental capital goods lies in the clean technology/end-of-pipe distinction. It is relatively easy to identify suppliers of end-of-pipe equipment which treats effluents or cleans up flue gases. With clean technology, environmental performance is intrinsic to the design of process plants, and the degree of investment in environmental protection is virtually impossible to identify. However, research carried out (Table 12.2) indicates that end-of-pipe technologies still account for a dominant share of the market.

The environmental services industry comprises a diverse range of enterprises and activities. The sector is very fragmented, though in the more mature markets for environmental protection (Germany and The Netherlands, for example) the degree of concentration is rising. Fragmentation arises because the risks of focusing exclusively on the supply of environmental capital goods are too high.

Table 12.2   Share of end-of-pipe technology in pollution control investment

Belgium	80%
Germany (Western Länder)	82%
France	87%

Source: Based on Recherche Développement International (1990).

For many suppliers environmental goods are a secondary and intermittent side market. The markets in many countries are dominated by small to medium-sized enterprises which have no long-term strategies for exploiting environmental opportunities.

As argued above, the demand side of the market has been defined largely by government regulation and is subject to huge political risks. While the environment was a priority in the early 1970s, the degree of political interest was much lower following the oil crises of the 1970s. The instability in the markets for environmental capital goods has been a direct result of this pattern of regulation. When a regulation is promulgated, there may be an initial burst of investment activity which lasts a small number of years. Thereafter, the rate of investment is likely to subside to a basic replacement level.

The larger players in the environmental services market tend to have diversified into related activities. For example, manufacturers of industrial boilers have played a leading role in the supply of flue gas cleaning equipment for power generation. In Japan, Mitsubishi and Babcock Hitachi have been major suppliers of sulphur dioxide and NO_x clean-up equipment, and have licensed their technology to suppliers in Germany and the USA as stringent emissions standards have spread internationally. This is a concrete example of the first-mover advantage principle in operation. Where governments have sent clear signals that they intend to pursue long-term, consistent policies with respect to environmental regulation, some companies have seen it as being to their advantage to expand their areas of environmental competence through internal growth, mergers or acquisitions. Companies such as Deutsche Babcock, the German market leader, have been able to hedge against changes in the emphasis of environmental policy by diversifying into air pollution control, effluent treatment and waste disposal (Recherche Développement International, 1990).

The recent, more proactive corporate environmental strategies, if sustained, may also help to create more reliable markets for environmental technologies. However, many corporate programmes consist of large numbers of relatively small, technically simple projects (the 'low-hanging fruit') rather than radical shifts in process technology (Ashford, 1993). The average savings per project in 3M's Pollution Prevention Pays programme, for example, are about $180 000.

Modest projects of this type are typically carried through in-house and may not provide any significant stimulus to the environmental services industry *per se.*

The broader trends towards the defragmentation of the environmental services industry have led some people to characterize markets for environmental technology as going through a three-stage evolution (ACOST, 1992). This is characterized by the interplay between the demand side of the market, as defined by government regulation, and the growing competencies of supplier firms. The three phases are:

- *Phase 1* – characterized by little environmental legislation, virtually no identifiable supply industry and only end-of-pipe controls;
- *Phase 2* – characterized by more, yet still reactive environmental legislation, with more focus on waste management issues;
- *Phase 3* – characterized by integrated, preventive approaches to environmental and industrial policy with a strong environmental services sector and an emphasis on cleaner as opposed to end-of-pipe technology.

However, the assumption that environmental markets in all countries will inevitably progress through these three phases deserves to be treated with caution. The characterization is broadly supported by comparisons across

Table 12.3   EU environmental services market, 1987

Member state	Market size (b ECU)	GDP (b ECU)	Market/GDP (%)	Market phase
Germany	14.4	1025.4	1.40	3
Netherlands	2.0	194.7	1.03	3
UK	6.8	686.5	0.99	2
France	7.7	804.2	0.96	2
Belgium	1.2	126.2	0.95	2
Denmark	0.8	90.9	0.88	2
Ireland	0.2	27.1	0.74	1
Italy	4.6	701.8	0.66	1
Greece	0.2	44.1	0.45	1
Spain	1.2	289.8	0.41	1
Portugal	0.1	35.1	0.28	1
EU total	39.3	4025.8	0.98	

Source: Based on Recherche Développement International (1990) and Commission of the European Communities (1993).

countries, but still represents an aspiration as much as an impartial analysis. Even in countries believed to have Phase 3 markets, such as Germany and The Netherlands (ACOST, 1992), end-of-pipe technologies are dominant, as Table 12.3 shows.

Table 12.3 shows the size of the environmental services market in EU member states in 1987. It also shows a set of judgements concerning the stage of development that each national market has reached. Only Germany and The Netherlands are at the final mature stage of market development, while the Mediterranean countries and Ireland are in Phase 1. Germany and The Netherlands together account for more than 40 per cent of the EU market for environmental services. In the longer term, there may be a convergence between national markets in terms of maturity and structure as EU environmental policy, led by countries such as Germany and The Netherlands, begins to take effect in other markets.

4. INTER-FIRM AND GOVERNMENT–FIRM RELATIONSHIPS

A simple supply side/demand side characterization does not do justice to the rich diversity of institutional and organizational forms associated with the development and diffusion of environmental technologies. Environmental markets are characterized by numerous instances of relationships between firms, as well as relationships between firms and public sector bodies. These arrangements are critical to the innovative process. This section illustrates a range of such relationships.

4.1 Supplier/Customer Relationships: Intermediate Goods

A commonly cited example of an important relationship between firms is that between large sophisticated firms (for example, automobile manufacturers) and their smaller satellite suppliers. In order to satisfy consumer and wider public demands for good environmental practice, the larger firm may need to ensure that its suppliers also have good standards of environmental performance. This will lead the large firm to seek assurances about production performance or sustainable sources of raw materials. Accreditation schemes with voluntary participation may have an important role to play in cementing this type of relationship. Participation in eco-labelling schemes, such as that introduced by the EU, may require a large company to ascertain the credentials of its suppliers. Eco-auditing schemes (see Chapter 11), such as the UK's BS 7750 Environmental Management Scheme, may provide evidence that a supplier is reaching adequate standards of environmental performance.

4.2   Supplier/Customer Relationships: Capital Goods

Many end-of-pipe technologies can be purchased more or less 'off the shelf' and added to existing process plants. However, new, cleaner technologies in which environmental performance is integral to the process may require a much closer technical relationship between capital goods suppliers and operators. The interaction between the petroleum refining industry, which operates complex, tightly integrated processes, and equipment suppliers provides a suitable example. Other examples include energy suppliers. For example, the UK gas industry develops furnace technology for the metals processing industry in order to reinforce its marketing strategy *vis-à-vis* electricity suppliers. Although capital cost reduction may be a major goal, the successful marketing of technology will involve consideration of factors such as fuel efficiency, waste reduction and the plant operating environment. Full consideration of these factors requires close interaction with potential customers.

4.3   Licensing Arrangements

Licensing arrangements have been particularly common for end-of-pipe abatement technology when stricter standards have evolved at different rates in different countries. For example, Japanese suppliers established an early lead in flue gas clean-up technology, which they were in a position to supply to other countries at a later date. However, local suppliers may be in a better position to apply these technologies in new countries because of their knowledge of technical conditions (for example, quality of combustion fuels) and because construction activity may be better managed by companies familiar with local practices and arrangements. Licensing arrangements can be used to allow local companies access to technology to the benefit of both parties.

4.4   Consortia

Sometimes responses to specific environmental challenges cut across sectors, demand industry-wide action or require integrated responses up and down a supply chain. In these circumstances, collaborative arrangements or more formal consortia may be an appropriate response. Numerous examples of such arrangements are already in existence. Major cross-cutting environmental problems, such as those in the transport domain, require more imaginative approaches. For example, vehicle emissions control is an issue that concerns both vehicle manufacturers and fuel suppliers. The UK Engine Emissions

Consortium has been put together to carry out collaborative work involving vehicle manufacturers and Exxon.

Recycling is another prime example of an area where coordinated responses are essential. The EU's action programme on the environment (Commission of the European Communities, 1992) specifies a number of priority waste streams, one of which is discarded motor vehicles. The current organization of disposal and dismantling activities means that a coordinated response from manufacturers is desirable. In the UK this has resulted in the formation of the Automotive COnsortium on Recycling and Disposal (ACORD) which is attempting to define, at the industry level, a proven strategy for dealing with this waste stream. This consortium also provides an interface between government and the industry as a whole.

4.5 Mergers and Acquisitions

Mergers and acquisitions have a role to play in the maturing of environmental technology markets. From the point of view of an individual firm, these developments may be motivated by: (1) the desire to access technology; or (2) to access markets for technology which it already possesses (Good, 1991).

4.6 Trade Associations

Many sectors are dominated by small to medium-sized companies which do not have the individual capacity to support significant amounts of R&D activity leading to successful environmental innovation. In such sectors, for example the foundry industry, trade associations and industry-wide research organizations often play a key role in fostering technological change. Indeed, it is often trade associations that act as the primary link between industry and regulatory authorities when it comes to negotiating or interpreting new regulations. Small to medium-sized firms tend to function reactively with respect to environmental issues. The degree to which they 'use' the trade associations and research organizations to which they are affiliated can have an important influence on their success in adapting to new regulatory demands.

4.7 Government Support for Research, Development and Demonstration

Most countries support research, development and demonstration (RD&D) activity intended to support cleaner technologies and foster the development of the environmental services industry. The motivation for such support may be to foster indigenous supply capabilities to take commercial advantage (or minimize the disadvantage) associated with differential standards of environmental control.

There are many examples of schemes which offer public support for new technologies. In the UK, for example, the Department of Trade and Industry (DTI) operates an Environmental Technology Innovation Scheme (ETIS) which provides grants of up to 50 per cent for the development of new technologies up to the proof-of-concept stage in the areas of cleaner production, recycling, waste treatment and environmental monitoring. For technologies that are closer to commercialization, the DTI's Environmental Management Option Scheme (DEMOS) provides assistance for companies installing 'state-of-the-art' technology and for collaborative ventures to assess the feasibility of new techniques. There are similar programmes in place at the EU level, including EUROENVIRON, which provides a mechanism for collaborative R&D across member states. The EU also runs more focused sectoral schemes, including JOULE (Joint Opportunities for Unconventional or Long-Term Energy Supply) and REWARD (REcycling and WAste Research and Development).

It is usually the case that this participation of government in the 'technology-push' is sponsored by sections of the administration other than those that are responsible for regulatory policy. Internal coordination of activity is essential if a government's 'technology-push' and 'demand-pull' policies with respect to the environment are to operate effectively.

Government support raises the important question of consistency with the 'polluter pays principle', which is discussed in Chapter 5. This question is most relevant in relation to near-market support (demonstration projects, for example). This issue has been considered by the European Commission in the context of competition policy. The Commission's view was that financial assistance given to facilitate compliance with environmental standards would be compatible with the common market, providing that the funding did not exceed 15 per cent of the total value and the facility had been in operation for more than two years before the standards became law. In addition, the Commission's view was that higher levels of subsidy would be acceptable if the project were intended to achieve higher standards of performance than required under legislation.

5.   ENVIRONMENTAL TECHNOLOGY AND POWER GENERATION: A CASE STUDY

This section presents a brief case study of environmental technology in relation to power generation. To some extent, this is an exceptional industry because of the degree of natural monopoly and the fact that plant operators tend to be subject to 'rate-of-return' economic regulation which may bias technological choice. Under 'rate-of-return' regulation, the prices that companies are permitted to charge are based on an allowed rate of return on capital invested, after allowing for depreciation. Nevertheless, there is now a long history of environmental control and investment and it illustrates many of the various forces and trends identified earlier in this chapter.

In many parts of the world, power generation systems rely on coal and, to a lesser extent, oil as input fuels. The inherent sulphur content of these fuels gives rise to sulphur dioxide emissions, which are associated with health effects, reduced visibility and acid rain. In conventional power generation systems, coal and oil are burned as boiler fuels and steam is raised to drive turbines. To reduce sulphur dioxide emissions, it is necessary to install end-of-pipe FGD technology. This can cut emissions by about 90 per cent but adds 15–20 per cent to the operating and capital costs of a power plant. Over 90 per cent of the world's FGD capacity is installed in three countries: the USA, Japan and Germany (Vernon and Soud, 1990).

But there are more radical alternatives which go under the heading of *clean coal technology*. These involve much more demanding combustion techniques (for example, pressurized fluidized bed combustion – PFBC or the gasification of coal prior to full combustion (integrated gasification combined cycle – IGCC). With clean coal technologies, sulphur dioxide emissions are reduced without recourse to end-of-pipe controls because sulphur can be absorbed by residual coal ash if limestone is added directly to the fluidized combustion bed. Conversion efficiencies are higher because electrical energy is extracted both from hot combustion gases/products and from steam (hence 'combined cycle'). With further development, the capital costs of clean coal technologies might also be lower, but this has yet to be demonstrated to the satisfaction of power producers.

The initial motive to clean up sulphur dioxide emissions from power stations came from the USA in the early 1970s. The principles underlying FGD technology had long been established but, by the end of the 1960s, only a few, relatively small-scale plants had been built. US regulators created New Source Performance Standards (NSPS), which were intended to force the further development of FGD technology in order to achieve higher levels of performance. A relatively low level of investment in FGD technology followed during the early/mid-1970s, driven mainly by the installation of new power plants (Table 12.4). Initial levels of performance were low, and to ensure compliance with standards enforced over very short 'averaging times', operators had to build 'spare' capacity in order to guard against equipment breakdowns. It was necessary, for example, to construct four FGD trains to clean up emissions from three power plant boilers. In Europe and Japan power plants were permitted to run for short periods without FGD in operation, resulting in much lower levels of capital investment. The level of compliance demanded in the USA resulted in high abatement costs, as measured in terms of $/per unit

Table 12.4　Build-up of flue gas desulphurization installations (GW coal plant equivalent)

Year	USA	Japan	Germany
1970	–	1.5	–
1975	3.9	22.7	–
1980	31.1	34.9	–
1985	60.3	44.1	4.5
1990	73.9	51.1	39.6

Source:　based on Vernon and Soud (1990) and Environment Agency Government of Japan (1990).

of sulphur abated. This example demonstrates some of the potential adverse effects of poorly formulated regulation.

Major Japanese investment in FGD followed very quickly (as Table 12.4 shows), allowing Japan to consolidate its position as a leader in power plant clean-up technology. Japanese investment was driven by two factors. The first was a national crisis over Minamata disease (linked to mercury poisoning) coupled with a wider concern about the effect of pollution on human health. The second was trade pressure from the Nixon administration in the USA which argued that lower standards of environmental control in Japan were giving it an unfair competitive advantage.

During the 1970s, Japan applied strict environmental standards to both new and existing plants and rapidly overtook the USA in terms of overall installed FGD capacity. This period of rapid investment, stimulated by a mixture of regulation and 'administrative guidance', gave Japanese firms such as Mitsubishi mastery of flue gas clean-up technology. During the 1980s this mastery extended to NO_x controls and controls on plant much smaller than power stations.

In the 1980s, concern about sulphur dioxide emissions in Europe and North America shifted away from human health towards the problem of acid rain. In 1981–83, Germany experienced a panic over forest dieback similar to the Japanese panic a decade before over Minamata disease. As a result, Germany engaged in a crash programme to reduce sulphur dioxide emissions by retrofitting its entire stock of coal and lignite power stations with FGD over a period of only five years. The first-mover advantage which Japanese suppliers enjoyed is apparent from examining the sources of technology for the German programme. Table 12.5 shows that approximately half of the German capacity was built using technology licensed from Japan. It may be that a more measured German programme would have allowed more use of indigenous technology.

Table 12.5 *Licensing of flue gas desulphurization technology (GW coal plant equivalent)*

Country of licenser	Country of licensee		
	USA	Japan	Germany
USA	52.2		†
Japan	1.1	51.1	20.1
Germany	12.2		17.1
Other	7.0		3.2
TOTAL	72.5	51.1‡	40.4

Notes:

† US licensed plant include in 'other'

‡ Japanese oil plant converted on the basis of the volume of flue gas treated.

Source: based on Vernon and Soud (1990) and Environment Agency Government of Japan (1990).

Certainly, the slower US build-up was largely based on domestic technology, though little US technology has been licensed abroad.

Higher standards of sulphur dioxide control are now spreading outside the USA, Japan and Germany, notably in Europe and South East Asia. This trend will provide new markets for companies which have mastered the technology in their domestic markets. Japan is particularly well placed to benefit. However, there are signs that the end-of-pipe response to sulphur dioxide controls may become less significant in the future.

The principle of fluidized bed combustion, the technique which underpins most clean coal technology, has long been understood. R&D expenditure grew rapidly during the 1970s when the oil crisis led to a search for cheaper and more efficient coal generation technologies to promote substitution for oil. The emergence of constraints on sulphur dioxide emissions during the 1970s also increased the attractiveness of clean coal technology. Another advantage of fluidized bed combustion is that it can be used to burn low-grade fuels that would be difficult to use in conventional boilers. During the 1970s and early 1980s, both the private sector and governments made significant R&D investments in fluidized bed combustion techniques.

Interest fell away when oil prices fell in the mid-1980s, but revived as concern about the climate change issue emerged in the late 1980s. Now a number of semi-commercial power plant retrofits and installations have been carried out based on clean coal technology designs. ABB, the Swedish-Swiss engineering group has built a handful of PFBC plants in the USA, Sweden and Spain. However, in the longer term IGCC plants may be more promising because they rely more heavily on gas turbine technology. Gas turbine technology is developing quite rapidly, whereas efficiency improvements in steam turbines have virtually saturated.

Although a modest amount of investment in clean technology has taken place, most power generators would argue that conventional coal combustion linked to FGD remains the market-leading technology. For clean coal technologies to become fully commercialized, capital costs will have to drop and guarantees of performance will have to be made by vendors.

The history of FGD and clean coal technology may provide evidence of a longer term dynamic linking end-of-pipe technologies with cleaner alternatives. The near commercialization of clean coal technology is largely due to the fact that environmental controls have pushed up the cost of conventional coal combustion. At a more generic level, it can be observed that regulatory compliance schedules seldom allow time for the development of cleaner alternatives, while the cost of existing technology is inevitably pushed up because of the need for end-of-pipe solutions. Over the long term, the higher cost of conventional technology creates enhanced incentives to search for more fundamental process changes. If these efforts ultimately succeed, the conditions are in place for a paradigm shift in the technologies employed. As the clean coal example shows, the time-scales for technology development are long and may be measured in decades rather than years. The political urgency of many environmental problems suggests that it is perhaps inevitable that end-of-pipe solutions play a 'bridging' role while more fundamental process changes are sought. This model suggests a legitimate role for both end-of-pipe and cleaner technologies. Indeed, within this framework, end-of-pipe technologies are an intrinsic part of the incentive structure which stimulates the development of cleaner alternatives.

However, market incentives and the action of private companies do not provide the whole story in relation to clean coal technology. Government-funded R&D played a vital supporting role. The development and proving of Texaco's IGCC concept relied heavily on US government funding for its Coolwater demonstration plant. The availability of such government funding is not fortuitous. In pluralistic market economies, regulation is negotiated with stakeholders rather than being handed down by government. To some extent, public sector R&D programmes may be seen as part of the bargain which governments must strike in order to pursue proactive environmental policies.

It is salutary to note, however, that the technological foresight of firms and governments is limited. Some paradigm shifts in technology are neither slow nor predictable. In the UK, for example, a combination of natural gas availability and progress in gas turbine technology has effectively rendered conventional coal combustion technology obsolete. Part of the attraction of the new combined-cycle gas turbine plants is that they are very clean, much more so than any 'clean coal' plant. This largely unforeseen development has undermined the value of much carefully formulated private and public sector R&D in the UK.

6.   CONCLUSIONS

This chapter has shown that the relationship between technological change, competitive forces and government environmental regulation is complex. The distinction traditionally made between end-of-pipe and cleaner technology, and the acknowledged linkage between the form regulation takes and incentives for technical change (notably the suggested superiority of market-based instruments), continue to have some validity. However, a range of other factors need to be taken into account if developments in environmental technology are to be more fully explained.

The concept of environmental technology itself is ill defined, and the first section of this chapter showed that the end-of-pipe-cleaner technology distinction is not sufficiently rich to describe the full range of technology that influences environmental performance. Research on the economics of technical change more generally was shown to have developed a vocabulary which could be used to describe and explain the processes through which environmental technology is developed and diffused.

In the past, government regulation was the major factor creating a 'demand-pull' for environmental technology. Since most end-of-pipe technologies are based on long-understood physical and chemical principles, the 'technology-push' factor has been of limited importance. More recently, the search for cost reductions, particularly in relation to waste, has promoted cleaner production practices. There have been specific circumstances in which first-mover advantage has operated in favour of firms and countries. However, this does not provide a sound basis for arguing that all firms should in all circumstances pursue proactive environmental strategies.

Markets for environmental goods and services evolve through a number of stages which are defined by interactions between government regulation and the growing competencies of supplier firms. At the earliest stages, the supply sector is very fragmented and dominated by small and medium-sized enterprises. As environmental regulation becomes more ambitious and established, markets become more assured and larger firms with a wide range of competencies play an important role. Inter-firm relationships (for example, licensing arrange-ments), various forms of consortia and links through trade associations play a vital role in the development of environmental technology. Government support for RD&D activity is also a significant factor.

Finally, a case study of technologies for cleaner electricity generation showed that there is a great deal more to environmental technology than a stark choice between end-of-pipe and cleaner technology. The development of end-of-pipe technology (FGD) and cleaner technology (clean coal technologies such as IGCC) were shown to be part of a single, longer-term dynamic relating to technical change in the industry. This case study illustrates a complex interplay of forces, including technology forcing, first-mover advantage at the firm and country levels, and interactions between private sector and government activity, taking the form of both regulation and RD&D support. The same type of story could be told in many other specific cases of environmental technology development.

REFERENCES

Advisory Council on Science and Technology (1992), *Cleaner Technology*, London: HMSO.

Ashford, N. (1993), 'Technological responses of industrial firms', in K. Fischer and J. Schot (eds), *Environmental Strategies for Industry: International Perspectives, Research Needs and Policy Implications*, Washington, DC: Island Press.

Ashford, N.A and G.R. Heaton (1979), 'The effects of health and environmental regulation on technological change in the chemical industry', in C.T. Hill (ed.), *Federal Regulation and Chemical Innovation*, ACS Symposium Series 109, Washington, DC: American Chemical Society.

Ausubel, J.H. and H.E. Sladovich (eds) (1989), *Technology and the Environment*, Washington, DC: National Academy Press.

Boehmer-Christiansen, S. and J. Skea (1991), *Acid Politics: Environmental and Energy Policies in Britain and Germany*, London: Pinter.

Commission of the European Communities (1992), 'Towards sustainability: a European Community programme of policy and action in relation to the environment and sustainable development', COM(92) 23 final, Brussels, March.

Commission of the European Communities (1993), 'Proposal for a Council Directive on integrated pollution prevention and control', COM(93) 423 final, Brussels, 14 September.

Dorfman, M., W. Muir and C. Miller (eds) (1992), *Environmental Dividends: Cutting More Chemical Waste*, New York: INFORM.

Dorfman, M., A. White, M. Becker and T. Jackson (1993), 'Profiting from pollution prevention: better environmental protection; improved economic competitiveness', in T. Jackson (ed.), *Clean Production Strategies: Developing Preventative Environmental Management in the Industrial Economy*, Boca Raton: Stockholm Environment Institute/Lewis.

Dosi, G. (1988), 'The nature of the innovative process', in G. Dosi et al. (eds), *Technical Change and Economic Theory*, London: Pinter, pp. 221–38.

ECOTEC (1992), 'The development of clean technologies: a strategic overview', *Business Strategy and the Environment*, **1**, Part 2, Summer, 51–8.

Environment Agency Government of Japan (1990), 'Quality of the environment in Japan 1989', Tokyo: Printing Bureau Ministry of Finance.

Freeman, C. (1982), *The Economics of Industrial Innovation*, London: Pinter.

Gabel, H. Landis (1995), 'Environmental management as a competitive strategy: the case of CFCs', in H. Folmer, H.L. Gabel and H. Opschoor (eds), *Principles of Environmental and Resource Economics: A Guide for Students and Decision-Makers*, Cheltenham, UK and Lyme, US: Edward Elgar, pp. 328–46.

Good, B. (1991), *Industry and the Environment: A Strategic Overview*, London: Centre for the Exploitation of Science and Technology.

Groenewegen, P. and P. Vergragt (1991),'Environmental issues as threats and opportunities for technological innovation', *Technology Analysis and Strategic Management*, **3** (1), 43–55.

Hirschhorn, J., T. Jackson and L. Baas (1993),Towards prevention: the emerging environmental management paradigm', in T. Jackson (ed.), *Clean Production Strategies: Developing Preventative Environmental Management in the Industrial Economy*, Boca Raton: Stockholm Environment Institute/Lewis.

Irwin, A. and P.D. Hooper (1992), 'Clean technology, successful innovation and the greening of industry: a case study analysis', *Business Strategy and the Environment*, **1**, Part 2, Summer, 1–12.

Irwin, A. and P. Vergragt (1989), 'Re-thinking the relationship between environmental regulation and industrial innovation', *Technology Analysis and Strategic Management*, **1** (1), 57–70.

Jackson, T. (ed.) (1993), *Clean Production Strategies. Developing Preventative Environmental Management in the Industrial Economy*, Boca Raton: Stockholm Environment Institute/Lewis.

Karadeloglou, P., T. Ikwue and J. Skea (1995), 'Environmental policy in the European Union', in H. Folmer, H.L. Gabel and H. Opschoor (eds), *Principles of Environmental and Resource Economics: A Guide for Students and Decision-Makers*, Cheltenham, UK and Lyme, US: Edward Elgar.

Mowery, D. and N. Rosenberg (1979), 'The influence of market demand upon innovation: a critical review of some recent empirical studies', *Research Policy*, **8**, 102–53.

Organization for Economic Cooperation and Development (1985), *Environmental Policy and Technical Change*, Paris: OECD.

Porter, M.E. (1990), *The Competitive Advantage of Nations*, London: Macmillan, pp. 647–9.

Recherche Développement International (1990), 'The environmental services industry in Commission of the European Communities', *Panorama of EC Industry 1990*, Brussels: CEC, 133–43.

Rothwell, R. (1992), 'Industrial innovation and government environmental regulation: some lessons from the past', *Technovation*, **12** (7), 447–58.

Schmidheiny, S. (1992), *Changing Course: A Global Business Perspective on Development and the Environment*, Business Council for Sustainable Development, Cambridge, MA: MIT Press.

Sorrell, S. (1994), 'Pollution on the market: the US experience with emissions trading for the control of air pollution', STEEP Special Report No. 1, Brighton: Science Policy Research Unit.

Vernon, J.L. and H.N. Soud (1990), *FGD Installations on Coal-Fired Plants*, IEACR/22, London: International Energy Agency Coal Research.

W.S. Atkins Management Consultants (1991), *Markets for Environmental Monitoring Instrumentation*, London: Department of Trade and Industry, HMSO.
Williams, J. (1992), *Environmental Opportunities: Building Advantage out of Uncertainty*, London: Centre for the Exploitation of Science and Technology.

13. Environmental marketing and public policy

Helmut Karl and Carsten Orwat

1. INTRODUCTION

This chapter examines some economic aspects of environmental marketing and related policy issues. We use the term 'environmental marketing'[1] to cover those activities and transactions of companies associated with the design, development, sale, distribution, and recycling of 'environmentally superior products',[2] or 'environmental products' for short. These activities, transactions, and products should cause less environmental damage than comparable alternatives. Thus, we refer to the operational marketing elements of producing companies, that is the traditional marketing mix with corporate product management, pricing, distribution, and recycling management, as well as corporate communication.[3]

The design of environmental products involves consideration of issues such as product life extension or optimization, change and substitution of materials, packaging selection, waste minimization, disassembly, repair, remanufacture and recycling. Product designers should consider the minimization of environmental impacts during products' consumption or use phases as well as during production, pre-production, and waste treatment (see Oosterhuis et al., 1996, for example). With regard to distribution and recycling options, companies may be able to act directly or use intermediaries. Indirect distribution and recycling necessitates cooperation with companies involved in different stages of the product life cycle. Decisions about the physical forward distribution and recycling, that is, the transportation and logistics, mainly involve choosing less environmentally damaging transportation systems in terms of energy use, emissions and transportation risk.

In certain circumstances, companies may be able to raise prices to cover the additional costs of product-related environmental measures. More often, they attempt to use environmental products to settle in attractive niches of otherwise fiercely competitive markets. These companies then advertise in a way that attempts to promote their environmental products and to create public trust in the environmental awareness and performance of the entire company.

The emergence and spread of environmental marketing is hampered by a variety of economic phenomena. These include positive externalities of environmentally superior products, asymmetric distribution of information, opportunistic behaviour of economic actors, and the public-good characteristics of certain types of environmental knowledge. These inefficiencies and market failures provide the rationale for public policies to foster the supply of environmentally superior products. Public policy can enhance the ability of companies to separate themselves from competitors with the environmental superiority of both individual products and the company as a whole. To accomplish this, public policy can provide incentives for environmental product innovation and promotion. The focus of these measures is the companies' environmental advertising. In addition, public policy can stimulate efficiency improvements in other marketing activities by addressing inefficiencies and failures which emerge in pricing, distribution and recycling. In the remainder of the chapter we examine potential policy responses to problems of externalities of environmentally beneficial behaviour (considered in section 2), credibility in environmental communication (section 3), definitions of environmental superiority (section 4), and cooperation and network benefits in environmental marketing (section 5). In addition, public policy itself may suffer from failures (for example, regulation capture), so we will also consider the cost of policy measures.

2. EXTERNALITIES

The production of many commodities is linked with negative externalities such as pollution. Positive externalities of environmental innovations are the spillovers of technological knowledge that can benefit the general public without a compensation of the producer of the knowledge via the price system. Moreover, positive externalities exist if the development and market supply of environmentally superior products raise the utility of externally affected parties. With the help of environmental innovations related to product design, distribution, recycling, and so on, companies can reduce environmental damages over the whole course of the product life cycle or in parts of it. The resulting benefits are not only obtained by the ('internal') purchaser of the specific product, but also by external individuals who cannot be excluded from the benefit from the reduction in environmental impacts. Because the external individuals can utilize the environmental benefits without necessarily paying for them, they do not offer their actual willingness to pay for the environmental benefits of environmental innovations. Therefore, this utilization of external benefits by other individuals is, in general, not reflected in the prices of environmentally superior products. In other words, the environmental products have some characteristics of a 'public good'.[4] Because consumers who are buying such products cannot fully internalize the external utility of their purchase, prices for environmental products and other environmental innovations may be insufficiently high to cover their costs (Kaas, 1993; Cleff and Rennings, 1999). As a result, fewer incentives for innovations are set and the level of environmental innovations is relatively low.

To solve this problem, companies may use environmental marketing to differentiate their environmentally superior products, to lower the price elasticity of demand, and to create a sufficient price premium for environmental products. However, many of the relevant consumer markets are fiercely competitive and possess a high price elasticity of demand, making it difficult for firms to charge price premiums or shift the costs of environmental innovations to customers. And even environmentally concerned consumers may be unwilling to pay a price premium for environmental products (Henion, 1976; Peattie, 1995; Kapelianis and Strachan, 1996). Environmental awareness and consciousness[5] may not result in corresponding buying behaviour for a number of reasons. First, the low prestige and recognition of environmentally conscious behaviour, the limited direct personal ability to perceive environmental effects, the additional transaction costs[6] related to changes in purchasing, and sometimes the relative unavailability of environmentally superior goods may outweigh the willingness of consumers to buy environmentally superior products (Hemmelskamp and Brockmann, 1997). Second, research studies show that a substantial proportion of consumers believe that environmental products are less effective in their function or technical performance and therefore seek a discount (Kapelianis and Strachan, 1996). Finally, some environmentally aware consumers are themselves willing to make significant efforts during purchase, consumption or disposal of products to behave in an environmentally responsible manner (for example, separate waste) but have a limited willingness to pay a price premium (Kaas, 1993).

Low consumer willingness to pay makes it difficult for firms to cover the costs of environmental innovations. Developing and marketing environmentally superior products often requires expensive and time-consuming research, changes in production processes or establishment of a recycling system, and 'explanation-intensive' environmental advertising. Whether such measures bring market success through higher prices or increased market share often remains uncertain. Solutions to this dilemma can be either market-endogenous or market-exogenous. The broad range of companies' environmental marketing strategies, explained in detail in the remainder of the chapter, is the market-endogenous attempt to resolve this problem. However, shortcomings and market failures hinder the market's ability to solve these problems itself. A market-exogenous public policy solution may be needed to remedy these failures or to support market-endogenous solutions. In particular, public policy can enhance the opportunities for environmentally superior firms to send credible signals of the superiority of their products to customers.

Another public policy objective is to provide incentives for all firms to improve the environmental quality of their entire marketing activities. The companies' product management, distribution and recycling are specific focuses of environmental policy due to their significant impacts on the natural environment. Economic instruments like emission licences or fees, for instance, for the use of virgin material, for specific hazardous substances used in products, or for waste disposal treatment, can create incentives for environmental marketing activities. Similar results can be obtained by combining economic instruments with environmental and technology policies such as direct governmental demand for environmental products, support for research and development, subsidization of pilot projects, and provision of technological infrastructure (see also Hemmelskamp, 1996; Cleff and Rennings, 1999; for a discussion of environmental policy see Barde, Chapter 6 in this volume).

3. CREDIBILITY IN ENVIRONMENTAL COMMUNICATION

3.1 The Adverse Selection Problem

The bulk of contractual relationships and market transactions involving environmental marketing feature asymmetrically distributed information[7] regarding the environmental attributes of the products, materials, or the environmental protection activities of the transaction partners. One of the reasons for asymmetric information in environmental marketing transactions is that the specific attributes of environmental products may lead to market situations of 'adverse selection' (or 'precontractual opportunism'). In general, commodities can have search, experience and credence attributes (for a taxonomy see Nelson, 1970, 1974; Darby and Karni, 1973), with the distinction hingeing on whether the quality of the good can be determined before or after purchase or not at all. Customers of goods with search attributes can identify the quality of the good before purchase, for example by inspection. The quality of goods with experience attributes can only be determined after purchase and during the consumption or use of the good (for example, the taste of food). Inability to observe quality either before or after purchase or use characterizes goods with credence attributes. Environmentally superior products are mainly characterized by credence attributes. Even after purchase and consumption, making judgements about environmental quality is generally impossible for consumers. For example, consumers can hardly gauge the environmental impacts of a product during its production process because such information is mainly available only to the producer. This means that this type of information is mainly a private good of firms.[8] Moreover, most consumers do not have sufficient ecological knowledge to evaluate environmental impacts even if such information is publicly available. The individual transaction costs of investigating, evaluating and comparing the wide range of environmental characteristics of different products are prohibitive in relation to the marginal benefits of environmental products for each consumer (Foss, 1996; Tietenberg, 1998).

The credence attributes of environmental products make it difficult for consumers to evaluate environmental advertising, resulting in opportunistic behaviour on the part of producers and increasing scepticism on the part of consumers (see for example, Zinkhan and Carlson, 1995). The reasons are manifold. Consumers have, in general, little or no knowledge, less comparative information, or limited understanding regarding the relevant environmental issues to evaluate the value or credibility of the environmental marketing claims. For example, consumer surveys show that many consumers do not fully understand the content of environmental marketing terms such as 'recyclable', 'source reduction' or 'biodegradable' (US EPA, 1993a). Moreover, many environmental advertising claims have proven to be inaccurate, unexplained, meaningless or excessive. Unexplained environmental claims of a single attribute such as 'phosphate free' are often understood by the consumer to imply overall environmental superiority. Terms such as 'environmentally friendly', 'degradable', or 'ozone friendly' are ambiguous (Kangun et al., 1991): up to now there is not a commonly accepted and widespread definition of the content or the underlying activities of environmental protection related to these terms. We consider the recent developments of defining and standardizing environmental terms below. Claims can be excessive if they emphasize the general 'environmental friendliness' of products when it is obvious that products have negative environmental impacts (Welford and Gouldson, 1993). Furthermore, some statements of product attributes are obviously false or misleading (Kangun et al., 1991; Kangun and Polonsky, 1995; Polonsky et al., 1998) and discredit environmental claims in general, for instance, when producers claim to sell a 'recyclable' product without having access to an appropriate recycling infrastructure (US EPA, 1993a). Additionally, environmental campaign organizations or consumers themselves often detect a less stringent company behaviour with respect to environmental responsibility when companies claim to sell environmentally superior products on the one hand, but cause significant environmental damages, for instance during natural resource extraction or waste disposal, on the other hand.

The problem of inaccurate environmental advertising worsens if new scientific knowledge makes existing claims of environmental superiority obsolete. This reflects the general problem of defining environmental superiority. Several obstacles in comparing environmental aspects of products over their life cycles make general statements of environmental superiority of products vulnerable to criticism (see section 4).

Information asymmetries regarding environmental quality may cause market failures and, in some cases, the breakdown of markets. Consumers have less product information than sellers, and therefore expect sellers to behave opportunistically by marketing as 'environmentally superior' products which are in fact of poor or average environmental quality. Consumers are only willing to pay a corresponding, average, market price. Hence, the equilibrium price only covers the average costs (see for example, Kaas, 1993; Caswell and Mojduszka, 1996; Morris, 1997). Under these market conditions, producers who offer products with high environmental quality have no chance to gain a price premium. Their costs of producing superior environmental quality are not rewarded and the high-quality producers cannot establish or sustain themselves in the market. Because their production costs are above the average level, the sellers of high-quality products will be driven out of the market. Since inferior-quality products remain on the market, the supply of quality is 'selected' adversely, and hence the market suffers from 'adverse selection' (Akerlof, 1970). To ameliorate these market failures some countervailing institutions are organized either endogenously by the market itself or exogenously by public policy intervention, which we describe in the following.

3.2   Market-endogenous Solutions and Self-regulation

The economics literature discusses a number of ways to mitigate problems arising from 'adverse selection', such as screening, signalling, non-salvageable assets, guarantees and warranties, and reputation. However, most of these approaches are not applicable to markets for products with credence attributes and strong information asymmetries (Caswell and Mojduszka, 1996). For example, guarantees, warranties, and repeated purchases are not appropriate because buyers of environmental products cannot form a complete judgement of the environmental quality of products even after purchase and consumption.

Since information regarding product quality attributes is of value to consumers, we might expect the development of a market in which firms act as reviewers and offer their judgements for sale (Faulhaber and Yao, 1989). This approach to overcoming market failure may itself fail if consumers are afforded public access to the review judgements and act as free-riders. In our search for a more realistic way to overcome the outlined dilemma we will encounter other 'counteracting institutions' which can signal high environmental product quality.

3.2.1 Sophisticated environmental communication

The 'adverse selection' problem cannot be resolved using image-oriented, 'non-informative' claims that do not reduce the asymmetrical distribution of information. Rather, environmental advertising must provide consumers with credible information about credence attributes so that consumers can identify products or brands with superior environmental performance. As a first step, environmental advertising could provide objective, factual information about specific environmental characteristics and benefits of the relevant product. For instance, the seller could explain the main environmental impacts and their relative level compared to other products. Armed with this information, consumers could better recognize the environmental benefits of their purchases (Davis, 1993). Such advertising could increase 'perceived consumer effectiveness', that is, the extent to which the environmentally concerned consumer believes that her or his individual action contributes effectively to matters of environmental protection (Scholder Ellen et al., 1991). Furthermore, detailed, fact-based and precise product information (for example, the detailed description of the product ingredients and substances used) creates the possibility for verification by third parties (for example, test institutes or consumer organizations).

Detailed, fact-based environmental advertising often involves a complex array of data. Sophisticated communication may necessitate extensive costs and may have the characteristics of a public good, for example, information about the health effects of product ingredients. Additionally, some studies have shown that consumers have a limited comprehension of detailed product-related environmental information (for example, see Morris et al., 1995). Detailed environmental information, especially at the point of purchase, may result in 'information overload', when limited ability to process information is confronted with large amounts of it. This may lead rational buyers simply to ignore information concerning the environmental characteristics of goods or the environmental behaviour of companies. Thus, there is a need for condensed information in the form of symbols, brands, and concise statements.

3.2.2 Guidelines and standards

Industry guidelines and standards for environmental communication are examples of private self-regulation, which tries to solve the problem of adverse selection on a voluntary basis. Self-regulators must solve the conflict between the goal of influencing buyers on the one hand and the necessity of conveying information that is reliable and accurate on the other hand. To that end, attributes of 'environmental terms' or 'environmental marketing claims' have been defined, standardized, and made verifiable. Various initiatives in numerous countries have established common guidelines and standards for environmental communication which allow suppliers to offer meaningful information to buyers and to distinguish themselves from suppliers with lower product quality.

These guidelines reduce the costs of information provision for producer and the costs of information processing for buyers.

Successful standards for communication and information require common rules about the way to report the credence attributes of products. Standards must be clearly defined and observable, and there must be monitoring to determine compliance, arbitration proceedings to address conflicts, and sanctions for violators. These tasks can be undertaken by state and/or private organizations. In practice, a number of hybrid groups have developed standards, including the International Chamber of Commerce, the Incorporated Society of British Advertising, and the International Advertising Association. Guidelines for environmental marketing claims, together with 'case-to-case' decisions, can also be found in the European Advertising Standard Alliance and in the British Advertising Standards Authority. The media associations decide on complaints made about companies' environmental advertising claims. On the international level, the International Organization for Standardization (ISO) covers the so-called type II environmental labelling in the ISO/DIS 14021 standard, which concerns direct environmental claims made by manufacturers, importers, distributors, or retailers without passing through any third-party organization (self-declaration). Frequently, the standard addresses only a single attribute, defining, for example, terms such as 'no use of ozone-depleting substances', 'recycled material', 'reduced resource use', 'energy-efficient', or 'designed for disassembly'.

3.2.3 Private environmental labelling

The overall purpose of environmental labelling is to overcome market failure caused by asymmetries of environmental quality information (for a detailed discussion, see Karl and Orwat, 1999). Environmental labelling or certification in general can act as a counteracting institution by establishing standards for product quality which inform the consumer about quality levels. The environmental labelling organization sets up a scale of measurements corresponding to current quality levels that applying products have to fulfil. The incentive for producers to demand environmental labelling is the extra revenue from selling environmental products at a higher price (that is, the rents of a separating high-quality equilibrium for environmentally superior products). However, increasing costs for screening and monitoring imply a reduced demand for such services (see also Leland, 1979; Shapiro, 1986; De and Nabar, 1991).

Signalling environmental superiority in terms of Spence (1974), by labelling products, requires a reputable certification agent, the accreditation agent, whom consumers consider trustworthy (Caswell and Mojduszka, 1996). For the sake of credibility and trustworthiness, these accreditation bodies must certify products which conform to a high environmental standard and maintain an efficient control and sanction system. The certification schemes must be based on clear pre-set environmental criteria, established by a competent body. Environmental criteria are scales of measurement such as quantitative thresholds or limit values for specific environmental impacts of the product during its life cycle or other qualitative product requirements (for example, production method requirements). Under these circumstances eco-labelling reduces evaluation and comparison costs for consumers at the point of sale (Foss, 1996) and enables consumers to discriminate between high- and low-quality products. The eco-labels turn the credence attributes of environmentally superior products into search attributes.

Once again, the International Organization for Standardization (ISO) strives for global harmonization of environmental labelling systems. Here, the relevant standard is the ISO 14024 for the so-called type I environmental labelling for voluntary third-party environmental labelling schemes. According to this standard, environmental labelling programmes have to fulfil certain characteristics, for example, to be based on available scientific methods that cover the entire product life cycle. This leads in most cases to the use of life-cycle analyses to determine the environmental impacts of the product under consideration. However, several methodological problems in defining environmental superiority (see section 4) put the credibility of such schemes at risk.

At this point, we can summarize some advantages and disadvantages of self-regulatory standards and guidelines as well as private eco-label programmes. These instruments have the potential to be effective in creating markets for goods that have a superior environmental performance if they are reliable, clearly defined, supervised and subject to sanctions. In contrast to governmental regulations, they have the advantage of greater flexibility: private standards, guidelines, and eco-label programmes can be adjusted more easily in response to new experiences and knowledge. One essential criticism of pure private self-regulation is that compliance is voluntary. Producers who do not apply the standard or eco-label will not be sanctioned and can therefore make misleading statements. Furthermore, the enforcement mechanisms are considered too weak because arbitration and legal proceedings are time-intensive and may be vested with too little authority.

3.2.4 Signalling with non-salvageable assets

Another possible solution to the problem of adverse selection is to provide certain kinds of signals to identify high-quality suppliers to customers. To this end, activities which function as signals need to be less costly for suppliers with high environmental quality than for suppliers with low environmental quality (Spence, 1974). Customers would recognize that the signal is associated with higher environmental quality. One signalling activity is the investment in non-salvageable capital assets, which are firm-specific costs that are not recoverable in uses outside the firm (Klein and Leffler, 1981). In the context of environmental marketing, non-salvageable assets include environmental brands or trade marks, logos, the company's own retail and service organization, or specific employee skills. A company's recycling activities are also an important instrument to signal environmentally superior performance because the high investments necessary to set up and run an extensive recycling infrastructure demonstrate the producer's interest in his products over all steps of the product life cycle. This may also be efficient, because the producer determines the opportunities and costs of recycling or final disposal by his decisions about the material composition of the product.

However, signalling via investments in non-salvageable assets is in some cases too costly in comparison with the profits gained by supplying environmental products. It may also result in losses in efficiency if the company takes on tasks that could be performed better by third parties. For instance, retail organizations specialized in supplying environmental products may realize greater economies of scale. Additionally, investments in non-salvageable assets are permanently threatened by the possible emergence of new knowledge about environmental attributes of products. For example, the good reputation of an environmental brand could be destroyed if consumers gain knowledge of a hazardous ingredient of only one product within the brand.

3.3 Public Policy Tasks Concerning Environmental Communication

3.3.1 Support and regulation of environmental advertising

Independent of the market-endogenous possibility to solve the adverse selection problem, from an economic perspective it is useful to ban misleading statements in environmental communication because misleading claims can destroy markets and induce misallocation (Beales et al., 1981; Shapiro, 1983a). Misleading advertising covers not only false statements but also vague claims, inaccuracies or omissions that cause customers to have false ideas about the environmental attributes of products and their life cycles. The resulting problems are aggravated if deceptive advertising confronts the bounded rationality of recipients (see, in general, Nagler, 1993).

The most obvious way to deal with misleading advertising is general legal regulations that prohibit false statements (Beales and Murris, 1993). We can find this approach in the majority of European countries. They mainly judge environmental advertising according to general rules of competition law rather than special advertising regulations. They all demand an extensive explanation of the claimed environmental benefits, and do not tolerate ill-defined advertising terms, especially concerning health issues. Potential violations are judged mainly in 'case-by-case' decisions. For instance, in Germany, no special legal regulation of environment protection claims or the use of environmental terms in advertisement exists. Instead, rules of the general competition law, in particular the 'law against unfair competition' ('Gesetz gegen den unlauteren Wettbewerb' – UWG) apply. In addition, there are the guidelines of the International Chamber of Commerce and the German Advertising Federation (Zentralverband der Deutschen Werbewirtschaft). All member firms of both organizations have to accept these guidelines as rules of advertising self-regulation, although they have no jurisdictional effects.

Regulations can also specifically address environmental claims. One example[9] can be found in the USA, where the Federal Trade Commission (FTC) regulates the advertising of environmental product attributes. Before 1992, diverse US states enacted individual statutes restricting environmental advertising. This decentralized approach created inconsistently standardized communication measures that became increasingly different, hampering the efficiency of markets, preventing economic scale effects, and increasing transaction costs. In response to the adverse effects of the plethora of sometimes conflicting environmental advertising statutes at the state level, the FTC issued its 'Guides for the Use of Environmental Marketing Claims' in July 1992, and modified them in 1996 and 1998.[10] Because the guides do not have the force of law, they do not pre-empt state and local regulations. However, some states have codified requirements to follow the FTC guidelines. Other states have stricter statutes, indicating that a race to the bottom does not exist. In some cases, the stricter standards set the *de facto* standard for environmental marketing claims. Nevertheless, some authors fear that inconsistent and potentially conflicting state and local regulations and standards will engender high information costs for the consumer (US FTC, 1992, 1998; Thomas, 1993; US EPA, 1993a; Gray-Lee et al., 1994). This is an argument for harmonizing public standards and influencing the process of private self-regulation[11] (Ruhnka and Boerstler, 1998).

The FTC directive has provided a framework for interpreting legal regulations issued for protection from misleading advertising. Companies can show their commitment by voluntarily adopting the directives. Thus, the directive is a hybrid form between solely private and solely governmental solutions. In detail, the FTC principles require that:

1. Environmental advertising cannot mislead consumers. Misleading environmental claims concern deceptive representation, omissions, or false details about material issues referring to the product life cycles or environmental behaviour of companies.
2. All statements, qualifications, and disclosures must be clearly understandable and the specific environmental benefit of the packaging, the distribution, or the product itself, should be clearly recognizable. Consequently, a product cannot just be marketed with the slogan 'recycled', but must indicate the

share of reused materials and differentiate information concerning the product and its packaging. In this sense, the directive gives specific requirements for the use of qualifications such as 'degradable', 'biodegradable', 'compostable', 'recyclable', 'ozone-safe', or 'ozone-friendly'.
3. Exaggerations must be omitted. These occur, for example, when a product is offered as 'recyclable' but a corresponding recycling system does not exist.
4. Clear criteria of environmental advertising must be used when making comparative claims. This is in order to increase the competition between suppliers (Beales et al., 1981; Wynne, 1991; Sellers, 1992; Thomas, 1993; Scammon and Mayer, 1993; Beales and Muris, 1993; US FTC, 1998).

General guidelines for environmental advertising encourage the production of beneficial, informative advertising because companies have a well-defined area in which to operate (Nagler, 1993). Additionally, the FTC directive treats communication measures on the basis of the analysis of marketing effects and scientific environmental criteria. The FTC's cooperation with the US Environmental Protection Agency (US EPA) offers the advantage of merging the FTC's specific knowledge concerning marketing issues with the ecological knowledge of the EPA (Sellers, 1992).

Both US and European types of regulation of misleading advertising depend on a time-consuming complaint procedure. Together with their inflexibility, the time requirements for screening and reviewing environmental claims on a 'case-by-case' basis makes it difficult for these regulations to curtail misleading advertising and thereby avoid 'adverse selection'. An alternative way of promoting accurate environmental advertising is to permit and encourage comparative advertising. Competitors with superior environmental performance and the necessary environmental and market knowledge can easily detect false statements and misleading information. Against this background, the prohibition of comparative advertising is inefficient. Competitive advertising gives competitors an opportunity to make a direct comparison with substitutable products and point out possible inappropriate claims of ecological qualities. Although Germany and other European countries have long-standing prohibitions against comparative advertising, it will be permitted Europe-wide in the future and will complement the European directive on protection from misleading advertising. According to this directive, comparative advertising is allowed if it is relevant in its contents and verifiable (Reader, 1995).

Additional public policy measures could encourage the coordination of environmental advertising among companies and increase the transaction costs of deceptive advertising (Nagler, 1993). First, public policy could initiate advertising self-regulation by encouraging advertising coordination among companies. To this end, governments could support the establishment and maintenance of market-endogenous councils and associations that monitor environmental advertising. These government-supported institutions could also provide environmental knowledge, such as analyses and evaluations of environmental product impacts, to build a common knowledge base for a fact-based environmental advertising. Antitrust regulators must ensure that coordination of advertising activities does not lead to inter-firm agreements that illegally reduce competition among companies. Second, public policy could increase the costs for deceitful companies by making it easier for misled consumers to bring complaints against them, for example, by offering free legal advice and relevant environmental product knowledge (Nagler, 1993). This is particularly necessary to increase consumers' ability to recognize and define the environmental damages of certain products due to the credence attributes of environmental products. The public-good characteristic of this type of environmental knowledge justifies its public production and provision.

Moreover, with the establishment of a system of metrics to measure environmental product characteristics, governments can reduce the search costs of consumers (Schwartz and Wilde, 1979), thereby creating a more competitive market situation and, hence, benefiting consumers. Displaying environmental product metrics near the product itself also helps to change credence attributes into search attributes which can be observed before purchase. These metrics are standardized scales for the measurement of environmental product performance, for example quantitative values of resource uses or environmental releases per product unit, values of minimum recycling quotes, or values of environmental efficiency regarding input factors such as fuel. The obvious public-good character of metrics establishes a reason for their provision by governments (see, in general, Shapiro, 1983a). However, standardization of environmental performance measures could also have negative side-effects. Due to the underlying complexity of environmental attributes, standards, indicators and other measures can only treat parts of them. Thus, installing particular standards and indicators may shift attention, activities and investments to specific product aspects. This may lead to the negligence of more environmentally efficient activities. Standard requirements for certain product attributes and for the use of certain technologies require companies to focus on specific research and development approaches. However, it is more efficient for companies' efforts to be more widely spread, potentially enabling them to uncover better alternatives that are not encompassed by the standards.

3.3.2 Public policy issues of third-party information provision

In addition to the buyer and seller, third parties could produce environmental information which is relevant in environmental marketing communication. These third parties could be environmental experts or eco-labelling organizations (see, in general, Shapiro, 1983a). Public policy tasks concerning third-party activities range from the establishment or subsidization of local information networks or experts to direct participation in environmental labelling programmes.

One example of a third-party information provider is a local information network such as a local market or a consumer information system that uses current information technologies. Such a network increases the consumer's ability to compare environmental products, to reduce their search costs, and to evaluate a company's reputation. The public-good nature of these benefits establishes the rationale for governmental subsidization. Other examples are third-party experts who can efficiently provide relevant product information based on their environmental expertise. They can gain economies of scale by inspecting and evaluating products for a large number of recipients. For instance, the German Foundation for Consumer Goods Testing (Stiftung Warentest) enlarged the scope of their product tests beyond the traditional quality focus to include environmental aspects. However, the difficulty of evaluating the advice of experts may lead to the governmental establishment of expert organizations (for example, consumer advice centres or the above-mentioned quasi-governmental Stiftung Warentest) or to regulation of professional experts (in general, Shapiro, 1983a).

Governments can also play a variety of roles in environmental labelling, ranging from the complete provision of an eco-labelling system to partial establishment and support of a programme to the provision of basic environmental research to complete absence (for a detailed discussion, see Karl and Orwat, 1999). Within eco-labelling programmes, the accreditation body is responsible for ensuring that eco-labelled producers achieve a specific level of environmental quality. The institutional system and background of the accreditation body therefore play a crucial role in determining the effectiveness of environmental labelling.

To decide whether governmental organizations are superior to private organizations, we have to address several issues. First, we note that a cooperation of private firms utilizing its own eco-label can be permanent and stable because the incentive to produce high environmental quality increases as the group's reputation improves and therefore enables the group to earn increased rent (Tirole, 1996). As a prerequisite for establishing group reputation, the group must apply a well-functioning mechanism of quality control (that is, monitoring and sanctions).

Second, we have to compare government and private provision of particular environmental criteria schemes. The quality of criteria schemes is determined by both the number of different environmental aspects being considered (for example, the set of environmental damages for which threshold values are defined) and the stringency of the criteria (for example, the level of each limit value). The quality of different criteria schemes can be compared by observing the different sizes of the criteria sets and the various threshold levels of each criterion. A private programme may install a broad set of environmental criteria with strict values in each category just as well as a government institution. The establishment of an environmental criteria scheme hinges mainly upon the participants and procedures of decision-making, which can be effective or ineffective for private as well as for governmental institutions. The mechanisms to prevent biased decision-making in favour of special interest groups are decisive. Private eco-label programmes installed by high environmental quality producers may have an advantage if the interests of the participants are more aligned to high environmental quality.

Third, a certification programme with the right to control entry, such as a (private) eco-labelling programme, may act like a monopoly. It may offer too few certificates, charge too high prices or set the standards for certification inefficiently high or low (Leland, 1979; Shaked and Sutton, 1981; Shapiro, 1983b). Additionally, as a monopoly, the certification body may increase its profits by pooling firms with high and low environmental quality, thus gaining the fees of low-quality producers (Lizzeri, 1994). This provides some rationale for public eco-labelling programmes. However, public monopolies for certifying environmental quality can also be used by producers as a barrier against competition (Stigler, 1971). Restrictive competition practices, however, become vulnerable to attack if the right to private eco-labelling programmes exists (Shaked and Sutton, 1981) and the price bonus for environmental quality is sufficiently high. Practical usage has shown that, under certain circumstances, producers with high environmental quality can establish and participate in their own eco-labelling schemes which, then, could put the credibility of governmental programmes at risk. Since government eco-labelling programmes generally have to give consideration to diverse interest and social groups in their eco-labelling procedure, a consensus-based procedure sets the environmental product standards in which the least environmentally advanced producers may influence the average results.

In general, the parallel existence and competition of diverse eco-labelling programmes can enhance the credibility of eco-label programmes if they compete on the basis of the quality of their environmental criteria schemes. The parallel existence offers opportunities of choice for both consumers and producers to determine the appropriate combination of labelled environmental quality and market segment. Furthermore, by making a greater variety of product alternatives eligible for eco-labels, multiple programmes provide a hedge against 'lock-in' effects. Lock-in effects are the possible path-dependencies if the eco-label scheme establishes, confirms and hardens specified product requirements which may favour inferior technologies and investments even when superior technologies exist (Morris, 1997).

However, the parallel existence and competition of eco-label programmes may also cause consumer confusion and situations of 'information overload' that make additional institutions (fourth parties) necessary. These institutions, such as test or research institutes, could support consumers in their buying decisions, for example, by investigating and comparing different eco-label schemes and providing scoring systems for the quality of eco-label programmes. Moreover, they can observe the internal procedures and participants, the utilization of environmental knowledge, monitoring and sanction procedures, and the financing of programmes, and thus can detect undue influences of certain interest groups.

To sum up the results concerning environmental advertising: we elaborated some measures that emerge from the market itself to overcome the credibility problem. However, several shortcomings of the private solutions (extensive costs, public-good characteristics of the measures, and missing standards and institutions) allow the application of such instruments only in exceptional market situations. This provides the general justification for public policy to support market-endogenous solutions by providing standards and metrics or by supporting the provision of information by third parties.

4.   DEFINING ENVIRONMENTAL SUPERIORITY

One of the most important obstacles to environmental communication is the difficulty of defining environmental superiority. In the context of environmental marketing, firms are often faced with decisions about the environmental superiority of the considered products. For example, during product development, comparison of product alternatives, partial or total optimization of existing products, and use of environmentally less damaging transport and waste treatment options, firms have to investigate the environmental impacts occurring within the course of the product life cycle to make proper environmental amendment decisions. This requires systematically investigating environmental impacts during different product life-cycle stages, as well as environmental product information from previous and subsequent life-cycle stages. To this end, analytical tools, in particular, life-cycle analyses, eco-balances, eco-profiles, or at least lists of product-related materials and other checklists, can be used (see also Freimann, 1995). However, the application of these tools by firms is hampered, especially by methodological problems and limitations of company budgets, knowledge or personnel resources.

4.1 Methodological Problems

The regular analysis of environmental impacts of products comprises defining the scope of the analysis, gathering quantitative data of environmental impacts in an environmental inventory, and qualitatively evaluating the data. These steps parallel those of a life-cycle assessment, which we therefore briefly describe (for the methodology of life-cycle assessment see SETAC, 1993; US EPA, 1993b, 1995; EEA, 1997).

An ideal environmental inventory investigation includes all material and energy inputs, outputs, flows and transformations for all stages of the product life cycle which occur before, during or after the manufacturing stage of the product. However, the extensive amount of data which would result requires limiting this scope to avoid unfeasible complexity. The investigation must concentrate on the intuitively expected, main environmental impacts within the selected stages and omit those which initially seem minor (see, in particular, SETAC, 1993). This necessary definition of analysis boundaries may lead to the neglect of important environmental effects and, hence, affect the accuracy of the life-cycle assessment (see Guinée et al., 1993, for example). Without clearly defined cut-off criteria, the consideration or non-consideration of certain feedstocks, materials, emissions, or other releases seems arbitrary. Moreover, the results of the life-cycle assessment become disputable if environmental impacts which were initially omitted become relevant when new environmental knowledge is acquired.

The environmental evaluation estimates the environmental effects of the quantitative material and energy inputs and outputs on ecosystems, human health and natural resources. For this purpose, environmental knowledge is linked to each inventory item in order to analyse the total contribution of the considered product to specific environmental problem areas (for example, resource depletion, pollution or human health effects, or degradation of ecosystems and landscape). However, the stage of environmental evaluation is also problematic (Wynne, 1994; US EPA, 1995), because it is hampered by uncertainties in environmental knowledge about the 'cause-and-effect' or 'dose–response' relationships between inventory items and ultimate impacts on human health or the ecosystem,[12] as well as by the non-comparability of different environmental impacts (Ayres, 1995). Non-comparability hinders the reduction of multiple environmental dimensions to a single evaluation measure such as eco-points.

4.2 Resource Problems of Companies

The production of the specific environmental knowledge concerning products under consideration can incur extensive costs. In particular, the acquisition of necessary data for an environmental inventory can be extremely cost-intensive or even impossible. Input materials can originate from anonymous resource markets, or it may be too difficult to follow the several stages of used products and their fractions up to final waste treatment. Other firms may be unwilling (proclaiming confidentiality) or unable to provide some or all of the vast amount of data required. Therefore, data sources are unverifiable and some parts of data are not available, necessitating the use of 'synthetic' or 'idealized' data from third-party sources. These 'data modules', which are mainly averaged data of environmental impacts belonging to comparable parts of the product life cycle (for example, averaged energy uses for different kinds of transport), may not be appropriate for all kinds of product groups or suitable in obviously similar life-cycle situations. In their place, Ayres (1995) emphasizes that firms should calculate missing data by applying the 'mass-balance principle', that is the first law of thermodynamics concerning the conservation of mass-energy. Since the mass of inputs equals the mass of (converted) outputs, the life-cycle analyst can calculate the missing inventory data or verify the measurements.

Another problem is the environmental evaluation step that requires the utilization of 'basic environmental knowledge' (for example, knowledge of ecology or 'cause-and-effect' relationships). The results of basic environmental research are, in general, available to the public because of their character as a public good and the fact that their provision is mostly state-subsidized. However, the gathering and processing of this kind of knowledge also incur costs. Moreover, the interpretation of the environmental inventory is difficult and often necessitates external expert judgements. In general, there is a lack of a stringent, commonly usable evaluation system that makes it possible for firms to make rational judgements and ranking decisions about the relative severity of the environmental impacts of products, production processes, and other elements of environmental marketing.

Due to the limitations of data collection and scientific methods and models, as well as obtainable data, the results of most environmental analyses are, at best, approximations. The resulting uncertainties often lead to radically different estimates of the environmental superiority of factors, products, production processes, and distribution and recycling systems. Moreover, (company) resources that are needed to conduct analyses to resolve the uncertainties are seldom adequate. As a consequence, declarations of environmental superiority are subjective, that is, dependent on the source of the analysis, which in the environmental marketing context is mainly the company. Therefore, it only seems possible to state environmental superiority under specific assumptions. Consequently, analysis results must be transparent, revealing the underlying methodological assumptions and omissions. Such disclosure may improve public confidence and understanding of the analysis results. Moreover, since omissions of parts of the product life cycle are often necessary, then only the declaration of the partial environmental superiority of the considered product seems reasonable and has to be sufficiently communicated to the customer. However, partial environmental improvements may lead to aggravation in other parts of the product life cycle.

4.3   Public Policy Issues

Facing these problems of defining environmental superiority by firms, there might be a call for public policy. In particular, it seems plausible that public policy tasks arise where results of individual activities have the characteristics of a 'public good', indicating a role for public policy to provide the public good itself or to support its provision by private firms.

Basic environmental research is one example of a public good. Here, the utilization of environmental knowledge can hardly be restricted and, as a normative issue, no one should be excluded from its utilization. Additionally, specific environmental knowledge implicitly created during environmental product analyses, as well as the methodology of environmental product analyses themselves, can have the characteristics of public goods. Therefore, the production of these different types of environmental knowledge can be seen as an issue of public policy and, hence, justify government support for universities, research institutes, governmental agencies, private companies and so on. The government itself can conduct life-cycle assessments or eco-balances (for the governmental comparative study of plastic and paper bags see, for example, UBA, 1988; for an overview see Rubik and Baumgartner, 1992). Additionally, there is a role for governments to play in developing the methods of environmental product analyses. In many countries, government agencies contribute to the development of methods of life-cycle analysis (for example, US EPA, 1993b, 1995; UBA, 1995; EEA, 1997). The methodological task is often related to efforts to standardize the methods and to make the results of different product analyses comparable. Here, an example would be the standardization work of the International Organization for Standardization (ISO) in cooperation with governmental agencies and governmentally supported research institutes.[13] An additional governmental task may be the establishment of a ranking system of environmental problems to aid company decisions about the relative seriousness of their environmental problems. This requires consensus-based decisions made with the use of democratic procedures and the involvement of different interest groups within society.

5.   COOPERATION AND VERTICAL INTEGRATION

5.1   Reasons for Cooperation and Vertical Integration

For many environmental marketing activities, inter-firm cooperation or collaboration between companies involved in 'downstream' or 'upstream' stages of a product's life cycle is economically efficient or even necessary. Such cooperation can address problems of information availability, information asymmetry and opportunistic behaviour, yield network benefits, and otherwise increase the efficiency of economic transactions.

Companies build up certain kinds of vertical cooperation to ensure a constant flow of information or input factors with a sufficient quality. Most of the activities of environmental product development and design require the involvement of other companies. Product developers must obtain as much information as possible about the environmental impacts of product ingredients and residuals and about disposal or recycling opportunities. This necessitates the exchange of information with companies from previous and subsequent stages of the product life cycle and may lead to types of cooperation. Additionally, if the company wants to improve environmental attributes in 'upstream' or 'downstream' parts of the product life cycle, it will have to influence the decisions of other firms. This is made possible in most cases by cooperation with relevant firms, also called 'environmental comakership' (Cramer and Schot, 1993; Wasik, 1996). For instance, the copier manufacturer Xerox cooperates with suppliers to develop materials with greater recycled content, create product designs that are more appropriate for re-manufacturing, and improve material recognition systems (Reinhardt and Vietor, 1996).

Cooperation with firms involved in previous stages of a product's life cycle engenders appropriate effort on the part of material suppliers to provide the necessary quantity and quality of inputs. Similarly, a substantial and continuous flow of potentially useful secondary materials is one of the prerequisites for a successful resource recovery system (Fuller et al., 1996). (The alternative to recycling, waste treatment and disposal, is discussed in detail by Turner in Chapter 22 of this volume.) Cooperation between recycling partners is needed to ensure a sufficient quantity and quality of the material and product flows. One example of such cooperation is the establishment of network relationships between automobile manufacturing firms and automobile dismantling and shredding companies to solve the problem of hazardous shredder waste (Hond and Groenewegen, 1993).

Cooperation is also observable in the distribution channels for environmental products. Close, long-term relations between manufacturers and intermediaries enable them to avoid opportunistic behaviour and to reduce transaction costs. Instead of direct distribution,[14] cooperation with intermediaries can be profitable if the relevant products can be sold within distribution systems, such as conventional retail channels or specialists such as The Body Shop, which make products available and accessible to target markets more efficiently. Distribution systems specializing in environmental products have an advantage in attracting customers with environmental preferences, and may have expertise concerning environmental product attributes and production processes. A producer's choice of distribution channels hinges upon the specifics of the relevant market segment, customers' desire for service, and transaction costs related to various distribution channels (see Picot, 1986).

Within distribution channels, some retailers set product standards for environmental quality and performance and put pressure on suppliers to enhance the environmental quality of their products. In a few cases, specialist 'green' retailers conduct investigations to evaluate the environmental attributes of products they are considering carrying. Retailers also often demand specific production methods or other efforts from suppliers, such as 'organic farming' or 'without animal testing'. These efforts require close cooperation between retailers and suppliers so that retailers can obtain some insights into the environmental performance of suppliers.

Another objective of inter-firm cooperation is to gain network benefits. These include economies of scale gained by the reduction of average costs of a commodity and economies of scope from the transfer of knowledge regarding products, materials, energy, releases, and so on. Cooperative partners in a knowledge exchange can gain by building the basis for further knowledge creation. In the environmental marketing context, network benefits are most visible in recycling and waste treatment systems (see also Turner, Chapter 22 in this volume). In general, recycling is economically attractive if the avoidance of waste treatment and disposal costs as well as the price premium for environmentally superior products cover the costs of collection, sorting, preparation and transformation of waste (Zikmund and Stanton, 1971; Fuller et al., 1996; Hecht and Werbeck, 1998).

Beyond cooperation between legally and economically separated companies, vertical integration within companies allows manufacturers to create integrated recycling and waste disposal systems. These systems are primarily installed for reusable and recyclable products, such as toner cartridges, bottles and so on, although it would be possible to use them for waste treatment and disposal. Vertical integration of recycling seems favourable if economies of scale exist, if high transaction costs (for example, for measuring uncertain quality of traded recycling goods) prevent cooperation with independent firms, and if the guarantee of an environmentally less damaging recycling or waste treatment and terminal disposal is decisive for the buyers.

The choice of the most efficient type of recycling network or channel is mainly determined by their costs and benefits, and by the institutional framework of waste disposal legislation. In general, the comparisons between the transaction costs required for cooperation and the network benefits favour a vertically integrated structure if a company's products need a specialized system of collection, transport and treatment because of their environmental risks, if the consciousness of the buyers about the recycling system and the final waste treatment and disposal is relevant for their decision to buy or not to buy, and if high transaction costs prevent the use of intermediaries (Williamson, 1985). Economies of scale may influence the scale of vertical integration. If the capacity of recycling channels is sufficient to collect and transport the material flows of many firms, inter-firm cooperation and joint use of these infrastructure systems are economically attractive.

5.2   Problems of Cooperation

In all types of environmental marketing cooperation, the success of each firm depends significantly on the efforts of the other firms. One major problem is that these cooperative channels are fragmented and complex systems involving a large number of independent parties with inherent potential for conflict (Peattie, 1995). Observing and monitoring the actions of cooperation partners can be difficult and may cause prohibitive transaction costs. For example, the efforts of recycling partners regarding the level of quality or purity of the secondary materials or reused products are hardly observable. As a result, asymmetrically distributed information, and therefore opportunistic behaviour, hampers inter-firm cooperation. Information concerning the environmental aspects of products, materials, ingredients, or production processes is often exclusively held by one participant. That company may fear that providing such information may make them liable for their products' environmental impacts (Cramer and Schot, 1993) or disclose confidential data that could benefit competitors. Information provision is, thus, less than what is optimal for cooperation.

In actual environmental marketing transactions with private (environmental) information and possibly unobservable actions of participants, no 'complete contracts', which would ideally specify the outcomes for each contingency, can be written, let alone enforced. Contract partners are confronted with limited foresight, imprecise language, costs of specifying reactions to contingencies, and the costs of writing detailed contracts ('bounded rationality'). Since contract specification incurs costs, the parties will write incomplete contracts that leave gaps and missing arrangements for some obligations or benefits of cooperation in some states of the world (Williamson, 1975, 1985; Klein et al., 1978). With incomplete contracts, participants may not always be motivated to act in the optimal way to achieve the common objectives of the cooperation. When unforeseen circumstances occur, there is a possibility for opportunistic behaviour ('moral hazard') (for example, Milgrom and Roberts, 1992). Each cooperation participant has independent economic interests which may conflict. For instance, certain ingredients of an environmental product may have different economic implications for each participant, because the material is, for example, less environmentally damaging during the manufacturing process but necessitates high recycling costs. Cooperation partners may act on private interests which are not necessarily aligned with the interests of other cooperation participants. They may attempt to influence the cooperation decisions in order to achieve their own objectives, for example, by lying about their environmental protection opportunities or about the environmental attributes of their products. The costs of measuring the characteristics and performance of cooperation participants and enforcing contracts may be extensive, leading to inefficient cooperation or even preventing potential participants from entering the cooperation.

Moreover, incomplete contracts require costly renegotiations or *ex post* bargaining when contingencies occur (Hart and Moore, 1988). Since contracts between cooperation participants are mainly incomplete, the interpretation of contracts and the renegotiations or the *ex post* bargaining is costly. This possibility impairs cooperative behaviour, especially of those requiring relationship-specific investments. If a cooperation partner invests in transaction-specific assets, such as the installation of an environmentally less damaging production process, the other partners would gain bargaining power to use during (re)negotiations (hold up' problem). Without complete contracts, participants cannot specify adequate protection against opportunistic behaviour ('post-contractual opportunism'). Foreseeing this potential vulnerability to opportunistic behaviour, cooperation participants are likely to underinvest or invest in relatively non-specific assets. Since efficient investments are not realized, cooperation outcomes will be suboptimal (Williamson, 1975, 1985; Hart and Moore, 1988; Milgrom and Roberts, 1992).

5.3 Market-endogenous Solutions

Some supposed market-endogenous solutions for the aforementioned co-operation problems, such as better specification of cooperation efforts, enhanced cooperative communication, or periodic reviews of each company's performance (Anderson and Narus, 1990, for example), are hampered by problems stemming from the specific characteristics of environmental performances of collaborating companies. They remain difficult to measure because environmental attributes of the supplied products, materials, services, or other environmental performances mainly have credence attributes. Furthermore, due to their limited monitoring abilities, cooperation partners may not gain sufficient information about the actual efforts of the other partners. Sophisticated contractual agreements are hard to verify as well as to enforce, and may involve prohibitive transaction costs.

Economic theory provides other solutions for problems of incomplete contracts, namely relational and implicit contracts, but they seem of limited applicability to environmental marketing cooperation. With relational contracting, the cooperation partners seek an agreement with general objectives, without providing a detailed plan of action, and provide decision criteria or dispute resolution mechanisms in cases of conflict (Milgrom and Roberts, 1992). For instance, the cooperation concerning product development could be based on a relational contracting agreement in which specific levels of commitment, mechanisms of sharing costs and benefits, or general consultation and bargaining processes are settled. However, in many cases, the underlying common mechanisms and processes are not developed for environmental marketing cooperation, and its development and spread could produce extensive transaction costs. Implicit contracts, which fill contractual gaps with unarticulated but (presumably) commonly shared expectations (Milgrom and Roberts, 1992), also seem less efficient in environmental marketing cooperation. Here, cooperation often involves completely new fields of product-related environmental protection measures in which common expectations, about, for example, information exchange or sharing of cooperation gains, are non-existent.

Another market-based solution to the cooperation problem is vertical integration by one company obtaining hierarchical control over the previous or subsequent stages of supply, production, distribution, and so on. This solution exceeds the concepts of cooperation among separate firms. Vertical integration can be especially advantageous if one party to the economic transaction has significant transaction-specific investments that create a significant threat for post-contractual opportunistic behaviour (Williamson, 1985). This happens, in particular, if manufacturing firms decide to invest in environmentally less damaging production processes. Since most environmental marketing transactions necessitate considerable information exchange over different stages of the product life cycle, vertical integration can improve the provision of relevant information. By vertically integrating the previous production stage, the producer gains more knowledge about the quality of the output of this stage since he can better observe the inputs of this stage as available proxies for measuring or estimating the output quality. Thus, vertical integration can reduce measurement costs (Barzel, 1982) and improve coordination and transfer of information, especially that associated with environmental credence attributes (see also Hennessy, 1997). However, vertical integration also has limits. Integration becomes inefficient if the company uses standardized inputs which are competitively supplied, if independent suppliers can realize economies of scale or scope, if transaction-specific investments do not exist, or if the increased costs of managing the integrated organization exceed its benefits (Milgrom and Roberts, 1992). Vertical integration can also concentrate power and reduce consumer choice, leading to possible legal sanctions. As a result, the choice of vertical integration of environmental marketing activities has to be decided in 'case-by-case' decisions taking the specific companies' situations into account.

5.4 Tasks of Public Policy

Public policies can support environmental marketing cooperation by reducing contract risks. This could be done by increasing opportunities for measuring the performance of cooperation partners. Establishing a common system of standards, metrics and indicators for environmental performance and quality may reduce transaction costs, such as costs of search and of performance and quality verification (see, in general, North, 1981). Furthermore, standardization of intermediate materials or products provides more market alternatives for suppliers and facilitates gains from economies of scale. More market alternatives also reduces the risk of specific investments. The standard system should comprise standards of environmental quality and performance that are related to materials, ingredients and products as well as companies' processes, activities and organization (see EEA, 1998, for example). For instance, specialized subsequent producers or retailers could require the application of metrics when advertising their environmental products.

Standards should be applicable to both forward distribution chains and recycling channels. They should be embedded in standards of environmental management systems such as ISO 14000. The international circulation of these standards secures economies of scale in their use by multinational firms. The standards could facilitate product-related information exchange by, for instance, formalizing and incorporating environmental data into material data sheets. However, standardization of environmental performance measures may lead to the previously mentioned adverse effects that occur when a standard takes into account only a limited number of environmental protection activities. Furthermore, requirements for environmental management systems, which are the main part of the certification procedure of the European Environmental Management and Audit Scheme (EMAS) or the ISO 14000 series, are less successful when it comes to obtaining information about actual environmental performance. These kinds of certification systems promote the establishment and maintenance of a management system rather than actual results in the form of reduced levels of environmental damage (Karl, 1994). Establishing standards which lay more stress on quantitative measures may limit these disadvantages.

Public policy can also support the provision of product-related information by establishing an information exchange system for gathering, aggregating, evaluating, and anonymizing the relevant product and material data (Cramer and Schot, 1993). Here, public policy plays a decisive role in conducting life-cycle assessments and applying other analytical tools. For instance, a system of knowledge about product ingredients and their environmental impacts, especially during the production stage, makes it easier for companies to specify their product information needs to their cooperation partners or suppliers. This would also help to verify the reliability of the suppliers' information by allowing it to be compared to the public knowledge system. Since the standard and information system mainly has the characteristics of a public good, the market-endogenous provision of the system seems unlikely and public provision seems justified.

In addition to these information-provision tasks, public policy could stimulate inter-firm cooperation by setting appropriate environmental policy incentives, most visible in recycling and waste treatment. In particular, waste disposal policy increases the incentives to reflect environmental impacts of waste disposal and encourages inter-firm cooperation to solve waste problems. Increasing costs of landfilling or incorporating waste service or product (packaging) charges at the point of purchase could lead to more attention being paid to environmental aspects of waste treatment and recycling (Cairncross, 1992).

In some cases, direct regulation of waste treatment and recycling activities may be needed to avoid free-rider behaviour and illegal waste disposal. From the point of view of environmental economics, a rationale for public regulation of all waste treatment and recycling measures of companies does not exist (for a discussion of this topic see Karl and Ranné, 1999). For example, free riders can be excluded from privately established deposit–refund systems (for example, for glass or polyethylene terephthalate (PET) bottles), and these and other recycling infrastructure networks work well. Government-imposed deposit–refund schemes and voluntary recycling programmes can offer incentives to increase recycling rates while leaving firms free to choose the most efficient way (Cairncross, 1992).

6.   CONCLUSION

In response to consumers' increased environmental awareness, companies may seek to gain competitive advantages with environmental marketing by developing, distributing, advertising, and selling environmental products. However, we have seen that the supply and demand sides of the market for environmentally superior products have some peculiar attributes. The development of environmentally superior products provides positive external-ities, resulting in inefficiently low supply. The externality problem could be solved if sellers were able to credibly advertise their environmental products and, thus, to skim off the higher willingness to pay for environmentally superior products. However, inaccurate environmental advertising and insufficient production of environmental knowledge to credibly define environmental superiority hinder the internalization of the externalities by the market itself.

Considering these inefficiencies and market failures of environmental marketing transactions, there are many issues for public policy to address. Public policy can support the resolution of credibility problems in environmental advertising, and, in this way, provide incentives for environmental product development and other innovations of environmental marketing. Public policy can also foster the large-scale supply of environmental products by facilitating the solution of certain economic problems in order to make environmental marketing transactions more efficient. To this end, public policy can provide certain kinds of environmental knowledge, product-related information, as well as metrics and standards of environmental performance measurement that mainly have the characteristics of public goods. With the help of these measures, companies should be able better to define the environmental superiority of their products and activities and develop more efficient cooperation.

ACKNOWLEDGEMENTS

We are grateful to Landis Gabel, Henk Folmer, Omar Ranné and Yoram Bauman for their helpful comments and suggestions. We assume complete responsibility for any remaining errors. We would like to thank the Volkswagen Foundation for the financial support of our research.

NOTES

1. Like the term 'marketing' itself, the term 'environmental marketing' is, in general, not precisely defined (see, for example, Henion, 1976; Peattie, 1995; Wasik, 1996; Ottman, 1998).
2. When we refer to 'environmentally superior products' or 'environmental products', it is understood that we are emphasizing the relative environmental superiority of the products. Since every product leads to certain kinds of environmental resource use and environmental damage, a product can only be relatively environmentally superior in comparison with others and not 'environmentally benign' in general terms. In this context, the product's environmental quality denotes its environmental superiority.
3. The term 'product' encompasses various types of utility services. We do not consider the special marketing of environmental non-profit organizations, the conventional marketing of environmental protection technology, or the environmental marketing of services.
4. In economic theory, public goods are characterized by the absence of excludability and rivalry. If no one can be excluded from the use of a commodity, service or other benefit, and if there is no rivalry in its use, the good will not be provided by individuals in private markets because nobody is willing to pay for it.
5. An overview of several studies regarding environmental consciousness can be found in Hemmelskamp and Brockmann (1997).
6. In economic theory, transaction costs encompass (a) costs of preparing contracts (search and information costs), (b) costs of concluding contracts (bargaining and decision costs), and (c) costs of monitoring and enforcing the performance of a contract (Williamson, 1985).
7. A host of economic research work, mainly assigned to the economics of information, considers 'asymmetric information'. If one party has or will have an information advantage regarding

the characteristics or variables of a contract (private information) before or in a contractual relationship, economists talk, in general, about asymmetrically distributed information. When one party holds private information before the relationship has begun and the other party does not, a situation arises that is generally referred to as a problem of 'adverse selection' or 'pre-contractual opportunism' (Akerlof, 1970). If the relationship has been initiated and one party then receives private information or if the action of the party is unverifiable, the situation is generally named 'moral hazard' or 'post-contractual opportunism' (Ross, 1973).

8. In many cases, knowledge is regarded as a durable public good, because knowledge does not lose validity due to its use or due to the passage of time, it can be used jointly, and the exclusion from access to it is costly. However, for some types of knowledge, intellectual property rights, like patents, copyrights or company and trade secret laws, can establish excludability. The purpose of intellectual property rights is to offer knowledge producers economic rents such as monopoly profits, and, hence, to set incentives for the production of knowledge (Dasgupta and David, 1994). These conditions are particularly relevant for the technical or organizational knowledge of companies, which include knowledge about the causes of environmental damages (for example, the releases of production processes) and about (technical) possibilities for environmental protection. These types of knowledge can be private goods unless they are released by the producers.

    In contrast to technical and organizational knowledge, scientific knowledge has more of the characteristics of a public good, because it is often costly or socially undesirable to exclude its use. The value of scientific knowledge is not depleted by joint use, and in fact use often adds to its value (Dasgupta and David, 1994). Scientific knowledge encompasses, for example, basic environmental research regarding the natural environment, the environmental impacts of certain released substances (for example, 'dose–response' relationships between pollutants and final environmental damage), and complex ecological processes.

    Within a market mechanism, producers of scientific knowledge are not sufficiently able to appropriate the value of their produced knowledge, because they cannot establish excludability (the 'free-rider' problem). To address the resulting underproduction of scientific knowledge, direct governmental involvement or priority incentive schemes have to be established. For instance, the scientific incentive scheme of priority induces fast disclosure of scientific knowledge by allowing producers to secure the (informal) intellectual property rights of their discoveries and inventions (Dasgupta and David, 1994).

9. Another example is Switzerland, which regulates environmental advertising in the 'directive of environmentally hazardous substances' ('Verordnung über umweltgefährdende Stoffe'). The directive prohibits vague environmental claims which are not explained in detail and mandates that terms such as 'environmental protecting detergent' must be replaced by the exact description of the detergent ingredients.

10. Additionally, a 'Joint Federal Task Force', a cooperation of the federal states with the US Environmental Protection Agency (EPA) and the 'Office for Consumer Affairs' should harmonize the guidelines for environmental claims (Sellers, 1992).

11. The US EPA offers a voluntary 'Environmental Leadership Program' in which companies with relatively less environmental damage can demonstrate their superior environmental performance. To this end, the US EPA evaluates and certifies the 'leading' environmental protection measures of participating companies.

12. Although there are commonly accepted dispersion and conversion models for the translation from emissions at the different stages of the product life cycle to the environmental impacts, these models are uncertain and the subject of much controversy (see also Gruenspecht and Lave, 1989).

13. Recently, several standards or draft standards for the life-cycle assessment have been embodied in ISO 14040 (Principles and framework), ISO 14041 (Goal and scope definition and inventory analysis), ISO 14042 (Impact assessment), and ISO 14043 (Interpretation).

14. Direct distribution by a producer itself may be advantageous if, for example, its internal sales organization does not require extensive financial support from the firm. Additionally, some environmentally superior products are 'explanation-intensive', and direct distribution can secure the appropriate conveyance of product information to the customer and may help in acquiring credibility and reputation. Furthermore, it is often profitable to simplify distribu-

tion channels, for example, by circumventing certain distribution levels and gaining the mark-ups of the intermediaries.

REFERENCES

Akerlof, G.A. (1970), 'The market for "lemons": quality uncertainty and the market mechanism', *Quarterly Journal of Economics*, **84** (3), 488–500.

Anderson, J.C. and J.A. Narus (1990), 'A model of distributor firm and manufacturer firm working partnerships', *Journal of Marketing*, **54** (1), 42–58.

Ayres, R.U. (1995), 'Life-cycle analysis: a critique', *Resources, Conservation and Recycling*, **14** (3/4), 199–223.

Barzel, Y. (1982), 'Measurement cost and the organization of markets', *Journal of Law and Economics*, **25** (1), 27–48.

Beales, J.H. and T.J. Muris (1993), *State and Federal Regulation of National Advertising*, American Enterprise Institute Studies in Regulation and Federalism, Washington, DC: AEI Press.

Beales, H., R. Craswell and S.C. Salop (1981), 'The efficient regulation of consumer information', *Journal of Law and Economics*, **24** (3), 491–539.

Cairncross, F. (1992), *Costing the Earth: The Challenge for Governments, the Opportunities for Business*, Boston: Harvard Business School Press.

Caswell, J.A. and E.M. Mojduszka (1996), 'Using informational labelling to influence the market for quality in food products', *American Journal of Agricultural Economics*, **78**, December, 1248–53.

Cleff, T. and K. Rennings (1999), 'Determinants of environmental product and process innovation', *European Environment*, Special Issue *Integrated Product Policy and the Environment*, **9** (5), 191–201.

Cramer, J. and J. Schot (1993), 'Environmental comakership among firms as a cornerstone in the striving for sustainable development', in K. Fischer and J. Schot (eds), *Environmental Strategies for Industry: International Perspectives on Research Needs and Policy Implications*, Washington, DC: Island Press, pp. 311–28.

Darby, M.R. and E. Karni (1973), 'Free competition and the optimal amount of fraud', *Journal of Law and Economics*, **16** (1), 67–88.

Dasgupta, P. and P.A. David (1994), 'Toward a new economics of science', *Research Policy*, **23** (5), 487–521.

Davis, J.J. (1993), 'Strategies for environmental advertising', *Journal of Consumer Marketing*, **10** (2), 19–38.

De, S. and P. Nabar (1991), 'Economic implications of imperfect quality certification', *Economics Letters*, **37** (4), 333–7.

European Environment Agency (EEA) (1997), 'Life Cycle Assessment (LCA): a guide to approaches, experiences and information sources', Final report to the European Environment Agency prepared by dk-TEKNIK and SustainAbility Ltd, Copenhagen: EEA.

European Environment Agency (EEA) (1998), 'Continuity, credibility and comparability. Key challenges for corporate environmental performance measurement and communication', Report prepared by Å. Skillius and U. Wennberg, Copenhagen: EEA.

Faulhaber, G.R. and D.A. Yao (1989), ' "Fly-by-Night" firms and the market for product reviews', *Journal of Industrial Economics*, **38** (1), 65–77.

Foss, K. (1996), 'A transaction cost perspective on the influence of standards on product development: examples from the fruit and vegetable market', Working Paper no. 96–9, Copenhagen: DRUID – Danish Research Unit for Industrial Dynamics.

Freimann, J. (1995), 'Environmental information systems and eco-auditing', in H. Folmer, H.L. Gabel and H. Opschoor (eds), *Principles of Environmental and Resource Economics: A Guide for Students and Decision-Makers*, Aldershot, UK and Brookfield, USA: Edward Elgar, pp. 362–88.

Fuller, D.A., J. Allen and M. Glaser (1996), 'Materials recycling and reverse channel networks: the public policy challenge', *Journal of Macromarketing*, **16** (1), 52–72.

Gray-Lee, J.W., D.L. Scammon and R.N. Mayer (1994), 'Review of legal standards for environmental marketing claims', *Journal of Public Policy and Marketing*, **13** (1), 155–8.

Gruenspecht, H.K. and L.B. Lave (1989), 'The economics of health, safety, and environmental regulation', in R. Schmalensee and R.D. Willig (eds.), *Handbook of Industrial Organization*, Vol. II, Amsterdam: North-Holland, pp. 1507–50.

Guinée, J.B. et al. (1993), 'Quantitative life cycle assessment of products. 2: classification, valuation and improvement analysis', *Journal of Cleaner Production*, **1** (2), 81–91.

Hart, O. and J. Moore (1988), 'Incomplete contracts and renegotiation', *Econometrica*, **56** (4), 755–85.

Hecht, D. and N. Werbeck (1998), 'Abfallpolitik', in P. Klemmer (ed.), *Handbuch Europäische Wirtschaftspolitik*, Munich: Vahlen, pp. 221–317.

Hemmelskamp, J. (1996), 'Environmental policy instruments and their effects on innovation', Discussion Paper no. 96–22, Mannheim: ZEW – Zentrum für Europäische Wirtschaftsforschung.

Hemmelskamp, J. and K.L. Brockmann (1997), 'Environmental labels – the German "Blue Angel" ', *Futures*, **29** (1), 67–76.

Henion, K.E. (1976), *Ecological Marketing*, Columbus, OH: Grid.

Hennessey, D.A. (1997), 'Information asymmetry as a reason for vertical integration', in A.J. Caswell and R.W. Cotterill (eds), *Strategy and Policy in the Food System: Emerging Issues*, Amherst: Food Marketing Policy Center, pp. 39–51.

Hond, F. den and P. Groenewegen (1993), 'Solving the automobile shredder waste problem: cooperation among firms in the automobile industry', in K. Fischer and J. Schot (eds), *Environmental Strategies for Industry: International Perspectives on Research Needs and Policy Implications*, Washington, DC: Island Press, pp. 343–67.

Kaas, K.P. (1993), 'Informationsprobleme auf Märkten für umweltfreundliche Produkte', in G.R. Wagner (ed.), *Betriebswirtschaft und Umweltschutz*, Stuttgart: Schäffer-Poeschel, pp. 29–43.

Kangun, N. and M.J. Polonsky (1995), 'Regulation of environmental marketing claims: a comparative perspective', *International Journal of Advertising*, **14** (1), 1–24.

Kangun, N., L. Carlson and S.J. Grove (1991), 'Environmental advertising claims: a preliminary investigation', *Journal of Public Policy and Marketing*, **10** (2), 47–58.

Kapelianis, D. and S. Strachan (1996), 'The price premium of an environmentally friendly product', *South African Journal of Business Management*, **27** (4), 89–95.

Karl, H. (1994), 'Better environmental future in Europe through environmental auditing?', *Environmental Management*, **18** (4), 617–21.

Karl, H. and C. Orwat (1999), 'Economic aspects of environmental labelling', in H. Folmer and T. Tietenberg (eds), *The International Yearbook of Environmental and Resource Economics 1999/2000: A Survey of Current Issues*, Cheltenham, UK and Northampton, USA: Edward Elgar, pp. 107–70.

Karl, H. and O. Ranné (1999), 'Waste management in the European Union: maintaining national self-sufficiency and harmonization at the expense of economic efficiency', *Environmental Management*, **23** (2), 145–54.

Klein, B. and K.B. Leffler (1981), 'The role of market forces in assuring contractual performance', *Journal of Political Economy*, **89** (4), 615–41.

Klein, B., R. Crawford and A. Alchian (1978), 'Vertical integration, appropriable rents and the competitive contracting process', *Journal of Law and Economics*, **21** (2), 297–326.

Leland, H.E. (1979), 'Quacks, lemons and licensing: a theory of minimum quality standards', *Journal of Political Economy*, **87** (6), 1328–46.

Lizzeri, A. (1994), 'Information revelation and certification intermediaries', Discussion Paper no. 1094, Evanston, IL: Northwestern University, CMSEMS – Center for Mathematical Studies in Economics and Management Science.

Mason, Ch.F. and F.P. Sterbenz (1994), 'Imperfect product testing and market size', *International Economic Review*, **35** (1), 61–86.

Milgrom, P. and J. Roberts (1992), *Economics, Organization and Management*, Englewood Cliffs, NJ: Prentice-Hall.

Morris, J. (1997), *Green Goods? Consumers, Product Labels and the Environment*, London: Institute of Economic Affairs, Environment Unit.

Morris, L.A., M. Hastak and M.B. Mazis (1995), 'Consumer comprehension of environmental advertising and labelling claims', *Journal of Consumer Affairs*, **29** (2), 328–50.

Nagler, M.G. (1993), 'Rather bait than switch. Deceptive advertising with bounded consumer rationality', *Journal of Public Economics*, **51** (3), 359–78.

Nelson, P. (1970), 'Information and consumer behavior', *Journal of Political Economy*, **78** (2), 311–29.

Nelson, P. (1974), 'Advertising as information', *Journal of Political Economy*, **82**, 729–54.

North, D.C. (1981), *Structure and Change in Economic History*, New York and London: Norton.

Oosterhuis, F., F. Rubik and G. Scholl (1996), *Product Policy in Europe: New Environmental Perspectives*, Dordrecht: Kluwer.

Ottman, J.A. (1998), *Green Marketing. Opportunities for Innovation*, Lincolnwood, IL: NTC Business Books.

Peattie, K. (1995), *Environmental Marketing Management. Meeting the Green Challenge*, London: Pitman.

Picot, A. (1986), 'Transaktionskosten im Handel', *Betriebs-Berater*, supplement, **13** (27), 2–16.

Polonsky, M.J., J. Bailey, H. Baker, C. Basche, C. Jepson and L. Neath (1998), 'Communicating environmental information: are marketing claims on packaging misleading?', *Journal of Business Ethics*, **17** (3), 281–94.

Reader, T.W. (1995), 'Is self-regulation the best option for the advertising industry in the European Union?', *Journal of International Business Law*, **16** (1), 181–215.

Reinhardt, F.L. and R.H.K. Vietor (1996), *Business Management and the Natural Environment. Cases and Text*, Cincinnati, OH: South-Western College Publishing.

Ross, S.A. (1973), 'The economic theory of agency: the principal's problem', *American Economic Review*, **62** (2), 134–9.

Rubik, F. and T. Baumgartner (1992), 'Evaluation of eco-balances', Strategic Analysis in Science and Technology (SAST), project no. 7, Brussels: European Commission.

Ruhnka, J.C. and H. Boerstler (1998), 'Government incentives for corporate self-regulation', *Journal of Business Ethics*, **17** (3), 309–26.

Scammon, D.L. and R.N. Mayer (1993), 'Environmental labeling and advertising claims: international action and policy issues', *European Advances in Consumer Research*, **1**, 338–44.

Scholder Ellen, P., J.L. Wiener and C. Cobb-Walgren (1991), 'The role of perceived consumer effectiveness in motivating environmentally conscious behavior', *Journal of Public Policy and Marketing*, **10** (2), 102–17.

Schwartz, A. and L.L. Wilde (1979), 'Intervening in markets on the basis of imperfect information: a legal and economic analysis', *University of Pennsylvania Law Review*, **127** (1), 630–82.

Sellers, V.R. (1992), 'Government regulation of environmental marketing claims', *Kansas Law Review*, **41** (2), 431–56.

Shaked, A. and J. Sutton (1981), 'The self-regulating profession', *Review of Economic Studies*, **48** (2), 217–34.

Shapiro, C. (1983a), 'Consumer protection policy in the United States', *Journal of Institutional and Theoretical Economics*, **136** (3), 527–44.

Shapiro, C. (1983b), 'Premiums for high quality products as returns to reputations', *Quarterly Journal of Economics*, **98** (4), 659–79.

Shapiro, C. (1986), 'Investment, moral hazard and occupational licensing', *Review of Economic Studies*, **53** (5), 843–62.

Society of Environmental Toxicology and Chemistry (SETAC) (1993), *Guidelines for Life-Cycle Assessment: A 'Code of Practice'*, Brussels: SETAC.

Spence, A.M. (1974), *Market Signalling: Informational Transfer in Hiring and Related Screening Processes*, Cambridge, MA: Harvard University Press.

Stigler, G.J. (1971), 'The theory of economic regulation', *Bell Journal of Economics and Management Science*, **2**, Spring, 3–21.

Thomas, R. (1993), 'A balanced approach to marketing regulation and self-regulation', *International Journal of Advertising*, **12** (4), 387–94.

Tietenberg, T. (1998), 'Disclosure strategies for pollution control', *Environmental and Resource Economics*, **11** (3/4), 587–602.

Tirole, J. (1996), 'A theory of collective reputations (with applications to the persistence of corruption and to firm quality)', *The Review of Economic Studies*, **63** (1), 1–22.

Umweltbundesamt (UBA – German Federal Environmental Agency) (1988), *Vergleich der Umweltauswirkungen von Polyethylen- und Papiertragetaschen*, (Texte/Umweltbundesamt, 88,5), Berlin: UBA.

Umweltbundesamt (UBA – German Federal Environmental Agency) (1995), *Methodik der produktbezogenen Ökobilanzen – Wirkungsbilanz und Bewertung*, (Texte/Umweltbundesamt, 95,23), Berlin: UBA.

US EPA (United States Environmental Protection Agency) (1993a), *Evaluation of Environmental Marketing Terms in the United States*, prepared by Abt Associates for Office of Pollution Prevention and Toxics, EPA/741-R-92–003, Washington, DC: US EPA.

US EPA (United States Environmental Protection Agency) (1993b), *Life-Cycle Impact Assessment: Inventory Guidelines and Principles*, prepared by Battle and Franklin Associates for Office of Research and Development, EPA/600-R-92–254, Washington, DC: US EPA.

US EPA (United States Environmental Protection Agency) (1995), *Life-Cycle Impact Assessment: A Conceptual Framework, Key Issues, and Summary of Existing Methods*, EPA/452-R-95–002, Washington, DC: US EPA.

US FTC (United States Federal Trade Commission) (1992), *Guides for the Use of Environmental Marketing Claims*, 57 Federal Register 36,363–69, codified at 16 C.F.R. Part 260, Washington, DC: US FTC.

US FTC (United States Federal Trade Commission) (1998), *Guides for the Use of Environmental Marketing Claims*, 63 Federal Register 84, 24239–51, codified at 16 C.F.R. Part 260, Washington, DC: US FTC.

Wasik, J.F. (1996), *Green Marketing and Management. A Global Perspective*, Cambridge, MA: Blackwell.

Welford, R. and A. Gouldson (1993), *Environmental Management and Business Strategy*, London: Pitman.

Williamson, O.E. (1975), *Markets and Hierarchies: Analysis and Antitrust Implications*, New York: The Free Press.

Williamson, O.E. (1985), *The Economic Institution of Capitalism*, New York: The Free Press.

Wynne, R.D. (1991), 'Defining "Green": toward regulation of environmental marketing claims', *University of Michigan Journal Law Reference*, **24** (3/4), 785–820.

Wynne, R.D. (1994), 'The emperor's new eco-logos?: a critical review of the scientific certification systems environmental report card and the Green Seal Certification Mark programs', *Virginia Environmental Law Journal*, **14** (1), 51–149.

Zikmund, W.G. and W.J. Stanton (1971), 'Recycling solid wastes: a channel-of-distribution problem', *Journal of Marketing*, **35** (3), 34–9.

Zinkhan, G.M. and L. Carlson (1995), 'Green advertising and the reluctant consumer', *Journal of Advertising*, **24** (2), 1–6.

14. Dealing with major technological risks

Bernard Sinclair-Desgagné and Carel Vachon

1. INTRODUCTION

In an era when technological progress is accelerating, one cannot avoid thinking about the level of risk and uncertainty it entails. For technological progress is ambivalent. On the one hand, it enhances economic growth and the quality of life; it shelters us from natural forces, contributing to the prevention and reduction of latent disasters such as epidemics; and it provides comforting replies to the advocates of pessimistic scenarios based on limited natural resources. On the other hand, it exacerbates the consequences of human error, and past experience also reveals that new industrial processes and products often hide lethal side-effects that show up only in the long run.

This chapter is concerned with the assessment, allocation and control of major technological risks. Such risks refer to the probability of occurrence of dreadful outcomes linked to an explosion, a fire, a leakage, or any sudden mal-functioning or misuse of technology (as in Chernobyl, Seveso or Bhopal, for example), as well as to the eventual outbreak of some general disease due to widespread exposure to hazardous industrial substances (like silicone or asbestos, for example). They belong to the category of catastrophic risks, which are characterized by small probabilities of large, collective and irreversible losses (Chichilnisky and Heal, 1992). They are also man-made and therefore endogenous to human activity (see Smith, 1996, ch. 13), unlike natural disasters such as earthquakes or landslides. But they pertain to activities or decisions linked to the production of goods, as opposed to other endogenous catastrophes such as bank runs, financial collapse, wars and riots.

Regulation and management practices in respect of major technological risks are now evolving rapidly. The Environmental Protection Agency, for instance, set new rules for 'risk management planning' only three years ago; these rules are currently being implemented and refined in approximately 66 000 industrial facilities across the USA. This chapter proposes a brief summary of the main difficulties and policy issues which arise when dealing with major technolog-ical risks.[1] The presentation unfolds as follows. The next section focuses on risk assessment; it includes topics such as the public's perception of industrial risk and the definition of acceptance thresholds. Section 3 is devoted to risk sharing, or the *ex ante* allocation of liability for damages and financial compensation should a disaster occur. In the fourth section, we cover the subject of risk control. This objective involves two complementary facets which are treated successively: the first – prevention – tackles what are *a priori* identified to be the sources of risk; the second – mitigation – aims instead at designing and implementing contingency plans in order to reduce damages *a posteriori*. Section 5 contains concluding remarks.

2. RISK ASSESSMENT

Risk assessment is the initial step before setting priorities and deciding on cost-effective measures to control risks. To assess major technological risk one must evaluate its two fundamental dimensions: (1) the magnitude of the potential adverse outcomes, and (2) the probabilities attached to them. Risk assessment is not only limited to the analysis of a single worst-case scenario. It can provide a global picture and may therefore be presented as a set of probability distributions over a full range of possibilities. The following is an overview of the approaches involved in risk assessment.

2.1 Qualitative and Quantitative Assessment Methods

Risk assessment is usually done in two steps. The first aims at identifying the sources of danger and at describing the extent of potential damages; it is essentially qualitative. For risks associated with engineering system failures, the assessment can rely on sophisticated identification methods such as HAZOP (Hazard and Operability studies) or FMEA (Failure Modes and Effects Analysis).[2] They may use techniques like *fault trees* and *event trees* to spell out the different scenarios. For example, one may want to examine how a discharge of toxic and corrosive slurry into the atmosphere via the stack could happen at a crystallization plant. A fault tree would then allow us to discover, working backwards, that the slurry might overflow into the pressure control valve header, that the operator might fail to take action upon a rising-level signal and not reduce the input, and that all this may have started with the level control valve on a discharge line being shut inadvertently.[3] An event tree would consider the other side of the coin and exhibit the possible consequences of a such an incident, each branch representing a particular outcome.

Estimating the physical effects and extent of damages of a particular release scenario involves the use of consequence or hazard models. Several systems have been developed, many of them computerized, to assess damages resulting from specific incidents such as spills, explosions, fires, toxic releases or other types of emissions. These hazard model systems include the population vulnerability models, the SAFETI computer code, the WHAZAN computer code, and the Yellow Book[4] models. All these make use of dispersion models that trace out the impact zones.

The assessment of latent risks linked to health and environmental hazards focuses on understanding the characteristics and effects on humans of hazardous substances. Uncertainty lies mainly in the extent of damages a substance can cause, given a certain level of exposure to it. Evidence of carcinogenicity of dioxins, for instance, is obtained from exposing animal bioassays to high doses and extrapolating from the findings to the situation of humans who are exposed to much smaller doses. Extrapolation involves making assumptions about the shape of the substance–disease relationship. Dose–response models are then used to capture this relationship.[5] They generally reduce to two distinct approaches: one that seeks some exposure threshold below which no harmful effects can be detected (the so-called NOAEL or 'no observed adverse effect level') and another that develops a positive relationship over the whole range.[6] Together with other parameters (nature, duration and spatial extent of exposure, size of the threatened population), this information often leads to norm-setting.

At the purely quantitative stage, probabilities are assigned to the different nodes in the chain of events. Probabilities are also associated with the extent of resulting damages. The difficulty lies of course in associating probabilities with events for which data do not exist. Hypothesis-setting and expert judgement can play a large role here. An example of a comprehensive risk assessment is provided by the Canvey Report. Public investigation leading to this report was triggered by the proposal of United Refineries Ltd to construct an additional refinery on Canvey Island in the UK. One objective was to investigate the overall risks to health and safety arising from any interactions between existing and proposed installations (Health and Safety Executive, 1978, 1981).

The assessment of major technological risk is rarely very precise, however. Inaccuracies in the system's description, lack of confidence in statistical data, the number of judgmental hypotheses being made, the diversity of assessment methods, and the fact that the scope of the analysis might have been limited *a priori* contribute altogether to set a significant margin of error. Risk assessment results therefore usually include an estimate of the uncertainty attached to them obtained from dispersion values or from sensitivity analysis. This uncertainty can dictate priority-setting. For example, one can decide to focus on the better-known risks in the name of efficiency and learning, or on the least-known risks instead, invoking the precautionary principle.

Another source of controversy in risk assessment is the approach taken to pricing human and environmental casualties. There are a number of methods that try to assign a monetary value to risk reduction, as well as to life, health and the environment: hedonic methods applied to the labour market (taking into account wage differentials, for instance), cost-of-illness methods, and contingent methods directly asking the question of the individuals.[7] The credibility of the figures obtained remains questionable, however, not only for ethical reasons, but also because the occurrence of an industrial catastrophe is likely to fuel public anger and to become a political event whose outcome is highly unpredictable.

2.2 Risk Perception

As mentioned above, the assessment of major technological risks is never exempt from subjectivity. Individual risk perceptions remain an indispensable input, due to lack of data concerning empirical frequencies, or because one usually needs also to consider the opinions and reactions of less informed stakeholders.

People's biases when dealing with uncertainty are now well documented.[8] For instance, some individuals directly relate the fact that an event or a chain of events seem reasonable to the probability of it happening: the easier it is to visualize, the higher is the assessed subjective probability of occurrence. The ease of identifying the victims and the attention given by the media to certain risks are also factors contributing to overestimation. This all relates to the so-called 'availability heuristic', whereby an event will be judged probable or frequent to the extent that instances of it are easily recalled or imagined. The degree of control one has over the risk is yet another factor likely to affect risk perception. The more control there is, the more underestimated is the actual risk. Moreover, risks assumed voluntarily are not perceived in the same way as those that are imposed. An agent willing to move near a toxic waste incinerator may not perceive the risk in the same way as one would if the owner of the incinerator chose to settle and work in the neighbourhood. Here, the perception of risk may also depend on the existence of benefits associated with risk exposure (for example lower real-estate prices). The presence of such benefits changes the point of reference from which people assess risks and thus may in that way alter their evaluation or perception of the risk. Finally, some people also tend to ignore probabilities that fall below some threshold, although the opposite is also true: on certain occasions, people overvalue small probabilities in proportion to the importance of potential damages and undervalue large probabilities. All these drawbacks make the use of expected utility as a unifying model to encode, aggregate and compare subjective perceptions quite problematic.[9]

The various ways of framing and communicating risk also have an effect on perception. Experimentation shows that different formulations of the same problem give way to opposite attitudes in decision-making. Choices framed in

terms of number of lives saved entail risk-averse behaviour or a preference for
certainty versus randomness in results; on the other hand, choices expressed in
terms of number of lives lost give rise to risk-taking behaviour or a preference
for an uncertain loss over a certain one.[10] In this context, risk communication
often has two conflicting goals to meet at once: to warn the people that some
immediate actions on their part are required while at the same time reassure
them that the whole situation is under control. The communicator implicitly
seeks to inform the public about the so-called 'objective' measure of risk and
lead them to update their beliefs.[11] Public trust in risk management institutions
is then crucial, for it does have a bearing on the way people perceive risks
(Groothuis and Miller, 1997). Risks are often perceived to be greater than they
truly are when institutions are less trustworthy.

2.3   The 'Acceptable' Level of Risk

Setting an acceptable or tolerable level of risk rarely emerges through
consensus. A firm will decide upon the risks it considers tolerable based on its
legal liability, its assets and revenues, its technological constraints and the
availability of insurance coverage. If the risk borne by third parties were totally
internalized by the firm, the level chosen would in principle be acceptable to
all stakeholders. This rarely happens, of course. Employees, environmental
groups, as well as the surrounding communities, might not see or assess some
major technological risk in a similar way. The chosen level of risk, or even the
approach used to reach it, might be a source of conflict. Whether the method
was some cost–benefit analysis or a benchmarking approach using levels of risk
tolerated elsewhere, some stakeholders might point to the limits of science,
calling into question the transparency of the process and the objectivity of the
experts involved.

For large industrial accidents, employees are more likely than external stakeholders to convey their interest further because of their close relationship with
the firm and the bargaining power they have through labour unions. Is this
mechanism sufficient to guarantee that the chosen level of risk will seem
acceptable to all the parties involved? The higher wages employees receive
due to their exposure to risk might raise their tolerance threshold. Furthermore,
employees might not know the exact level of risks they are exposed to. Finally,
some selection bias in recruiting and the effect of training might make the pool
of employees constitute a bad representation of the exposed population.

When a new firm is about to settle nearby, surrounding communities and
local residents often engage in lobbying. In this case, public hearings in the
process of environmental impact assessment certainly provide for more transparency and for the revelation of preferences. In most cases, however, the plant
and its accompanying risks are already present in the neighbourhood. This *fait*

accompli leaves little room for dialogue and compromise. Communities are thus generally subject to negative externalities. They have little negotiating power, apart from the threat of legal suits which, as we will see, also present some difficulties. Furthermore, they are often ill informed and unable to reach a proper assessment of the risks.

Setting an acceptable level of risk is thus inevitably a political process, which may be guided by economic tools (Moatti, 1989). Economic efficiency and cost-effectiveness prescribe an optimal level where the marginal cost to reduce risk is equal to the marginal benefit of having a more secure environment. This approach was supported, for instance, by the International Commission of Radiological Protection and is embedded in popular criteria such as ALARA (as low as reasonably achievable) or ALARP (as low as reasonably practicable). In a wider multi-criteria approach, however, other factors can be given more weight and may prevail. Society might want to give priority to employment or regional development, for example, and the acceptable level of risk will then be that minimal level compatible with technological or financial objectives. In other circumstances, society might instead choose a certain threshold of risk, without being overly concerned with the economic or opportunity costs that the attainment of such a level implies. Most practical approaches are of course combinations of the above. In addition to some technically and economically feasible lower bound, they usually prescribe some upper level above which a risk is considered intolerable and must be reduced. Risks that fall between the two boundaries are deemed acceptable only if all practical and reasonable measures have been taken; some calculation towards an optimal solution is thereby asked for. As an illustration, the Canadian Council for Major Industrial Accident (CCMIA) considers, for instance, that with a probability of damages above 10^{-4} a risk is unacceptable, but with a probability below 10^{-6} it is. Between those two thresholds, acceptability depends on the use of land and on the feasibility of emergency measures.

A complement to the above is to decompose the chosen risk level further into specific safety goals. After satisfying explicit rules and regulations, a firm may set some threshold for the probability of a severe accident, and then formulate distinct objectives concerning what is the acceptable probability of casualty for an individual worker (for instance 10^{-3}) and for someone from the public (say 10^{-5}). This procedure is often followed in Europe, particularly in Holland (Paté-Cornell, 1994).

Finally, the precautionary principle provides another guiding tool to establish the proper level of risk (Gollier et al., 2000). In its best-known formulation this principle says that one should not await greater scientific certainty before adopting protective measures. The precautionary principle thus embodies the fact that when risks are not well known, preserving flexibility of action – or the possibility of adjusting or relaxing stringent standards as new information becomes available – has a value that must be taken into account when assessing the benefits of reducing the risk. The same type of reasoning holds when damages are totally irreversible. The precautionary principle currently lies at the foundation of recent European regulations concerning global warming and genetically modified crops.

3.   RISK-SHARING

Sharing technological risks means allocating *a priori* amongst the agents the financial liability for the potential damages. Who will be responsible for the restoration of the environment and for the compensation of victims? The firm and its insurers? The victims' insurers? Other partners of the firm? The government? The allocation of liability by law and by contract between the different agents is essential for many reasons. First, sharing the risk allows for the sustainability of different activities that would otherwise be abandoned. Most firms could not support alone the burden of liability without running an excessive risk of going bankrupt. They must therefore share the risk with agents – insurance companies in most cases – willing to add these risks to their portfolio of diversified risks. Risk-sharing also contributes to making other agents who are benefiting from the risky activities aware of their responsibilities and accountable for their decisions. By making the surrounding communities or consumers support some fraction of the damages (denying them a total compensation), and by making the partners of the firm – business or financial ones – support some of the risks, one might increase prevention and mitigation efforts, thereby reducing everyone's exposure. Of course, optimal risk-sharing needs to take into account the respective interests and degree of risk aversion of all stakeholders, and the means they have to supervise and change the prevailing level of risks.

3.1   Civil Liability

The first risk-sharing instrument is the degree of civil liability of the firm and of its partners.[12] It is given by tort law and by statutory extensions or limitations of this liability. From these rules, shareholders, lenders, insurers and other business partners make decisions that will have an impact on the prevailing level of risk. The state has two objectives in mind when establishing civil liability rules. First it wants to spread risk so that social cost is internalized, negligence is deterred, and the risk is brought to an acceptable level. Second, the legislator wants eventual innocent victims to be fairly compensated whenever possible.

The general civil liability rule imposes on individuals or firms the duty to restore or compensate for damages caused by their negligence. In principle, such a rule gives incentives to the firm to control its risks tightly and to prevent any damages to third parties, without the need for legislation on particular control measures. In practice, however, there are several well-known obstacles to the application of this general rule in the context of major technological risks.

First, the burden of proof can easily become overwhelming for any plaintiff. Negligence can be difficult to establish in a context of innovation, for instance, or where industrial standards of safety are yet to be defined or are too difficult to verify. The legislator may then decide to enact presumptions of negligence and, when certain conditions are met, the onus of proof will be on the firm to show that it took the reasonable care expected in the circumstances and adhered to established safety standards. To this end, conformity to ISO standards like the 14000 series on environmental management, the upcoming 18000 ones for health and safety in the workplace, or the Responsible Care guidelines for the chemical industry may provide a successful defence. The legislator can also establish a strict liability rule where the plaintiff only has to prove a damage as well as the causal link with the firm's activities, but not negligence on the firm's part. In that case, the firm will not defend itself by simply proving reasonable care and the respect of all recognized standards: only an 'act of God' – the fact that the damage was totally unforeseeable or the fault of a third party (or of the victim) – would exonerate a defendant. In the case of strict liability, victims are more likely to be fully compensated than under a negligence rule. Regimes of strict liability rules were adopted in the USA notably with the Comprehensive Environmental Response, Compensation and Liability Act (CERCLA). The Council of Europe also adopted such a regime in 1993 in the Convention on Civil Liability for Damages Resulting from Activities Dangerous to the Environment (ETS No. 150). This type of regime may lead, however, to excessive prevention, or push certain firms to simply exit the industry. If the firm bears all the risk of an accident and cannot show that it was caused by a random factor, it will become much more conservative, and the accrued precaution is likely to be reflected in price increases and a loss in competition if firms leave (Shavell, 1979; Manning, 1994). Finally, the proof of damage itself may not always be easily made. This is especially true of latent diseases. Showing a causal link between an activity and some occurring damage may be difficult when the damage could be attributed to a combination of many factors, such as the climate or the victim's health. The success of the plaintiff and the effectiveness of the liability rule will depend on the conclusiveness of the proof that is required from the plaintiff. Chapter 15 provides a more in-depth analysis of the efficiency of different liability rules for promoting safety behaviour and victim compensation.

Transaction costs can also jeopardize both the incentive mechanism and the compensation objectives. Litigation costs – including time and expertise costs – preclude the victims from being totally compensated and discourage some proper use of the system. The dispersion of damages among a large group of victims can present some further difficulties when each person is affected in a small way and nobody alone has enough incentive to bring the case to court. Class action suits may then alleviate this problem.

Whether the goals of safety and full compensation can always be met by a single liability rule is therefore unlikely.[13] But perhaps the most critical aspect of liability rules in the case of major technological risks is the fact that the liability of a corporation is limited to its assets. When damages are much larger than the assets of the company, incentives for risk reduction are more limited: to the eyes of the firm a large-scale catastrophe is the same thing as one that just makes it go bankrupt. The level of prevention will therefore not differ past a certain point. Some existing solutions to this problem are presented in the next subsections.

3.2   Extended Liability to the Firm's Partners

The firm that holds the risk-inducing technology rarely constitutes the only node in the production chain. Financial institutions provide funds to support the firm's activities, and other commercial partners either consume the firm's hazardous products or participate in the production process as input providers.

A firm may be tempted to outsource risky activities and make subcontractors bear the responsibilities associated with them. In this case, potential subcontractors will naturally demand a risk premium and the size of that premium will determine in part whether the activity will be subcontracted or not (as exemplified, for instance, in a recent study by Aubert, et al. 1998). For activities occurring in a highly competitive market, like transportation, outsourcing is all the more appealing since the premium that can be extracted is limited by the market structure. But transferring risky activities to competitive subcontractors may result in less effort devoted to safety. Subcontractors cannot generally manage these types of risks nor insure themselves as easily as larger firms. Furthermore, smaller contractors may be more reckless since they have much less to lose. This may lead them to take fewer precautions and to underinvest in their processes in order to shelter their assets from major technological risks, for, in the event of an accident, they may always benefit from the protection of bankruptcy laws.

One way out of this is to make several nodes in the production chain (subcontrators and subcontractees, lenders and debtors) jointly and severally liable in case of a major industrial accident. One hopes thereby to facilitate victims' compensation by going into the 'deeper pockets', insuring that the latter do not let others with 'shallow pockets' run unreasonable risks. The presumption is also that the external parties involved will put pressure on the firm to make sufficient investments in safety. The courts will trace the participation of firms linked to the risky activities either by the fact that they possess critical information concerning safety, or by the fact that they are the owner, operator or manufacturer of the processes or products at stake.

The economic downside of an extended liability regime, however, is that the targeted firm might change its pattern of transactions or expose less capital to liability when it cannot invest in safety nor control the risk (Boyd and Ingberman, 1997). For instance, toxic waste producers may be held liable for damages due to a leak in the landfill operated by another firm in which their waste is disposed of. By wanting to limit the wealth they are exposing to liability, targeted waste producers, especially smaller ones, may exhibit distorted capital investment and output choices. Furthermore, this regime might encourage contractual relations or affiliation between firms with similar degrees of solvency or safety standards: deep-pocketed firms will avoid contracts or affiliations with shallow-pocketed firms, even when it is not socially optimal, and small firms will get together without due care about the risk they generate.[14] So while extended liability may improve social cost internalization and deterrence, it may not necessarily improve welfare and a trade-off must be made.

Legislation like CERCLA in the USA and other regulations on the allocation of clean-up costs for contaminated sites are used to extend liability to lenders. The decision power of secured creditors in the firm management or the fact that they become owners of certain assets when the firm is in default can lead to their liability. Here again, extended liability may have downsides. It may affect the availability of credit, the cost of capital and the level of investment. Research results show, among other things, the importance of the information structure and of asymmetric information phenomena such as 'moral hazard' – not observing the firm's efforts on prevention and mitigation – and 'adverse selection' – not knowing the firm's initial risk profile – on the optimal extended liability rule. They suggest that lender's liability be only partial.[15]

3.3 Insurance

Firms facing major technological risks will seek to insure themselves whenever such insurance exists at a reasonable cost. Demand for insurance against liability claims by industrial firms results in part from risk aversion on the part of concerned firms and their shareholders or lenders; it may also be required by the law. The Convention on Civil Liability adopted by the Council of Europe requires that firms have a financial security scheme to cover liability. This scheme may take the form of an insurance contract or other financial arrangements among an industrial pool, for example.[16] In the USA, the same is required from facilities that produce or handle hazardous chemicals by the Resource Conservation and Recovery Act. Compulsory liability insurance enhances the compensation of victims who would otherwise face a bankrupt firm.

Other benefits can be derived from insurance with respect to major techno-logical risks. By design, the terms of an insurance policy, namely the premium, the extent of coverage, restrictions, exclusions and deductibles, should separate and deal with the various sizes and types of risks involved. Insurance contracts then become a mechanism that provides incentives to reduce risks. The insurer thereby takes the role of a surrogate regulator. The case of industrial boilers is a good illustration of the role insurers can play in risk reduction (see Paté-Cornell, 1996; Er et al., 1998).

For most major technological risks, however, insurance is not readily available, so insurers cannot fulfil a role in risk-sharing and reduction. Tech-nological risks that are too uncertain for a firm to bear may also be too uncertain for an insurance company that typically shows ambiguity aversion (Kunreuther et al., 1995). Lack of actuarial data and their public-good nature, dramatic con-sequences that can amount to enormous costs, the uncertain duration of adverse effects or of the latency period, and the fact that liability rules can change over time can deter insurers from entering the market. Moreover, the increasing complexity of technology, which makes the causal relationship between safety measures and risk reduction difficult to grasp, tends to exacerbate both the classical problems of adverse selection and moral hazard.

Under adverse selection, when insurance companies cannot assess precisely the respective risk of their potential clients before agreeing on the terms of a policy, insurance becomes less efficient as a means to redistribute risk (Borch, 1990). An average rate coupled with cross-subsidies between low and high risks is no longer sustainable because it is not attractive to low-risk agents. Different policy packages are then offered – high premium/large coverage and low premium/partial coverage – so agents will implicitly reveal their risk profile by the choice they make. The most likely outcome is then under-insurance of firms that generate lower risks, since only those firms will choose a partial insurance contract. Hence when adverse selection is too severe, as may be the case for major risks, there can actually be no insurance available: no package will be profitable at current insurance premiums, and raising premiums would only attract the worst risks, reducing profits further.

Moral hazard, or the possibility that the firm, once insured, takes fewer prevention measures, will also reduce the available coverage (Shavell, 1979). Unless the level of safety and prevention is perfectly observable by the insurance company, the insured agent has less incentive to be prudent, once insured, and is therefore more likely to cause harm. In this case the only way to provide some incentive for prevention and damage mitigation is to offer an incomplete coverage (or a large deductible), thereby making the insured firm bear some of the risk. There is thus a trade-off between optimal risk-sharing and incentives to prevention and mitigation. Experience rating – when subsequent premiums depend on the track record of the firms – is sometimes invoked to alleviate this trade-off. It is not, however, a system that insurance companies can rely on for major technological risks, since data in this case are so rare. An alternative route is *ex post* supervision with coverage and premium depending upon the observed prevention and mitigation levels. Such inquiries, however, are often very costly.

Finally, insurance availability is also limited in some areas due to the correlation of risks. If the risks of the whole pool of insured agents are not statistically independent, the probability increases for an insurance company that it may have to pay out indemnities all at once; some insurers might then find this too large a risk to bear. This may be the case for widespread substances that prove to be hazardous at the same point in time (like asbestos), triggering massive toxic torts. The year 2000 computer bug was another example of the kind of risk uninsurable for high correlation reasons. Another source of correlation can come from changes in liability rules that make all insured agents liable at once.[17]

Insurability of major technological risks is thus problematic. However, it holds an important key to proper internalization of those risks: insurance contracts can provide incentives for risk reduction by aligning their terms with good risk control measures. One important improvement in the management of major technological risks would therefore be better techniques to monitor and appraise initiatives in risk control. For this, one needs some means of references for recognizing the application of reliable measures. Er et al. (1998) propose third-party inspection to improve risk estimates and thereby enhance the role insurance can play in risk reduction and risk-sharing. Risk retention groups – where insurance funds are held by industrial pools of similar policy-holders – may also provide a solution. These groups are in a better position to monitor managerial performance than an external insurance company and may do it at lower costs.[18]

4.   RISK CONTROL

Risk control measures include self-protection; that is, activities affecting the probability of a loss; and self-insurance, that is activities aimed at lowering the loss itself when it occurs.[19] The firm's or the risk-maker's problem is to choose an optimal combination of the two approaches to risk control. Boyer and Dionne (1983) have shown that a risk-averse agent would prefer self-insurance to self-protection even when they both reduce the expected loss to the same extent and at the same cost. Intuitively, self-insurance is more efficient because it increases the wealth in the bad state where the marginal utility of income is higher. However, in the context of major technological risks, the irreversibility of losses often makes both types of activities indispensable and equally important, if not mandatory. This section reviews the literature on both subjects, starting with the former. To be consistent with the current literature, self-protection is called prevention, while self-insurance refers to mitigation efforts.

4.1   Prevention

Preventive measures involve both public and private means of intervention. Some of the possible strategies will now be discussed.

4.1.1   Public measures

State intervention in the field of safety with respect to major technological risks is quite extensive.[20] It is justified on the grounds of classical market imperfections such as imperfect information and, of course, negative externalities. Control of activities generating risks through command and control regulation, legal liability rules or economic incentive instruments such as Pigouvian taxes, tradable permits or refundable deposits all offer advantages and drawbacks. While economic instruments provide more room for efficiency and the implementation of cost-effective measures, they are not easily applicable to actions that are (1) discrete and (2) difficult to monitor, as is often the case for actions leading to major accidents. Legal liability rules, like economic instruments, also provide incentive to reduce risk as well as securing some compensation for victims should the damage occur. Furthermore, they do not require that the firm's behaviour be monitored. Liability rules have none the less their limitations, as we saw. They are thus invariably complemented with safety regulation. Defining safety standards and obligations, together with fines and other sanctions for non-compliance, remains the most common approach to regulating hazardous processes and products. Table 14.1 lists existing command-and-control legislations designed to reduce risks.

The difficulty with command-and-control intervention, on the other hand, is that the legislator must be omniscient. She must know everything about technology and about the performance of different risk reduction measures. This knowledge acquisition may turn out to be very costly. Furthermore, the government must carry out inspections to ensure that legislation is enforced. The actions likely to lead to accidents must therefore be observable at a reasonable cost in order to be efficiently regulated.[21] Command-and-control regulation is nevertheless often preferred, for it addresses problems more directly than economic incentives generally do.

Banning some products or processes is another, albeit radical, avenue that is often taken. The fact that society in this case loses some benefits it would otherwise reap from technology can be justified by invoking the precautionary

Table 14.1   Command-and-control legislation to reduce risk

- Occupational safety and health legislation
- Public health legislation (food and drugs, etc.)
- Environmental legislation, itself vast: air, water, ground quality, impact assessment, etc.
- Flammable, explosive and fire legislation
- Toxic substances legislation
- Labelling legislation
- Storage legislation
- Waste disposal legislation
- Transportation legislation
- Consumer product safety legislation
- Ports and waterway safety legislation
- Nuclear installations legislation
- Other energy specific legislation

principle, or because the irreversible nature of the damages (say the potential losses of hundreds of lives) forbids any cost–benefit trade-off, or finally because it is not in the firm's interest to find out at its own costs the true risks involved (Shavell, 1993).

State intervention to prevent damage can also take the form of subsidy for the development of safer technology. It can actually be more efficient to have particular agreements between the government and the firm in order to meet the goals of regulation. This is the case, for instance, when enhanced safety requires the development of new technology or when research results have a public-good nature. In this case, the government wants both to control behaviour and to stimulate innovation, two goals that can be more easily achieved by a contract that sets certain standards on the one hand and that partially subsidizes innovation on the other (Carraro and Siniscalco, 1996).

Many official reports and inquiries have brought up the need for a 'goal-setting' type of regulation instead of the standard-setting type.[22] With goal-setting regulation, operators must demonstrate safe design and operation to the regulator rather than mere compliance with prespecified technologies and checklists. In keeping with this, both the USA and the EU have adopted major hazard legislation to control these risks. In Europe, in the aftermath of the Seveso disaster in Italy, where an accidental release of dioxin shook the whole continent, the European Council adopted the 1982 Seveso Directive, which was reinforced in 1988 and 1996. It essentially requires that there be an obligation for firms to adopt safety measures and emergency plans, and that this information be made available to the public. Similarly, the US Environmental

Protection Agency has recently strengthened the control of risks by developing performance-based (or goal-setting) regulations also aimed at preventing and mitigating major accidental chemical releases. These new rules are commonly referred to as the risk management planning requirements or RMP.[23] RMP imposes on firms producing or handling certain chemical substances the obligation to conduct an offsite consequence analysis assessing the worst-case scenario and to develop and implement risk management programmes, including emergency plans. All this information must be submitted thereafter to a central location and be made available to the local authorities and the public. One goal here is to appeal to market mechanisms to induce risk reduction, in particular to capital markets believed to be sensitive to this kind of information (Kleindorfer and Orts, 1998; Lanoie et al., 1998).

4.1.2   Private measures

Once a firm meets safety standards imposed by law and regulation, it may still seek to reduce its residual risk. Actions firms can take to control the source of risks and reduce the probability of damages include the adoption of inherently safer technology and of technical safety features (additional safety valves, detection devices, and so on), and the reduction of hazardous material inventories. Increased emphasis has also recently been put on management systems, such as specific training to promote workers' reflexes and awareness concerning safety, task division and clear definition of responsibilities, information and control systems keeping track of interventions, and audit schemes to detect gaps and suggest remedies.[24]

Table 14.2 gives an overview of the typical elements of process safety management.[25]

Table 14.2   Elements of process safety management

- Review and documentation of the plant's chemicals, processes, and equipment
- Detailed process hazard analysis to identify hazards, assess the likelihood of accidental releases, and evaluate the consequences of such releases
- Development of standard operating procedures
- Training of employees on procedures
- Implementation of a preventive maintenance programme
- Management of changes in operation that may have an impact on the safety of the system
- Reviews before initial start-up of a process and before start-up following a modification of a process
- Investigation and documentation of accidents
- Periodic safety audits to ensure that procedures and practices are being followed

---

When these elements are implemented and emergency plans (to be discussed later) are put in place, however, several questions remain to be answered. What is the best strategy to reduce risk further or insure it as it is? What is the optimal level of investment in safety? Is the so-called 'human error' entirely controlled? In the next subsection we relate these to the observations of several studies and expand on the importance of organizational means.

The safety versus productive investment   All members of the firm face this apparent trade-off, from the bottom hierarchical levels to intermediate managers up to the board of directors. High-ranked executives must decide on the financial resources that will be devoted respectively to safety and market research, whereas the foreman must decide whether or not he should spend an extra day double-checking safety procedures instead of spending time on more productive (and often more visible) activities.

The safety budget decision – upgrading older equipment, hiring extra people, improving maintenance, and so on – should in principle be related to the marginal productivity of such investment and the marginal productivity of other inputs. How does further investment in safety translate into reduced liability, lower insurance premium, better access to capital, stronger partnerships, and the like? Measuring this, however, poses problems, for it is difficult to establish the effects of some prevention measures (especially organizational ones) on low probability levels. When dealing with recurrent workplace accidents with relatively small consequences (albeit very significant, when workers die or when a whole plant is shut down for several days), the marginal productivity of safety investments might be easier to measure. This is, however, not the case for low probability events with very large consequences. It is therefore not surprising that safety budgets are often dictated by safety regulation, industrial standards or insurance companies. Empirical studies actually note an overemphasis on insurance as opposed to actual risk factors and the lack of communication and coordination between the financial division of the firm, which usually deals with insurance matters, and the production staff, who generally take care of safety (see Paté-Cornell, 1996). Furthermore, it has been observed that firms tend to focus on short-term production goals as opposed to long-term safety issues. This is especially true for companies experiencing financial difficulties. It was the case for the Union Carbide plant at Bhopal, although other factors also contributed to the disaster (Lees, 1996).

Human error   Be it in design, in construction, or during operation and maintenance, human error is often seen as the culprit after a major industrial accident occurs. And for good reasons: in a study of marine systems such as offshore platforms, for instance, it was found that only 5 per cent of the failure probability could be truly attributed to random factors or 'bad luck', 40 per

cent to design errors and the rest to operation errors (Paté-Cornell, 1990).
Human errors can be classified under the following headings: slips and lapses,
mistakes, misperceptions, mistaken priorities and straightforward violations.
Causes of human errors can be some external events or distractions, the
operator's inability or poor training, excessive demands and pressure being put
on personnel, and biased incentives. Several observers have noticed that the
allocation of resources between technical and organizational or managerial
measures is not well balanced, and that if more attention were devoted to
management, then the occurrence of human errors might diminish (Paté-Cornell,
1996; Warner et al., 1992). But firms typically prefer to add physical redundancy
or to use stronger materials rather than rely on better training, hire more
competent managers and operators, or have external reviews (audits) of technological design. The report following the Three Mile Island incident actually
pointed out this bias in the allocation of resources.

Organizational measures   Poor involvement of high executives in risk
management is often mentioned as a factor contributing to higher levels of risk.
It was one of the main criticisms in a report leading to the shut-down of seven
nuclear reactors in Canada in 1997. It is also one of the lessons learned from
the Seveso accident, where the directors of the corporation ultimately
responsible were unfamiliar with the hazards. More involvement of high-ranked
officials in routine risk management should allow for a stronger control of
intermediate management decisions. On the other hand, by limiting the decision
power on issues that intermediate managers often master best, the firm might
lose some opportunities that do not necessarily compromise safety. Furthermore,
better monitoring by a higher hierarchical level will be futile if the actions of
employees or lower-ranked managers are not readily observable or if one would
need to be close to them at all times to detect problems and to prevent them.

   Other mistaken organizational arrangements can contribute to increased risk
levels. For example, when the distribution of tasks is such that the responsibility for risk management is separated for highly dependent subsystems, the lack
of coordination can have unforeseen repercussions. The explosion of the
Challenger space shuttle and the Eurotunnel 1995 fire are illustrations of this
point. Task design, distribution and compensation can lead to consistent biases
away from safety activities. Different arrangements are then needed to realign
employees' incentives with the firm's safety goals. It might be worthwhile, for
instance, to delegate different maintenance activities to different divisions when
those activities cannot be monitored equally well. Otherwise, a division in charge
of both tasks would be tempted to allocate more effort to the more easily
monitored (usually financially) one, in order to signal diligent work, and neglect
the safety one (Holmstrom and Milgrom, 1991). When the tasks cannot be easily
separated, a special audit and compensation scheme may not only promote an

efficient allocation of effort in both safety and production but also induce synergies between otherwise substitutable tasks (Sinclair-Desgagné, 1999). It might also be safer to avoid letting a single division decide on the adoption of a new technology when the choice involves technologies characterized by different risk levels and different maintenance requirements. If the division is in charge of maintenance, safety could be neglected and the ultimate decision would not be in the best interest of the firm (Hirao, 1993; Itoh, 1994; Vafaï, 1998).

Information disclosure   Efficiency and learning about loss control measures require that information concerning near misses, alerts and other deficiencies be disclosed instead of remaining in a private circle. Information demonstrating reliability of the engineering system and of the risk management system should also be disclosed, as it promotes the reputation of the firm and may enhance its value. However, the implementation of any system aimed at revealing key information is likely to face fierce resistance. The fear of reprisal naturally leads employees to dissimulate their own problems, mistakes and errors. But loss control measures cannot improve without their collaboration on this. Hence, several experts favour a forgiving approach rather than a carrot-and-stick one with respect to individual performance in risk management; they believe this will encourage information revelation (Warner et al., 1992). It is certainly necessary to take into account all market features that can have a direct impact on the firm's value and the executive's career prospects in order to find ways by which executives would voluntarily submit the firm to safety audits or any system that discloses information.

4.2   Mitigation

Containing the scale of adverse events through *ex ante* and *ex post* mitigation measures is the other route that leads to risk reduction. It can be a very effective strategy, especially when there is a lot of uncertainty about the probabilities of failures or about some particular effects. The extent of damages in a given industrial accident is a function of two essential elements: (1) the number of people and the value of resources exposed to the risk, and (2) the effectiveness of emergency intervention. These are under the partial control of public authorities and the firm through complementary means that are presented below.

4.2.1   Siting and urban planning
Zoning regulation is certainly one of the oldest and most obvious form of risk reduction. By splitting the territory and isolating hazardous plants, public exposure to risk is diminished. Environmental assessment procedures may also require proper risk analysis that defines a transition zone, helping thereby to determine a location minimizing the potential damages. The solution is not

always easy to implement, however. First, firms may be reluctant to locate at a distance that raises their transportation costs or affects the availability of inputs. Linking risk performance and zoning is used more and more frequently to circumvent this problem; it allows more flexibility in land use as long as the firm controls the risk with other measures. This of course defeats the purpose of using mitigation measures to further reduce the risk. This alternative is also more costly in terms of monitoring and emergency planning and may shift the cost from the firm and its particular clients to the local community. Second, zoning regulation typically categorizes industries into different types – light, heavy or general – and locates them accordingly. These categories are based on historical data and can rapidly become outdated due to innovations in products and processes.

More critically, relatively few local communities take or have taken into account major technological risks in their zoning decisions. Their analyses are usually confined to common nuisances like noise and odours. Another difficulty comes from the strong lobby of developers who do not see a problem in encroaching on transition zones that should normally be prohibited for residential purposes. This was actually one of the main problems at Seveso; it was also particularly acute in Mexico City when the petrochemical terminal of PEMEX exploded, as well as in Bhopal where shanty-towns extended up to the plant's boundary. Local authorities in financial difficulties are less likely to resist this pressure. Finally, grouping several hazardous plants within one area may entail another trade-off: the population might be less exposed to each risk taken separately, but the likelihood of a domino effect and much larger damages can rise with the geographic concentration of risks.

In 1992, the OECD set some guiding principles for zoning decisions: there should be general zoning criteria as well as a case-by-case assessment of any new industries and any new development near hazardous installations. It is, however, recognized that risk assessment is still largely absent from land use planning and zoning regulation, a problem that the latest amendments to the Seveso Directive have sought to address. One reason explaining this problem is the lack of clear and accepted guidelines on both the methodology for risk assessment and on the definition of an acceptable level of risk (Canadian Council for Major Industrial Accidents, 1995).

4.2.2 Emergency planning

The other approach to damage mitigation consists in preparing in advance the interventions of the different parties in case of a disaster in order to prevent further escalation of the original incident. In a study done by the Reactor Safety Study of the Atomic Energy Commission, it was estimated that for a particular scenario, early fatalities would be reduced from 6200 to 350 if there were effective evacuation (Atomic Energy Commission, 1975). However, although emergency planning is usually required by regulations on hazardous substances and processes, technical and organizational uncertainty in the firm and the lack of proper contingency plans are factors that often prevent damages from being properly contained.

The essential elements of an emergency plan are the control systems, personnel with specified responsibilities, communication scenarios, clear rules and procedures, and coordination/cooperation between various external and internal services. Communication is of particular importance in the very first stages of a crisis since it is at that time that key interventions are made. Nevertheless, delays in reaction and in communication are often observed. Typically, each level waits until the situation is locally out of control before alerting other divisions all the way to public authorities and the population. The level of preparedness and coordination of each party involved – the firm, the public security teams and the population – is thus crucial and will determine to a large extent the scale of damages.

Of course, it is not sufficient that emergency plans be thoroughly designed. The main lesson from the past is that these plans should be kept simple and flexible, and be capable of being scaled up or down according to circumstances (Lees, 1996, vol. 2). They must also be put to trial and reassessed regularly. This requires time and resources since the operations will often be interrupted. It also requires that the firm accepts some transparency *vis-à-vis* its workers and the surrounding communities. Unless a culture of safety is well embedded in the organization and there is prior coordination with public security and with the community, damages are bound to be large. This culture largely bears on a voluntary basis, but legislation like the new RMP rules in the USA reinforcing the Emergency Planning and Community Right to Know Act and the Seveso Directive in Europe certainly contribute to tighter relationship and coherence between stakeholders. Both of these regimes require that firms dealing with hazardous substances develop emergency response programmes including procedures for informing the public and coordinating with the local agencies responsible for emergency intervention.

5.   CONCLUSION

This chapter summarized the main traditional facets of dealing with major technological risks: assessment, insurance, prevention and mitigation. It is probable that each of those aspects will change significantly over the next decades, following the pace of technological innovation. Changes will be triggered by the spread of computer viruses and the consequent realization by the public of the current over-reliance on larger and larger computer networks, and also by the proliferation of new drugs, products and livestock born from genetic manipulations. We believe, however, that the categories and trade-offs emphasized above (following Warner, 1992) – quantitative versus qualitative assessments, preventive versus mitigating expenses, no-fault versus carrot-and-stick approaches, narrow versus broad stakeholder involvement – are inescapable and will therefore prevail. It is the answers to those trade-offs that will adjust, according to the evolution of society and of technology.

ACKNOWLEDGEMENTS

We wish to thank the editors, Henk Folmer and Landis Gabel, for helpful comments and suggestions on earlier drafts. We also benefited from several conversations with our colleagues Hélène Denis on risk perception and management, Marcel Boyer, Karine Gobert and Sandrine Spaeter on liability and insurance, and Erwann Michel-Kerjan on catastrophic risks, and with Robert Lapalme of the Ministère de la Sécurité Publique du Québec on the regulation and public management of industrial hazards and risks.

NOTES

1. Comprehensive surveys are also available. See Lees (1996), or the recent book by Hélène Denis (1998) and the references therein.
2. For a detailed description of the numerous risk identification and assessment methods, see Lees (1996), vol. 1.
3. This example is taken from Lees (1996), vol. 1.
4. 'Methods for the calculation of the physical effects resulting from release of hazardous material', developed in The Netherlands by the Committee for the Prevention of Disasters.
5. For a brief guide on health risk assessment methods, see the American Chemical Society (1998).
6. For a more detailed analysis of the different dose–response models, their underlying assumptions and the political implications for the regulatory process of toxic substances, see Harrison and Hoberg (1994).
7. For a detailed discussion of these methods, see Chapters 2 and 3 of this volume. See also Landefeld and Seskin (1982) on the economic value of life, Moatti (1989) on the willingness to pay for safety, and Viscusi (1993) on evaluation methods using labour market data.
8. For a survey of risk perception issues and the decision process for low probability events, see Camerer and Kunreuther (1989). See also Slovic (1987) and Viscusi (1992) for models incorporating biases in risk perception, Smith (1992) on the relationship between risk perception, information on risk and behaviour under uncertainty, and Lopes (1992) on misconceptions about the public's ability to perceive risks adequately.
9. For a survey on the topic of expected utility theory and alternative models of choice under uncertainty, see Machina (1987).
10. See the famous experiment results given in Tversky and Kahneman (1981).
11. But if communication fails, correcting for public biases will remain contentious as long as people's disagreement is rooted in their preferences. For more on this, see Smith (1992).
12. Pathbreaking work on this topic was accomplished by Calabresi (1970). Here we distinguish civil liability rules or tort law, whereby victims may claim compensation for the damages

suffered, from penal or statutory liability rules where corporations, directors or officers are exposed to sanctions (fines or imprisonment, but not compensation) if proven guilty of an offence. For a discussion on penal liability rules, see Chapter 15 of this volume.

13. For the necessity of a combination of instruments depending on the characteristics of the risks, see Katzman (1987) and Segerson (1992). To illustrate further, consider torts where several several injurers may have contributed to a single damage. A joint and several liability regime will foster the compensation goal by permitting the plaintiff to sue all or any of the injurers. But the cost of poor practice is then spread amongst many firms who then have lower incentives, individually, to take good care.

14. Affiliation between firms is recognized when several contractors or clients do business with a common producer.

15. For a survey on lender's liability, see Boyer and Laffont (1996). Gobert and Poitevin (1997) and Pitchford (1995) also present different approaches to derive the lender's optimal liability rule. For a discussion of lender's liability within the general corporate landscape, see Boyer and Sinclair-Desgagné (2000). For empirical evidence of the effect of such legislation on the cost of capital, see Garber and Hammitt (1998).

16. See section 12 of the Convention on Civil Liability for damages resulting from activities dangerous to the environment (ETS No. 150).

17. For an analysis of liability insurance and catastrophic environmental risk, see Katzman (1987).

18. For other solutions to insurability problems, see Dionne (1992).

19. See Ehrlich and Becker (1972).

20. For a good overview of the role government can play in the management of environmental risks and an analysis of the efficiency of different policy instruments, see Segerson (1992).

21. See Shavell (1984) for the characteristics risks must show in order for the regulatory approach to be appropriate.

22. The reports following the Three Mile Island and Piper Alpha disasters both insisted on this aspect.

23. EPA rules on Chemical Accident Prevention and Risk Management Planning were adopted in 1996, pursuing the Clean Air Act amendments of 1990, section 112(r). Firms had until June 1999 to submit their plan.

24. See also Chapter 10 in this volume for a discussion of these issues within the framework of operations strategy.

25. These elements are part of the OSHA Process Safety Management Standard. The Center for Chemical Process Safety, established as a Directorate of the American Institute of Chemical Engineers following the Bhopal disaster, proposes similar elements in its safety process management guide.

REFERENCES

American Chemical Society (1998), *Understanding Risk Analysis, A Short Guide for Health, Safety, and Environmental Policy Making*, Internet edition available at www.rff.org.

Atomic Energy Commission (1975), 'Reactor safety study: an assessment of accident risks in U.S. commercial nuclear reactors', Rep. WASH-1400, Washington DC.

Aubert, B., M. Patry and S. Rivard (1998), 'Assessing the risk of IT outsourcing', mimeo, CIRANO Working Paper.

Boyd, J. and D.E. Ingberman (1997), 'The search for deep pockets: is "extended liability" expensive liability?', *Journal of Law, Economics and Organization*, **13** (1), 232–58.

Boyer, M. and G. Dionne (1983), 'Variations in the probability and magnitude of loss: their impact on risk', *Canadian Journal of Economics*, 411–19.

Boyer, M. and J.-J. Laffont (1996), 'Environmental protection, producer insolvency and lender liability', in A. Xepapadeas (ed.), *Economic Policy for the Environment and Natural Resources: Techniques for the Management and Control of Pollution*, Cheltenham, UK and Lyme, USA: Edward Elgar, pp. 1–29.

Boyer, M. and B. Sinclair-Desgagné (2000), 'Corporate governance of major technological risks', in Henk Folmer, Landis Gabel, Shelby Gerking and Adam Rose (eds), *Frontiers of Environmental Economics*, Cheltenham, UK and Northampton, USA: Edward Elgar (forthcoming).

Calabresi, G. (1970), *The Cost of Accidents. A Legal and Economic Analysis*, New Haven, CT: Yale University Press.

Camerer, F.C. and H. Kunreuther (1989), 'Decision processes for low probability events: policy implications', *Journal of Policy Analysis and Management*, **8** (4), 565–92.

Canadian Council for Major Industrial Accidents (1995), *Risk-Based Land Use Planning Guidelines*.

Carraro, C. and D. Siniscalco (1996), 'Voluntary agreements in environmental policy: a theoretical appraisal', in A. Xepapadeas (ed.), *Economic Policy for the Environment and Natural Resources: Techniques for the Management and Control of Pollution*, Cheltenham, UK: Edward Elgar, pp. 80–94.

Chichilnisky, G. and G. Heal (1992), 'Global environmental risks', *Journal of Economic Perspectives*, **7** (4) 65–86.

Denis, H. (1998), *Comprendre et gérer les risques sociotechnologiques majeurs*, Montréal: Éditions de l'École polytechnique.

Dionne, G. (ed.) (1992), *Contributions to Insurance Economics*, Boston: Kluwer Academic Press.

Ehrlich, I. and G.S. Becker (1972), 'Market insurance, self-insurance and self-protection', *Journal of Political Economy*, **80**, 623–48.

Er, J., H.C. Kunreuther and I. Rosenthal (1998), 'Utilizing third-party inspections for preventing major chemical accidents', *Risk Analysis*, **18** (2), 145–53.

Garber, S. and J.K. Hammitt (1998), 'Risk premiums for environmental liability: does Superfund increase the cost of capital?', *Journal of Environmental Economics and Management*, **36**, 267–94.

Gobert, K. and M. Poitevin (1997), 'Environmental risks: should banks be liable?', mimeo, Université de Montréal.

Gollier, C., B. Jullien and N. Treich (2000), 'Scientific progress and irreversibility: an economic interpretation of the precautionary principle', *Journal of Public Economics*, **75**, 229–53.

Groothuis, P.A. and G. Miller (1997), 'The role of social distrust in risk–benefit analysis: a study of the siting of a hazardous waste disposal facility', *Journal of Risk and Uncertainty*, **15**, 241–57.

Harrison, K. and G. Hoberg (1994), *Risk, Science, and Politics: Regulating Toxic Substances in Canada and the United States*, Montréal and Kingston: McGill-Queen's University Press.

Health and Safety Executive (1978), 'Canvey: an investigation of potential hazards from operations in the Canvey Island / Thurrock area', London: HMSO.

Hirao, Y. (1993), 'Task assignment and agency structure', *Journal of Economics and Management Strategy*, **2**, 325–32.

Holmstrom, B. and P. Milgrom (1991), 'Multitask principal–agent analyses: an incentive perspective', *Journal of Law, Economics and Organization*, **7**, 24–52.

Itoh, H. (1994), 'Job design, delegation and cooperation: a principal–agent analysis', *European Economic Review*, **38**, 691–700.

Katzman, M. (1987), 'Pollution liability insurance and catastrophic environmental risk', *Journal of Risk and Insurance*, 75–100.

Kleindorfer, P. and E.W. Orts (1998), 'Informational regulation of environmental risks', *Risk Analysis*, **18** (2).

Kunreuther, H., R. Hogarth and J. Meszaros (1995), 'Insurer ambiguity and market failure', *Journal of Risk and Uncertainty*, **7**, 71–87.

Landefeld, S.J. and E.P. Seskin (1982), 'The economic value of life : linking theory to practice', *American Journal of Public Health*, **72**, 555–61.

Lanoie, P., B. Laplante and M. Roy (1998), 'Can capital markets create incentives for pollution control?', *Ecological Economics*, **26**, 31–41.

Lees, F.P. (1996), *Loss Prevention in the Process Industry: Hazard Identification, Assessment and Control*, 2nd edn, Oxford: Butterworth-Heinemann, 3 vols.

Lopes, L. (1992), 'Risk perception and the perceived public', in D.W. Bromley and K. Segerson (eds), *The Social Response to Environmental Risk*, Kluwer Academic Publishers, pp. 57–74.

Machina, M.J. (1987), 'Choice under uncertainty: problems solved and unsolved', *Journal of Economic Perspectives*, **1**, 121–54.

Manning, R.L. (1994), 'Changing rules in tort law and the market for childhood vaccines', *Journal of Law and Economics*, **37**, p. 247.

Moatti, J.-P. (1989), *Économie de la sécurité: De l'évaluation à la prévention des risques technologiques*, Paris: Institut de la santé et de la recherche médicale.

Paté-Cornell, E. (1994), 'Quantitative safety goals for risk management of industrial facilities', *Structural Safety*, **13**, 145–57.

Paté-Cornell, E. (1996), 'Global risk management', *Journal of Risk and Uncertainty*, **12**, 239–55.

Pitchford, R. (1995), 'How liable should a lender be? The case of judgement-proof firms and environmental risk', *The American Economic Review*, **85**, 1171–86.

Segerson, K. (1992), 'The policy response to risk and risk perception', in D.W. Bromley and K. Segerson (eds), *The Social Response to Environmental Risk*, Kluwer Academic Publishers.

Shavell, S. (1979), 'Risk sharing and incentives in the principal and agent relationship', *Bell Journal of Economics*, **10**, 55–75.

Shavell, S. (1984), 'Liability for harm vs. regulation of safety', *Journal of Legal Studies*, **9**, 1–25.

Shavell, S. (1993), 'The optimal structure of law enforcement', *Journal of Law and Economics*, **36**, 255–87.

Sinclair-Desgagné, B. (1999), 'How to restore higher-powered incentives in multitask agencies', *Journal of Law, Economics and Organization*, **15**, 418–33.

Slovic, P. (1987), 'Perception of risks', *Science*, **236**, 280–85.

Smith, V. Kerry (1992), 'Environmental risk perception and valuation: conventional versus prospective reference theory', in D.W. Bromley and K. Segerson (eds), *The Social Response to Environmental Risk*, Kluwer Academic Publishers, pp. 23–57.

Smith, Keith (1996), *Environmental Hazards: Assessing Risk and Reducing Disaster*, London: Routledge.

Vafaï, K. (1998), 'Délégation et hiérarchie', *Revue économique*, **49**, 1199–225.

Viscusi, K. (1992), *Fatal Tradeoffs: Public and Private Responsibilities for Risk*, Oxford: Oxford University Press.

Viscusi, K. (1993), 'The value of risks to life and health', *Journal of Economic Literature*, **31**, 1912–46.

Warner, Sir Frederick, et al. (1992), *Risk: Analysis, Perception and Management*, London: The Royal Society.

15. Liability for environmental damages
Kathleen Segerson

1. INTRODUCTION

Traditional economic analyses of environmental policy design focus on the use of regulation (for example, discharge limits), emission taxes (that is, Pigouvian taxes), or marketable permits as alternative instruments for inducing efficient investments in pollution abatement (see for example, Baumol and Oates, 1988). These instruments are applicable to environmental contaminants that are emitted continuously, as a known and anticipated by-product of some production process. Examples include sulphur dioxide emissions and continuous waste discharges into water bodies. For these pollutants, even when firms invest efficiently in pollution abatement, there is likely to be some positive discharge and hence the imposition of a limit or tax on that discharge or the creation of a permit market for that discharge is feasible.

However, many important environmental concerns stem from the unintentional and unanticipated release of substances, or 'environmental accidents'. Examples include oil spills, unintended chemical releases, leaking underground storage tanks, and leaching of pesticides or landfill wastes into soil and surface or groundwater. In such cases, neither emission taxation nor marketable permits are generally feasible. Regulation of activities contributing to the likelihood and magnitude of a release is possible and frequently used.[1] In addition, taxes on the activities that lead to potential damages (for example, waste generation or pesticide use) can be used to create incentives for reductions in potential damages. However, some actions that affect the likelihood or magnitude of an environmental accident, such as the care taken in handling materials or maintaining structures, are not readily observed by regulators and hence not easily subject to regulation. Similarly, while taxes on dangerous activities may reduce the amount of that activity that is undertaken (for example, the amount of waste generated or the amount of oil transported), they fail to provide incentives for increasing the amount of care taken in conducting the activity (for example, the care taken in ensuring safe disposal or transport).

Instead of using regulation or taxes, policy-makers can attempt to influence the behaviour of potential polluters (and hence the likelihood and/or magnitude of an accident) by imposing legal liability for the damages that result if a spill or release occurs. As distinct from regulation or taxes, which are imposed *ex ante* or before any environmental damages are realized, liability is an *ex post* policy instrument, which is imposed only after it is determined that damages have occurred. None the less, the anticipation of liability for damages that might occur as a result of a given activity can provide incentives for polluters to undertake actions *ex ante* in an attempt to reduce the likelihood or extent of future liability payments.[2]

The two main types of legal liability are strict liability and negligence-based liability. Under strict liability, a polluter would be liable for damages resulting from his activities regardless of the amount of care he exercised in conducting them. Strict liability has historically been applied in cases where a particular product or activity has been deemed to be ultra-hazardous, although it has been increasingly applied to liability for environmental damages.[3] For example, in the USA both the Comprehensive Environmental Response, Compensation and Liability Act (CERCLA or 'Superfund') and the Oil Pollution Act impose strict liability on polluters.[4] Strict liability is consistent with the 'polluter pays principle', which states that polluters should be responsible for environmental damages resulting from their activities. In contrast, under a negligence rule, a polluter would be held liable for damages only if he were deemed to have been negligent in conducting the activity, that is, if he had not exercised a sufficient amount of care (the 'due standard' of care). In the absence of negligent behaviour, the polluter is not liable for damages that result from his activities. Under strict liability, a polluter essentially pays a price for conducting a particular activity, while under negligence he pays a price for failure to comply with a given standard of conduct. Thus, strict liability is often viewed as a 'price' instrument, while negligence is effectively a 'quantity' instrument (Cooter 1984). The distinction between the two parallels the distinction between price and quantity instruments that has been made in the literature on *ex ante* policy instruments (for example, Weitzman, 1974).

In evaluating the use of liability as an environmental policy tool, economists have considered the incentives for efficient pollution reduction created by both strict liability and a negligence liability rule. Most of this literature has been theoretical. However, the effectiveness of either liability rule in inducing pollution abatement depends not only on the theoretical incentives it creates but also on the way in which it is actually applied in practice. Although one might in principle hold a polluter liable for damages resulting from his activities, in practice there may be a number of factors that insulate the polluter from ultimate payment, such as difficulties in proving causation and limited assets. A complete examination of the use of liability as an environmental policy tool must consider both the theoretical properties of this policy instrument (in its various forms) and the empirical evidence regarding the incentive effects it creates.

This chapter provides an introduction to both the theoretical and empirical literature on the incentive effects resulting from the imposition of legal liability for environmental damages. We limit consideration primarily to the two basic forms of liability, strict liability and negligence. The first section of the chapter is devoted to an overview of some basic results regarding the theoretical impact of liability. We begin with a discussion of the alternative efficiency criteria that can be used to compare policy instruments. We then use those criteria to evaluate the efficiency properties of a strict liability rule. This is followed by a comparison of the impacts of strict liability with those of a negligence rule. Finally, we briefly review some of the empirical literature on the incentive effects of liability. There have been relatively few empirical liability studies, perhaps because of the difficulties inherent in obtaining the data necessary to test hypotheses about the impact that liability has had on behaviour. None the less, the emerging literature suggests that, while in theory liability can induce efficient behaviour, in practice its impact is likely to be limited except in cases where damages are large, easily proven and concentrated. In addition, even in these cases, liability can have unintended effects, as firms seek to avoid (rather than reduce) their expected payments. Both of these results suggest that sole reliance on liability is not likely to lead to adequate control of environmental accidents. An approach that combines liability with *ex ante* regulation or taxation is likely to be more effective.

2.   EFFICIENCY CRITERIA: SOME BASIC PRINCIPLES

An economic evaluation of alternative environmental policy instruments generally focuses on their efficiency properties, that is, the extent to which they promote efficient decisions or resource allocations. When evaluating liability as a policy instrument, a number of different types of efficiency have received attention, and in many cases trade-offs among them exist. These stem from the fact that the possible environmental damages associated with a given activity depend on a number of factors, including (i) the amount of care exercised by the polluter in conducting the pollution-generating activity, (ii) the amount of that activity that the polluter conducts, (iii) the amount of mitigation or care exercised by the potential victim to avoid or reduce damages through reduced exposure, and (iv) the amount of the exposure-generating activity that the victim engages in. For example, the ultimate damages from contamination of groundwater from the use of agricultural chemicals depend on (i) the care used in the application of the pesticides (for example, timing and method), (ii) the amount of the pesticide used, (iii) the extent to which the victim invests in filtration to reduce the contamination level of the water, and (iv) the extent to which the victim reduces exposure by reducing consumption of the contaminated water. In evaluating the efficiency of alternative liability rules, we should consider the effect of the rule on each of these four decisions, although in any given context some of these decisions may be more important than others.

In addition, to the extent that different policies imply different allocations of risk and parties are not risk neutral, an evaluation of alternative approaches should also consider a fifth type of efficiency, namely, the efficiency of the implied risk allocation, which varies across different rules. For example, a strict liability rule places all of the risk associated with the uncertain future liability on the polluter. In contrast, under a negligence rule, as long as the polluter is non-negligent, he will not face any liability-related risk.[5] Instead, the risk would be borne by the victim or possibly by a third party responsible for victim compensation (such as the government).

In evaluating alternative approaches in terms of these five types of efficiency, four basic principles are generally applied. The first principle is that efficient care incentives for a party (either the polluter or the victim) can be created by making that party bear the full amount of damages (either directly or financially) at the margin. In other words, a party's incentive to exercise care to reduce damages will be efficient if, for every one-dollar increase in damages, the damage or financial cost borne by that party increases by one dollar. This forces the party to internalize the damages, thereby creating an incentive for him to reduce damages efficiently through increased care. This basic principle underlies the incentive effects of Pigouvian taxes and the effects of strict liability (as will be seen below).

A second principle is that efficient care can also be induced by creating a sufficiently large (discrete) difference between the amount the party pays (or receives) if he engages in an efficient amount of care, and the amount he pays (or receives) if he does not. By imposing a sufficiently high payment or penalty for failure to exercise efficient care, the party can be induced to choose an efficient amount of care in order to avoid the penalty. This is the principle underlying the use of negligence-based liability rules. In addition, it underlies the use of financial penalties to induce compliance with environmental regulations.

In contrast to efficient care levels, efficient activity choices (by polluters or victims) depend on total costs rather than marginal or incremental costs. The third principle, which is used to evaluate incentives regarding activity levels, is that a party will engage in the efficient amount of an activity if it fully internalizes the total costs (and benefits) of that activity. If a party engaging in an activity does not bear the total social costs associated with that activity, he will have an incentive to engage in an inefficiently high activity level.

The fourth principle relates to the efficient allocation of risk. The standard literature on efficient risk-sharing shows that risk should be borne by the risk-neutral party (if one party is risk-neutral and the other is not) or allocated such that at the margin the cost imposed by the risk is equal for both parties (Shavell, 1979). Thus parties that are better able to bear risk (because of different risk preferences or greater access to risk-spreading mechanisms such as insurance) should bear a greater portion of the risk.

These four basic principles can be used to evaluate the efficiency properties of various policy instruments, including both *ex ante* tax and regulation policies and *ex post* liability.

3.   STRICT LIABILITY

As noted above, strict liability is similar to a price-based rather than a quantity-based instrument for pollution control. Because strict liability imposes the full costs of any pollution that occurs on the polluter, it essentially makes polluters pay a price for pollution. In this sense, it is similar to the imposition of a Pigouvian tax. Although under strict liability the payment is not determined until after damages occur (if they occur at all), at the time the polluter is making decisions regarding potentially polluting activities, he has some expectation about what those damages will be (based on both the probability of a release and the damages that result from a release) and hence some expectation about what his likely liability will be. This is analogous to a polluter knowing what his tax payments will be under a Pigouvian tax. Thus, when applied to stochastic pollution, many of the *ex ante* incentive effects of strict liability are similar to the incentive effects of Pigouvian taxes applied to continuous emissions of pollutants. However, there are also some important ways in which even the *ex ante* effects of these two policy instruments differ. Although the two instruments are designed for different contexts (continuous versus stochastic releases), because the incentive effects of Pigouvian taxes are well known and often used as a benchmark, we note some of the similarities and differences between the properties of the two instruments below.

3.1   Polluter's Choice of Care

The effect of strict liability on polluter care can be seen from a simple model of environmental accidents.[6] Let x denote the polluter's expenditure on care or pollution abatement. We assume that the polluter's care can affect either the probability of an accident or the magnitude of the damages that result if an accident occurs. For example, the care used in construction and operation of an oil tanker can affect both the probability that an oil spill will occur, and the magnitude of a possible spill. Let $p(x)$ denote the probability that an accident will occur and let $D(x)$ denote the damages that the victim will suffer if an accident occurs, where $p'(x) < 0$ and $D'(x) < 0$. At the time that the polluter makes his care decision, the expected damages are thus $ED(x) = p(x)D(x)$. The socially efficient choice of x (x^*) then minimizes total social costs $x + ED(x)$, which are the sum of the cost of care and the expected environmental damages.[7,8] If the sufficient second-order conditions are met, then x^* is defined by the first-order condition

$$1 + ED'(x) = 0. \tag{15.1}$$

The polluter, on the other hand, chooses a level of x that minimizes his private costs, which are the sum of the cost of care and the expected liability payment. Let $L(D(x))$ denote the polluter's liability payment, which depends on the damages that the victim suffers as a result of the accident. Expected liability is thus given by $EL(x) = p(x)L(D(x))$. The polluter seeks to minimize $x + EL(x)$. The first-order condition for the polluter's choice of care is

$$1 + EL'(x) = 0. \tag{15.2}$$

Under a strict liability rule, the polluter is liable for all damages that occur, that is, $L(D(x)) = D(x)$. Clearly, under such a rule, $EL(x) = ED(x)$, which implies $EL'(x) = ED'(x)$ for all x. Thus, marginal private costs equal marginal social costs and the polluter is induced to choose the efficient level of care. In other words, the polluter is forced to internalize the expected damages that result given his choice of care. This is the same principle that underlies the use of a Pigouvian tax, under which pollution-generating activities (such as emissions of a given pollutant) are taxed at a rate equal to the marginal social damages that result from that activity (Baumol and Oates, 1988).

The efficiency of strict liability requires that polluters believe they will pay for any environmental damages that result from their activities. However, polluters may perceive that the probability of being held liable for the full amount of damages is less than one. One reason a polluter might not be held liable even under a strict liability rule is the difficulty of proving causation when damages are uncertain. This is particularly problematic for risks with long latency periods. For example, it may be difficult to prove that a given cancer case was caused by exposure to a toxic substance many years ago. Similarly, even if held liable, a polluter may not make the full damage payment if the damages exceed the assets available for payment. In cases with long latency periods, a polluting firm may go out of business before damages are realized. Alternatively, victims may not bring suit if legal fees are high and/or damages are widely dispersed across individuals. If the polluter perceives the probability of a successful suit to be less than one for any of these reasons, then even under strict liability he will not expect to pay the full amount of damages and hence will not choose an efficient amount of care.[9] However, if the expected damages are known (or can be estimated statistically), then use of an *ex ante* tax based on expected damages would ensure that the firm pays the full expected social costs of an activity before it is allowed to engage in that activity.

3.2 Polluter's Choice of Activity/Output Level

Recall that efficient activity or output choices occur when a firm pays the total expected cost, including total environmental damages, associated with that activity. Under a Pigouvian tax, total expected payments by the polluter equal total expected damages only if the damage function is linear (over the relevant range for the firm) (Spulber, 1985; Baumol and Oates, 1988).[10] However, under strict liability total expected payments by the polluter equal total expected damages even if the damage function is non-linear. Thus, unlike a Pigouvian tax, strict liability creates efficient activity level or output incentives for the polluter, regardless of the form of $D(x)$.

To understand this result, we must extend the simple model of care used above to incorporate the choice of activity level as well. Let q be the output or activity level of the injurer and assume that both the care level (x) and damages (D) are defined per unit of output.[11] Let $B(q)$ be the benefits from the production of q and let $c(x)$ be the per unit production costs, which are assumed to increase with the firm's investment in care (that is, $c'(x) > 0$). Given the efficient level of care (x^*), the socially efficient choice of q (q^*) maximizes the net benefits from the activity, which are the gross benefits minus total costs, including both the production costs and the expected damages. Thus, q^* solves

$$\max B(q) - [c(x^*) + p(x^*)D(x^*)]q. \tag{15.3}$$

The associated first-order condition is

$$B'(q) - [c(x^*) + p(x^*)D(x^*)] = 0. \tag{15.4}$$

Given q^*, the polluter should engage in the activity (or enter the industry) if and only if the net benefits (given the efficient choices of q and x) are non-negative, that is, if and only if

$$B(q^*) - [c(x^*) + p(x^*)D(x^*)]q^* \geq 0. \tag{15.5}$$

The above conditions characterize the efficient polluter decisions, that is, the decisions that maximize net social benefits. However, in making his actual decisions, the polluter seeks to maximize net private benefits, $B(q) - [c(x) + p(x)L(D(x))]q$. The corresponding first-order condition is

$$B'(q) - [c(x) + p(x)L(D(x))] = 0. \tag{15.6}$$

Similarly, the polluter will choose to engage in the activity (or enter the industry) if and only if his net profits from doing so are non-negative, that is, if and only if[12]

$$B(q) - [c(x) + p(x)L(D(x))]q \geq 0. \tag{15.7}$$

Comparing (15.6) with (15.4) and (15.7) with (15.5) implies that the care and output choices, as well as the decision about whether or not to engage in the activity at all, will be efficient if $L(D(x)) = D(x)$, that is, if the polluter's liability payment is equal to the total damages that result from the accident. Since under a strict liability rule polluters pay the full amount of damages for all x, this rule will induce an efficient choice of activity level, as well as an efficient entry/exit decision. In other words, since polluters bear the full social costs of all of their actions (choice of care and activity level), those choices will be efficient. Note that, unlike in the case of Pigouvian taxes, efficiency results here even if marginal damages are not constant since under strict liability total payments always equal total damages.

3.3   Victim Incentives

For some environmental accidents, it is possible for the victim to take steps to reduce potential damages, either by investing in direct mitigation measures (for example, installing filters to remove contaminants from drinking water) or by reducing the level of the activity that creates exposure to the contaminants (for example, drinking less water from the contaminated source). Accidents where the care levels of both the injurer and the victim can affect damages are termed 'bilateral care' accidents.

It is well known that victim incentives for both care and the choice of activity level will be efficient if victims cannot affect the amount of compensation they receive for any damages they suffer, that is, if the compensation they receive (if any) is lump-sum (Baumol and Oates, 1988). To see this, we extend the simple model of care presented above to allow for the possibility that the victim can invest in mitigation that will reduce the damages that result from an accident. Thus, the damages will depend not only on the care choice of the polluter but also on the mitigation or care choice of the victim.[13]

Let y denote the care choice of the victim (measured in dollars) and write the expected damages as a function of the care choices of both the polluter and the victim, that is, $ED(x,y) = p(x)D(x,y)$. Total social costs are now given by the sum of care expenditures by both the polluter and the victim and expected damages, that is, $x + y + ED(x,y)$. The first-order conditions for the efficient levels of x and y are

$$1 + ED_x(x,y) = 0 \tag{15.8}$$

$$1 + ED_y(x,y) = 0 \tag{15.9}$$

where subscripts denote partial derivatives. Let $C(D(x,y))$ denote the amount of compensation that the victim receives when he suffers damages of $D(x,y)$. His expected compensation is thus $EC(x,y) = p(x)C(D(x,y))$. In making his care choice, the victim will choose a level of y that minimizes his expected total costs, net of any compensation he receives, that is, a level that minimizes $y + ED(x,y) - EC(x,y)$. Given x, the first-order condition for the victim's choice of y is

$$1 + ED_y(x,y) - EC_y(x,y) = 0. \tag{15.10}$$

Comparing (15.10) with (15.9) implies that, for a given x, victim incentives will be efficient if and only if $EC_y(x,y) = 0$, that is, if and only if the victim's care choice does not affect the amount of compensation, implying that the compensation is lump-sum. Of course, a special case of lump-sum compensation is zero or no compensation.[14]

Since under a Pigouvian tax policy tax payments are paid to the government rather than to victims, victims receive no compensation for the damages they suffer. This lack of victim compensation under Pigouvian taxes ensures that victim mitigation incentives will be efficient under this policy. However, when strict liability is imposed by the courts, the liability payment from the polluter is paid directly to the victim, that is, $C(D(x)) = D(x)$. Thus the victim is fully compensated (at least in principle) for any damages that he suffers. This compensation offsets the damages, thereby removing any incentive for the victim to reduce damages through mitigation.[15] Hence, under a strict liability rule, victim mitigation incentives are inefficient.[16] For example, if employers are strictly liable for damages to workers from exposure to toxic substances in the workplace, workers will face inefficient incentives to exercise care in handling these substances.[17]

The inefficiency of strict liability in the case of bilateral care stems from the transfer of polluter payments to victims (in the form of victim compensation). It should be noted, however, that while transfer is an integral part of strict liability when imposed by a court under the law of torts, the same is not necessarily true if it is imposed legislatively. In this case, payment is not necessarily made to specific individuals who may have suffered damages. For example, strict liability under CERCLA covers only response and clean-up costs and damages to public resources. In particular, it does not provide for any transfer or direct compensation to adversely affected individuals. To obtain compensation for damages, these individuals would have to seek redress through the courts.[18]

3.4   Uncertainty

Up to this point, the discussion of the impact of strict liability has focused on its ability to create incentives for risk reduction. However, when polluters are risk-averse, the socially optimal choice of care may involve a trade-off between risk reduction incentives and efficient risk allocation (see Shavell, 1979; Segerson, 1986, 1987). Although strict liability creates efficient incentives for polluter care, it also imposes all of the risk associated with the uncertainty of damages on polluters. This is in contrast to the allocation of risk under an *ex ante* tax (for example, a Pigouvian tax or a tax on waste generation or chemical use). Under the tax, the polluter's payment is certain (given, for example, the level of waste generation or chemical use). Thus the polluter bears no risk regarding his payment under the tax. In contrast, under strict liability, the polluter's payment is uncertain *ex ante* since it depends on the uncertain level of damages. Thus, in the absence of any mechanism for shifting risk (such as insurance), all of the risk regarding the level of damages is borne by the polluter. When damages are potentially very large, as for some environmental accidents, the uncertainty regarding the level of damages (and hence the amount that the polluter will have to pay) generates a considerable amount of risk for the polluter.[19]

Placing all of the risk on polluters can be inefficient if polluters are risk-averse. An efficient allocation of risk requires that risk be shared or placed on the party that is better able to bear that risk (Shavell, 1979). If society as a whole is better able to bear risks than individual polluters (because they can be spread across a large population), then shifting some (or all) of the uncertainty associated with damages to the public would yield a more efficient allocation of risk.[20] Thus, even though strict liability would provide efficient risk reduction incentives, it would not yield efficient risk allocation and hence would not be socially optimal. A socially optimal policy would balance risk reduction and risk allocation objectives.

4.   STRICT LIABILITY VERSUS NEGLIGENCE

As noted above, an alternative to the use of strict liability is the use of a negligence rule. Both rules are *ex post* in the sense that they are triggered only after an accident occurs. In addition, both can be designed to induce efficient care decisions by polluters (for example, Shavell, 1980). As shown above, strict liability induces polluters to invest efficiently in care by making them responsible for all damages that result from their activities, thereby forcing them to internalize all environmental damages. In contrast, under a negligence rule, provided the polluter complied with the 'due standard of care', he would not be held liable for damages. None the less, if the due standard of care is set at the efficient level, the firm will have an incentive to meet that standard in order to avoid liability. As long as the cost of meeting the standard is less than the expected cost of liability for failure to meet it (as is the case if the standard is set at the efficient level of care and negligent parties are liable for all damages), it will be cheaper for the polluter to meet the standard than not to meet it and be liable for damages. Hence a properly designed negligence rule can induce efficient care as well. However, unlike strict liability, a negligence rule will not create an incentive for firms to respond to an accident efficiently (that is, take steps to contain a spill or clean up after it) unless the definition of negligent behavior includes failure to respond appropriately when an accident occurs.

While both liability rules can create similar incentives for polluter care, they differ in the incentives they create for polluters to choose an efficient output or activity level. Under strict liability, polluters pay not only for care but also for any damages that result despite the care they have undertaken in conducting the activity. In other words, they pay the full social costs of their activities. As a result, both the prices of their products and the corresponding output levels will reflect all costs associated with production and will thus be efficient. In contrast, under a negligence rule, the firm's costs will be less than the full social costs whenever the firm is non-negligent. Since product prices reflect private rather than social costs, under a negligence rule product prices will tend to be too low (that is, below the social opportunity cost of production, which determines the efficient price) and output will be too high (Polinsky, 1980). Thus, while a strict liability rule induces efficient output/activity levels, a negligence rule does not.

A negligence rule might, however, be preferred on the basis of victim incentives. As noted above, victim incentives are inefficient under a strict liability rule that includes transfer of payments from the polluter directly to the victim. However, under a negligence rule, victims would receive no compensation when polluters are non-negligent.[21] As a result, they would bear the full amount of damages and would thus have an incentive to undertake mitigation to reduce those damages. Although the lack of victim compensation under a negligence rule can induce efficient victim incentives, this feature of the negligence rule can be criticized on fairness grounds. Since victims are not directly responsible for the activities that led to the accident, it can be argued that on the basis of fairness they should not bear the resulting damages. Even if one takes the view that the production activities that led to the accident are socially desirable and thus society should bear the costs, in most cases the associated benefits will be widely distributed while the costs will be concentrated on a small number of victims.

Strict liability and negligence differ not only in terms of their allocation of costs, but also in their allocation of risks. Because strict liability imposes uncertain liability on polluters, it also imposes considerable risk on them. In contrast, the negligence rule imposes a much smaller risk on polluters, since compliance with the due standard absolves the polluter of liability. The risks are instead borne by victims or by the government if public victim compensation funds exist. As noted above, the efficient allocation of risk depends on both the risk preferences of the parties (that is, whether they are risk-neutral or risk-averse) and their opportunities for shifting or spreading risks. In general, victims have little opportunity to spread risks associated with exposure to contamination, but the government can spread compensation costs across taxpayers. Similarly, while large firms may be able to spread risks through self-insurance, small firms may not be able to spread risks unless commercial environmental liability insurance is readily available. Thus a negligence rule will impose very costly risks on risk-averse victims if no form of public victim compensation exists, while a strict liability rule could impose costly risks on small, risk-averse firms if environmental liability insurance is not available.

Finally, the two rules can be compared on the basis of the transactions costs (that is, information and litigation costs) they are likely to generate. Because a negligence rule requires a showing of negligence to establish liability, the transactions costs associated with a given lawsuit are likely to be higher than those under a strict liability rule. However, these higher costs will also serve to deter some potential lawsuits. Thus, even though the cost per suit may be higher under a negligence rule, the number of suits might be lower. Whether total transactions costs are higher or lower under a negligence rule than under strict liability will depend on the relative strengths of these two opposing effects.

The above analysis of strict liability and negligence is in the context of third-party victims, that is, victims who have no interaction with the polluter other than through the imposition of damages.[22] In some cases, the victim of an accident may interact directly with the polluter through a market transaction as well, that is, as a buyer or seller of a product or service. For example, with industrial accidents, the victims may be employees of the polluter. Similarly, in cases of environmental hazards associated with the use of products, the victim may be the purchaser of the product. In such cases, the victim and polluter have a contractual relationship (through the employment contract or the purchase contract), and the price of the transaction (the wage or the product price) provides a mechanism for transferring or shifting liability from one party to the other.

When one party can shift some of its costs on to the other party through changes in the contract price, the initial allocation of liability becomes 'irrelevant'.[23] The polluter effectively bears the social costs of his actions either directly (if he is liable for damages) or indirectly (through a change in the price the victim is willing to pay or accept if the victim is liable). The polluter is thus induced to choose efficient levels of care and output even if he is not directly liable for damages.[24]

We have also assumed above that there is a single polluter. In some contexts, the actions of several polluters may combine to determine the likelihood or magnitude of an environmental accident. For example, many different polluters may dispose of waste in a hazardous waste disposal facility, which might result in contamination of groundwater. If the damages are attributable to the combined actions of all of the parties, then some means of allocating liability among the parties must be determined. If the relative contributions of each can be readily determined, then a court can apportion the damages based on these relative contributions. However, in some cases, such an apportionment may not be possible, or there may be 'orphan shares' (that is, shares attributable to parties that are no longer in existence or unable to cover their share of liability). In these cases, an alternative approach is the use of joint and several liability, under which any one of the polluters can be held liable for the full amount of damages. A joint and several liability rule can be based on the principles of strict liability or negligence. In addition, it might or might not be coupled with a right of contribution.[25]

In theory, either an apportionment rule or strict joint and several liability (with or without contribution) can provide efficient incentives under certain conditions, although in practice none of them is likely to do so (Miceli and Segerson, 1991).[26] The factors determining the allocation of liability under these rules differ from those determining each polluter's incremental damage. For example, polluters with 'deep pockets' may be more likely to be held liable for damages, regardless of the magnitude of their contributions.[27] Thus, in practice these rules for determining liability when there are multiple polluters are not likely to be efficient.

5. EMPIRICAL EVIDENCE

While considerable attention has been devoted to the theoretical effects of alternative liability rules on behaviour, relatively little has been done to test whether in practice the imposition of liability actually creates incentives for reductions in risks. The main empirical question to be answered is the extent to which anticipated liability for damages affects a potential polluter's decisions regarding pollution-generating or reducing activities.[28,29] As noted above, the incentive effects of liability are reduced if polluters perceive that they may not have to pay the full amount of damages for which they would otherwise be liable either because a suit is not brought or the payment they are required or able to make is less than total damages.

Empirically estimating the incentive effects of liability directly requires observations both on the polluter's expectations regarding the liability rule that would be applied if damages occurred and on the decisions that could potentially affect the probability or level of damages. Unfortunately, in many cases neither of these will be readily observable. For this reason, empirical verification of the incentive effects created by liability has been limited, and those studies that have been done generally employ imperfect proxies for one or both of these variables.

For example, because observations on polluter care are generally not available, some studies have examined the impact of liability on damages. While this approach provides information on the net effect of liability on damages, it does not necessarily answer the question of the extent to which liability is creating incentives for polluter care. In cases of bilateral care where damages depend on the behaviour of both polluters and victims, a change from no liability to strict liability will not necessarily change the level of damages despite the fact that it changes polluter incentives. In the absence of liability, victims can be expected to take steps to reduce damages. If strict liability is imposed, this incentive is reduced (or eliminated). The net effect of the decrease in victim care and the increase in polluter care may be a relatively small change in total damages, despite the fact that the imposition of strict liability may have been quite effective in changing the behaviour of both parties. Thus, at least in cases of bilateral care, it is difficult to infer anything about the effectiveness of liability by simply considering the impact on damages.

Even when damages are a suitable proxy for the polluter's decisions, it may be difficult to obtain an accurate measure of damages. Two possible proxies for actual damages are the number of accidents of a particular type that occur and the dollar amounts awarded in a particular type of case. However, use of the former measure ignores differences in damages across accidents, while use of the latter ignores the fact that actual awards often reflect factors other than simply damages.

In addition to the above data problems, satisfactory hypothesis-testing regarding the effects of liability may be hampered by the confounding effects of regulation (Dewees et al., 1996). In some cases, changes in liability have been coupled with changes in regulation. Examples include product safety, where the move toward greater producer liability has been accompanied by increased regulation, and hazardous waste management in the USA, where increased liability under CERCLA followed closely after the regulatory changes embodied in the Resource Conservation and Recovery Act. In fact, several authors have argued that in some cases the combined use of liability and regulation to control externalities is preferred to the use of either alone (for example, Shavell 1984a,

1984b; Segerson 1986, 1987; Kolstad et al., 1990). Since both policies are generally designed to increase precaution or care, it is difficult to isolate the effect of either individual policy change when the two are changed concurrently.

Because of these difficulties, the empirical literature on the effect of liability is much smaller than the theoretical literature. The early studies were not in the context of environmental liability. Rather, they examined accidents in the contexts of workplace safety and product safety.[30] However, this literature is relevant for understanding the likely effectiveness of liability for controlling environmental risks, since in some recent cases (for example, asbestos and Agent Orange) the workplace or product risk stems from exposure to a toxic substance.

In the USA, a change in the liability for workplace hazards came about when workers' compensation was introduced during the first half of the twentieth century. Several studies have examined the impact that increases in the amount of workers' compensation have had on safety. A number of these studies are outlined in Ehrenberg (1988). In general, they use accident or claim rates as a proxy for damages. The conclusion from these studies is that observed accident rates and claims rose (instead of falling) when workers' benefits were increased.[31] While some of this may simply reflect increased incentives to report accidents, to the extent that the number of accidents has actually increased, it implies that increased liability can lead to less rather than more safety. The likely explanation is the response of victims. Because industrial accidents are examples of bilateral care in which the actions of both the employer and employee can affect the probability and/or magnitude of damages, any additional precaution taken by employers (injurers) in response to greater liability can be offset by reduced care by victims due to greater compensation. More recent evidence based solely on fatal accidents shows, however, that workers' compensation has been effective in reducing death risks (Moore and Viscusi, 1989, 1990). It has been less effective, though, in addressing disease-related claims where there are long latency periods and causation is more difficult to prove (Viscusi, 1991a).

A second related area where the empirical effects of liability have been examined is product liability. In fact, because of the limits on the amount of compensation that a worker receives under workers' compensation, many workers exposed to asbestos sought relief from the manufacturers under product liability (Viscusi, 1991a). In the USA the scope of product liability has expanded in the last several decades, and a number of researchers have attempted to evaluate the impact that this expansion has had.[32] For example, in an analysis of trends in product-related accidents, Priest (1988) found no evidence of a change in the accident rate as a result of increased product liability. This is not necessarily inconsistent with the predictions of the theoretical models. The 'irrelevance' result discussed above suggests that, when injurers and victims have a contractual relationship and there is perfect information, a change in liability will not affect safety incentives. With misperceptions or other imperfections in the legal system, however, one would expect to see some response to a liability change. None the less, it appears that the safety gains from increased product liability have been modest (Dewees et al., 1996).

Since one way to increase safety is through changes in a firm's product line, a number of studies have examined the impact of product liability on product innovation.[33] The evidence is mixed. For example, Viscusi and Moore (1993) conclude that liability costs have a positive effect on innovation at low to moderate levels of liability but a negative effect when liability costs are very high. The likely explanation is that, at relatively low levels of liability, production is still profitable and firms seek to improve product design (and hence reduce liability) through innovation. However, with high levels of liability, the impact on profitability can be significant and further investment in the associated products may not be worthwhile. In fact, there is considerable anecdotal evidence of firms withdrawing products from the market because of potential liability (Viscusi and Moore, 1993; Dewees et al., 1996).

Overall, the evidence on the impacts of workplace and product liability is mixed. When measurable impacts have been observed, it is generally in a context where the link between injurer behaviour and damages is clear and immediate, so that causation and responsibility can be readily established. This suggests that liability is most likely to be effective in controlling environmental risks with the same characteristics. However, to the extent that polluters can shield themselves from liability through mechanisms other than increased safety, they will have an incentive to do so. As seen below, the limited literature on the effect of liability on environmental risks supports this conclusion.

One of the earliest empirical studies of the impact of environmental liability was by Opaluch and Grigalunas (1984). They examined the effect of the liability provisions of the US Outer Continental Shelf (OCS) Lands Act of 1978, which made firms strictly liable for the damages from offshore oil spills. They tested the hypothesis that producers would reduce their bids for OCS leases in environmentally sensitive areas in anticipation of greater liability for spills in such areas. According to their estimates, total high bids for tracts declined by 20 per cent in response to perceived environmental risks. Opaluch and Grigalunas (1984) argue that their results provide evidence to suggest that liability has promise as a mechanism for encouraging polluters to exercise care when conducting activities that can lead to environmental damages. However, the effect of liability on bids does not provide any information about its effect on damage-avoidance behaviour in the sense of increased care or reduced activity level. Even if firms did not change their care or activity levels at all, we would still expect to see bids decrease in response to greater environmental sensitivity since bids reflect expected returns from the lease, which are lower with increased liability. Thus, while it may be true that the winning firm both adjusted its bid and in addition engaged in greater care during development of the tract, such a response in the level of care cannot be inferred from the results on bids presented by Opaluch and Grigalunas.

Dewees et al. (1996) review more direct evidence regarding the deterrence effects of environmental liability. This evidence includes both responses to industry surveys regarding the impact of liability and case studies of individual industries and pollutants.[34,35] They conclude that, while there is little evidence of a general response to liability, there is anecdotal evidence that firms have responded to statutory liability imposed under CERCLA. Most CERCLA cases have the characteristics that Dewees et al. suggest are necessary in order for liability to be effective, namely, they involve large amounts of pollutants discharged from a single source that harm property (mainly land) or a small group of individuals. In cases where the damage is to health and/or it is spread thinly over a large group of individuals, the difficulty of proving causation and the limited incentive to bring suit dampen the deterrence effect of liability.

While anecdotal evidence suggests that firms have responded to CERCLA liability, the responses have not necessarily focused on increased safety. There are other ways that firms can limit their liability exposure. In the context of land contamination, one approach is simply not to purchase land that carries with it potential liability, since under CERCLA that liability is transferred with ownership.[36] Alternatively, firms can shield themselves from liability through changes in corporate structure. For example, in anticipation of potential liability, firms can spin off hazardous parts of their business into small firms that can avoid liability through divestiture and bankruptcy. Recent studies suggest that this has, in fact, been an observed response. Using cross-sectional data on firm structure across industries that vary in their degree of hazard,[37] Ringleb and Wiggins (1990) and Merolla (1998) find evidence of corporate restructuring in response to expected liability. In particular, they find that more hazardous industries have more small, private independent firms and firms with shorter life-spans. Both of these findings suggest that firms may seek to avoid liability by concentrating hazardous activities in firms that can easily hide behind the protection of bankruptcy. This conclusion is also consistent with anecdotal evidence presented by Wiggins and Ringleb (1992).

The desire to avoid liability for environmental damages also creates an incentive for polluters to invest heavily in fighting liability claims, which leads to large litigation and other related transaction costs. Perhaps the most notable example is CERCLA, where critics have claimed that litigation costs associated with legal battles over CERCLA liability consume a large share of the financial resources that would otherwise be available for clean-up. For example, one study estimated average transaction costs under CERCLA to be 32 per cent of total expenditures by responsible parties.[38] A key issue in CERCLA reform has been the perceived need to reduce the associated transaction costs (for example, Probst et al., 1995).

6. CONCLUSION

Economists typically advocate the use of Pigouvian taxes or marketable permits for controlling environmental pollutants. While these instruments can be effective in controlling continuous emissions, they are not generally applicable to the control of stochastic 'emissions' or environmental accidents. The likelihood or magnitude of environmental accidents can be reduced through the use of regulation or taxes on the activities that generate the potential for accidents, but these instruments typically fail to provide efficient incentives for those dimensions of polluter care that are not readily observable and hence cannot be easily regulated or taxed. Environmental accidents can alternatively be reduced through the use of legal liability for any environmental damages that result from a given activity. In fact, strict liability is the *ex post* analogue of the standard Pigouvian tax. Although strict liability is used for environmental accidents while Pigouvian taxes are applicable to continuous emissions of pollutants, both instruments create incentives by internalizing the marginal social costs associated with a pollution-generating activity.

While strict liability replicates some of the properties of a Pigouvian tax in the context of environmental accidents, there are several important differences between the two. Unlike Pigouvian taxes, strict liability induces efficient output/activity levels even when damages are non-linear. However, when liability awards are paid directly to victims, strict liability can reduce victim incentives to invest in mitigation (a problem that does not exist with Pigouvian taxation). Victim incentives can be restored through use of a negligence rule rather than strict liability, but under a negligence rule non-negligent firms do not pay the full social costs associated with their activities and hence tend to overproduce or over-engage in the pollution-generating activity.

Strict liability also imposes considerable risk on polluters. Firms can be shielded from some of the risk of strict liability by using a negligence rule, although it is not clear whether the resulting allocation of risk would be efficient. This would depend upon the extent to which polluters and victims can diversify risks and the availability of other victim compensation mechanisms.

Although the theoretical literature on liability suggests that it has the potential to create efficient incentives for polluters to invest in safety or care to reduce the likelihood or magnitude of an environmental accident, the *ex ante* deterrence effect of liability hinges on polluters' expectations with regard to the liability payment that would be imposed if an accident occurred. The barriers to bringing a successful suit against a responsible polluter, including the difficulty in proving causation, the limited assets of firms, and the disincentive to file suit when damages are dispersed, all serve to reduce the expected liability payment and hence to dampen the incentive effects of liability.

Empirical evidence on the actual deterrence effect of environmental liability is sparse. Much of it is anecdotal, and the statistical analyses that have been done generally provide at best only indirect evidence of the impact of liability on deterrence. The empirical literature on workers' compensation and product liability is somewhat larger. It provides evidence regarding the impact of liability in these contexts. Since in recent years both workers' compensation and product liability have involved environmental health risks, this literature provides some insight into the likely effects of environmental liability. Again, however, the direct effect on investment in safety has been difficult to measure.

Despite these difficulties, the empirical analysis that has been done suggests that environmental liability is most effective when it is applied to measurable contamination problems where the damages are large and concentrated. In such cases, it is easier to prove causation and the incentives to sue are greater. Examples include land contamination from hazardous waste disposal and oil spills. When damages take the form of increased health risks due, for example, to exposure to toxic substances, causation will be more difficult to establish and the deterrence incentives of liability will be correspondingly reduced.

However, even in cases where responsibility might be easily established, the threat of liability may have unintended consequences that do not promote safety. For example, empirical evidence suggests that firms may divest of hazardous operations in an attempt to shield themselves from liability. Liability can create an incentive to concentrate hazardous operations in small firms that can hide behind bankruptcy in the event of an accident. Thus, instead of reducing their liability exposure by investing more in care, firms may reduce it through corporate restructuring. In addition, the large liabilities associated with some environmental hazards, coupled with uncertainties regarding causation and fault, create incentives for firms to fight liability claims. In such cases, the liability system generates large transaction costs, which consume resources that would otherwise be available for victim compensation or clean-up.

Two research issues emerge from this analysis. First, concerns about the actual impact of liability suggest that, despite its theoretical appeal as an instrument to internalize pollution externalities, it would be unwise to rely solely on liability as an environmental policy instrument, even in cases where it is likely to be most effective. Rather, it seems that the most useful role that environmental liability could play is as a complement to, instead of a substitute for, a more traditional approach to pollution control. Thus, rather than considering instruments in isolation, research on environmental policy design should instead focus on the design of an optimal policy package, explicitly incorporating the role of multiple instruments and their interactions.[39]

Second, it is clear from the empirical literature that firms can respond to liability in a myriad of ways, only one of which is reducing expected damages by increasing care or reducing output. Yet, to date the literature on liability has focused primarily on care and output decisions. To capture the impacts of liability more fully, the behavioural assumptions that underlie models of liability should be expanded to allow for a more complete range of possible responses. Unless the theoretical literature on liability incorporates these other responses, it will continue to generate rather naïve predictions regarding both the impact and the desirability of using liability to control environmental accidents.

NOTES

1. For example, in the USA hazardous waste disposal is regulated under the Resource Conservation and Recovery Act.
2. Liability can have important implications not only for incentives but also for the allocation of costs and risks. See Dewees et al. (1996) for a discussion of these alternative effects of liability.
3. See Epstein (1980) for a historical description of product liability law and Opaluch (1984) for a description of the use of strict liability in environmental law.
4. See Grigalunas and Opaluch (1988) for a description of CERCLA and Dunford (1992) for a description of the Oil Pollution Act.
5. It is possible that there will be some uncertainty about what constitutes negligent behaviour. In this case, a polluter could face risk even under a negligence rule. See Craswell and Calfee (1986) for a discussion of this type of uncertainty.
6. See Shavell (1987) for more detailed discussion of alternative models of liability for accidents and the basic incentive results discussed below.
7. This assumes risk neutrality (constant marginal utility of income) or that independent income distribution mechanisms are available. When such mechanisms are not available, then the liability rule must simultaneously try to achieve cost minimization and income distribution goals. See Miceli and Segerson (1995) and Shavell (1982a) for discussions of efficient care in this context.
8. In this simple model we ignore litigation costs. In practice, litigation or, more generally, transaction costs can be very large. For example, a major criticism of CERCLA is that it generates very large transaction costs. See Acton and Dixon (1992) and Dixon et al. (1993) for discussions of the transaction costs associated with CERCLA, Shavell (1982b) for a theoretical model and discussion of efficiency in the presence of litigation costs, and Shavell (1984b) for the role of transaction costs in determining the relative desirability of using regulation or liability to control stochastic damages.
9. See Shavell (1984b), *Harvard Law Review* (1986), Menell (1991), and Dewees et al. (1996) for discussions of these issues, and Shavell (1984a) for a model incorporating them.
10. To see this, let total damages be written as a function of emissions, that is, $D = D(e)$, where e is the level of emissions. Under the Pigouvian tax, the tax rate t is set equal to marginal damages from emissions evaluated at the efficient level of emissions e^*, that is, $t = D'(e^*)$. The total tax payment T is simply marginal damages times emissions, that is, $T = D'(e^*)e^*$. This is equal to total damages $D(e^*)$ if and only if D is linear.
11. Defining care and damages in this way implies that the care level can be chosen independently of the output level. The efficient level of care then simply minimizes expected per unit costs, $c(x) + p(x)D(x)$. The results below would differ somewhat under a more general specification.

12. This assumes that there are no externalities that result from the activity other than the possible environmental damages, so that private and social benefits from the activity are equal.

13. For simplicity, we focus solely on the victim's choice of care and do not explicitly model the victim's activity level. In addition, we assume that the victim can only affect the damages from an accident, that is, he cannot affect the probability that an accident will occur. The model could be extended to allow the victim's choice to affect the probability of an accident. In this case, the results would have to be modified slightly.

14. If the victim can affect the probability of an accident, that is, if $p = p(x,y)$, then the only lump-sum compensation that will induce efficient incentives is zero compensation. This can be seen by noting that in this case $EC_y(x,y) = p_yC + pC_y$. Given lump-sum compensation, that is, $C_y = 0$, the only compensation rule that ensures $EC_y = 0$ is $C = 0$.

15. This is analogous to the standard moral hazard problem created by insurance.

16. Victim care incentives would be efficient if the strict liability rule were coupled with a defence of contributory negligence. See Shavell (1987).

17. For a discussion of empirical evidence relating to the incentive problem created by employer liability, see section 5. Note, however, that in the workplace context the inefficiency would not necessarily exist if wages adjust to the allocation of liability. See Segerson and Tietenberg (1992) and related discussion below.

18. See *Harvard Law Review* (1986) for a discussion of personal injury recovery for damages from hazardous wastes.

19. In fact, the desire to reduce the amount of risk borne by polluters under CERCLA was a major force behind the move to overhaul the liability provisions of the statute. See Probst et al. (1995).

20. This could be done through use of an *ex ante* tax with publicly provided victim compensation (funded, for example, through tax revenues).

21. This assumes that there is no alternative mechanism for victim compensation, provided, for example, through the government.

22. Shavell (1987) terms these 'accidents between strangers'.

23. The 'irrelevance' result was originally discussed by Landes and Posner (1985) in the context of products liability. See Segerson (1995) for an overview of this argument and applications in the context of environmental liability.

24. The effect on victim incentives depends on whether the polluter can adjust his price to reflect the care decision of the victim. If he is not able to do so, he will not be able to 'penalize' the victim (through a price change) for a low level of care and will hence not be able to induce the victim to invest in an efficient amount of care. In this case, the liability rule will matter, since (as discussed above) in the absence of shifting the choice of a liability rule will affect victim mitigation incentives.

25. 'Contribution' is the process by which parties held liable for damages can seek reimbursement from other responsible parties in a separate action.

26. Kornhauser and Revesz (1989) compare joint and several liability based on negligence to joint and several liability based on strict liability principles. They conclude that a negligence-based rule is generally preferred for providing incentives to invest in care, since the sharing inherent in a joint and several liability rule based on strict liability creates a moral hazard problem.

27. See Tietenberg (1989) for a discussion of the efficiency implications of targeting deep pockets.

28. Of course, it is possible for the allocation of resources to be efficient even if polluters do not change their behaviour in response to potential liability. For example, lack of polluter response is efficient if polluters are not the least-cost avoiders. We assume throughout the remainder of the discussion, however, that the imposition of polluter liability reflects a determination that efficiency requires some change in polluter behaviour.

29. Liability can have other effects as well. For example, Dewees et al. (1996) review the effectiveness of tort liability in providing victim compensation and corrective justice. There have also been a number of studies of the effect of increased liability on the insurance industry in a number of different contexts (see, for example, Viscusi, 1995; Viscusi and Born, 1995; and Born and Viscusi, 1994).

30. In addition, an early study by Landes (1982) examined the impact of no-fault automobile insurance laws, which effectively remove or reduce liability for injuries arising from motor vehicle accidents. Similarly, White (1989) compared automobile accident rates under contributory and comparative negligence rules. Other evidence regarding the impact of liability in this context is reviewed in Dewees et al. (1996). Automobile accidents are unique in that every driver is a potential victim as well as a potential injurer. For this reason, it is difficult to generalize results from this context to other contexts, such as environmental risks.

31. Chelius (1976) found that accident rates decreased when workers' compensation was introduced. However, as argued by Fishback (1987), his results are subject to potentially significant measurement errors.

32. See Epstein (1980) and Viscusi (1991b) for discussions of product liability in the USA.

33. See Dewees et al. (1996) for a review of empirical studies of the effect of product liability on innovation and R&D.

34. Dewees et al. (1996) also examine more aggregate indicators of environmental improvement, such as pollution control expenditures, emissions, and direct measures of environmental quality, to determine whether there is any evidence that liability has contributed to any improvement. They find no evidence of a significant impact of liability. However, these measures capture primarily the effects of traditional air and water pollutants, which are not typically governed by liability.

35. There do not appear to have been any econometric studies of the impact of environmental liability on safety, perhaps because of the difficulty in disentangling the effects of increased liability and regulation, which often go hand in hand.

36. See Segerson (1993, 1997) for a discussion of the impact of liability transfers under CERCLA on the incentives to buy and sell property.

37. Hazardousness is a proxy for expected liability. It is measured by the worker exposure to carcinogens in a given industry.

38. See Dixon et al. (1993). This figure is based on costs up through 1992. In addition, it reflects the distribution of firm sizes within the sample. The report found higher transaction cost shares for smaller companies than for large ones. This is consistent with an earlier study of large firms (Acton and Dixon, 1992), for which transaction costs were 21 per cent of total expenditures. Seventy-five per cent of these transaction costs were legal costs.

39. For example, the existence of a regulatory structure can generate information regarding polluting activities that would be useful in determining causation and fault. The availability of this information could improve the incentive effects of liability.

REFERENCES

Acton, Jan Paul and Lloyd S. Dixon (1992), *Superfund and Transaction Costs: The Experience of Insurers and Very Large Industrial Firms*, Santa Monica, CA: RAND Institute for Civil Justice.

Baumol, William J. and Wallace E. Oates (1988), *The Theory of Environmental Policy*, Cambridge: Cambridge University Press.

Born, Patricia and W. Kip Viscusi (1994), 'Insurance market responses to the 1980s' liability reforms: an analysis of firm-level data', *Journal of Risk and Insurance*, **61**, 192–218.

Chelius, James R. (1976), 'Liability for industrial accidents: a comparison of negligence and strict liability systems', *Journal of Legal Studies*, **5**, 293–309.

Cooter, Robert (1984), 'Prices and sanctions', *Columbia Law Review*, **84**, 1523–60.

Craswell, Richard and John E. Calfee (1986), 'Deterrence and uncertain legal standards', *Journal of Law, Economics and Organization*, **2**, 279–303.

Dewees, Don, David Duff and Michael Trebilcock (1996), *Exploring the Domain of Accident Law: Taking the Facts Seriously*, New York and Oxford: Oxford University Press.

Dixon, Lloyd S., Deborah S. Drezner and James K. Hammitt (1993), *Private-Sector Cleanup Expenditures and Transaction Costs at 18 Superfund Sites*, Santa Monica, CA: RAND Institute for Civil Justice.

Dunford, Richard (1992), 'Natural resource damages from oil spills', in T.H. Tietenberg (ed.), *Innovation in Environmental Policy: Economic and Legal Aspects of Recent Developments in Environmental Enforcement and Liability*, Cheltenham, UK and Lyme, USA: Edward Elgar.

Ehrenberg, Ronald G. (1988), 'Workers' compensation, wages, and the risk of injury', in John F. Burton, Jr (ed.), *New Perspectives in Workers' Compensation*, Ithaca, NY: Cornell University ILR Press.

Epstein, Richard (1980), *Modern Products Liability Law*, Westport, CT: Quorum Books.

Fishback, Price V. (1987), 'Liability rules and accident prevention in the workplace: empirical evidence from the early twentieth century', *Journal of Legal Studies*, **16**, 305–28.

Grigalunas, Thomas A. and James J. Opaluch (1988), 'Assessing liability for damages under CERCLA: a new approach for providing incentives for pollution avoidance?', *Natural Resources Journal*, **28**, 509–33.

Harvard Law Review (1986) 'Developments in the law: toxic waste generation', **99**, 1458–661.

Kolstad, Charles D., Thomas S. Ulen and Gary V. Johnson (1990), 'Ex post liability for harm vs. ex ante safety regulation: substitutes or complements?', *American Economic Review*, **80**, 888–901.

Kornhauser, Lewis A. and Richard L. Revesz (1989), 'Sharing damages among multiple tortfeasors', *The Yale Law Journal*, **98**, 831–84.

Landes, Elisabeth M. (1982), 'Insurance, liability, and accidents: a theoretical and empirical investigation of the effects of no-fault accidents', *Journal of Law and Economics*, **25**, 49–65.

Landes, William and Richard Posner (1985), 'A positive economic theory of products liability', *Journal of Legal Studies*, **14**, 535–67.

Menell, Peter S. (1991), 'The limitations of legal institutions for addressing environmental risks', *Journal of Economic Perspectives*, **5**, 93–113.

Merolla, A. Todd (1998), 'The effect of latent hazards on firm exit in manufacturing industries', *International Review of Law and Economics*, **18**, 13–24.

Miceli, Thomas J. and Kathleen Segerson (1991), 'Joint liability in torts: marginal and inframarginal efficiency', *International Review of Law and Economics*, **11**, 235–49.

Miceli, Thomas J. and Kathleen Segerson (1995), 'Defining efficient care: the role of income distribution', *Journal of Legal Studies*, **24**, 189–208.

Moore, Michael J. and W. Kip Viscusi (1989), 'Promoting safety through workers' compensation: the efficacy and net wage costs of injury insurance', *Rand Journal of Economics*, **20**, 499–515.

Moore, Michael J. and W. Kip Viscusi (1990), *Compensation Mechanisms for Job Risks: Wages, Workers' Compensation, and Product Liability*, Princeton: Princeton University Press.

Opaluch, James J. (1984), 'The use of liability rules in controlling hazardous waste accidents: theory and practice', *Northeastern Journal of Agricultural and Resource Economics*, **14**, 210–17.

Opaluch, James J. and Thomas A. Grigalunas (1984), 'Controlling stochastic pollution events through liability rules: some evidence from OCS leasing', *Rand Journal of Economics*, **15**, 142–51.

Polinsky, A. Mitchell (1980), 'Strict liability vs. negligence in a market setting', *American Economic Review*, **70**, 363–7.

Priest, George L. (1988), 'Products liability law and the accident rate', in R.E. Litan and C. Winston (eds), *Liability: Perspectives and Policy*, Washington, DC: The Brookings Institution.

Probst, Katherine N., Don Fullerton, Robert E. Litan and Paul R. Portney (1995), *Footing the Bill for Superfund Cleanups: Who Pays and How?* Washington, DC: The Brookings Institution and Resources for the Future.

Ringleb, A.H. and S.N. Wiggins (1990), 'Liability and large-scale, long-term hazards', *Journal of Political Economy*, **98**, 574–95.

Segerson, Kathleen (1986), 'Risk sharing in the design of environmental policy', *American Journal of Agricultural Economics*, **68**, 1261–5.

Segerson, Kathleen (1987), 'Risk-sharing and liability in the control of stochastic externalities', *Marine Resource Economics*, **4**, 175–92.

Segerson, Kathleen (1993), 'Liability transfers: an economic assessment of buyer and lender liability', *Journal of Environmental Economics and Management*, **25**, S46–S63.

Segerson, Kathleen (1995), 'Liability and penalty structures in policy design', in Daniel W. Bromley (ed.), *The Handbook of Environmental Economics*, Cambridge, MA: Blackwell Publishers.

Segerson, Kathleen (1997), 'Legal liability as an environmental policy tool: some implications for land markets', *Journal of Real Estate Finance and Economics*, **15**, 143–59.

Segerson, Kathleen and Tom Tietenberg (1992), 'The structure of penalties in environmental enforcement: an economic analysis', *Journal of Environmental Economics and Management*, **23**, 179–200.

Shavell, Steven (1979), 'Risk sharing and incentives in the principal and agent relationship', *Bell Journal of Economics*, **10**, 55–73.

Shavell, Steven (1980), 'Strict liability versus negligence', *Journal of Legal Studies*, **9**, 1–25.

Shavell, Steven (1982a), 'On liability and insurance', *Bell Journal of Economics*, **13**, 120–32.

Shavell, Steven (1982b), 'The social versus private incentive to bring suit in a costly legal system', *Journal of Legal Studies*, **11**, 333–9.

Shavell, Steven (1984a), 'A model of the optimal use of liability and safety regulation', *Rand Journal of Economics*, **15**, 271–80.

Shavell, Steven (1984b), 'Liability for harm vs. regulation of safety', *Journal of Legal Studies*, **13**, 357–74.

Shavell, Steven (1987), *Economic Analysis of Accident Law*, Cambridge, MA: Harvard University Press.

Spulber, Daniel F. (1985), 'Effluent regulation and long-run optimality', *Journal of Environmental Economics and Management*, **12**, 103–16.

Tietenberg, Tom H. (1989), 'Indivisible toxic torts: the economics of joint and several liability', *Land Economics*, **65**, 305–19.

Viscusi, W. Kip (1991a), 'Product and occupational liability', *Journal of Economic Perspectives*, **5**, 71–91.

Viscusi, W. Kip (1991b), *Reforming Products Liability*, Cambridge, MA: Harvard University Press.

Viscusi, W. Kip (1995), 'Insurance and catastrophes: the changing role of the liability system', *Geneva Papers on Risk and Insurance Theory*, **20**, 177–84.

Viscusi, W. Kip and Patricia Born (1995), 'The general-liability reform experiments and the distribution of insurance-market outcomes', *Journal of Business Economics and Statistics*, **13**, 183–88.

Viscusi, W. Kip and Michael J. Moore (1993), 'Product liability, research and development, and innovation', *Journal of Political Economy*, **101**, 161–84.

Weitzman, Martin (1974), 'Prices vs. quantities', *Review of Economic Studies*, **41**, 477–91.

White, Michele J. (1989), 'An empirical test of the comparative and contributory negligence rules in accident law', *Rand Journal of Economics*, **20**, 308–30.

Wiggins, Steven N. and Al H. Ringleb (1992), 'Adverse selection and long-term hazards: the choice between contract and mandatory liability rules', *Journal of Legal Studies*, **21**, 189–215.

PART III

Selected Topics

16. International environmental problems and policy

Henk Folmer and Aart de Zeeuw

1. INTRODUCTION

In Chapters 1–6 in Part I of this volume it was shown that the nature of the environmental problem is one in which economic agents through consumption or production impose external costs on society in the form of air, soil and water pollution, landscape degradation, health risks and loss of biodiversity. Moreover, it was argued that in contrast to conventional economic goods and services, environmental functions and the assets that provide them usually do not involve market transactions. Hence, explicit market-determined valuations and, consequently, prices do not exist for environmental goods and services.

An important reason for the absence of prices for environmental commodities is that they are typically public goods characterized by non-rivalness. This means that once an environmental good, for example clean air, is provided, consumption by one economic agent does not interfere with another agent's consumption.[1] In other words, the additional costs of another economic agent consuming the environmental good is zero. Most environmental goods are also non-excludable. This implies that it is impossible or very expensive to prevent anyone from consuming the environmental commodity who is not willing to pay for it. A consequence of the public-good characteristics is the risk of free-riding, that is, that economic agents enjoy the environmental goods and services without paying for them. For instance, if one firm decided to reduce its emissions (and hence incurs the corresponding costs), other firms would have an incentive not to abate. Since this holds in general, everybody has an incentive to wait for others to provide the environmental good and to free-ride. This in its turn means that there are usually no incentives to produce and supply these goods and services. The reason is that each firm expects the others to free-ride.

As is true in the case of other public goods such as defence, the government assumes a role in the provision of environmental commodities by means of environmental protection. For this purpose a wide variety of instruments has been developed including command and control measures, environmental taxes, tradable emission permits, subsidies, education, deposit–refund systems, damage compensation, voluntary agreements and information disclosure.[2] In the absence of markets the government decides about the optimal level of provision of environmental protection on the basis of cost–benefit analysis. As described in Chapter 4, this is a decision-support technique based on the comparison of the advantages and costs of a given project. In order to obtain monetary values for environmental assets, that is, to estimate their prices, valuation methods like the travel cost method, hedonic pricing and contingent valuation can be applied (see Chapter 3).[3]

At first sight the above framework of domestic environmental policy is also applicable to environmental problems that occur internationally. International environmental problems such as ozone layer depletion and climate change also impose external costs on society. Moreover, there usually exist no markets for these 'commodities' either, so that valuation methods have to be used to estimate their prices (endnote 3 applies here too). Finally, in policy analyses and debates of, for example, global warming, the use of such instruments as tradable emissions permits is frequently discussed. So, there seems to be nothing new under the sun, except for the geographical scale of the problems. In spite of this, the analysis of international environmental problems has almost become a sub-discipline of its own in environmental economics. What is the rationale for this paradox?

As mentioned above, the government plays a crucial role in a national setting in the sense that it intervenes in the market system to correct for the negative technological externality that gives rise to an environmental problem.[4] However, in the case of an international environmental problem, the impacts of the externality are not confined to the country of origin. For instance, sulphur dioxide and nitrogen oxides emissions generated in one country are deposited in other countries and lead to acidification there. CO_2 emissions produced in any country contribute to global warming, that is, increases in temperature worldwide, and can cause damage in any country. Typical of an international environmental problem is the absence of an institution or 'government' with the jurisdiction to enforce environmental policy internationally. For instance, there exists no institution or 'world government' that can enforce a global CO_2 emissions reduction policy. Any international environmental policy is ultimately national environmental policy in the sense that independent states decide whether or not to adopt a common policy aimed at solving an international environmental problem. Moreover, the policy, if adopted, is implemented and enforced domestically.[5] For instance, an internationally accepted global warming policy would ultimately come down to CO_2 emissions abatement in the signatory countries under the same conditions as the execution of a domestic environmental policy.

The following observation applies. Under customary law, countries are supposed to comply with the agreements to which they are signatories. In case of deviation, they can be expected to be punished. Usually an international agreement specifies sanctions for deviation and a punishment mechanism. The enforcement power of an 'international court', however, is limited. In principle a country can ignore the sanctions or get around them, a practice not uncommon in the international arena. However, there also exist additional, though more diffuse, punishments in international relationships. For instance, a deviant can be punished by retaliation in another area of interest. Trade sanctions are probably most common in this connection. Moreover, the punishment can be more diffuse, with other countries being more reluctant to engage in relations with the deviant in the same or other areas (see section 4.2 for further details).

A second and related aspect that distinguishes an international environmental problem from a domestic one is the restrictiveness of national environmental policy in an international setting. Because of the sovereignity of independent nations, a country's policy is restricted to its own jurisdiction. For instance, a victim country where depositions take place cannot intervene in other countries where the emissions are generated without the consent of the latter. In some cases the situation is even more extreme: there also exist international environmental problems that occur in a geographical space where there is no authority at all with the jurisdiction to control. Examples are the pollution of international seas, space and the atmosphere.

To sum up, any international environmental policy must be voluntary. This has some far-reaching consequences. First, there is a considerable risk that the policy is foiled because of free-riding behaviour. Second, if a policy has been agreed upon, participating countries may defect. This is in contrast to domestic environmental policy where free-riding and defection behaviour can be controlled by the government. In other words there are fundamental differences between domestic and international environmental problems, which warrant a treatment of the latter on its own.

The purpose of this chapter is to present an introduction into the main aspects of international environmental problems. Section 2 surveys the nature and main characteristics of this kind of problem. In section 3 three approaches to international environmental problems are presented: the market approach, the non-cooperative and the full cooperative approach. The main obstacles to achieve the last, which from an effectiveness and efficiency point of view is usually the most desirable one, will also be discussed in this section. Instruments to achieving the full cooperative approach will be examined in section 4. Section 5 reviews instruments of international environmental policy. We end with a brief summary.

2.   MAIN CHARACTERISTICS

In the preceding section the absence of an institution with the jurisdiction to enforce environmental policy internationally has been identified as the main characteristic of an international environmental problem. However, there are several other features that are important for a good understanding of this kind of problem. We begin with a classification.

International environmental problems can be divided into physical and non-physical problems. The former comprise those situations where pollutants actually move across borders as in the case of global warming, ozone layer depletion and acid rain. Non-physical environmental problems can take different forms. For instance, individuals or organizations in one country may be concerned with pollution, natural resource exploitation or the lack of protection of rare species in other countries.[6] Another non-physical problem relates to international trade. International trade and trade policies have impacts on the environment through altering the volume and international location of production and consumption (see, among others, Anderson and Blackhurst, 1992, and Whalley, 1991). However, not only does trade affect the environment; there is also a reverse relationship: environmental policy may also affect international trade and capital movements. For instance, stringent environmental policy in one country may induce firms to locate in or relocate to other countries with lax environmental policy.[7] Another link between environmental policy and trade is that environmental policy in one country may restrict imports into that country. For instance, the introduction of product norms may lead to an increase of import prices.[8]

In subsequent sections we shall concentrate on physical international environmental problems. The other problems mentioned above will not be dealt with or only incidentally. However, the notions presented in connection with physical international problems also hold for most non-physical problems, although modifications may be required with respect to formal modelling. For instance, in the case of non-physical problems there is no need to take the geographical direction of pollution flows into account (see below).

In the context of international environmental problems, it is important to distinguish between source and victim country. The former relates to the country where emissions are generated and the latter to the country where they are deposited. It should be observed that a country can simultaneously be a source and victim country, as in the cases of global warming and acid rain. In fact, in most international environmental problems this is more common than situations where sources and victims are clearly separated. The latter may occur when there is a physical separation between an upstream and downstream country, such as the pollution of international rivers where the pollution is generated at the border of the upstream country.

As mentioned in the preceding section, at least two countries are involved in an international environmental problem. Combinations of the number of countries involved with the distinction between source and victim country lead to the following typology:

- one source – one victim;
- one source – several victims;
- several sources – one victim;
- several sources – several victims.

The last category is the most general and most complicated to solve. The other categories can be viewed as special cases. Therefore we shall primarily focus on this category in what follows.

Not only is the number of countries and the distinction between source and victim countries relevant, but also in many cases the direction of pollution. In this regard a distinction is usually made between uniformly mixing and non-uniformly mixing pollutants (Tietenberg, 1985). In the former case each unit of pollution contributes to the same extent to the accumulation of pollution independently of the location where it was generated. An example is global warming, where the contribution to the accumulation of greenhouse gases in the atmosphere of each unit of CO_2 is the same wherever it was produced. In the case of non-uniformly mixing, the origin of the pollutant matters: emissions of different sources do not accumulate uniformly. An example is acid rain. A given amount of SO_2 emissions generated in, for example, Scandinavia contributes less to the accumulation of acid substances over North-Western and Central Europe than the same amount generated in, for example, the United Kingdom. The reason is that because of the predominant south-west winds in Western Europe the former pollution is partly dispersed over Arctic regions and the latter primarily over North-Western and Central Europe (Amann and Schopp, 1993).[9]

It should be observed that although the contribution of uniformly mixing pollutants to accumulation is independent of location, the impacts in terms of environmental damage usually differ geographically, both in physical and monetary terms. Although a unit of CO_2 generated in Canada or in Africa contributes to the same extent to the accumulation of greenhouse gases in the atmosphere, the impacts of global warming are likely to differ dramatically between the regions. For instance, agriculture in Canada is expected to benefit from global warming, whereas it is likely to suffer in Sub-Saharan countries. Similarly, the environmental impacts of acid depositions in Scandinavia differ from those in, for example, The Netherlands because of differences in the composition of the soil. This implies that from the perspective of environmental *damage* uniformly mixing and non-uniformly mixing pollution problems may be similar.

The number of countries and the direction of pollution affect the source–victim configuration with respect to non-uniformly mixing pollution problems. This in its turn may lead to serious information problems regarding each country's emissions and depositions. For instance, when there is only one polluting country the emissions can be attributed unequivocally whereas in the case of several polluters uncertainty about the origins of pollution may prevail. Moreover, it may affect the incentive structure to cooperate (see sections 3 and 4 below). In the case of several victims, the incentives for abatement are likely to be stronger than in the case of one victim.

The foregoing discussion implies that in the case of non-uniformly mixing pollutants it is important to distinguish between source and victim countries as well as their geographical positions. This is done by means of a dispersion matrix, say T. A typical element of this matrix, say T_{ji}, indicates the proportion of pollution generated in country i and deposited in country j.

In the case of uniformly mixing pollutants there is no need to take the geographical positions of the sources into account. Hence, the dispersion matrix T can be ignored.

We end this section by considering the three most important reasons for countries involved in an international environmental problem to cooperate, that is, to conclude an agreement with respect to an overall emissions reductions programme including an abatement specification per country.

1. Effectiveness. Unilateral actions or actions by a small proportion of the countries involved in an international environmental problem are usually futile. For instance, in the case of global warming, abatement involvement of the less developed countries (LDCs) is a prerequisite. The reason is that the major growth in energy demand between 2000 and 2020 will occur in these countries. If the trend in energy use in the LDCs continues and if the more developed countries (MDCs) succeed in reducing or stabilizing their CO_2 emissions, the share of the LDCs in global CO_2 emissions will exceed that of the MDCs before 2010.[10]

2. Efficiency. In many instances there are substantial differences in abatement costs among the various countries. Efficiency requires that abatement takes place where the least-cost option exists. For instance, if prevention of emissions is cheaper than cleaning up depositions, abatement should take place in the countries where pollution is generated.

3. Welfare. The foregoing implies that cooperation leads to higher welfare or total net benefits for all the countries involved together in comparison with the non-cooperation outcome. An individual country's welfare, however, may suffer from cooperation (see below).

3.   THE MARKET, NON-COOPERATIVE AND FULL COOPERATIVE APPROACH

In this section we shall describe and compare three approaches that countries can adopt with respect to an international environmental problem (see also van der Ploeg and de Zeeuw, 1992). For this purpose we present a simple model that relates to non-uniformly mixing pollutants. Problems relating to uniformly mixing pollutants can be viewed as special cases of this general model.

Consider N countries denoted by subscripts $j = 1, 2, ..., N$. Let Y be the set of country j's emissions with elements y_j. Since production and consumption cannot take place without emissions, we have a gross benefit function B_j, defined as

$$B_J = B_j(y_j), \quad j = 1, 2, ..., N. \tag{16.1}$$

For instance, equation (16.1) could relate to the benefits of CO_2 emissions generated in order to produce the gross domestic product. It is usually assumed that B_j is twice continuously differentiable, that the benefits increase with emission (that is, $B_j' > 0$) but that the marginal benefits decrease ($B_j'' < 0$).

Pollution causes not only benefits but also damage in the form of environmental degradation. We consider a typical country whose emissions generate damage at home and abroad. This is represented by means of a damage function D_j. In the context of an international environmental problem the damage is caused by the pollution generated at home and in other countries. As mentioned in the preceding section, in the case of non-uniformly mixing pollutants, sources and victims and the geographical dispersion of pollution among them have to be taken into account. This is done by means of the dispersion matrix $\mathbf{T}$. Hence, the damage function reads as

$$D_j = D_j \left(\sum_{i=1}^{N} \mathbf{T}_{ji} y_i \right), \quad j = 1, 2, ..., N. \tag{16.2}$$

Combining (16.1) and (16.2) gives the net benefit function W_j:

$$W_j = B_j(y_j) - D_j \left(\sum_{i=1}^{N} \mathbf{T}_{ji} y_i \right), \quad j = 1, 2, ..., N. \tag{16.3}$$

The three types of approaches mentioned above can be illustrated as follows. First, under the market approach the benefit function (16.3) is maximized ignoring the damage component. That is, the market outcome is given by

$$\max_{y_j} B_j(y_j), \quad j = 1, 2, ..., N. \tag{16.4}$$

The market approach is rather rare in the industrialized countries nowadays because of the growing environmental concern. More common is the non-cooperative approach. Typical of this approach is that both the benefit and damage component of (16.3) are taken into account. However, a given country, say j, only considers its *own* benefits and damage and ignores the effects of its emissions on other countries. Moreover, the emissions of the other countries are taken as given by country j. This means that country j will continue increasing its pollution as long as the benefits of each additional unit of pollution exceed the damage to country j itself. This implies that the optimal level of pollution under the non-cooperative approach, say Q_N, is determined by the equality between the marginal benefits and marginal damage in the home country. Formally, Q_N is determined by

$$B_j'(y_j) = \mathbf{T}_{jj} D_j' \left(\sum_{i=1}^{N} \mathbf{T}_{ji} y_i \right), \quad j = 1, 2, \ldots, N. \tag{16.5}$$

In the case of the full cooperative approach country j not only takes its own marginal benefits and marginal damage into account but the marginal damage of its emissions in other countries as well. This implies that it equates its marginal benefits to the total world or social marginal damage. Hence the optimal level of pollution under the full cooperative approach, Q_S, is determined by

$$B_j'(y_j) = \sum_{k=1}^{N} \mathbf{T}_{kj} D_k' \left(\sum_{i=1}^{N} \mathbf{T}_{ki} y_i \right), \quad j = 1, 2, \ldots, N. \tag{16.6}$$

A comparison of (16.4) and (16.5) shows that under the market approach there are no restrictions on emissions whereas under the non-cooperative approach emissions in the home country are restricted by the damage they cause in the country itself. Under the full cooperative approach they are even further restricted because the damages in other countries are taken into account as well. This implies that under the full cooperative solution emissions by country j are usually (but not always!) smallest, followed by the non-cooperative and market outcome.[11] This result is further illustrated in Figure 16.1 for *linear* marginal benefit and cost functions.[12]

In Figure 16.1 the horizontal axis represents the amount of emissions produced in a given country while the vertical axis denotes the marginal costs (MC) and marginal benefits (MB) of pollution.[13] The market, non-cooperative and full cooperative outcome are indicated by subscripts M, N and S, respectively. Since the marginal costs curve under the full cooperative approach

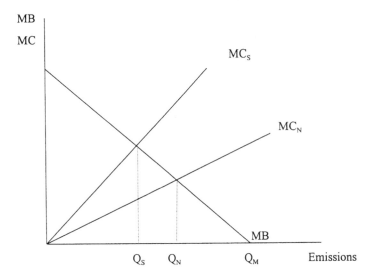

Figure 16.1 The market, non-cooperative and cooperative outcome

comprises both the marginal costs in the home country and those in other countries, MC_S coincides with or lies above MC_N. It follows that emissions under the full cooperative approach (Q_S) are equal to or lower than emissions under the non-cooperative approach (Q_N). Emissions under the market outcome are found where the marginal benefits of pollution are equal to zero. They are equal to or exceed emissions under the non-cooperative approach.

The following observations apply. First, the full cooperative outcome does not necessarily imply that each country's emissions decrease or remain stable; in some 'boundary' solutions a country's emissions may increase. As an example, consider the pollution of a transboundary river passing through two countries. The full cooperative approach requires the upstream country to take the damage in the downstream country into account and to reduce its emissions according to (16.6). The emission reduction upstream may make it possible for the downstream country to increase its emissions according to (16.5). For linear damage functions, however, we find that under the full cooperative approach the emissions for each country are smaller than or equal to the emissions under the non-cooperative outcome. Second, under the full cooperative solution the emissions for each country cannot exceed those under the non-cooperative outcome. Third, total emissions under the full cooperative approach need not necessarily be smaller than under the non-cooperative approach. (For further details see Folmer and van Mouche, 2000.) Finally, the full cooperative approach belongs to the set of cooperative approaches that are characterized by Pareto efficiency. Under the cooperative approach countries negotiate and sign a treaty. In addition to the full cooperative approach the set of cooperative or Pareto-efficient outcomes comprises several other allocations such as the Nash bargaining solution. In this chapter we mainly consider the full cooperative approach since it has received most attention in the environmental economics literature so far.

From the foregoing it follows that the full cooperative solution is most desirable because it leads to the highest net social benefits. In spite of this, it is often difficult for countries to achieve the full cooperative approach. Moreover, even cooperation or Pareto efficiency is often difficult to achieve, judging by, for example, the considerable problems involved in reaching an agreement on global warming abatement. This raises the question: what are the obstacles to the (full) cooperative approach?

We first address the question why countries would refuse to cooperate, that is, refuse to adopt a Pareto-efficient outcome. After all, international law requires countries to negotiate and discuss their problems openly. One reason for a country to opt for a Pareto-inefficient outcome is that such an outcome would be more favourable to the country concerned than a cooperative equilibrium. A possible strategy for a country in such a situation is to claim to have preferences that differ from its true preferences. By under-reporting its true benefits or over-reporting its true costs it could try to escape some of its abatement obligations. Such a strategy is facilitated by the fact that preferences of countries involved in negotiations on international problems often differ widely. They range from those in the OECD countries to those in low-income countries. In high-income countries such as the OECD countries, there is a growing demand for environmental quality. This has led to the introduction of environmental policies in many areas and a growing awareness of the need to cooperate internationally. In low-income countries, on the other hand, the situation is quite different. They face a strong need to provide for basic necessities, and to stimulate the economic development that can alleviate poverty and stabilize populations. Moreover, the average consumer's willingness to pay for environmental quality is low. All this will put restrictions on environmental policy including participation on an equal footing with the industrialized countries in international environmental agreements. This reluctance is strengthened by the awareness of the asymmetry between the industrialized and developing countries with respect to resource utilization and pollution generation over time.[14]

The following impediments to the *full* cooperative approach can be identified. First, the full cooperative approach may imply net welfare losses for some countries and, at the same time, substantial gains to others. This is most obvious in the case of a two-country unidirectional externality where the pollution is generated right at the downstream border of the upstream country. The full cooperative approach would require the upstream country to completely clean up its act and hence incur all the costs, whereas all the benefits would accrue to the downstream country. However, in the case of reciprocal externalities also, where each country is both a source of a given type of pollution and a victim, the distribution of net benefits over the countries involved may be highly skewed. Those countries that incur net negative benefits would have an incentive not to cooperate or to defect from a concluded agreement.[15]

The foregoing is empirically illustrated in Table 16.1, which relates to acidification in Europe.[16]

The first column of Table 16.1 gives the absolute reduction per country under the full cooperative approach. The second gives the absolute reduction as a percentage of the total emissions of a given country in 1984. For instance, under the full cooperative approach the United Kingdom is to abate 1 494 000 tons of SO_2, which is 81 per cent of its total in 1984. The last column gives the net benefits per country under the full cooperative approach. For the UK the net benefits are negative: –DM 336 million.

The full cooperative approach would require the total emissions to be reduced by about 40 per cent relative to the situation in 1984. As can be seen in the second column, the full cooperative outcome implies widely varying reduction percentages. They deviate substantially from the non-cooperative solution for the individual countries. Most countries would incur positive net benefits from the full cooperative solution, except Italy, Spain, and, notably, the UK which would lose. The main reason for their losses is that these coutries are located upstream so that most of the pollution generated at home is deposited elswhere in the continent whereas they themselves receive relatively little pollution from other countries. In particular, the substantial loss for the UK explains why it used to be so reluctant to participate in European sulphur emissions reduction programmes.

A second impediment to the full cooperative approach is that even if the net benefits of cooperation are positive, a country has an incentive to free-ride. The reason is that by staying out of an agreement or by defecting from a concluded one it may be possible for a country to reap virtually the same benefits of pollution control as by joining it, without incurring abatement costs. Hence it will be better off because the net benefits will be larger than when it cooperates fully. Free-riding is an especially attractive option in the case of global environmental problems because under these circumstances each country's contribution is a relatively small proportion of total pollution. This implies that each country's loss of environmental quality is small or even negligible.[17] Note that an important prerequisite for the benefits of free-riding to hold is that not too many countries decide to free-ride or to defect because then the desired level of environmental quality would not materialize. (See section 4 for further details on this issue.)

Table 16.1   Emissions reduction under the full cooperative approach in the acid rain game

	Emission control (1000 tons of SO$_2$)	% reduction	Benefits (DM million)
Albania	10	42	22
Austria	31	21	324
Belgium	112	36	191
Bulgaria	179	36	28
Czechoslovakia	1219	75	152
Denmark	130	86	119
Finland	25	14	–2
France	104	10	879
German Dem. Republic	1040	80	11
Federal Rep. of Germany	1183	86	328
Greece	303	86	52
Hungary	635	77	5
Ireland	27	38	71
Italy	634	33	–84
Netherlands	105	62	565
Norway	3	6	272
Poland	560	27	599
Portugal	15	19	10
Romania	83	83	420
Spain	231	14	–29
Sweden	6	4	606
Switzerland	10	23	192
Turkey	299	62	0
UK	1494	81	–336
USSR	107	2	1510
Yugoslavia	465	79	346
TOTAL	9011	39	6248

Source: Mäler (1989).

Free-riding is especially a problem in situations where an international environmental treaty is concluded for a limited period of time and will be revised a limited number of times (finitely repeated game) or will not be revised at all (one-shot game). The reason that commitment is a problem under these conditions is that there are no credible punishments for free-riding or defection in the international arena.[18] This implies that in the final period and each preceding period each country will choose the allocation with the highest private net pay-off rather than the full cooperative outcome.

The free-riding problem is usually modelled as a prisoners' dilemma game. As a simple example consider two countries, A and B, that have two actions,[19] that is, to cooperate (C) or not to cooperate (D).[20] The costs associated with cooperation in the form of reduction of a unit of pollution are 5 for both A and B. Moreover, the benefits of reduction of a unit of pollution are 4 in both A and B, regardless of which country makes the reductions.[21]

Associated with each combination of actions are pay-offs (or net benefits) which are given in the so-called bi-matrix stage game in Table 16.2. If country A cooperates and country B does not, A's benefits will be 4 but its costs will be 5, so that it will incur a net negative benefit (–1). B on the other hand, will only incur benefits and no costs. Hence its net benefits are 4 (cell (–1,4) in Table 16.2). If B cooperates and A does not, the pay-offs are reversed. If both countries cooperate, each will incur the benefits from its own abatement plus those from the other's action (8). However, each incurs costs equal to 5, so that the net benefit is 3 for each country. Non-cooperation leads to neither benefits nor costs, so that the net benefits are 0 for each country.

Table 16.2   *An international environmental problem as a prisoners' dilemma game: pay-off matrix*[22]

		Country B	
		D	C
Country A	D	(0,0)	(4,–1)
	C	(–1,4)	(3,3)

What actions will the countries choose? If A decided to cooperate, then B would incur a net benefit of 3 if it also cooperated. However, it could do better by not cooperating because its net benefits would be 4. So, it would choose D. A is aware of this and knows that it will incur a loss of –1 in this situation. Hence, it will choose D. Along the same lines it can be shown that country A will choose not to cooperate, whatever action B chooses. So the outcome of this game is that both countries will decide not to cooperate. This outcome (D, D) is the so-called Nash equilibrium. It is defined as that pair of actions such that A's choice is optimal given B's choice, and B's choice is optimal given A's choice.[23]

The superiority of defection for country B is even stronger in the sense that, regardless of the action of A, B does better by not cooperating because the pay-off 0 is better than −1 and 4 is better than 3. So action C is strictly dominated by strategy D. Similarly for country A.

From Table 16.2 it also follows that the joint pay-offs would be maximal (3,3) if both countries cooperated (that is, if the outcome were (C, C)). However, given the *present* structure of the problem, this outcome cannot be reached. The reason is that we are in a static situation where the game is only played once (that is, a one-shot Nash equilibrium).[24] This implies that there is a need for mechanisms to induce countries to choose the cooperative solution rather than the Nash outcome (D,D). We will return to this problem below.

The following observations apply. First, Hoel and Schneider (1997) assume that countries have preferences to commit whereas Carraro and Siniscalco (1993) assume different kinds of partial commitment. However, this begs the question why countries make commitments. Second, as commitment is a problem in a finitely repeated game, the question arises under what conditions a finitely repeated treaty could be concluded. The prerequisites of such a so-called self-enforcing agreement have been described by amongst others Barrett (1994). He shows that if

(a)   the signatories choose their abatement levels to maximize their collective pay-off;
(b)   the signatories invariably comply with the obligations they have signed up to;
(c)   the pay-offs are such that, as the number of signatories increases, the level of provision demanded by (a) increases;

then a treaty will be self-enforcing and sustain some level of cooperation. The reason is that if one party withdraws, the other parties, needing to obey (a), will lower their abatement levels and so will punish the deviant.

It follows from the foregoing that strong tendencies undermine the full cooperative approach. However, the difference in abatement levels for the full cooperative and non-cooperative outcomes need not necessarily be very large. Barrett (1990) shows that in the case of mildly innocuous pollutants that can only be abated at high costs, the cooperative approach will not call for large abatement levels relative to the non-cooperative approach. The same applies to the case of very damaging pollutants that can be abated at relatively low costs. In this situation countries will initiate substantial abatement programmes uni-laterally, that is, in a non-cooperative setting. The discrepancy between the abatement levels will tend to be large, however, in the cases of damaging pollutants that are costly to abate and mildly innocuous pollutants that can be abated at little cost. The former causes the greatest concern because of the great risks involved. An example is global warming. This explains why a great deal of research has been devoted to design mechanisms to adopt the full cooperative approach under unfavourable circumstances. We turn to these mechanisms in the next section.

4. INSTRUMENTS TO STIMULATE THE ADOPTION OF THE FULL COOPERATIVE APPROACH

In the previous section it was argued that two of the main impediments to reaching full cooperation to cope with international environmental problems are the following. First, some countries may be worse off in the full cooperative outcome than in the non-cooperative outcome, and second, countries normally have an incentive to free-ride on the efforts of other countries. Several authors, such as Mäler (1989), argue that the first impediment can be overcome if the countries that gain compensate the countries that lose. This instrument is usually referred to as 'side-payments'.

Free-riding is a more difficult issue that can only be tackled by moral persuasion or by threatening to punish the countries that free-ride. The latter option derives from the fact that countries are aware of the disadvantages of the non-cooperative outcome relative to the full cooperative outcome (see section 3, in particular Table 16.2). Hence they have an interest in ensuring that international environmental agreements materialize and that existing agreements are sustained. By threatening not to cooperate or to defect from a concluded agreement, the cooperating countries have an instrument to punish the free-riders. This mechanism is usually referred to as 'retaliation' or 'self-enforcement'.

A third mechanism derives from the fact that countries are usually involved in several areas of negotiations, both environmental and non-environmental. If the interests in the various areas are reversed, there exist possibilities for an exchange of concessions in the fields of relative strength. This mechanism is referred to as 'interconnection' or 'issue linkage'.

Below we shall discuss these instruments in more detail. The basis will be non-cooperative behaviour but note that a substantial part of the literature is based on cooperative game theory.[25] For a comparison between these two approaches see Tulkens (1998).

4.1 Side-payments

Side-payments are transfers to countries whose net benefits from the full cooperative approach are negative.[26] As an example, consider the acid rain problem described in the preceding section. As can be seen in Table 16.1, most countries would gain under the full cooperative approach. Moreover, total net benefits would be more than sufficient to cover the net losses from cooperation of the UK, Finland, Italy and Spain (the 'losers'). So, in order to induce the 'losers' to cooperate, the countries that would gain from cooperation (the 'winners') could offer to compensate the losers and still be better off.[27]

Side-payments can also be considered as a possible instrument to induce countries to join an existing coalition, even if they do not incur a net loss. The problem we have in mind here is the one in which the benefits of joining the coalition do not outweigh the benefits of free-riding on that coalition. The trade-off between joining or not has been modelled by means of the concept of a stable coalition (Carraro and Siniscalco, 1993; Barrett, 1994). It comes down to the following. Assume a group of similar countries, some of which form a coalition whereas the rest of the group does not cooperate and just takes advantage of the efforts of the countries inside the coalition. If a country leaves the coalition, the efforts of the countries remaining in the coalition will be reduced because of reduced pay-offs. If a country joins the coalition, the efforts of the countries already in the coalition will be increased (see also section 3). A coalition is called stable if no country has an incentive to leave or to join the coalition. The size of a stable coalition is generally very small, which gives rise to the idea that the countries inside the coalition may consider offering a side-payment to the countries outside the coalition to bribe them to join.

Side-payments look like a powerful instrument to stimulate cooperation because they open the possibility for the winners to compensate the losers without turning their net benefits into a net loss. In spite of this, the instrument has only been used to limited extent in practice (Mäler, 1990). Possible reasons are the following (Folmer et al., 1993). First, there is the problem of allocating the net benefits. Should the losers only be compensated for their losses or should they also share in the remaining gains? And how much should each winner contribute to the compensation? The allocation of the side-payments is an entirely new game for which generally accepted rules have yet to be developed.

Second, the anticipation of side-payments may induce losers to act strategically and implement environmental policy even below the level determined by the non-cooperative outcome. The rationale is that the potential beneficiaries may not only have the discrepancy between the full cooperative and non-cooperative outcome covered by side-payments but also part of the costs they would incur on the basis of the non-cooperative approach. The risk of strategic behaviour will be particularly relevant in the case of imperfect information about the countries' preferences for environmental quality and abatement costs, which is typical of international environmental problems. Similarly, the winners have an incentive to downplay their net gains and hence their contribution to the side-payments scheme.

Strategic behaviour also applies in the case of bribing countries to join an existing coalition. Hoel and Schneider (1997) show that if countries realize that they will be bribed, they have an incentive to stay out of the initial coalition so that this one will be even smaller. Therefore, the net result of the option to bribe may be negative.

Third, Mäler (1990) argues that side-payments may have a prejudicing effect of characterizing the compensating country as a 'weak negotiator'. The loss of reputation is not only relevant with respect to future negotiations on the same problem, but also with respect to negotiations on other problems, both environmental and non-environmental. Hence, loss of reputation may imply substantial future costs. Finally, side-payments signify application of a 'victim pays' principle rather than a 'polluter pays' principle, which is against international guidelines.[28]

Side-payments with respect to international environmental problems in the form of financial payments from one country to another are rarely seen in practice.[29] It is more common that a given country that has an incentive to defect cooperates for reasons of expected punishments or loss of reputation or in return for the cooperation of other countries on some other issue. We shall return to the latter instrument in the next subsection.

4.2 Interconnection

Countries are usually simultaneously engaged in several areas of negotiation. For instance, most countries in the world are engaged in negotiations about trade liberalization in the context of the World Trade Organization (WTO) and about CO_2 abatement to reduce global warming in the context of the 1997 Kyoto Protocol. At regional levels similar developments take place. For instance, in the context of the European Union the member states are simultaneously involved in negotiations on issues regarding monetary integration, environmental problems, defence, foreign policy, agricultural policy, cultural affairs, and so on.

Simultaneous involvement in negotiations on several issues of interest opens up the possibilities for exchanging concessions in fields of relative strength. A prerequisite for such an exchange or 'interconnection' is that the net benefits of cooperation are reversed in the problems in which the countries are involved. Using a two-country example, consider country A that is located downstream of country B and suffers from the latter's pollution. Thus country A would like to see country B abate its emissions. However, at the same time, country A limits imports from country B; a practice that country B would like to see discontinued. The countries, being aware of the asymmetry of their predicament, could base negotiations implicitly or explicitly upon some exchange of concessions across the two arenas. Country A increases imports from country B, and in exchange the latter reduces the amount of transboundary pollution generated within its borders.[30]

As a simple illustration, consider again the two countries, A and B, that have a choice, that is, to cooperate (C), or not to cooperate (D). The costs associated with cooperation in the form of reduction of a unit of pollution are 6 for A and 5 for B. Moreover, the benefits of reduction of a unit of pollution are 5 in A and 2 in B, regardless of which country makes the reductions. Associated with each combination of actions are pay-offs which are given in the bi-matrix game in Table 16.3.

Table 16.3   The international   Table 16.4   The international
environmental game   trade game

	B D	**B** C
D	0,0	5,–3
C	–1,2	4,–1

		B D	**B** C
A	D	0,0	2,–1
	C	–3,5	1,4

The difference with the symmetric prisoners' dilemma of Table 16.2 is that the asymmetries in costs and benefits lead to the situation that country B is worse off under full cooperation (C,C) (–1) than in the Nash equilibrium (D,D) (0). The gain (4) for the winner, country A, is however large enough to compensate the loser, country B, and still have positive net benefits. Moreover, total net benefits are largest under full cooperation (3).

Suppose that the same two countries are also involved in a trade dispute with net benefits that are an exact mirror image of the net benefits of the environmental game. This international trade game is represented in Table 16.4. It basically has the same problem that one of the countries (B) would have to compensate the other country (A) to induce cooperation. In both games a monetary transfer may be considered problematic for the reasons mentioned above. However, the trade and environmental game can be interconnected in the sense that the interconnected game comprises simultaneous play of the two games such that each country plays a strategy containing actions for both games rather than one strategy for each game separately. Pay-offs in the interconnected game are unweighted sums of the pay-offs from the constituting isolated games.[31] Interconnection yields the symmetric bi-matrix game represented in Table 16.5.

Table 16.5   The interconnected game

		B			
		D,D	D,C	C,D	C,C
A	D,D	0,0	2,–1	5,–3	7,–4
	D,C	–3,5	–1,4	2,2	4,1
	C,D	–1,2	1,1	4,–1	6,–2
	C,C	–4,7	–2,6	1,4	3,3

The interconnected game should be read as follows. The actions for each country are a combination of an action from the environmental game and one from the trade game. For instance, the action (C,D) means that the country concerned cooperates in the environmental game but defects in the trade game. The pay-offs are obtained by simply adding the pay-offs for each country in each game. For instance, the pay-offs (7,–4) for the action pair ((D,D), (C,C)) are the sum of the pay-offs (5,–3) for the action pair (D,C) in the environmental game and the payoffs (2,–1) for the action pair (D,C) in the trade game.

The action (D,D) is the best action for each country, regardless of what the other country does, so that the action pair ((D,D),(D,D)) is the Nash equilibrium with pay-offs (0,0). It is the combination of the Nash equilibria of the isolated games. The full cooperative outcome in the interconnected game is ((C,C),(C,C)) with pay-offs (3,3). It is the largest total or sum of pay-offs. By linking the issues, the full cooperative outcome is now better for both players than the Nash equilibrium, so that there is no need for side-payments. Of course, issue linkage is in fact a form of reciprocal side-payments but one that may be preferred to monetary transfers in international agreements. How to achieve the full cooperative outcome will be discussed in the next section.

A real-world example of interconnection is the 1961 Columbia River Treaty between the USA and Canada. Krutilla (1975) finds a gain of approximately US$250 million to Canada and a loss of US$250 to 375 million to the USA. The author suggested that the USA signed the agreement in exchange for concessions involving North American continental defence.

Interconnection has some drawbacks. First, it is likely to complicate negotiations. This holds in particular if the number of issues that are being linked increases. Along the same lines, Tollison and Willett (1979) and Sebenius

(1983) argue that issue linkage typically increases the number of decision-makers and thus the costs of decision-making. Second, the situation described in the example is one in which the pay-offs in the two games are completely reversed. In practice, the mirror image may be skewed. This will result in a situation in which the pay-offs in the full cooperative outcome are unequal, which will change the incentive structure to reach the cooperative outcome. In particular, the country with the smaller pay-off will be less inclined to cooperate, though not completely opposed to it. (For further details see Folmer and van Mouche, 2000.) Third, interconnection may be hampered by existing international agreements. For instance, the most favoured nation clause of the World Trade Organization (WTO) implies that if a WTO party grants an advantage with respect to trade conditions to any country, it must immediately and unconditionally extend this to all WTO parties. This clause may undermine interconnection. Interconnection is further hampered by the fact that the use of trade restrictions, which are often used to influence some other aspect of a targeted nation's behaviour,[32] is restricted by the WTO.[33] In the light of the foregoing observations, Keohane (1986) stresses the importance of regimes to link issues efficiently. Regimes are institutions with the purpose of detecting issues that are useful to link without unnecessarily complicating the negotiations.

We conclude this section by observing that interconnection is common in many areas of policy-making. For instance, in countries like The Netherlands and Germany, which typically have coalition governments made up of two or more parties, interconnection is a standard procedure. Similarly, Tsebelis (1990) shows that individual voting decisions may seem irrational at first sight, but they appear to be rational when viewed in a larger context of party politics. Finally, Bernheim and Winston (1990) essentially use an interconnected game structure in their analysis of the impacts of multi-market contact on oligopolistic behaviour. To sum up, the analysis of interconnection in international environmental policy-making deserves further attention.

4.3 Retaliation

As argued in the preceding section, free-riding behaviour is the main impediment to full cooperation. Also, after side-payments have been used by the winners to compensate the losers or after issues have been linked, incentives still remain to defect from an agreement. Countries may feel a moral obligation to stick to the agreement but an agreement becomes stronger if mechanisms can be built in that neutralize the incentives to defect.

One such mechanism, called retaliation, is based on the idea that the game is played forever (or for a period which may be assumed to be forever). In such a dynamic context strategies can be constructed in which the countries retaliate if one of them deviates from the cooperative path. If the countries use these strategies, the incentives to deviate may be outweighed by future punishments. This is known in the literature as the Folk Theorem, which states that, for small enough values of the discount rate, each feasible pair of Pareto-improving pay-offs can be sustained as a subgame-perfect Nash equilibrium of the infinitely repeated game, with this type of strategies (see for example Fudenberg and Maskin, 1986).[34]

A problem is that the punishments may hurt the punishing countries as much as the punished ones, so that all countries may have an incentive to reconsider their strategies after some country has defected. If this is foreseen, the threat is not credible and will not have the desired effect. It is, however, possible to construct strategies for the repeated prisoners' dilemma that are renegotiation-proof, which means that the countries will *not* have an incentive to renegotiate their strategies after a country has defected (van Damme, 1989). The intuition is as follows. Consider the bi-matrix game of Table 16.2. If country A does not cooperate at some point in time but country B still cooperates, country A gets 4 instead of 3. Country B gets –1, however. At the next point in time country B could retaliate by not cooperating. This is the well-known tit-for-tat strategy (Axelrod, 1984). However, tit-for-tat will not restore cooperation; the countries continue playing the strategy (D,D). The basic idea for the alternative strategy is that country B not only retaliates at this point in time but also announces its intention to return to cooperation at the next point in time, if country A returns to cooperation now. This leads to the following pay-offs. By defecting, country A realizes the pay-offs (4,–1). Country B then announces it is willing to restore cooperation but first it gets even with country A by realizing the pay-offs (–1,4) by defecting while A cooperates again. When both countries employ this strategy, two important properties result (for small enough values of the discount rate). First, cooperation is sustained since it is not profitable to defect because of the retaliation. Second, the threat to retaliate is credible since the punishing country will not accept an offer to restore cooperation immediately because it is better off if it gets even first.

The notion of retaliation can also be applied to the interconnected game of Table 16.5. Each country has an incentive to defect on both issues, because 7 is the highest payoff if the other country still cooperates on both issues. If one country defects, the other will then retaliate by defecting on both issues as well. If the first country cooperates again, the second country gets even by realizing the pay-offs (–4,7), after which full cooperation is restored.

Interconnection also creates possibilities for sustaining cooperation by punishing defection in one game by means of deviation in the other game. To continue the example given in section 4.2, if B defected in the environmental game, then A could retaliate by means of defection in the trade game. For further details see Folmer et al. (1993).

The renegotiation-proof equilibria discussed above sustain full cooperation for a two-country bi-matrix game. When the idea is applied to a game with more than two countries, the question is how large the resulting self-enforcing coalition will be. Barrett (1994) investigated this for a game with specific pay-off functions and his conclusion is that the coalition can be large but only if the difference in global net benefits between the full cooperative and the non-cooperative outcomes is small. If this difference is large, only cooperation by a few countries can be sustained.

5. INTERNATIONAL ENVIRONMENTAL POLICY INSTRUMENTS

As was mentioned in the introduction, international environmental agreements are ultimately implemented nationally. This implies that in the context of international environmental policy, use is made of the same set of instruments as in a national setting, in particular, regulations and standards, taxes and tradable permits.[35] However, some new instruments have been developed that are specifically used in the context of international environmental problems, that is, joint implementation (JI) and clean development mechanisms (CDM). These instruments can be seen as predecessors of genuine permit-trading at the international level. They were not dealt with in Chapter 6 and will be discussed below (section 5.2).

In section 4.2 it was mentioned that issue linkage might be hampered by existing international agreements. Similarly, environmental policy, whether motivated by purely domestic or international problems, may interfere with international conventions, particularly relating to free trade. This aspect will be discussed in section 5.1.

Before proceeding we will briefly discuss the optimal level of international environmental policy-making. From Tinbergen's (1954) theory of international economic integration it follows that the optimal policy level is determined by the geographical spread of externalities. The policy level should be such that the externality under consideration is geographically internalized but that countries not affected are excluded from the policy-making process. This implies that in, for example, global environmental problems all countries in the world should be involved. In the case of a transboundary pollution problem between two countries, only those two countries should be included in the policy-making process.

In the EU this optimal policy principle shows up in the subsidiarity principle, which states that the primary responsibility and decision-making competence should rest with the lowest possible level of authority of the political hierarchy capable of handling a particular public policy problem (see also Chapter 5).[36] It implies that decision-making which can adequately be handled by member states should not be handled by, for example, the European Commission. The rationale of the subsidiarity principle is that national preferences and information can be more adequately taken into account and that the complex process of regulation on an EU level can be substantially reduced. According to the subsidiarity principle, domestic problems of the member states, such as land use, should be handled at the national level, except when community interests are involved, such as the protection of the European heritage. However, in the case of transboundary pollution, externalities arise that restrict a member state's discretion. In principle, the countries directly involved should resolve the distortion. If this does not lead to a solution, EU involvement is called for. Product standards are not at a member state's full discretion either because of the risk that the free movement of goods and services may be hampered (see also section 5.1 and Folmer and Howe, 1991).

5.1 Environmental Policy and Free Trade[37]

With respect to free trade we make a distinction between free trade in the context of the WTO and free trade within a federation such as the EU. We start with the former.[38]

The WTO principle that is relevant for environmental policy is the non-discrimination or national treatment principle. It requires that imported goods be treated no less favourably than domestically produced goods. This implies that

- domestic taxes or other charges, laws, product norms and technical regulations may not be applied to imported products so as to protect domestically produced goods;
- an unequal treatment of similar domestic and imported products on the basis of the method of production is not allowed;
- trade-distorting subsidies are forbidden.

The foregoing imposes restrictions on environmental policy. In particular, the non-discrimination principle does not allow restrictions on imports of goods that have been produced in an environmentally harmful way. Nor does it allow subsidies that compensate for price differentials because of environmentally friendly but relatively expensive methods of production. However, the WTO allows measures to protect human, animal or plant life or health as well as measures relating to the conservation of exhaustible natural resources if such measures are made effective in conjunction with restrictions on domestic production or consumption. The rationale of the provision is that the measures are not applied in a manner that would constitute a means of arbitrary or unjustifiable discrimination between countries where the same conditions prevail, or a disguised restriction on international trade. Hence, there is scope for environmental policy in the WTO framework, although substantial uncertainty exists as to what can or may be done.

Given the ambiguity of the WTO rules with respect to environmental policy, several conflicts have arisen, in particular with respect to the use of trade measures for environmental protection. One of the best-known trade disputes is probably the USA–Mexico tuna–dolphin conflict. The US Marine Mammal Protection Act sets limits to the allowable number of dolphin kills for its domestic fishing fleet. Furthermore, it embargoes tuna imports from countries that harvest tuna in the eastern tropical Pacific and cannot meet the US dolphin protection standard. Mexico filed a complaint against the US embargo. The GATT's dispute settlement committee agreed with Mexico's complaint because the national treatment principle requires a comparison of the products of the exporting and importing countries and not of the production methods, that is, the catching techniques.

The situation in the EU exhibits some similarities as well as some differences compared to the WTO.[39] They have in common the emphasis on free trade. However, in the EU the removal of trade barriers has progressed much further than in the WTO. Whereas the WTO still focuses on the elimination of tariff trade barriers and other discriminatory obstacles to free trade, the EU has been in the process of eliminating non-tariff trade barriers in the context of the Single European Act which came into force in 1987.[40] More importantly, in the present context, in contrast to the WTO, the Single European Act provides an explicit legal basis for environmental policy since one of its objectives is protection of the environment, which should have a high priority. In particular, in the context of the Single Market with its emphasis on the free movement of goods and services, imports may be restricted on grounds of certain public policies and interests, including environmental protection.[41] A prerequisite is that the restriction is not a hidden trade barrier or measure of discrimination. This implies, *inter alia* that the policy measure also applies to domestically produced goods and services.

5.2 Joint Implementation and Clean Development Mechanisms

In the international negotiations on the reduction of greenhouse gases, two new instruments were introduced: joint implementation (JI) and clean development mechanisms (CDM). The rationale is to exploit the differences in abatement costs by country. For instance, greenhouse gas abatement can be less expensively undertaken in developing countries than in industrialized countries, and thus efficiency in global resource allocation can be obtained through cooperation. The underlying idea with both instruments is the following. Suppose that country A has agreed to reduce the emissions of greenhouse gases but that it is very expensive to abate in that country and that a cheaper option exists in country B. JI and CDM open the possibility that the abatement takes place in country B and that country A compensates country B for fulfilling country A's obligation. The difference between JI and CDM is the position of country B. If this country is a signatory to the agreement, it also has an obligation to reduce emissions. In that case, we speak of JI. If B is a country outside the agreement, which means that B has not agreed to a reduction target, we speak of CDM. In the case of CDM, B will generally be a less developed country arguing that it cannot participate in an agreement on the reduction of greenhouse gases before it has caught up with the developed countries.

It should be observed that there are substantial differences among countries with respect to greenhouse gas abatement targets. At the Kyoto meeting in December 1997, where 160 nations gathered, the following emission reduction targets were agreed upon: USA: 7 per cent; EU: 8 per cent; Japan: 6 per cent; developing countries: 0 per cent. The reductions should be realized by 2010 and are relative to 1990 levels.

Both JI and CDM can be seen as first steps in the direction of a system of tradable permits. By abating more than what it is obliged to do, a country creates an 'emission reduction credit' that it can 'sell' to another country for a price agreed upon in bilateral bargaining. In a full-blown tradable permit system, all countries with emission reduction credits are suppliers on the permit market whereas in the context of JI and CDM only a limited set of countries is allowed to supply. In particular, the USA and EU are excluded.

Experience with tradable permit systems in the USA (Foster and Hahn, 1995) shows that permit markets will not emerge automatically but have to be guided by setting up market intermediaries. In the case of greenhouse gases, clearing houses need to be introduced that administer supply and demand of emission reduction credits.

We end this section with an overview of the main pros and cons of CDM.[42] Before going into detail, we observe that this mechanism is still in an experimental phase in the sense that neither host nor donor countries currently receive abatement credits against current or future requirements. It is actively encouraged by the United Nations Framework Convention on Climate Change and various international organizations. Many private companies, NGOs and national governments in both developing and industrialized countries are participating. Government motivations on both sides include the desire to help solve a global environmental problem, moving up the learning curve in anticipation of crediting at a future date, fostering good public relations, and promoting and obtaining new technology (Rose et al., 1999).

Although CDM improves efficiency, it is criticized on various grounds. The first ground is fairness. The main argument is that the rich developed countries can buy out their obligations, which is considered to be unfair. The counter-argument is of course that the less developed countries will only agree to the trade if they benefit from it. The second critique is geared towards technological innovation. It is clear that the development of new technologies is very important for solving environmental problems in the long run (see Chapter 12). It is also well known that most technological innovation takes place in the developed countries. CDM may reduce the pressure on developed countries to develop new technologies.[43] On the basis of this argument the EU has proposed in the 1997 Kyoto Protocol that countries are only allowed to buy credits up to 50 per cent of their reduction target. The third critique is strategic behaviour. If (developing) countries know that they can sell emission credits, they have an extra incentive to keep their obligations at a low level.

Despite CDM's positive benefits, in particular financial compensation and transfer of technology, developing countries are apprehensive about entering into agreements because CDM will use up most of their low-cost mitigation options. Consequently, they will be left with only high-cost options to meet their own abatement requirements in the future. It might also result in lost opportunities to earn revenues if a full-fledged tradable permits programme were eventually implemented (Rose et al., 1999). Other reasons for developing-country scepticism about CDM include a perception of donor-country market power, and loss of sovereignty and concerns about the disruptive effects of new technology in the host country. Other concerns relate to the risk that standard development aid will be turned into CDM, with its more restrictive conditions. CDM is also assumed to contribute to the preservation of the *status quo* between developing and industrialized countries because it gives the latter the opportunity to circumvent domestic abatement policies that might slow economic growth.

CDM also has major (additional) advantages for the developing countries. It generates employment, has positive impacts on the balance of trade and stimulates economic development. Furthermore, it may contribute to an improvement of local and regional environmental quality through reduced air pollution. Finally, CDM may lead to an earlier involvement of developing countries in climate change policies, and hence enlarge their influence in these policies.

In addition to low-cost mitigation options, CDM may offer industrialized countries export options of 'cleaner' technology. It also reduces the risk that under time pressure suboptimal technology is being developed and that some industries have too little time to adapt themselves to greenhouse gas abatement policies. On the other hand, the donor country (partly) loses control over the implementation and development of the project. It may also slow down investments in energy-saving programmes in the donor countries. Finally, CDM may have negative employment effects and, because of a slowing down of technological development, affect a country's competitiveness. For instance, it may reduce a country's opportunities to obtain first-mover advantages (see Chapter 12).

6. SUMMARY

In this chapter we have argued that the absence of an institution with the jurisdiction to enforce environmental policy internationally is the main characteristic of an international environmental problem. It implies that international environmental policy must be voluntary. Consequently, there is a risk of free-riding. Moreover, a policy that has been agreed upon may be foiled. We have reviewed the market outcome as well as the non-cooperative and full cooperative approaches to international environmental problems. We have shown that the last is most desirable but also difficult to achieve because it may lead to a welfare loss for some countries and to free-riding behaviour. Three instruments to achieve the full cooperative approach have been discussed, that is, side-payments, interconnection and retaliation. The last two have been identified as the most powerful.

We have argued that environmental policy that has been agreed upon internationally is ultimately implemented domestically, and that in that connection use is made of the standard instruments discussed in Chapter 6, such as taxes, regulations and standards and tradable permits. We have also shown that environmental policy may interfere with free trade, both globally and regionally. However, there is also a growing consensus that environmental policy may necessitate restrictions on free trade provided that they are not hidden trade barriers or measures of discrimination. Finally, we have reviewed Joint Implementation and Clean Development Mechanisms as instruments of international environmental policy in the context of global warming abatement.

ACKNOWLEDGEMENT

The authors thank Landis Gabel for his valuable comments and suggestions.

NOTES

1. This does not apply generally because beyond a certain level of congestion, rivalry may arise.
2. See Chapter 6 for detailed information about the instruments mentioned here.

3. It should be observed that, in many cases, one need not rely solely on valuation methods to obtain monetary values. Consider, for instance, the costs of climate change or ozone layer depletion. For some components, such as damage to agricultural production and the construction of defence works, market-determined prices can be calculated. A complication is that future prices are needed, which usually introduces substantial uncertainty.

4. In Chapter 1 a distinction was made between technological and pecuniary externalities. In contrast to the former, the latter do not require policy intervention (see also Baumol and Oates, 1988). In this chapter we will only use the notion externality because we will only be dealing with technological externalities.

5. It should be observed that international institutions exist, in particular the United Nations, that have been authorized to coordinate international environmental policy. These institutions, however, cannot enforce policy.

6. The distinction between use, existence and option values (see Chapters 2 and 3 for definitions) is relevant in this connection.

7. This phenomenon is usually referred to as environmental capital flight (see Chapters 17, 18 and, for instance, Kuhn, 1998 and the references therein).

8. For a discussion of trade and the environment the reader is referred to Chapter 17.

9. A major difference between global warming and ozone layer depletion on the one hand and acidification on the other is that for the latter to become effective the emissions need to be deposited whereas for the former the emissions are effective as long as they remain in the atmosphere.

10. Important reasons are high population growth and efforts to stimulate economic growth in the LDCs. Another reason is that the energy sources used in the LDCs (especially coal) have unfavourable emission coefficients. For instance, the major commercial energy source in China has been coal, and by the beginning of the next century coal will still account for more than 70 per cent of its energy production. Finally, the LDCs lack the financial means to invest in technology to control emissions even at elementary levels or to substitute low-emission energy sources for high-emission sources. Economic growth is one of the main instruments to combat these factors. This gives rise to the following paradox: in order to reduce their CO_2 emissions which are associated with economic growth, LDCs need to grow!

11. For a detailed comparison between the non-cooperative and full cooperative approach see Folmer and van Mouche (2000).

12. For many environmental problems the assumption of linear marginal benefit and cost functions does not hold.

13. Figure 16.1 can also be formulated in terms of abatement. In that case the marginal benefits from abatement curve under the full cooperative outcome comprises the marginal benefits from abatement both in the home country and in the other countries. Hence it coincides or lies above the marginal benefits from abatement curve corresponding to the non-cooperative approach. The marginal cost of abatement curve is one single curve. The abatement level under the full cooperative approach is equal to or larger than the abatement level under the non-cooperative approach, which in its turn is equal to or larger than that under the market approach.

14. The perceptions of the benefits and damage components in economies in transition and rapidly industrializing countries differ from the perceptions in both the high-income countries and the less developed countries, which further complicates achievement of the full cooperative approach. (See Żylicz, 1998, for further information about East European economies in transition.)

15. An intermediate case between the two-country, unidirectional case and the reciprocal instances is the multi-country, unidirectional occurrence where each upstream country pollutes all the downstream countries but not vice versa. An example is an international river such as the River Rhine. The country where the river originates would have an incentive *not* to cooperate. Similarly, each downstream country would have an incentive to ignore its own emissions in so far as they cause damage in the downstream countries and at the same time it would like the upstream countries to clean up their acts.

16. The geographical configuration relates to 1984. For details see Mäler (1989).

17. The similarity to the 'small country' case in, for example, international trade should be observed.
18. This is in contrast to infinitely repeated games that do involve possibilities for punishing defection (see section 3.2). See Friedman (1991) for further details on punishment in a game-theoretical setting.
19. Action and strategy will be used as synonyms.
20. Cooperation means abatement here. Abatement and cooperation will be used as synonyms. Moreover, 'not to abate', 'not to cooperate' and 'defection' will be used interchangeably.
21. The present example is highly artificial and is presented primarily for illustrative purposes. For somewhat more realistic examples, see below.
22. The game corresponding to Table 16.2 is a symmetric prisoners' dilemma game because the off-diagonal elements are reversed and the diagonal elements are the same for each country.
23. A game may have several Nash equilibria. Moreover, every finite-player, finite-strategy game has at least one Nash equilibrium, if mixed strategies are admitted. Mixed strategies are a randomization of a player's strategies (Friedman, 1991). An easy way to find a Nash equilibrium is to identify the maximum for B in each row and the maximum for A in each column. Those matrix elements, for which both a row and a column maximum occur, are Nash equilibria.
24. This gloomy outcome may change in other settings. In particular, in infinitely repeated, or more generally, infinite dynamic games, cooperation can be achieved under certain conditions (see, for example, Friedman, 1991).
25. The difference is that in the latter it is assumed that the countries cooperate fully. The main theme is the analysis of mechanisms to divide the gains in such a way that sub-coalitions are deterred from stepping out of the coalition so as to do better for themselves outside the coalition. The former, on the other hand, focuses on explaining how cooperation can emerge from self-interested individual behaviour within a given set of rules.
26. The use of side-payments with respect to international environmental problems was first brought up by Mäler (1989).
27. Side-payments could also induce countries to cooperate in general rather than adopt a Pareto-inefficient approach as a means of influencing the outcome in their favour. Moreover, in the case of strong asymmetries as between rich and poor countries, side-payments may be instrumental in transforming the cooperation problem from one in which every country undertakes abatement to one in which the rich countries make the money available to fund abatement by the poor countries (see section 5).
28. See Chapter 5 for detailed information about these principles.
29. An exception is a case between The Netherlands and Germany on the one hand and France on the other with respect to the River Rhine in 1972 (Kneese, 1988).
30. This kind of problem is usually modelled by means of suasion games. For an application to environmental problems see Cesar and de Zeeuw (1996).
31. It is possible to introduce weights to represent the relative importance of each game (Folmer et al., 1993).
32. A recent example is formed by the trade sanctions against Iraq.
33. According to the Montreal Protocol on the reduction of CFCs, signatories should ban products produced with CFCs from non-signatories, but according to the GATT, trade barriers are not allowed, and the GATT had a larger group of signatories (see Wirth, 1992).
34. A subgame-perfect Nash equilibrium is a Nash equilibrium for the game that also gives a Nash equilibrium in every proper subgame of the game. When a game has a unique subgame-perfect equilibrium, it is usually held that this equilibrium is the outcome of the game because of its uniqueness.
35. Within the international context, the introduction of a uniform CO_2 tax to abate global warming has been proposed by, among others, Barrett (1991). The tax would be levied by the national governments but the (uniform) tax rate would be decided internationally. The main obstacles to such an international tax are that it would be viewed by some countries as an impingement on sovereignty and that it would result in very different costs in different countries because of the heterogeneity across countries. The latter would require large transfer payments. Since the idea has never been discussed seriously on a political level, we will discard it here.
36. In the USA a similar principle prevails, which is called federalism.

37. This section is complementary to Chapter 17.
38. The following description is based on Verbruggen (1995).
39. This part is based on Folmer and Howe (1991).
40. The types of barriers that have been removed in the context of the completion of the Single Market are: (1) technical barriers in the form of different technical regulations and product norms, market entry barriers, nationally protected procurement markets and different regulations concerning the protection of intellectual property; (2) fiscal barriers consisting of differences in VAT and excise duties; (3) physical barriers caused by border controls.
41. An example is the Danish bottle case. This case concerns the approval of the Danish refusal to import beer in aluminium cans.
42. Most of the results discussed below also apply to JI. Because of the stronger asymmetry between the countries involved in CDM (that is, industrialized and developing countries), the pros and cons under CDM are clearer than in the case of JI.
43. A counter-argument is that the demand for environmental technology in the developing countries may stimulate the production and development of cleaner technology, both in the developing and developed countries.

REFERENCES

Amann, M.and W. Schopp (1993), 'Reducing excess sulphur depositions in Europe by 60 percent. Further analysis of an international reduction scheme suggested as a basis for a new sulphur protocol in Europe', background paper prepared for the UN/ECE Working Group on Abatement Strategies, IIASA, Laxenburg, Austria.

Anderson, D. and R. Blackhurst (1992), *The Greening of World Trade Issues*, Hemel Hempstead: Harvester Wheatsheaf.

Axelrod, R. (1984), *The Evolution of Cooperation*, New York: Basic Books.

Barrett, S. (1990), 'The problem of global environmental protection', *Oxford Review of Economic Policy*, **6**, 1–24.

Barrett, S. (1991), 'Economic instruments for climate change policy', in OECD, *Responding to Climate Change: Selected Economic Issues*, Paris: OECD.

Barrett, S. (1994), 'Self-enforcing international environmental agreements', *Oxford Economic Papers*, **46**, 878–94.

Baumol, W.J. and W.E. Oates (1988), *The Theory of Environmental Policy*, 2nd edn, Cambridge: Cambridge University Press.

Bernheim, B. and M. Winston (1990), 'Multimarket contact and collusive behavior', *Rand Journal of Economics*, **21**, 1–26.

Carraro, C. and D. Siniscalco (1993), 'Strategies for the international protection of the environment', *Journal of Public Economics*, **52**, 309–28.

Cesar, H. and A. de Zeeuw (1996), 'Issue linkage in global environmental problems', in A. Xepapadeas (ed.), *Economic Policy for the Environment and Natural Resources*, Cheltenham, UK and Brookfield, USA: Edward Elgar, pp. 158–73.

Damme, E. van (1989), 'Renegotiation proof equilibria in repeated prisoners' dilemma', *Journal of Economic Theory*, **47**, 206–17.

Folmer, H. and C. Howe (1991), 'Environmental problems and policy in the Single European Market', *Environmental and Resource Economics*, **1**, 17–39.

Folmer, H. and P. van Mouche (2000), 'Transboundary pollution and international cooperation', in T. Tietenberg and H. Folmer (eds), The *International Yearbook of Environmental and Resource Economics 2000/2001: A Survey of Current Issues*, Cheltenham, UK and Northampton, USA: Edward Elgar.

Folmer, H., P. van Mouche and S. Ragland (1993), 'Interconnected games and international environmental problems', *Environmental and Resource Economics*, **3**, 315–35.

Foster, V. and R.W. Hahn (1995), 'Designing more efficient markets: lessons from Los Angeles smog control', *Journal of Law and Economics*, **38**, 19–48.

Friedman, J. (1991), *Game Theory with Applications to Economics*, Oxford: Oxford University Press.

Fudenberg, D. and E. Maskin (1986), 'The folk theorem in repeated games with discounting and with incomplete information', *Econometrica*, **54**, 533–54.

Hoel, M. and K. Schneider (1997), 'Incentives to participate in an international environmental agreement', *Environmental and Resource Economics*, **9**, 153–70.

Keohane, R.O. (1986), 'Reciprocity in international relations', *International Organization*, **40**, 1–27.

Kneese, A.V. (1988), 'Environmental stress and political conflicts: salinity in the Colorado river', paper presented at the conference Environmental Stress and Security, Stockholm.

Krutilla, J.V. (1975), 'The international Columbia river treaty: an economic evaluation', in A.V. Kneese and S.C. Smith (eds), *Water Research*, Baltimore: Johns Hopkins University Press, pp. 69–97.

Kuhn, M. (1998), 'Going green or going abroad? Environmental policy, firm location and green consumerism', in N. Hanley and H. Folmer (eds), *Game Theory and the Environment*, Cheltenham, UK and Northampton, US: Edward Elgar, pp. 34–91.

Mäler, K.G. (1989), 'The acid rain game', in H. Folmer and E. van Ierland (eds), *Valuation Methods and Policy Making in Environmental Economics*. Amsterdam: Elsevier, pp. 231–52.

Mäler, K.G. (1990), 'International environmental problems', *Oxford Review of Economic Policy*, **6**, (1) 80–108.

Ploeg, F. van der and A.J. de Zeeuw (1992), 'International aspects of pollution control', *Environmental and Resource Economics*, **2** (2), 117–39.

Rose, A., E. Bulte and H. Folmer (1999), 'Long-run implications for developing countries of joint implementation of greenhouse gas mitigation', *Environmental and Resource Economics*, pp. 19–31.

Sebenius, J.K. (1983), 'Negotiation arithmetic: adding and substracting issues and parties', *International Organization*, **37**, 281–319.

Tietenberg, T.H. (1985), 'Emission trading: an exercise in reforming pollution policy', report, Resources for the Future, Washington, DC.

Tinbergen, J. (1954), *International Economic Integration*, Amsterdam: Elsevier.

Tollison, R.D. and T.D. Willett (1979), 'An economic theory of mutually advantageous issue linkage in international negotiations', *International Organization*, **33**, 425–49.

Tsebelis, G. (1990), *Nested Games*, Berkeley: University of California Press.

Tulkens, H. (1998), 'Cooperation versus free-riding in international environmental affairs: two approaches', in N. Hanley and H. Folmer (eds), *Game Theory and the Environment*, Cheltenham, UK and Northampton, US: Edward Elgar, pp. 30–44.

Verbruggen, H. and H.M.A. Jansen (1995), 'International coordination of environmental policy', in H.Folmer, H.L.Gabel and H. Opschoor (eds), *Principles of Environmental and Resource Economics*, Cheltenham, UK and Lyme, US: Edward Elgar, pp. 228–52.

Whalley, J. (1991), 'The interface between environmental and trade policies', *Economic Journal*, **101**, 180–89.

Wirth, D.A. (1992), 'A matchmaker's challenge: marrying international law and American environmental law', *Virginia Journal of International Law*, **32** (2), 377–420.

Żylicz, T. (1998), 'Environmental policy in economies in transition', in T. Tietenberg and H. Folmer (eds), *The International Yearbook of Environmental and Resource Economics 1998/1999*, Cheltenham, UK and Northampton, US: Edward Elgar, pp. 119–52.

17. Environment and trade

Alistair Ulph

1. INTRODUCTION – THE ISSUES

What I am going to be concerned with in this chapter is the possible link between environmental policy and trade policy. There are two main reasons why such policies may be linked. The first is that environmental problems are international because of transboundary pollution or global pollution such as acid rain or climate change. It is well known that when countries act non-cooperatively in their own self-interest they will ignore the effect of their pollution on other countries (the 'free-riding' problem), and there is a need for some form of international environmental agreement (IEA) to ensure that countries take account of the global impact of their pollution. However, there needs to be some form of enforcement mechanism in these IEAs and it is sometimes proposed that trade sanctions be used against countries which violate these agreements – the Montreal Protocol for dealing with CFCs had such trade sanctions. I shall not be concerned with these issues – they are covered in Chapter 16 by Folmer and de Zeeuw. So I shall be assuming that pollution generated in one country causes damages only in that country. I shall also focus exclusively on the case where pollution is linked to production of goods.

The second linkage is that environmental policy may affect trade and trade policy may affect the environment. Thus policy-makers frequently worry about the effect of environmental policy on costs of production of domestic industry and the effect this might have on the competitiveness of domestic producers in world markets, and in the extreme case with the possibility that firms (particularly transnational corporations) may choose to relocate production facilities to countries with weaker environmental policies (so-called 'pollution havens'). Conversely, many environmentalists are concerned about the effect that globalization – the liberalization of trade and foreign investment – may have on the environment. This concern has been particularly prominent in the discussions on the Single European Market, NAFTA and the role of the World Trade Organization (see Anderson and Blackhurst, 1992 and Low, 1992 for early collections of papers discussing these concerns). The direct reason for this concern is that if trade liberalization acts to expand consumption, production and transportation of goods, this may increase pollution and the environmental damage caused by this extra pollution may outweigh any gains from trade. A more important aspect of this concern, and on which I will focus much attention in this chapter, is that precisely because of the concerns policy-makers have about the impact of environmental policy on competitiveness, countries may have incentives to set weaker policies than they would have done in the absence of fears about competitiveness – what is sometimes called 'environmental dumping' (see Rauscher, 1994 for a discussion of different concepts of environmental dumping). What environmentalists fear is that governments have incentives to weaken their environmental policies for strategic trade reasons, so that there will be a form of policy competition between governments of different countries which is sometimes characterized as a 'race to the bottom' in environmental policies. To prevent policy competition, environmentalists have argued that, if countries can only act individually, then those that set tough environmental policies should be allowed to impose 'countervailing tariffs' on imports from countries with weaker environmental policies, while, if international action is to be taken, then environmental policies should be harmonized, or at the very least there should be a set of 'minimum standards' set for environmental policies in different countries. Industrialists often support such policies on the basis that they provide a 'level playing field' for international trade.

Now much of the conventional analysis of environmental policy ignores the impact of environmental policy on trade while conventional analysis of trade policy often ignores the impact of trade policy on the environment. It is well known from the theory of the second best that such partial welfare analyses[1]_ of policies can be justified if it is assumed either that there are no other distortions in the economy other than the ones being analysed or that if there are, then the government has got other policy instruments it is using to address these distortions. Thus suppose that trade takes place in perfectly competitive markets with no trade barriers. Then while it may be true as a matter of positive economics that the imposition of environmental policy to correct an environmental externality may cause a country's share of some world markets to fall (either through lower exports or higher imports), that has no welfare significance – it is simply the consequence of correctly dealing with the externality, and it is quite correct for the analysis of environmental policy to ignore the trade impacts. Conversely, if a 'small country' (that is, one that cannot influence world prices) removes a trade distortion which causes production of some goods and pollution to rise, then, if nothing is done about the pollution it may well be the case that the benefits of eliminating the trade distortion may be outweighed by the increased environmental damage. But the problem is the absence of environmental policy, not trade liberalization *per se*, and if the government is operating an optimal environmental policy which reflects the costs to society of environmental damage, then if trade liberalization, combined with optimal environmental policy, causes increased pollution, that has no welfare significance, and the usual arguments in favour of trade liberalization apply (Markusen, 1975b, Long and Siebert, 1991, among many). So with competitive markets, small countries will have no incentives to engage in environmental dumping. Moreover, countries which differ in their environmental characteristics (for example whether their rivers are fast flowing and can easily disperse pollutants, the preferences of their citizens for a clean environment) will differ in the stringency of their environmental policies, and attempts at harmonization of environmental policies could rightly be resisted by some countries without any implication that they are seeking to exploit any trade advantage.

Suppose now that while markets are competitive, a country is not small so governments have an incentive to manipulate terms of trade in their favour. The first-best policies will involve trade taxes (for example an 'optimal export tax') to manipulate the terms of trade and the usual first-best environmental policies to address the environmental distortion (Markusen, 1975a, b; Panagariya et al., 1993, among many). If governments are not allowed to use trade instruments such as export taxes, they may well use environmental policies to address both sets of distortion, in which case environmental policies will not be set using the usual partial first-best rule (for example an emission tax equal to marginal damage costs or emission standards set so that marginal damage cost equals marginal abatement cost). A country that is a net importer will wish to set too weak an environmental policy in order to expand domestic production, reduce its demand for imports and hence the price it pays for its imports. But a country that is a net exporter of a good whose production causes pollution will wish to set too tough environmental policies, essentially as a proxy for the optimal export tax (Anderson, 1992; Krutilla, 1991; Rauscher, 1994). So the environmentalists' fear that with trade liberalization all countries will engage in 'environmental dumping' is not borne out if markets are competitive.

However, matters become more interesting when markets are not perfectly competitive, so that because of economies of scale there are a small number of producers who engage in imperfect competition. The last two decades have seen the development of 'strategic trade theory' to take account of imperfect competition. This can give quite different policy predictions from conventional trade theory based on competitive markets – for example, that it might be optimal for countries to subsidize exports. However, as long as governments are allowed to use trade policy instruments for strategic trade reasons, it will remain the case that environmental policy can be set ignoring trade considerations. But if, because of trade liberalization, countries cannot use trade instruments for strategic trade reasons, then they may turn to environmental policies for strategic trade reasons. I will show that there are circumstances in which governments may well engage in 'environmental dumping' for strategic trade reasons, but these results are by no means robust. The introduction of strategic behaviour by governments will also allow me to address another claim, known as the 'Porter hypothesis' (Porter, 1991), that governments acting strategically would set policies which are too tough (relative to the first-best rule) as a way of inducing their producers to innovate new 'green technologies' ahead of their rivals and thus gain a long-term competitive advantage.

Even if governments engage in environmental dumping, it does not follow that the policy responses frequently advocated – harmonization or minimum standards – are appropriate policies, because, as already noted, there may be perfectly legitimate reasons why countries would want to set different environmental policies.

In the rest of this chapter I will provide the analytical support for the arguments I have sketched out in this introduction. Section 2 considers the case of perfectly competitive markets. Section 3 introduces imperfectly competitive markets and the notion of strategic environmental policy for the case where firms have fixed locations. In section 4 I allow for firms to be internationally mobile, and ask how this affects incentives for environmental dumping. In section 5 I survey some of the empirical evidence on whether 'ecological dumping' is a major issue. Finally in section 6 I review the policy implications of the previous sections.

2.   TRADE AND ENVIRONMENTAL POLICIES WITH PERFECT COMPETITION

Throughout this chapter I conduct a partial equilibrium analysis of a single homogeneous-good industry. Consider a particular country, called the home country, and suppose that there is a single firm belonging to this industry located in the home country.[2] Production of this good causes a particular form of pollution which is unique to this industry and again, for simplicity, assume that one unit of the good produces one unit of pollution, there is no abatement technology, and the pollution generated damages only the inhabitants of the home country, so there is no transboundary pollution. Figure 17.1 shows the marginal private cost curve (MC) and the marginal social cost curve (MSC) for production of this good, where the difference between the two curves represents the marginal damage cost of the pollution caused by production of the good (that is, $MSC = MC + MDC$). I assume that the country imposes a 100 per cent profits tax so that all profits accrue to the home country.

There are two stages of decisions. In the first stage the government of the home country sets its trade and environmental policy for the firm in this industry. For what follows I do not need to be very explicit about environ-

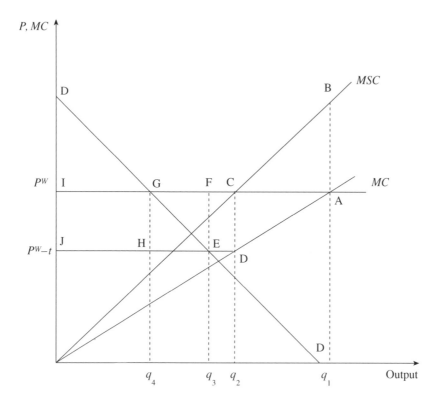

Figure 17.1 Competitive market

mental policy, and shall characterize it simply by the extent to which the policy causes the firm to internalize the damage costs of pollution; in the absence of any environmental policy the firm would operate with its private marginal cost curve. I shall call a first-best environmental policy one which causes the firm to operate as if its marginal cost curve were the marginal social cost curve; a lax environmental policy is one which would make the firm operate as if its marginal cost curve were below the social marginal cost curve, while a tough environmental policy is one which would make the firm operate as if its marginal cost curve were above the marginal social cost curve. In the second stage the firm chooses how much output to produce, and it will do this so as to maximize profits, setting marginal revenue, in this case the price facing the producer, equal to whatever marginal cost curve the government has faced it with. In the first stage, the government knows how its environmental policy will determine the output of the firm, and will choose its environmental policy (implicitly the output of the firm) so as to maximize welfare, which is consumer surplus plus the profits of the firm minus the costs of the damage caused by the firm's pollution.

2.1 The Small-country Case

I shall begin by assuming that the country is a small one, in the sense that this firm is just one of a very large number located elsewhere in the world and so its output can have no influence on the world price for this good (that is, the country's terms of trade are given). The situation is shown in Figure 17.1, where DD is the home country's demand for this good, and P^w is the world price for this good. I now analyse various policy scenarios.

Suppose we start with the assumption that the government follows a free trade policy, so that, because the firm is a price-taker, it sells to home and foreign consumers at the same price – the world price. Suppose initially that the government imposes no environmental policy, so the firm uses its private marginal cost curve. The firm produces q_1 (where $P^w = MC$) sells q_4 at home, and exports $q_1 - q_4$. If the government now introduces a first-best environmental policy, so that the firm operates as if its marginal costs are the marginal social cost curve MSC, then output will fall to q_1 (where $P^w = MSC$) and exports fall to $q_2 - q_4$. This loss of exports will reduce the firm's profits by ADC, but will also reduce environmental damage costs by ABCD, so the home country gains by ABC. I argue that this combination of policies – free trade and first-best environmental policy – is the best outcome for the home country. For any greater reduction in domestic output would lose the country more in marginal profits than it gains in reduced marginal damage costs; any smaller reduction in output would cost the country more in marginal damage costs than it gains in marginal profits. So as long as the firm is acting competitively and the country is pursuing a free trade policy, then it should just implement the usual first-best environmental policy. Although there is an impact on trade, the government can ignore this in terms of welfare.

Second, it might be thought that the government could achieve the same outcome by not imposing environmental policy but instead interfering in trade by imposing a tariff on exports $t = CD$ (tariff equal to marginal damage costs). This would have the effect of reducing the price faced by the producer to $P^w - t$ and, with no environmental policy, the firm will reduce output to q_2, where $P^w - t = MC$. While this has the same effect on output, and hence, in this very simple model on pollution,[3] it does not have the same effect on exports or welfare. For the firm will also have to sell to domestic consumers at the price,

$P^w - t$, and this will expand domestic consumption to q_3 and so reduce exports to $q_2 - q_3$. But while domestic consumers gain EGH from this expansion of domestic consumption, the firm loses EFGH in lost export profits, so there is a net welfare loss of EFG relative to the outcome that can be achieved by having free trade and first-best environmental policy. This is a standard result in the theory of policy-targeting. Although, in the absence of an environmental policy, exports are undoubtedly exacerbating pollution in the home country, the problem is not due to free trade as such but to the lack of an appropriate environmental policy. Taking action against exports targets the wrong variable – it is pollution emissions that need to be reduced, and while, in this case, reducing emissions will indeed reduce exports, the use of an export tariff is a much less efficient way of dealing with pollution than acting directly on pollution by implementing a first-best environmental policy.[4]

Third, the above story can be told another way round. Suppose we now start with no environmental policy but the government has imposed an export tariff $t = CD$, perhaps in order to reduce prices to domestic consumers. If we ignore environmental damages for the moment, then the usual analysis shows that this export tax is not desirable. By getting rid of the export tax and allowing the price to rise to the world price, the domestic firm would gain ADJI in extra profits, domestic consumers would lose EGIJ in consumer surplus and the government would lose CDEF in export tariff revenues. There would thus be a net welfare gain of ACD plus EFG, essentially the additional profits the firm makes by expanding exports. This is the usual argument for getting rid of trade distortions. But if we now take account of environmental damages, then trade liberalization, with no environmental policy, by increasing output from q_2 to q_3, has increased environmental costs by ABCD, and if the area ABC exceeds the area EFG, then the increase in environmental costs will have outweighed the conventional gains from trade liberalization. Again, this is just the standard second-best result that what looks like a good move from the perspective of trade policy may not be so if there is an uncorrected distortion elsewhere in the economy. But again, this is not an argument against trade liberalization. For the sensible policy is both to get rid of the trade distortion and to impose the usual first-best environmental policy; in that case output will be held at level q_2, exports will increase from $q_2 - q_3$ to $q_2 - q_4$, so while we do not get the gain from trade ACD, we do not suffer the extra environmental damage costs ABCD and so we are just left with the welfare gain from trade EFG.

In summary, with competitive markets and a small country, the optimal policy mix is free trade plus first-best environmental policy.

2.2 The Large-country Case

I now suppose that the firm in the home country is the only firm producing this good, so that it is a monopolist, and, for simplicity, I shall now assume that there are no domestic consumers, so all the firm's output is exported. Again the government imposes a 100 per cent profits tax so that all profits accrue to the home country. The situation is shown in Figure 17.2 where *DD* is now the world demand curve, or the country's export demand curve. *MR* is the corresponding marginal revenue curve. We now need to distinguish between world welfare, which is consumer surplus plus the profits of the firm minus damage costs, and home-country welfare, which is just profits minus damage costs. I begin by assuming that, although the firm is a monopolist, it continues to act as a price-taker. Again I consider a number of scenarios.

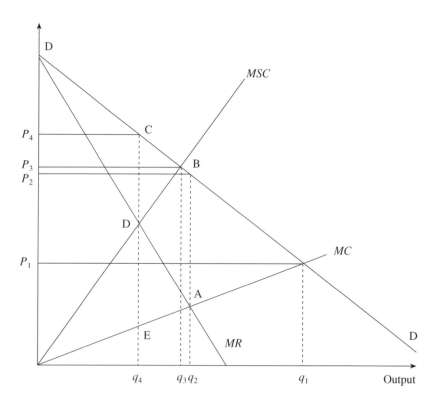

17.2   Pure monopoly

Suppose, first, that we ignore environmental damage costs for a minute. Then in the absence of any trade or environmental policy, equilibrium will be at output q_1 and price P_1 where price equals marginal cost and price clears the market. This maximizes world welfare (ignoring environmental considerations), so the optimal policy from the point of view of world welfare is free trade. However, from the point of view of welfare, the home-country would like to exploit its market power for exports, and so it would prefer that output were set at q_2, where $MR = MC$, with price P_2, and it can achieve this by imposing the optimal export tariff AB on its exports, so that its firm produces where $P_2 - AB = MC$. Thus, ignoring environmental considerations, the optimal policy for the home country is no longer free trade but an export tax.

Second, let us take account of environmental damages. From the point of view of world welfare, the optimal policy will be to have output restricted to q_3 with price $P_3 = MSC$. This can be achieved by the home country just imposing first-best environmental policy and free trade. But from the perspective of the welfare of just the home country the optimal policy will be to set output at level q_4 with price P_4 where $MR = MSC$. This can be achieved by the home country imposing the first-best environmental policy on its firm (so that it operates as if its marginal cost is MSC) combined with the optimal export tariff CD so that its domestic firm sets output at level q_4 where $P_4 - CD = MSC$. However, if the government cannot set the optimal export tariff, because such trade instruments are outlawed by a trade liberalization agreement, say, then the government would have an incentive to set a tougher environmental policy than the first-best policy in such a way as to ensure that at output level q_4 the firm acted as if its marginal cost were $MSC + CD$. For example, if the government used an emission tax as its policy instrument, then while the optimal policy would be an emission tax DE = marginal damage cost plus an optimal export tariff CD, if the government cannot impose an export tariff, it should raise its emission tax from DE to CE, that is, the optimal emission tax will be the usual first-best tax MDC plus the optimal tariff CD.

Thus we have a similar message to that of the small-country case. Provided the home country sets its optimal trade policy, then its optimal environmental policy can ignore trade considerations; similarly, provided the country sets its optimal environmental policy, then the country can set its optimal trade policy ignoring environmental considerations. But if, for example, the home country cannot set its optimal trade policy, then it will want to move its environmental policy away from the usual first-best environmental policy, and in the case where the country is a net exporter this will mean setting a tougher environmental policy than would be warranted by the usual first-best rule.

Finally, suppose now that the domestic firm realizes that it can exploit market power, and so will always set its output where MR equals what it perceives its marginal cost to be. Then, from the point of view of the home country, there is no longer any need to worry about a trade policy, for its domestic firm acts to exploit its market power. In this case, the optimal policy from the perspective of the home country is just free trade plus first-best environmental policy, for the domestic firm will produce output q_4 where $MR = MSC$.

Thus the only scenario in which the home country would have any need to set environmental policy different from the simple first-best rule is when the domestic producer does not exploit its market power and it is not allowed to set an optimal trade policy to compensate for this distortion in its output market.

3. TRADE AND ENVIRONMENTAL POLICIES – IMPERFECT COMPETITION

To introduce the modelling of strategic environmental policy with imperfect competition I shall extend the simple model of monopoly introduced in the last section to the case of oligopoly, for which the simplest case is duopoly. Suppose that there is another firm located in some other country, called the foreign country. The foreign firm and country are identical to the home firm and country, except that I shall assume for the moment that this other firm produces no pollution, so that it just operates with its marginal private cost curve. Output is determined by means of Cournot competition, that is, each firm takes as given the output of its rival and chooses its own output to maximize profits.

I begin by showing how equilibrium output is determined. Assume for the moment that the government in the home country sets first-best environmental policy, then the situation is shown in Figure 17.3(a), which is very similar to Figure 17.2. The firm in the home country takes as given the output of the foreign firm, Q^*, say, and this yields the marginal revenue curve for the home firm $MR(Q^*)$; the profit-maximizing choice of output by the home firm is q^*, where $MR(Q^*) = MSC$. By considering different levels of output for the foreign firm we generate the home firm's reaction function $q = R^h(Q)$, which gives the home firm's optimal choice of output for any level of output of the foreign firm. A similar analysis for the foreign firm results in the foreign firm's reaction function $Q = R^f(q)$. These reaction functions are shown in Figure 17.3(b). Equilibrium outputs q^* and Q^* for the home and foreign firms are where these reaction functions intersect, so that each firm is choosing its profit-maximizing output level, given the choice of the other firm.

But is it the case that the optimal policy is for the home government to impose the first-best environmental policy? If the government also operates on the Cournot assumption that the output of the rival firm is fixed at Q^*, then it is again the case that the government's optimal policy is to impose the first-best

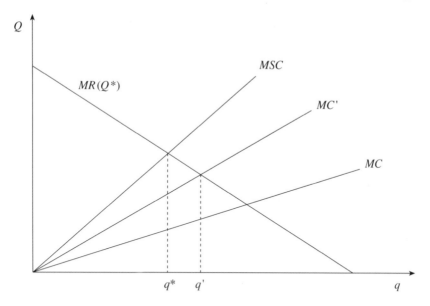

Figure 17.3(a)   Imperfect competition

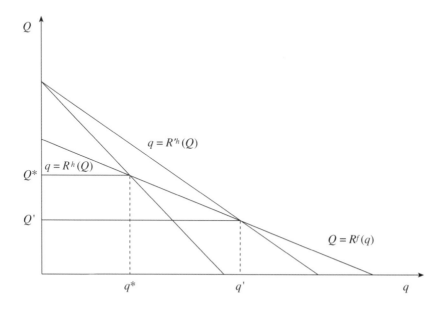

Figure 17.3(b)   Firms' reaction functions

environmental policy, for exactly the same reason that was given for the monopoly case, that is, the firm is choosing the optimal output level (the profit-maximizing output level) from the perspective of the welfare of the home country, so the only market distortion is the environmental externality and the optimal policy for the government is just to correct the externality using the usual first-best environmental policy.

However, suppose the government sets its environmental policy before the firms choose their output levels (that is, the government can commit to its environmental policy), then the government can use its environmental policy to change the equilibrium in the output market. Thus, suppose the government relaxes its environmental policy from first-best, and sets the home firm the marginal cost curve MC' in Figure 17.3(a). Then, for any given output level, Q^*, say, by the foreign firm, the home firm will choose a higher level of output; this will shift out the home firm's reaction function to $q = R^{h'}(Q)$ in Figure 17.3(b), so the equilibrium outputs will now be q' and Q'. So the new equilibrium will involve higher output (and hence pollution) by the home firm but lower output by the foreign firm. Starting from the first-best environmental policy (where, by definition, marginal damage costs of a little bit more pollution are equal to the marginal profits of a little bit more output), the costs of the additional pollution would be equal to the additional profits earned by expanding the output of the home firm, for a given output by the foreign firm. But the reduction in the output of the foreign firm will give a further increase in profits to the home firm. So, starting from first-best environmental policy, in this simple model, the government of the home country has a strategic incentive to relax its environmental policy in order to reduce the equilibrium output of foreign rivals.[5] There is no such strategic incentive in competitive markets, since the world price cannot be manipulated, nor in the pure monopoly case since there are no rivals whose output can be manipulated.

I want first to draw out a number of points from this analysis, then analyse the effect of dropping some of the simplifying assumptions, and finally analyse the effect of changing or extending the model.

First, as emphasized in the previous section, the strategic incentive to relax environmental policy depends crucially on the assumption that the only policy instrument available to government is environmental policy. The model outlined above is a simple extension of the Brander–Spencer model from strategic trade theory which showed that in imperfectly competitive markets governments would have incentives to use export subsidies to shift profits to their domestic producers by trying to reduce the output of rival producers. If the home government were able to use trade policies, such as export subsidies, then, as in the previous section, the optimal choice of policies would be to use export subsidies to achieve its strategic trade objective and first-best environmental policy to internalize the externality. It is only if trade policies are outlawed, say by trade liberalization agreements, that governments might use their environmental policies for strategic trade reasons.

Second, if the foreign firm also generates pollution, then its government will also have an incentive to relax its environmental policy. This generates a form of policy competition between the two governments which I analyse as follows. In doing this I shall generalize the model used so far by assuming that the firms are able to abate some of the pollution their output generates, but at a cost. I suppose that the governments can use one of two environmental policy instruments – an emission limit or an emission tax. Any given choice of policy instruments by the two governments will determine the marginal cost curves used by the two firms, hence the reaction functions of the two firms, and hence the equilibrium set of outputs of the two firms as set out in Figures 17.3(a) and (b). Knowing the equilibrium outputs of the two firms, the governments can calculate the profits the firms will earn, the pollution damage they will cause, and hence the welfare of the two countries.

Figure 17.4(a) shows for any combination of emission limits by the home and foreign governments (denoted e and ε respectively) the iso-welfare contours of the two countries.[6] Assuming again that each government imposes 100 per cent profits tax, and that there are no consumers in either country, welfare in each country is just profits minus damage costs. If the two countries set their environmental policies independently, then we look for a non-cooperative equilibrium in environmental policies between the two countries. In particular, as with the two firms, we can construct the reaction functions of the two governments (denoted $e = \rho^h(\varepsilon)$, $\varepsilon = \rho^f(e)$) which shows the welfare-maximizing choice of emission limit by the home (foreign) government for any given choice of emission limit by the foreign (home) government. These reaction functions must slope down for the following reason. Suppose the foreign government toughens its environmental policy (reduces its emission limit). That would reduce the output of the foreign firm, and allow the home firm to expand output, making more profit. If the home country keeps its emission limit fixed, then the home firm will have to clean up all the extra pollution it generates by expanding output. But, in general, it will be more sensible for the home country to allow some of the extra pollution to be emitted because it is being compensated by increased profits. So the home government should respond to a toughening of environmental policy by the foreign government by relaxing its policy. This is shown in Figure 17.4(a), where the reaction functions are downward sloping. The non-cooperative equilibrium set of emission limits (denoted e^N, ε^N) is where the reaction functions intersect, so each government makes the best choice of emission limit given the choice of emission limit by the other government.

A similar analysis can be conducted if governments use emission taxes as their policy instruments, and this is shown in Figure 17.4(b), where t (τ) denotes

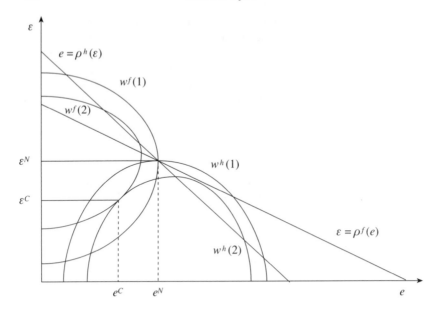

17.4(a)   *Governments' reaction functions – emission limits*

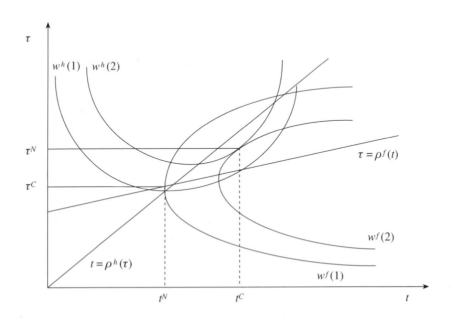

17.4(b)   *Governments' reaction functions – emission taxes*

the emission tax of the home (foreign) government. In this case the reaction functions slope upwards.[7] The reason is that, again if the foreign government toughens its environmental policy (raises its emission tax), this will reduce foreign output and increase domestic output and pollution. If the home country keeps its emission tax unchanged, then all of the extra pollution generated will be emitted. But it would pay the home country to clean up a bit of this extra pollution, and to give the home firm an incentive to do a bit more pollution abatement, the home country should raise its emission tax in response to the increase by the foreign government. Obviously the home government will increase its emission tax by less than the foreign government because it wants to encourage some expansion of output by the home firm. So the reaction functions, denoted $t = \rho^h(\tau), \tau = \rho^f(t)$, slope upwards and their intersection represents the non-cooperative choice of emission taxes by the two countries, denoted t^N, τ^N.

Note that although there is policy competition between the two governments, which results in all governments relaxing their environmental policies (confirming environmentalists' fears about 'ecological dumping'), this does not result in a 'race to the bottom' in which no environmental policies are implemented at all. There is a cost to the governments in trying to increase the market share of the domestic firms in terms of increased pollution damages, and there is a limit to how much they are willing to pay in order to increase the profits of their firms.

Notice that while each individual government has an incentive to expand its domestic firm's output in the expectation that other firms will reduce their output, when all governments act this way the aggregate effect is to drive up total output, which reduces total industry profits and also increases pollution in each country. If countries are roughly similar, then they will all be worse off than if they had stuck to first-best environmental policies. The countries would be better off if they could agree collectively not to engage in ecological dumping. Indeed, there is a stronger conclusion that can be drawn. For it is in the collective interests of the producing governments to reduce industry output, since imperfect competition yields industry output above the monopoly level. Thus if governments were able to act cooperatively, the optimal policy would be for governments to set environmental policies which were tougher than first-best (see for example, Barrett, 1994). These cooperative policies are denoted (e^c, ε^c) and (t^c, τ^c) in Figures 17.4(a) and 17.4(b) respectively. In a sense the cooperative equilibrium is like the case discussed in section 2 of a single firm which acted as a price-taker, where, if the government were only able to use its environmental policy it would set policy tougher than first-best to reduce the output of the firm (industry) closer to the monopoly level.

Figures 17.4(a) and (b) show that governments acting non-cooperatively have an incentive to relax their environmental policies relative to both the first-best environmental policy and the cooperative policies, and this is true no matter what policy instrument governments use. However, the size of the strategic effect can depend on the nature of the policy instrument, so that the choice of policy instrument has a strategic element. To understand this, return to the two-country example, and consider the situation where there is no technology for abating pollution, so the only way to reduce pollution is to reduce output. Suppose now that the foreign government sets an emission limit, and this emission limit is effective. That means that the level of output of the foreign firm is effectively determined by the environmental policy of the foreign government, irrespective of the output produced by the domestic firm. This implies that in the first-stage game between governments, where the domestic government takes as given the emission limit set by the foreign government, there can be no strategic incentive for the domestic government to distort its environmental policy from first-best (whatever environmental policy the domestic government uses), because it cannot affect the output level of the foreign firm. On the other hand, if the foreign government uses an emission tax, then the output of the foreign firm will respond to variations in the output of the domestic firm, and in the first-stage game between governments there will be an incentive for the domestic government to distort its environmental policy, since by affecting the output of the domestic firm it can indirectly affect the output of the foreign firm. For further details see Ulph (1992, 1996c).

The analysis has assumed that there are no consumers located in the producing countries and no transboundary pollution. Relaxing these assumptions will reinforce the conclusion that non-cooperative governments will engage in ecological dumping. Imperfect competition means that firms produce less output than they would under perfect competition and this harms consumers; to counteract this effect, governments wish to encourage their firms to expand their output. When there is transboundary pollution, governments have an additional incentive to reduce foreign production since that reduces the pollution damage caused by the foreign production. Both these arguments reinforce the incentive for governments acting non-cooperatively to relax environmental policy. The conclusions are more ambiguous when governments act cooperatively. Transboundary pollution means that all governments should set environmental policies that are tougher than simple first-best since they should take account of the pollution damage caused by their domestic production to foreign countries as well as to themselves. But the desire to protect consumers by raising output conflicts with the desire to raise profits by restricting output. Again, these issues arise because of missing instruments: ideally governments would deal with protection of consumers through industrial policy, leaving environmental policy to address externalities (see Conrad, 1993a, b, Kennedy, 1994, Ulph, 1996c for further discussion).

The simple analysis with no consumers assumed there was a single firm in each country. If there are several domestic firms, then the government has a conflicting objective. Because the domestic firms compete with each other, they collectively produce too much output for any given output from foreign firms, and this should lead the government to toughen its environmental policy relative to the first-best. However, the government has the same strategic incentive to expand domestic output at the expense of foreign output. So even when governments act non-cooperatively, it can no longer be concluded that they will have an incentive to set environmental policy that is laxer than simple first-best (Barrett, 1994). Indeed, as noted in section 1, in the limit as the market becomes perfectly competitive, the incentive is for the government to set environmental policies tougher than first-best as a proxy for the optimal export tax.

A crucial assumption of the duopoly model outlined above was that the product was homogeneous and that firms competed taking as given the output of their rivals (Cournot competition). If the model is changed to allow for the products of the firms to be imperfect substitutes and for firms to compete by taking the prices of their rivals as given, then the conclusion about ecological dumping is overturned: if governments act non-cooperatively they will set environmental policies that are tougher than first-best. In the case of Cournot competition firms took as given the output of their rivals, while each government realized that if its domestic firm expanded its output then rival firms would cut their output, assuming foreign governments did not change their environmental policies. In the case of Bertrand competition each firm takes as given the prices set by their rivals. But if one firm raises its price, that will increase the demand for its rivals' products, and they will respond by also raising their prices. So in this case the strategic incentive is to induce domestic firms to raise their prices so that foreign firms will also raise their prices, and if environmental policies are the only weapons available to governments, then governments achieve their strategic objectives by setting environmental policies that are tougher than first-best. It remains the case that if governments act cooperatively they will set tougher environmental policies than if they act non-cooperatively, for the same reason I gave for Cournot competition. For further discussion see Barrett (1994), Ulph (1996d). Obviously other oligopolistic concepts could be used, and the general point is that the form of market interaction between firms affects the direction that strategic distortions to environmental policy will take. An important question is which oligopolistic concept is appropriate for any particular market – a question that is the subject of much debate amongst industrial economists. The implication for policy-making, discussed later, is whether governments could know which form of oligopolistic interaction would be used in any particular market where they may seek to set their environmental policies strategically.

An important structural feature of all the models of strategic environmental policy discussed so far is the assumption that governments set their environmental policies before firms set their outputs or prices. It is implicit that governments can commit themselves to an environmental policy, and it is this commitment that allows them to influence the outcome of the subsequent market game and hence provides the basis for strategic behaviour. This raises two obvious issues. First, is it reasonable to suppose that governments can make such commitments? This has more force in conjunction with the second issue – since if governments can make such commitments to influence markets, so too can firms. The obvious mechanisms available to firms are investments in plant capacity or R&D which are designed to lower operating costs (including costs of emissions of pollution) and hence give a competitive advantage in the subsequent competition for market share. This raises the question whether, if firms can make such strategic investments, this reduces the need for governments to distort their environmental policies for strategic reasons. For, as I have just noted, the argument for governments to set their environmental policies strategically is the assumption that they can make commitments which change the outcome in subsequent market competition. But if firms can also make such commitments there may be no need for governments to get involved. Ulph (1996a) shows that to the extent that firms' strategic behaviour is a substitute for government strategic behaviour, then indeed this will reduce the incentive for governments to distort their environmental policies. However, this is not the end of the story, for governments' environmental policies will also affect the incentives for firms to act strategically, and the important question is the direction of this effect. The 'Porter hypothesis' referred to in the introduction assumes that tougher environmental regulations will increase the incentives for firms to invest in R&D. But as shown by D. Ulph (1994) and Ulph and Ulph (1996), this need not be the case. There are two effects of tougher environmental policy on incentives to invest in R&D. First, to the extent that R&D reduces emissions per unit of output, then tougher environmental policies will stimulate R&D. But tougher environmental policies also reduce the profits earned by firms, and this reduces the incentives to undertake R&D. It is not clear which of these effects will dominate. But it is clear that for R&D which is designed only to reduce costs, not emissions of pollution, only the second effect applies, and so tougher environmental policies will reduce domestic producers' incentives to invest in R&D. Under these circumstances, the incentive is for governments to relax their environmental policies. Thus theoretical analysis cannot provide unambiguous support for the 'Porter hypothesis'. For further discussion of this issue see Oates et al. (1994), Palmer et al. (1995) and Porter and van der Linde (1995).

4. TRADE AND ENVIRONMENTAL POLICIES – IMPERFECT COMPETITION WITH FOOTLOOSE FIRMS

The analysis so far has assumed that the number and location of firms is fixed. However, there are a number of papers which allow for the possibility that firms can respond to tough environmental policies in one country by relocating plants to countries with laxer environmental policies (see Markusen, 1999; Ulph and Valentini, 1998 for recent surveys). While this literature leads to the same broad conclusion as for the case of fixed location that there may be strategic trade incentives for governments acting non-cooperatively to set weaker or tougher policies than the first-best policies, in this case it is often supposed that where the incentives are to weaken environmental policies these incentives will be greater when firms are 'footloose'. Underlying this view is a belief that governments have more to lose when firms can respond to environmental policy by delocating. With fixed location, a government considering toughening its environmental policy has to trade off the benefit of reduced pollution damage against the marginal loss in profits from increasing the market share of rival producers. But if the firm delocates in response to a tougher policy, then it is not just the marginal profits the country loses, but the entire profits of the firm. Of course this is based on the assumption made in sections 2 and 3 that governments impose a 100 per cent profits tax and so capture all the profits of the firms located in their territories. There may be other benefits from having firms located domestically: for example, domestic consumers may benefit from having goods produced locally by not having to pay prices charged by firms for trade costs (such as transport costs). Thus the usual view is that there may be more intense competition between countries when firms are footloose and it is this that really engenders a fear about a 'race to the bottom' in environmental policies. I briefly discuss some models which throw some light on these issues.

4.1 A Simple Model

I begin with the simplest possible model which would seem to generate the 'race-to-the-bottom' outcome. It is based on Hoel (1997) and Ulph and Valentini (1998). So consider the model of the last two sections in which there is a single firm and two countries in which it can locate. Both governments impose a 100 per cent profits tax, so the country in which the firm locates gets all the profits, but also experiences any pollution the firm generates. Governments use a simple emission limit (e) to regulate pollution. Welfare of the country where the firm locates is thus given by profits of the firm less environmental damage, shown as $V(e)$ in Figure 17.5, while welfare of the other country is zero.

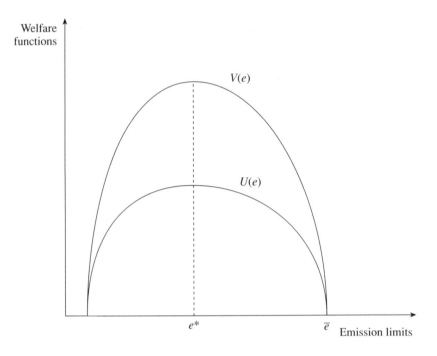

Figure 17.5   Race to the bottom – single firm

If the firm chooses its location before the government sets its policy, then the government in which the firm locates will simply set the emission limit, e^*, which maximizes welfare. This will be the usual first-best emission limit such that marginal abatement cost equals marginal damage cost, so there is no strategic element to environmental policy.[8] Since the policy is the same for both countries, the firm will randomize where it locates, so each country will get expected welfare $U(e^*) = 0.5V(e^*)$. If governments choose their policies first, then if governments set the same emission limit, e, we assume that the firm randomizes where it locates so that each government gets expected welfare $U(e) = 0.5V(e)$, shown in Figure 17.5. If governments set different emission limits, the firm locates in the country with the higher limit, and that country gets welfare $V(e)$. The equilibrium of the game in emission limits will be a simple 'race to the bottom' in which both governments set emission limit $\bar{e}$ where welfare gets driven to zero. It cannot be an equilibrium for the governments to set the same emission limit below $\bar{e}$ because by setting a marginally higher emission limit a government could get welfare $V(e) > U(e)$, and it cannot be an equilibrium for governments to set different emission limits if the government with the higher emission limit gets strictly positive welfare, since the other government could set a marginally higher emission limit and get positive rather than zero welfare. This very simple model would seem to confirm the fears outlined above that competition between governments to attract capital induces them to weaken their environmental policies and this takes the form of a 'race to the bottom'. Moreover, environmental policies are weaker when governments have to worry about the location of firms than when they do not, that is, $\bar{e} > e^*$; and the countries are worse off with footloose firms than when firms are not footloose, in the sense that $U(e^*) > U(\bar{e}) = 0$.

However, even within the context of this very simple model, not all these results are robust. For the argument depends on the assumption that $V(e^*) > 0$, so that there are some emission limits for which damage costs are less than the profits which the firm earns. But suppose environmental damage costs are so high that $V(e^*) < 0$, then while the outcome with fixed location will be as before (the government in the country with the firm sets emission limit e^*) with endogenous location both governments will set such tough environmental policies that no firm would want to locate in their countries – the NIMBY (not in my back yard) outcome. This would immediately overturn the claims in the previous paragraph.

It might be argued that the NIMBY case is only relevant for a few extreme cases (for example disposal of nuclear waste) so that the general conclusion from this simple model is to confirm many of the concerns and claims outlined above. I now turn to various ways in which the simple model might be extended.

4.2   Allowing for Multinational Production

A key feature of the simple model is that there are no transport (trade) costs so that, even if we take the more general Hoel (1997) version of the model which allows for consumers in both countries, the firm would only operate one plant. Markusen et al. (1995) use a model which has a very similar structure to the simple Hoel model except that they have transport costs,[9] so that the firm has to decide whether to have a single plant, from which it can sell to both countries, and if so where to locate it, or to have a plant in each country (that is, to go multinational). Note that an immediate implication is that if, in the absence of any environmental policies in either country, the equilibrium choice is for the firm to locate plants in each country, because profits are strictly greater with the multinational equilibrium than with an equilibrium with a single plant exporting to the other country, then if one country introduces an environmental policy there will be a range of values for the environmental policy before it would pay the firm to switch to the equilibrium with a plant located in the country with no environmental policy. Thus the introduction of transport costs, which is needed to rationalize a multinational pattern of production, provides a degree of protection to a country to set a tougher environmental policy than other countries without fear of losing plants to rival countries.

Markusen et al. again compare the policies governments would set after the firm had made its choice of plant location, with those they would set before such a decision. Markusen et al. reach the same conclusion as Hoel about the possibility of a NIMBY outcome – with high enough damage costs both governments will set prohibitive environmental policies to deter any plant being located in their countries, despite the fact that in terms of global welfare it would be desirable that the product be produced. But there is an interesting twist to the 'race-to-the-bottom' case. When governments set their policies after the firm has chosen its plant locations (so that, as in the simple model, there is no strategic competition between governments), there will be two possibilities – the firm chooses a single plant and exports to the other country, or it locates a plant in each country, with the first outcome being chosen when the fixed cost of setting up a plant is relatively high. In both cases, when we switch to having the governments set environmental policies before the firm chooses plant locations there will be competition to weaken environmental policies. But if, in the non-strategic case, the outcome involved the firm setting up a single plant, then in the process of competition the firm might decide to switch to having two plants, while if the non-strategic outcome involved the firm having two plants, this would remain the outcome when the governments competed strategically. Thus strategic competition may lead the firm to proliferate plants, but, except in the NIMBY outcome, not to reduce the number of plants. The rationale is this. The firm is trading off the fixed costs of setting up plants against the transport costs of having to export. Suppose in the non-strategic case governments set tough environmental standards so that production costs are high; then output will be relatively low, transport costs will be low relative to total production costs and it will not be economic for the firm to carry two sets of fixed plant costs; however, as the governments compete and weaken environmental policies this will reduce production costs relative to transport costs, expand sales in each country and make it more attractive for the firm to set up a second plant. Thus allowing for the possibility of multinational production means that, if again we exclude the NIMBY outcomes, in addition to governments setting weaker environmental policies when they take account of plant location decisions, this may lead to excessive numbers of plants being set up – too many multinational plants. In other words, the link between weak environmental policies and multinational firms may be the opposite of what environmentalists suppose – it is because governments set weak environmental policies that this may allow multinational patterns of production to come into being; multinational firms are a response to weak environmental policies rather than weak environmental policies being a response to multinational firms.

4.3 Allowing for Many Firms

In subsection 4.2 I extended the simple model by allowing a single firm to set up more than one plant. In this subsection I consider what happens if we revert to the assumption of no transport costs, so that each firm has a single plant from which it can sell to any country, but now assume there may be more than one firm. As the simplest possible extension to the simple model of subsection 4.1 I take the model of Ulph and Valentini (1998) in which there are two firms which engage in Cournot competition. The key difference this makes to the conclusions of the simple model is that even if we ignore the NIMBY case, environmental policy when governments set policy before firms choose to locate may be tougher than when they set policy afterwards. There are four reasons why introducing more firms changes the conclusions of the simple model.

First, with fixed locations there is now the possibility that the two firms locate in separate countries. As shown in section 3, and contrary to the previous two subsections, there will be strategic incentives for governments to engage in environmental dumping and set weaker environmental policies than they would set if they cooperated.[10] To see why this might mean that policies are weaker when locations are fixed than when firms are footloose, note that it is possible that, for some parameter values, the non-cooperative equilibrium between governments when firms have already decided to locate in separate countries involves such intense competition that governments set environmental policies so loosely that countries get negative welfare. When governments set their policies before firms locate, they would never choose to end up with negative welfare; so, for these parameter values, even if there were a 'race to the bottom' in which countries got zero welfare with endogenous locations, this might involve governments setting tougher policies than in the game where firms' locations are fixed.

Second, precisely because there is now competition between the firms, it may no longer be the case that relaxing environmental policies always leads to higher profits for firms; in the absence of environmental policies total output would be higher than that which maximizes profits, so there will be cases (with low environmental damage costs) where toughening environmental policies may raise profits and this may limit the 'race to the bottom'.

Third, if damage costs are strictly convex, then, for any given level of output and pollution by each firm, while having both firms locate in one country will double the profits that country can earn, it will more than double the environmental damage costs that country has to bear. Now if we think of the two-firms analogue of the race-to-the-bottom argument set out in Figure 17.5, we want to compare the welfare a country gets if it sets a higher emission limit than its rival and hence attracts both firms, $V(e)$, with the expected welfare it gets if it sets the same emission limit as its rival and both firms randomize where to locate, $U(e)$; in calculating this expected welfare we now include the possibility that the two firms locate in different countries. Because of the convex damage-cost argument it may no longer be the case that $V(e) > U(e)$; indeed Ulph and Valentini show that there must always be some values of e below $\bar{e}$ for which $V(e) < U(e)$ and indeed this may be true for all e. This introduces the possibility of multiple equilibria for the game where firms are footloose, and while these will include the race-to-the-bottom equilibrium, they may also include equilibria that have tougher emission limits than when firm locations are fixed. Hoel (1997) makes a similar argument when extending his model from one to many firms.

Fourth, a further implication of the convex damage-cost argument is that when we consider the environmental policies governments will set when firms' locations are fixed, it is quite natural to assume that they will set different environmental policies depending on whether one or two firms locate in their countries; in other words we can think of environmental policies being conditioned on the number of firms that locate in those countries. However, the argument sketched out in the previous paragraph, and which is used by other authors when considering models of endogenous firm location with more than one firm,[11] assumes that governments set a single environmental policy independent of the number of firms, so that if governments set different emission limits then all firms locate in the same country. But if we want to compare the difference in policies when firms have fixed or endogenous locations, and we do this by varying the move structure of the game, then if we allow a government to condition its policy instrument on the number of firms located in its country under one move structure, we should do so under both. This means that when governments set policies before firms locate, governments can separate the emission limits they set to attract one firm to locate from those they set to attract both firms to locate. Speaking loosely, this means that governments are not driven into an all-or-nothing race to the bottom but can settle for sharing the firms between them. Perhaps not surprisingly, if governments know they can secure an equilibrium where one firm will locate in each country, they will set the same level of emission limits as if these locations were fixed, so we get exactly the same outcome irrespective of whether firms' locations are fixed or endogenous. This occurs for a wide class of parameter values. This is illustrated in Figure 17.6 where $W(e)$ is the welfare a country gets when the two firms locate in separate countries and $V(e)$ is the welfare a country gets when both firms locate in a single country. I denote by e^N the Nash equilibrium emission limits the governments would set after the firms have chosen to locate in separate countries, and suppose it is located at the point shown in Figure 17.6. If the configuration of W and V is as shown in Figure 17.6, which is true for a wide range of parameters, then e^N would also be an equilibrium when governments set policies before firms choose their

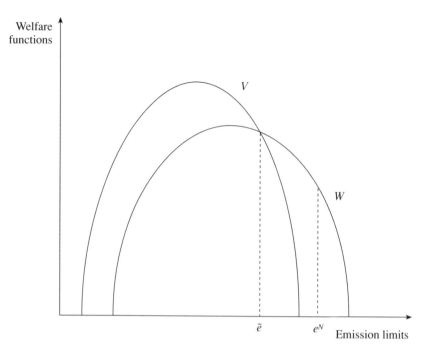

Figure 17.6   Location decisions – many firms

location, because it would not pay a government to try to attract both firms to locate in its country. Note that at this Nash equilibrium point welfare in both countries remains strictly positive, so we do not get the destructive all-or-nothing competition that drives welfare to zero.

In summary, introducing many firms means that, even excluding the NIMBY outcome, it need no longer be the case that governments engage in more environmental dumping when firms choose their locations in response to government policies than when government policies are set after firms have fixed their locations, and indeed for a wide class of cases the move structure makes no difference. Ulph and Valentini (1998) showed that the greater the degree of substitution between firms' products (and hence the greater the degree of market competition), the more likely it was that environmental policy would be tougher with endogenous locations with fixed locations. The reason is that with more substitution between the outputs of firms the more intense is the competition for market share and rent-shifting by governments with fixed locations of plants.

4.4   Many Firms and Plants

Markusen (1999) extends the analysis of the two previous sections by considering a general equilibrium model with two identical countries (denoted h and f for home and foreign) and two sectors – a competitive sector and a non-competitive sector. Within the non-competitive sector firms may be national (that is, a single plant in h or a single plant in f) or multinational (type m). The number of each type of firm and the amount that each firm produces is determined endogenously, using a zero-profit condition, so that, for example, if some configuration of firm types meant that h firms made positive profits and m firms made losses, then some additional h firms would enter the market and some m firms would leave until all firms just made zero profits. Given the complexity of the model, Markusen does not analyse the non-cooperative setting of environmental policies by the two governments, but just studies the impact of the foreign government unilaterally introducing an environmental policy which can affect either the marginal or fixed cost of production in country f. However, there are results from his model which allow us to test whether multinational firms encourage the switching of production between countries in response to environmental policies. Figure 17.7 shows the types of configurations of firms that exist in equilibrium for different combinations of trade costs and environmental cost penalties in country f. The top row shows what would happen in the absence of any environmental policy in f; for low transport costs (below 0.09) only national firms exist, while for high transport costs (above 0.09) only multinational firms exist. For low transport costs, as production costs in country f rise, production will be switched away from f firms to h firms and eventually only h firms survive. With high transport costs, as costs in country f rise, multinational firms will also switch production from their f to h plants, and as costs in f rise it is possible for national firms in h to enter the market and export to f. Because of general equilibrium effects (essentially lower wages in country f), type f firms can also emerge. With high enough production costs, multinational firms shut down (this is just the converse of the argument in subsection 4.2 that saw multinational activity expand as environmental polices weakened) and eventually only h firms survive.

   Note first that the cost differential at which production in f shuts down completely is (slightly) higher when we start with multinational production than when we start with solely national firms (the cost differential is 2.25 or 2.5 in the first case and 2.0 in the second). Markusen also reports that a detailed analysis of production shows that production switches more slowly from f to h when we start with multinational firms than with only national firms. Both these findings would seem to contradict the claim that multinational firms exacerbate the process of switching production out of countries with high environmental costs. However, Markusen noted that these findings are not due to

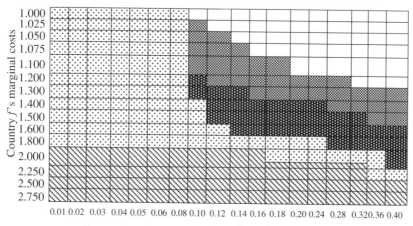

Transport costs as a proportion of marginal production costs

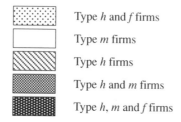

Type *h* and *f* firms

Type *m* firms

Type *h* firms

Type *h* and *m* firms

Type *h*, *m* and *f* firms

Figure 17.7   Patterns of production

multinational firms *per se* but rather to the fact that the existence of multinational firms can only be rationalized when there are high transport costs and it is this that protects production in country *f* from increases in its production costs due to environmental policy. However, in welfare terms, the higher transport costs that rationalize multinational production raise the costs of tougher environmental policies in *f* for the obvious reason that they increase the cost to consumers in *f* having to buy more of their consumption from country *h*. This effect outweighs the welfare benefits of a slower loss of production from *f* to *h* plants as environmental costs in *f* rise, at least for Markusen's model. Thus the fact that multinational production may slow down the loss of production in country *f* in response to tougher environmental policies in country *f* may not be beneficial to that country. A similar point was made in Ulph (1994), where it was shown that using tax rebates to reduce the incentives for firms to relocate abroad in response to tougher environmental policy (that is, reducing the extent to which domestic firms are footloose) may be counterproductive if that leaves domestic firms faced with higher costs (because of the tougher environmental policies they face compared to firms that have relocated abroad) and hence domestic consumers with higher prices than would otherwise be the case. Motta and Thisse (1994) make a similar point with respect to the use of protectionist policies to reduce the incentives for firms to relocate abroad.

4.5   Agglomeration Effects

In all the models studied in the previous subsections, environmental policy has affected location decisions through its impact on costs of production and hence on profits. To focus attention on the impact of environmental policies on location we have assumed that countries are identical (so there are no comparative advantage factors affecting location decisions). In the models in subsections 4.1 and 4.3 with no transport costs, small differences in environmental policies would be sufficient to induce firms to locate in the country with weaker environmental policies. In the models in subsections 4.2 and 4.4 transport costs, which are necessary to rationalize multinational production, provided a degree of protection for a country to set a tougher environmental policy than its rivals without losing all its production. Indeed, Figure 17.7 shows that as environmental costs rise in country f there will be a steady decline in the number of plants and firms located in country f rather than any sudden exodus of production. The reason for this is that if a small toughening of environmental policy in f makes it marginally profitable for a plant to switch from country f to country h, then that switch will marginally raise the profitability of firms that remain in f and reduce the profitability of plants located in h, thus reducing the incentive for any other plant to switch location.

Consider what happens to this argument if what matters in making location decisions is more than just costs of production, but also proximity to markets or sources of supply. Thus suppose that because of the input–output structure of production for producers in a particular sector, a significant fraction of their market will be producers in other sectors who use the output of this particular sector as inputs to their production processes; similarly, a significant fraction of the inputs used by producers in the particular sector will be the outputs of producers in yet other sectors. Thus, because sectors are linked in the structure of production, the location decisions of producers in different sectors become interdependent. This provides incentives for agglomeration of producers. Consider then what happens if a producer in a particular sector decides to close a plant in a particular location. As noted above, within the sector itself that has the usual effect that by reducing supply in that sector it will raise the profits of the producers who remain in that sector in that location. But it will also have two knock-on effects. It will reduce the demand for the products it used as inputs, and so reduce the profits of plants which supplied that producer, which will typically be plants located close to the original producer. Second, it will raise the input costs of plants which used the output of the original plant as inputs, since they will now have to get their inputs from more distantly related producers. Again, these customers will have been located close to the original plant. If these reductions in profits in related sectors were sufficiently strong to cause the closure of some of the plants in those sectors, that would in turn have negative impacts on the profits of the plants remaining in the original sector, which, if intersectoral linkages were strong enough, could offset the original boost to profits of those plants caused by the closure of the original plant. Venables (1994) and Ulph and Valentini (1997) analyse models of strategic environmental policy when there are agglomeration effects due to intersectoral linkages of production.

There are two implications of this analysis of agglomeration. First, there is the possibility that with strong intersectoral linkages there is the scope for quite catastrophic effects of policy on location decisions of producers when critical thresholds are reached. This can be characterized by the concept that a country can lose its manufacturing base in a particular set of related industries. Thus even if there are transport costs which would be expected to give countries a degree of isolation of their production from increases in domestic costs, agglom-eration effects may reintroduce the possibility that there could be critical thresholds at which a small toughening of environmental policy in one country triggers a substantial exodus of production. Second, when agglomeration effects are strong, what matters to producers is being located close to producers in related sectors; where that happens to be is less important. This can mean that for a range of parameter values, including policy parameters, there can be multiple possible equilibria; for example, it is perfectly consistent with a particular set of parameters that a particular set of industries be located either in *h* or *f*, while outside that range of parameters there may be a single equilibrium. This has an important implication for policy in that it introduces a kind of 'hysteresis effect'.[12] Suppose that at a very low level of environ-mental taxes, say, the only equilibrium is for a set of industries to locate in *f*. As environmental policy in *f* gets stricter, there may emerge another equilibrium in which the industries could locate in *h*. But given that the industries are already located in *f*, no individual producer would wish to switch to *h*. When environ-mental policy in *f* becomes strict enough, it is no longer possible to sustain the industries in *f*, and production switches to *h*. But now if *f* subsequently relaxes its environmental policy, by the same argument, the producers will not switch back to *f* unless the environmental policies reverted to the very low level at which location in *f* was the only possible equilibrium. Figure 17.8, from Ulph and Valentini (1997) illustrates this possibility for a two-country, two-sector (upstream and downstream) model in which there are two firms in each sector which have to decide how many plants to locate in each country. For a wide class of parameter values, in the absence of any environmental policy, agglomeration effects lead to all firms locating a single plant in country 1. Country 1 introduces an emission tax but as long as it lies below 1.5, the strength of agglomeration effects means that it remains a unique equilibrium for all firms to locate in country 1. For taxes between 1.5 and 2.0 there is a second equilibrium in which three firms relocate in country 2; for taxes above 2.0 this second equilibrium is unique. So an emission tax above 2.0 would trigger a rapid exodus of firms from country 1, but country 1 would have to cut its tax below 1.5 to attract these firms back again.

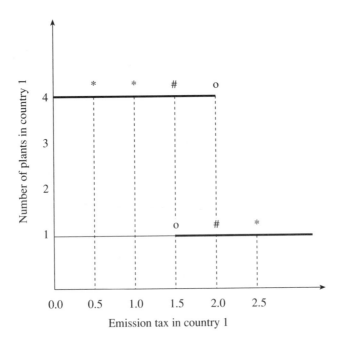

*	single equilibrium
#	multiple equilibria
o	chosen equilibrium

Figure 17.8   Hysteresis effects

4.6 Time Structure Revisited

As D. Ulph (1995) notes, it is not really appropriate to use the term 'hysteresis' for the above discussion, for there are no real dynamics in which environmental policies change and firms relocate. Agglomeration effects simply introduce multiple equilibria in the policy game between governments when firms are footloose. A proper analysis of hysteresis would require a multi-period interaction between governments and firms in which governments can change their policies from one period to the next and firms can change their locations in response to these changes in policy. As he notes, it is then important to distinguish between sunk costs, which are incurred when a plant is initially established and would have to be incurred again if a plant were relocated, from recurrent fixed costs of producing a positive output level in any period. It is the need to incur this sunk cost which gives a degree of commitment to firms' location decisions and which may mean that locations selected in previous periods may not be changed in response to policies which would have induced an alternative location choice by firms making that location choice from scratch.[13] For such a multi-period model of hysteresis to work, one would also need to explain why governments would wish to change environmental policies from one period to the next, and whether there are any factors (analogous to sunk costs) which might lead governments to commit to environmental policies (reputation effects might be a candidate). In his paper, the dynamics used by D. Ulph to motivate a change in environmental policy is the opening up of countries to trade. This has the usual effects – an increased market size effect which acts to increase profits, an increased competition effect which acts to reduce profits, and a relocation effect of production switching from countries with high autarkic costs to those with low autarkic costs. In addition, there will be an induced change in government environmental policies. He shows that while the opening up of trade will lead governments to set weaker environmental policies than under autarky, for a wide range of parameters the number of firms will be exactly the same as under autarky. This is because the gain in profits due to the net effect of increased market size and weaker environmental policies less the impact of increased competition is insufficient to compensate for the sunk costs needed to establish new firms.

However, it should be noted that the trade liberalization which drives the change in environmental policy is unanticipated by firms, for otherwise this would have influenced their initial location decisions. In the context of environmental policy we know of no fully specified multi-period analysis in which governments calculate their environmental policies each period and firms calculate their location decisions each period, with firms and governments acting strategically and with rational expectations, and with a proper account of what might determine the relative degrees of commitment by firms and governments which would allow a proper analysis of hysteresis effects.

4.7 Summary

If, in addition to the complexities outlined in the previous paragraph, we add the desirability of including transport costs and the simultaneous determination of multinational and national firms, and the possibility of intersectoral linkages with agglomeration effects, it is clear that there could be no single model which could address all the issues involved in thinking about strategic environmental policy with footloose firms. However, from the review of the literature provided in this section I want to draw out a number of conclusions that contradict some of the popular wisdom that informs policy-making.

1. Allowing for transport costs, agglomeration effects and sunk costs all means that even with no comparative advantage effects there could be significant differences in environmental policies between countries without inducing firms to switch plants to countries with weaker environmental policies.
2. Even if firms are tempted to relocate abroad in response to difference in environmental policies, it does not follow that a country is better off having fewer footloose firms, because if that leaves domestic firms with higher costs and domestic producers with higher prices, welfare may be lower than if firms had relocated abroad and exported back to the home country.
3. While there are certainly circumstances under which governments have incentives to weaken environmental policies when acting non-cooperatively, as we have shown there are other cases where governments will want to set too tough policies (for example NIMBYism, where governments seek implicitly to tax foreign profits).
4. While there are models in which governments will set much weaker environmental policies when they are trying to influence locations than when they set policies with fixed locations, this is by no means always the case; the discussion in subsection 4.3 showed that there may be many cases where environmental policies are unaffected by the timing of government policy-setting relative to firms' location decisions; when policies differ, the more intense is market competition (as measured by the degree of substitution between firms products), the more likely it is that environmental policy will be tougher when governments take account of the location decisions of firms in setting their policies.
5. Finally the discussion in subsections 4.2 and 4.4 emphasized that because multinational patterns of production are most likely to be competitive against national production when transport costs are high relative to production costs, these high transport costs will also reduce the sensitivity of domestic

production to differences between domestic environmental costs and foreign environmental costs. Moreover, it may be that multinational firms are a response to weak environmental policies (and hence transport costs are high relative to production costs) rather than weak environmental policies being a response to multinational firms.

5. THE EMPIRICAL EVIDENCE

In this section I review some of the empirical literature that attempts to assess whether environmental legislation has a significant impact on international trade and particularly the plant location decisions of firms. Because there are several excellent recent surveys of this literature (Cropper and Oates, 1992; Markusen, 1996; Rauscher, 1997 and Levinson, 1996a), I shall be relatively brief, drawing heavily on the survey by Levinson (1996a). He begins by quoting a number of sources from international organizations such as the OECD, international and national industrial associations, US politicians of all parties who all believe that industrial delocation in response to stringent environmental legislation is a major issue and have proposed steps to try to limit its effect. However, he then surveys a wide range of different kinds of evidence which suggest that these concerns are not borne out in practice.

The first kind of evidence reviewed by Levinson (1996a) is surveys, from different countries, of factors which businesses say influence their international location decisions, and in the vast majority of cases environmental regulations are unimportant; there is some evidence that in particular industries, such as chemicals, environmental regulations feature more importantly (Knogden, 1979 in a survey of West German firms that invested in developing countries), although these industries were also more sensitive to all cost factors. One possible explanation for this apparent lack of importance of environmental regulations in location decisions is an UNCTAD survey of multinational companies which suggested that such companies were concerned with environmental regulations in their home countries rather than their host countries – that is, they applied the same (tougher) environmental regulations wherever they located.

The second form of evidence is data on trade patterns. Most of these studies use various aggregate indicators of trade to see whether they are influenced by environmental variables. For example, Grossman and Krueger (1993) studied USA–Mexico trade patterns for a wide range of industries and showed, as Heckscher–Ohlin would suggest, that the USA tends to import from Mexico goods that have relatively low-skilled labour and capital content; they also included a variable capturing US pollution abatement costs by industry and showed that this had a positive effect on imports from Mexico, but the variable was quantitatively small (and statistically insignificant) so that whatever effect US environmental legislation had in encouraging imports from Mexico was trivial. As Levinson (1996a) notes, a problem with almost all these studies is that they fail to control properly for all the other factors that might influence trade patterns. An exception is a study by Tobey (1990) of trade in five products which are pollution-intensive; he regresses net exports of these five products for a range of countries against 11 factor-endowment variables (the other factors which might explain trade patterns) and a variable which measures the strictness of the countries' environmental policies on an index of 1 to 7. The environmental strictness variable is never significant, but Levinson (1996a) comments that the other variables do not have sensible patterns either, so it may be that the data are just not adequate to address the question.

The final set of studies surveyed by Levinson (1996a) are studies of location decisions by US firms across US states, which again consist of survey data and econometric studies of establishment-level decisions. Of the latter, the most comprehensive to date is one by Levinson himself (Levinson, 1996b).[14] This is a study of the locations of new plants (those that appeared in the 1987 quinquennial Census of Manufactures but not the 1982). The use of new plants gets round the problem of sunk costs noted in the last section; another reason for focusing on new plants is that many environmental regulations apply specifically to new plants. A major difficulty with studies of this type is the construction of appropriate measures of environmental stringency, and Levinson confronts this issue by using six different measures of stringency – three being various indicators of stringency of legislation, one being number of employees involved in state environmental agencies (to capture stringency of enforcement rather than just what is on the statute book) and two measuring abatement costs. The model follows a standard conditional logit model of plant location in which the probability of a plant locating in a particular state is related to a whole set of state characteristics – business taxes, employment costs, energy costs, unionization, infrastructure and so on, and the environmental stringency variable. Levinson first analysed the full sample of new firms and showed that the location decisions of new plants which were branch plants of large companies were more sensitive to 'manufacturing climate' than new plants in general, which would be consistent with the view that multinational firms are more sensitive to environmental legislation than other firms, and in the rest of his analysis he concentrates on the new branch plants opened by the largest 500 multi-plant manufacturing firms. The results of the conditional logit analysis show that while the environmental stringency variable is always negative, it is significant in only two cases: an index of legislative stringency constructed by the Fund for Renewable Energy and the Environment and an index of abatement costs. However, even where these variables were significant, an analysis of the effects of an increase in environmental stringency (by one standard deviation) shows that the quantitative impact would be small (the probability of a plant locating in a state would drop by 1.73 per cent). Levinson then studied the location decisions by individual industries (17 different SIC codes) and compared the impact of the environmental stringency variable with the overall pollution abatement costs to see if 'dirty' industries were more likely to be adversely affected by environmental legislation than clean industries; he found no significant pattern.

Similar results can be found in analyses of location decisions in other countries; an interesting recent example is a World Bank study (Mani et al. 1997) of location decisions in India since studies for developing countries have been rare. They apply the same methodology as Levinson to all new large (over Rs 500 million) industrial projects in India in 1994, choosing large projects on the presumption that they would be more footloose. Stringency of environmental regulation is captured by the number of prosecutions in a state under the Air and Water Acts normalized by the number of medium- and large-size plants in the state. They find that environmental stringency actually has a positive effect on location choices, although this is not significant. Restricting attention only to the five most polluting industries confirms the result.

The accumulation of evidence from many different kinds of studies and many different data sets all points to the same conclusion that environmental regulations either have no significant effect on trade patterns and plant locations, or, where there is such an effect, it is quantitatively small. In either case there seems to be a discrepancy between the public perception that capital flight caused by environmental legislation is sufficiently serious to warrant policy action and the available evidence. I offer five possible explanations why the empirical evidence shows such small effects, and ask whether this suggests that the studies have not addressed the real issue.

Levinson dismisses the standard argument that environmental costs are too small to have an effect – in some industries in the USA they can account for up to 15 per cent of costs and this should be large enough to influence location decisions. However, this could ignore a consideration that is particularly relevant to transnational companies which operate plants in many different countries. The additional factor would be that there may be substantial sunk costs involved in designing a plant. While it may pay a firm considering where to locate a single plant to take account of differences in environmental policies in different countries and locate its plant in a country with weak environmental policies (*ceteris paribus*), with its plant designed to meet those regulations, it may not pay a transnational company which wants to operate plants in several countries to incur such costs in designing different plants for different countries. In that case plants may be designed to meet the toughest regulations the firm expects to face, and transnational firms may be relatively insensitive to differences in environmental policies. In short, for transnational firms, differences in operating costs may be outweighed by large sunk costs in redesigning plants to take advantage of such differences.

A second possibility is that the various studies do not properly control for the different degrees of 'footlooseness' across types of firms or industries. I noted that Levinson focused on branch plants of large companies and Mani et al. concentrated on large projects in both cases because it was believed that these would be more footloose (Levinson had evidence to support this). But these may not really capture footlooseness. A recent study of trade data by van Beers and van den Bergh (1997) splits industries into resource-based and non-resource-based, with the latter being presumed to be more footloose, and finds that there is a more significant effect of environmental regulation in footloose industries.

A third possibility is that the studies are picking up the wrong variables to measure environmental policy. In particular, current environmental policies in different states/countries are being used to explain current location decisions. If we believe that governments can commit themselves to environmental policies before firms choose their locations, and that current policies reflect these commitments, then there would be some justification for this empirical approach. But if either governments cannot commit themselves to environmental policies, or can commit themselves to different policies at different time-periods, then it is not current environmental policies that matter, but what firms expect environmental policies to be in the future over the lifetime of their plants. If firms believe that current differences in policies are unlikely to be sustained in the future, and that there will be some convergence of environmental policies in all countries towards the higher standard of policies currently in place in different countries, then their location decisions will be little influenced by current differences in environmental policies. Only if such differences are well correlated with expected future differences in environmental policies will the empirical approach be appropriate.

Another aspect of the same issue is that if there are other factors driving growth of firms in a country, and governments cannot commit themselves to future tightening of environmental regulations, but only respond once growth has taken place, then any correlation between numbers of firms locating in a country and current toughness of environmental policy will show a positive correlation. What is required is a proper simultaneous model of how governments set their environmental regulations (whether they can commit to policies based on expected future emissions or respond to current or past emission levels), and how firms make their location decisions (whether these are based on expectations of future environmental policy or past policy announcements). In brief, empirical analysis needs to pay careful attention to the dynamics of the link between environmental policy and location decisions.

A further argument, which relates to discussion of policy in the next section, is that there may be omitted political economy dimensions. Levinson (1996a) refers to his 'cynical interpretation' that it would pay industry and politicians to exaggerate the threat that environmental legislation poses to local employment to justify other forms of assistance given to industry. Frederikson (1997b) has a theoretical model which supports this view (that is, in a political-economy equilibrium tough environmental legislation is offset by other subsidies offered to industry); in a personal communication he says this is being confirmed by empirical modelling for US states. This suggests that studies may not be properly picking up all the state taxes and subsidies offered by state governments.

Finally, there may be offsetting comparative advantage aspects which are not being properly picked up by the variables used to control for other factors affecting location decisions. Almost all of these other factors are cost-related. A particular aspect of this argument would relate to agglomeration effects discussed in the last section. This could be a possible explanation of the discrepancy between rhetoric and evidence; for the theory suggested that with strong agglomeration effects there could be a wide range of differences of environmental policies which would have no effect on location decisions, but then a critical threshold could be reached where a small further difference in policies has a 'catastrophic' effect; the empirical evidence is picking up the former effect while the policy concern is picking up the latter. It is obviously impossible to test this conjecture using conventional econometric modelling. To assess whether in practice intersectoral linkages are strong enough to provide this kind of catastrophic effect, Venables (1994) used a calibrated model of the world chemical industry, which is one which is always identified as highly polluting and thought to be particularly vulnerable to environmental legislation. The industry is split into two sectors: basic chemicals and other chemicals; and there are four country groups: North America, Far East (Japan, Australia, New Zealand), Europe (EU + EFTA), and Rest of the World (other versions of the model have used different industrial sectors and intra-EU countries). The linkage between the sectors is that basic chemicals contribute 25 per cent and 17 per cent of the gross costs of producing basic chemicals and other chemicals respectively, while the corresponding figures for other chemicals are 2 per cent and 9 per cent. The policy instrument he uses is an energy tax imposed unilaterally by Europe (energy accounts directly for about 14 per cent of the gross costs of basic chemicals and 3.5 per cent of other chemicals). Table 17.1 shows the impacts of different levels of taxes on the number of plants (N) and the unit operating costs of production (C) in the two industries in the three main blocks.

Table 17.1 shows that when the energy tax rate reaches 50 per cent, this will close down the European basic chemicals industry, with most of the production shifting to North America. Notice that given the moderate strength of the intersectoral linkages, there is no catastrophic decline in the industry at a particular threshold (nor was there any hysteresis effect), but the decline in plant numbers

Table 17.1 Impacts of a European energy tax on plants and costs (index form, no tax case 100)

Tax, %	Basic chemicals						Other chemicals					
	North America		Far East		Europe		North America		Far East		Europe	
	N	C	N	C	N	C	N	C	N	C	N	C
10	106	100	101	100	83	102	101	100	100	100	94	101
20	113	99	101	100	64	105	102	100	101	100	87	102
30	122	99	102	100	44	107	103	99	101	100	81	104
40	135	98	102	100	18	110	104	99	101	100	73	105
50	145	98	103	100	0	112	105	98	102	100	67	106

does accelerate as the tax rises. To understand the importance of the plant location decisions, note that at the 50 per cent tax rate unit costs have risen by 12 per cent in Europe and declined by 2 per cent in North America, so European competitiveness has declined by 14 per cent relative to the USA. Just under half of this can be accounted for by the effects of the energy tax on costs (both directly and indirectly through the higher costs of intermediate inputs). The rest of the cost increase is accounted for by the fact that suppliers are relocating to North America. Thus agglomeration effects have doubled the impact of the energy tax, which supports the claim that conventional models may understate the impact on competitiveness of environmental policies.

In summary, the evidence to date provides little support for the concerns expressed by environmentalists and policy-makers about the influence of stringent environmental legislation on trade patterns, and particularly the location decisions of firms. However, I have argued that there may be short-comings in the current literature. I suggest that more attention to capturing properly the footlooseness of industries, to recognizing the political dimensions and hence ensuring that all forms of industry assistance are captured, and to allowing for agglomeration effects may help to reconcile the difference between empirical evidence and political rhetoric, although I do not exclude the possibility that popular debate is simply blind to proper evidence.

6. POLICY IMPLICATIONS

From the review of the economic analysis in sections 3 and 4 I concluded that if governments act non-cooperatively they may seek to manipulate their environmental policies for strategic trade reasons in markets which are imperfectly competitive, but this need not always take the form of setting too lax environmental policies. From the review of the empirical literature in section 5, I concluded that there was no very strong empirical evidence that either trade patterns or firms' location decisions were influenced by environmental policies. From this it might be concluded that policy concerns about environmental dumping are significantly exaggerated and so there is little need to do anything about it. This is reinforced by the argument that what lies behind the environmental dumping argument is essentially a 'missing instruments' problem. When markets are imperfectly competitive, governments may have incentives to engage in strategic trade policies. If such policies are outlawed by trade liberalization agreements, then governments may turn to other policies, such as environmental policies, as proxies. But the same argument would apply to other policies, such as employment protection policies, and following the discussion of the empirical evidence, labour costs are in general more significant than environmental abatement costs and so environmental policy may not be the main focus of strategic behaviour.

For the purpose of this section, however, I suppose that strategic manipulation of environmental policies is an issue to be taken seriously and ask what should be done about it. I shall address this question mainly in the context of the model of strategic competition with fixed location introduced in section 3, but the arguments would also apply to models with footloose firms reviewed in section 4.

Since the problem of strategic competition arises from governments setting their environmental policies non-cooperatively, the first issue is what institutions might induce international coordination of domestic environmental policies. Three possibilities might be considered. The first is to allow individual governments to take action against countries who they believe are engaging in environmental dumping, for example by reforming GATT articles to allow the use of countervailing tariffs against environmental dumping. There are many reasons to oppose this approach and I do not pursue it.[15] A second possibility is the use of international environmental agreements as proposed for transboundary pollution.[16] However, this raises a whole set of other issues I do not wish to explore here. So I will simply assume that there exists some supranational agency which can be given the power to set national environmental policies, which for concreteness I shall refer to as the 'federal government' with national governments being 'state governments', but recognizing that this covers arrangements which are not formally federal, such as the EU. For simplicity, I shall consider a single federation consisting of just two states, denoted 1 and 2.

The next question is what form of intervention the federal government might make in state governments' environmental policies. As I said in the introduction, a commonly proposed approach is harmonization of environmental policies supported by environmentalists to prevent a 'race to the bottom' and by industrialists to provide a 'level playing field'.[17] For the purpose of this section I shall take a strict definition of harmonization to mean imposing either the same environmental standards or the same equiproportionate tightening of environmental standards.

Harmonization is neither necessary nor sufficient to ensure the absence of distortions to policy. It is not sufficient because if all countries were identical they would all impose the same environmental policy, but that would still differ from either the first-best or the cooperative level of policy. It is not necessary because if countries differ in marginal damage costs or marginal abatement costs, then first-best or cooperative environmental policies should differ between countries. Indeed, if countries differ significantly, then harmonization cannot achieve even a Pareto improvement over the non-cooperative outcome (see Kanbur et al.,1995; Ulph, 1997b). This is illustrated in Figure 17.9, simply a modified version of Figure 17.4, which shows the state governments' reaction functions in terms of emission standards $e_1 = R^1(e_2)$, $e_2 = R^2(e_1)$ as well as their iso-welfare contours. As with Figure 17.4, there are two versions of this diagram depending on whether environmental policies are strategic substitutes (17.9(a)) or strategic complements (17.9(b)) (refer to discussion in section 3, especially note 5). Note that in both cases I have shown the outcome where there is 'environmental dumping' – there is a set of policies in the shaded area which would make both countries better off than in the non-cooperative equilibrium (point N), and these would involve both states having tougher (lower) emission standards than in the non-cooperative equilibrium. But, crucially, note also that I have assumed a significant asymmetry between the two states (for example different damage costs), so that in the non-cooperative equilibrium between state governments, emission standards are laxer (higher) in state 1 than in state 2.

Harmonization involves setting equal emission standards for both states, and thus choosing a point on the 45-degree line. With the degree of asymmetry I have shown in Figure 17.9, any point on the 45-degree line lies above the iso-welfare contour for state 1 passing through the non-cooperative equilibrium point N. So harmonization would make state 1 worse off than in the non-cooperative equilibrium. The reason is obvious. Harmonization involves two aspects. It attempts to reduce total emissions, and since the non-cooperative equilibrium involves total emissions that are too high in terms of the total welfare of the two countries, such a move will in general raise total welfare. But it also involves changing market shares, with the high-emissions country losing market share to the low-emissions country. This harms the high-emissions country, and if countries are sufficiently different, this second effect outweighs the first. As shown in Ulph (1997b), countries would only have to differ by about 50 per cent in damage costs for harmonization not to yield a Pareto

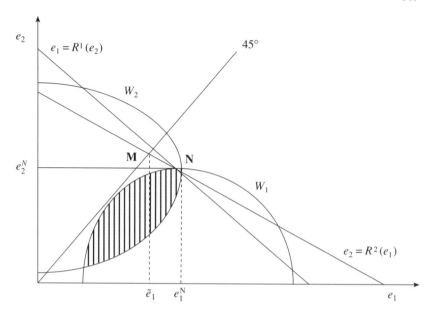

Figure 17.9(a)   Harmonization and minimum standards – strategic substitutes

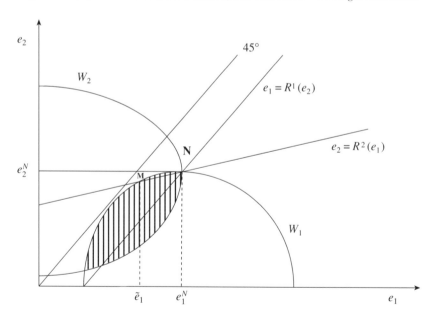

Figure 17.9(b)   Harmonization and minimum standards – strategic complements

improvement over the non-cooperative equilibrium. If harmonization involves either equal absolute or proportionate reductions in emission standards, then this would involve choosing a point on a line with a 45-degree slope passing through point N, but below point N. It is clear from Figure 17.9 that, in general, this form of harmonization will give both countries higher welfare than in the non-cooperative equilibrium.

While it is obvious that with sufficient asymmetries between countries the strict form of harmonization of environmental policies will not work, it is sometimes thought that a policy of minimum environmental standards would be desirable, on the grounds that it would raise environmental standards in countries which fell below the minimum standard, and if other countries chose to respond by also raising their standards, it would only be because they were better off by doing so. The argument is that one 'ratchets up' environmental standards across nation states. But this argument will also fail to deliver a Pareto improvement over the non-cooperative equilibrium if environmental policies are strategic substitutes, as shown in Figure 17.9(a). If state 1 is compelled to reduce its emission standard below the level e_1^N but above $\tilde{e}_1$, state 2 would respond by raising its emission standard to a point on its reaction function between N and M. This clearly makes the state 1 worse off. Any minimum standard tougher than (that is, lower than) $\tilde{e}_1$ would be equivalent to strict harmonization.[18] However, Figure 17.9(b) shows that if environmental policies are strategic complements, then the 'ratchet effect' works, and any combination of policies on state 2's reaction function between N and M would be a Pareto improvement on the non-cooperative outcome.

Thus neither of the policies frequently discussed – strict harmonization or minimum standards – may yield improvements over the outcome where state governments are just left to set their own policies. Even if they do yield Pareto improvements over the non-cooperative equilibrium, there is no reason in general to believe that they will be Pareto-optimal for the two states. The obvious approach is for the federal government simply to impose a cooperative solution. That raises the standard question when consideration is given to moving powers from state to federal level of whether the federal government would have enough information to calculate such an equilibrium. Ulph (1997b) assumes that damage costs are private information to state governments, so that any set of environmental policies imposed by the federal government would need to satisfy incentive compatibility constraints. The obvious constraint here is to prevent countries with high damage costs pretending to be low-damage-cost countries in order to be allowed to set lax environmental policies and hence obtain larger market shares. As Ulph (1997b) showed, this can lead to environmental policies in countries that have different damage costs being more similar to each other than would be the case if the federal government had full information. The reason is simply that the need to satisfy the incentive compatibility constraint means that countries with high damage costs have to be rewarded for revealing that information by being allowed to produce more output, and pollution, than would be the case with full information. However, this falls short of full harmonization.

So far in this chapter I have assumed that all governments are welfare-maximizing. But there is another reason why state governments may not implement first-best environmental policies, and that is because they are responding to political influence exercised by powerful lobby groups. There is now a small literature applying political-economy models of electoral competition or political influence to trade and environment.[19] As with strategic trade arguments, these models can explain why, even in a small country, a government may not implement first-best environmental policies, or pursue free trade, but deviations from first-best could involve either too lax or too tough environmental policies depending on the relative strengths of lobby groups. This literature also explains why environmentalists may support protectionist groups. However, it does not provide any support for a policy of harmonization, for two reasons. First, the fact that policies in some countries are set as a result of political influence does not, in itself, provide a rationale to coordinate reforms of environmental policies. To see this, go back to the discussion of the 'small-country' case in section 2.1. It may well be that other countries set their policies for all sorts of 'political motives', and that may affect the world prices a 'small country' faces. But as long as that 'small country' cannot affect those prices, the optimal policies are as set out in section 2.1. There is no need to coordinate, let alone harmonize, environmental policies. So there have to be other reasons, such as those provided by the analysis of strategic trade in section 3, for coordinating environmental policies. Second, while the literature discusses how political influence may affect policies set by governments, it does not address the issue of whether or how to limit political influence on environmental policies, and in particular whether harmonization may play a role in limiting political influence.

Johal and Ulph (1998) address this latter question in a model which builds on work of Boyer and Laffont (1996) and extends the model of Ulph (1997b) to include political-economy elements. Thus suppose that federal and state governments can be elected to be either green or industrial in the sense that a green government uses a utility function which gives environmental damages a greater weight than in a true welfare function, while an industrial government uses a utility function which gives environmental damage too little weight. There is no transboundary pollution and it is only when the state government comes into power that it learns a key parameter of its damage cost function (which determines the level of total and marginal damage cost for any given level of emissions). If environmental policy is to be set at the federal level, then the federal government will have to provide incentives for state governments to reveal this information. There are two prior constitutional choices that the people in the two states face: whether to delegate the setting of environmental policy to the states (in which case they will act non-cooperatively, so we get environmental dumping) or to the federal government; and whether or not to 'tie governments' hands', that is, to mandate the appropriate government (state or federal) to implement a specific environmental policy, that which maximizes expected social welfare. The sense in which welfare is expected is that at the time the constitutional choice is made society will not know the true value of environmental damages, and so has to set policies based on expected value of environmental damages (with expected value being the same for both states). Thus society essentially has a choice between allowing governments to come into power and learn the true value of environmental damages before setting environmental policies, but recognizing that elected governments will pursue objectives which reflect the interests of the party in power, not social welfare; or else mandating governments to pursue policies which maximize expected welfare, but based only on the expected value of damage costs, not the actual value of damage costs. Note that in the latter case, because expected damage costs are the same in both countries, tying governments' hands will mean that environmental policies will be harmonized.

Johal and Ulph (1998) show that whether or not it is decided to tie governments' hands, it is better to set environmental policy at the federal rather than the state level. This is because the usual gains to coordinating environmental policies, to eliminate strategic policy competition between countries, outweigh any welfare costs of asymmetric information. They also show that when policy is set at the federal level it is more likely that society will want to tie governments' hands. This is essentially because when policy is set at the federal level the gain to having policy set by governments who know the true value of environmental damage costs is reduced by the asymmetry of information between state and federal governments. This might provide some explanation as to why, as trade has become liberalized and hence the need to coordinate domestic environmental policies has increased, there have been increasing calls for harmonization of environmental policies; the explanation provided here is that harmonization is designed to limit the extent of political influence on federal policy-making.

To summarize, in this section I have taken seriously the issue of non-cooperative nation state governments engaging in environmental dumping and asked what could be done to prevent this. I have presumed the existence of some supranational body ('federal government') to whom powers can be given to implement policies to maximize the joint welfare of nation states, and I have shown that widely canvassed policies such as harmonization or minimum standards may not give Pareto improvements over the non-cooperative outcome depending on the degree of asymmetry between nation states and on whether environmental policies are strategic complements or strategic substitutes. In any case such policies are unlikely to be Pareto-efficient; and I then investigated two possible limitations on the federal government implementing the cooperative solution – asymmetric information between state and federal governments, which does not justify policies such as harmonization, and political influence, which, within a very special model, may provide some justification for harmonization. However, if one is considering the possibility of restricting what governments do, then it may be more sensible to mandate state governments not to engage in strategic environmental policy in the first place (see Grossman and Maggi, 1998 for related discussion in the context of strategic trade policy).

7.   CONCLUSIONS

In this chapter I have addressed a number of concerns raised in recent debates on globalization that in more liberal markets for trade and foreign direct investment nation states acting independently will have incentives to use 'environmental dumping', which in the extreme case would be a 'race to the bottom', and that to counter this possibility there should be harmonization of environmental policies, or at least the imposition of a set of 'minimum standards' for environmental policies.

I have reviewed some recent economic models and some empirical investigations and have shown that, as matters of both theory and evidence, there is little substance to the fears about a 'race to the bottom' and that even if there were concerns about environmental dumping the usual policy prescriptions cannot be sustained in general.

NOTES

1. By partial welfare analyses I mean analyses that consider the optimal policy rule for dealing with one market distortion, such as emissions of a particular pollutant, on the assumption that there are either no other market distortions, or that all other market distortions have been optimally regulated. On that assumption, the optimal policy rule leads to a 'first-best' outcome. The theory of the 'second-best' says that if there are other market distortions, some of which have not been optimally regulated, then the use of the 'first-best' rule may actually reduce welfare, not increase it, because the policy rule may make the unregulated market distortion worse and this may offset the direct effects of the first-best rule. In such circumstances one has to design 'second-best' policy rules which take account of the other distortions that cannot be regulated.
2. For the first part of this section it would not matter if we considered a large number of firms such that the industry supply curve corresponds to the assumed single firm's marginal cost curve.

3. This depends crucially on the assumption that production is equivalent to output. If we allowed for abatement activity by the firm, then environmental policy should be targeted on emissions, not output.

4. Following on from note 2, in this very simple example, it turns out that a production tax would be equivalent to the optimal first-best environmental policy, because emissions are assumed to be equivalent to output. In a more general model which includes abatement this equivalence breaks down and so a production tax, while better than an export tax for the reasons given, would not be as efficient as a properly designed environmental policy.

5. This does not mean that the government will set no environmental policy at all. There will be an optimal degree of relaxation, for as the output of its domestic firm expands and the output of the rival firm contracts, the gain in terms of additional profits to the domestic firm will decline, and the cost in terms of additional pollution will increase.

6. An iso-welfare contour for, say, the home country plots combinations of emission limits for the home and foreign country which yield the home country the same level of welfare. I have shown examples of these contours as $W^h(1)$ and $W^h(2)$ ($W^f(1)$ and $W^f(2)$) for the home (foreign) country, with the higher number representing the higher level of welfare. The shape of the contour reflects the fact that for a given level of emission limit for the foreign country, welfare will first of all rise as the home-country emission limit rises (the increased profits from rising output outweigh the increased pollution damage) but beyond a critical level of the home emission limit, further increases in the home country's emission limit will cause a greater increase in pollution damage than in profits, so welfare will fall. For any given level of emission limit by the foreign country, the home country's reaction function shows this critical level of home-country emission limit at which home-country welfare is maximized.

7. If reaction functions slope upwards, then the policy instruments are said to be 'strategic complements' as opposed to 'strategic substitutes' when the reaction functions are downward-sloping (Bulow et al., 1985).

8. This depends crucially on the assumptions that there are no consumers in each country and that the country in which the firm locates earns all the profits. So although the firm is a monopolist, the government is quite content for it to maximize profits. The only distortion as far as the government in which the firm locates is concerned is the environmental distortion. If there were consumers in the country, the government would set policy weaker than first-best to offset the monopoly distortion; if the country did not capture all profits, the government would set policy tougher than first-best as a way of capturing foreign profits.

9. There are some other differences which do not affect the general point we make; thus there is no third set of countries to which the firm can export; where the firm sets up a single plant in one country the governments can use an export tax. Because, as pointed out in note 2, of the discontinuities this introduces in the firm's pay-offs and hence welfare pay-offs, they have to rely on special functional forms and some numerical examples to illustrate their argument.

10. In particular the assumptions of Cournot competition and the fact all profits accrue to the country in which the firm is located lead to environmental dumping. (See Ulph, 1997a for more discussion.)

11. See Hoel (1997) and Markusen et al. (1993), although in the latter case the authors do not study policy competition between governments.

12. Hysteresis effect means that 'history matters', that is, the equilibrium one ends up in depends on where one started; thus reversing a policy may not take the economy back to where it started; that is, starting from an equilibrium A, introducing a policy may move the economy to B; but reversing the policy may not take the economy back to A, but to a different equilibrium, C.

13. Motta and Thisse (1994) also note that because firms have prior locations in which they have incurred sunk costs, the extent of delocation in response to environmental policies may be less than suggested by models that ignore such sunk costs.

14. For example the study by McConnell and Schwab (1990) considers only the motor vehicle industry.

15. These reasons include: it is governments not firms that are 'dumping'; the difficulty of one government establishing what should be the 'right' environmental policies of another

government against which to measure 'dumping'; if governments are engaging in environmental dumping for strategic trade reasons or at the behest of industrial lobby groups, what reason is there to believe that the countervailing tariff will not be used for similar purposes? For further discussion see Rauscher (1997), Bhagwati (1996).

16. Throughout this section I continue to ignore problems of transboundary pollution.
17. Bhagwati (1996) critiques various arguments that have been proposed for harmonization of environmental and labour policies, and Leebron (1996) discusses different senses in which policies might be harmonized.
18. Because country 2's optimal response, as given by its reaction function, would involve setting an emission limit laxer than the minimum standard, and so both countries will be constrained to set their emission limits at the minimum standard, and hence policies will be harmonized.
19. See Hillman and Ursprung (1992, 1994), Frederikson (1997a, 1997b), Rauscher (1997); Ulph (1998) provides an overview.

REFERENCES

Anderson, K. (1992), 'The standard welfare economics of policies affecting trade and the environment', in K. Anderson and R. Blackhurst (eds), *The Greening of World Trade Issues*, Hemel Hemstead: Harvester Wheatsheaf.

Anderson, K. and R. Blackhurst (1992), (eds), *The Greening of World Trade Issues*, Hemel Hempstead: Harvester Wheatsheaf.

Barrett, S. (1994), 'Strategic environmental policy and international trade', *Journal of Public Economics*, **54** (3), 325–38.

Bhagwati, J. (1996), 'The demands to reduce domestic diversity among trading nations', in J. Bhagwati and R. Hudec (eds), *Fair Trade and Harmonization*, Cambridge, MA: MIT Press, ch. 1.

Bhagwati, J. and H. Daly (1993), 'Debate: does free trade harm the environment?', *Scientific American*, November, 17–29.

Boyer, M. and J.-J. Laffont (1996), 'Toward a political theory of environmental policy', *Nota di Lavoro 56.96*, FEEM, Milan.

Brander, J. and B. Spencer (1985), 'Export subsidies and international market share rivalry', *Journal of International Economics*, **18**, 83–100.

Bulow, J., J. Geanakoplos and P. Klemperer (1985), 'Multi-market oligopoly – strategic substitutes and strategic complements', *Journal of Political Economy*, **93**, 488–511.

Conrad, K. (1993a), 'Taxes and subsidies for pollution-intensive industries as trade policy', *Journal of Environmental Economics and Management*, **25**, 121–35.

Conrad, K. (1993b), 'Optimal environmental policy for oligopolistic industries in an open economy', Department of Economics Discussion Paper 476–93, University of Mannheim.

Cropper, M. and W. Oates (1992), 'Environmental economics: a survey', *Journal of Economic Literature*, **30**, 675–740.

Frederikson, P. (1997a), 'The political economy of pollution taxes in a small open economy', *Journal of Environmental Economics and Management*, **33**, 44–58.

Frederikson, P. (1997b), 'Why don't environmental regulations influence trade patterns?', mimeo, World Bank.

Grossman, G. and A. Krueger (1993), 'Environmental impacts of a North American free trade agreement', in P. Garber (ed.), *The Mexico–US Free Trade Agreement*, Cambridge, MA: MIT Press.

Grossman, G. and G. Maggi (1998), 'Free trade versus strategic trade: a peek into Pandora's Box', CEPR Discussion Paper 1784, London.

Hillman, A. and H. Ursprung (1992), 'The influence of environmental concerns on the political determination of trade policy', in K. Anderson and R. Blackhurst (eds.) *The Greening of World Trade Issues*, Hemel Hempstead: Harvester-Wheatsheaf, pp. 195–220.

Hillman, A. and H. Ursprung (1994), 'Greens, supergreens and international trade policy: environmental concerns and protectionism', in C. Carraro (ed.), *Trade, Innovation, Environment*, Dordrecht: Kluwer, pp. 75–108.

Hoel, M. (1997), 'Environmental policy with endogenous plant locations', *Scandinavian Journal of Economics*, **99** (2), 241–59.

Johal, S. and A. Ulph (1998), 'Tying governments' hands: why harmonisation of environmental policies may be desirable', Southampton Discussion Paper in Economics and Econometrics 9802.

Kanbur, R., M. Keen and S. van Wijnbergen (1995), 'Industrial competitiveness, environmental regulation and direct foreign investment', in I. Goldin and A. Winters (eds), *The Economics of Sustainable Development*, Paris: OECD, pp. 289–301.

Kennedy, P.W. (1994) 'Equilibrium pollution taxes in open economies with imperfect competition', *Journal of Environmental Economics and Management*, **27**, 49–63.

Knogden, G. (1979), 'Environment and industrial siting', *Zeitschrift für Umweltpolitik*, **2** (24), 407–34.

Krutilla, K. (1991), 'Environmental regulation in an open economy', *Journal of Environmental Economics and Management*, **20**, 127–42.

Leebron, D. (1996), 'Lying down with Procrustes: an analysis of harmonisation claims', in J. Bhagwati and R. Hudec (eds), *Fair Trade and Harmonization*, Cambridge, MA: MIT Press, ch. 2.

Levinson, A. (1996a), 'Environmental regulations and industry location: international and domestic evidence', in J. Bhagwati and R. Hudec (eds), *Fair Trade and Harmonization*, Cambridge, MA: MIT Press, ch. 11.

Levinson, A. (1996b), 'Environmental regulations and manufacturers' location choices: evidence from the census of manufactures', *Journal of Public Economics*, **62**, 5–29.

Long, N.V. and H. Siebert (1991), 'Institutional competition versus ex-ante harmonisation – the case of environmental policy', *Journal of Institutional and Theoretical Economics*, **147**, 296–312.

Low, P. (ed.) (1992), *International Trade and the Environment*, Washington, DC: World Bank.

Mani, M., S. Pargal and M. Huq (1997), 'Is there an environmental "race to the bottom"? Evidence on the role of environmental regulation in plant location decisions in India', mimeo, Washington, DC: World Bank.

Markusen, J. (1975a), 'Cooperative control of international pollution and common property resources', *Quarterly Journal of Economics*, **89**, 618–32.

Markusen, J. (1975b), 'International externalities and optimal tax structures', *Journal of International Economics*, **5**, 15–29.

Markusen, J. (1999), 'Location choice and environmental quality and policy', in J. van den Bergh (ed.), *Handbook of Environmental and Resource Economics*, Cheltenham, UK and Northampton, USA: Edward Elgar.

Markusen, J., E. Morey and N. Olewiler (1993), 'Environmental policy when market structure and plant location are endogenous', *Journal of Environmental Economics and Management*, **24**, 69–86.

Markusen, J., E. Morey and N. Olewiler (1995), 'Noncooperative equilibria in regional environmental policies when plant locations are endogenous', *Journal of Public Economics*, **56**, 55–77.

McConnell, V. and R. Schwab (1990), 'The impact of environmental regulation on industry location decisions: the motor vehicle industry', *Land Economics*, **66**, 67–81.

Motta, M. and J.-F. Thisse (1994), 'Does environmental dumping lead to delocation?', *European Economic Review*, **38**, 563–76.

Oates, W., K. Palmer and P.R. Portney (1994), 'Environmental regulation and international competitiveness: thinking about the Porter hypothesis', Discussion Paper 94–02, Washington, DC, Resources for the Future.

Palmer, K., W. Oates and P. Portney (1995), 'Tightening environmental standards: the benefit–cost or no-cost paradigm?', *Journal of Economic Perspectives*, **9** (4), 119–32.

Panagariya, A., K. Palmer, W. Oates and A. Krupnick (1993), 'Toward an integrated theory of open economy environmental and trade policy', Working Paper no. 93–8, Department of Economics, University of Maryland.

Porter, M.E. (1991), 'America's green strategy', *Scientific American*, **264**, 168.

Porter, M.E. and C. van der Linde (1995), 'Toward a new conception of the environment–competitiveness relationship', *Journal of Economic Perspectives*, **9** (4), 97–118.

Rauscher, M. (1994), 'On ecological dumping', *Oxford Economic Papers*, **46**, 822–40.

Rauscher, M. (1995), 'Environmental policy and international capital allocation', University of Kiel Working Paper.

Rauscher, M. (1997), *International Trade, Factor Movements and the Environment*, Oxford: Clarendon Press.

Tobey, J. (1990), 'The impact of domestic environmental policies on patterns of world trade: an empirical test', *Kyklos*, **43**, 191–209.

Ulph, A. (1992), 'The choice of environmental policy instruments and strategic international trade', in R. Pethig (ed.), *Conflicts and Cooperation in Managing Environmental Resources*, Berlin: Springer-Verlag.

Ulph, A. (1994), 'Environmental policy, plant location and government protection', in C. Carraro (ed.), *Trade, Innovation, Environment*, Dordrecht: Kluwer, pp. 123–63.

Ulph, A. (1996a), 'Environmental policy and international trade when governments and producers act strategically', *Journal of Environmental Economics and Management*, **30**, 265–81.

Ulph, A. (1996b), 'Strategic environmental policy, international trade and the single European market', in J. Braden, H. Folmer and T. Ulen (eds), *Environmental Policy with Economic and Political Integration: The European Community and the United States*, Cheltenham, UK and Brookfield, USA: Edward Elgar, pp. 235–56.

Ulph, A. (1996c), 'Environmental policy instruments and imperfectly competitive international trade', *Environmental and Resource Economics*, **7** (4), 333–55.

Ulph, A. (1996d), 'Strategic environmental policy and international trade – the role of market conduct', in C. Carraro, Y. Katsoulacos and A. Xepapadeas (eds), *Environmental Policy and Market Structure*, Dordrecht: Kluwer, pp. 99–130.

Ulph, A. (1997a), 'International trade and the environment: a survey of recent economic analysis', in H. Folmer and T. Tietenberg (eds), *The International Yearbook of Environmental and Resource Economics 1997/1998: A Survey of Current Issues*, Cheltenham, UK and Lyme, USA: Edward Elgar, pp. 205–42.

Ulph, A. (1997b), 'Harmonisation, minimum standards and optimal international environmental policy under asymmetric information', Discussion Paper in Economics and Econometrics no. 9701, University of Southampton.

Ulph, A. (1997c), 'International environmental regulation when national governments act strategically', in J. Braden and S. Proost (eds), *Economic Aspects of Environmental Policy Making in a Federal State*, Cheltenham, UK: Edward Elgar, pp. 66–96.

Ulph, A. (1998), 'Political institutions and the design of environmental policy in a federal system with asymmetric information', *European Economic Review*, **42**, 583–92.

Ulph, A. and D. Ulph (1996), 'Trade, strategic innovation and strategic environmental policy – a general analysis', in C. Carraro, Y. Katsoulacos and A. Xepapadeas (eds), *Environmental Policy and Market Structure*, Dordrecht: Kluwer, pp. 181–208.

Ulph, A. and. L. Valentini (1997), 'Plant location and strategic environmental policy with intersectoral linkages', *Resource and Energy Economics*, **19**, 363–83.

Ulph, A. and L. Valentini (1998), 'Is environmental dumping greater when firms are footloose?', mimeo, University of Southampton.

Ulph, D. (1994), 'Strategic innovation and strategic environmental policy', in C. Carraro (ed.), *Trade, Innovation, Environment*, Dordrecht: Kluwer, pp. 205–28.

Ulph, D. (1995), 'Globalisation and environmental dumping: firm location and environmental policy', paper presented to Workshop on Environmental Capital Flight, Wageningen University.

van Beers, C. and J. van den Bergh (1997), 'An empirical multi-country analysis of environmental policy on foreign trade', *Kyklos*, **50**, 29–46.

Venables, A. (1994), 'Economic policy and the manufacturing base – hysteresis in location', paper presented to CEPR Workshop on Environmental Policy, International Agreements and International Trade, London.

Wilson, J. (1996), 'Capital mobility and environmental standards: is there a theoretical basis for a race to the bottom?', in J. Bhagwati and R. Hudec (eds), *Fair Trade and Harmonization*, Cambridge, MA: MIT Press, ch. 10.

18. Green taxation

Eirik Romstad and Henk Folmer

This chapter takes a look at environmental, also known as green, taxes. The rationale for such taxes is to reduce pollution caused by production or consumption. Environmental taxes, like the other instruments of environmental policy, are aimed at making economic agents internalize the costs of the environmental damages they cause.

There are several interesting side-effects of environmental taxes. One of the most controversial issues is the double dividend, that is, that in addition to improved environmental quality, environmental taxes open up the possibility of a welfare improvement via a green tax swap (the substitution of environmental taxes for distortionary taxes such as a labour tax). Another, less desirable, side of environmental taxes is that they may lead to capital flight, so that regulated firms may relocate from countries with stringent environmental policies to countries with lax environmental regulations.

Environmental taxes can come in many forms.[1] The classic case is a direct tax on emissions (such as a tax on carbon dioxide emissions). However, in many circumstances direct emissions taxes are difficult to implement. If that is the case, the regulator frequently resorts to alternatives that are easier to implement but only indirectly relate to the emissions that the policy is intended to reduce. Several forms of indirect environmental taxes exist. For instance, the regulator may decide to tax consumption (passenger seat taxes on airplanes), inputs (taxes on gasoline), or charge the firms causing a deterioration in environmental quality – for example, water quality going below a pre-set standard (so-called ambient taxes).[2] In this chapter we shall pay attention to both direct and indirect environmental taxes.

The main question regarding an environmental tax is: has it or will it be successful in terms of contributing to improved environmental quality? This issue has already been considered in Chapter 6. In this chapter we shall reconsider this problem, although in a more formal way. Moreover, we shall pay attention to the side-effects mentioned above, that is, the double dividend, competitiveness and environmental capital flight.

The structure of this chapter is as follows. The first part (sections 1–4) deals with the 'traditional' issues in environmental taxation. In section 1 we shall discuss an example to illustrate that environmental taxes work in practice. The incentives that an environmental tax provides to firms will be paid attention to in a formal way in section 2. In sections 1 and 2 we argue that environmental taxes tend to reduce emissions, which has important consequences for the feasibility of a revenue-neutral green tax swap. This brings up the issues of erosion and stability of green taxes in section 3. In section 4 we take a closer look at indirect environmental taxes. The second part of the chapter deals with the above-mentioned side-effects, that is, competitiveness and environmental capital flight in section 5 and the double dividend in section 6. Conclusions follow in section 7.

1.   DO ENVIRONMENTAL TAXES WORK IN PRACTICE?

Many environmentalists are generally sceptical towards environmental taxes, claiming that it is immoral to buy oneself some right to pollute.[3] Environmental economists would argue that environmental taxes change the behaviour of firms and consumers in an environmentally friendly direction. This section aims at demonstrating that there is much merit to the economists' position.

Even though reference to specific cases constitutes no proof, a close look at lead emissions in gasoline in Sweden provides some interesting insights into the effects of environmental taxes.[4] In the period 1986–94 the Swedish government introduced several measures to reduce lead emissions from the Swedish transportation sector. It all started in 1986 when a differentiated tax on gasoline was introduced with a higher rate tax on leaded than on unleaded gasoline. The higher tax more than compensated for the extra costs of making unleaded gasoline. The differentiated gasoline tax was combined with stricter emissions standards on automobiles. These standards were voluntary from 1987 and mandatory from 1989 onwards. At that time only cars with catalytic converters could operate on unleaded gasoline. However, cars with catalytic converters cost more than cars without, not only because of the cost of the catalytic converter, but also because catalytic converters necessitated fuel injection. In addition to imposing differentiated taxes, consumers were further induced to buy cars with catalytic converters via a reduced sales tax on such cars in 1987 and 1988. The sales tax reduction was more or less the same as the extra costs of fuel injection and of having the catalytic converter installed.

In 1985 the market share of leaded gasoline in Sweden was nearly 100 per cent. Four years later, this market share was reduced to about 50 per cent. For the next three years the drop in the market share for leaded gasoline was far less. The primary reason for this was that older cars without the catalytic converter could not run on unleaded gasoline. In 1992 one oil company introduced gasoline where the lead was replaced by sodium, allowing older cars to run on this 'new' kind of unleaded gasoline. Other oil companies soon followed suit, introducing unleaded gasoline with sodium or potassium replacements for lead, and by 1994 leaded gasoline had vanished from the Swedish market.

The tax on leaded gasoline was the main driving force behind the new unleaded gasoline, inducing consumers to change their behaviour and the oil companies to search for substitutes for lead. It should be observed, however, that the tax incentives were strengthened by the impacts from complementary measures such as the reduction of the sales tax and regulatory measures with respect to emissions standards.

The following observations apply. First, environmental taxes do not usually eliminate all pollution they are targeted at. Nor is this their intent. Rather, environmental taxes intend to correct for negative externalities to the extent that marginal social abatement costs are equal to marginal social environmental benefits. In some cases this implies complete elimination of the pollutant; in other cases only a partial reduction. As explained in Chapters 1, 5 and 6, violation of the 'marginal social abatement costs equal marginal social environmental benefits' rule would entail a loss of welfare to society. In terms of the morality issue raised at the beginning of this section, it is tempting to ask if overinvestment in environmental quality would not be immoral when there are multiple other important objectives to pursue in society. Examples of such objectives include improved schooling, better health care and reduction of poverty.

Second, environmental taxes are not as frequently used in practice as one would expect on the basis of their theoretical properties (cost efficiency, correct dynamic incentives, relative ease of administration and so on; see Chapter 6 for details). One reason for this is that environmental taxes lead to increased costs to those facing the regulation (firms' profits are reduced, and consumers' consumption bundles become more expensive). Therefore, those subject to environmental taxes are usually opposed to them, which makes it difficult for politicians to implement the tax. Opponents to environmental taxes are also quick to point to other regulatory alternatives (fixed standards, tradable permits,[5] or voluntary agreements[6]) or to other groups to be targeted (for example farmers versus industry). Despite industry lobbying and opposition from interests groups, several environmental taxes have been implemented, particularly in the Scandinavian countries, The Netherlands and Germany. For an overview see, among others, The Swedish Green Tax Commission (Swedish Ministry of Finance, 1997).

2. THE INCENTIVES OF AN ENVIRONMENTAL TAX

This section first looks at emission taxes from a representative firm's perspective. It shows how an emissions tax induces firms to reduce their emissions. Assume that a representative firm seeks to maximize its profits π in a competitive market. It has three choice variables, y (the amount produced), z (the amount of pollution emitted), and θ (the technology). Let the firm's short-term profits be given by the following expression:

$$\begin{Bmatrix} \text{Max} \\ y,z,\theta \end{Bmatrix} \pi (y,z,\theta) = \begin{Bmatrix} \text{Max} \\ y,z,\theta \end{Bmatrix} (py - tz - C_\theta(y,z)) \qquad (18.1)$$

where (in addition to the above-defined variables):

p is the market price of the product y;
t is the per unit tax on z, and
$C_\theta(y, z)$ is the cost of production for technology θ.

The introduction of the tax would induce firms to look for ways of reducing their emissions that would hurt firm profits the least. In principal, the firm has three options,[7] ranked in the order they normally would be considered:

1. Examining current operating practices to see if emissions could be reduced by minor adjustments in the way the firm operates. Such changes in firm operations may lead to net benefits.[8]
2. Once 'wasteful emission practices' have been removed, output is reduced until the marginal profits of production (which equal marginal revenues minus marginal costs of production) equal the marginal costs of emissions (which equal t, the tax rate on emissions).
3. Undertaking investments to change the production technology (θ) so that emissions and hence tax payments, are reduced.[9]

Figure 18.1 illustrates these steps. The shaded area is the joint production possibility area for output and emissions for technology $\theta = 1$. Note that emissions increase at an increasing rate with increased production.

   The question arises as to what is the optimal level of abatement for the firm. In the appendix we show that a firm would abate until the net marginal benefits of abatement (marginal revenues minus marginal abatement costs) equal the tax rate t. Formally:

$$t = p\frac{\partial y_n}{\partial z} - \frac{\partial C_\theta}{\partial z} \qquad (18.2)[10]$$

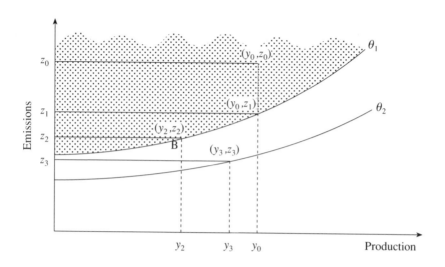

Steps:
1. Changing wasteful emission treatment practices, $(y_0, z_0) \rightarrow (y_0, z_1)$
2. Reducing output to achieve reductions in emissions, $(y_0, z_1) \rightarrow (y_2, z_2)$
3. Investment in new technology to further reduce emissions, $(y_2, z_2) \rightarrow (y_3, z_3)$.

Figure 18.1   Steps in adjusting emissions for a firm

Once the firm has undertaken the low-cost adjustments, that is, moved from a point such as (y_0, z_0) towards the frontier of the shaded area, for a given technology reductions in emissions are linked to reductions in production levels. This makes it possible to express the overall costs of reducing emissions from this level onwards in terms of two variables, the emission level, z, and the choice of abatement technology, θ. Assume that there are two abatement technologies, θ_1 (the current technology) and θ_2 (a new abatement technology that lowers the marginal abatement costs, but incurs extra investment costs to the firm). Which of the technologies should the firm choose in light of the emission tax, t? The answer to this question depends on two factors:

*   the difference in the sum of the reduction of abatement costs and taxes paid for the two technology alternatives, and
*   the investment costs associated with technology choice θ_2.

The shaded area in Figure 18.2 depicts the difference between the two technologies in terms of effect on abatement costs and taxes paid.

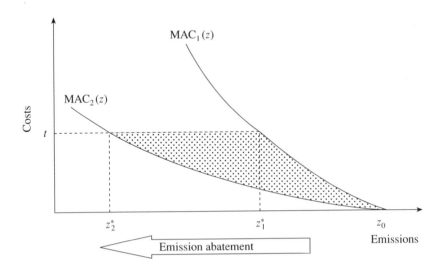

Notes:
$MAC_1(z)$ and $MAC_2(z)$ denote the firm's technology-dependent marginal abatement costs functions, and z_0 denotes the firm's pre-tax emission level. Note that with the new technology, θ_2, the firm's optimal emission level drops from z_1^* to z_2^*.

Figure 18.2   *The firm's optimal emissions levels, z_1^* and z_2^*, for technologies θ_1 and θ_2 under an emission tax, t*

Since the cost savings are being realized over time, we need to compare the net present value of cost savings of the two technology alternatives. This also involves taking the total investment costs into consideration. Denote the cost savings as a consequence of reduced tax payments (benefits) ΔB_τ and the investment costs I. Moreover, let T denote the lifetime of the new investment, r the interest rate and let τ be the time index, $\tau = \{1, 2, ..., T\}$. The net present value[11] of the investment decision then becomes:

$$NPV = \sum_{\tau=1}^{T} \left(\frac{1}{1+r}\right)^{\tau} \Delta B_\tau - I \tag{18.3}$$

If the net present value in (18.3) is positive, the investment in the new abatement technology is profitable for the firm. Suppose that the emission tax rate is increased from t^a to t^b. To see the effects of this increase, consider Figure 18.3. The optimal emission level decreases from $z_{1,2}^a$ to $z_{1,2}^b$, respectively, for the two technology alternatives. With the higher emission tax rate the cost savings from the new technology increase, as illustrated by the light-shaded area in Figure 18.3.

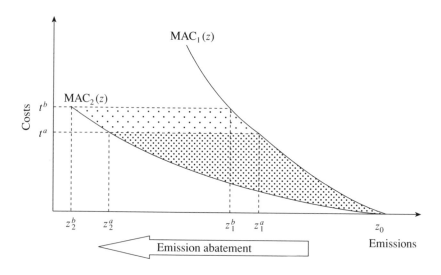

Figure 18.3 *The effect on the firm's optimal emissions level from an increase in the emission tax rate from* t^a *to* t^b

3. EROSION AND STABILITY OF ENVIRONMENTAL TAXES

From the preceding two sections it follows that a properly designed environmental tax produces incentives for firms to reduce their emissions by examining their current wasteful operations, or by installing abatement equipment or changing inputs, or by reducing their output, or by investing in new technologies (see Figure 18.2).[12] This means that environmental taxes tend to reduce emissions over time, which undermines a revenue-neutral green tax swap. The decline in revenues implies that if the condition of revenue neutrality is to be retained, erosion effects of the green taxes have to be compensated by revenues from other taxes or by an increase of the tax rate of the green taxes. The latter will, however, further contribute to erosion of the tax revenues generated by the green tax. It may also violate the marginality conditions. Moreover, frequent changes in tax rates and frequent introduction of new taxes creates inconsistencies in the overall tax base.

In many industrialized countries tax reforms are under consideration in which green tax swaps play an important role. An important incentive for the tax reforms is to reduce labour taxes because of the widespread theoretical and empirical evidence that labour taxes have induced firms to substitute capital for labour or to (re)locate their operations to countries with relatively low labour taxes (capital flight). These developments in their turn have contributed to increased unemployment and erosion of the labour taxes which in their turn necessitated an increase of the tax rate, and consequently, more lay-offs, further increases in unemployment, more tax erosion, and so on. It is astonishing that given the well-documented and widespread knowledge of erosion of labour taxes so little attention has been paid to erosion of environmental taxes. This is the more surprising since it is well known that the ultimate goal of environmental taxes is to reduce emissions!

Environmental taxes are subject to another type of inconsistency that relates to the information problems inherent in the implementation of an optimal Pigouvian tax. As described above and in Chapter 6, both the marginal benefits and marginal costs of abatement need to be known in order to determine the optimal tax rate. Moreover, information with respect to non-convexities is required and the future optimal level of production needs to be estimated (see also Chapter 1). If these information requirements are not fulfilled and the regulator wants to adhere to the use of environmental taxes, a standards and charges procedure can be adopted. In such a framework the regulator formulates a predetermined set of environmental standards that is to be achieved by means of pollution charges.[13]

The standards and charges approach is not free from information problems either. In order to fix the charges at the right level the price elasticity needs to be known. This, however, is seldom the case in practice. To solve this information problem one could resort to an iterative 'trial and error' procedure where the pollution charge is determined in a number of rounds. Initially, the charge is determined on the basis of existing knowledge or a 'guesstimate'. Next, the environmental effect is determined. In the case of discrepancy between the actual effect and the predetermined standard, the charge is adjusted. In the second round the environmental effect is estimated and, if necessary, adjustment takes place again, and so on.

This iterative procedure leads to inconsistencies in the tax base. Such inconsistencies are strongly opposed by the business community. Moreover, they are undesirable from a public finance point of view because of the variation in tax revenues they create. For these reasons the number of adjustments is limited. This in its turn is undesirable from the viewpoint of environmental policy because one may be stuck with charges fixed at incorrect levels. In other words, there is a trade-off between environmental and tax objectives.

The following observations apply. First, in addition to the above-mentioned points, tax rate adjustments may be necessitated by general economic developments, such as economic growth leading to an increase of emissions. Second, from Keynesian macroeconomic theory[14] we know that governments should run surplus budgets in periods of economic expansion and deficit budgets in periods when the economy is slowing down. In such a perspective, the *short run* public budget problems associated with the stability effects of the introduction of environmental taxes would be smaller when the general economy is expanding.[15] Moreover, the opposition of the business community might be smaller if the introduction of environmental taxes or changes in the tax rates took place during an economic upswing. The reason is that in such a period the willingness to pay for environmental quality is likely to be relatively high and the funds for investment in clean technology relatively large.

4. INDIRECT ENVIRONMENTAL TAXES

According to the standard models of environmental taxation and regulation economics, an emission tax should directly relate to the emissions the tax is targeted at. This requires monitoring of the emissions which may be technically difficult or costly, as in the case of nutrient run-offs from individual farms into waterways. In the case of monitoring problems direct emissions taxes could be replaced by taxes that indirectly affect emissions. Examples are taxes on inputs or products. More details on indirect environmental taxes are discussed in the following subsections (see also Chapter 6).

4.1 Taxes on Inputs

Taxes on inputs are appropriate substitutes for direct taxes when there is a clear linkage between input use and pollution. Such taxes alleviate the need for costly monitoring of emissions. Rather the emissions per unit of input are determined and regulation of input is used to control the emissions. Taxes on polluting inputs generate incentives to reduce input use rather than emissions. How serious this is depends on:

(a) how strong the linkage between input use and pollution is, and
(b) what kind of incentives the input tax provides in terms of reducing the targeted emissions rather than input use.

Car emissions have already been mentioned as one example where the input is taxed rather than emissions. Other examples include:

- fertilizer taxes to reduce nutrient run-offs from agricultural fields where some of the nutrients leach into waterways or groundwater
- oil and kerosene taxes to reduce emissions from energy use and heating of private houses.

4.1.1   Non-point source pollution from agriculture[16]

Nutrient run-off from agriculture is an example of what is often referred to as 'non-point source pollution'. This kind of pollution involves severe information problems, as it is difficult to monitor each individual farmer's contribution to the aggregate (see Braden and Segerson, 1993). The technical difficulties – or high costs – of tracing pollution to the point of origin seriously hamper the implementation of a direct emissions tax. In such settings the regulator could resort to some other tax with similar environmental effects at lower administrative costs, such as a fertilizer tax.

Taxing the use of fertilizers leads to a reduction in fertilizer use and a more efficient utilization of animal manure through substitution or changes in agronomic practices. More specifically, a tax on nitrogen fertilizers increases the implicit value (shadow price) of animal manure, which means that it pays the farmer to utilize the manure more efficiently. Improved manure storage (with reduced losses of nutrients), reduced time between manure spreading and incorporation of the manure into the soil (with reduced ammonia losses to the atmosphere) are examples of practices that may become profitable for the farmer due to a fertilizer tax. These changes in agricultural practices in their turn would reduce nutrient run-offs (see Vatn et al., 1997, for details). Moreover, there are direct environmental effects related to reduced fertilizer use.

The environmental performance of fertilizer taxes has been found to be mixed. A recent study by Vatn et al. (1997) concluded that to reach the necessary reductions in nitrogen leaching, nitrogen taxes needed to be substantially increased. However, such high taxes would have undesirable distributional consequences. The tax would penalize grain farmers – with generally lower nutrient leaching – more than intensive livestock units generating higher nutrient leaching. At such high nitrogen tax rates this policy was found to be not the least costly policy option. For example, combining a nitrogen tax with a catch crop requirement would yield the desired reductions in nitrogen leaching at less cost in private as well as societal terms in some regions. This combination of policies would also provide substantial reductions in the variability of nutrient leaching between years (Vatn et al., 1997).

In agriculture one is far from a one-to-one relationship between input use and emissions. Other factors such as tillage, crop rotation and other agronomic practices and their interlinkages are of importance. For example, a fertilizer tax may increase the use of nitrogen-fixing plants (legumes, clover in meadows, and so on) that could increase rather than reduce nutrient run-offs. The reason for this is that these plants release nitrogen into the soil. With large amounts of such plants the concentration of soluble nitrogen in the soil increases, thereby increasing the risk of nitrogen leaching under certain conditions. Another side-effect of changes in relative profitability between crops pertains to tillage. For example, certain types of grain respond well to lower fertilization levels, but are difficult to combine with reduced or spring tillage. This increases the share of the land that is tilled in the autumn, which implies that the risk of erosion goes up. Although this would not lead to increased nitrogen leaching, phosphorus losses may increase, which adversely affects water quality, particularly in shallow lakes and slow-moving waterways. The reason erosion leads to increased losses of phosphorus is that phosphorus binds to soil particles.

Detailed and integrated studies like Vatn et al. (1997), that are targeted at specific farming systems are needed to be able to predict the direct and indirect effects of input-based regulations in agriculture. To conclude, non-point source pollution in agriculture is a complex area. In general, there is no easy and quick fix to these problems.

4.1.2 Fuel taxes

Fuel taxes have been applied in a wide variety of circumstances. We shall restrict ourselves to taxes on heating oil, motor fuel taxes and taxes on heavy fuel oils for industry.

When it comes to the heating of houses, high taxes on heating oil not only provide incentives to reduce the use of energy by, for example, improved insulation, but also incentives to switch to other heating materials, such as firewood. This switch need not necessarily have positive impacts. For example, improper use of firewood produces large amounts of carbon monoxide, which oxidizes to CO_2, and other gases where the polluting effects and implications for human health are not yet properly understood.

The rationale behind motor fuel taxes is to make private car use more expensive, thereby inducing people to reduce their automobile use.[17] Figure 18.4 shows that for most OECD countries, the share of the price of unleaded gasoline that is environmentally motivated is more than 60 per cent. Notable exceptions are the USA, Canada and Japan. The last has a much higher pre-tax price than the other OECD countries. Similar taxes exist for other automotive fuels, such as diesel.

In terms of environmental impacts of these taxes, the crucial question is: what have the effects been on fuel consumption and emissions from the transport sector? It is not straightforward to capture these effects. For example, time series data on fuel consumption cannot be used as an indicator without correcting for other factors (economic growth, changes in land use patterns, and so on) that also affect fuel consumption. In order to estimate the tax effects, the other variables that impact on fuel consumption have to be controlled for. In this connection, the Swedish Green Tax Commission pursued several modelling

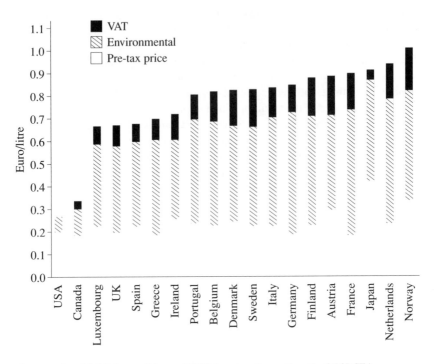

Source: Swedish Ministry of Finance (1997), based on figures from the OECD/IEA

*Figure 18.4   Pre-tax prices, value-added taxes and environmentally motivated
            taxes on gasoline in 1995*

strategies (various pooled sector models as well as computable general
equilibrium models). The results from these analyses all indicated a 1–2 per cent
decline in gasoline consumption in the short run and a 3–5 per cent decline in
the long run from a doubling of a tax on gasoline related to CO_2 emissions in
Sweden. The primary reason that the short-run estimates are lower than the
long-run estimates is that the number of consumers who trade in their cars as
a result of such taxes grows over time. Few consumers will trade in their cars
immediately after the introduction of the tax. In the long run, however,
consumers will consider the current CO_2 tax and their expectations regarding
future CO_2 taxes when deciding when to buy a new car and what kind.

   As mentioned above, for an input tax there needs to be a clear linkage between
input use and pollution. For a gasoline tax this feature holds with respect to
carbon dioxide emissions. The less gasoline used, the lower these emissions. The
linkage is not equally clear for emissions of nitrogen oxide, where the combustion
process is more important than the amount of fuel used. Due to catalytic

converters, new cars have more efficient combustion than older cars when it comes to nitrogen oxide. In order to reduce these emissions the automotive tax on old cars or cars with poor performance could be increased. This will not be a tax on the margin, but it will lead to faster replacement of old cars.

Other environmentally motivated taxes exist in the transport sector. One such tax is an entry toll into large cities and metropolitan areas. Such a tax increases the cost of using automobiles and makes public transportation less expensive in relative terms. The environmental benefits from such taxes are primarily linked to reduced car emissions and congestion, particularly during rush hours.

The energy sector is another area where indirect taxes have been used. However, as illustrated in Figure 18.5, the environmentally based tax component is not as high as in the case of gasoline and heating oils for households.

One explanation for the lower tax share in fuel oil prices for industry than in gasoline and heating oil prices is concern about competitiveness and (re)location behaviour of firms.[18] We shall return to this issue in section 5.

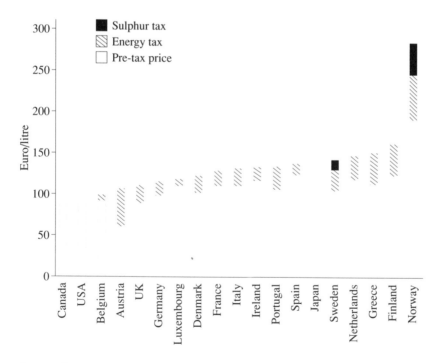

Source: Swedish Ministry of Finance (1997), based on figures from the OECD/IEA

Figure 18.5   Pre-tax prices, energy taxes and sulphur taxes on heavy fuel oils for industry in 1995

Two countries – Sweden and Norway – have a specific sulphur dioxide tax. The rationale of such a tax is to induce firms to switch to lighter oil qualities containing less sulphur. It should also be noted that Norway's total price (including taxes) far exceeds the price in the other countries. With most of Norway's exporting and energy-demanding heavy industries (aluminium and other metals) running on cheap hydroelectric power, the adverse effects of high taxes on heavy fuel oils on the competitiveness of these industries are likely to be minor.

4.2   Taxes on Polluting Products and Resource Use

Suppose that consumption of a given product creates pollution. By issuing a tax on the product, the price of the product increases and will have a depressing effect on consumption and hence on pollution, *ceteris paribus*.

The tax could also be imposed on the producer rather than on the consumer. For instance, the producer may be charged for packaging waste (see Chapter 22 for details). Such a tax comes down to an increase in the marginal costs of production. This is illustrated in Figure 18.6 by a counter-clockwise shift in the firm's marginal production cost curve from MC_0 to MC_1.

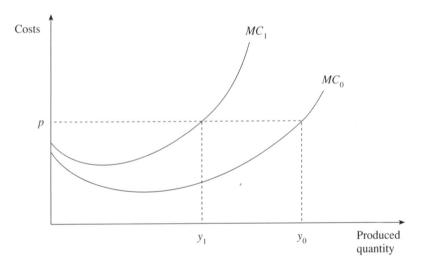

Note: y_0 and y_1 – without and with a tax on the production process, respectively. p denotes the market price of the product

Figure 18.6   *The effects of increasing marginal production costs on a firm's market supply of a product,* y

In the short run, the firm will reduce its supplied quantity from y_0 to y_1. In the longer run, the firm has more options. One alternative is to change the product so that the pollution caused by the product is reduced. An example of this is that some car manufacturers have increased the share of parts of cars that are recyclable, partly by changing the use of materials, and partly by the way materials are combined in various components of the car (see Chapter 10 for further details).

From the firm's perspective, the primary benefit from changing the product is that it reduces environmental tax payments, that is, it leads to a smaller tax-induced movement of the marginal cost curve to produce y. Changing the product is not without costs for the firm, however, as it may require additional investments or may increase other production cost components. What the firm decides to do depends on which of the two alternatives – continuing with the old and more polluting product, or investing in a less polluting substitute – yields the highest discounted expected profits for the firm for the presumed lifetimes of the production technologies. Finally, note that taxes on polluting products levied on the producer may result in higher market prices for the commodities, thereby shifting (some of) the costs to consumers.

Taxes on resource use are similar to those on products. The objective of such taxes is to reduce the use of the resource concerned. An example is the Dutch groundwater tax that was introduced in 1995 (Vermeend and van der Vaart, 1998). This tax operates with different tax rates depending upon the purpose of the use, with households being charged the highest rates and industry the lowest per cubic metre of groundwater used. The official justification for this difference is that industry is undertaking costly water-saving measures to reduce its use of groundwater. From a theoretical perspective this argument appears strange, however. After all, the objective of a tax on resource extraction or use is that it induces households and industry to undertake investments that reduce usage so as to meet certain policy objectives. If a tax succeeds in achieving this objective, there is no reason to lower it.

We observe that the tendency in many industrialized countries to shift from fixed fees to user charges is desirable from the perspective of environmental and resource management. The reason is that the user charge forces the user to trade off the benefits of an additional unit used versus the charge. The analysis of the impacts of a user charge is similar to the analysis of a direct emission tax, as outlined in section 2.

5.   COMPETITIVENESS AND CAPITAL FLIGHT[19]

The impacts of environmental taxes (and other instruments) on competitiveness are anything but univocal. The business community usually claims that such taxes may lead to substantial cost hikes for the targeted firms and, consequently, to a loss of market shares. Environmental policy is also claimed to induce capital flight to countries with lax regulations. Loss of competitiveness and capital flight in their turn will have serious economic impacts including loss of employment and of private and public incomes. On the other hand, there is the Porter hypothesis, which states that 'Strict environmental regulations do not inevitably hinder competitive advantage against foreign rivals; indeed, they often enhance it' (Porter, 1991, p. 96). According to the Porter hypothesis, domestic environmental policy does not lead to a loss of competitiveness; rather it enhances it.

In this section we shall first address the Porter hypothesis and next environmental capital flight. The two are logically related as environmental capital flight is the ultimate response to (the fear of) loss of competitiveness.

5.1   The Porter Hypothesis

The Porter hypothesis implies that properly designed environmental policies can trigger innovation and production efficiency gains that may lead to an absolute advantage over non-regulated firms. The hypothesis is controversial and has been extensively debated in the economics and management literature (see for example Palmer et. al., 1995, and Porter and van der Linde, 1995). In this section we present a brief review of the literature on the Porter hypothesis.

Porter and van der Linde (1995) formulated the following conditions for the Porter hypothesis to hold:

> If environmental standards are to foster the innovation offsets that arise from new technologies and approaches to production, they should also adhere to three principles. First, they must create the maximum opportunity for innovation. Second, regulations should foster continuous improvements, rather than locking in any particular technology. Third, the regulatory process should leave as little room as possible for uncertainty at every stage. (p. 110)

Gabel and Sinclair-Desgagné (1998), on which this section is based, distinguished three different ways in which the Porter hypothesis might show itself (See also Gabel and Sinclair-Desgagné, 2000):

1. Enhanced competitiveness of producers of complementary products and services. This type of competitiveness is caused by environmental-policy-induced demand. For instance, taxes on leaded gasoline have stimulated the development of catalytic converters which could stimulate exports and international competitiveness, if other countries were to adopt the same technology later. [20]
2. Relatively enhanced competitiveness of the regulated firms. The rationale is that strict domestic regulations will raise the costs of domestic firms

subject to them, but they will raise the costs of foreign competitors subject to the regulations by even more. In particular, domestic firms may develop a first mover advantage (see Chapter 12 for details).

The following observations apply. First, this variant does not lead to a win–win situation, as is usually claimed to be typical for the Porter hypothesis. The reason is that the costs burden on the entire private sector rises even though some firms (and possibly countries) benefit at others' expense. Second, for the first-mover advantage to work it is necessary that analogous regulations be adopted in other countries. If this were not the case, then the first mover might be left at a competitive disadvantage.

3. Absolute cost reduction for the regulated firm. The rationale in this case is that strict regulation will prompt the firm to find so much 'low-hanging fruit' that it will reduce its private costs at the same time as it will improve its environmental performance.[21] This would clearly be a typical win–win situation. This variant of the Porter hypothesis is the most controversial because it implies that firms should adopt environmental policies voluntarily and unilaterally since it is in their narrow interest to do so. In fact, one would expect firms to be ahead of the regulator!

We now turn to the reason why firms usually are not ahead of the regulator. A prerequisite for the third variant of the Porter hypothesis to hold is the existence of 'organizational failure' within the firm so that it is not producing efficiently, *ex ante*. In other words, it is operating inside the production possibility area rather than on its frontier (see Figure 18.1). The reason that the firm would not be on the production frontier is a consequence of its organizational structure and operational procedures. With respect to the former, it is well known that there exist discrepancies between the objectives of management, shareholders and employees that could contribute to organizational failure in several ways. For instance, because of expected losses of jobs in certain sectors, employees could oppose changes in the production process proposed by management. Limited interest of management in the direct production process could also contribute to organizational failure. In particular, management is likely to be unaware of all opportunities for cost-saving. Operational procedures relate to information exchange between management and employees and control of task performance of employees, in particular with respect to production. It is well known that information exchange and control of task performance may be subject to several kinds of imperfections.

It should be observed that initially a firm may be at the cost frontier but with the passage of time it will become less efficient because relative prices, technology, regulatory and environmental conditions and the firm's competitive situation change. If the organizational structure and operational procedures could be changed frequently, marginally and at negligible costs, there would be no organizational failure. However, in the short and medium run they are essentially fixed because the (perceived) benefits of reorganization do not outweigh their costs. Under these circumstances the introduction of environmental policy including environmental taxes may act as an exogenous shock that changes the benefit/cost ratio of a reorganization of the firm's structure and operational procedures.

Under what circumstances would this third variant of the Porter hypothesis show up? First, in a rigid organization with inflexible procedures the 'low-hanging fruit' is likely to be less scarce than in a small and flexible organization. Consequently, the amount of low-hanging fruit could be hypothesized to vary with age and size of the firm. Second, the exogenous shock of environmental policy needs to be sufficiently strong to change the cost/benefit ratio of reorganization. If the environmental-policy-induced costs are only minor, they will be easily absorbed by organizational failures.

So far there exists little empirical support for the three variants of the Porter hypothesis. In particular, systematic evidence is lacking. With respect to the first variant, Porter (1991) gives several examples such as German exports of air emission abatement to the USA and US exports of relatively benign pesticides, an area in which the USA seems to be ahead of many other countries. However, Oates et al. (1994) questioned the accuracy of these examples. Support for the second variant can be found in Gabel (1995), who refers to the ban on CFCs to explain DuPont and ICI's activities in the profitable CFC-replacement business. Finally, there is some anecdotal evidence for the third variant. Best known is probably the 3M company that between 1975 and 1990 eliminated 500 000 tons of waste and pollutants and saved US$482 million in doing so and another US$650 million by energy conservation in the framework of its 'pollution prevention pays' programme.

There is also counterfactual evidence. For instance, Brännlund et al. (1996) estimated the effects of environmental policy on firms' profits in the Swedish pulp and paper industry using non-parametric methods. They found that as environmental regulations became more stringent, firms' profits declined. Their finding contradicts the Porter hypothesis. Moreover, Jaffe et al. (1995) found that there is little evidence that at its current level US environmental policy has increased the competitiveness of the regulated industries.

To sum up, so far there exists little support for the three variants of the Porter hypothesis. Further empirical research in this area therefore seems to be desirable.

5.2 Environmental Capital Flight[22]

In the literature on environmental capital flight a distinction is usually made between macro and micro approaches. We shall consider the former in section

5.2.1 and the latter in section 5.2.2. Before proceeding we observe that environmental capital flight may lead to a loss–loss situation for a given region.[23] This would be the case if environmental capital flight not only led to loss of employment and income in a given region but also to an increase of pollution. The latter would occur if the relocated firms via transboundary pollution increased environmental degradation in the region they left.[24] Because of its serious economic impacts, environmental capital flight has played an important role in recent policy debates, for instance, in The Netherlands and Denmark in the context of the introduction of an energy tax. It was also a major argument launched by opponents to an EU carbon energy tax.[25]

5.2.1 Macro approaches[26]

The macro approach relates to international trade and international capital movements.[27] Moreover, there are models that combine international trade and capital mobility.

Theoretical trade models usually start from the Heckscher–Ohlin model that analyses international trade in terms of differences in factor endowments, that is, land, capital and labour. Countries with relative abundance of a given factor have a comparative cost advantage in that respect. For fixed resources trade serves to reallocate production so that the marginal costs of production are equalized among countries.[28]

The basic model of international capital mobility is the MacDougall–Kemp model (MacDougall, 1960; Kemp, 1964). According to this model, in the absence of trade, capital relocates internationally on the basis of marginal returns. Consequently, factor prices converge over countries. From these standard models of international trade and capital movement it follows that international trade and factor movements are substitutes.[29]

The simplest possible theoretical models of international capital movement that include environmental and resource endowments and environmental policy ignore environmental externalities in production and consumption as well as transboundary pollution. In these models the basic result is that a country repels mobile capital by imposing restrictive environmental policy. However, in more realistic models with external environmental effects in production and consumption and transboundary pollution results become ambiguous. Then, no clear-cut relationship between the strictness of environmental policy and capital movement can be found: the effects on international capital mobility can be positive, negative or zero depending on the parameter configuration. (For further details see Rauscher, 1997.)

Similar results hold for trade models.[30] If environmental and resource endowments are taken into account, relative price differentials among countries are not only dependent on the relative scarcity of the conventional factors but also on the marginal tendency to pollute, the marginal social damage of pollution and the demand for and supply of environmental commodities. This implies that for countries with identical production, pollution and abatement functions, the country with the largest assimilative capacity will specialize in the production of the polluting commodity (Siebert, 1974). By means of a simple Heckscher–Ohlin model McGuire (1982) showed that unilateral environmental policy would lead to a loss of competitiveness. Moreover, factors will exit the regulated industry. However, in more realistic models with different technologies, transboundary pollution or external environmental effects on production and consumption, the impacts of stricter environmental policy on trade flows are ambiguous and dependent on specific parameter constellations (Rauscher, 1997).

Theoretical models that simultaneously consider international trade and capital mobility basically come to the same conclusions as the above-mentioned studies: the policy effects can be positive, zero or negative depending on the specific parameter configuration.

The empirical macro literature on environmental capital flight also gives mixed results.[31] Murell and Ryterman (1991) estimated a Heckscher-Ohlin model for 46 market and 9 centrally planned economies. They found that the difference in stringency of environmental policy between the two groups of countries had no impact on international trade. Tobey (1990) also obtained an insignificant effect on international trade for the 24 most polluting industries in the USA in 1975. Van Beers and van den Bergh (1997) analysed bilateral trade flows. For Tobey's 1975 data set they obtained similar results except for a significant and positive relationship between environmental policy and exports. For 1992 data, however, they found a significant negative impact of environmental policy on trade, in particular for industries that are highly mobile. (For an overview of the methodological flaws of these studies see below.)

Empirical research with respect to capital movement does not give much support for environmental capital flight either. Rather, the results are mixed. Walter (1982) and Leonard (1988) rejected the hypothesis. Hettige et al. (1992) and Lucas et al. (1992) examined whether environmental regulation in the OECD countries had displaced toxic industrial production to less developed countries with lax environmental policy. They found some support for the environmental capital flight hypothesis. Birdsall and Wheeler (1992) reached a similar conclusion. In a study relating to the USA Rowland and Freilock (1991) also found support. The relationship, however, turned out to be non-linear: capital tends to relocate, if a state's environmental policy exceeds a given threshold.

The conclusions that emerge from the macro literature are that highly simplified theoretical models of international trade and capital movement support trade effects and large-scale international capital movement. However, when these models are made more realistic, the unambiguous conclusions disappear. If, for instance, externalities on production or consumption are included, or other differences among countries than environmental policy are considered, then environmental policy does not necessarily lead to negative trade effects or capital movement. The empirical studies are also mixed in their conclusions. The majority of the studies find an insignificant relationship between environmental policy and capital flight. Some studies even find a significant, positive relationship; others a significant negative relationship.

The empirical studies suffer from many methodological problems that hamper their comparability. First of all there is scarcity of data. Second, different types of, and often inadequate, definitions of environmental policy are used throughout the literature. An adequate definition should directly relate to the private costs for the regulated industry, that is, taxes paid, additional number of people employed in the firms on the basis of the regulations, and so on. Many studies, however, use measures that (at best) indirectly relate to the regulated industries' costs, for example, a dummy whether an environmental tax is in force or not in a region, or the number of state employees involved in monitoring an environmental regulation. Third, many studies suffer from spec-ification errors or differ in terms of underlying theoretical models. For instance, many studies are characterized by missing variables or inappropriate proxies or by inadequate time lags between the introduction of environmental policy and its possible effects (see also section 5.2.2 below). The models often also differ in terms of explanatory variables or types of environmental effects included. For instance, as mentioned above, the simplest theoretical models ignore external-ities on production or consumption whereas others do not. Consequently, the results obtained differ. Similar results would emerge for empirical models based on different theoretical models. Another specification aspect is that the level of aggregation varies considerably. As is well known, aggregation might blur significant effects in certain sectors. Finally, some of the studies relate to years when environmental policy was still in its infancy and others to years in which the costs of environmental policy were much larger.

This brings us to the more general conclusion that the costs of environmen-tal policy need to exceed some threshold to have an impact on capital movement and trade. In other words, with a continued increase in the strictness of envi-ronmental policy in the future, impacts on trade and capital movement will increase.

5.2.2   Micro and regional approaches[32]
In this section we shall pay attention to the micro and regional approaches to environmental capital flight.[33] In the former the unit of analysis is the individual firm; in the latter the region. Both types of analysis are closely related, however. The basic question in the micro approach is to what regions firms tend to (re)locate; in the regional approach which regions tend to attract firms.

Environmental capital flight is usually associated with relocation of firms from a region with strict regulations to regions with more lax environmental regulations. However, environmental capital flight may also show up in several other forms. First, there is termination of production or exit of the industry. Another form is related to firm birth: new firm start-ups may be deterred in regions with stringent environmental policies. Finally, it may take the form of partial shifting production from one region to another, without complete termination in the former.

A basic theoretical micro model is Markusen et al. (1993). They considered a two-region two-firm situation. In the model, location and market structure are endogenous. They showed that an increase in the stringency of environmental policy in one region might induce firms to relocate to the other region in spite of a loss of competitiveness due to a change in the market structure in the region of out-migration. Motta and Thisse (1993) showed that substantial fixed sunk costs have a mitigating effect on environmental capital flight. Folmer and Howe (1991) argued that environmental policy is only one out of a set of location factors including the quality of the labour market, the wage rate, geographical location, state of the business cycle, cultural environment, relationships to local authorities, and so on. Moreover, in the case of relocation, relocation costs have to be taken into account. Relocation is rational only if the difference between discounted costs associated with compliance with environmental policy at the present and an alternative location minus relocation costs outweighs the discounted sum of the differences in costs and benefits of all other location factors at both locations. Similar observations apply to the other forms of environmental capital flight, though relocation costs are not or are less relevant in these cases.

In addition to location factors, location arbitrage has to be taken into account. If firms move their polluting activities to other regions, pollution in these regions of in-migration will go up. This will induce the regulator to increase the stringency of its environmental policy. On the other hand, pollution in the regions of out-migration will go down, *ceteris paribus*. This will be an incentive for the regulators in these regions to relax or not to increase environmental policy. Expectations of such a scenario will have a mitigating effect on environmental capital flight.

Environmental policy accounts on average for only 2–3 per cent of total production costs in most industrialized countries. This contrasts sharply with labour and capital costs that are usually a multiple of the costs induced by environmental policy. Hence there is support for the hypothesis that at the present level of intensity of environmental policy environmental capital flight is not likely to be a large-scale phenomenon. It should be observed, however, that the costs associated with environmental policy and therefore the likelihood of environmental capital flight may vary widely across sectors.

The above-mentioned hypothesis is supported by several empirical studies. Stafford (1985, 1991), using surveys among large US corporations, found that traditional variables such as the quality of the labour market and transport costs were the decisive variables affecting location behaviour and that environmental policy did not play a significant role. On the basis of a sample of all new establishments in the USA in 1987 Levinson (1992), found that the costs of environmental policy per worker did not have an impact on location behaviour. However, he did find a significant effect for the most polluting industries (plastics, chemicals and electronics). In a sample of 49 steel plants Deily and Gray (1991) found that firms that faced more stringent environmental policy are more likely to close down than firms that face less stringent regulations. Henderson (1996) found that firms tend to move from more to less regulated counties in the USA. On the other hand, McConnell and Schwab (1990) found that US automobile firms were not deterred from locating in regions with stringent environmental policy. Rather, the opposite seemed to hold: firms were deterred from locating in regions with poor environmental quality. One possible explanation for this finding is that environmental quality is seen as a positive location factor with positive impacts on, for example, health. Another reason is that poor environmental quality is expected to lead to an increase in stringency of environmental policy (see above).

The empirical micro and regional studies are characterized by methodological problems similar to those observed in the preceding section, that is, inappropriate measures of stringency, missing explanatory variables, inappropriate aggregation and misspecification, in particular of time lags between the introduction of environmental policy and possible responses. The latter type of misspecification may lead to spurious correlation and wrong conclusions. This can be seen as follows. From the foregoing it follows that the causal chain between environmental policy and location behaviour is: increase of the number of polluting firms at time t followed by an increase of pollution at a later stage, say $t + k$. This in its turn will lead to an increase of the stringency of environmental policy in due time, say $t + k + l$, which, at a later stage, say $t + k + l + m$, may deter firm location behaviour ($k, l, m > 0$). If the time lags in the causal chain are not taken into account and, for example, firm birth at s is regressed on environmental policy at s, a positive correlation between environmental policy and, for example, firm birth will be found!

The upshot of this section is similar to the main conclusion of the previous section: at the present level of stringency of environmental policy in most industrialized countries there is not much support for large-scale environmental capital flight. However, in certain industries where the policy-induced costs exceed a given threshold, capital flight may not be ruled out. Moreover, international capital flight seems to be less likely than domestic, since domestically many location factors, such as cultural differences, are constant. Finally, possible positive impacts of environmental policy on location behaviour should not be ignored.

6.   THE DOUBLE DIVIDEND

The basic idea behind the double dividend is that environmental taxes generate revenues that can give room for reducing other distortionary taxes (labour taxes, capital taxes and so on). The first dividend is the environmental benefit from introducing environmental taxes. The second dividend is the benefit that emerges from reducing other distortionary taxes that only are there to generate the revenues needed to cover the government's expenses for purposes such as education, health care, defence, and so on.

From a policy perspective, the existence of a double dividend could make life much easier for policy-makers as it implies that environmental improvements come at low costs to society. More specifically, assume that the social environmental benefit from an environmental tax is non-negative. If there is a positive second dividend, this then ensures that the net social benefit from introducing the tax is positive.

The double dividend comes in two different forms (Goulder, 1994, p. 4):

(1) *Weak double dividend*: By using revenues from the environmental tax to finance reductions in marginal rates of a distortionary tax, one achieves cost savings relative to the case where the tax revenues are returned to tax-payers in a lump-sum fashion.
(2) *Strong double dividend*: The revenue-neutral substitution of the environmental tax for *a typical or representative distortionary tax involves* a zero or negative gross cost.

The weak double dividend has a sound theoretical basis and has received support in various simulation studies (for example Jorgenson and Wilcoxen, 1994, or Shah and Larsen, 1992).

The theoretical foundation of the strong dividend is weak (Bovenberg and de Mooij, 1993; Parry, 1994; Goulder, 1994). Goulder (1997) summarizes the arguments as follows:

(a) A tax on the environmentally harmful consumption good components lowers the after-tax wage and generates distortions in the labour market. These distortions are at least as great in magnitude as the labour market distortions from the labour tax. Therefore, a revenue-neutral change from labour taxation to an environmental tax cannot lead to reductions in the labour market distortions.

(b) The environmental tax changes consumer behaviour, introducing distortions in the commodity market.

In Goulder's own words:

> These two distortionary effects – in labor and commodity markets – imply that, apart from environmental considerations, the revenue-neutral combination of an environmental tax and reduction in labor tax involves a reduction in the non-environmental component of welfare. In fact, the distortions in the commodity and labor markets are connected. To the extent that the environmentally motivated commodity tax leads households to substitute other commodities for the taxed commodity, there is a reduction of the gross revenue yield of the tax. This limits the extent to which the environmental tax can finance a reduction in the labor tax, and augments the overall gross costs of the tax initiative. (Goulder, 1997, p. 34)

Still, under extremely distortionary taxes and special assumptions about the elasticity of labour supply, even the strong form of the double dividend cannot be ruled out. Generally, however, one would not expect the strong double dividend to hold.

Goulder (1997) presents an overview of 11 empirical models that deal with the welfare effects of a revenue-neutral swap of an income tax for an environmental tax. The main result is that in most cases the green tax swap involves a reduction in welfare, that is, it entails positive gross costs. Proost and van Regemorter (1996) obtained similar results. In a dynamic general equilibrium model they analysed the recycling effects of a CO_2 tax under various assumptions. The welfare effects ranged from very negative to positive, though very small.

Similar results hold for an employment dividend. In this connection a distinction should be made between an intersectoral and an intrasectoral employment effect. In the former case the revenues from environmental taxes are used to reduce labour taxes in labour-intensive sectors. The burden reduction in the latter, however, cuts across a burden increase in sectors facing high environmental taxes (the polluting sectors). The ultimate employment effect is dependent on a variety of factors, such as input–output relationships and interactions among the labour and commodity markets.

In the case of a possible intrasectoral employment dividend, the employment effects are to be realized within the sector itself via substitution of labour for resource use, for example energy. As is well known, such substitution possibilities are very limited in the short and medium run. In the long run, because of path dependency, the tax swap is likely to lead to the development of alternatives for the taxed resources within the same area or factor, such as solar energy for energy generated by fossil fuels. This will undoubtedly have employment effects, notably in research and development. It is unlikely, however, that this will have large-scale intrasectoral employment effects, for example within the energy sector.

There are some empirical studies of the employment double dividend. For instance, Brunello (1996) simulated the employment effects in 12 EU member states of a reduction of a tax on labour financed by the revenues of ECU 19 per ton carbon dioxide equivalent. The main outcome was that the employment effect was positive, though very small, whereas the environmental effect was negative in the sense that CO_2 emissions increased. Proost and van Regemorter (1996) found similar results for Belgium.

The empirical evidence of the existence of the strong double dividend is mixed and very sensitive to the underlying assumptions. For instance, Parry and Bento (1999) found in some of their general equilibrium simulations that if the tax system distorts consumption in addition to the labour market, the welfare gain from using environmental tax revenues to reduce labour taxes can be significantly higher than implied in previous studies (see for example Goulder et al., 1997 or Feldstein, 1999). However, Parry and Bento (1999) were careful to note the stringent conditions for their result to hold.

The following observations apply. First, in the presence of distortionary taxes the optimal tax rate changes. In Chapter 6 the optimal Pigouvian tax was defined as follows (rewritten to be consistent with the notation used in this chapter):

$$t = MAC(Z^*) = MED(Z^*) \tag{18.5}$$

where Z^* denotes the optimal emission level, $MAC(Z^*)$ marginal abatement costs and $MED(Z^*)$ marginal environmental damages from emissions. Goulder (1997) showed that in the presence of other tax effects in the economy, the optimal emission tax rate is given by:

$$t^e = \frac{t}{\mu} = \frac{MED(Z^*)}{\mu} \tag{18.6}$$

where μ denotes the marginal costs of public funds. If μ is greater than one, which is usually the case, the optimal emission tax rate, t^e, is lower than the tax rate implied by (18.5). Second, reduction of distortionary taxes is not dependent on environmental taxes but can also be undertaken in other settings. In many countries general tax reforms are under consideration, which lend themselves to reductions of distortionary taxes. However, in these general settings greening of taxes and double dividends play important roles. Third, absence of a double dividend, in particular lack of the strong form, does not invalidate environmental taxes as such. Usually their welfare effects in terms of improvement of environmental quality are sufficient to warrant their introduction. Finally, Goulder (1997) observed that the double dividend has received much attention in policy debates to facilitate the introduction of environmental tax to achieve environmental goals. This applies in particular to situations of controversy about the desirability of an environmental tax, such as a carbon tax. Double dividends are proclaimed to compensate the uncertainties as to the likely environmental benefits.

7. SUMMARY AND CONCLUSIONS

This chapter has dealt with green taxes. First we discussed the standard core of environmental taxation. We showed that environmental taxes form a permanent incentive to reduce emissions. This in its turn leads to erosion of the tax base that hampers a large-scale green tax swap. The stability of environmental taxes is also negatively affected by the fact that environmental taxes are often used in a charges and standards framework. The implementation of such a framework requires knowledge of price elasticities. This information is usually not available or becomes dated because of general economic developments, like economic growth. Under such conditions the charges are determined in an iterative trial and error procedure. Since this kind of instability is opposed by the business community and undesirable from a tax policy point of view, there exists a trade-off between environmental and taxation objectives. Introducing the tax or changing the tax rates in periods of economic upswing could mitigate the stability problem.

We also paid attention to environmental taxes in practice. Because of high monitoring costs direct emission taxes are frequently replaced by indirect taxes on inputs. Moreover, we paid attention to polluting products. We have argued that an important condition for the substitution of an indirect input tax for a direct emission tax is the linkage between input use and emissions. The stronger the linkage, the better the substitute.

The chapter then dealt with recent and widely discussed issues related to green taxation. Section 4 discussed competitiveness and capital flight. In this connection we first paid special attention to the Porter hypothesis which states that environmental policy often enhances rather than hinders competitiveness. We distinguished three ways in which environmental policy might enhance competitiveness. The first two forms, that is, enhanced competitiveness of producers of complementary products and services and relatively enhanced competitiveness, in particular due to a first-mover advantage, are fairly undisputed, although empirical support is still scarce. For the third form, absolute cost reduction for a regulated firm, which would lead to a win–win situation with improved environmental quality in addition to private cost reduction, we described the conditions under which it may hold. For this form there only exists anecdotal evidence so far.

Nor is there much support for the opposite of the Porter hypothesis, that is, that environmental policy leads to a substantial loss of competitiveness or large-scale environmental capital flight. However, possible differences among industries should be taken into account. For those industries for which environmental-policy-induced costs are large relative to other factor costs, such as labour and capital costs, and that exceed a critical threshold, loss of competitiveness and environmental capital flight may not be ruled out. However, empirical studies in this area suffer from data problems and methodological pitfalls that hamper firm conclusions.

The last issue considered in this chapter is the double dividend. This is an issue that arises in second-best settings. Two forms of the double dividend are usually distinguished. First, the weak form which comes down to the following: by using revenues from an environmental tax to reduce distortionary taxes instead of returning them to taxpayers in lump-sum fashion, cost-savings and welfare improvement can be achieved. Second, the strong form that states that the revenue-neutral substitution of environmental taxes for typical distortionary taxes, such as labour taxes, involves positive benefits. The weak form is hardly disputed since it follows almost directly from the definition of a distortionary tax. The strong form, on the other hand, has been criticized from a theoretical point of view. Moreover, there is very little empirical support for it. Most empirical studies show that the revenue-neutral green tax swap involves a reduction in welfare. Similar results hold for the employment double dividend. Moreover, if positive employment effects show up, they usually go together with an increase in pollution.

The main conclusion of this chapter is that environmental taxes should be evaluated on their environmental merits and not so much on the basis of their side-effects. As instruments of environmental policy they have been found to perform well, although their implementation is not straightforward. Moreover, environmental taxes are unlikely to solve environmental problems alone. Usually combination with other instruments into an environmental programme or package is required. For example, tollgates in metropolitan areas could be combined with automotive fuel taxes, increased parking fees and capacity increases for transportation alternatives (more train and bus departures). Such packages have been shown to slow down the growth of private car use. Similarly, environmental taxes have been combined with regulations as in the case of the control of infrequent, serious cases of pollution whose occurrence is unpredictable, such as smog.

ACKNOWLEDGEMENT

The authors would like to thank Landis Gabel for his valuable comments.

APPENDIX

Let a representative firm's short-term profits in a competitive market be represented by the following expression:

$$\begin{Bmatrix} \text{Max} \\ y,z,\theta \end{Bmatrix} \pi\,(y,z,\theta) = \begin{Bmatrix} \text{Max} \\ y,z,\theta \end{Bmatrix} \left(py - tz - C_\theta(y,z) \right) \qquad (18\text{A}.1)$$

where: y is the product produced;
  z is the emissions caused by the production of y;
  θ is the technology, which is a discrete variable, i.e. $\theta \in \{1,2, ..., k\}$;
  p is the market price of the product y;
  t is the per unit tax on emitting z, and
  $C_\theta(y,z)$ is the cost of production for technology θ.

Polluting without adjusting output or technology pays until

$$\frac{\partial \pi(y,z,\theta)}{\partial z}\,|\,(y = y_0) = -t - \frac{\partial C_\theta(y,z)}{\partial z} \le 0$$

$$\Downarrow \qquad\qquad (18\text{A}.2)$$

$$-\frac{\partial C_\theta(y,z)}{\partial z} \le t$$

As long as y is kept constant,

$$C_{\theta z} = \frac{\partial C_\theta(y,z)}{\partial z} \le 0 \qquad (18\text{A}.3\text{a})$$

$$C_{\theta zz} = \frac{\partial^2 C_\theta(y,z)}{\partial z^2} > 0 \qquad (18\text{A}.3\text{b})$$

(18A.3a) implies that costs can be reduced by increasing emissions, everything else constant. The rationale for this is that by, for example, using more polluting inputs or taking less care, costs are reduced. Put differently, emission reduction is costly, all other things equal.

Next we consider abatement via output reduction for the firm at its production emissions frontier. At the frontier of a given technology, there is a one-to-one relationship between emissions and production, so that it is possible to write output as a function of emissions, that is:

$$y = y_\theta(z), \quad \text{where} \quad \frac{\partial y_\theta(z)}{\partial z} > 0 \qquad (18A.4)$$

Then, the cost function $C_\theta(y, z)$ can be written as $C_\theta(y_\theta(z), z)$, which for simplicity is written as $C_\theta(z)$. The standard assumption is that the cost function is increasing in y, that is:

$$C_{\theta y} = \frac{\partial C_\theta(y, z)}{\partial y} > 0 \qquad (18A.5a)$$

$$C_{\theta yy} = \frac{\partial^2 C_\theta(y, z)}{\partial y^2} > 0 \qquad (18A.5b)$$

Note that while the emission rate still is a continuous variable (and hence differentiable), the firm's technology choice is discrete. For given technology θ the first-order condition for profit maximization is:

$$\frac{\partial \pi}{\partial z} = p\frac{\partial y_n}{\partial z} - t - \frac{\partial C_\theta}{\partial z} = 0 \qquad (18A.6)$$

which can be rearranged as

$$t = p\frac{\partial y_n}{\partial z} - \frac{\partial C_\theta}{\partial z} \qquad (18.2)$$

$$\underset{\text{revenue}}{\text{marginal}} \quad \underset{\substack{\text{abatement} \\ \text{costs}}}{\text{marginal}}$$

NOTES

1. Environmental taxes should not be confused with fines. The latter are related to violations of laws. In the case of environmental taxes there is no violation of laws; the polluter is allowed to emit. The tax is an incentive to reduce emissions.

2. In the case of ambient taxes, the tax rate is determined by the marginal damages caused by the emission. For emissions into, for example, waterways this implies that the tax rate could vary throughout the year depending upon the actual level of damage. In theory, ambient taxes or standards are interesting, but in practice they cause several problems including time inconsistency and increased transaction costs on behalf of affected agents and the regulator. Because of their limited applicability, we will not consider them any further here.
3. Similar objections are often raised in regard to other instruments of environmental policy, particularly tradable permits.
4. A review of the effects of the Swedish lead tax is found in the report of the Swedish Green Tax Commission (Swedish Ministry of Finance, 1997, pp. 25–8).
5. The Norwegian Association of Business Enterprises (NHO) has argued in favour of tradable permits with free initial allocation of permits (grandfathered tradable permits) as an alternative to environmental taxes. See Chapter 6 for a further discussion of tradable permits.
6. Voluntary agreements imply that industry, together with representatives for the regulator, comes up with a plan for emissions reduction over time. See Chapter 6 for further details.
7. In addition to the three steps distinguished here there exists a fourth option, that is, abatement at positive costs without changing output or technology. In this case one might think of using less polluting inputs or the instalment of special abatement equipment. This step would usually be intermediate between 1 and 2. It is not considered in the context of Figure 18.1.
8. For further details see Chapter 10, particularly Figure 10.2 and the discussion of the Porter hypothesis in section 4 below.
9. See also Figure 10.3.
10. The derivation of (18.2) can be found in the appendix.
11. Calculation of the net present value involves discounting. See Chapter 5 for further details on discounting.
12. See also Chapter 6.
13. This approach is satisficing rather than socially optimal (Baumol and Oates, 1988).
14. The validity of Keynesian macroeconomic policy has been questioned with the emergence of rational expectations models in modern macroeconomics. The rational expectations model predicts the failure of monetary policy to achieve an increase in demand via monetary expansion. The reason is that the increase in the price level following monetary expansion will be offset immediately by increases in money wages. The rational expectations model is not relevant here, however. The reason is that in contrast to monetary policy, in the case of environmental policy there are no possibilities for people to take (legal) actions that nullify the policy's goals. In particular, the analogue of increases in money wages does not exist here.
15. This does not imply that environmental taxation or environmental policies should be made dependent upon the state of the economy in general. Rather, it suggests that the timing of the introduction of environmental taxes or other environmental policies may have some welfare effects.
16. A recent discussion of issues linked to nutrient leaching in agriculture can be found in Romstad et al. (1997).
17. The environmental justification of the taxes is sometimes questioned. There is a popular belief that these taxes are primarily used to generate public funds and that the environmental rationale is only secondary, (at best).
18. Regarding possible migration of households income and wealth taxes are supposed to have a bigger effect than environmental taxes.
19. Competitiveness and environmental capital flight are not unique for green taxes, but apply to other instruments of environmental policy as well.
20. Chapter 12 describes how poor formulation and implementation of environmental policy may inhibit innovation.
21. The 'low-hanging fruit' is the wasteful pollution in Figure 18.1 that can be abated at negative costs. The notion of 'low-hanging fruit' or unrealized business opportunities is counterintuitive to mainstream microeconomists. However, it has been in the limelight in the management literature.
22. This section is complementary to and elaborates upon section 5 of Chapter 17.

23. Environmental capital flight may occur domestically and internationally. In the former case capital migrates from one region to another within one country; in the latter from one country to another. Below we shall only use the notion of region to refer to both regions and countries, unless stated otherwise.
24. Environmental capital flight may also lead to loss of employment and income and have positive environmental impacts. This would be the case if the in-migrating region had a larger assimilative capacity than the out-migrating region.
25. The lobbying efforts seem to have been successful, witnessing the fact that the Dutch and Danish energy taxes have been made applicable to households and small firms only. The EU carbon energy tax was also abandoned.
26. This section is based on Jeppesen et al. (1999).
27. Macro approaches mainly, though not exclusively, deal with international environmental capital flight.
28. For a recent summary of the Heckscher–Ohlin model see Krugman and Obstfeld (1997).
29. We observe that the standard models are highly simplified. For instance, they assume perfect competition and no scale economies. In the recent literature these simplifications have been abandoned so that these issues are in the limelight.
30. It should be observed that trade models are more complicated than models of international capital movement because they include at least two commodities.
31. We only discuss some typical studies here. For a more comprehensive overview see Jeppesen et al. (1999).
32. This section is based on Jeppesen and Folmer (1999).
33. It should be observed that the regional literature comprises both micro and macro studies. The vast majority of the regional studies are micro, however. Therefore, the micro and regional approaches are combined in this subsection.

REFERENCES

Baumol, W.J. and W.E. Oates (1988), *The Theory of Environmental Policy*, Cambridge: Cambridge University Press.

Birdsall, N. and D. Wheeler (1992), 'Trade policy and industrial pollution in Latin America: where are the pollution heavens?', in P. Low (ed.), *International Trade and the Environment*, World Bank Discussion Papers, Washington, DC: World Bank.

Bovenberg, A.L. and R.A. de Mooij (1993), 'Environmental levies and distortionary taxation', *American Economic Review*, **83** (4), 1085–9.

Braden, J.B. and K. Segerson (1993), 'Information problems in the design of nonpoint-source pollution policy', in C.S. Russell and J.F. Shogren (eds), *Theory, Modeling and Experience in the Management of Nonpoint-Source Pollution*, Boston, MA: Kluwer Academic Publishers, pp. 1–36.

Brännlund, R., L. Hetemäki, B. Kriström and E. Romstad (1996), 'Command and control with a gentle hand: the Nordic experience', final report from the NERP project 'Economic Instruments in Environmental Policy: The Nordic Forest Sector', Swedish University of Agricultural Sciences, Umeå, Sweden.

Brunello, G. (1996), 'Labour market institutions and the double dividend hypothesis: an application of the WARM model', in C. Carraro and S. Siniscalco (eds), *Environmental Fiscal Reform and Unemployment*, Boston, MA: Kluwer Academic Publishers.

Deily, M.E. and W.B. Gray (1991), 'Enforcement of pollution regulations in a declining industry', *Journal of Environmental Economics and Management*, **21**, 260–74.

Feldstein, M. (1999), 'Tax avoidance and the deadweight loss of the income tax', *Review of Economics and Statistics* (forthcoming).

Folmer, H. and C.W. Howe (1991), 'Environmental problems and policy in the Single European Market', *Environmental and Resource Economics*, **1** (1), 17–41.

Gabel, H.L. (1995), 'Environmental management as a competitive strategy; the case of CFCs', in H. Folmer, H.L. Gabel and H. Opschoor (eds), *Principles of Environmental and Resource Economics: A Guide for Students and Decision Makers*, Aldershot, UK and Brookfield, USA: Edward Elgar, pp. 328–46.

Gabel, H.L. and B. Sinclair-Desgagné (1998), 'The firm, its routines and the environment', in T. Tietenberg and H. Folmer (eds), *The International Yearbook of Environmental and Resource Economics 1998/1999: A Survey of Current Issues*, Cheltenham, UK and Northampton, USA: Edward Elgar.

Gabel, H.L. and B. Sinclair-Desgagné (2000), 'The Firm, its procedures, and win–win environmental regulations', in H. Folmer, H.L. Gabel, S. Gerking and A. Rose (eds), *Frontiers in Environmental Economics*, Cheltenham, UK and Northampton, USA: Edward Elgar, (forthcoming).

Goulder, L.H. (1994), 'Environmental taxation and the "double dividend": a reader's guide', paper presented at the Public Finance 50th Congress 'Public Finance, Environment, and Natural Resources', 22–25 August 1995, Cambridge, MA.

Goulder, L.H. (1997), 'Environmental taxation in a second-best world', in H. Folmer and T. Tietenberg (eds), *The International Yearbook of Environmental and Resource Economics 1997/1998: A Survey of Current Issues*, Cheltenham, UK and Lyme, USA: Edward Elgar, pp. 28–54.

Goulder, L.H., W.H.I. Parry and D. Burtraw (1997), 'Reverse ranking vs. other approaches to environmental protection: the critical significance of pre-existing tax distortions', *RAND Journal of Economics*, **28**, 708–31.

Henderson, J.V. (1996), 'Effects of air quality regulation', *American Economic Review*, **86**, 789–813.

Hettige, H., R.E.B. Lucas and D. Wheeler (1992), 'The toxic intensity of industrial production: global patterns, trends, and trade policy', *American Economic Review*, **82**, 478–81.

Jaffe, A.B., S.R. Peterson, P.R. Portney and R.N. Stavins (1995), 'Environmental regulations and the competitiveness of U.S. manufacturing: what does the evidence tell us?', *Journal of Economic Literature*, **33** (1), 132–63.

Jeppesen, T. and H. Folmer (1999), 'The confusing relationship between environmental policy and location behavior of firms: a methodological review of selected case studies', *Environment and Planning A* (forthcoming).

Jeppesen, T., H. Folmer and R. Komen (1999), 'Impacts of environmental policy on international trade and capital movement: a synopsis of the macroeconomic literature', Working Paper, Department of Economics, Odense University, Denmark.

Jorgenson, D.W. and P.J. Wilcoxen (1994), 'Reducing U.S. carbon emissions: an econometric general equilibrium assessment', in D. Gaskins and J. Weyant (eds), *The Costs of Controlling Greenhouse Gas Emissions*, Stanford, CA: Stanford University Press.

Kemp, M.C. (1964), *The Pure Theory of International Trade*, Englewood Cliffs, NJ: Prentice-Hall.

Krugman, P.R. and M. Obstfeld (1997), *International Economics. Theory and Policy*, 4th edn, New York: Addison-Wesley.

Leonard, H.J. (1988), *Pollution and the Struggle for the World Product*, Cambridge: Cambridge University Press.

Levinson, A. (1992), 'Environmental regulations and manufacturers' location choices: evidence from the census of manufacturers', mimeo, Columbia University.

Lucas, R., D. Wheeler and H. Hettige (1992), 'Economic development, environmental regulation and international migration of toxic industrial pollution: 1960–1968', in P. Low (ed.), *International Trade and the Environment*, World Bank Discussion Papers, Washington, DC: World Bank.

MacDougall, G.D.A. (1960), 'The benefits and costs of private investments from abroad', *Economic Record*, **13**, 13–35.

Markusen, J.R., E.R. Morey and N.D. Olewiler (1993), 'Environmental policy when market structure and plant locations are endogenous', *Journal of Environmental Economics and Management*, **24**, 69–86.

McConnell, V. and R. Schwab (1990), 'The impact of environmental regulation on industry location decisions: the motor vehicle industry', *Land Economics*, **66**, 67–81.

McGuire, M.C. (1982), 'Regulation, factor rewards, and international trade', *Journal of Public Economics*, **17**, 335–54.

Motta, M. and J.F. Thisse (1993), 'Does environmental dumping lead to relocation?', *Nota di Lavoro 77.93*, Fondazione Enrico Mattei, Milan.

Murell, P. and R. Ryterman (1991), 'A methodology for testing comparative economic theories: theory and application to East–West environmental policies', *Journal of Comparative Economics*, 582–601.

Oates, W., K. Palmer and P. Portney (1994), 'Environmental regulation and international competitiveness: thinking about the Porter hypothesis', mimeo, University of Maryland and Resources for the Future, Washington, DC.

OECD (1985), *Environmental Policy and Technical Change*, Paris: OECD.

Palmer, K., W.E. Oates and P.R. Portney (1995), 'Tightening environmental standards: the benefit–cost or the no-cost paradigm?', *Journal of Economic Perspectives*, **9** (4), 119–32.

Parry, I.W.H. (1994), 'Pollution taxes and revenue recycling', working paper, Economic Research Service, US Department of Agriculture, Washington.

Parry, I.W.H. and A. Bento (1999), 'Tax deductions, environmental policy, and the "double dividend" hypothesis', World Bank Working Paper Series, paper 2119, World Bank, Washington DC (downloaded from www.worldbank.org/nipr/work_paper/wps2119.htm as of 20 May 1999).

Porter, M.E. (1991), 'America's green strategy', *Scientific American*, April.

Porter, M.E. and C. van der Linde (1995), 'Toward a new conception of the environment–competitiveness relationship', *Journal of Economic Perspectives*, **9** (4), 97–118.

Proost, S. and D. van Regemorter (1996), 'The double dividend hypothesis, the environmental benefits and the international coordination of tax recycling', in C. Carraro and S. Siniscalco (eds), *Environmental Fiscal Reform and Unemployment*, Boston, MA: Kluwer Academic Publishers.

Rauscher, M. (1997), *International Trade, Factor Movements and the Environment*, Oxford: Oxford University Press.

Romstad, E., J.W. Simonsen and A. Vatn (eds) (1997), *Controlling Mineral Emissions in European Agriculture: Economics, Policies and the Environment*, Oxford: CAB International.

Rowland, C.K. and R. Freilock (1991), 'Environmental regulation and economic development: the movement of chemical production among states', in M.J. Dubnick and A.R. Gitelson (eds), *Public Policy and Economic Institutions*, Greenwich, CT: JAI Press.

Shah, A. and B. Larsen (1992), 'Carbon taxes and greenhouse effect and developing countries', World Bank Policy Research Working Paper Series no. 957, World Bank, Washington, DC.

Siebert, H. (1974), 'Environmental protection and international specialization', *Weltwirtschaftliches Archiv*, 494–508.

Stafford, H.A. (1985), 'Environmental protection and industry location', *Annals of the Association of American Geographers*, **75**, 227–40.

Stafford, H.A. (1991), 'Manufacturing plant closure selections within firms', *Annals of the Association of American Geographers*, **81**, 51–65.

Swedish Ministry of Finance (1997), 'Taxation, environment and employment, a report from the Swedish Green Tax Commission', Ministry of Finance, Stockholm, Sweden.

Tobey, J.A. (1990), 'The effects of domestic environmental policy on patterns of world trade: an empirical test', *Kyklos*, 191–209

Van Beers, C. and J.C.J.M. van den Bergh (1997), 'An empirical multi-country analysis of the impact of environmental regulations on foreign trade flows', *Kyklos*, 29–46.

Vatn, A., L.R. Bakken, P. Botterweg, H. Lundeby, E. Romstad, P.K. Rørstad and A. Vold (1997), 'Regulating nonpoint source pollution from agriculture: an integrated modeling analysis', *European Review of Agricultural Economics*, **24** (2), 207–29.

Vermeend, J. and J. van der Vaart (1998), *Greening Taxes: The Dutch Model*, Deventer: Kluwer Academic Publishers.

Walter, I. (1982), 'Environmentally induced industrial relocation to developing countries', in S.J. Rubin and T.R. Graham (eds), *Environment and Trade. The Relation of International Trade and Environmental Policy*, Allenheld and Osmund.

19. Social accounting and national welfare measures

Thomas Aronsson

1. INTRODUCTION

The questions of how to design and use the national accounts have been subject to a considerable amount of both debate and research during the last two decades. Historically, one may identify (at least) three areas of use: (1) the national accounts provide information to policy-makers, (2) they provide data for empirical research and (3) the net national product (NNP) has sometimes been used as an indicator of welfare or 'standard of living'. The first two examples of use are, perhaps, obvious to most readers. The national accounting system was founded in the 1940s to provide a basis for macroeconomic (stabilization) policy, which is in line with the ideas of Keynesian economics. In addition, as computational facilities have improved considerably during the last twenty years, the national accounts have also become an important data source for economic research.

However, the third example of use may seem surprising at first glance. Since their first course in macroeconomics, students are normally taught that the NNP is not a suitable indicator of welfare. This is so for a variety of reasons. One has to do with the 'narrow' definitions of consumption and net investments in the national accounts. The only type of consumption included in the conventional NNP refers to goods and services, and the net investment concept is limited to physical, man-made, capital. A more comprehensive consumption concept, which actually reflects consumer preferences, may not only include goods and services; it is also likely to include other 'utilities' such as leisure and environmental quality. Similarly, net investments should reflect all capital formation undertaken by society and not just changes in the stock of physical capital. This suggests that changes in other stocks of importance for production or consumption, such as natural resource stocks, environmental stocks and the stock of human capital, should also qualify as capital formation, since they are part of the 'investment policy' undertaken by society. Therefore, since the conventional NNP neither reflects consumption nor capital formation in an accurate way, it cannot be used as a welfare indicator. Another criticism of the welfare interpretation is that the NNP does not reveal how consumption possibilities are distributed across individuals, households or generations.

There is a rapidly growing literature on what is sometimes called 'social accounting', where one of the purposes is to augment, or extend, the conventional NNP measure so as to obtain a better indicator of welfare. Such a measure may be called 'a national-product-related welfare measure'. The idea of making the national accounts a better indicator of welfare has been recognized in several areas of economic research. One such example is the discussion of how to 'green' the national accounts. The basic issue here is that production depletes natural resources and causes environmental damage. Changes in these stocks of 'natural' capital are part of society's investment policy and should, therefore, be included in a correct NNP measure. Another example is the recent attempt to measure the value of the net investments in human capital and to augment the NNP with these net investments.

At the same time, even if one may know what a correct NNP measure looks like, it is important to point out the additional valuation problems arising from market imperfections. In a 'distorted' market economy, the market data on which the (extended) NNP is based do not reflect socially optimal decisions. In other words, the *observed* resource allocation does not maximize social welfare and is, therefore, insufficient as a basis for welfare analysis. As I will show below, the latter turns out to have important implications for welfare measurement in decentralized market economies.

Welfare measurement is also connected with sustainability. The basic concern here is intergenerational equity, which may involve planning over very long time horizons. It may also require that greater weight be placed on the well-being of future generations than is often the case in the utilitarian framework, where the utilities of future generations are subject to discounting. In line with the emphasis on sustainable development, one would also like to have an indicator of sustainability, preferably an easily observed static measure. Intuitively, an augmented NNP measure may seem to be such an indicator, since the NNP is often interpreted as the maximum consumption one can afford at present without reducing the capital stock. However, this idea is not correct when there are several types of capital, which means that an NNP measure does not, in general, provide a suitable indicator of sustainability.

I shall in this chapter use the term 'green' NNP to mean that the conventional NNP measure is extended to reflect the actual consumption and capital formation in society. The purpose is to address five questions, which are all related to the concept of green NNP:

1. Under what conditions can we measure welfare by observables related to the green NNP?

2. What does the appropriate welfare measure look like in an imperfect market economy with, for example, uninternalized external effects and unemployment?
3. How will policy objectives, such as distributional concern, and restrictions on the set of available policy instruments, such as the necessity to raise revenues by means of distortionary taxes, affect the national welfare measures?
4. What is the relationship between the green NNP and sustainability?
5. To what extent are global environmental problems, such as transboundary pollution, important in the context of social accounting?

The outline of the chapter is as follows. Section 2 analyses the foundation for measuring welfare by using the green NNP. This is then followed by a discussion of the social accounting problem in an imperfect market economy. In section 3, I shall address the questions of whether the complications arising in the market economy are empirically relevant, and if there is an 'easy' way of solving at least some of these additional problems. Section 4 analyses the social accounting problem from a policy perspective by studying the implications of distributional objectives and distortionary taxes. Section 5 addresses sustainability and its relationship with the green NNP. Finally, in section 6, I extend the analysis to a global economy with transboundary pollution.

2.   WHAT IS MEASURED BY THE GREEN NNP?

The welfare economic foundation of the green NNP originates from an influential paper of Martin Weitzman.[1] What Weitzman meant by NNP is not the conventional measure; it is, instead, an extension of that measure, which contains information about all relevant aspects of consumption and capital formation during a period. Naturally, the exact definition of such a measure depends on consumer preferences as well as on the production technology. Therefore, to be able to perform the welfare analysis, one needs to make assumptions about the characteristics of preferences and technology. I will formulate a 'reference' model on which most of the analysis in this chapter is based.

  To keep the analysis simple (without losing generality), I assume that the 'correct' consumption concept consists of three parts: goods, leisure and 'environmental quality'. Also for purposes of simplification, the measure of environmental quality is one-dimensional: it consists of the stock of pollution, which affects the consumers' utility negatively. At this stage of the analysis, I disregard any distriburional objectives relevant for welfare measurement. Distributional objectives are, instead, discussed in section 4. For the time being, and to avoid unnecessary notations, I assume that all consumers are identical, disregard population growth and normalize the population to equal one. Finally, I abstract from any renewable and non-renewable natural resources, since these do not add to the principal findings.[2]

Given these assumptions, the instantaneous utility of the (only) consumer at time t will be written

$$u(t) = u(c(t), L(t), x(t)) \qquad (19.1)$$

where $c(t)$ is consumption of goods, $L(t)$ leisure time and $x(t)$ the stock of pollution at time t. I impose the (conventional) assumptions that the instantaneous utility is increasing in c and L decreasing in x, and strictly concave.

The production side of the economy is characterized by a stationary technology. This assumption will be relaxed in section 3, where technological progress is introduced. Net output is produced by labour, physical capital and emissions (through the use of energy input). The net output at time t, $y(t)$, is given by[3]

$$y(t) = f(l(t), k(t), g(t)) \qquad (19.2)$$

where $l(t)$ is labour, $k(t)$ the stock of physical capital and $g(t)$ emissions at time t. The production function – or net production function[4] – is increasing in l and g as well as strictly concave. Note also that, since we are measuring net output, the depreciation of physical capital has been accounted for. The net investment concept in this economy consists of two parts; physical capital and pollution. Net investments in physical capital are measured as net output less the consumption of goods, that is,

$$\dot{k}(t) = f(l(t), k(t), g(t)) - c(t) \qquad (19.3)$$

The stock of pollution accumulates through the release of emissions. This means that the accumulation equation for the stock of pollution can be written

$$\dot{x}(t) = g(t) - \gamma x(t) \qquad (19.4)$$

where γ is the (natural) rate of depreciation of pollution. Equation (19.4) means that the net additions to the stock of pollution (which are also interpretable in terms of net investments in environmental capital) equal emissions less natural depreciation.

With this model at my disposal, I will now turn to the social accounting problem.

Welfare Measurement in the 'First-best'

The welfare foundation of the green NNP is fundamentally related to a first-best optimal resource allocation. This either means that the markets themselves allocate the resources in the best possible way for society or, in case markets fail, that economic policy can be used to achieve the same outcome as that of a perfect market economy. I will not go into technical detail about the first-best optimization problem here. The interested reader can, instead, find these details in the Appendix. The purpose is here to derive a national welfare measure in a first-best setting, and show that this measure is interpretable in terms of the green NNP.

What do we mean by economic welfare? For the time being, I have chosen to disregard distributional objectives and normalized the population to equal one. An implication is that the concepts of social welfare and individual utility coincide. In the context of a dynamic economy, this suggests that the most natural definition would be the present value of future utility facing the consumer.[5] Given the form of the instantaneous utility function in equation (19.1), the present value of future utility at time t can be written as a discounted sum (integral) of all future utilities

$$V^*(t) = \int_t^\infty u(c^*(s), L^*(s), x^*(s))e^{-\theta(s-t)}ds \tag{19.5}$$

where θ is the rate of time preference, that is, the utility discount rate. The superscript * will be used throughout this chapter as a notation for the first-best optimal resource allocation. This means that equation (19.5) measures the present value of future utility along the first-best optimal path.

Is it possible to measure future utility solely by means of an indicator, which is based on information that is available at the time the measurement is conducted? In a first-best setting, where the resources are allocated optimally from society's point of view, the answer is yes. This is the major result of Weitzman (1976). For the economy discussed here, I show in the Appendix that this welfare measure can be written as

$$\theta V^*(t) = u(c^*(t), L^*(t), x^*(t)) + \lambda^*(t)\dot{k}^*(t) + \mu^*(t)\dot{x}^*(t) \tag{19.6}$$

where $\lambda^*(t)$ and $\mu^*(t)$ are shadow prices, measured in utility terms, of physical capital and pollution, respectively, in the first-best optimum. Equation (19.6) means that the present value of future utility is proportional to something that looks very much like an NNP measure, where the factor of proportionality is given by the utility discount rate. It follows that the right-hand side of equation

(19.6) constitutes a static equivalent (or annuity equivalent) of future utility. The first term on the right-hand side can be interpreted as the 'utility consumption' at time t: it measures the utility from consuming goods, leisure and pollution at that time. The second and third terms constitute, together, the utility value of the current net investments (note that the capital concept in this example includes physical capital and pollution).

I shall refer to the right-hand side of equation (19.6) as the utility value of the green NNP at time t and use the short notation $GNNP_u^*(t)$. With this notation at my disposal, I summarize Weitzman's result as follows:

Proposition 1: *With a stationary technology, and if the economy follows the first-best optimal path, then* $GNNP_u^*$ (t) *is directly proportional to the present value of future utility.*

This is a remarkable result. It means that one can measure future utility by means of an indicator, which is based on observable variables. Note also that the welfare interpretation of a green NNP measure is not particular for the economy set out here; it would equally well apply in economies where the consumption and net investment concepts have components other than those discussed above. The only difference would be that the definition of $GNNP_u^*$ (t) will change in order to reflect the correct measures of consumption and capital formation. The welfare interpretation of the green NNP originates from the efficiency properties of a first-best resource allocation. An implication of these efficiency properties is that one cannot make society better off by reallocating the resources either between fields of use or over time. This means, among other things, that the shadow prices attached to different capital stocks measure the future social welfare consequences of today's net investments. With these properties of the first-best resource allocation, it becomes possible to prove Weitzman's result.

From a practical point of view, a possible shortcoming of the analysis so far is that the green NNP is measured in utility terms. What is the relationship between the utility value of the green NNP and the green NNP measured in real terms? To transform the green NNP into real terms, it has become conventional in the literature on social accounting to approximate the instantaneous utility by a linear function.[6] This approximation, which is illustrated in the Appendix, means that one can derive the following linearized welfare measure:

$$\theta V^*(t) \approx \lambda^*(t)[c^*(t) + \dot{k}^*(t) + w^*(t)L^*(t) + \rho^*(t)x^*(t) - \tau^*(t)\dot{x}^*(t)] \quad (19.7)$$

where the terms within the bracket, together, constitute the green NNP in real terms at time t for the model set out above, and will be denoted $GNNP_r^*(t)$. Equation (19.7) is based on the assumption that the linear approximation of the instantaneous utility function is reasonably accurate. It means that $GNNP^*_u(t)$ can be approximated by $GNNP^*_r(t)$ times the shadow price of physical capital, $\lambda^*(t)$. This shadow price is, in turn, equal to the marginal utility of consumption along an optimal path. Dividing equation (19.7) by $\lambda^*(t)$, one finds that the welfare level in real terms times the rate of time preference is approximately equal to $GNNP^*_r(t)$.

The first two terms of $GNNP^*_r(t)$ constitute, together, the conventional NNP at time t, that is, consumption of goods plus net investments in physical capital. The third term is the value of leisure time and w^* is the real wage rate, which is the correct marginal valuation of leisure time in a competitive labour market. The occurrence of leisure in equation (19.7) steams from the assumption that leisure is an argument in the utility function. The fourth term can be interpreted as reflecting the value of the environment as a 'consumption good'. It measures the value of the existing stock of pollution at time t, and the real shadow price of this stock is the marginal rate of substitution between x and c, that is,

$$\rho^*(t) = u_x(c^*(t), L^*(t), x^*(t)) / \lambda^*(t) < 0$$

where I have used that the shadow price of physical capital is equal to the marginal utility of consumption along an optimal path, while $u_x(c^*, L^*, x^*)$ is the marginal utility of pollution. The marginal rate of substitution between x and c is interpretable as the marginal willingness to pay – in terms of reduced consumption of goods – for a small decrease of the stock of pollution. Finally, the fifth term on the right-hand side of equation (19.7) measures the value of additions to the stock of pollution (the value of investments in environmental capital), and the real shadow price is defined as the shadow price in utility terms divided by the marginal utility of consumption;

$$\tau^*(t) = -\mu^*(t) / \lambda^*(t).$$

For future reference, it is important to point out that *the shadow price of additions to the stock of pollution is forward-looking* in a dynamic economy. The reason is that emissions at time t will affect the stock of pollution at all future dates. This is illustrated by deriving the shadow price of additions to the stock of pollution in utility terms:

$$\mu^*(t) = \int_t^\infty u_x(c^*(s), L^*(s), x^*(s)) e^{-(\theta+\gamma)(s-t)} ds < 0 \qquad (19.8)$$

Equation (19.8) means that the shadow price of pollution at time t, measured in utility terms, is defined as the sum (integral) of all future marginal utilities of pollution discounted back to time t.

Note that, to reach the first-best resource allocation in a market economy, it is necessary to fully internalize external effects. In this model, the uncontrolled market solution would imply a negative externality from pollution, because the producers do not take into account that their use of emissions affects the stock of pollution and, therefore, the consumer's utility. As we saw in Chapter 1 of this volume, one way of internalizing an external effect is to use Pigouvian taxes. In the context of a market economy, the real shadow price of pollution, $\tau^*(t)$, is also interpretable as the Pigouvian emission tax at time t, that is, it is part of the emission tax path that brings the market economy to the first-best optimum. The Pigouvian tax provides the same information as a market price would do in a competitive economy and is, therefore, an important part of $GNNP^*_r(t)$. This means that Pigouvian taxes play two distinct roles here: first, they bring the economy to the first best optimum and, second, they provide information that is directly useful from the point of view of social accounting.

The analysis conducted above provides an important reference case. To summarize, we have found that, in a first-best setting, the present value of future utility at time t can be measured by using $GNNP^*_u(t)$. If, in addition, it is possible to closely approximate the instantaneous utility by a linear function, then $GNNP^*_r(t)$ becomes the natural welfare measure. This result is very convenient and may also explain some of the recent interest in green accounting by suggesting that welfare comparisons over time and across nations can be based on observable market data. However, it is important to point out once again that the analysis is based on a very restrictive assumption: the observed resource allocation solves the first-best optimization problem. This means, among other things, that there are no uninternalized external effects, no disequilibrium problems (for example unemployment) and that there is no need for policy-makers to use distortionary taxes. In addition, I have neglected distributional concern. It is, therefore, important to extend the welfare analysis to a framework where some of these assumptions are relaxed.

The Importance of Imperfections

Real-world economies usually deviate from the first-best for a variety of reasons. Examples are uninternalized external effects, other market imperfections, as well as (possible) restrictions facing policy-makers which make the first-best unattainable. I shall here address market imperfections by means of two examples: external effects and unemployment.

The analysis of uninternalized external effects is interesting because, even if policy-makers have understood the source of the externality and want to correct for its presence, it requires a great deal of information for policy-makers to be able fully to internalize an external effect. This is so because the correct social shadow price for an investment, at a given point in time, must reflect the present value of all future welfare effects (at the margin) caused by this investment. As I mentioned above, an implication is that Pigouvian taxes are forward-looking. Therefore, to be able to monitor emissions correctly by means of Pigouvian taxes, the policy-makers need information about the future welfare effects caused by today's polluting behaviour. This makes it relevant to address the question of what happens if the external effect caused by pollution has not become fully internalized.

To illustrate, suppose that we are trying to monitor pollution in the market economy by means of an emission tax, which will be denoted $\tau^0(t)$ for all t. Suppose also that, even if this emission tax provides the best available estimate of the value of additions to the stock of pollution is real terms, it still differs from its Pigouvian counterpart. Nevertheless, since $\tau^0(t)$ is the best available estimate, one would presumably use this information for the purpose of computing (a best estimate of) the green NNP. An important question is: what does the correct welfare measure look like when the external effect from pollution has not become fully internalized?

I will use the superscript '0' as a notation for the imperfect market solution (so as to be able to distinguish it from the first-best). In the Appendix, I present the conditions obeyed by the market equilibrium with externalities and show that the welfare measure takes the form

$$\theta V^0(t) = GNNP^0_u(t) + \Omega^0(t) \tag{19.9}$$

where the superscript '0' indicates that all entities are evaluated along the market equilibrium path. The first term on the right-hand side of equation (19.9) is analogous to its counterpart in the first best optimum, that is,

$$GNNP^0_u(t) = u(c^0(t), L^0(t), x^0(t)) + \lambda^0(t)\dot{k}^0(t) - \lambda^0(t)\tau^0(t)\dot{x}^0(t)$$

where $-\lambda^0(t)\tau^0(t)$ is the (implicit) shadow price of pollution in utility terms.[7] The second term on the right-hand side of equation (19.9) measures the present value of the marginal external effect. It turns up in the welfare measure because the shadow price of pollution used is not correct, which leaves part of the external effect uninternalized.

It is important to note that $\Omega^0(t)$ is forward-looking: it measures the part of the future welfare effects of today's pollution that is not captured by the incorrect estimate of the shadow price $\tau^0(t)$. The present value of the marginal external effect is interpretable as a weighted sum of future changes in the stock of pollution, in which the weights reflect the marginal utility value of pollution as well as the emission tax. In the Appendix, I show that the marginal external effect can be written as

$$\Omega^0(t) = \int_t^\infty [u_x^0(s) + \lambda^0(s)\tau^0(s)\{f_k^0(s) + \gamma\} - \lambda^0(s)\dot{\tau}^0(s)]\dot{x}^0(s)e^{-\theta(s-t)}ds$$

where u_x^0 and f_k^0 are short notations for, respectively, the marginal utility of pollution and the marginal product of physical capital evaluated at the decentralized equilibrium. The marginal external effect is forward-looking in the sense that it depends on the future equilibrium path of the economy. In the special case when the emission tax is Pigouvian, it is possible to show – as I do in the Appendix – that the terms within the bracket will cancel out.

In summary, I have derived the following result:[8]

Proposition 2: *In a decentralized economy with imperfect pollution control, the present value of the marginal external effect becomes part of the national welfare measure.*

The practical problem here is that, even if $GNNP_u^0(t)$ is, in principle, observable (it can at least be approximated by using the observable green NNP in real terms), we cannot observe the present value of the marginal external effect. Therefore, the presence of externalities means that there will be no simple connection between the present value of future utility and the utility value of the green NNP, where the latter is based on a biased estimate of the shadow price of pollution. For example, the green NNP may increase as time passes, whereas the welfare actually declines, which points at the danger of using a 'best estimate' of green NNP as a welfare indicator.

It may, of course, sound trivial to say that market data fail to measure welfare outside the first-best. However, to go from that conclusion to welfare analysis, it is important to know what the exact welfare measure looks like under imperfect pollution control, and equation (19.9) tells us what to look for. Note that, to evaluate the welfare measure in equation (19.9), we must actually compute (or estimate) the present value of the marginal external effect. This requires knowledge of *future willingness to pay* to reduce the stock of pollution, which for obvious reasons is very difficult to obtain. In fact, such information appears not to be more accessible than the information one would need to be able to implement the first-best. This clearly calls for simpler methods. One possible approximation method for designing what might be called 'close to Pigouvian taxes' is discussed in the next section.

Disequilibrium in one or several markets gives rise to problems reminiscent of those caused by uninternalized external effects. What immediately comes to mind is unemployment. In addition, since unemployment is a severe economic problem in Europe, it is important to address its implications for social accounting. In the context of the model set out above, introducing unemployment means assuming that the real wage rate is set such that the marginal product of labour exceeds the marginal value of leisure time (the reservation wage rate).

This has at least two important implications for welfare measurement.[9] First, it means that the real wage rate does not reflect the marginal value of leisure time. Instead, to value leisure time so as to obtain an analogue to the third term on the right-hand side of equation (19.7), it is necessary to collect information about the reservation wage rate. Second, and more important, the present value of future changes in employment becomes part of the welfare measure. To see this, let me define $\beta^0(t)$ to measure the difference between the marginal product value of labour and the marginal utility value of leisure at time t, that is,

$$\beta^0(t) = \lambda^0(t) f_l(l^0(t), k^0(t), g^0(t)) - u_L(c^0(t), L^0(t), x^0(t))$$

Then, with reference to equation (19.9), it is possible to show that the introduction of unemployment changes the national welfare measure to read

$$\theta V^0(t) = GNNP_u^0(t) + \Omega^0(t) + \int_t^\infty \beta^0(s) \dot{l}^0(s) e^{-\theta(s-t)} ds \qquad (19.10)$$

where $\dot{l}^0(s) = dl^0(s) / ds$ is the change of employment at time s, and $\beta^0(s) > 0$ with excess supply of labour at time s (it is zero when supply equals demand in the labour market). The last term on the right-hand side measures the present value of future changes in employment. From a technical point of view, therefore, unemployment affects social accounting in a way similar to external effects by adding forward-looking terms to the welfare measure. This means that the occurrence of the last term on the right-hand side of equation (19.10) is a natural consequence of imperfections in the labour market in the context of a dynamic economy.

In summary:

Proposition 3: *With excess supply of labour at each instant, welfare measurement requires us to add the present utility value of future changes in employment to the utility value of the green NNP. In addition, since the market wage rate and the reservation wage rate will differ under unemployment, it is not possible to value leisure time at the margin by using the observed wage rate.*

To go further into the analysis of social accounting and unemployment, it is necessary to know what is causing the excess supply of labour. In fact, such knowledge is likely to make the information collection problem somewhat less difficult. For instance, under monopoly union wage-setting, we know that the difference between the marginal product of labour and the reservation wage rate is proportional to the inverse of the wage elasticity of the labour demand. This elasticity is estimable by means of econometric analysis. Therefore, if monopoly union wage-setting is a reasonable assumption, at least the qualitative information provided by this estimate is important in the sense that it gives guidance as to the 'severity of the bias' of the green NNP as a welfare indicator. The smaller the wage elasticity of the labour demand in absolute value, the more biased the welfare measure if we neglect union wage setting and treat the labour market as if it is competitive.[10] Similarly, if the wage elasticity is large in absolute value, then neglecting the present value of future changes in employment is likely to be a less important omission.

3. ON THE STEP FROM THEORY TO APPLICATION

The purpose of this section is to try to relate the theory of social accounting to practical applications. An important question is whether the additional complications arising in imperfect market economies (some of which were addressed above) are empirically relevant, or if the first-best accounting practices can also serve as a reasonable approximation in the more or less imperfect market economy. I shall also analyse 'practical' means of information collection; more specifically, the contingent valuation method as a means of collecting information for the purpose of measuring the value of additions to the stock of pollution.

Are the Imperfections Empirically Relevant?

There are to date a large number of empirical studies concerned with augmenting the traditional national accounts with different kinds of 'natural capital'. Recent reviews include Sheng (1995), Hamilton and Lutz (1996), and Vincent and Hartwick (1997). According to Vincent and Hartwick (1997), the number of studies has increased more or less steadily since Repetto et al. (1989), which is the most cited work on natural resources and national accounts. Vincent and Hartwick list a dozen studies from 1996, and they review about thirty studies covering accounts for 20 countries. The greatest number of studies pertains to countries in Asia. Most of the studies covered are concerned with augmenting the national accounts with the present and future benefits of more than one natural resource. The most frequently occurring resource is the forest.[11]

There are also studies which introduce estimates of the true output from the educational sector – the value of net investments in human capital. The first of these studies was Jorgensen and Fraumeni (1992) for the USA, which was followed by Ahlroth et al. (1997) for Sweden.

Without going into detail, it is fair to say that most of these studies attempt to follow the first-best valuation principles described by equations (19.6) and (19.7) above. This means that they add the value of the consumption of 'non-market goods', and/or add the value of net investment in, for example, natural and environmental capital to the conventional NNP. In many cases, however, they do not indicate clearly the theoretical framework guiding the adjustments they make. Moreover, most material has been published outside refereed journals. As the field is newly established, this raises the risk of inappropriate accounting procedures and valuation techniques being applied. Vincent and Hartwick (1997) do a good job in pointing out the errors in the studies pertaining to forest resources.

The cited studies do not address the complications created by externalities and other deviations from the first-best. As should be clear from the analysis in section 2, such omissions will imply that the green NNP provides a biased measure of welfare. Numerical simulations presented by Aronsson et al. (1997) show that the bias could be considerable. I shall briefly summarize their results. They use a dynamic model with an externality related to human capital. This framework serves as a complement to the reference model set out in section 2. Instead of focusing on negative external effects from pollution (as in section 2), this model addresses a positive external effect arising from human capital accumulation. To make the analysis simple, both the instantaneous utility and production functions are of Cobb–Douglas type. Formally, the utility and production functions are written

$$u(c,L) = c^{\omega}L^{(1-\omega)}, \, 0 < \omega < 1$$

$$f(a(h)l,k,h) = [a(h)l]^{\kappa_1}k^{\kappa_2}h^{(1-\kappa_1-\kappa_2)}, \, 0 < \kappa_1,\kappa_2 < 1 \text{ and } \kappa_1 + \kappa_2 \leq 1$$

where ω is a utility parameter, while κ_1 and κ_2 are parameters of the production function.

As before, c is consumption of goods, L leisure time, l the time spent in market work (which reduces the leisure time available) and k the physical capital stock. The term h is the human capital stock created by the utility-maximizing consumer through time spent in education, and $a(h)$ is a concave and increasing function, which affects labour productivity. This means that $a(h)l$ is interpretable as measuring 'effective labour'. The final term in the production function represents the positive externality created by the human capital stock. Since this argument is not connected to labour productivity, it will not directly influence the wage rate paid to consumers in a decentralized economy. This creates a difference between the private and social value of human capital, which is what causes the external effect. Finally, the model also contains a standard accumulation equation for physical capital, which is similar to equation (19.3) above, and an accumulation equation for human capital, where the net investments in human capital depend on the time the consumer spends in education. A more detailed description of the model, including the choice of parameter values, is given by Aronsson et al. (1997, ch. 5).

Let us now turn to welfare measurement and compare the first-best welfare measure with that arising in the decentralized economy. A particular concern here will be the importance of the externality for measuring welfare in the decentralized economy. As in the theoretical analysis in section 2, welfare is measured by the present value of future utility times the rate of time preference. In the context of the first-best, this measure is accurately captured by the utility value of the green NNP (in the same way as in the first part of section 2). For the decentralized equilibrium, the equality between welfare and green NNP does not apply, so I will present both the actual welfare level (the rate of time preference times the present value of future utility) and the green NNP. The results are given in Table 19.1.

Table 19.1   Welfare in the Cobb–Douglas example

κ_1	κ_2	$1 - \kappa_1 - \kappa_2$	First-best welfare	Decentralized solution		
				Welfare	$GNPP_u$	MEE/welfare
0.45	0.30	0.25	1212.47	1104.53	729.74	0.33
0.55	0.30	0.15	962.86	929.16	709.08	0.24
0.35	0.30	0.35	1565.35	1315.56	721.27	0.45

The figures in the first three columns of Table 19.1 indicate the weights given to effective labour, physical capital and human capital, respectively, in the production function. Since this production function is characterized by constant returns to scale, it follows that the lower (higher) the weight on effective labour, given the weight on physical capital, the higher (lower) the weight on the separate human capital argument. When the resource allocation is determined in a decentralized economy, meaning that the external effect from human capital remains uninternalized, I present three columns of figures: the welfare level (measured as suggested above), the utility value of the green NNP and, finally, the marginal externality's share of the welfare measure (MEE/welfare). The last is calculated by using information about the welfare level and the utility value of the green NNP.

In addition to the obvious conclusion that welfare is greater in the first-best than in the imperfect market economy, the results imply that the utility value of the green NNP underestimates the welfare level in the decentralized version of the model. The reason is that the external effect arising from human capital is positive. Naturally, the importance of the externality depends on the weight given to human capital, in comparison with the weights on effective labour and physical capital, in the production function. It is, therefore, interesting to relate the welfare contribution of the marginal external effect to the weight given to the separate human capital argument in the production function. In the first row of Table 19.1, the weight given to human capital is 0.25. In the second row this weight has decreased to 0.15, and in the third row it has increased to 0.35. It is clear that, by reducing the weight on human capital, the difference between the welfare level in the first-best optimum and the decentralized economy will decrease, and the welfare contribution of the external effect in the decentralized equilibrium becomes less important. Increasing the weight on human capital gives the opposite result: it makes the welfare contribution of the external effect more important and, as a consequence, the green NNP a less accurate indicator of welfare.

Briefly on Technological Change

The human capital model is also interesting from another point of view: it introduces technological change into the welfare analysis. To what extent does technological change contribute to welfare? The importance of technological change in the context of social accounting has been addressed in several previous studies.[12] In an attempt to estimate the effects from technological progress on future welfare, one can use the fact that the utility value of the green NNP, under ideal conditions, is an annuity equivalent of future utility at the prevailing rate of time preference. By assuming that technological progress proceeds at a constant rate (at an average historical rate), one obtains an estimate of the downward bias of a green NNP measure, which neglects technological progress. Recent estimates,[13] using available US historical data, imply that this bias can be up to 40–50 per cent. In other words, omitting technological progress may bias the estimates of future consumption possibilities to a considerable extent.

Is There a Practical Step Towards Green Accounting?

If market imperfections are part of the general equilibrium, welfare measurement will, in general, require us to evaluate forward-looking terms. From a practical point of view, this is what makes social accounting much more complicated in 'distorted' market economies than in the first-best. In a first-best setting, such additional terms would vanish from the welfare measure, because the shadow prices (and/or market prices) measure social opportunity costs of today's actions. As mentioned in section 2, if the market failure has to do with external effects, then Pigouvian taxes are particularly interesting to study, since they play multiple roles. First, they bring the market economy to the social optimum. Second, they are directly relevant from the point of view of social accounting, as they provide the same information as a market price would do under perfect competition.

Clearly, most 'non-Pigouvian' taxes will not accomplish this task. This makes most real-world emission taxes less useful as measures of the value of changes in the stocks of environmental capital. However, non-Pigouvian taxes may, under certain conditions, be closely related to their Pigouvian counterparts and, as such, provide close enough approximations of the value of depletion of environmental capital. Instead of trying to capture future preferences, what happens if we try to design emission taxes on the basis of the willingness-to-pay to reduce pollution at present? This has a pure practical purpose: we can only hope to collect willingness to pay information from the generations currently alive. It is, therefore, important to study the usefulness of willingness-to-pay information for accounting purposes.[14]

Following Aronsson and Löfgren (1999b), I shall address two questions with reference to the model set out in section 2. First, if we were to design emission taxes on the basis of the current willingness to pay for a better environment, will these taxes improve the welfare level in comparison with the uncontrolled market economy? Second, if we were to use these taxes to value additions to the stock of pollution in the accounting system, will the resulting green NNP provide a reasonable approximation of the correct welfare measure?

To answer these questions, suppose we were to ask the consumer how much he/she is willing to pay to reduce the stock of pollution temporarily by one unit at time t, and that this question is repeated as time passes. I also assume that the consumer reveals his/her true willingness to pay, which means that the answer to the willingness-to-pay question measures the marginal rate of substitution between pollution and consumption of goods. If we treat the marginal utility of pollution as being constant, until new willingness-to-pay information becomes available (that is, until new information is collected), and if it takes dt units of time to collect new information, the implied approximation of the Pigouvian tax in the time interval $(t, t + dt)$ takes the form

$$\tau_a^0(t) = -\bar{u}_x(t) / [(\theta + \gamma)\lambda^0(t)] \tag{19.11}$$

where $\bar{u}_x(t)$ is a constant and equal to $u_x(c^0(t), L^0(t), x^0(t))$. At first glance, equation (19.11) looks exactly like the formula for the Pigouvian tax in the special case when the marginal utility of pollution is constant,[15] which may seem to be a very restrictive assumption. However, note that equation (19.11) only holds on the time interval $(t, t + dt)$ after which new willingness-to-pay information is collected and the emission tax is revised accordingly. This repeated information collection is likely to make the errors smaller than they would have been had equation (19.11) been used as a basis for emission taxation along the whole future equilibrium path.

It is easy to show that, if this approximation of the Pigouvian tax does not underestimate the future marginal utilities of pollution and the instantaneous utility function has the properties specified in section 2, then the emission tax is welfare-improving in comparison with the uncontrolled market economy. A somewhat simplistic interpretation is that the emission tax is welfare-improving unless it is set 'too high'. For example, if the pollution is increasing during the initial part of an uncontrolled equilibrium path, then the approximation of the Pigouvian tax is likely to improve the welfare level. The answer to the second question is somewhat less satisfying: even if the repeated revisions of the basis for the emission tax may bring us closer to the Pigouvian tax path than would otherwise be possible, there will still remain errors in general. These will, in turn, affect the welfare interpretation of the estimate of the green NNP. At the same time, it is not possible to say, on theoretical grounds, whether these predication errors are practically important or, as one may expect, that their magnitude will decrease if willingness-to-pay information is collected more often. The latter is particularly important to explore, since one would like to find welfare indicators that are both reasonably accurate and empirically manageable. Numerical simulations may shed light on these issues.

4. POLICY OBJECTIVES AND CONSTRAINTS

The analysis so far has focused attention on market imperfections and their implications for welfare measurement. By using a representative-agent model, I have neglected other objectives than those facing the representative consumer. This may seem to be a very restrictive basis for welfare analysis. For example, since distributional concern is often an important objective underlying economic policy, a more comprehensive welfare measure should also reflect these objectives. In addition, restrictions on the set of available policy instruments will have implications for social accounting, since they may prevent the economy from reaching a first-best outcome. I shall in this section briefly address the implications of distributional objectives and distortionary taxes.

Distributional Objectives

A criticism of most previous studies on social accounting is the neglect of objectives for the distribution of consumption (or utility) across consumers.

For example, one may argue that, since the NNP (broadly defined) contains no information about this distribution, then the NNP is likely to fail as a welfare measure if society has such distributional objectives. Following Aronsson and Löfgren (1999a), I will show that equality objectives do not, themselves, invalidate the welfare interpretation of an NNP concept. Instead, what matters is that these objectives are fully implemented in a first-best setting. Otherwise, if the resource allocation is not optimal from society's point of view, it is not possible to measure welfare by observables. Therefore, it turns out that a suboptimal distribution affects the welfare analysis in a way similar to other market imperfections.

To illustrate the basic implications for social accounting following from distributional concern, there is no need to use a model as complicated as that in section 2. I shall, therefore, disregard both the valuation of leisure time and the disutility of pollution. In addition, to simplify as much as possible, I assume a two-person economy, where both agents act as if they have infinite time horizons. The instantaneous utility function facing agent i takes the form $u_i(t) = u_i(c_i(t))$, where $i = 1,2$. In addition, suppose that society's preferences for the distribution of utility at time t can be represented by the instantaneous social welfare function $\Gamma(u_1(t),u_2(t))$.

Since the economy consists of two consumers, and as the labour supply is completely inelastic (because the agents do not value leisure time), the accumulation equation for physical capital can be written

$$\dot{k}(t) = f(k(t)) - c_1(t) - c_2(t)$$

where the constant labour input has been suppressed for notational convenience. Since the consumers do not value pollution in this example, I have also relaxed the assumption that emissions constitute a production factor.

The first-best optimization problem and its solution are presented in the Appendix. I will here examine what the appropriate welfare measure looks like in this two-person economy. If the economy operates in the first-best equilibrium, which is (again) denoted by the superscript '*', it is possible to derive the following national welfare measure for time t:

$$\theta W^*(t) = \Gamma(u_1(c_1^*(t)),u_2(c_2^*(t))) + \lambda^*(t)\dot{k}^*(t) \tag{19.12}$$

where

$$W^*(t) = \int_t^\infty \Gamma(u_1(c_1^*(s)),u_2(c_2^*(s)))e^{-\theta(s-t)}ds.$$

Except that the economy now consists of two consumers, equation (19.12) looks exactly like a simplified version of equation (19.6), where the main simplifications are that I here disregard the values of leisure time and pollution. The left-hand side of equation (19.12) measures the present value of future social welfare times the rate of time preference. The first term on the right-hand side represents society's 'utility consumption' at time t, and the second term is the utility value of the current net investments.[16] We can interpret the right-hand side of equation (19.12) as measuring $GNNP_u^*(t)$ for this economy. In summary:

Proposition 4: *Within the given framework, where the distribution across agents is part of a first-best policy, welfare is appropriately measured by the utility value of the green NNP.*

Therefore, *concern for the distribution of utility across agents does not, itself, invalidate the results from representative-agent models that the utility value of the green NNP can be used as a welfare indicator in a first best-setting.* To facilitate the interpretation of the welfare measure in terms of the green NNP, one can linearize the welfare measure in the same way as in section 2:

$$\theta W^*(t) \approx \lambda^*(t)[c_1^*(t) + c_2^*(t) + \dot{k}^*(t)] \qquad (19.13)$$

This linearized welfare measure has the same general interpretation as equation (19.7): the present value of future social utility is approximately proportional to $GNNP_r^*(t)$ times the marginal utility value of capital. There are, however, two important differences between equations (19.7) and (19.13). First, equation (19.13) is based on the assumption that distributional concern is part of the social welfare function, whereas equation (19.7) is not. Second, since the model used here abstracts from leisure time and pollution, it turns out that $GNNP_r^*(t)$ coincides with the conventional NNP at time t.

If, on the other hand, the actual distribution does not reflect the distributional objectives at each instant, it is not possible to measure welfare solely by using the utility value of the green NNP. To see this without going into technical detail about what might cause a suboptimal distribution in real-world market economies, let us use the first-best optimal consumption as a starting-point, and then redistribute the consumption across agents over a future time interval, (t_1, t_2). The new consumption paths become

$$c_1^0(t) = c_1^*(t) + \delta \text{ and } c_2^0(t) = c_2^*(t) - \delta \text{ for } t \text{ in } (t_1, t_2), \text{ while}$$
$$c_1^0(t) = c_1^*(t) \text{ and } c_2^0(t) = c_2^*(t) \text{ otherwise,}$$

where $0 < \delta < c_1^*(t), c_2^*(t)$. This means that the distribution of consumption is suboptimal during a future time interval, (t_1, t_2), whereas output, the capital stock and aggregate consumption remain as they were in the first- best. Aronsson and Löfgren (1999a) then derive the following welfare measure for time $t < t_1$:

$$\theta W^0(t) = \Gamma(u_1(c_1^0(t)), u_2(c_2^0(t))) + \lambda^0(t)\dot{k}^0(t) + \int_{t_1}^{t_2} \sum_{i=1}^{2} \alpha_i^0(s)\dot{c}_i^0(s)e^{-\theta(s-t)}ds$$

(19.14)

In equation (19.14), the superscript '0' is again used to denote that the resource allocation deviates from the first-best. The first two terms on the right-hand side constitute, together, the utility value of the green NNP, whereas the third term is interpretable as a weighted sum of future changes in consumption. The variable $\alpha_i^0(t)$ measures the difference at time t between the social marginal utility of consumption for consumer i and the shadow price of capital. This term is generally non-zero, when consumption is not optimally chosen. Equation (19.14) suggests the following result:

Proposition 5: *If the distribution of consumption is suboptimal, a weighted sum of future changes in consumption, which occur during the time interval of suboptimal distribution, becomes part of the welfare measure.*

With the analysis of market imperfections in mind, Proposition 5 should come as no surprise to the reader: a suboptimal distribution affects the welfare measurement problem in a way similar to other imperfections by adding forward-looking terms to the welfare measure. In other words, neglecting distributional considerations in social accounting may neither be a greater nor a lesser omission than the neglect of other imperfections in the market economy.

Distortionary Taxes

So far, I have not explicitly addressed public policy. However, if I were to introduce public expenditures into the model (or try to implement distributional objectives in the context of a market economy), it is easy to show that most of the previous results would hold, provided the public expenditures are financed by lump-sum taxes. As is shown by Aronsson (1998a), what actually matters is the option of using lump-sum taxes: if lump-sum taxes are replaced by distortionary taxes, a welfare loss will arise which is, in turn, important for social accounting.

To see this without going into technical details, suppose a labour income tax is introduced into the model in section 2. This tax will create a difference between the marginal product of labour and the social value of leisure time at the margin. This means that the consequences for social accounting following from labour income taxation are reminiscent of those of unemployment, which were discussed above. Accordingly, the presence of a labour income tax makes the present value of future changes in employment become part of the welfare measure. The implications of capital income taxation are similar to those of labour income taxation. The only difference is that capital income taxation introduces a distortion in the capital market. A capital income tax creates a difference between the marginal product of capital and the post-tax real interest rate, where the latter is what determines the consumer's saving decision. As a consequence of this tax wedge, the present value of future net investments in physical capital will become part of the national welfare measure.

Therefore, basic intuition has leaded us to conclude:

Proposition 6: *Distortionary taxes make the green NNP fail as a welfare indicator. With a labour income tax, future changes in employment become part of the welfare measure because of a tax wedge in the labour market, while a capital income tax will imply that future changes in the capital stock affect the welfare measure via a tax wedge in the capital market.*

A natural extension of the welfare measurement problem under distortionary taxes is to use the second-best as a reference case. Such a model would imply that the resources are allocated in an optimal way from society's point of view, conditional on tax revenues being raised by distortionary taxes. Aronsson (1998a) analyses welfare measurement problems in the context of the second-best and finds, among other things, that the marginal excess burden becomes part of the national welfare measure.

5. SUSTAINABILITY

The previous sections have focused on national-product-related welfare measures, as well as on why such welfare measures are likely to be biased in imperfect market economies. There is a conventional wisdom[17] that a correct welfare indicator should, in some way, be connected to the concept of 'sustainable development' first popularized in the report of the Brundtland Commission, chaired by Gro Harlem Brundtland, at the time the Prime Minister of Norway. The report, issued by the World Commission on Environment and Development, argues for sustainable development defined as 'development that meets the needs of the present without compromising the ability of future generations to meet their own needs'.[18] The underlying concern of the Commission was that humanity is consuming its natural endowments too rapidly.

Ideas about sustainability in terms of sustainable income are much older than the Brundtland Commission. They originate from economists such as Irving Fisher, Erik Lindahl and John Hicks. As Nordhaus (1995) points out, Irving Fisher was the first to make a clear distinction between income and wealth.[19] The modern discussion dates back to Lindahl (1933) and Hicks (1939). Both defined income as the maximum amount you can consume and still keep the capital intact (interest on the capital). This income concept is interpretable as current consumption plus net capital accumulation. More fundamentally, however, Hicks realized that there is an intertemporal dimension involved. He writes: 'Income must be defined as the maximum amount of money which the individual can spend this week, and still be able to spend the same amount in real terms in each ensuing week.'[20] In other words, Hicks comes very close to a theoretically reasonable definition of income as the sustainable level of consumption. An even more demanding measure of sustainable welfare was suggested by Nordhaus and Tobin (1972), which acknowledged the existence of technological progress. Under special conditions, the path along which society can consume without short-changing the future is one with per capita consumption growing steadily at the rate of technological progress.

Along the lines of Hicks, I will say that development is sustainable if there exists a non-declining utility (or consumption) path. This is equivalent to requiring that the current utility level must not exceed future utilities. Development is then sustained if the utility path actually chosen is non-declining. It has been suggested[21] that Weitzman (1976) reconciled the ideas of Fisher, Lindahl and Hicks with modern optimal growth theory, in the sense that the green NNP along a first-best optimal path measures the maximum sustainable utility level. This idea is based on the interpretation of NNP as the maximum utility one can afford at present without reducing the capital stock. It is, then, a short step to conclude that the economy is on a sustainable utility path, if the value of net investment is non-negative. This argument is obviously correct if capital is homogeneous, that is, when there is only one type of capital. However, it is not in general correct in economies with multiple capital goods. As shown by Asheim (1994),[22] even if the value of net investment – measured as the sum of values of net investments in all capital goods – is non-negative, the utility may actually exceed its maximum sustainable level. With multiple capital goods, it is generally not possible to construct an exact indicator of sustainability based on accounting entities at a given point in time. Therefore, even if the green NNP constitutes a welfare measure under first-best conditions, it does not measure the maximum sustainable utility level.

To address sustainability more formally, I shall assume that the economy has reached a first-best resource allocation. The utility value of the green NNP – measured at time t along the optimal path – will be written as

$$GNNP^*_u(t) = u^*(t) + \Lambda^*(t)'I^*(t) \tag{19.15}$$

where $u^*(t)$ is a short notation for the instantaneous utility at time t. The term $\Lambda^*(t)$ can be interpreted as a vector whose elements are the marginal utility values of different kinds of capital, while $I^*(t)$ is a vector whose elements are the net investments into these capital stocks. In the context of the reference model in section 2,

$$\Lambda^*(t)'I^*(t) = \lambda^*(t)\dot{k}^*(t) + \mu^*(t)\dot{x}^*(t)$$

In a more general framework, the value of net investment may also reflect the value of changes in other capital stocks (for example natural resource stocks) as well as the value of marginal technological progress.[23] This means that the net investment concept to be considered here is not limited to the reference model.

With this concept of net investment at my disposal, I will now turn to the conditions under which utility is constant along the optimal path. A natural starting-point is the pioneering work of Hartwick (1977), which gave rise to the so-called 'Hartwick's rule'. It provides a sufficient condition for utility to be constant along an optimal path, and is summarized as follows:

Hartwick's rule: If $\Lambda^*(t)'I^*(t) = 0$ for all t along the optimal path, then $u^*(t)$ is constant for all t.

Note that if $u^*(t)$ is constant for all t, and since the resource allocation is optimal by assumption, it follows that $u^*(t)$ is also the maximum sustainable utility level. Dixit et al. (1980) showed that $\Lambda^*(t)'I^*(t) = 0$ for all t is also a necessary condition for utility to be constant along an optimal path. I summarize the result of Dixit et al. as follows:

Dixit–Hammond–Hoel: If $u^*(t)$ is constant for all t along the optimal path, then $\Lambda^*(t)'I^*(t) = 0$ for all t.

These two results, together, mean that $\Lambda^*(t)'I^*(t) = 0$ for *all* t along an optimal path is both necessary and sufficient for $u^*(t)$ to be constant and equal to the maximum sustainable utility level. However, $\Lambda^*(t)'I^*(t) \geq 0$ at *some* t is no indication of sustainability.

What is then measured by the value of net investment at a given point in time? Following Aronsson et al. (1997), one can use that $GNNP_u^*(t)$ is proportional to the present value of future utility and then derive the following expression for the value of net investment at time t;[24]

$$\Lambda^*(t)'I^*(t) = \int_t^\infty \frac{du^*(s)}{ds} e^{-\theta(s-t)} ds$$

which means that the value of net investment at time t is positive (negative) if, and only if, a weighted sum of future changes in utility along the optimal path happens to be positive (negative). This holds irrespective of the appropriate capital concept, and it has nothing to do with whether or not the current utility level is sustainable.

6. SOCIAL ACCOUNTING AND TRANSBOUNDARY POLLUTION

Adding global external effects, caused by, for example, transboundary pollution, to the welfare analysis creates certain very important valuation problems. The purpose of this section is to extend the analysis in section 2 to a global economy, where the pollution caused by the production in one country affects the well-being of consumers in other countries. To be able to focus exclusively on how to handle global external effects in the context of social accounting, I shall neglect international trade.[25]

The framework for studying global external effects is well known from previous work on international pollution control. Global external effects are routinely analysed in terms of Nash-non-cooperative games in open-loop or feedback-loop form.[26] The conventional assumption in the environmental economics literature is that the games are played between nations. Since a nation allocates its resources via markets, the game-theoretical approach presupposes that Pigouvian-related taxes are used to implement the non-cooperative solution.[27] Since the solution is not first-best, these taxes are suboptimal and the welfare measurement problem is reminiscent of that arising in one-country economies with externalities.

The analysis in this section follows Aronsson and Löfgren (2000). To simplify as much as possible, I assume a two-country economy, where each individual economy consists of one agent. With one minor (although important) modification, each individual economy is assumed to coincide with the framework set out in section 2, and all notations used are those of section 2 except that instantaneous utilities and accumulation equations are now country-specific. The modification has to do with the instantaneous utility function for country i, which is now written

$$u_i(t) = u_i(c_i(t), L_i(t), z_i(t)) \text{ for } i = 1, 2$$

where $z_i(t) = z_i(x_1(t), x_2(t))$ is an indicator of environmental quality in country i. It depends on the pollution accumulated by emissions in both countries. This means that the model allows for transboundary pollution in the sense that the environmental quality and, therefore, the well-being of country i depend on the pollution accumulated in both countries. To be specific, I assume that the environmental quality of country i is negatively affected by both x_1 and x_2.

The purpose is here to derive both national and global welfare measures, and to relate these measures to the functioning of the economic system. As it turns out, the forms of the welfare measures are very sensitive to whether or not the countries coordinate their environmental policies so as to internalize the global external effects. Suppose, to begin with, that *each country allocates its resources in an optimal way conditional on the path of the part of the stock of pollution created by the other country*. A solution concept based on this assumption is the Nash-non-cooperative open-loop solution. A feature of this solution concept is that only the domestically created parts of the external effects are internalized. The resource allocation is, therefore, suboptimal from society's point of view in the sense that each country neglects the impact of its pollution on the other country's well-being. Even if such a resource allocation is very difficult to implement in the context of actual market economies,[28] it enables me to focus explicitly on the welfare consequences of transboundary pollution.

If we denote the Nash-non-cooperative open-loop solution by superscript 'n', so as to distinguish it from other suboptimal equilibria in market economies, and in line with the model in section 2, the utility value of the green NNP facing country i at time t can be written

$$GNNP_{u,i}^n(t) = u_i(c_i^n(t), L_i^n(t), z_i^n(t)) + \lambda_i^n(t)\dot{k}_i^n(t) + \mu_i^n(t)\dot{x}_i^n(t)$$

which is analogous to, and has the same interpretation as, its counterpart in the one-country economy. The important thing to note here is that the utility value of additions to the stock of pollution in country i, $\mu_i^n(t)$, only reflects the welfare effects in country i following from pollution accumulation in that country. This means that the welfare consequences for the other country are not included in $\mu_i^n(t)$.

The national welfare measure is defined as in section 2, that is, by the present value of future utility, which is usually referred to as the 'value function'. In a similar way, I define the global welfare level by the sum of the countries' value functions. When there are uninternalized external effects in the general equilibrium solution, it should come as no surprise to the reader that the utility value of the green NNP, as defined above, cannot be used as a welfare indicator. More specifically, one can show that the national welfare measure for country i takes the form

$$\theta V_i^n(t) = GNNP_{u,i}^n(t) + \Psi_i^n(t) \tag{19.16}$$

where

$$V_i^n(t) = \int_t^\infty u_i(c_i^n(s), L_i^n(s), z_i^n(s)) e^{-\theta(s-t)} ds$$

The term $\Psi_i^n(t)$ is the marginal external effect following from transboundary pollution. It measures the welfare effect in country i following from pollution accumulation in the other country. All other external effects are internalized in the Nash-non-cooperative solution, which is what makes it possible to relate the marginal external effect exclusively to transboundary pollution. This marginal external effect is, of course, forward-looking for the same reason as in section 2.

Measuring the global welfare level gives rise to a similar conclusion. Adding the two national welfare indicators gives

$$\theta \sum_{i=1}^2 V_i^n(t) = \sum_{i=1}^2 [GNNP_{u,i}^n(t) + \Psi_i^n(t)] \tag{19.17}$$

Equations (19.16) and (19.17) can be summarized as follows:

Proposition 7: *If the countries follow the Nash-non-cooperative open-loop solution, each national welfare measure is affected by external effects caused by pollution accumulation in other countries. These external effects also remain uninternalized at the global level. The implication is that observable market data do not contain all relevant information for measuring national and global welfare.*

What happens if *the countries coordinate their environmental policies* and reach a first-best outcome? Such an equilibrium is usually referred to as the 'cooperative solution'. This solution would internalize all external effects at the global level, and is (at least in theory) implementable in market economies by means of 'full' Pigouvian taxes. This means that the emission tax imposed on country *i* reflects *all* welfare effects caused by that country's polluting behaviour. By using the superscript '*' to denote the first-best cooperative solution, it is possible to show that the global welfare measure takes the form

$$\theta \sum_{i=1}^{2} V_i^*(t) = \sum_{i=1}^{2} GNNP_{u,i}^*(t) \qquad (19.18)$$

in which $GNNP_{u,i}^*(t)$ is defined in the same general way as $GNNP_{u,i}^n(t)$ except that it is here evaluated along the cooperative solution, where the shadow price of pollution is correct from society's point of view. The interpretation of equation (19.18) will be summarized as follows:

Proposition 8: *If the economies follow the cooperative solution, then the sum of the countries' green NNPs, measured in terms of utility, constitutes the correct global welfare measure.*

Proposition 8 is a logical consequence of the fact that the cooperative solution internalizes all external effects at the global level. It is, therefore, analogous to the first-best welfare measures derived in section 2. By linearizing the welfare measure, it is also possible to relate the global welfare level to the sum of the green NNPs in real terms.

   In the context of a cooperative solution with several countries involved, it is important to realize that these countries act as one decision-maker. It is, therefore, not straightforward to split the observable global welfare measure into two observable national welfare measures. The reason is that the marginal benefits and costs of pollution control only balance at the global level in the cooperative solution. From the point of view of each individual country, there is still a discrepancy between what the country pays, in pollution charges, and the benefits the country receives from pollution control. As we learned in section 2, such discrepancies are precisely what make market data fail to measure the national welfare level. Therefore, basic intuition suggests the following result:

Proposition 9: *If the economies follow the cooperative solution, each national welfare measure contains more information than is provided by the country's contribution to the global welfare measure.*

Proposition 9 contains a very important message. Even if the global welfare level can be measured by the sum of the countries' green NNPs, each national welfare measure will, in general, contain forward-looking terms, which are reminiscent of those analysed in section 2. The welfare contributions of these 'nation-specific externalities' will cancel out at the global level. Therefore, transoundary pollution clearly weakens the welfare-economic foundations for the green NNP, since it suggests that the national welfare level can never be measured solely by means of observables.

7. CONCLUSIONS

One of the most important aims of the literature on green accounting has been to augment, or extend, the conventional NNP measure so as to obtain a better indicator of welfare. A simplified summary of this research is that, while the early literature primarily concerned the potentials of green accounting, by deriving green NNP welfare indicators in more or less complicated economic environments, the recent literature has been more oriented towards complications arising in imperfect market economies. In this chapter, I have tried to summarize the main messages of this research, even if much of the analysis has concentrated on the recent developments in the literature.

The welfare interpretation of the green NNP depends, in a fundamental way, on the economic environment in which green NNP is measured. If the economy follows a first-best optimal path, and with a stationary technology, future utility can be measured by an indicator based on observable variables, which is interpretable as the green NNP. This means that the welfare interpretation of a green NNP measure is based on the assumption of a first-best resource allocation. An interesting implication is also that distributional concern does not invalidate this welfare interpretation: the green NNP (appropriately defined) is still the correct welfare measure, provided the distributional objectives are fully implemented in a first-best setting.

Welfare measurement in decentralized market economies usually implies a number of complications, which do not arise in the first-best. By relaxing the first-best assumption, observable market data will no longer provide all information needed to measure future utility. This also explains why welfare measures corresponding to imperfect market economies contain forward-looking terms that represent the future welfare effects of today's actions that are not captured by market data. A typical example is the occurrence of uninternalized externalities, implying that the present value of marginal external effects becomes part of the welfare measure. I have shown that similar complications arise as a consequence of unemployment, or if distributional objectives have not become fully implemented. Distortionary taxes will also give rise to forward-looking terms in the welfare measures, as the existence of such taxes prevents the economy from reaching the first-best resource allocation.

Most practical attempts to do green accounting have failed to handle the complications created by externalities and other market imperfections. The researcher typically does not even acknowledge the problem, which suggests that there remains much work to be done in this area. However, the difficulties are not easily solved, and the 'practical step' discussed in section 3 gives rise to a biased welfare measure, even if the magnitude of this bias remains to be studied.

The green NNP cannot, in general, be used as an indicator of sustainability. As pointed out by Asheim (1994), even if the value of net investment (appropriately measured) is non-negative, utility (or consumption) may actually exceed its maximum sustainable level. I have tried to emphasize this result by showing that the value of net investment at a given point in time only reflects a weighted sum of future changes in utility, which has nothing to do with whether the current utility level is sustainable or not. Necessary and sufficient conditions for a constant utility path have been provided by Hartwick (1977) and Dixit et al. (1980). The basic message from these studies is that utility is constant along the optimal path if, and only if, the utility value of net investment is always zero along the optimal path.

Transboundary pollution complicates welfare measurement. If the individual countries do not cooperate in order to control pollution, external effects will remain uninternalized at both the national and global levels. As a consequence, neither national nor global welfare can be measured solely on the basis of observables. If, on the other hand, the countries were able to implement a cooperative equilibrium, all externalities would become internalized at the global level, which means that the global welfare level is appropriately measured by a weighted sum of the countries' green NNPs. However, it is not straightforward to split this global welfare measure into static national welfare measures. This means that, even if the economies follow the cooperative equilibrium path, each national welfare measure contains forward-looking components. In other words, the existence of transboundary pollution weakens the relationship between national welfare and the green NNP.

The literature on social accounting has evolved rapidly during the last decade, and many of the difficult valuation problems have been solved at a theoretical level. Yet, there is much more to learn about the relationship between national (and global) welfare measures and the functioning of the economic system. Despite the recent focus on complications that may arise as a consequence of, for example, externalities and/or unemployment, the first-best is commonly used as a reference case by which to compare the accounting procedures relevant in imperfect market economies. At present, there are very few studies dealing with social accounting in second-best economies. Such an extension of the theory would be particularly relevant in the context of distributional objectives, which are often implemented by means of distortionary taxes. In addition, there is a huge gap between theoretical analysis and practical application, and there is a need for simpler accounting procedures that are reasonably accurate in terms of capturing values as well as being empirically manageable. Numerical simulation might be a useful tool in the search for these accounting practices.

FURTHER READING

Aronsson, T., P.O. Johansson and K.G. Löfgren (1997) *Welfare Measurement, Sustainability and Green National Accounting*, Cheltenham, UK and Lyme, USA: Edward Elgar.

Asheim, G.B. (1994), 'Net national product as an indicator of sustainability', *Scandinavian Journal of Economics*, **96**, 257–65.

Hartwick, J. (1977), 'Intergenerational equity and the investing of rents from exhaustible resources', *American Economic Review*, **66**, 972–4.

Vincent, J. and J. Hartwick (1997), 'Forest resources and the national income accounts: concepts and experience', mimeo, Harvard University.

Weitzman, M.L. (1976), 'On the welfare significance of national product in a dynamic economy', *Quarterly Journal of Economics*, **90**, 156–62.

ACKNOWLEDGEMENTS

I would like to thank Henk Folmer, Landis Gabel and Karl-Gustaf Löfgren for helpful comments and suggestions. A research grant from HSFR is also gratefully acknowledged.

APPENDIX

The First-best 'Reference' Model

The utility maximization problem can be written

$$\underset{c(t),l(t),g(t)}{\text{Max}} \int_0^\infty u\big(c(t), T - l(t), x(t)\big) e^{-\theta t} dt$$

subject to

$$\dot{k}(t) = f(l(t), k(t), g(t)) - c(t)$$
$$\dot{x}(t) = g(t) - \gamma x(t)$$

$$k(0) = k_0 > 0$$
$$x(0) = x_0 > 0$$
$$\lim_{t \to \infty} k(t) \geq 0$$

$$\lim_{t \to \infty} x(t) \geq 0$$

where leisure time, L, is defined as a time endowment, T, less the time in market work, l. The present-value Hamiltonian takes the form

$$H_p(t) = u(c(t), T - l(t), x(t))e^{-\theta t} + \lambda_p(t)\dot{k}(t) + \mu_p(t)\dot{x}(t) \qquad (19A.1)$$

where λ_p and μ_p are present-value shadow prices. We obtain the current-value shadow prices in the text by multiplying by $e^{\theta t}$, that is, $\lambda^*(t) = \lambda_p^*(t)e^{\theta t}$ and $\mu^*(t) = \mu_p^*(t)e^{\theta t}$.

If we neglect the time indicator for notational convenience, and in addition to the restrictions on the optimization problem above, the necessary conditions are written

$$u_c(c^*, L^*, x^*)e^{-\theta t} - \lambda_p^* = 0 \qquad (19A.2)$$
$$-u_L(c^*, L^*, x^*)e^{-\theta t} + \lambda_p^* f_l(l^*, k^*, g^*) = 0 \qquad (19A.3)$$
$$\lambda_p^* f_g(l^*, k^*, g^*) + \mu_p^* = 0 \qquad (19A.4)$$
$$\dot{\lambda}_p^* = -\lambda_p^* f_k(l^*, k^*, g^*) \qquad (19A.5)$$
$$\dot{\mu}_p^* = -u_x(c^*, L^*, x^*)e^{-\theta t} + \mu_p^* \gamma \qquad (19A.6)$$

where the superscript '*' is used as a notation for the first-best optimal path. In addition to equations (19A.2)–(19A.6), there are also transversality conditions, which are necessary provided that the optimization problem obeys certain growth conditions.[29] By substituting the optimal control, state and costate variables into the present-value Hamiltonian, differentiating with respect to time and using the necessary conditions, we have

$$\frac{dH_p^*(t)}{dt} = -\theta u\left(c^*(t), L^*(t), x^*(t)\right)e^{-\theta t} \qquad (19.A7)$$

Solving this differential equation and transforming the outcome to current value gives the welfare measure[30]

$$\theta \int_{t}^{\infty} u(c^*(s), L^*(s), x^*(s)) e^{-\theta(s-t)} ds = H^*(t) \qquad (19.A8)$$

where $H^*(t) = H_p^*(t) e^{\theta t}$ is the current-value Hamiltonian, which is the correct welfare measure and interpreted as $GNNP_u^*(t)$ in the main text. To go from equation (19A.8) to the linearized welfare measure, note that by linearizing the instantaneous utility function, while using the necessary conditions given by equations (19A.2) and (19A.3), we obtain

$$u(c^*(t), L^*(t), x^*(t)) \approx \lambda^*(t) c^*(t) + \lambda^*(t) w^*(t) L^*(t) + u_x^*(t) x^*(t)$$

where $w^* = f_l(l^*, k^*, g^*)$ and $u_x^* = u_x(c^*, L^*, x^*)$.

Welfare Measurement and External Effects

The main difference between the first-best, if obtained by solving a social-planner problem, and the decentralized economy is that the accumulation equation for the stock of pollution is not a restriction in the latter case. It is, instead, a side-effect of the behaviour of the pollutant, and its path is exogenous to the consumer. To take a short cut to the decentralized solution, suppose that an emission tax, $\tau^0(t)$, is imposed on the firms to improve the resource allocation, and that this emission tax differs from the Pigouvian tax, that is, $\tau^0(t) \neq -\mu^*(t) / \lambda^*(t)$. It is, nevertheless, the best estimate available of the real shadow price of pollution. Conditional on this emission tax, the decentralized solution obeys, among other things, the following conditions (the time indicator has been neglected):

$$u_c(c^0, L^0, x^0) e^{-\theta t} - \lambda_p^0 = 0 \qquad (19A.9)$$

$$-u_L(c^0, L^0, x^0) e^{-\theta t} + \lambda_p^0 f_l(l^0, k^0, g^0) = 0 \qquad (19A.10)$$

$$f_g(l^0, k^0, g^0) - \tau^0 = 0 \qquad (19A.11)$$

$$\dot{\lambda}_p^0 = -\lambda_p^0 f_k(l^0, k^0, g^0) \qquad (19A.12)$$

where the superscript '0' is used to denote the decentralized path, which is derived conditional on the emission tax path $\{\tau^0(t)\}_0^{\infty}$. Note also from equation (19A.10) that this example presupposes that the labour market is in equilibrium. The necessary conditions given by equations (19A.9)–(19A.12) look as if they are derived from the following pseudo-Hamiltonian

$$H_p^0(t) = u(c^0(t), T - l^0(t), x^0(t)) e^{-\theta t} + \lambda_p^0(t) \dot{k}^0(t) - \lambda_p^0(t) \tau^0(t) \dot{x}^0(t) \qquad (19A.13)$$

which measures the utility value of the green NNP, discounted to present value, and $-\lambda_p^0(t)\tau^0(t)$ is interpretable as the shadow price of pollution in utility terms. By differentiating equation (19A.13) with respect to time and rearranging, we have

$$\frac{dH_p^0(t)}{dt} = -\theta u(c^0(t), L^0(t), x^0(t))e^{-\theta t} + [u_x^0(t)e^{-\theta t} + \lambda_p^0(t)\tau^0(t)\{f_k^0(t) + \gamma\}$$
$$- \lambda_p^0(t)\dot{\tau}^0(t)]\dot{x}^0(t)$$

where $u_x^0 = u_x(c^0, L^0, x^0)$ and $f_k^0 = f_k(l^0, k^0, g^0)$. By solving this differential equation and transforming the solution to current value gives the welfare measure

$$\theta \int_t^\infty u(c^0(s), L^0(s), x^0(s))e^{-\theta(s-t)}ds = H^0(t) + \Omega^0(t) \qquad (19.\text{A}14)$$

where

$$\Omega^0(t) = \int_t^\infty [u_x^0(s)e^{-\theta s} + \lambda_p^0(s)\tau^0(s)\{f_k^0(s) + \gamma\} - \lambda_p^0(s)\dot{\tau}^0(s)]e^{\theta t}\dot{x}^0(s)ds.$$

Equation (19A.14) corresponds to equation (19.9) in the text.

Finally, note that if the emission tax is Pigouvian, that is,

$$\tau^0(t) = \tau^*(t) = -\frac{\mu_p^*(t)}{\lambda_p^*(t)} \quad \text{for all } t$$

where μ_p^* and λ_p^* are determined by solving equations (19A.5) and (19A.6) subject to the appropriate transversality conditions, then equations (19A.9)–(19A.12) will look exactly like their counterparts in the first-best. Therefore, the Pigouvian emission tax path will imply that the outcome of private optimization coincides with that of the first-best optimization problem: $c^0(t) = c^*(t)$, $l^0(t) = l^*(t)$, $g^0(t) = g^*(t)$, $k^0(t) = k^*(t)$, $\lambda_p^0(t) = \lambda_p^*(t)$ and $x^0(t) = x^*(t)$ for all t. It will also imply that $H_p^0(t) = H_p^*(t)$ and $\Omega^0(t) = \Omega^*(t) = 0$ for all t. To fully understand the last result, use equations (19A.5) and (19A.6) to derive

$$\dot{\tau}^*(t) = \frac{u_x^*(t)e^{-\theta t}}{\lambda_p^*(t)} + \tau^*(t)[f_k^*(t) + \gamma]$$

By substituting this time derivative of the Pigouvian emission tax into the formula for the marginal external effect:

$$\Omega^*(t) = \int_t^\infty [u_x^*(s)e^{-\theta s} + \lambda_p^*(s)\tau^*(s)\{f_k^*(s) + \gamma\} - \lambda_p^*(s)\dot{\tau}^*(s)]e^{\theta t}\dot{x}^*(s)ds$$

it follows that the terms within the bracket cancel out and, as a consequence, $\Omega^*(t) = 0$ for all t.

Welfare Measurement and Distributional Objectives

The first-best optimization problem for the model used in the text can be written as follows:

$$\underset{c_1(t),c_2(t)}{\text{Max}} \int_0^\infty \Gamma\big(u_1(c_1(t)), u_2(c_2(t))\big)e^{-\theta t}dt$$

subject to

$$\dot{k}(t) = f(k(t)) - c_1(t) - c_2(t)$$
$$k(0) = k_0 > 0$$
$$\lim_{t\to\infty} k(t) \geq 0$$

The necessary conditions for this problem include the following equations (in which the time indicator has been neglected)

$$\frac{\partial \Gamma(u_1^*, u_2^*)}{\partial u_1} \frac{\partial u_1^*}{\partial c_1} e^{-\theta t} - \lambda_p^* = 0 \qquad (19A.15)$$

$$\frac{\partial \Gamma(u_1^*, u_2^*)}{\partial u_2} \frac{\partial u_2^*}{\partial c_2} e^{-\theta t} - \lambda_p^* = 0 \qquad (19A.16)$$

$$\dot{\lambda}_p^* = -\lambda_p^* f_k(k^*) \qquad (19A.17)$$

where the superscript '*' is again used to denote the first-best optimal path and λ_p^* is the present-value shadow price of capital.

By using the methods discussed previously in this Appendix, it is possible to show that the current-value Hamiltonian corresponding to this problem gives the correct welfare measure. This welfare measure is given by equation (19.12).

NOTES

1. Weitzman (1976).
2. Human capital is analysed in section 3.
3. This is based on Brock (1977). See also Tahvonen and Kuuluvainen (1993).
4. Since net output is defined as gross output less the depreciation of physical capital, it follows that the net output does not necessarily increase monotonically with the physical capital stock.
5. See also, for example, Samuelson (1961) for a useful discussion of this subject.
6. See, for example, Hartwick (1990) and Mäler (1991). See also Weitzman (1998) for an interpretation of the linearized welfare measure in terms of a normalization of the utility function.
7. Recall from the first-best optimum that $\mu^*(t) = -\lambda^*(t)\tau^*(t)$.
8. See Aronsson and Löfgren (1993, 1995).
9. The analysis of unemployment is based on Aronsson (1998b).
10. See Aronsson and Löfgren (1998).
11. See Hultkrantz (1992) for an application to the Swedish forest sector. See also Hartwick (1992) for a theoretical analysis of deforestation in the context of social accounting.
12. See, for example, Kemp and Long (1982), Löfgren (1992) and Aronsson and Löfgren (1993).
13. See Weitzman (1996) and Weitzman and Löfgren (1997). In the first paper future growth is driven by a time-dependent residual shift factor that increases productivity, although it does not show up anywhere in national income accounts. In the latter paper it is driven by labour-augmenting technological progress. The technological premium is of approximately the same magnitude in both cases.
14. For a survey of the willingness-to-pay technique as a means of capturing values, see Hanemann (1994). See also Chapter 3 of this volume. The use of the willingness-to-pay technique in the context of social accounting has been discussed by, for example, Peskin and Peskin (1978).
15. This is seen from equation (19.8). By evaluating equation (19.8) under the additional assumption that the marginal utility of pollution is constant, and denoted by $\bar{u}_x^*$, we have $\mu^*(t) = \bar{u}_x^* / (\theta + \gamma)$. The formula for the Pigouvian tax will be

$$\tau^*(t) = -\bar{u}_x^* / [(\theta + \gamma)\lambda^*(t)].$$

16. Note that the only capital concept here is physical capital.
17. See, for example, Solow (1986), Mäler (1991) Hulten (1992), Solow (1992) and Nordhaus (1995). For a recent survey of the sustainability issue, the reader is referred to Hartwick (1997).
18. The World Commission on Environment and Development, *Our Common Future*, Oxford: Oxford University Press, p. 43.
19. See Fisher (1906).
20. *Value and Capital*, 1939, p. 165.
21. See, for example, Hulten (1992), Dasgupta and Mäler (1991) and Mäler (1991).
22. Pezzey (1995) proved a similar result.
23. See Aronsson et al. (1997).
24. Recall from section 2 that

$$\theta \int_t^\infty u^*(s)e^{-\theta(s-t)}ds = GNNP_u^*(t).$$

Integrating the left-hand side by parts and solving for the value of net investment gives the formula in the text.

25. Asheim (1996) analyses terms of trade effects and their complications for welfare measurement.
26. The reader is referred to Mäler (1989), Tahvonen (1994), and Mäler and de Zeeuw (1995) to mention a few. More details are available in a recent survey by Missfeldt (1996).
27. See, for example, van der Ploeg and de Zeeuw (1992).
28. One way of implementing a Nash-non-cooperative solution concept in market economies would be to impose 'local' Pigouvian taxes, which only reflect how pollution caused by country i affects the utility of consumers in country i. The reader is referred to Aronsson and Löfgren (2000) for details.
29. The reader is referred to Seierstad and Sydsaeter (1987, Theorem 16 of ch. 3) for further details.
30. I have used the result that the present-value Hamiltonian approaches zero when time goes to infinity, which is due to Michel (1982).

REFERENCES

Ahlroth, S., A. Björklund and A. Forslund (1997), 'The output of the Swedish education sector', *Review of Income and Wealth*, **43**, 89–104.
Aronsson, T. (1998a), 'Welfare measurement, green accounting and distortionary taxes', *The Journal of Public Economics*, **70**, 273–95.
Aronsson, T. (1998b), 'A note on social accounting and unemployment', *Economics Letters*, **59**, 381–4.
Aronsson, T. and K.G. Löfgren (1993), 'Welfare consequences of technological and environmental externalities in the Ramsey Growth Model', *Natural Resource Modeling*, **7** (1), 1–14.
Aronsson, T. and K.G. Löfgren (1995), 'National product related welfare measures in the presence of technological change, externalities and uncertainty', *Environmental and Resource Economics*, **5**, 321–32.
Aronsson, T. and K-G. Löfgren (1998), 'Green accounting in imperfect market economies – a summary of recent research', *Environmental and Resource Economics*, **11**, 273–87.
Aronsson, T. and K-G. Löfgren (1999a), 'Welfare equivalent NNP under distributional objectives', *Economics Letters*, **63**, 239–43.
Aronsson, T. and K-G. Löfgren (1999b), 'Pollution tax design and green national accounting', *European Economic Review*, **43**, 1457–74.
Aronsson, T. and K-G. Löfgren (2000), 'Green accounting and green taxes in the global economy', forthcoming in H. Folmer, L. Gabel and A. Rose, (eds), *Frontiers of Environmental Economics*, Cheltenham, UK and Northampton, USA: Edward Elgar.
Aronsson, T., P.O. Johansson and K.G. Löfgren (1997), *Welfare Measurement, Sustainability and Green National Accounting*, Cheltenham UK and Lyme, USA: Edward Elgar.
Asheim, G.B. (1994), 'Net national product as an indicator of sustainability', *Scandinavian Journal of Economics*, **96**, 257–65.
Asheim, G.B. (1996), 'Capital gains and "net national product" in open economies', *Journal of Public Economics*, **59**, 419–34.
Brock, W.A. (1977), 'A polluted golden age', in V.L. Smith (ed.), *Economics of Natural and Environmental Resources*, New York: Gordon & Breach.

Dasgupta, P. and K.G. Mäler (1991), 'The environment and emerging development issues', Beijer Reprint Series No. 1. The Royal Swedish Academy of Sciences.

Dixit, A., P. Hammond and M. Hoel (1980), 'On Hartwick's rule for regular maxmim paths of capital accumulation', *Review of Economic Studies*, **47**, 551–6.

Fisher, I. (1906), *The Nature of Capital and Income*, New York: Macmillan.

Hamilton, K. and F. Lutz (1996), 'Green national accounts: policy uses and empirical experience', Paper no. 039, Environmental Economic Series. Environmental Department, World Bank, Washington, DC.

Hanemann, M. (1994), 'Valuing the environment through contingent valuation', *The Journal of Economic Perspectives*, **8**, 19–43.

Hartwick, J. (1977), 'Intergenerational equity and the investing of rents from exhaustible resources', *American Economic Review*, **66**, 972–4.

Hartwick, J. (1990), 'Natural resources, national accounting and economic depreciation', *Journal of Public Economics*, **43**, 291–304.

Hartwick, J. (1992), 'Deforestation and national accounting', *Environmental and Resource Economics*, **2**, 513–21.

Hartwick, J. (1997), 'National wealth, constant consumption and sustainable development', in T. Tietenberg and H. Folmer (eds), *International Yearbook of Environmental and Resource Economics: 1997/1998: A Survey of Current Issues*, Cheltenham, UK and Lyme, USA: Edward Elgar.

Hicks, J.R. (1939), *Value and Capital* (2nd edition), Oxford: Clarendon Press.

Hulten, C. (1992), 'Accounting for the wealth of nations: the net versus gross output controversy and its ramifications', *Scandinavian Journal of Economics*, **94**, supplement, 9–24.

Hultkrantz, L. (1992), 'National accounts of timber and forest environmental resources in Sweden', *Environmental and Resource Economics*, **2**, 283–305.

Jorgenson, D.W. and B. Fraumeni (1992), 'Investment in education and U.S. economic growth', *Scandinavian Journal of Economics* **94**, supplement, 51–70.

Kemp, M.C. and N. van Long (1982), 'On the evolution of social income in a dynamic economy: variations on a Samuelsonian theme', in G.R. Feiwell (ed.), *Samuelson and Neoclassical Economics*, Boston: Kluwer-Nijhoff.

Lindahl, E. (1933), 'The concept of income', in G. Bagge (ed.), *Economic Essays in Honor of Gustaf Cassel*, London: George Allen & Unwin.

Löfgren, K.G. (1992), 'Comments on C.R. Hulten, "Accounting for the Wealth of Nations: The Net versus Gross Output Controversy and its Ramifications" ', *Scandinavian Journal of Economics*, **94**, supplement, 25–8.

Mäler, K.G. (1989), 'The acid rain game', in H. Folmer and E. Van Ireland (eds), *Valuation Methods and Policy Making in Environmental Economics*, Amsterdam: Elsevier.

Mäler, K.G. (1991), 'National accounts and environmental resources', *Environmental and Resource Economics*, **1**, 1–15.

Mäler, K.G. and A.J. de Zeeuw (1995), 'Critical loads in games of transboundary pollution control', *Nota di Lavora 7.95*, Fondazione Eni Enrico Mattei, Milan.

Michel, P. (1982), 'On the transversality condition in infinite horizon optimal control problems', *Econometrica*, **50**, 975–85.

Missfeldt, F. (1996), 'Game theoretic modelling of transboundary pollution: a review of the literature', Economics Department, Stirling University.

Nordhaus, W.D. (1995), 'How should we measure sustainable income?', Cowles Foundation Working Paper, Yale University.

Nordhaus, W.D. and J. Tobin (1972), 'Is growth obsolete?', in *Economic Growth*, New York: National Bureau of Economic Research.

Peskin, H.M. and J. Peskin (1978), 'The valuation of nonmarket goods in income accounting', *The Review of Income and Wealth*, **24**, 71–91.

Pezzey, J. (1995), 'Non-declining wealth is not equivalent to sustainability', mimeo, Department of Economics, University College, London.

van der Ploeg, F. and A.J. de Zeeuw (1992), 'International aspects of pollution control', *Environmental and Resource Economics*, **2**, 117–39.

Repetto, R., W. Magrath, M. Wells, C. Beer and F. Rossini (1989), *Wasting Assets: Natural Resources in the National Income Accounts*, Washington, DC: World Resources Institute.

Samuelson, P.A. (1961), 'The evaluation of social income: capital formation and wealth', in F. Lutz and R.C. Hague (eds), *The Theory of Capital*, Proceedings from the IEA Conference, New York: St Martin's Press.

Seierstad, A. and Sydsaeter, K. (1987), *Optimal Control Theory with Economic Applications*, Amsterdam: North-Holland.

Sheng, F. (1995), *Real Value of Nature*, Gland, Switzerland: World Wildlife Fund International.

Solow, R.M. (1986), 'On the intergenerational allocation of natural resources', *Scandinavian Journal of Economics*, **88**, 141–9.

Solow, R.M. (1992), 'An almost practical step towards sustainability', Resources for the Future Invited Lecture, Washington, DC.

Tahvonen, O. (1994), 'Carbon dioxide abatement as a differential game', *European Journal of Political Economy*, **10**, 685–705.

Tahvonen, O. and J. Kuuluvainen (1993), 'Economic growth, pollution, and renewable resources', *Journal of Environmental Economics and Management*, **24**, 101–18.

Weitzman, M.L. (1976), 'On the welfare significance of national product in a dynamic economy', *Quarterly Journal of Economics*, **90**, 156–62.

Weitzman, M.L. (1997), 'Sustainability and technical progress', *Scandinavian Journal of Economics*, **99**, 1–13.

Weitzman, M.L. (1998), 'Comprehensive NDP and the sustainability–equivalent principle', Harvard University.

Weitzman, M.L. and Löfgren, K.G. (1997), 'On the welfare significance of green accounting as taught by parable', *Journal of Environmental Economics and Management*, **32**, 139–53.

Vincent, J. and Hartwick, J. (1997), 'Forest resources and the national income accounts: concepts and experience', mimeo, Harvard University.

20. Economic growth and environmental quality

Sjak Smulders

1. INTRODUCTION

Can economic growth go on without deteriorating the quality of the environment? Is economic growth still desirable if we take its adverse consequences for the environment into account? What are the effects of environmental policy on economic growth?

These questions are typically asked when thinking about the interaction between economic growth and environmental quality. On the one hand, the (in itself desirable) huge improvements in the standard of living during the past decades have not been without a dark side. Air pollution (smoke and noise), municipal waste problems, loss of wilderness areas, habitat destruction, threats to biodiversity, resource depletion and the global greenhouse problem seem to be linked to economic growth. Growing awareness of these problems raises questions as to whether economic growth is still desirable. Doomsday scenarios become imaginable in which the success of growth leads to its own demise and to the collapse of the world economy because of environmental problems. On the other hand, economic growth has created richer and more productive economies which have access to more advanced levels of technological knowledge. Productivity per unit of natural resource use has increased which allows, in principle, larger volumes of production at lower rates of environmental degradation. Technological progress and economic growth have created the opportunities and resources to finance investments in new environmentally friendly technologies, to solve waste problems, and to reduce material and resource use.

This chapter uses analytical tools from environmental economics and the theory of economic growth to shed some light on how to assess these two opposing views. It provides a theoretical perspective on the above questions. In particular, we extend the modern theory of economic growth to incorporate economy–environment interactions. We concentrate on the link between economic and environmental dynamics at a high level of aggregation by considering growth in GDP and changes in an aggregate index of environmental quality. We formulate a unifying framework that is general and flexible enough to study the common elements and main mechanisms that are present in more specific situations where economic growth and environmental change interact.

Sections 2 and 3 outline the basic framework. A core model of five equations suffices for our purposes. We examine how 'first principles' from production and utility theory, as well as from physics and biology, restrict the specifications of these equations. Sections 4 and 5 confront the optimistic and pessimistic views of economic growth and the environment. Within the framework of the sections we examine some conditions under which sustainable growth becomes infeasible, and some necessary conditions for the more optimistic scenario of feasible unlimited sustainable growth. We also examine when growth may become undesirable even when sustainable growth is feasible. Sections 6–8 are devoted to the impact of environmental policy on standards of living and economic growth. In these sections we assume that unbounded growth without hurting the environment is feasible, but not necessarily desirable. A distinction is made between the positive and normative analysis of environmental policy. The former deals with the effects of a more or less arbitrarily chosen change in the level of pollution in the economy, while the latter deals with the optimal reduction of pollution, given preferences and the structure of the economy. Furthermore, we explore the role of technological change in more detail by distinguishing between exogenous and investment-driven endogenous technological change.

2. GROWTH–ENVIRONMENT INTERACTIONS

Economic growth and physical conditions of the environment interact. Economic activity may be the cause of environmental problems, but so also might a deterioration in physical conditions hamper economic processes. Environmental change and economic growth interact because of many environment–economy links and feedbacks. First, the environment is a sink for wastes and, second, a source of resources for the economy. Third, society may have a preference for a clean environment, because environmental quality has an amenity value or an existence value (see Chapter 2 for a detailed discussion). Fourth, a clean environment boosts productivity of production factors, so that it has a productive value. Finally, part of economic activity may be directly devoted to cleaning up spoilt parts of the environment, that is, abatement and recycling may take place.

In order to analyse these interactions, it is useful to focus on the essential distinguishing features of ecological and economic processes and their links. In the tradition of economic growth models, we take an aggregate view, that is, we consider national production (GDP) without distinguishing between the ouputs generated in different sectors of the economy, and we consider a single index for environmental quality rather than distinguishing between different natural resources and indicators of the state of the environment.

The interplay of supply (production technology), demand (preferences), and market institutions (regulation and intervention) forms the economic sphere in which production and allocation are determined. In particular, it determines at what rate natural resources are used for production, how much pollution is generated in the economy, and how much of total output in the economy is used for investment. Natural resource use and pollution affect the environment, investment creates new capital inputs for future use and thus creates opportunities for economic growth.

How exactly resource use and pollution affect the environment depends on ecological considerations. Changes in environmental quality are subject to complex processes that in general take place gradually over time. Hence, it is useful to see the environment as a renewable natural resource stock that may grow or decline over time, depending on whether resource use falls short or exceeds the natural growth of the resource.[1]

Economic growth and environmental quality improvements over time thus depend on two types of investments. First, investment in physical capital and other man-made production assets expands the available endowments of factors of production (provided that investment exceeds depreciation), allowing for growth in output. Second, by limiting pollution and natural resource use, the environment improves. It is these two types of investments, investments in man-made assets and in natural assets, that determine the interaction between economic growth and the environment.

The fundamentals of growth–environment interactions can be studied by linking in a dynamic model a macroeconomic production function, a utility function, a natural resource growth function, and assumptions about government regulation and institutions. The simplest model one could think of consists of the following set of equations:

$$Y = C + I \qquad \text{market equilibrium} \qquad (20.1)$$

$$Y = F(N, P, K, T) \qquad \text{technology} \qquad (20.2)$$

$$\dot{K} = I - \delta K \qquad \text{accumulation} \qquad (20.3)$$

$$\dot{N} = E(N) - P \qquad \text{natural resource growth} \qquad (20.4)$$

$$W = \int_0^\infty U(C, N) \exp(-\theta t) \, dt \qquad \text{(intertemporal) utility} \qquad (20.5)$$

where N is an indicator of environmental quality, P is the use of services from the environment in production, $E(\cdot)$ is the capacity of the environment to absorb pollution, Y is aggregate economic activity (production), K is the stock of man-made capital, T is the state of technology, C is consumption of man-made goods, $U(\cdot)$ is instantaneous utility, and θ is utility discount rate; all variables depend on the time index t. The following natural assumption are made (where notation is abreviated by the use of subscripts attached to function symbols to denote partial derivatives):

- $F_N \geq 0$, $F_P > 0$, $F_K > 0$, $F_T > 0$ inputs contribute non-negatively to production;
- $U_C > 0$, $U_N \geq 0$ consumption and amenities are not disliked;
- $N \geq 0$, $P \geq 0$, $C \geq 0$, $K \geq 0$, $Y \geq 0$ non-negativity constraints;
- Initial values $N(0)$ and $K(0)$ are given, as well as $T(t)$.

Equations (20.1)–(20.3) represent the production block of the model, equation (20.4) models ecological processes as growth and depletion of a renewable resource, and equation (20.5) specifies preferences.

The goods market equilibrium condition (20.1) states that supply of goods (Y) is equated to demand for goods, which consists of demand for produced consumption goods (C) and demand for investment goods (I). Supply is determined by the production function $F(\cdot)$. There are two types of inputs, produced capital inputs K and natural inputs P and N. Produced capital goods comprise all kinds of reproducible productive assets like physical capital, knowledge (or human) capital, and infrastructure. Equation (20.3) captures the fact that this stock of man-made capital results from cumulated investment. Environmental quality N affects productivity, so that environmental quality acts as an input in production. This might happen because the health of workers is improved, which boosts labour productivity, or because wear and tear of buildings diminishes with improved air quality. Note that with respect to these services the environment acts like a public good. All workers and firms benefit from the same environmental quality and its services are therefore non-rival in nature. Natural inputs P are inputs like mineral and energy use. They are extractive (or rival) in nature as can be seen from equation (20.4) that models the change in environmental quality (or the stock of environmental resources) N. Each unit of resource use P correspondingly reduces the available stock of natural resources N. Also pollution can be interpreted as extractive use of the environment: each unit of pollution generated by production reduces environmental quality. Hence, by P we capture not only extractive resource use but also pollution and accordingly we will interchangably use the terms 'resource use', 'pollution' and 'polluting inputs' for it.[2] Similarly, the variable N stands for both the stock of environmental resources and the quality of the environment. After all, environmental quality (like clean air or water) is a valuable resource that can be depleted. The environment provides services to production, both in the form of directly productive inputs and in the form of media (soil, water, air) in which to dump pollution.

According to equation (20.4), pollution and extraction of resources P can be counteracted by ecological processes captured by the term $E(N)$. The latter represents nature's capacity to renew itself and to assimilate pollution. As long as the economy uses less environmental services than are provided by ecological processes, that is, $P < E(N)$, environmental quality improves over time. Nature is able to absorb a certain amount of pollution without deteriorating equal to $E(N)$, so that we may call $E(N)$ the absorption capacity of the environment. An ecological equilibrium (defined by $\dot{N} = 0$) can only be maintained if pollution P is constant and does not exceed the maximum absorption capacity.

Society's preferences are modelled by the utility function in (20.5) with produced consumption (C) and environmental amenities (measured by N) as the arguments. The latter also allows taking into account the existence value of the environment. Note that environmental quality contributes directly as well as indirectly to welfare in the model. It contributes directly because of amenity and existence values. It contributes indirectly because of its productive value (N enters the production function so that environmental quality boosts the production of consumption goods) and also because its ecological value (N affects nature's capability to absorb pollution so that environmental quality affects the availability of natural inputs to produce consumption goods).

The model presented so far only gives a rough picture of the structure of the economy. We need to specify more exactly the properties of the production, utility and absorption functions. Moreover, we need to specify economic behaviour that determines, for example, consumption, investment and natural resource use. Obviously, both elements crucially determine the interaction between growth and the environment. We proceed as follows. First we study alternative specifications of the three mentioned functions. In the next section we describe how elementary principles from physics (thermodynamics) and biology are likely to restrict these functions. By considering the specification for the production function in section 4, we may find out whether sustained long-run growth is feasible. In particular, this allows us to study whether it is possible to choose C and P in such a way that Y grows forever. The specification of preferences determines whether long-run growth (if feasible) is desirable. Second, we will make assumptions about savings behaviour and resource use. This allows us to investigate which of the feasible growth paths actually occur and whether actual growth paths are desirable. We contrast economies with different degrees of government intervention in order to investigate whether the market grows too fast and what the effects of environmental regulation are for economic growth.

3. HOW THERMODYNAMICS LAWS RESTRICT FEASIBLE ECONOMIC GROWTH

3.1 How Large was the Garden of Eden?

The environment can be seen as a natural resource that is valuable because it provides four types of services to human beings in the form of amenity services, productive services and ecological services. The total of services that the environment may provide is ultimately limited. The reason is that the state of the environment is ultimately constrained by biophysical principles. The environment is a highly ordered structure that is able to use and transform energy. In fact, all services by the environment can be reduced to (some form of) energy. Different parts of the environment create and use different forms of energy (think of a pool where big fishes grow by eating small fishes). Hence, ecological services are 'produced' by the environment, using its own services. However, in this process of using services and transforming or reusing energy, energy becomes dissipated and less and less useful. This can be understood by the 'entropy law' which states that the transformation and rearrangement of material and energy inevitably implies an irreversible process from free or available energy into bound or unavailable energy.

If the environment had to rely on its own services only (the energy it makes available itself), it would be doomed to decay. The environment is preserved thanks to the constant inflow of energy from outside, that is, solar energy. This inflow offsets the entropy process and allows for a steady 'production' of ecological services. Figure 20.1 illustrates this. The concave curve represents the 'supply' of ecological services, as the result of the transformation of solar energy by the environment. The richer the environment (higher N), the more services can be produced. However, diminishing marginal returns apply since the input of solar energy is fixed. The convex curve represents the 'demand' for ecological services that is needed to maintain a given level of environmental quality. More complex ecosystems (higher N) require more inputs to be maintained.

The difference between the supply curve and the replacement demand curve is excess supply of ecological services (energy) that can be used to grow the environment, making it richer and more complex. Hence, this difference exactly equals $E(N)$, that was introduced in equation (20.4), and represents the net amount of energy available for rival use. Processes of environmental change ($\dot{N}$) and pollution or extractive resource use (P) are the rival users of this available amount of energy, that is, $E(N) = \dot{N} + P$.

We may draw several conclusions. First, there is an upper bound to environmental quality. This upper bound may be reached if all available ecological

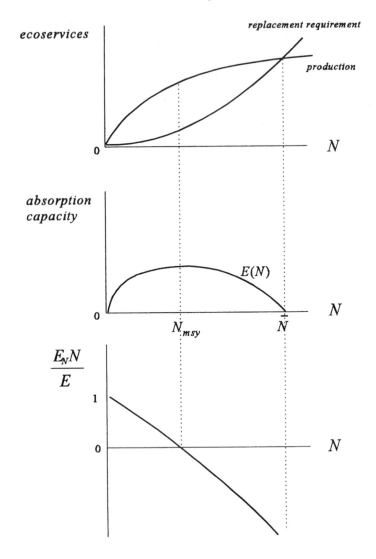

Note: A richer environment (indicated by a higher N) not only produces but also uses more eco-
services for maintenance (upper panel). The difference between production and use for maintenance
is the net available amount of resources to improve environmental quality, denoted by E(N) in the
middle panel. It equals nature's absorption capacity, that is the amount of pollution that can be
assimilated without a change in environmental quality. For $N > \bar{N}$, the inflow of solar energy is insufficient to maintain environmental quality, so that $\bar{N}$ is the maximal (virgin or garden of Eden) level.
The lower panel depicts the elasticity of the absorption capacity with respect to environmental
quality which monotonically decreases and becomes negative for $N > N_{msy}$.

Figure 20.1   How ecological processes determine absorption capacity

services are exploited by nature to grow (and nothing of it is used up in the economy, $P = 0$), so that $\dot{N} = E(N)$. Given the limited inflow of solar energy, the environment is never able to produce eco-services to maintain a higher level of environmental quality than $N = \bar{N}$. The basic reason is that the higher the quality of the environment, the more eco-services are needed to sustain this level, whereas the supply of these services is ultimately limited by solar energy because of the entropy law. The maximal level of environmental quality $\bar{N}$ can be called the virgin state of the environment or the garden of Eden level of environmental quality.

Second, the absorption capacity of the environment is a hump-shaped function of environmental quality; see middle panel of Figure 20.1. That is, when environmental quality improves, the net supply of ecological services E first increases, but decreases if environmental quality grows large. Intuitively, at low environmental quality, few ecological services are provided but also few are needed because the complexity of the ecosystem is low. When the environment improves, it not only produces more services but it also grows more complex so that a larger and larger fraction of the services it generates are needed to maintain at least this quality and complexity level. At $N = \bar{N}$ all eco-services produced are needed to maintain environmental quality.

Third, it immediately follows that there is an upper bound to the absorption capacity E. No pollution level can be mainained above this upper level without reducing environmental quality to zero. Hence, a feasible growth path requires a long-run pollution level below this. We will denote the maximal sustainable pollution level by P_{msy} and the associated level of environmental quality for which absorption capicity is at this maximal level by N_{msy}.[3]

Fourth, environmental quality cannot fall below a critical level without destroying ecosystems. For simplicity we assume that N should remain positive for ecosystems to keep functioning. If no eco-services are provided ($N = 0$), regeneration of nature as well as absorption of pollution stops. (In terms of production theory, N is a necessary input in the production of eco-services.)

To sum up, we have found the following properties of the ecological function:

- $E(0) = 0$: environmental quality is necessary for eco-services.
- $E_{NN} < 0$: the entropy law applies.

     That is, the absorption capacity first increases in N (from 0 to P_{msy} if N increases from 0 to N_{msy}), and then decreases (from P_{msy} to 0, if N increases from N_{msy} to $\bar{N}$).
- $N \leq \bar{N}$: environmental quality is bounded.
- $\partial(E_N N/E)/\partial N < 0$: the elasticity of nature's absorption capacity declines in environmental quality.

Note that the last property immediately follows from the second one. We will frequently use this property in section 6. The middle panel of Figure 20.1 depicts the shape of nature's absorption capacity that we will use in the rest of this chapter. For later use, the lower panel depicts the associated elasticity of the absorption capacity $E_N N/E$.[4]

Obviously, our assumptions imply a drastic, but powerful simplification. A more complex picture (with several local maxima, for instance) may be justified if we take into account interaction between different parts of the real-world environment. For example, the temperature of the oceans affects the temperature of the different layers of the atmosphere and hence growth of plants and forests in complex, non-linear ways (see Nordhaus, 1994 for an accessible description). Similarly, in a more general model we could assume that there is a threshold level of environmental quality below which ecosystems are irreversibly damaged, that is $E(N) = 0$ for all levels of environmental quality N below some positive level $N_{ssp} < \bar{N}$, where N_{ssp} is the 'silent spring level of environmental quality'.[5] Notwithstanding, most results in the rest of this chapter will go through (or can be easily modified to accommodate more complex shapes of the absorption capacity function), provided that we maintain the key assumption on ecological process, that is, that environmental quality is bounded and that absorption capacity is bounded.

3.2   How Large is Plato's World of Ideas? (Production)

No production is possible without energy and material use. We will assume that P is a necessary input in production. This is obvious in the case of producing a well-defined object, say the paper on which this chapter is printed. It is also true in general if we realize that all production for which we care (that is all output of economic activity that enters utility), including any service, is in some sense basically 'work', or something that pleases the brain, that changes the state of our body. No physical change can occur without energy use, so there is no consumption without energy use. Since it is the environment that makes energy available, production necessarily uses natural inputs.

However, no valuable production is possible without knowledge as to how to produce; no enjoyment from produced consumption goods is possible without knowledge of how to enjoy. This also seems trivial, but it points out two things. First, man-made inputs and natural inputs alike are necessary. Second, consumable (or valuable) produced goods embody both energy and knowledge. Hence the variables K, Y, and C are not of a strictly physical dimension. This implies that it should be possible in principle to produce more and more that pleases the brain without necessarily increasing the input of energy, just by increasing the knowledge content of production. This has strong implications for the amount of energy, or more general natural inputs, that is necessary for a certain amount of production. While there may be a minimum energy and material requirement to produce a given product using a given process technology, there is in principle *no* minimum requirement of energy to reach a certain level of (aggregate) production or utility. In other words, while at a process level energy requirements impose strict constraints, at the more aggregate level, which is more relevant from an economic perspective, substitution between knowledge and energy makes minimum energy requirements less important. The time dimension helps to relax energy requirement constraints. Over time, new technologies, processes and ways to organize the economy may become available. In short, new ideas shifts minimum energy requirements for the economy as a whole (see Cleveland and Ruth, 1997).

While thermodynamics laws can be invoked to argue that environmental quality is bounded, it is not immediately clear whether the stock of human knowledge is bounded over time. Production of new knowledge is not subject to a law comparable to the entropy law. That is, there is no reason to assume that using existing knowledge to create new knowledge reduces the availability of useful knowledge. In contrast, the exploitation of knowledge is non-rival (whereas the use of ecological services is crucially rival). A single idea can be used over and over again by many persons without degrading. The stock of available knowledge does not become depleted by the use of it. On the contrary, the more widespread knowledge is, the more productive it may be (by some kind of network externality). Available knowledge is not only used to produce goods and services, but also to produce new knowledge. Availability, dissemination and use of knowledge may stimulate the generation of new knowledge. It remains a philosophical question whether the total number of useful ideas that can be generated is bounded (as in Plato's metaphor where human beings can only capture a shadow of the Ideas that exist in the ideal world of Ideas) or unbounded. We cannot know how much is unknown at present.

In the rest of this chapter we will see that sustainable economic growth (ongoing increases in economic output) requires an ongoing process of creation of new knowledge. The process of knowledge creation is usually called technological progress in growth models, but it should be clear that this process not only encompasses the development of new technologies but also changes in organization, management and marketing, not only in firms, but in all value-creating entities (including schools or universities and public institutions). What we have stressed here is that we have no theory to predict whether unbounded technological change is possible, but in any case, thermodynamic laws do not directly restrict the process of technological change, whereas they do play a crucial role in ecological processes.

To sum up, we have found the following properties of the production and utility function which state that to produce and enjoy we need both natural and man-made inputs:

- $F(0, P, K, T) = F(N, 0, K, T) = F(N,P, 0, T) = F(N, P, K, 0) = 0$: all inputs are necessary in production;
- $U(0, N), U(C, 0) \leq U(\tilde{C}, \tilde{N})$ for and $\tilde{C}, \tilde{N}$: all arguments are necessary in utility.

4.   DOOMSDAY MODELS

Many economists, as well as researchers from other disciplines and popular press writers, have been sceptical about the possibility of unbounded economic growth without environmental collapse. The best-known representation of this view is the Club of Rome's 1972 report *The Limits to Growth* (Meadows et al., 1972).[6] This section investigates some cases that support this doomsday view. To be more precise, it presents cases in which no time paths for resource use P and investment I exist such that output Y keeps growing in the long run. It also identifies some necessary conditions under which doomsday may be avoided.

4.1   Doomsday I: No Substitution

Suppose the economy's production possibilities can be described as follows. If environmental quality is below a certain threshold level $\underline{N}$ (where $\underline{N} < \bar{N}$), no production is possible. If it is above the threshold level, production requires natural inputs P and man-made inputs in a fixed proportion. Man-made inputs comprise reproducible capital K and exogenously determined technology capital T. In particular, the technology level is measured in such a way that TK measures the effective input level of man-made inputs, that is, technology T represents the productivity of the capital stock K. Formally, the profuction function reads:[7]

$$F(N,P,K,T) = \begin{cases} 0 & \text{if } N < \underline{N} \\ \min(P,TK) & \text{otherwise.} \end{cases} \qquad (20.6)$$

The main feature of this production function is that there is no substitution between environmental and man-made inputs.[8] Given our assumptions in the previous sections, unbounded long-run growth is infeasible. Growth requires increases in both P and TK. However, if P grows unboundedly, it will exceed the upper bound that is required to maintain a positive level of environmental quality, which in turn is required to keep production viable. Hence, independent of how fast capital is accumulated or technology improves, output is bounded.

The same conclusion applies in less extreme cases in which environmental and man-made inputs are not perfect complements but (poor) substitutes. Substitution means that we may reduce one input and increase the other without changing output levels. Hence, we may increase man-made inputs and reduce environmental inputs and still produce the same amount. Or, equivalently, we may increase man-made inputs, keep environmental input the same and produce more. The crucial issue is now how much more output results from increasing only capital inputs. If substitution is poor, more capital yields less and less additional output such that output never exceeds a certain upper bound, no matter how large capital grows (for a formalization of the relation between substitution and boundness of production see Dasgupta and Heal, 1978, ch. 7).

Feasible long-run growth requires good substitution between man-made inputs that can be reproduced and environmental inputs that ultimately are constant. With good substitutability, output per unit of the input that is kept constant may grow without bound by letting the other input grow without bound.

Technological change does not prevent doomsday in the specification in (20.6). The reason is that technological change does not affect the relationship between pollution and output, but only that between capital and output. Technological progress is capital augmenting. If it were environmental-input-augmenting instead, that is, if T multiplied P, constant environmental inputs could be reconciled with unbounded growth, provided that technological change was unbounded.

4.2 Doomsday II: Malthusian Stagnation (Decreasing Returns without Technological Progress)

Now suppose that environmental and man-made inputs are good substitutes, but there are decreasing returns to the accumulation of reproducible capital, that is, one additional unit of capital contributes proportionally less and less to production. Moreover, there is no technological change. In particular, let's assume the following Cobb–Douglas specification:

$$F(N,P,K,T) = \begin{cases} 0 & \text{if } N < \underline{N} \\ P^{\omega}T^{\gamma}K^{\beta} & \text{otherwise.} \end{cases} \tag{20.7}$$

where $0 < \beta < 1$ and T is a positive constant. Since T is constant and P has an upper limit, unbounded growth, if feasible, has to be driven by capital accumulation. Clearly, the maximal feasible long-run growth rate is attained if P is set at the maximal level (to be denoted by P_{msy}) and if capital accumulation is maximal, that is, if total output is invested $I = Y$. The growth rate of capital is then, from (20.3):

$$\dot{K}/K = Y/K - \delta = (P_{msy})^\omega T^\gamma K^{\beta-1} - \delta \tag{20.8}$$

Hence the growth rate of K falls with the level of capital. For small levels of the capital stock, the output/capital ratio Y/K is large enough to exceed the rate of depreciation δ, so that the economy generates enough output to both replace worn-out capital and expand the capital stock. The higher the capital stock, however, the lower productivity of capital as measured by the output/capital ratio. As a result very high levels of K necessarily yield a falling capital stock since total output at these levels is insufficient to replace all worn-out capital ($Y < \delta K$).

Figure 20.2 illustrates this. The downward-sloping curve is the output/capital ratio that depends negatively on the capital stock because of diminishing returns. For levels of K below $\bar{K}$, the output/capital ratio exceeds the rate of depreciation so that a growing stock of capital can be supported. For $K > \bar{K}$, capital falls.

The maximal long-run capital stock $\bar{K}$ can be calculated from (20.8) by setting $\dot{K} = 0$, which gives:

$$\bar{K} = (P_{msy}^{\ \omega} T^\gamma/\delta)^{1/(1-\beta)} \tag{20.9}$$

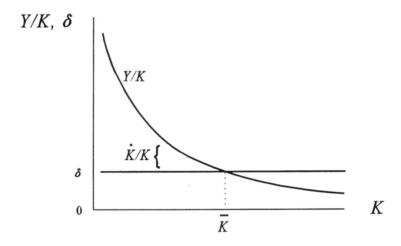

Note: When capital is relatively scarce ($K < \bar{K}$), its productivity is high and enough production is available to expand the capital stock. When the capital stock is large ($K > \bar{K}$), depreciation requirement δ is larger than available production per unit of capital (Y/K) and the capital stock necessarily falls. The basic reason is diminishing returns, implying that marginal capital productivity falls to zero when capital grows large.

Figure 20.2   Capital accumulation with diminishing returns

Since the capital is stock is bounded, capital accumulation cannot keep growth going. The basic reason is diminishing returns, that is, the phenomenon that output per unit of capital decreases as the capital stock is expanded. Under this assumption, a growing economy has less and less investment opportunities available and growth peters out. The classical economists Malthus and David Ricardo stressed the same source of limits to growth. In their view, an expanding population is forced to exploit land with lower and lower yields, food production per head falls and starvation slows down population growth.

In the presence of diminishing returns and without technological change, there is only one escape from stagnation, that is, boundedness of capital productivity. In the example above, the Cobb–Douglas specification of the production function implies that the output/capital ratio falls to zero when capital grows infinitely large. However, if the output/capital ratio were bounded from below such that it always exceeded δ, unbounded growth would become feasible (see Jones and Manuelli, 1990). The following generalization of the production function in (20.9) allows for this:

$$F(N,P,K,T) = \begin{cases} 0 & \text{if } N < \underline{N} \\ P^{\omega} \cdot T^{\gamma} \cdot h(K) & \text{otherwise,} \end{cases} \qquad (20.10)$$

where $h(\cdot)$ is an concavely increasing function of K, such that when K grows large, $h(\cdot)$ increases linearly with K, that is:

$$h_K(K) > b > 0, \ h_{KK}(K) < 0, \text{ and } \lim_{K \to \infty} h(K) = bK.$$

The upper panel of Figure 20.3 depicts the production function. The lower panel confronts the output/capital ratio, or capital productivity, to depreciation requirement. Returns to capital still fall in a growing economy, but since capital productivity is bounded below by $bP^{\omega}T^{\gamma}$, they do not fall to 'starvation levels' provided that $bP^{\omega}T^{\gamma} > \delta$.[9] Despite diminishing returns, the economy remains fairly productive.

Diminishing returns may be offset by increases in productivity through technological progress. An increase in T in (20.7) captures technological progress: it improves output for any given level of other inputs. Equation (20.9) shows that the maximal sustainable capital stock unboundedly grows if technology grows without bound.

4.3 Discussion

To sum up the preceding sections, we find that stagnation will inevitably occur if in the long run we face particularly unfavourable combinations of poor

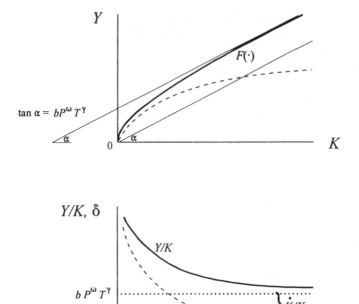

Note: If capital productivity (*Y/K*) never falls below replacement requirement δ, production exceeds depreciation needs and an unbounded expansion of the capital stock can be supported. The production function (20.10), depicted by the solid line in the upper panel, features (average and marginal) capital productivity that is bounded from below. The basic reason is that diminishing returns to capital no longer hold when capital grows large. For ease of comparison with Figure 20.2, the broken lines correspond to the case in which diminishing returns apply for all levels of capital, as in production function (20.7).

Figure 20.3   Bounded capital productivity

substitutability between produced and natural inputs, diminishing returns and absence of technological progress.   •

Can we say something about the plausibility of the doomsday models sketched here? Since we are talking about technology and opportunities in the future, we basically do not know. Although for current technologies diminishing returns may apply and substitution possibilities may be limited, technology may change over time. Not only is the time dimension important; so too is the distinction between substitution and technological change at firm level and at more aggregate level. While for an individual firm diminishing returns abound and technological progress in its own area may become difficult, on the macro-economic level, substitution across different products, processes and sectors

may occur and technological change in one field may cross-fertilize technological change elsewhere, thus offsetting diminishing returns (this phenomenon
is referred to as technology 'spillovers' in the growth literature). Furthermore,
the economy may go through phases of growth and stagnation because
technology develops in a discontinuous way. In growth theory this is typically
disregarded. Instead, we may rely on small models to capture some aspects
that may be relevant for some sub-periods.

In sum, it is useful to contrast doomsday models with models in which
unbounded growth is feasible. In the next section, we study the desirability of
growth when unbounded growth is feasible. This requires a discussion of the
structure of households' preferences. In sections 6–8 we study the consequences
of environmental policy on growth and standards of living when unbounded
growth is feasible.

5. UNDESIRABLE GROWTH

In the previous section we discussed feasible growth paths. We concluded that
under some conditions there exist allocations of pollution and investment (P and
I) such that consumption C grows unboundedly and the environment N does
not become depleted. Now the question arises whether it is desirable to live in
an economy in which investment and pollution levels actually sustain
unbounded economic growth. Might situations in which the economy stops
growing be more desirable than situations in which growth lasts forever?
Among others, Mishan (1993) and Hirsch (1977) have argued that the more
affluent a society grows, the less desirable further economic growth becomes.
People care less about material production and more about non-material and
non-produced values, one of which is environmental quality. Others have
stressed the consequences of current decisions on investment and environmental policy for future generations (see Brundtland, 1987). They have argued
that intergenerational fairness is a crucial criterion by which to assess whether
economic growth is desirable.

5.1 Patience, Greenness and Flexibility: the Structure of Preferences

Within the formal framework of this chapter, the (un)desirability of growth
clearly depends on the structure of preferences (individual utility and social
welfare criteria). Hence we need to explore the consequences of different specifications of preferences. It will be argued that four crucial parameters determine
the desirability of economic growth: time preference (patience), preference for
a clean environment (greenness), intratemporal substitution and intertemporal
substitution (flexibility).

To introduce these four parameters in an informal way, we compare four different hypothetical growth paths and ask which one is preferred under alternative specifications of preferences (in sections 6–8 we turn to a more formal modelling of preferences). Figure 20.4 depicts four hypothetical feasible growth paths A–D in a particular economy that is characterized by a certain production function and natural resource growth function. All paths start at the same initial level of environmental quality, N_0. However, the paths differ in the choice of investment and resource use levels over time. In general, higher levels of investment I reduce contemporaneous consumption levels, but speed up the rate of growth and hence increase future consumption levels. Higher levels of resource use P result in higher levels of consumption, but at the cost of smaller improvements (or larger deteriorations) in the environment.

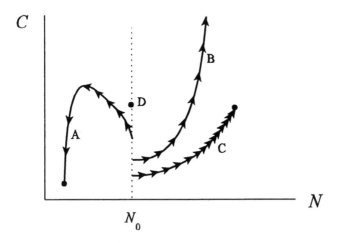

Note: Each of the four paths depicts the evolution of consumption (C) and environmental quality (N) over time, starting at N_0 and evolving over time in the direction of the arrows. The dots at the end of paths A, C, and D represent stationary states with C and N constant. All paths are feasible for one and the same economy, depending on the strategy of investment and environmental policy it chooses.

Figure 20.4   Four feasible growth paths

Path A results from high investment and pollution levels. Consumption initially grows rapidly and then falls, but the environment deteriorates. Pollution is lower in path B, resulting in lower consumption levels but improving environmental quality and ongoing economic growth. Path C has even lower pollution levels and also lower investment outlays. As a result, the environment improves more and consumption grows slower; consumption growth stops in the end. Finally, a stationary economy is depicted by point D, where investment equals depreciation and pollution equals absorption capacity at each moment in time.

Now we may ask which path is preferred. Does society prefer the path with ongoing growth (path B), or does it prefer one of the other growth paths on which long-run growth is absent? This clearly depends on preferences. Two trade-offs are basically present: the intratemporal trade-off between produced services and services provided by nature at each moment in time, and the intertemporal trade-off between utility now and utility in the future.

Path C is preferred over path B only if people care relatively little about produced consumption goods and most about a cleaner environment, that is, if the 'greenness' of preferences is high. In the extreme situation that people care about the environment only, C dominates B if at any moment in time environmental quality is higher at C than at B. Hence, if preferences are sufficiently green, growth may become undesirable.

Path A may be preferred to paths B and C if people do not care very much about environment and care very little about what happens in future. That is, if society is very 'impatient', or, more formally stated, if society discounts future events at a high rate. Path A has higher levels of consumption than B and C at early dates. The environment rapidly deteriorates. After some date, consumption starts declining and environmental degradation gradually comes to a halt. Since environmental quality has become very low, the environment's absorption capacity is very small and pollution has to be severely restricted. Output and consumption are accordingly low. Although these latter developments are undesirable *per se*, path A as a whole may be desirable: the decline in living standards occurs in a far future and may be outweighed by the high consumption levels at earlier dates. A society with a high discount rate sacrifices long-run growth and environmental quality for high growth in the short run.[10] Long-run growth is undesirable in this case.

Path D, with both consumption and environmental quality constant over time, is also characterized by zero growth. This path may be preferred over the other three paths if society cares very much about an egalitarian distribution of utility over time, that is, if it has very egalitarian preferences when comparing the utility levels attained by different generations. All other paths have lower utility levels $U(C, N)$ at early dates compared to D, but higher utility levels at (some) later dates. Hence, utility is more equally distributed over time on path D. If society finds it very unfair that people living at one moment in time are better off than those living at another moment, path D is clearly preferred. In other words, society dislikes economic growth if it dislikes trading off low utility today against high utility tomorrow, that is, if intertemporal substitution is low. A low rate of intertemporal substitution can also be loosely called a low degree of 'flexibility' over time. It can also be considered as a high preference for intergenerational equity.[11]

Finally, we introduce the concept of intratemporal substitution, which is closely (and inversely) linked to 'satiation'. Compare again path C with path B. Along path B, produced consumption becomes more and more abundant relative to environmental quality, whereas along path C relative scarcity is more balanced. Path B is less desirable if satiation in consumption is important, that is, if the marginal utility of consumption falls rapidly when consumption becomes abundant. Satiation occurs when consumption levels of the goods that become relatively abundant (in this case C) are poor substitutes for the goods that become relatively scarce (in this case N). Figure 20.5 illustrates this for the extreme case that produced consumption goods and environmental amenities are perfect complements, that is, the intratemporal elasticity of substitution between the two arguments in utility is zero. The figure depicts path B and C from Figure 20.4 as well as iso-utility curves, which are rectangular. It is clear that instantaneous utility on path C is lower at early dates, but is higher at later dates when satiation becomes important. Hence, if the discount rate is not too large, C is preferred over B.[12]

The discussion so far has been quite informal, in two respects. First, we did not show that if a path without growth was the preferred one among the four paths in the figure, there was no other (fifth) feasible path that was preferred

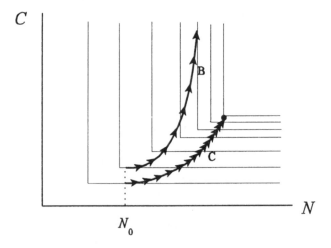

Note: The rectangular iso-utility curves reflect the case of perfect complementarity (that is, absence of substitution) between produced consumption goods (C) and environmental amenities (N) in utility. Development path C, on which the environment improves more at the cost of zero consumption growth in the long run, reaches higher levels of utility than path B, on which consumption keeps growing at the cost of smaller environmental improvements.

Figure 20.5   Intratemporal substitution and the desirability of growth

over the other four paths depicted and characterized by positive long-run growth. That is, we did not attempt to pick the *optimal* growth path among *all* feasible paths. To do so requires a careful analysis of preferences in combination with the production structure of the economy. In sections 6–8 we will study optimal growth for certain specifications of production and preferences. Second, we did not formally define 'greenness', 'impatience', 'flexibility' and intratemporal substitution. We will do this in the next section.

To sum up, we have found that growth may become undesirable if society is impatient, if society cares a lot about intergenerational equity or if it cares a lot about the environment, especially when produced consumption goods become relatively abundant.

5.2 Sustainability and Balanced Growth

Sustainability or sustainable development is a much-used concept in discussions about economic growth and the environment. Many feel that growth is desirable only if it does not come at the cost of generations in the (far) future. The desire for intergenerational justice is often expressed by using the notion of 'sustainable development' to assess the desirability of growth (or any investment project or economic development). Although many definitions circulate (see Pezzey, 1989 and 1992), the most-cited definition of sustainability reads: 'development that meets the needs of the present without compromising the ability of future generations to meet their own needs' (Brundtland, 1987). We will adhere to the definition that is more precise and easier to formalize in growth theory which reads: 'non-declining utility of a representative member of society for millennia into the future' (Pezzey, 1992).

In our formal framework, if the economy grows along a balanced growth path in the long run, the economy is also characterized by sustainable development as defined by Pezzey. 'Balanced growth' is a situation in which all variables grow at a constant rate that may be zero: economic variables (output, consumption, investment, man-made capital stocks) grow at a constant rate, and environmental variables (pollution and environmental quality) remain constant over time. Since utility depends positively on consumption, which grows, and environmental quality, which remains constant, utility is increasing over time.

Whether sustainable development along a balanced growth path is actually desirable depends on the four key characteristics of preferences discussed above. A sufficiently impatient society (with a high discount rate) finds sustainability as defined by Pezzey undesirable. To a large extent, it favours utility today at the cost of utility tomorrow, so that utility levels optimally decline over time. Sustainability therefore requires a certain amount of patience. Note also that desirable growth requires patience. In general, growth and sustainability may optimally go together. What makes sustainability difficult to achieve, however, are market imperfections that cause actual developments to differ from optimal developments. We will return to this in section 6.5.

Perhaps surprisingly, sustainability does not necessarily require 'greenness'. If, for instance, a clean environment has only a small weight in utility, and produced consumption and environmental amenities are good substitutes, a patient society opts for growing utility perhaps by compensating decreases in environmental quality by rapid consumption growth. Indeed, declines in environmental quality need not imply declines in utility. The crucial parameter is intratemporal substitution between produced goods and the environment. The opposite case arises if intratemporal substitution between consumption and amenities is absent: then non-declining utility requires non-declining environmental quality (as well as non-declining produced consumption). In general, when intratemporal substitution is rather poor, increasing consumption at the cost of environmental degradation will not increase utility any more in the end because of satiation.

It is sometimes argued that two types of sustainability are relevant. First, 'strong sustainability' is said to occur if environmental quality (or the stock of natural resources) does not decline over time. Second, 'weak sustainability' allows for declines in environmental capital provided that compensating increases in man-made capital prevent utility levels from declining. In the approach taken here, strong sustainability is a special case of weak sustainability (which in itself always satisfies the definition of sustainability above): if substitution is poor, only strong sustainability (non-declining environmental capital) implies non-declining utility. In fact, it is intratemporal substitution not only in utility but also in production that matters. If substitution in production between non-rival environmental services and man-made capital is poor, an ongoing decline in environmental capital will irrevocably lead to lower production levels in the end. Lower production must lead to lower consumption of produced goods at some time and utility necessarily declines.

We have assumed that it is the maximization of intertemporal welfare, the discounted sum of utilities as in equation (20.5), that provides the criterion by which to judge the desirability of sustainability. This so-called utilitarian principle implies that utility at some date can be traded off against utility later or earlier on. Some criticism has been raised against the principle and alternative criteria have been proposed which are worth mentioning. First, Rawls (1971) argued that it may be unfair to make one generation suffer for the well-being of other generations. He reasons that the only (intertemporally) fair situation[13] is the 'infinitely egalitarian society' in which only gains accruing to the poorest generation yield an improvement in intertemporal welfare (the Rawlsian criterion can be formalized as maximization of the minimum level of undiscounted utility over time, which implies a zero discount rate and a zero rate of intertemporal substitution). The far-reaching implications of this are that future generations are not only protected against falls in utility; they are also deprived of possibilities of growth. Growth in utility does not add to welfare in this perspective as it would be unfair to previous generations.

The second alternative criterion is that of the 'infinitely altruistic society' that only considers the welfare of future generations. Only the utility levels that are reached in the infinite future determine intertemporal welfare. This criterion expresses a moral obligation to the the best we can for our children's children. These preferences make any improvement in the far future desirable irrespective of the short-run costs involved.[14] This criterion also seems too extreme: it may involve great suffering for many generations in the not-so-distant future.

The sustainability criterion defined above is in some respects in between the egalitarian and the altruistic extremes. However, sustainability has implications that are similarly counter-intuitive as is the Rawlsian criterion. Declines in utility are ruled out, even if they lead to huge improvements in utility in later phases.

We may conclude that we do not need to replace the utilitarian approach by a sustainability criterion nor by a Rawlsian or infinitely altruistic criterion to address issues of intergenerational concern. Indeed, the utilitarian approach already allows for varying degrees of altruism by permitting low discount rates. It allows for varying degrees of egalitarianism by varying rates of intertemporal substitution (the lower the intertemporal substitution, the higher the intergenerational equity). Moreover, relying on the utilitarian approach avoids the problem associated with the sustainability criterion that the latter is not a sufficient criterion to choose between several feasible growth paths. For instance, paths B, C, and D in Figure 20.4 all meet the criterion of sustainability. Intertemporal welfare associated with each of these paths is the most natural criterion to select the optimal path (see Solow, 1993 and Nordhaus, 1994b).

In the remainder of this chapter, we will focus on the maximization of intertemporal utility. However, it remains useful to check whether this goes hand in hand with non-declining environmental quality (strong sustainability, or ecological sustainability) or with non-declining utility (weak sustainability) and to investigate its implications for long-run utility levels (from an altruistic perspective).

6. EXOGENOUS TECHNOLOGICAL PROGRESS

6.1 Basic Model

This section presents a stylized model to study the interaction between economic growth and the environment. In particular, the model is a specific version of the basic model (see section 2) devised to examine the effects of environmental policy on aggregate income and growth. Environmental policy entails measures to improve environmental quality, which takes time. Meanwhile, in the short run, the policy implies that the economy has to cut back pollution levels at the cost of lower output: to reach a lower pollution level, production has to fall and less production is available for consumption and investment activities. This may hurt economic growth. In the medium or long run, however, obvious gains materialize. Society not only benefits directly from a higher environmental quality, it may also benefit indirectly as a better environment may feed back into higher harvest rates from natural resources and higher productivity of workers. The model in this section allows us to analyse the trade-off between the short-run costs and long-run gains of environmental policy and their implications for material standards of living and economic growth.

Applying our insights from the previous sections of this chapter, we specify the production and preference function in such a way that ecologically sustainable growth is both feasible and desirable. Using specific forms allows us to study explicitly how investment behaviour and pollution affect the economy over time. We make the following distinction. We first study the economy for a constant savings rate ($s \equiv I/Y$) and a constant level of pollution (P). Then we turn to the situation in which both variables are optimally chosen so as to maximize welfare, that is, we study optimal growth. Throughout this section we consider technological change as exogenous.

Production of final goods (20.2) is given by:

$$Y = (aN^{\chi}) (T_L L)^{\alpha} K^{\beta}(T_p P)^{\omega}, \ \alpha + \beta + \omega = 1, \qquad (20.11)$$

where L is labour input, T_L (T_P) is labour-augmenting (resource-augmenting) technological progress, aN^{χ} is the total factor productivity term that depends positively on the quality of the environment, and α, β and ω are the production elasticities of labour, capital and resources respectively (they are all positive). We disregard population growth and assume full employment, so that L is a positive constant. The two indexes of technology T_L and T_P evolve exogenously over time. A useful aggregate index of technology turns out to be defined by:

$$T \equiv (aT_L{}^{\alpha}T_P{}^{\omega})^{1/(1-\beta)} \qquad (20.12)$$

The production function can then be rewritten as

$$Y = N^{\chi} L^{\alpha} K^{\beta} T^{1-\beta}P^{\omega} \qquad (20.13)$$

We will assume that this technology index grows at a given rate g:

$$\dot{T}/T = g \qquad (20.14)$$

Recall from our discussion about feasibility of long-run growth that we need technological progress ($g > 0$) to offset the diminishing returns with respect to man-made capital (as reflected by $\beta < 1$). Note also that our Cobb–Douglas specification implies that substitution between man-made assets and natural inputs is large enough to guarantee feasible long-run growth.[15]

As explained in the discussion of the basic framework, output is used for consumption and investment in man-made capital, see (20.1) and (20.3):

$$Y = C + I \tag{20.15}$$
$$\dot{K} = I - \delta K \tag{20.16}$$

and environment quality evolves as a renewable resource, see (20.4):

$$\dot{N} = E(N) - P \tag{20.17}$$

Firms maximize profits in perfectly competitive markets by choosing labour input, capital input and natural resource input (pollution). This implies that the marginal products of each of these three inputs equals their prices:

$$\alpha Y/L = \omega \tag{20.18}$$
$$\beta Y/K = r + \delta \tag{20.19}$$
$$\omega Y/P = \tau \tag{20.20}$$

where w, r and τ are the wage, interest rate and price of a pollution permit (or price of one unit of the resource) respectively. The wage and interest rate adjust endogenously so as to balance demand and supply of labour and capital respectively. The government issues a certain number (P) of pollution permits each moment in time. The price of pollution permits τ adjusts endogenously so as to equate firms' total demand for polluting resources and the total number of available pollution permits. Alternatively, we may say that the government impose a tax τ and firms choose the level of pollution. Hence, government regulation (directly or indirectly) determines the aggregate level of pollution P.

Changes in environmental policy stance require changes in the equilibrium amount of pollution. If the government employs a system of tradable pollution permits, it can implement such a policy change by buying or selling pollution permits. If the government employs environmental taxes, environmental policy changes involve changes in environmental tax rates. In what follows we will not refer to these specific institutional details of policy, but simply study the effects of changes in pollution levels directly. We study the situation in which the government reduces the level of pollution so as gradually to increase environmental quality to a certain target level N_∞. This models the tightening of environmental policy. For expositional reasons, we assume that the economy starts from a steady state in which pollution and environmental quality are constant, that is, $P = E(N)$. As a result pollution has to fall initially below the actual absorption capacity level $E(N_0)$ in order to induce improvements in the environment, that is, $\dot{N} > 0$ only if $P < E(N)$.

To analyse the long-run effect, we need to distinguish between two initial situations, as is illustrated in Figure 20.6. First, assume that environmental quality is already rather high, such that $N_0 > N_{msy}$. Then, when the environment improves, absorption capacity E falls and a higher stable level of environmental quality will be reached once absorption capacity has fallen to the new level of pollution. See Figure 20.6 upper panel, where the policy reform implies a reduction in pollution from P to P' and enviromental quality improves from N_0

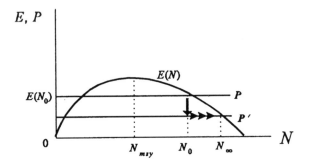

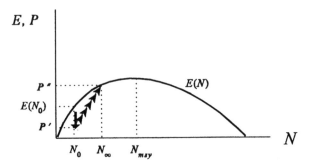

Note: To improve long-run environmental quality, short-run pollution level P has to be reduced below absorption capacity levels $E(N_0)$. Once environmental quality has changed, absorption capacity also changes. Environmental improvements stop once the pollution level matches absorption capacity. In the uper panel, the long-run pollution level has to fall below the initial level $E(N_0)$ since absorption capacity has fallen. In the lower panel, absorption capacity has improved with environmental quality and the long-run pollution level can be increased relative to its initial level.

*Figure 20.6   How environmental policy brings about environmental quality
            improvements*

to N_∞. A second situation arises if initial environmental quality is below N_{msy}. Then, the absorption capacity improves once environmental quality improves. Hence, in the long run a higher level of pollution can be maintained (unless, of course, the target level for environmental quality N_∞ is very ambitious ($N_\infty > N_{msy}$) and implies a lower absorption capacity $E(N_\infty) < E(N_0)$). See Figure 20.6, lower panel, where pollution is reduced from P to P' on impact but gradually increases to P'' in the long run.

In the analysis that follows, we are mainly interested in the immediate effects and those in the long run, and we need not make any assumption about the precise path of pollution over time. We shall analyse not only the effects of small changes in long-run levels of pollution and environmental quality, given the initial levels, but also the determinants of the optimal levels of pollution and environmental quality, given society's welfare function.

Finally, we have to specify household behaviour. Here we consider two alternative routes. First, some useful insights can be gained by assuming that consumers save a constant fraction of income s, which follows the standard neoclassical theory of economic growth (Solow, 1957). Alternatively, we may assume that households maximize intertemporal utility. In that case we specify preferences of the representative agent, see (20.5), by:

$$W = \frac{\sigma}{\sigma - 1} \int_0^\infty \left(C \cdot N^\phi\right)^{\frac{\sigma-1}{\sigma}} e^{-\theta t} dt, \tag{20.21}$$

where $(1 - 1/\sigma)(C \cdot N^\phi)^{1-1/\sigma}$ represents instantaneous utility, θ the utility discount rate ('impatience'), ϕ the preference for the environment ('greenness'), and σ the intertemporal elasticity of substitution ('flexibility').[16]

6.2   Solowian Growth

Households save a fraction of income s, so that consumption equals $C = (1-s)Y$ and capital accumulation in (20.16) can be written as

$$\dot{K} = sY - \delta K \tag{20.22}$$

Substituting (20.13) into (20.22), we solve for the growth rate of the capital stock:

$$\dot{K}/K = s\, N^\chi P^\omega L^\alpha (T/K)^{1-\beta} - \delta \tag{20.23}$$

Because of diminishing returns, the growth rate of capital falls with the stock of capital. Technological progress, however, offsets diminishing returns: an increase in the technology level T increases the growth rate of capital. The growth rate of capital can only be constant if T/K is constant, that is, if technology and capital grow at the same rate. Since technology grows at the exogenous rate g, see (20.14), capital also grows at rate g in the long run.[17] Setting $\dot{K}/K$ in (20.23) equal to g, we can solve for the capital technology ratio to which the economy converges:

$$(K/T)_\infty = [sL^\alpha P_\infty^\omega N_\infty^\chi/(g + \delta)]^{1/(1-\beta)} \qquad (20.24)$$

where the subscript ∞ is used to denoted long-run values.

In the long run, pollution is determined by absorption capacity so as to maintain environmental quality at a constant level:

$$P_\infty = E(N_\infty) \qquad (20.25)$$

Substitution of (20.24) and (20.25) into the production function gives the following expression for per capita income:

$$(Y/TL)_\infty = [s/(g + \delta)]^{\beta/(1-\beta)} L^{-(1-\alpha-\beta)/(1-\beta)} [E(N_\infty)^\omega N_\infty^\chi]^{1/(1-\beta)} \qquad (20.26)$$

This expression clearly indicates the long-run effects of a change in environmental quality (N) on the standards of living (per capita income Y/L). Environmental policy that is aimed at improving environmental quality affects output, first, through changes in absorption capacity ($E(N)$) and, second, through the link between environmental quality and total factor productivity (N^χ). Higher environmental quality may improve the capacity of the environment to assimilate pollution (E). The economy benefits from this improvement since it allows the economy to pollute more without adverse effects in the long run. However, the absorption capacity can only be improved if initial environmental quality was critically low. Figure 20.7 reproduces two panels of Figure 20.1. If $N > N_{msy}$, the absorption capacity falls if environmental quality is improved. Investment in the environment then implies a richer natural environment but the sustainable pollution level declines. Thus, in the long run, the economy has to cut back pollution and production falls. By the second effect, however, environmental quality improvement directly affects total factor productivity (for example by reducing illness of workers). Hence, for N close enough to N_{msy}, the productivity effect offsets the reduction in absorption capacity and standards of living still increase in environmental quality; see the lower panel of Figure 20.7.

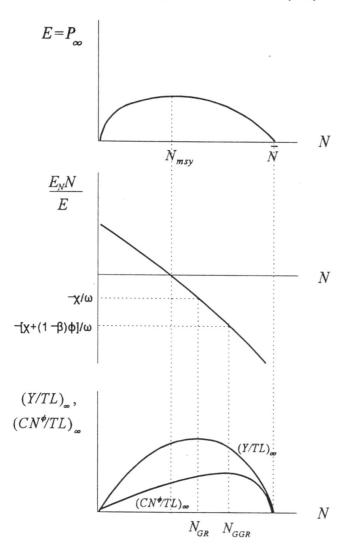

Note: The curves in the upper two panels are reproduced from Figure 20.1. The lower panel depicts long-run material standards of living (per capita output, scaled by productivity) as a function of environmental quality (with $s = \beta$). The level of environmental quality for which long-run material living standards are maximized is given by the golden rule (N_{GR}) which requires the elasticity of the regeneration function to be equal to $-\chi/\omega$, see middle panel. The level of environmental quality for which long-run utility levels are maximized is given by the green golden rule (N_{GGR}). The larger the preference for a clean environment (measured by ϕ), the larger is the 'green' golden level of environmental quality and the lower are long-run material living standards.

Figure 20.7 The (green) golden rule

By differentiating (20.26) with respect to N, we find that environmental policy maximizes the long-run standard of living (as well as consumption levels) if the following condition holds:[18]

$$\text{Golden rule } E_N N/E = -\chi/\omega \qquad (20.27)$$

that is, the elasticity of the regeneration function E should equal minus the ratio of the production elasticity of environmental quality and that of pollution. Since the elasticity of the regeneration function is a negative function of N, see middle panel of Figure 20.7, this condition determines a unique level of environmental quality that can be called the 'Golden stock of natural capital', denoted by N_{GR}. The associated pollution level can be said to characterize the 'golden rule of environmental policy', P_{GR}.[19] The shape of the regeneration function and two parameters of the production function determine the golden stock: ω, the production elasticity of rival use of the environment, and χ, the production elasticity of non-rival services from the environment.[20]

There are two useful interpretations of condition (20.27) which will be called the 'golden rule of environmental policy'. First, the golden rule has a positive interpretation and indicates in which situation environmental policy improves long-run standards of living. A more ambitious environmental policy standard improves long-run production and consumption levels if $E_N N/E > -\chi/\omega$, that is, if initial environmental quality was relatively low ($N < N_{GR}$). Vice versa, standards of living worsen if $E_N N/E < -\chi/\omega$, and $N > N_{GR}$. Note that this result again underlines that a more ambitious environmental policy does not necessarily conflict with long-run material welfare.

Second, the golden rule has a normative implication. If society wants to maximize long-run standards of living (ignoring short-run costs), it should set long-run pollution levels according to the golden rule. In an economy in which production heavily relies on natural resource use (ω large), the golden rule implies that pollution should be close to the maximum sustainable pollution level P_{msy}. However, in an economy that relies relatively heavily on non-rival services from the environment (χ large, ω small), pollution standards under the golden rule should be substantially lower than the maximum sustainable pollution level P_{msy}.

In this model, environmental policy has no effect on the long-run growth rate of the economy, but only on production levels. Environmental policy affects growth in the short run, but in the long run capital cannot grow at a faster rate then exogenous technological change because of diminishing returns with respect to capital accumulation. Indeed, in the long run, output, consumption and capital grow at the same rate (g) as the technology index (T).[21]

What happens in the short run is worth mentioning briefly. In the short run, production levels necessarily fall if a policy is implemented to improve environmental quality. This can be derived directly from (20.13) by evaluating production in the short run (denoted by time subscript zero):

$$(Y/TL)_0 = (K_0/T_0)^\beta \, (P_0{}^\omega N_0{}^\chi) \, L^{\alpha-1} \tag{20.28}$$

In the short run, K, T, and N are given. In order to increase environmental quality, pollution has to be reduced, and output falls. Hence, while environmental policy may boost output in the long run, it necessarily harms production in the short run.

6.3   The Green Golden Rule

The golden rule of environmental policy that was derived in the previous subsection has the single purpose of maximizing consumption levels in the long run. This is not necessarily the most desirable strategy for society as a whole. In fact, it completely neglects (intertemporal) preferences (note that preference parameters do not show up in the golden rule). To go from the golden rule to the most desirable (that is, optimal) environmental policy, two modification have to be taken into account. First, it has to be recognized that society cares about not only consumption but also environmental quality as an amenity. Second, the long-run effects of the golden policy may take a very long time to materialize and society may care about the short-run effects as well.

To address the first issue, let us find out what the level of environmental quality should be in order to maximize long-run utility levels rather than consumption levels. This level is the goal of a society that is infinitely altruistic, in which current generations are willing to sacrifice whatever is needed to attain the best for the future (formally, such a society has a zero discount rate and an infinite elasticity of substitution).

Instantaneous utility is given by (a monotone transformation of) $C \cdot N^\phi = (1 - s) Y \cdot N^\phi$. Eliminating Y using (20.26) and maximizing with respect to s and N, we find respectively:

$$s = \beta \tag{20.29}$$

$$\text{Green golden rule} \quad \frac{E_N N}{E} = -\frac{\chi + \phi(1 - \beta)}{\omega} \tag{20.30}$$

To distinguish condition (20.30) from condition (20.27), we refer to it as the 'green golden rule of environmental policy', defining the level N_{GGR}.[22] Again, there is a positive and a normative implication. If the actual stock of environmental quality is below the green golden level, a more ambitious environmental policy raises long-run utility levels. If society wants to maximize long-run utility levels, it should set environmental policy according to the green golden rule. This policy would be the optimal policy in an infinitely altruistic society; see section 5.2.

First, consider the role of environmental amenities (as parametrized by ϕ). The more society cares about the environment as an amenity or the larger its existence value, the larger is the green golden stock of environmental capital (N_{GGR} increases in ϕ). As can be seen in Figure 20.7, such a 'greener' economy has lower material standards of living than a society that is less 'green'. The former economy sacrifices material production for the enjoyment of a cleaner environment.

Second, consider the interaction between investment in man-made capital (as indicated by s) and investment in the environment as a consumption good (as parametrized by ϕ). According to the green golden rule, the more productive capital is, the more should be saved for future generations and the less should be invested in environmental quality for amenity reasons (N_{GGR} falls and s rises with β). The amenity value of the environment is the reason for society to optimally invest in the environment beyond the level that maximizes economic output. Then not only output is below its maximum, but also investment in man-made capital. The higher that productivity of man-made capital is, as reflected in high values of β, the more costly it is to reduce man-made capital investment in favour of investing in the environment as a consumption good (amenity). Hence higher returns to capital call for lower long-run environmental quality and higher savings rates in order to reach the best steady state for future generations.

6.4 Optimal Growth

To address the trade-off between short-run costs and long-run benefits of environmental policy, the second issue that was ignored by the golden rule, let us determine the fully optimal growth path. Society maximizes intertemporal utility of the representative agent as given by (20.21), subject to (20.13)–(20.17). This maximization problem is only well behaved if the intergral in (20.21) is bounded. This requires that discounted instantaneous utility approaches zero for $t \to \infty$. Since N is constant and C grows at rate g in the steady state, the discounted value of instantaneous utility asymptotically grows at rate $(1 - 1/\sigma)g - \theta$. Hence we need to make the following assumption:

$$\theta + g(1 - \sigma)/\sigma > 0. \tag{20.31}$$

The following Hamiltonian characterizes the maximization problem:

$$H^0 = (1 - 1/\sigma)^{-1}(CN^\phi)^{1-1/\sigma} + \mu \cdot [N^\chi L^\alpha K^\beta T^{1-\beta} P^\omega - \delta K - C] + v \cdot [E(N) - P]$$

where μ and v are the co-state variables (shadow prices) of the capital stock and environmental quality. The first-order conditions are:

$$\partial H^0/\partial C = C^{-1/\sigma} N^{\phi(1-1/\sigma)} - \mu = 0 \qquad (20.32)$$
$$\partial H^0/\partial P = \mu\omega Y/P - v = 0 \qquad (20.33)$$
$$\partial H^0/\partial K = \mu\beta Y/K - \mu\delta = \mu\theta - \dot{\mu} \qquad (20.34)$$
$$\partial H^0/\partial N = \phi C^{1-1/\sigma} N^{\phi(1-1/\sigma)-1} + \mu\chi Y/N + vE_N = v\theta - \dot{v} \qquad (20.35)$$

Eliminating the shadow price μ by differentiating (20.32) with respect to time and substituting the result into (20.34), we find:[23]

$$\beta Y/K - \delta = \theta + (1/\sigma) \cdot [\dot{C}/C + (1 - \sigma)\phi\dot{N}/N] \qquad (20.36)$$

This expression equates the net rate of return to capital (left-hand side of equation 20.36) to the required rate of return on forgone utility (on the right-hand side) and is known as the 'Keynes Ramsey rule'.[24] Note that society requires a higher rate of return if it is more impatient and inflexible (that is, if θ is large and σ is small). The term in brackets represents the rate of decrease in marginal utility of consumption over time $(-\dot{U}_C/U_C)$. The faster marginal utility of produced consumption goods falls, the lower is the value of an increase in production capacity in terms of utility. Households only keep investing if they are compensated for this loss by a higher rate of return in terms of output. Hence, the faster marginal utility of produced consumption goods falls, the higher the required rate of return on investment is.

In the long run, consumption grows at rate g and environmental quality is constant so that the Keynes Ramsey rule boils down to the so-called 'modified golden rule'.

$$\beta Y/K = \delta + \theta + g/\sigma \qquad (20.37)$$

From this expression we can calculate the long-run optimal savings policy:[25]

$$s^* = \frac{\beta(g + \delta)}{\delta + \theta + g/\sigma}. \qquad (20.38)$$

Society optimally saves less in the steady state the more impatient it is (that is, the higher its θ) and the lower its rate of intertemporal substitution ('flexibility', σ) is. It invests more if the returns to capital (measured by β) are larger.

To determine the optimal environmental policy, we eliminate the shadow prices v and μ by substituting (the time derivative of) (20.32–34) into (20.35) and find:[26]

$$\beta Y / K - \delta = \frac{\omega Y \dot{/} P}{\omega Y / P} + E_N + \left(\frac{\chi + \phi C / Y}{\omega} \right) \frac{P}{N} \tag{20.39}$$

This expression equates the net return to capital (on the left-hand side) to the return on investment in environmental quality (on the right-hand side). Investment in environmental capital yields a return to society for four reasons. First, preserving the environment ensures the availability of a sink for wastes and a source of resources in future. The faster the productivity of polluting and natural resource inputs in production grow, the more attractive it is to preserve the environment, as reflected in the first term on the right-hand side (note that $\omega Y/P$ is the marginal product of P). Second, improving environmental quality may improve the absorption capacity of the environment, as is reflected in the second term. Third, the environment improves productivity of man-made assets with elasticity χ. Fourth, the environment has an amenity value that is more important the larger ϕ is.

In the long run, Y, C and K grow at rate g, and pollution equals absorption capacity ($P = E$), which are both constant. Substituting these results, and eliminating the net rate of return to capital between (20.37) and (20.39), we find:[27]

$$\frac{E_N N}{E} = -\frac{\chi + \phi\left(1 - s^*\right)}{\omega} + \frac{N}{E(N)} \left(\theta + \frac{1 - \sigma}{\sigma} g \right) \tag{20.40}$$

If this condition is satisfied in the long run, environmental policy is optimal and environmental quality takes its optimal long-run level, to be denoted by N^*. Figure 20.8 determines the optimal level of environmental quality graphically. The middle panel depicts the left-hand side and right-hand side of equation (20.40) by the downward-sloping LL cuve and upward-sloping RR curve respectively. The point of intersection determines N^*.

A balanced growth path leading to a positive long-run level of environmental quality is optimal only if there exists a solution to (20.40), that is, if the point of intersection in the figure exists. It can be seen immediately that if the rate of discount θ is very large, such a point of intersection does not exist (the RR curve is then always above the LL curve). This confirms our intuition from section 5.2 that sustainability requires some degree of patience. We can be more precise now. There is a point of intersection for positive N if the intercept

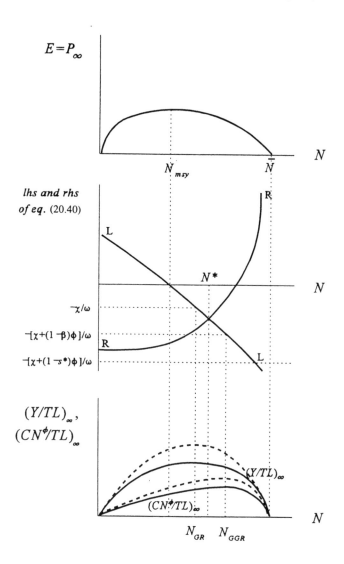

$E = P_\infty$

N

N_{msy} $\bar{N}$

lhs and rhs of eq. (20.40)

L

R

N^*

N

$\lnot\chi/\omega$

$\lnot\{\chi+(1-\beta)\phi\}/\omega$

$\lnot\{\chi+(1-s^*)\phi\}/\omega$

R

L

$(Y/TL)_\infty$,

$(CN^\phi/TL)_\infty$

$(Y/TL)_\infty$

$(CN^\phi/TL)_\infty$

N_{GR} N_{GGR}

N

Note: The optimal level of environmental quality trades off long-run benefits and short-run costs of investment in a clean environment. It is determined by the point of intersection in the middle panel, which corresponds to equation (20.40). The lower panel shows the corresponding long-run material standard of living (with $s = s^*$). Since the optimal savings rate is below the golden rule savings rate ($s = \beta$), long-run optimal living standards are below their golden rule levels which are indicated by the broken lines.

Figure 20.8   Optimal environmental policy

of the LL curve exceeds that of the RR curve. By evaluating (20.40) for $N = 0$, we find that this corresponds to the following condition:[28]

$$\theta < \left(\frac{\omega + \chi + \phi(1 - s^*)}{\omega} \right) E_N(0) - \frac{1 - \sigma}{\sigma} g.$$

According to this inequality, a balanced growth path (which is also a sustainable development path) is optimal in the long run if the discount rate (θ) is sufficiently small, or if environment quality is sufficiently important as a source of productive and amenity services (as measured by χ and ϕ) or if environmental quality improves quickly if it is (almost) completely depleted (as measured by $E_N(0)$). Intuitively, even an impatient economy is willing to invest in environmental quality provided that the returns to this investment materialize quickly and the returns have a large value in terms of production and utility. If polluting inputs are highly productive (as measured by a high value of ω), sustainability is less likely optimal. Intuitively, it makes excessive depletion for the sake of short-run gains attractive relative to the loss of long-run environmental quality. In the rest of this section we assume that the above condition holds in order further to analyse optimal sustainable growth paths.

The positive implication of the optimal policy rule in (20.40) is that as long as $N < N^*$, a more ambitious environmental policy will improve intertemporal welfare. The normative implication is that in order to maximize intertemporal welfare, society should aim at a long-run level of environmental quality equal to N^*.

The optimal environmental policy rule in (20.40) can be compared to the green golden rule of environmental policy in (20.30). While the latter maximizes *long-run* utility levels, the former maximizes *intertemporal* utility. The difference between the two rules can be decomposed in a difference in savings rate (the green golden rule savings rate equals β while the optimal savings rate is lower; see (20.29) and (20.38)) and a difference that stems from the second term in (20.40).

The first term on the right-hand side of (20.40) is similar to the green golden rule, but now the savings rate s differs. Investment in man-made capital involves a short-run cost in terms of forgone consumption. The optimal savings rate trades off the short-run cost against the long-run gain and accordingly arrives at a lower savings rate than the (green) golden rule which only considers the long-run impact of savings on utility (s^* falls short of β under condition (20.31)). A lower stock of man-made capital results, which also causes the productivity of complementary inputs to be lower. The value of polluting inputs in production is accordingly lower, which makes it less costly to expand environmental quality beyond N_{msy}) at the cost of long-run sustainable pollution levels. We will call this the 'investment shifting effect'.

The second term in (20.40) modifies the green golden rule so as to incorporate the trade-off between short-run costs and long-run benefits of environmental policy. This term reduces the optimal level of environmental quality in the long run as compared with the green golden rule. Higher environmental quality requires a reduction in pollution and an accompanied fall in output in the short run. The second term reflects this short-run cost of maintaining a high level of environmental quality in terms of forgone output and consumption. Note that the short-run cost weighs more heavily if impatience (θ) is larger and intertemporal flexibility (σ) is smaller.

Whether the optimal stock of environmental quality is larger or smaller than the green golden stock depends on the balance of the two opposing effects. On the one hand, impatience reduces society's total investment efforts; on the other hand impatience shifts investment from physical capital that is only indirectly useful for welfare towards environmental capital that has a direct impact on welfare through its amenity value. The second effect dominates if society's preferences are relatively heavily biased towards a clean environment (that is, if the 'greenness' parameter ϕ is large).

Optimal environmental quality increases with the greenness of preferences (ϕ) and the productivity value of the environment (χ); it decreases with the degree of dependence on polluting inputs (ω). This can be seen from the fact that increases in θ/ω and χ/ω imply the right-hand side of (20.40) to be smaller (for a given value of N) and shift down the RR curve in the middle panel of Figure 20.8 so that the point of intersection shifts to the right. The preference parameters θ and σ have an ambiguous effect on optimal environmental quality. To illustrate, an increase in the impatience parameter (discount rate) on the one hand reduces overall investment, which implies a fall in the optimal level of environmental quality, but on the other hand, it will shift investment from physical capital accumulation to environmental improvements by the investment shifting effect explained above.[29] Normally, higher discounting implies lower environmental quality in the optimum steady state. The environment can be seen as a productive asset (yielding ecological and productive services). Impatient societies tend to invest less in productive assets. Only when environmental quality is an important source of direct utility (that is, if ϕ is large), the investment shifting effect may dominate the overall reduction in investment, and optimal environmental quality increases if society starts discounting more. In this latter case, the environment acts like a consumption good rather than a capital good, and any shift that makes investment more attractive reduces optimal environmental quality.

Finally, let us examine the effect of a higher rate of growth on optimal environmental quality. This effect also depends on whether the environment is mainly a productive asset or a consumption good (measured by ϕ). Furthermore, it depends on intertemporal preferences (measured by σ).

Consider first the role of intertemporal preferences by setting $\phi = 0$ for convenience. Then, the rate of growth affects optimal environmental quality through the second term in (20.40) only. A higher rate of technological improvements (g) implies that both physical capital and natural inputs (pollution) become more productive at a faster rate, thereby increasing future production and consumption opportunities. On the one hand, these higher returns make investment more attractive. On the other hand, consumers want to anticipate some of the future productivity gains by increasing consumption now and smoothing their consumption over time. The less willing they are to substitute intertemporally (that is, the smaller σ), the more important this investment reduction effect. Indeed, if $\sigma < 1$, the latter effect dominates the former effect and faster technological improvements reduce overall investment (see the term $(1 - \sigma)g$ on the right-hand side of (20.40)). Intuitively, society likes to use the windfall profits from faster technological improvements for consumption purposes rather than for investment in order to smooth consumption over time. Higher growth is associated with lower long-run environmental quality through this channel (the RR curve shifts up). If, on the other hand, intertemporal substitution is large, society optimally invests more since it is flexible enough to postpone the benefits of technological advance to later dates. In this case, higher growth tends to be associated with higher environmental quality.

Now consider the role of the environment as a consumption good by allowing for positive values of ϕ. A higher rate of technological improvements increases returns to investment and accordingly increases the fraction of output devoted to investment s^*; see (20.38). This makes investing in environmental amenities more costly, by the investment shifting effect described above. Hence, through this channel higher growth tends to be associated with a lower level of optimal environmental quality in the long run.

Taking the effects together, we may conclude that higher growth is bad for the environment in the long-run social optimum unless intertemporal substitution is large and the environment is an investment good rather than a consumption good.

6.5   The Decentralized Economy: Open Access and Externalities

Up to now we have assumed that the government fully controls the level of pollution through an appropriate system of pollution permits or environmental taxes. This section explores what happens if this government control is imperfect or even absent. We will see that the '*laissez-faire* economy' tends to pollute too much and to experience rapid degradation of the environment. The basic reason is that environmental quality has a public-good character and private agents

have insuffient incentives to invest in it. In particular, environmental quality has
a public-good character in providing ecological services, since many individual
parts of the environment, like separate species or areas, may benefit from the
overall improvements in environmental quality. Similarly, firms and households
benefit from environmental quality improvements, which makes the environment
a public capital good that provides productive services and amenities.

Excessive pollution levels may have two types of consequences. First, and
most dramatically, pollution may exceed sustainable levels in the market
economy such that environmental quality deteriorates steadily. These high
levels of natural inputs and resource exploitation may allow material standards
of living to increase in the short run. However, the accompanying deterioration
of environmental quality may cause output to fall in the long run. No steady-
state balanced growth path will arise in such a market economy.

A second possibility is that pollution is excessive in the market economy, but
still at sustainable levels. In this case, environmental quality will be below the
optimal level because of the insufficient investment incentives. From Figure
20.8, lower panel, we can derive immediately that this lower level of environmental quality (N) may result in either higher or lower long-run material
standards of living (the former happens if the optimal level N^* is much larger
than N_{GR} while the suboptimal level of in the market is close to N_{GR}). In any
case, of course, welfare will be lower than possible in the economy suffering
from uninternalized externalities.

To study the market economy without any government intervention, we
assume that there is no cost associated with polluting the environment. The
price of pollution (τ) is zero since there are no taxes levied by the government;
nor are firms required to hold pollution permits. Firms would choose an infinite
level of pollution, as is shown by the firms' first-order condition for maximizing
profits, equation (20.20), with $\tau = 0$. Intuitively, natural resources can be used
for free (firms have free access to natural resources), so that firms demand as
much of them as they can use.

In equilibrium, pollution cannot be infinite, however. First, the supply of
natural resources is limited by the actual state of the environment. Second, the
amount that can be extracted from nature depends on (extraction) technology.
If we think of P as the amount of rival inputs harvested from nature (see section
2), this amount cannot exceed the 'maximal harvest rate', denoted by P_{max}. It
seems natural to assume that this amount depends positively on the total stock
of natural resources N (a larger stock allows for larger harvest) and the state of
technology (more advanced technology may give access to larger parts of
natural resources). We choose the following simple specification:

$$P_{max} = \rho \cdot N \cdot T^{\psi}. \tag{20.41}$$

Alternatively, if we think P as the level of pollution disposed in the environment, there is likely to be a similar maximum P_{max}. The richer the environment, the larger the maximum amount of pollution that can be disposed of. More advanced technologies may lead to ways more easily to use environment as a sink for wastes. With infinite demand for rival environmental resources and supply bounded by (20.41), actual pollution levels will equal P_{max}.[30] We may characterize this economy as an 'open access resource economy', in which each polluter pollutes as much as he can.[31]

Sparsely populated economies can be often characterized as an open-access area, in particular the world economy in the earliest pre-historical times. Man depended on food-gathering and hunting, using primitive techniques. Thus, natural resource input was extremely important, but labour input, capital (tools) and technology (hunting pratices and knowledge of plants and herbs) also were essential to determine living standards (which is captured by the production function in (20.13)). Our stylized model sheds some light on the interaction between open access and technological change from the beginning of history. Suppose that the world started at a virgin level of environmental quality, $\bar{N}$, and a stationary technology level T_0. How the environment evolves over time is now determined by the ecological function (20.17) and the open-access level of pollution given by (20.41). Both are depicted in Figure 20.9. Prehistoric man collected as much food (natural resources) as he could, $P_{max} = \rho \bar{N} T_0^{\psi}$. This level is fairly small as hunting and gathering technologies are still underdeveloped; only a very small fraction of the total natural environment was of use in this society (e.g. mammoths but not offshore oil). Nevertheless, this level necessarily exceeds absorption capacity initially (since $E(\bar{N}) = 0$; see section 3) and environmental quality gradually declines from $\bar{N}$ to N_{he}.

The transition from hunting to agriculture implied a major jump in technology which allowed society to exploit a larger part of nature's resources. In Figure 20.9, the advent of more advance technology (an increase in T) rotates the ray of maximal pollution to the left, pollution increases and environmental quality falls (to N_{ae}).

The lower panel of Figure 20.9 displays the consequences of ongoing technological progress, as man's history has witnessed. The small arrows indicate that, for a long period, pollution increases over time (because of technological advances) and environmental quality falls (because of pollution levels that exceed absorption capacity). However, technological progress and environmental degradation interact, since they both affect pollution levels; see (20.41). In early phases the improvement in technology dominates the decrease in environmental quality and pollution increases. However, the larger pollution is, the more it exceeds absorption capacity and the faster environmental degradation takes place. Hence, at a certain moment in time, environmental quality becomes so low that smaller and smaller amounts of natural resources become available

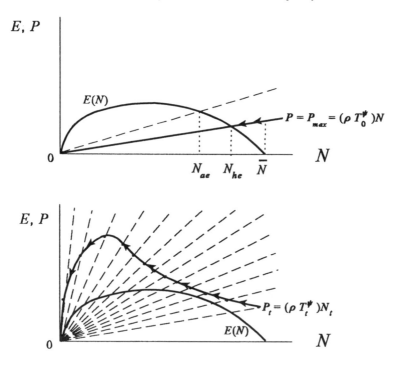

Note: If resource use is unpriced (because property rights on resources are not defined), society pollutes as much as it is can, as represented by the P_{max} line, defined by equation (20.41). As long as maximal pollution levels are not too large, a stable steady-state environmental quality level is reached. A jump in technology rotates the P_{max} line upward. This results in higher pollution levels and environmental degradation. Ongoing technological improvements give rise to the path of pollution in the lower panel.

Figure 20.9   The open-access economy

for the economy despite high levels of resources extraction technology. This explains the fall in pollution in later stages. The open-access economy leads to a race to the bottom, where technological improvements allow producers to deplete the environment completely in the end.

History has not entirely proceeded along the lines of the open-access economy. Many societies started to regulate the use of natural resources soon enough to prevent the doomsday scenario that emerges in Figure 20.9.[32] The pure *laissez-faire* economy has hardly existed anywhere. This is not to say that environmental management always leads to the optimal environmental policy, which we studied in the previous subsection. Without spelling out a detailed model of institutional change, we will argue that intervention in market economies is likely to be imperfect because of coordination problems and transaction costs. It implies that externalities that are present in the economy are only partly internalized. In the rest of this section we will identify three externalities in our basic growth model, and will investigate how the subsequent internalization of these externalities through appropriate environmental policy will affect environmental quality and living conditions in the long run, relative to the optimal environmental policy (that by definition internalizes *all* externalities).

The first step in avoiding the undesirable consequences of open access is to define property rights over natural resources. Once a single person or agency is responsible for (or owns) a part of the environment, for example a forest, a lake or any other site, the robbery of the environment that happens under open access stops. The resource-owner charges a price for the use of services derived from the natural resource and excludes – as much as possible – users that refuse to pay. To ensure a steady flow of revenues earned in this way, the resource-owner has an incentive to keep the resource from deteriorating. In the model spelled out in section 6.1, producers are charged for the use of the environment. Implicitly, we have assumed that the government holds the property rights for the entire environment. Firms pay a price τ to the government for the rival use of natural resources (they pay to discharge wastes on the site, to fish in a certain lake, and so on). As a result, resource exploitation will be limited and environmental quality can be maintained.

Let us now consider a decentralized economy in which there are many (symmetric) environmental agencies, each managing a certain part of the environment. To fix ideas, let us assume that there is a fixed amount of land which is split up into many sites, indexed i, each managed by a separate agency. The sites serve as a landfill for firms. Any site can serve any firm (which is consistent with our earlier assumption of a single natural resource), so that there is a single price for resource use (τ) and the market for pollution disposal is competitive. Let us normalize total land size by 1, denote the environmental quality of site i by N_i and the amount of pollution per unit of land that is dumped on site i by P_i, to be distinguished from aggregate environmental quality N and pollution P. The quality of each site evolves in a similar manner as aggregate environmental quality (cf. (20.17):

$$\dot{N}_i = \varepsilon \cdot E(N) + (1 - \varepsilon) \cdot E(N_i) - P_i, \qquad 0 < \varepsilon < 1, \qquad (20.42)$$

where we have now assumed that the absorption capacity of a certain part i of the environment not only depends on aggregate environmental quality N, but also on its own quality N_i. Parameter ε measures how important aggregate environmental quality is relative to its own environmental quality.

Resource-owners choose the amount of services they supply to firms, P_i. They take into account that a larger supply degrades the resource they manage according to (20.42). Since each resource-owner is small, she takes aggregate environmental quality and the market price for resource use τ as given. She maximizes the present value of revenues per unit of land:

$$R_i = \int_0^\infty \tau(t) \cdot P_i(t) \exp(-rt) dt \qquad (20.43)$$

where r is the market rate of interest as before. The Hamiltonian associated with the resource-owner's maximization problem reads:

$$H^r = \tau(t) \cdot P_i(t) + \lambda_i(t) \cdot [\varepsilon \cdot E(N) + (1 - \varepsilon) \cdot E(N_i) - P_i] \qquad (20.44)$$

where λ_i is the costate variable. The first-order conditions read:

$$\partial H^r / \partial P_i = \tau - \lambda_i = 0, \qquad (20.45)$$
$$\partial H^r / \partial N_i = \lambda_i (1 - \varepsilon) E_{Ni} = \lambda_{ir} - \dot{\lambda}_i. \qquad (20.46)$$

Eliminating λ gives the following condition:

$$\text{Hotelling rule } \dot{\tau}/\tau + (1 - \varepsilon) E_{Ni} = r, \qquad (20.47)$$

This is a version of the well-known Hotelling rule. It states that efficient exploitation of a renewable resource requires that the rate of resource price increases plus the 'own rate of return' should equal the market rate of interest. If the left-hand side of the equation were larger than the interest rate, the resource-owner would prefer not to sell any resources today. Rather, he would sell tomorrow, when he faces a larger amount (since the resource has expanded at a rate $(1 - \varepsilon) E_{Ni}$) and/or a higher price, such that the gain from selling tomorrow rather than today exceeds the amount that could be earned by investing the returns from selling today at the market interest rate r. If the left-hand side were smaller than the interest rate, selling today the maximal amount of resources and investing it against r would be optimal. In equilibrium, equality must hold.[33]

In a symmetric equilibrium, each resource-owner chooses the same amount of pollution per land area and the same level of quality arises, which implies $P_i = P$ and $N_i = N$. Combining (20.47) with (20.19) and (20.20), we find:

$$\beta Y / K - \delta = \frac{\omega \dot{Y} / P}{\omega Y / P} + (1 - \varepsilon) E_N = r \qquad (20.48)$$

The first equality states that in the market the rate of return to capital (lhs) and the private rate of return to investing in the resource (rhs) are equalized. By comparing this equation with equation (20.39) which governs arbitrage between capital investment and resource investment in the optimum, we see that the private rate of return differs from the social rate of return: in (20.48) the third term of (20.39) does not show up and the private rather than the aggregate marginal absorption capacity shows up. The reason is that the private resource-owner (the decentralized competitive environmental agency in charge of a site) ignores that own-resource exploitation affects aggregate environmental quality. Since the resource-owner controls only a small part of the total environment, it takes aggregate environmental quality as given. This gives rise to three separately distinguishable externalities. First, aggregate environmental quality affects quality improvements on individual sites; see (20.42), but resource-owners only internalize the effects of own-site quality on own-site ecology (so that $(1 - \varepsilon)E_N$ enters (20.48) instead of E_N). This is the ecological externality, parametrized by ε. Second, aggregate environmental quality affects firms' productivity through non-rival services. Resource-owners have a negligible effect on aggregate environmental quality and therefore cannot internalize this effect (so that the parameter χ does not enter (20.48)). It is the productivity externality, parametrized by χ. Third, resource-owners neglect their impact on amenity value of aggregate environmental quality (so that the parameter ϕ does not enter (20.48)). This is the consumption externality.[34]

To find out the consequences of these externalities in general equilibrium, we have to confront the producers' decisions as summarized in (20.48) by household decisions. Households maximize utility in (20.21) subject to their budget constraint

$$r \cdot A + w \cdot L = C + \dot{A}, \tag{20.49}$$

where A is the amount of financial assets households hold. The budget constraint states that total income from asset holdings and wage income equals total consumption plus savings. Also, households take environmental quality as given. The Hamiltonian of the household maximization problem reads

$$H^h = (1 - 1/\sigma)^{-1}(C \cdot N^\phi)^{1-1/\sigma} + \lambda^h \cdot [r \cdot A + w - C], \tag{20.50}$$

where λ^h is the costate variable (shadow price) associated to the budget constraint. The first-order conditions are:

$$\partial H^h / \partial C = C^{-1/\sigma} N^{\phi(1-1/\sigma)} - \lambda^h = 0, \tag{20.51}$$

$$\partial H^h / \partial A = \lambda^h r = \lambda^h \theta - \dot{\lambda}^h. \tag{20.52}$$

Eliminating the shadow price λ^h by differentiating (20.51) with respect to time and substituting the result into (20.52), we find:

$$r = \theta + (1/\sigma) \cdot [\dot{C}/C + (1 - \sigma)\phi\dot{N}/N]. \tag{20.53}$$

Note that this equation is the same as the optimal savings rule in (20.36), which implies that for given rates of resource exploitation, savings behaviour is optimal; that is, there are no externalities in savings behaviour.

Equations (20.48) and (20.53) represent the two sides of the capital market. On the demand side, firms demand funds up to the point at which the return to physical capital and natural capital equals the market rate of interest according to (20.48). On the supply side, households supply funds (through saving) up to the point where the market rate of interest exactly compensates for impatience and declines in marginal utility of consumption according to (20.53). Capital market equilibrium follows from eliminating r from these equations. In the steady state (in which $\dot{N} = \dot{P} = 0$ and $\dot{C}/C = \dot{Y}/Y = g$), this yields:

$$(1-\varepsilon)\frac{E_N N}{E} = \frac{N}{E(N)}\left(\theta + \frac{1-\sigma}{\sigma}g\right). \tag{20.54}$$

This is the counterpart of (20.40). It determines the long-run level of environmental quality in the economy with decentralized environmental management, N_{DC}, which differs from the optimal long-run level because of the externalities discussed above. In Figure 20.10, both the market level and the optimal level of environmental quality are determined by depicting the left-hand and right-hand sides of (20.54) by the solid lines and those of (20.40) by the broken lines. The left-hand side of (20.54) is smaller in absolute value for any level of environmental quality than the left-hand side of optimality condition (20.40) as long as there is an ecological externality ($\varepsilon > 0$). The right-hand side of (20.54) is larger than that of (20.40) because of the productivity externality ($\chi > 0$) and the consumption externality ($\phi > 0$). As a result, environmental quality in the decentralized economy is lower than in the optimum ($N_{DC} < N^*$). Also, for a wider range of parameters, no balanced growth plan with a stable level of environmental quality exists in the decentralized economy. Unsustainable development in the decentralized economy is more likely since individual agents underinvest in environmental quality.

To compare long-run living standards in the decentralized economy and social optimum, note that optimal and decentralized savings rates are equal,[35] but that the level of environmental quality is below the golden rule level (because the right-hand side of (20.54) is positive under the assumption (20.31) so that $E_N > 0$ and $N < N_{msy} < N_{GR}$). Nevertheless, if optimal environmental quality is close to N_{GR}, long-run living standards may be below their optimal level. This happens if the ecological externality is large (causing N to be small in the decentralized economy) and the consumption externality is small (causing

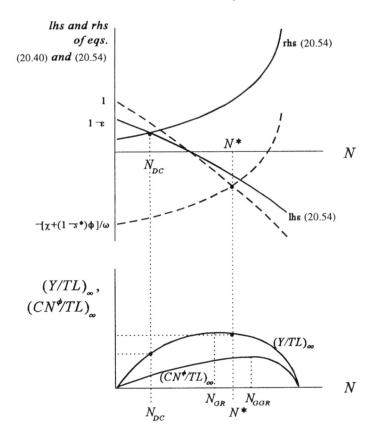

Note: A great number of independent profit-maximizing environmental agencies are in charge of the environment. They charge a price for the use of the environment, thus limiting resource use and pollution, thereby protecting environmental quality. The situation is suboptimal compared to the social optimum, which is depicted by the broken lines reproduced from Figure 20.8. Too low levels of environmental quality arise from the public-good character of environmental quality. Decentralized environmental agencies fail to internalize their impact through aggregate environmental change on ecological services, non-rival productive services and amenity values.

Figure 20.10   Decentralized environmental management

N^* to be close to N_{GR}). Starting from this situation, a shift to optimal environmental policy is not in conflict with higher long-run material standards of living. However, if society cares a lot about a clean environment and as a result the consumption externality is large, long-run material standards of living are too high. The internalization of externalities then implies a fall in material welfare to reach higher overall intertemporal welfare.

7. ENDOGENOUS TECHNOLOGY

7.1 Technology as Man-made Capital

Up to now we have assumed that technological progress occurs independently of what happens in the economy or what happens to the environment. Technological progress is as 'manna from heaven', which is the usual assumption in neoclassical growth theory. However, technological progress may stem from costly R&D projects and publicly financed research projects deliberately aimed at developing new technologies. Technological progress can be regarded in a way similar to capital accumulation: R&D outlays are the investment outlays that increase the stock of knowledge. A larger knowledge stock has similar effects as a larger stock of capital – both increase output. Hence, technological progress becomes subject to similar incentives as capital accumulation and thus technology becomes an endogenous variable. It is along this line of reasoning that we explore the consequences of endogenous technology in this section.

Let us first assume that technology T is partly the result of R&D efforts, while the remaining part depends, as before, on exogenous developments in science and engineering, luck, and so on. We model this by making T a function of exogenous technology T_x and '(re)producible knowledge' H:

$$T = T_x^{1-\gamma} H^\gamma, \qquad 0 \leq \gamma < 1 \tag{20.55}$$

Substituting this expression in the production function (20.13) we find:

$$Y = N^\chi L^\alpha K^\beta H^{\gamma(1-\beta)} T_x^{(1-\gamma)(1-\beta)} P^\omega. \tag{20.56}$$

Exogenous technology grows at a given rate:

$$\dot{T}_x / T_x = g. \tag{20.57}$$

The stock of producible knowledge increases by devoting part of investment to R&D. Hence, total investment has now to be split up between investment in capital and investment in technology (that is, R&D outlays). Hence we replace (20.16) by:[36]

$$I = (\dot{K} + \delta K) + (\dot{H} + \delta H), \tag{20.58}$$

where we have assumed that physical capital depreciates at the same rate as knowledge capital.

7.2 Solowian Growth

Let us again assume that the fraction spent on investment is constant. Since there are two types of investment in man-made assets (physical capital and knowledge capital), two investment rates are relevant. Hence, we write (cf. 20.22):

$$\dot{K} = s_K Y - \delta K \tag{20.59}$$

$$\dot{H} = s_H Y - \delta H \tag{21.60}$$

where s_K (s_H) is the investment rate in physical (knowledge) capital. We can now follow the same procedure as in the previous section to calculate the growth rates of H and K. Because of diminishing returns, the long-run growth rates of these stocks equal the exogenous rate of technological change g. Hence, we solve $\dot{H}/H = s_H Y/H - \delta = g$ and $\dot{K}/K = s_K Y/K - \delta = g$ to find the long-run ratios H/T_x and K/T_x. Substituting these ratios in the production function we find the long-run standard of living:

$$(Y/T_x L)_\infty = [s_{KH}/(g + \delta)]^{\beta'/(1-\beta')} L^{-(1-\alpha-\beta')/(1-\beta')} [E(N_\infty)^\omega N_\infty{}^\chi]^{1/(1-\beta')} \tag{20.61}$$

where $\beta' \equiv \beta + \gamma(1 - \beta)$ and $s_{KH} \equiv (s_K{}^\beta \cdot s_H{}^{\gamma(1-\beta)})^{1/(\beta + \gamma(1-\beta))}$. Note that this expression is the same as the expression without endogenous technological change in (20.26) except that s is replaced by a weighted average of the two savings rates and that β is replaced by $\beta' > \beta$.[37] Hence, the introduction of endogenous technological progress is equivalent to an increase in the weight of man-made capital β. Intuitively, part of technology now becomes man-made also, just like physical capital.

Two very important implications of endogenous technological progress can be derived directly. First, the long-run effects of environmental policy become magnified as compared with the case without endogenous technological progress. Second, the short-run costs of environmental policy become also magnified. The first claim can be checked by inspecting (20.61). Any change in N has larger effects whenever β' is larger. The second claim can be checked as follows. Environmental policy requires a reduction in P, which reduces output Y; see (20.56). The fall in output hurts investment in both types of man-made capital (H and K); see (20.59)–(20.60), and future stocks of capital will be smaller. The more important endogenous technology is for the economy (that is, the larger γ and β'), the larger the effect of reduced investment on future output. While in the case of exogenous technological change output is reduced because of lower polluting input levels and reduced physical capital stocks, in a world of endogenous technological change, environmental policy also hurts the accumulation of new technology.

7.3   Optimal Environmental Policy

Now we know that endogenous technological progress is equivalent to an increase in β in the model without endogenous technological progress, we can easily explore the effects of endogenous technology on optimal growth and optimal environmental policy. Condition (20.38) characterizes optimal saving, where now we have to realize that the total savings rate equals $s = s_K + s_H$. Condition (20.40) defines optimal environmental policy. An increase in β increases the optimal savings rate s^*, increases the right-hand side of (20.40) for any value of N and shifts up the RR curve in Figure 20.8. Hence, optimal environmental quality falls. The reason is that environmental policy is more costly as it crowds out not only physical capital accumulation but also technology investment.

8.   LONG-RUN ENDOGENOUS GROWTH AND ENVIRONMENTAL POLICY

8.1   Growth in the Medium and Long Run

The peculiar outcome of the models in the previous two sections is that the long-run growth rate of output and consumption is exogenously determined by the rate of exogenous technological progress g (see section 6, and equation (20.26) in particular). As we have seen, the reason is that there are diminishing returns to man-made assets. No matter how much we invest in man-made assets, their rate of growth will fall over time as long as technology grows at a slower pace than man-made capital. Hence, increased investment efforts boost growth in the economy in the short run only. We have, however, also seen in the previous section that the larger the share of man-made capital in production (for example because technology is largely endogenous, that is, γ is large), the longer-lasting are the effects of environmental policy. This applies to all other shocks to investment, for instance, a change in savings rates also has longer-lasting effects. In other words, it may take a very long time before growth rates are back at the long-run exogenous level. If we are mainly interested in what happens in the long but not too long run, the long-run results of the neoclassical model of growth are not very informative.

Table 20.1 summarizes the transitional impacts that arise in neoclassical growth models driven by exogenous technological progress.

To analyse the medium-run impact of environmental policy, we now turn to a model that does not feature the diminishing returns with respect to man-made capital which causes long-run growth rates to fall back to the exogenous rate g.

*Table 20.1   Growth effects of environmental policy in (non-endogenous)
              neoclassical growth models*

1. *On impact*:	pollution P falls;
	capital stocks K, H, N unchanged;
	output Y falls.
2. *Medium run*:	growth rates of K, H, N change;
	output growth changes.
3. *Long run*:	diminishing returns start to dominate;
	growth rates of K and H back to their old level;
	output growth back to g.

We assume that technological progress is entirely driven by R&D and other forms of endogenous investment in technical knowledge accumulation. Exogenous technological no longer plays a role. We therefore consider a special case of the model of the previous section, that is, the case with $\gamma=1$. Production can now be written as:

$$Y = N^{\chi}L^{\alpha}K^{\beta}H^{1-\beta}P^{\omega} \qquad (20.62)$$

The assumption $\gamma = 1$ implies that there are constant returns with respect to man-made capital goods: if technology capital H and physical capital K increase by 1 per cent, output also increases by 1 per cent. Intuitively, technological change opens up new investment opportunities and a larger stock of physical capital provides the right scale of operation at which new technologies can be succesfully developed. Technological investment and investment in productive capacity reinforce each other such that diminishing returns are offset.

8.2   Endogenous Growth with Fixed Savings Rates

If the economy invests a fraction s_K (s_H) of output in physical (technology) capital, the growth rates of K and H are:

$$\dot{K}/K = s_K Y/K - \delta = s_K B(K/H)^{\beta-1} - \delta \qquad (20.63)$$

$$\dot{H}/H = s_H Y/H - \delta = s_H B(K/H)^{\beta} - \delta \qquad (20.64)$$

where $B \equiv P^{\omega}N^{\chi}L^{\alpha}$. Subtracting these two equations, we can express the growth rate of the capital knowledge ratio K/H as:

$$\dot{K}/K - \dot{H}/H = [s_K - s_H(K/H)] B(K/H)^{\beta-1}. \qquad (20.65)$$

This differential equation is stable. If $K/H < s_K/s_H$, the left-hand side is positive and K/H increases over time. The opposite happens if $K/H > s_K/s_H$. Hence, in the long run, the capital knowledge ratio converges to:

$$(K/H)_\infty = s_K/s_H. \tag{20.66}$$

Substituting (20.66) into (20.63)–(20.64) we find the long-run growth rates of K and H. Since B is constant in the long run, output Y also grows at this rate in the long run. Taking into account that in the long run pollution equals absorption capacity $P = E(N)$, we find:

$$g_\infty = (s_K^\beta s_H^{1-\beta}) \, L^\alpha \, (E(N)_\infty)^\omega \, N_\infty^\chi - \delta \tag{20.67}$$

where g_∞ denotes the long-run growth rate of output. This expression clearly shows that the long-run growth rate is endogenous and depends on environmental quality through two effects. First, changes in environmental quality determine long-run sustainable pollution levels $E(N_\infty)$. Higher pollution levels allow for higher output levels, which stimulates investment and growth. Second, environmental quality directly affects productivity of the economy (N^χ), so that for given savings rates investment is higher. Differentiating (20.67) with respect to N, we see that long-run growth increases (falls) with environmental quality if:

$$\partial g_\infty/\partial N_\infty > 0 \quad \text{if} \quad E_N N/E > -\chi/\omega \tag{20.68}$$

In other words, the growth rate is maximal if $N = N_{GR}$ (see section 6, equation (20.27) in particular). Environmental policy stimulates both environmental quality and growth if initially $N < N_{GR}$. If initial environmental quality exceeds the golden level, there is a trade-off between long-term growth and environmental quality.

8.3 Optimal Endogenous Growth

We now examine how much should be invested in man-made capital and in the environment to maximize intertemporal welfare. The maximization problem is the same as in section 6.3, with the only difference that $T = H$ is now an endogenous variable. The first-order conditions (20.32)–(20.35) have to be supplemented by the condition for optimal knowledge capital accumulation, which reads:

$$\partial H^0/\partial H = \mu(1 - \beta)Y/H - \mu\delta = \mu\theta - \dot{\mu}. \tag{20.69}$$

Combining (20.34) and (20.69) we find that $\beta Y/K$ should equal $(1-\beta)Y/H$ in the optimum. Intuitively, each dollar of investment should yield the same return, so that the rate of return on physical capital investment should equal the return to investment in new technologies. The implied optimal capital knowledge ratio is given by:

$$(K/H)^* = \beta/(1 - \beta). \tag{20.70}$$

Multiplying the production function (20.62) by β/K or by $(1 - \beta)/H$ and substituting (20.70), we can express the marginal return to man-made capital as

$$\beta Y/K = (1 - \beta)Y/H = \beta^\beta (1 - \beta)^{1-\beta} L^\alpha P^\omega N^\chi. \tag{20.71}$$

Because of the assumption of constant returns with respect to man-made capital, the rate of return does not fall with the level of any of the stocks of man-made capital.

In the long run, pollution matches absorption capacity, $P = E(N)$, so that the above expression boils down to

$$\beta(Y/K)_\infty = \beta^\beta (1 - \beta)^{1-\beta} L^\alpha E(N_\infty)^\omega N_\infty{}^\chi \equiv r^M{}_\infty, \tag{20.72}$$

where r^M denotes the rate of return on man-made assets. Again, this rate of return depends on environmental variables. First, if the economy is allowed to pollute more, productivity of man-made capital is higher since capital can be run with more polluting inputs; see the term $E(N_\infty)^\omega$ in (20.72). Second, higher environmental quality directly contributes to the productivity of capital because it affects total factor productivity; see the term N^χ in (20.72).

The long-run rate of return r^M depends on N in a similar way as $(Y/TL)_\infty$ depends on N in the exogenous growth model in section 6 (see Figure 20.7): $r_\infty{}^M$ increases (decreases) with N_∞ if $N < (>) N_{GR}$, where N_{GR} solves (20.27). The long-run rate of return increases with environmental quality if environmental quality is low ($N < N_{GR}$), since higher levels of environmental quality permit higher sustainable levels of pollution and since environmental quality boosts total factor productivity. However, if environmental quality is already high ($N > N_{GR}$), improving the environment further requires substantial reductions in pollution levels and implies only modest direct productivity gains so that on balance the long-run productivity of man-made assets falls.

Changes in the rate of return directly affect the incentives to invest and grow. Substituting $\beta Y/K = r^M$ from (20.72) into optimality condition (20.36), setting $\dot{N}/N$ equal to zero and denoting the long-run growth rate of consumption and output by g_∞, we find the relation between the long-run growth rate and the rate of return:

$$g_\infty^* = \sigma(r_\infty^M - \delta - \theta). \tag{20.73}$$

The expression shows that the growth rate is affected by environmental variables to the extent that the rate of return is affected. The upper panel of Figure 20.11 depicts the long-run growth rate as well as the rate of return as a function of environmental quality. Again we see that a 'win–win' situation is possible in which improvement of the environment and an increase in economic growth go together in the long run. In particular, this situation arises if $N < N_{GR}$. Intuitively,

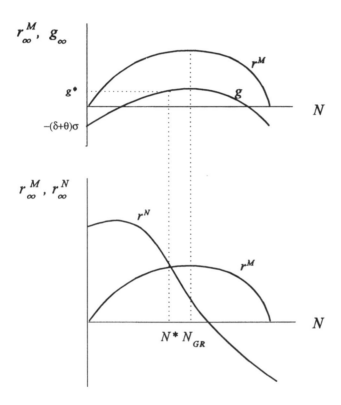

Note: Due to the absence of diminishing returns with respect to man-made capital, the long-run rate of growth depends on environmental quality. In the upper panel, the r^M curve shows how environmental quality affects the rate of return to investment in man-made capital. The g curve has a similar shape, expressing that a high rate of return stimulates investment. In the lower panel, the optimal level of environmental quality is determined by the equality of the rate of return to investment in man-made capital and that in environmental assets, corresponding to the point of intersection between the r^M and r^N curves. These curves correspond to the right-hand sides of equations (20.72) and (20.74), respectively.

Figure 20.11 Optimal endogenous growth and environmental quality

when society invests in the environment it invests at the same time in enhancing productivity of the economy, since the environment provides productive inputs (P) and it is directly productive. As long as a better environment makes economic capacity (that is, man-made capital and labour inputs) more productive, economic growth is stimulated. However, for high levels of environmental quality, further environmental improvements come at the cost of the economy's productivity. Investment in the environment then requires taking away some of the productive resources that flow from the environment to the economy and to use these natural resources for improvements in the environment.

In the long run, optimal environmental policy is determined by condition (20.39), where now the marginal product of capital equals r^M, the growth rate of $\omega Y/P$ is given by g_∞, while as before $C/Y \equiv 1 - s$ and $P = E(N)$, so that we may rewrite the condition as:

$$r_\infty^M - \delta = g_\infty + E_N(N) + \left(\frac{\chi + \phi(1-s)}{\omega}\right)\frac{E(N)}{N} \qquad (20.74)$$

As before, the right-hand side of (20.74) can be interpreted as the long-run rate of return to investment in environmental quality, to be denoted by r^N. Condition (20.74) states that investment in the environment is optimal if its return equals the opportunity cost which is the net rate of return to investment in man-made assets. The right-hand side can be written as a function of N by substituting (20.72), (20.73) and[38]

$$s = (g + \delta)/(\beta Y/K) \qquad (20.75)$$

The lower panel of Figure 20.11 depicts the right-hand side of (20.74), that is, the rate of return on natural capital, as the r^N curve.[39] The panel also depicts the rate of return to man-made assets; see the r^M curve. Since in the optimum the rates of return on all types of investment should be equal, the point of intersection between the r^N and r^m curve determines the optimal level of environmental quality N^*. Once N^* is determined in the lower panel, the optimal long-run growth rate g^* can be determined in the upper panel.

What makes this model interesting compared with the models with exogenous technological change is that the long-run growth rate is no longer an exogenous parameter, but depends on technology parameters, preference parameters and environmental parameters (the parameters of the regeneration function). This allows us to revisit the issue of desirable growth. Suppose that the rate of impatience θ becomes large (similar results apply if the rate of intertemporal substitution becomes small). A more impatient economy tends to grow at a slower pace; see (20.73), as is expressed by a downward shift of the g curve in the upper panel of Figure 20.11. As a result, a larger part of the curve implies negative growth rates; that is, economic growth becomes undesirable for a wider range of environmental quality levels. Whether an impatient society actually wants to stop growing depends on the level of environmental quality it desires. Indeed, if it prefers either relatively low or relatively high levels of environmental quality, growth becomes undesirable (see the g curve in the figure). A very environmentally minded society (with high ϕ) will choose a high level of environmental quality (a high value for ϕ implies that the r^N curve in the lower panel of Figure 20.11 is situated far to the right). Hence a green, but impatient society optimally gives up growth in exchange for a clean environment. Intuitively, impatience implies a low willingness to invest, but environmental quality requires investment. By reducing overall investment but devoting most of it to investment in environmental amenities, thus forgoing output growth, society can reconcile the two conflicting goals. An impatient economy with small preference for environmental amenities (θ large, ϕ small) also finds growth undesirable. This society not only gives up investment in the economy but also investment in environmental amenities. Only an impatient society with moderate preferences for environmental amenities desires to grow. On the one hand it opts for low investment rates because of its impatience; on the other hand, it invests (moderately) in environmental quality to enhance amenities, thereby offsetting reduced investment because of impatience and boosting long-run productivity of the economy.

8.4 Endogenous Growth in the Decentralized Economy

Only a 'benevolent dictator' that optimally determines pollution levels can guide the economy towards the social optimum analysed in the previous subsection. If instead the economy is decentralized, with many separate environmental agencies (or with many national governments in a world economy and global environment), market imperfections will cause deviations from optimal growth and environmental quality. The incentives to protect the environment are lower in the decentralized economy because of the public-good character of the environment, as explained in section 6.5. Figure 20.12 illustrates this for the case of endogenous growth. Externalities and impaired investment incentives are reflected in a rate of return to environmental capital that is lower in the decentralized economy (solid r^N curve) than in the centralized economy (broken r^N curve).

A second type of externalities is likely to arise in economies with endogenous technological change. Technology has in many respects a public-good character. First of all, technology and knowledge (or ideas) are a non-rival good. One idea can be used by many users. Second, it is difficult to establish a market for

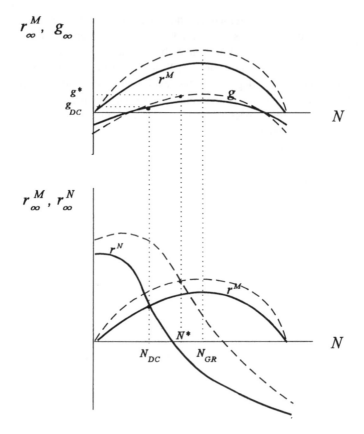

Note: The solid lines represent the decentralized economy; the broken lines are reproduced from Figure 20.11 and represent the social optimum (centralized economy). The public-good character of the environment causes rates of return to environmental capital (r^N curve) to be lower in the decentralized economy, while the public-good character of technology reduces the rate of return to man-made capital (r^M) in the decentralized economy.

Figure 20.12   Decentralized economy and endogenous growth

technology through which returns to innovation can be appropriated. Whenever a firm has developed a new technology, it may write it down and try to sell the 'blueprint' to other potential users of the technology. However, a well-functioning market requires – among other things – well-informed buyers. In product markets, buyers need to be informed about the characteristics of the goods supplied; that is, they must have knowledge of the products before they buy the product. In markets for technology, however, the sellers of technology cannot fully inform potential buyers. Once the information is transmitted, the potential buyer no longer wants to pay for the blueprints that are for sale, since a blueprint is nothing more than the knowledge itself in codified form. So we end up with technology markets in which either buyers have problems in assessing the value of new technolgies, or investors are not (fully) rewarded because potential buyers learn about technology without paying for it. In both cases the market equilibrium will generate suboptimally low levels of technology investment. In practice, patent protection mitigates some of the problems, but full intellectual property right protection proves to be impossible. As a result, appropriability of technological knowledge is imperfect and so-called technology spillovers cause knowledge to 'leak' from investors to users without compensation for the former. Appropriability problems cause rate of return to innovation to be too low.

Figure 20.12 reflects the low innovation incentives by depicting a rate of return to man-made capital (including technology capital H) that is lower in the decentralized economy than in the centralized economy. A complex interaction between environmental and technology externalities arises. Environmental externalities tend to reduce long-run environmental quality (as in section 6.5). The larger the ecological externality, the smaller both environmental quality and long-run growth in the decentralized economy. The long-run rate of growth may be either below or above the optimal one, depending on how close optimal environmental quality is to N_{GR}.

Second, technology externalities tend to reduce returns to investment in man-made assets and the rate of growth in the long run. Whether growth is suboptimally low depends again on specific parameters. Somewhat paradoxically, technological externalities may move growth rates closer to their optimal levels. For example, if society cares a lot about a clean environment, the optimal growth rate may be rather low (see previous section). However, the amenity value of the environment is not internalized in a decentralized economy and results in growth rates that are too high. Negative technological externalities may mitigate this since they give rise to lower growth rates and higher environmental quality levels. The intuition behind the latter is that the rate of return to man-made assets is reduced, which implies a lower opportunity cost for investment in the environment.

It is, however, not necessarily desirable to have growth rates closer to their optimal level when other variables are still suboptimal. Welfare (appropriately defined) should be the single criterion to assess economic outcomes. The social optimum with maximized welfare is reached only if all externalities are internalized. This requires a government that determines pollution levels and innovation strategies, or that introduces a well-thought-out system of subsidies to environmental protection as well as to research and development.

9. CONCLUSIONS

This chapter has combined neoclassical growth theory and renewable resource theory to study the interaction between economic growth and environmental change. We conclude by summarizing some of the main conclusions.

A first insight from our theoretical exercises concerns the *sources of growth*. The environment provides inputs and services that are indispensable to support production activities, but the environment cannot contribute positively to growth in the long run. Our basic assumption has been that accumulation of environmental capital is restricted by biophysical laws, implying that it is limited and subject to diminishing returns. As a result, continuous economic growth can only be driven by other types of capital accumulation. Any strategy of growth based on resource depletion must come to a halt unless it is accompanied by investment in man-made assets like physical, human, organizational and institutional capital. Neoclassical theory assumes that diminishing returns apply to the accumulation of physical capital as well. Sustained growth requires technological change. Economic growth is ultimately driven by knowledge accumulation, which may fuel accumulation of various kinds of man-made productive assets. We have studied both exogenous and endogenous (accumulation-driven) technological change. Growth can only be sustained indefinitely if technological change is unbounded. Although it is impossible to assess whether this condition applies in the real world, there are no compelling reasons to think that knowledge accumulation has a limit.

Another condition for unbounded growth is that natural inputs (which are fundamentally limited) and man-made inputs (mainly knowledge) are good enough substitutes. Also with respect to this condition, theory cannot give definite answers, but it seems that in the long run this condition can be satisfied. A drying-up of human creativity and poor substitutability are lethal conditions in environmental growth models. New ideas and technological solutions that come as manna from heaven and make nature inessential would be an easy road to bliss. Reality is probably somewhere in between: limited substitutability and costly, time-consuming knowledge and capital accumulation constrain growth without necessarily limiting growth.

A second set of insights regards *desirability* of economic growth. Society's preferences determine whether it is optimal to support a positive growth rate and non-declining environmental quality, given that growth is feasible. Patience, that is, low discounting, makes (high rates of) growth as well as conservation of (large parts of) the environment desirable. Optimal growth also increases with the willingness to suffer short-run costs in exchange for long-run gains (that is, high intertemporal substitution or flexibility) and concern for environmental quality as a direct source of happiness (which we called 'greennness'). Our formal analysis has made these arguments more precise.

Impatience, flexibility and greenness interact. An impatient economy tends to invest few resources for future well-being, but if it cares a lot about a clean environment, it may still end up with a high stock of environmental capital and high levels of utility (see section 6.4).

The last sections of the chapter are devoted to the long-run effects of *environmental policy* on GDP and economic growth. By environmental policy we mean interventions that deliberately increase long-run environmental quality. With diminishing returns to the accumulation of man-made capital, environmental policy affects growth in the short run, but only GDP *levels* are affected in the long run. With endogenous technology such that constant returns to man-made capital apply, long-run *growth rates*, too, depend on environmental quality. In the latter case, economic growth is endogenous (see section 8). Endogenous growth models can be usefully applied to study the medium-term effects of environmental policy; that is, their outcomes come close to the transitional dynamics of neoclassical growth models with diminishing returns (see section 7).

Environmental policy has three main effects on long-run output, consumption, utility and endogenous growth rates. First, environmental improvements change nature's capacity to absorb pollution and grow resources. Starting from a seriously damaged environment, environmental improvement leaves room for higher sustainable pollution levels and rates of resource extraction. This favours production possibilities, thus stimulating material standards of living, welfare and growth. Starting from a relatively clean environment, however, maintaining environmental quality on higher levels requires lower pollution levels and less resource extraction. The opposite effect on material production, growth and welfare then results. The level of environmental quality that yields the highest material productive services is the maximum-sustainable-yield level of environmental quality.

Second, environmental improvements increase total factor productivity levels by reducing workers' sickness, reducing wear and tear of machines and buildings, or improving soil fertility. This stimulates GDP and welfare as well. The level of environmental quality for which productivity of man-made capital is maximized is the golden rule level, which is in general larger than the maximum-sustainable-yield level. Since beyond the maximum-sustainable-yield level of environmental quality sustainable pollution levels fall, but total factor productivity increases if the environment improves, the relationship between productivity and environmental quality is inverted-U- shaped, upward-sloping when the total factor productivity improvements dominate, downward-sloping when lower pollution levels dominate. Starting from the top, that is, from the golden rule level, any change in environmental quality lowers material standards of living (it lowers growth in an endogenous growth setting). This underlines our insight that the effect of environmental policy on

GDP and growth is ambiguous and depends on the initial level of environmental quality.

Finally, higher environmental quality contributes directly to welfare because of the amenity values associated with environmental quality. To maximize long-run welfare levels, it is optimal to give up some material productivity by investing in a level of environmental quality beyond the golden rule level, in exchange for higher amenity values. The resulting level of environmental quality for which long-run productivity losses are traded off against long-run amenity values is called the green golden stock level. Endogenous growth rates at this level are lower than maximally feasible.

Environmental improvement requires reductions in pollution levels in the short run. In general, it is therefore not optimal to aim at the green golden rule level of environmental policy, but to trade off short-run costs and long-run gains. This trade-off determines the optimal level of environmental quality.

Decentralized economies suffer from externalities that prevent investment levels from being at their optimal level. Since environmental quality acts as a public good, there are insufficient private investment incentives to conserve environmental quality. The resulting GDP levels (or endogenous growth rates) may be higher or lower than in the optimum, since the relationship between environmental quality and GDP (or endogenous growth in the constant return case) is hump-shaped. This implies that environmental policies that aim at the internalization of environmental externalities may indeed either increase or reduce economic growth.

NOTES

1. We ignore the role of non-renewable resources. Doing so implies that we focus on pollution problems and other environmental issues, rather than issues of material and energy scarcity. For the latter isues, see the older literature in the tradition of Dasgupta and Heal (1978) or more recent literature, for example Scholz and Ziemes (1999) and Schou (1999).

2. Pollution acts as an input in production since the more a firm is allowed to pollute, the higher its output can be. Reducing pollution at given levels of other inputs requires abatement measures (changes in the production process) which are generally costly and which reduce output. Hence, modelling pollution as an input implicitly models abatement activities. For an explicit modelling of abatement in growth models, see, for example, Gradus and Smulders (1993), Huang and Cai (1994), Den Butter and Hofkes (1995).

3. Hence, $E(N_{msy}) = P_{msy}$ and $E(N) \leq P_{msy}$ for all N. The subscript *msy* is used to recall the concept of 'maximum sustainable yield' from the natural resource literature; see the chapter by Tahvonen and Kuuluvainen in this volume (Chapter 21).

4. Note that, by construction, absorption capacity its maximum at $N = N_{msy}$, so that $\partial E/\partial N = E_N = 0$ and the elasticity of E with respect to N is zero in this point. Hence the curve in the lower panel cuts the horizontal axis at $N = N_{msy}$. Since $E(0) = 0$, we apply L'Hospitâl's rule to find $\lim_{N \to 0} E(N)/N = E_N(0)$, which implies that the elasticity equals unity for $N = 0$.

5. Rachel Carson's book *Silent Spring* (1962) played a very influential role in pointing out the damage to ecosystems by the use of pesticides.

6. See Nordhaus (1992) for a critical evaluation of the reports by the Club of Rome.

7. Note that we can generalize the production function by replacing TK by $f(K,T)$ without changing the conclusions. By choosing $f(K,T)$ to be a constant returns to scale function with $T = hL$, the labour force L multiplied by labour-augmenting technology h, the example boils down to a variant of the well-known Solow–Swan model extended with pollution as a side-product.

8. The fixed input requirement has a useful alternative interpretation. For $N > \underline{N}$, we may write $Y = KT$ and $P = Y$, that is, pollution P is a side-product of production (pollution is modelled as an output rather than an input). This shows that the assumption that pollution is a joint output is equivalent to the assumption that there is no substitution between environmental and man-made inputs.

9. When K becomes infinitely large, capital productivity (Y/K) becomes $\lim_{K \to \infty} P^\omega T^\tau h(K)/K = P^\omega T^\tau b$. This level is the asymptote in Figure 20.3. Growth is unbounded if $Y/K > \delta$, see the first equation in (20.8).

10. High discount rates may lead to more extreme situations. Aalbers (1995) assumes that if environmental quality becomes lower than a critical value $(N < \underline{N})$, output irreversibly falls to a positive level $\underline{Y}$ for T periods, and only thereafter drops to zero (note that this is a slightly modified version of (20.7)). He shows that if the discount rate is sufficiently high, society may find it optimal to deplete environmental quality below $\underline{N}$ and thus cause the economy to collapse totally, that is, for the human race to go extinct.

11. The work of Rawls (1971) is usually associated with the extreme case in which society does not allow any trade-off between utilty levels at different time periods (that is, for different generations) and only cares about the level of utility of the generation that is worst off.

12. Satiation can be interpreted in terms of shifts in 'greenness'. As consumption becomes more abundant and satiation occurs, society cares more about the environment, that is, greenness increases.

13. Rawls himself was more interested in (intratemporal) distribution between individuals than in distribution over different generations. Moreover, uncertainty plays a major role in his work. In resource and environmental economics, however, it is the intertemporal aspect under certainty that is stressed. The classical question is to find the maximum sustainable level of consumption in a non-renewable resource economy, see for example Solow (1974) and Hartwick (1977). Since in a model of renewable resources the constant consumption (or constant utility) path is trivial – it just implies zero net investment for all types of capital – this route is not pursued further in this chapter.

14. This approach is associated with the 'golden rule of accumulation'; see Phelps (1961). We will pursue this route further in sections 6–8.

15. We choose a Cobb–Douglas production function to simplify the analysis. All results go through if the production function is replaced by $Y = a(N) \cdot F(T_L L, K, T_p P)$ where $a(\cdot)$ is a non-decreasing function of N and $F(\cdot)$ is a (nested) CES function. To show this is left as an exercise for the reader.

16. The specification implies an intratemporal elasticity of substitution equal to one, which is a necessary condition for balanced growth to be optimal; see Bovenberg and Smulders (1995).

17. Subtracting (20.14) from (20.22), we find $\dot{K}/K - \dot{T}/T = s N^\chi P^\omega L^\alpha (K/T)^{-(1-\beta)} - (\delta + g)$, where the left-hand side of this equation represents the growth rate of K/T. Hence, the equation is a differential equation in the single variable K/T. All values of K/T converge to the value given in (20.24). Note that a similar picture can be drawn as in Figure 20.2, with K/T – rather than K – on the horizontal axis, and sY/K rather than Y/K as well as $\delta + g$ rather than δ on the vertical axis. The difference between the sY/K curve and the $\delta + g$ line determines the growth rate of K/T rather than of K.

18. Taking logs in (20.26), we find $\ln Y/TL = [\omega \cdot \ln E(N) + \chi \cdot \ln N]/(1 - \beta) + \text{constant}$. Differentiating with respect to $\ln N$ gives $\partial \ln(Y/TL)/\partial \ln N = [\omega \cdot (\partial \ln E(N)/\partial \ln N) + \chi]/(1 - \beta)$. Note that $\partial \ln E(N)/\partial \ln N = E_N N/E$ is the elasticity of E. We find the maximal value for Y/TL by setting $\partial \ln(Y/TL)/\partial \ln N = 0$.

19. Phelps (1961) introduced the notion of the 'Golden rule of accumulation'. This was defined as the savings rate that maximizes long-run per capita income. Note that this savings rate can be found by maximizing $(1 - s)Y/TL$ with respect to s. This yields $s = \beta$. Hence, long-run per capita consumption is maximized if $s = \beta$ and if $P = E(N_{GR})$, where N_{GR} solves (20.27).

20. See section 2 on the distinction between rival and non-rival natural inputs.

21. This can be checked immediately from (20.26): since all variables on the right-hand side and L on the left-hand side are constant, Y grows at the same rate as T. Since consumption C is a fixed fraction $1 - s$ of output, it grows at the same rate.

22. Chichilnisky et al. (1995) introduced the term 'green golden rule'. Our discussion generalizes their work by allowing for substitution between polluting inputs and other inputs: Chichilnisky et al. assume $P = C$ and $Y = F(K,N)$. The label 'green' indicates the link to the 'green accounting' literature (see the chapter by Aronsson – Chapter 19 – in this volume). Green national income refers to a concept of income that is a more encompassing index of welfare because it takes into account, among other things, environmental amenities.

23. Differentiation with respect to time of the second equality in (20.32) gives: $\dot{\mu}/\mu = -(1/\sigma)\dot{c}/c + (1 - 1/\sigma)\,\dot{N}/N$. From the second equality in (20.34), we have $\dot{\mu}/\mu = \theta - \beta Y/K + \delta$. Elimination of $\dot{\mu}/\mu$ between these two equations gives (20.36).

24. See Blanchard and Fischer (1989, p. 45) for a more detailed discussion of the technicalities of the optimization procedure for the model without environmental issues.

25. Note that $I = (g + \delta)K$ in the steady state, so that $s = I/Y = (g + \delta)/(Y/K)$.

26. First, divide both sides of the second equality in (20.35) by v. Second, use $v = \mu\omega Y/P$ and $\dot{v}/v = \dot{\mu}/\mu + (\omega\dot{Y}/P)(\omega Y/P)$ from (20.33) to eliminate v and $\dot{v}/v$ respectively. Next, use $\mu = C^{-1/\sigma}N^{\theta(1-1/\sigma)}$ from (20.32) to eliminate μ. Finally, use $\dot{\mu}/\mu = \theta - \beta Y/K + \delta$ from (20.34) to eliminate $\dot{\mu}/\mu$.

27. First, note from (20.37) that the left-hand side of (20.39) equals $\theta + g/\sigma$. Second, note that the growth rate of $\omega Y/P$, that is, the first term on the right-hand side of (20.39), equals g since ω is a parameter and P is constant in the steady state. Finally, note that $C/Y = 1 - s$.

28. Since $E(0) = 0$, we apply L'Hopitâl's rule to find $\lim_{N\to 0}E(N)/N = E_N(0)$.

29. The two effects show up in condition (20.40) in the following way. An increase in θ directly increases the right-hand side of (20.40) for given N. This is the investment reduction effect (recall that an increase in the right-hand side shifts up the RR curve in Figure 20.8 and decreases N^*). An increase in θ reduces the right-hand side (and shifts down the RR curve) indirectly through a decrease in s^*, see (20.38). This is the investment shifting effect. A decrease in σ has similar effects.

30. Formally, we had to include the restriction $P \leq P_{max}$ in the former subsections. By ignoring this constraint for simplicity, we implicitly assumed that the restriction never binds under the golden rule and optimal environmental policy rules. Note that this must be true in the long run in an economy in which T grows without bound, which we have assumed.

31. Alternatively, this economy can be labelled a 'cowboy economy' in which firms and households imagine the environment as an limitless plain, the frontier of which can be pushed back indefinitely (Boulding, 1966).

32. Ponting (1991) masterfully surveys how in history societies managed (or not) their environment. For example, institutional change in Easter Island failed, with disastrous consequences for the environment, while Egypt was pretty successful.

33. See the chapter by Tahvonen and Kuuluvainen for more details (Chapter 21 in this volume).

34. To avoid the externalities, there should be a single agency in charge of total environmental quality. A (world) government could act as such.

35. From (20.48) we have $r = \beta Y/K - \delta$. In the steady state, (20.53) implies $r = \theta + g/\sigma$. Solving for Y/K gives $Y/K = [\delta + \theta + g/\sigma]/\beta$. In the steady state, gross investment equals savings according to $(g + \delta)K = sY$. Hence, $s = (g + \delta)/(Y/K) = (g + \delta)\beta/[\delta + \theta + g/\sigma] \equiv s^*$.

36. This is a very simplified way of modelling technological progress. Mankiw et al. (1992) take the same approach. In more sophisticated models, technology development requires specific inputs, that is, the final goods production sector in the economy is separated from the R&D sector of the economy. Moreover, the literature on R&D-driven growth stresses that knowledge is different from physical capital since it is a non-rival good: one idea can be non-rivalrously

exploited by many producers. See Romer (1990), Grossman and Helpman (1991), and Jones (1995) for R&D-based growth models that elaborate these two ideas.

37. This directly implies that the golden rule of environmental policy remains the same as in (20.27) and the green golden rule as in (20.30) with β replaced by β'. The golden rates of savings become $s_K = \beta$ and $s_H = \gamma(1-\beta)$, so that the aggregate savings rate $s = s_K + s_H$ equals β'.

38. In the steady state we have: $s = (\dot{K} + \delta K + \dot{H} + \delta H)/Y = (g + \delta)(K + H)/Y = (g + \delta)[1 + (1 - \beta)/\beta]K/Y$.

39. To figure out the shape of the r^N curve derived from the right-hand side of (20.74), note that this expression consists of three terms: first, the long-run growth rate which is hump-shaped in N (see the r^M curve), second, E_N which is declining in N (and becomes negative for large enough N; see section 3), third a term in E/N which is also declining in N and is always positive).

REFERENCES

Aalbers, R.B.T. (1995), 'Extinction of the human race: doom-mongering or reality?', *De Economist*, **143**, 141–61.

Blanchard, O.J. and S. Fischer (1989), *Lectures on Macroeconomics*, Cambridge, MA: MIT Press.

Boulding, K.E. (1966), 'The economics of the coming spaceship Earth', in H. Jarrett (ed.), *Environmental Quality in a Growing Economy*, Baltimore, MD: Johns Hopkins University Press.

Bovenberg, A.L. and S. Smulders (1995), 'Environmental quality and pollution-augmenting technological change in a two-sector endogenous growth model', *Journal of Public Economics*, **57**, 369–91.

Brundtland (1987), The World Commission on Environment and Development (WCED), *Our Common Future*, New York: Oxford University Press.

Butter, F.A.G. den and M.W. Hofkes (1995), 'Sustainable development with extractive and non-extractive use of the environment in production', *Environmental and Resource Economics*, **6**, 341–58.

Carson, R. (1962), *Silent Spring*, Boston, MA: Houghton Mifflin.

Chichilnisky, G., G. Heal and A. Beltratti (1995), 'The green golden rule', *Economics Letters*, 49, 175–9.

Cleveland, C.J. and M. Ruth (1997), 'When, where and by how much do biophysical limits constrain the economic process? A survey of Nicolas Georgescu-Roegen's contribution to ecological economics', *Ecological Economics*, **22**, 203–23.

Dasgupta, P.S. and G.M. Heal (1978), *Economic Theory and Exhaustible Resources*, Cambridge: Cambridge University Press.

Gradus R. and S. Smulders (1993), 'The trade-off between environmental care and long-term growth; pollution in three proto-type growth models', *Journal of Economics*, **58** (1), 25–51.

Grossman, G.M. and E. Helpman (1991), *Innovation and Growth in the Global Economy*, Cambridge MA: MIT Press.

Hartwick, John M. (1977), 'Intergenerational equity and the investing of rents from exhaustible resources', *American Economic Review*, **67**, 972–4.

Hirsch, F. (1977), *Social Limits to Growth*, London: Routledge and Kegan Paul.

Huang, Chung-huang and Deqin Cai (1994), 'Constant returns endogenous growth with pollution control', *Environmental and Resource Economics*, **4**, 383–400.

Jones, C.I. (1995), 'R&D based models of economic growth', *Journal of Political Economy*, **103**, 759–84.

Jones, L. and R. Manuelli (1990), 'A convex model of equilibrium growth: theory and policy implications', *Journal of Political Economy*, **98**, 1008–38.

Mankiw, N.G., D. Romer and D. Weil (1992), 'A contribution to the empirics of economic growth', *Quarterly Journal of Economics*, **107**, 407–37.

Meadows, Donella H. et al. (1972), *The Limits to Growth*, New York: Universe Books.

Mishan, E.J. (1993), *The Costs of Economic Growth* (rev. edn of 1967 publication), London: Weidenfeld and Nicolson.

Nordhaus, W.D. (1992), 'Lethal Model 2: the limits to growth revisited', *Brookings Papers on Economic Activity*, **2**, 1–59.

Nordhaus, W.D. (1994a), *Managing the Global Commons: The Economics of Climate Change*, Cambridge, MA: MIT Press.

Nordhaus, W.D. (1994b), 'Reflections on the concept of sustainable economic growth', in L. Pasinetti and R. Solow (eds), *Economic Growth and the Structure of Long-term Development*, New York: St Martins Press. pp. 309–25.

Pezzey, J. (1989), 'Economic analysis of sustainable growth and sustainable development', Environmental Department Working Paper no. 15, Washington, DC: World Bank.

Pezzey, J. (1992), 'Sustainability: an interdisciplinary guide', *Environmental Values*, **1**, 321–62.

Phelps, E.S. (1961), 'The golden rule of accumulation: a fable for growthmen', *American Economic Review*, **51**, 638–43.

Ponting, C. (1991), *A Green History of the World: Environment and the Collapse of Great Civilizations*, Harmondsworth: Penguin.

Rawls, J. (1971), *A Theory of Justice*, Cambridge, MA: Oxford University Press.

Romer, P.M. (1990), 'Endogenous technological change', *Journal of Political Economy*, **98**, s71–s102.

Scholz, C.M. and G. Ziemes (1999), 'Exhaustible resources, monopolistic competition, and endogenous growth', *Environmental and Resource Economics*, **13**, 169–85.

Schou, P. (1999), 'Endogenous growth, nonrenewable resources and environmental problems', PhD thesis, Copenhagen University.

Solow, R. (1956), 'A contribution to the theory of economic growth', *Quarterly Journal of Economics*, **70**, 65–94.

Solow, R. (1974), 'Intergenerational equity and exhaustible resources', *Review of Economic Studies*, Symposium, May, 29–45.

Solow, R. (1993), 'An almost practical step towards sustainability', *Resources Policy*, September 162–72.

21. The economics of natural resource utilization

Olli Tahvonen and Jari Kuuluvainen

1. INTRODUCTION

It is common to divide natural resources into stocks that are capable of regenerating, such as fish populations, and those which are non-renewable, such as coal or oil. The central feature underlying the distinction between different natural resources is the variation in resource utilization possibilities over time. Some resources, such as agricultural products, solar radiation and the ability of the environment to absorb non-persistent pollution, may be assumed to be expendable or constant flow resources. The consumption of these resources at a particular point in time will not affect the amount that can be used in the future.

Table 21.1 presents one possible classification of natural resources. For example, salt is included in expendable resources because of its large amount and its easy availability; it is difficult to imagine that there will ever be a shortage. In contrast with using expendable resources, using renewable resources such as fish populations and forests usually affects future utilization possibilities. This means that rational utilization policy must take into account the time dimension needed by the resource for regeneration. Biologically regenerating resources are often characterized by emphasizing that they are 'renewable but exhaustible'. This refers to the minimum viable population size. Harvesting a population that is smaller may cause extinction. The other threat to these resources is the deterioration of the environment in which they are regenerating.

In the case of non-renewable or depletable resources, consuming a unit of the resource implies that the stock for future consumption is reduced for ever. However, most depletable resources, such as oil, coal and peat, are in fact regenerating but, from the human time horizon point of view, at a regeneration rate of virtually zero. It is evident that when using these kinds of resources the main question is how the benefits from the resources should be allocated rationally and equitably to different generations.

Inclusion of the time dimension implies that natural resources are considered as capital assets in economic terms. Allowing a renewable resource stock to

Table 21.1 Classification of natural resources

Availability	Physical properties			
	Biological	Non-energy minerals	Energy	Environmental
Expendable	Most agricultural products, e.g. corn, grains	Salt	Solar radiation Hydropower Ethanol	Noise pollution Non-persistent air and water pollution
Renewable	Forest products Fish stocks Livestock Harvested wild animals Wood Whales Flowers Insects		Wood for burning Hydropower Geothermal power	Groundwater Air Persistent air and water pollution Forest environment
Depletable	Endangered species, Peat*	Most minerals, e.g. iron ore, gold, bauxite Topsoil	Petroleum Natural gas Coal Uranium Oil shale	Virgin wilderness Ozone layer Water in some aquifers

* not included in the original table.

Source: Sweeney (1993).

grow is investing in future harvesting possibilities; reducing the stock size is dis-investing. Rational decision-making requires the comparison of the costs and benefits accruing at different moments of time.

Natural resource utilization is closely related to pollution problems. This is due to 'materials' balance, which means that human production activity ultimately leads to a depositing of the utilized material back into the environment as 'pollution'. One implication is that efficient pollution control is impossible if the rate of natural resource utilization is too high. An example of this is the former Soviet Union, where low prices of natural resources made recycling unprofitable and did not provide any incentives for emission abatement. Another close connection between natural resources and pollution problems is that the economic analysis of both problems requires a long time horizon; that is, the welfare of future generations must be accounted for in the present environmental policy. How this can be done is one of the most complicated but most studied questions in natural resource economics. Under-standing how natural resources can be allocated efficiently among different generations gives direct insight into long-term pollution problems as well.

One can take many different points of view in studying questions of natural resource utilization. We study the issue from the point of view of economics. It is interesting to compare this perspective with that of ecology. An ecology textbook by Begon et al. (1996, p. 664) explains that biologists can take three different attitudes towards natural resource management problems. According to the first, ecological interactions are too complex for ecologists to make pro-nouncements of any kind. The second view holds that ecologists should concentrate exclusively on ecology and give recommendations designed to satisfy purely ecological criteria. According to the third view, ecologists should make ecological assessments that are as accurate as possible, taking into account that the ecological interactions they address include humans as one of the interacting species and that humans are subject to social and economic forces. Our approach is in line with the third view, which Begon et al. (1996) also find to be the only sensible alternative.

Economists have been studying the scarcity of natural resources since David Ricardo (1772–1823) and John Stuart Mill (1806–73), with an abundance of literature as a result. To present the most essential principles, we have chosen three typical examples of natural resources. We will first study non-renewable resources such as minerals and fossil fuels. Second, we will consider the economics of fisheries and the problem of open access. Finally, we will discuss forest economics. However, before proceeding it is necessary to take a close look at the role of property rights in natural resource utilization. As we will see, the difficulty of assigning property rights to nature is the key economic explanation for excessively fast depletion of natural resources.

2.   PROPERTY RIGHTS AND NATURAL RESOURCES

Property rights can be understood as characteristics that define the rights and duties in using a particular asset or resource. According to Bromley (1991), natural resources can be utilized under any of the following property rights regimes:

1. Under a *state property* regime the ownership and utilization of the resource is controlled by the state. Individuals may be allowed to use the resource, but only according to the rules imposed by the state. Examples are state-owned national forests, parks and mines.
2. Under a *private property* regime, the right to utilize the resource and to buy or sell it is controlled by individuals. Examples are private forests and meadows.
3. In a *common property* regime a group of owners can control the use of the resource and prevent others from using the resource. The members of the group have specified rights and duties. Examples are common land, in some cases the harvesting of animal populations in ancient societies and, perhaps, 'everyman rights'[1] in Nordic countries. So-called communal resource management also belongs to this regime (see, for example Ligon and Narain, 1999).
4. Under an *open- or free-access* regime, each potential user of the resource has complete autonomy to utilize the resource since no one has the legal right to prevent anyone from using it. One cannot speak of property since there are no property rights. An example is whale populations before countries signed international agreements on the regulation of harvesting.

It is obvious why property rights, or the absence of them, have played a central role in natural resource economics. A particular natural resource stock creates an economic surplus, which is the difference between the market price of the resource and the costs incurred when the resource is extracted or harvested. This difference represents the value of a particular natural resource unit and is called 'economic rent'. When this rent is received by a particular resource-owner who can be sure that the situation will continue in the future (as in the case with private or common property regimes),[2] it is in the interest of utilizers to manage and harvest the resource carefully. Under the free-access regime, the situation is completely different. There is no resource-owner and those who utilize the resource have no incentive to pursue careful management or conservation of the natural asset. What is absent is a binding agreement which assures every user that, if he stops his overexploitation, the other users will behave similarly.

Biologically renewable resources are often examples of free-access resources. In eighteenth-century Sweden, wood-based industries had free access to forest resources (Johansson and Löfgren, 1985). As a consequence, the condition of forests was worse than at present. North Sea herring was harvested under free access in the 1970s until fishing was temporarily prohibited by an international agreement (Björndal and Conrad, 1987). American bison were exploited to near extinction under free access. At present the reindeer pastures in Finnish Lapland are free-access or badly managed common property resources, although the reindeer are privately owned.[3]

This chapter emphasizes that understanding property rights is important for explaining the behaviour of a natural resource industry and resource markets, and also in planning resource and environmental policy. In a market economy the behaviour of firms is characterized by the profit motive which, in the case of natural resources, entails the desire to maximize the economic rent from resource utilization. The definition of property rights may completely determine the outcome of profit maximization. We will see, especially in the section on fishery resources, that intervention by public authorities can easily fail to be efficient and equitable if the interplay of ill-defined property rights and the profit motive are not carefully taken into account.

3. NON-RENEWABLE RESOURCES

It is difficult to overemphasize the importance of non-renewable resources for industrialization and the modern economy. Energy production in developed countries is heavily based on oil, coal and uranium. Similarly, it is difficult to imagine present industrial production without aluminium, lead, plastic or iron, to mention a few examples. As a consequence, there has been serious concern as to whether and when the limited availability of these resources will set an upper bound to economic growth and welfare. Another frequent debate is whether the market economy, with economic growth as one of its main objectives, will exhaust these resources in a myopic manner, that is, without taking into account the welfare of future generations. In other words, is the rate of extraction of non-renewable resources by profit-maximizing firms appropriate from a social point of view? We next consider some economic principles underlying the analysis of non-renewable resource scarcity.

3.1 Non-renewable Resource Use According to the Model by Hotelling

In a classic article published in 1931, Hotelling defined the question of non-renewable resource use as that of allocating a given amount of resource stock over different moments of time in order to maximize the utility or benefit from consuming the resource. During the past 60 years the economic analysis of this question has become much more complicated than that of Hotelling. However, it is fair to say that the basic insight and results of Hotelling are still included in nearly all economic analyses of non-renewable resources (see, for example, Sweeney, 1993). Hotelling's analysis employed sophisticated mathematics, which prevented many economists of his time from understanding his ideas, although the basic economic logic of his analysis was intuitive.

The first notion in Hotelling's analysis is that the size of a non-renewable resource stock is fixed. Thus consuming and extracting a unit of the resource now implies that there is less of the resource available in the future. This means that, in addition to extraction costs, there is another special kind of cost: the reduced level of future benefits due to fewer resources being available. In the context of non-renewable resources, the amount of lost benefit is called a 'royalty' or 'user costs'. These costs reflect the scarcity of the resource and must be taken into account in determining an extraction policy. Hotelling assumed, as is usual in theoretical economic analysis, that the marginal utility of consuming the resource is decreasing.[4] In addition, he assumed the marginal extraction cost to be constant. This means that, along an economically optimal extraction path, the marginal utility of consuming the resource must be equal to the sum of the constant unit extraction cost and the royalty. Thus the marginal utility exceeds the marginal cost of extracting the resource. The difference, that is, the royalty, reflects the value of an unextracted marginal resource unit with respect to future consumption possibilities. The existence of royalties means that society must be more conservative in consuming non-renewable resources compared with ordinary goods, whose production costs do not include royalty.

The idea of a royalty and optimal utilization decision is explained in Figure 21.1. The vertical axis measures the marginal utility from consuming the resource, the marginal cost of extracting the resource and the price of the resource. The horizontal axis measures the annual level of resource utilization. As is shown, the marginal utility of consuming the resource is declining. For a normal commodity, the optimal production level is reached where the marginal utility equals the marginal production cost. This occurs at level q^{**}. However, in the case of a non-renewable resource, consumption today implies a special kind of opportunity cost, that is, a royalty. If the size of the royalty equals $A - B$, then the optimal level of resource extraction and consumption is q^*.

The next question is how the size of a royalty evolves over time. Hotelling derived the result that a royalty must increase at a rate equal to the rate of discount (Hotelling rule). This means that the net marginal utility of consuming the resource must also increase at a rate equal to the rate of discount. The interpretation of this result is intuitive: it implies that the discounted value of net utility is the same in all periods.[5] In other words, from the current point of view

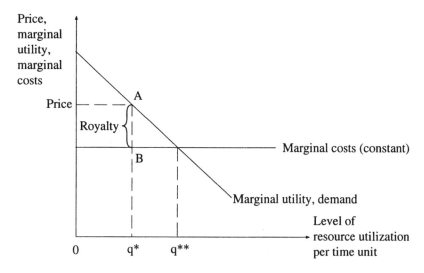

Figure 21.1   Royalty and the optimal utilization decision

the net benefits from marginal units consumed in each period are equalized. This equality implies that it is impossible to increase the total amount of discounted net utility from resource consumption by changing the timing of the extraction of the resource. The Hotelling rule implies that a royalty increases exponentially (an increase of, for example, 5 per cent every year) and the level of resource utilization decreases over time. The higher the rate of discount, the higher the rate at which the level of resource consumption falls over time.[6]

So far our discussion has described optimal non-renewable resource utilization when society can directly control the rate of utilization. In a market economy, resources are usually utilized by profit-maximizing firms. Does the profit maximization of private mine-owners lead to accelerated resource utilization? According to Hotelling the answer is no. Note that the marginal utility curve in Figure 21.1 shows the maximum amount that consumers (or firms who use the resource as an input) are willing to pay for consumption of an additional unit of the resource. Thus the marginal utility curve equals the demand curve of the mining industry in the market. For the mining industry the level of a royalty reflects the net marginal profit from extracting the resource, just as a royalty reflects the net marginal benefit to society as a whole. To maximize the present value of profits, the mining industry must apply such a rate of extraction that the royalty increases exponentially over time. But this means that a resource extraction policy that maximizes profits for the mining industry is also the socially optimal resource utilization policy. In addition, as Figure 21.1 indicates, the higher the level of royalty, the higher the market price of the resource, which implies that the market price of a non-renewable resource must increase over time.

3.2 Extensions to the Hotelling Approach

Following the work by Hotelling, several additional features have been incorporated into the above analysis. Models that aim to explain empirical observations in resource markets include technological development in resource extraction and the discovery of new deposits. Both of these imply that the market price of non-renewable resources may have a U-shaped form (see Slade, 1982), that is, from a historical perspective, the market price may first fall and later start to increase. This occurs because technological development and new deposits dominate the increase in the royalty at the beginning of resource extraction. Later, increases in the royalty and increases in extraction costs may dominate, causing prices to increase (Tahvonen and Salo, 2000).

That resource extraction by profit-maximizing firms equals the socially optimal policy seems to hold only under restrictive assumptions. There are at least two situations in which profit-maximizing firms may extract resources too rapidly. First, private firms may discount future profits at a rate of discount that is higher than the preferred one from a social point of view. Second, extraction of non-renewable resources usually causes environmental damage, that is, external effects (see, for example, Tahvonen, 1997).[7] If these problems are taken into account, then the rate of optimal resource utilization will be lower than that in a private mining industry. How can society influence the rate of resource extraction? One possibility is to apply a tax per unit of resource extracted. This kind of tax, if accurately gauged (Sweeney, 1993), may shift the resource extraction from the present to the future and thus promote better conservation of resources.

Natural resource industries are often characterized by monopolies, cartels and oligopolistic market structures. The best-known examples of this are OPEC, oil markets and the energy crisis during the 1970s and 1980s. Economic models for oligopolistic natural resource markets are studied by differential game models that analyse the strategic interaction of resource suppliers simultaneously with the Hotelling type stock flow dynamics of resource extraction (Salo and Tahvonen, 2000).

3.3 Some Historical Debates on the Scarcity of Non-renewable Resources

Historically, both public and scientific discussion about the scarcity of non-renewable resources has often been dominated by gloomy predictions. In the United Kingdom during the nineteenth century, it was predicted that there would be enough coal for heating for the next 30 years. In 1874 a US geologist predicted that petroleum reserves would last four years. In 1936 a group of geologists predicted that world copper reserves would be depleted in 40 years. However, in 1974 the same prediction method indicated that there was still enough copper left for 57 years. The famous *Limits to Growth* report of the Club of Rome, published in 1972, predicted that the world economy would reach its physical boundaries during the twenty-first century. We next investigate some historical debates on natural resources.

The first debate: the British classical economists

The first professor of economics, Thomas Malthus, published his well-known essay on the principles of population in 1798. Malthus argued against the growth optimists and some philosophers of his time (like the French philosopher Nicolas de Condorcet) who believed that the human mind and technological development would solve all obstacles to future progress and economic growth. Malthus believed instead that the human race will always breed until the limits of natural resources are met, and at that equilibrium societies are characterized by misery, starvation and a subsistence level of wages. Technological development only produces a short-term increase in well-being until the limits of nature are again met. Long-term development would be possible only if mankind had better morals so as not to breed during happier times when wages exceed the subsistence level. This, however, Malthus takes to be impossible.

Other classical economists were not as pessimistic. For example, John Stuart Mill emphasized (1862) that the limited quantity of natural resources forms real limits to the increase of production. However, according to Mill's views these limits had not yet been reached and would never be reached in any country at any time. Mill based his argument on future developments in agricultural knowledge and because social institutions and increases in economic welfare may slow down population growth. An interesting feature in Mill's thinking was the argument that the quality of living space is an important part of economic well-being. According to Mill a world where the environment is totally in industrial and agricultural use is a bad ideal.

The second debate: the US conservation movement, 1890–1920, and the first neoclassical studies on natural resources

The conservation movement was a highly successful political ideology in the USA between 1890 and 1920, with President Theodore Roosevelt among its leaders. According to its doctrines, economic growth has clear physical boundaries which cannot be avoided by technological development. Too rapid use of non-renewable resources was taken to be a major threat to future generations. It was argued that the lower the use of non-renewable resources, the better. Economic competition as well as monopolies were seen as major enemies to the wise use of natural resources, defined in physical and ethical terms. It was stated that the government should control the use of natural resources. Needless to say, many of the ideas being discussed in the present-day debate on nature conservation and sustainability were conceived during this period.

Partly as a reaction to the conservation movement, Harold Hotelling published the study 'The Economics of Exhaustible Resources' in 1931. In contrast to the conservation movement, he argued that in a market economy profit-maximizing mining firms may well extract non-renewable resources at the socially optimal rate.

Thirty years later there were data available for studying the question of natural resource scarcity empirically. In the study *Scarcity and Growth*, two US economists (Barnett and Morse, 1963) collected price and cost time series data on minerals, agriculture and renewable resources. Their purpose was to test whether the hypothesis of increasing natural resource scarcity obtains empirical support. The results were quite surprising: for agriculture and minerals, price and production costs fell or remained constant over the period from 1870 to 1957. Only in forestry had the price level shown an upward trend (see Figure 21.2). According to the study, these findings can be explained by technological development, which produces substitutes for scare resources, reduces extraction costs of minerals, and thus expands the size of economic reserves. In general, the authors strongly question many of the basic premises of the conservation movement as well as the pessimistic Malthusian view.

The third debate: the *Limits to Growth* report to the Club of Rome

It took only nine years after the previous discussion was forgotten before a group of scientists published the *Limits to Growth* report to the Club of Rome (Meadows et al., 1972). This study sold nine million copies in 29 languages. It was based on new digital computers and on a modelling method called 'system analysis'. The study presented a large and new type of model designed to predict the future development of five global variables: population, food, industrialization, non-renewable resources and pollution. The prediction of the study was highly pessimistic. The future world population level, food production and industrialization will first grow exponentially but then collapse during the twenty-first century. The collapse follows because the world economy will reach its physical limits in terms of non-renewable resources, agricultural production and excessive pollution. The study also predicted that 11 vital minerals would be exhausted before the end of the twenrieth century. Among these were copper, gold, lead, mercury, natural gas, oil, silver, tin and zinc.

As is now clear, these predictions have failed. Figure 21.3(a–c) shows the actual development of oil production and reserves as a comparison. Due to new discoveries and technological change, the level of proven reserves has increased in spite of the fact that oil production has also increased. The lowest

Ratio scale

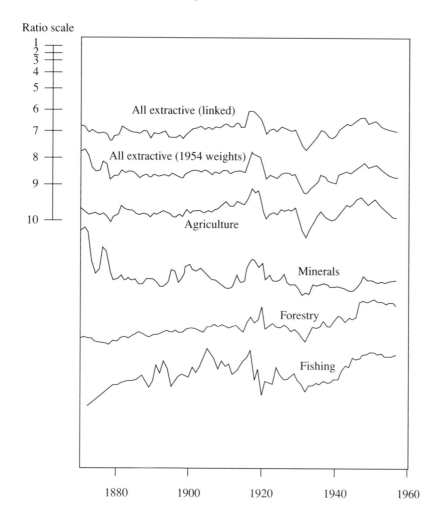

Source: Barnett and Morse (1963).

*Figure 21.2   Trends in natural resource prices relative to other prices in the
            USA, 1879–1957*

panel shows that the static reserve index, which is the ratio of existing reserves
to annual production, has increased as well, proving that such an index cannot
be used for prediction purposes. Figure 21.4 shows examples for several
different non-renewable resources. Typically their real prices have shown
downward trends.

(a) World crude oil production in million barrels per day

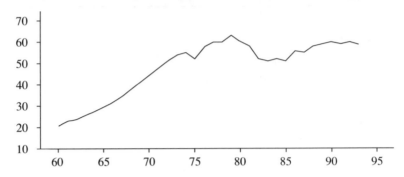

(b) World proven oil reserves in billion barrels

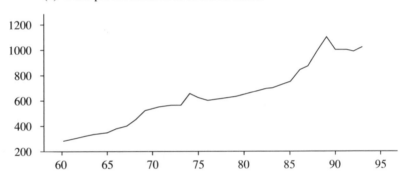

(c) Reserves to production ratio, years

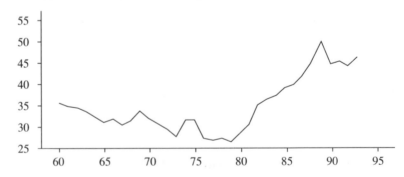

Data source: OECD (1995), *Middle East Oil and Gas*

Figure 21.3   Development of oil prices and reserves

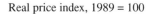

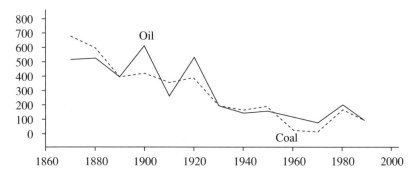

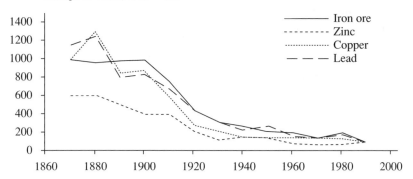

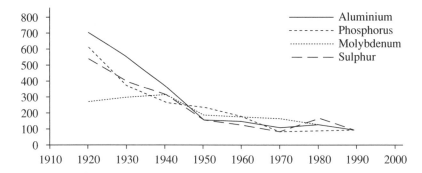

Source: Nordhaus (1992).

Figure 21.4 Development of some non-renewable resource prices

In 1992 the *Limits to Growth* group published a new, slightly modified version of the model (Meadows et al., 1992). Economists have strongly argued against both studies. One problem with these models is that they are not based on any specific statistical data. Instead the model-builders rely on their own intuition about how, for example, population growth depends on other variables. Thus there is a tendency to overlook scientific work in many fields of social sciences and economics. Among other problems, the studies neglect the price system and dynamics of the market economy and thus have a strong Malthusian tendency. In 1977 the United Nations asked an economist and Nobel prizewinner, Wassily Leontief, to carry out a study on whether natural resources will be exhausted before the end of the twentieth century. Leontief (1977) applied equally pessimistic assumptions as the *Limits to Growth* study except that he took into account that demand may respond to higher prices. According to his results, only two minerals were in danger of being exhausted. Unfortunately, compared to the *Limits to Growth* report, this study has been rather neglected outside economics.

One reason for the fortunate failure of these predictions is that the scarcity of non-renewable resources is based too much on physical factors. This perspective has led to the use of the static reserve index (or reserve-to-use ratio), which is the ratio of current reserves to current consumption. Current reserves are the known resources that are economically extractable. The index expresses the number of years until the resource is depleted, given that there will be no additions to the known reserves and that the future annual use of the reserve remains at the current level. Both of these assumptions seem to be seriously flawed. First, because of discoveries of new deposits, the size of reserves may increase over time despite continuing extraction. In addition, the size of reserves increases due to rapid technological development, which makes the extraction of known subeconomic stocks less expensive. Second, the static reserve index neglects technological development in recycling and the possibility of substituting scarce materials for more abundant resources. From this it follows, as in the case of oil and gas, that reserves have increased over time.

The efficiency of the market mechanism seems to be one reason why the most gloomy predictions for non-renewable resources depletion have thus far failed. Environmental and natural resource economists have emphasized that it is not possible to rely on this same argument in the case of pollution and many free-access resources like open-sea fisheries (Clark, 1973). We turn next to this issue.

4.   ECONOMICS OF FISHERIES

The economics of fisheries includes a particularly vast collection of problems in natural resource utilization. Fish stocks are populations with complex biological reproductive dynamics. The growth and productivity features of these natural assets must be known and incorporated into economic analysis before rational utilization decisions or the behaviour of the fishermen can be understood. This means that the economic analysis of fisheries should be interdisciplinary, using models which combine biological and economic points of views.

One important result of regarding fish populations as natural assets is that a long-term perspective is inherent in the economic analysis of fisheries. In particular, the literature contains an interesting debate between the maximum sustainable harvest of fish populations and the economically efficient utilization policy. The economics of fisheries also shows how aspects other than the raw material value of natural resources can be incorporated into rational utilization policy.

The main issue in this area follows from the gap between the nature of human institutions and the biological nature of fish populations. These populations are usually very mobile, and it has been difficult to assign property rights to individuals or even nations. As a consequence, fish stocks are harvested in many places in the world in situations with open-access features. One main theme in the economics of fisheries has been the analysis and development of public regulatory measures that guarantee sustainable harvesting policies and positive net revenue for the fishing industry.

4.1 The Debate Concerning Maximum Sustainable Yield versus Economic Optimality

Fish populations can be harvested indefinitely if the size of the population or the environment in which they are reproducing is not in danger. However, a given fish population can be harvested on a sustainable basis by applying various different harvesting intensities. This can be demonstrated by a very simple growth model shown in Figure 21.5. The diagram depicts the growth of a fish population over a year as a function of the size of the population, measured as the weight of its biomass. According to this biological model, the growth of the population is low when the size of its biomass is low and when the size of its biomass is near the carrying capacity level, represented by symbol K. If there is no harvesting, then the population grows until it reaches its carrying capacity level. The carrying capacity is the maximum level of population that the given habitat can support.

Perhaps the most traditional approach to the utilization of fish resources, often promoted by fishery biologists, is to apply the maximum sustainable harvesting policy, that is, the 'full utilization' of the resource. In terms of Figure 21.5, this is a policy which maintains the stock at the level represented by X_{msy}. Thus the annual harvest of the resource can be kept at the level H_{msy}. This kind of utilization policy seems to be the most preferable policy because it gives the largest possible material flow that is sustainable over time. Note that any harvesting level above

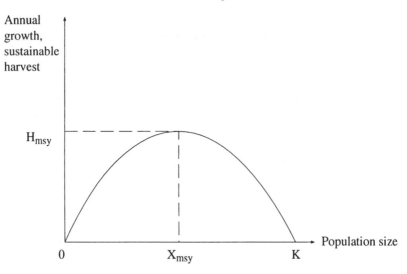

Figure 21.5   Maximum sustainable yield

H_{msy} will cause the population to become extinct. This follows since rate of harvesting will then always exceed the population growth rate.

However, there are at least three reasons why the policy of maximum sustainable yield is not optimal from an economic point of view. First, because the fish population is regarded as a capital asset, all units of the population must yield a positive rate of interest, just as other assets in the economy. To yield interest, an asset must 'grow'. If the fish population is kept at level X_{msy}, then the marginal or last unit of the population does not have a positive contribution to the growth of the stock. Note this from Figure 21.5: if the population size equals X_{msy} and we reduce the size by a small amount, the loss in the total annual growth of the population is approximately zero. This is because the growth curve is flat when the population equals X_{msy}. Thus, the last unit of the population yields a zero rate of interest and if the actual interest rate in the economy is positive the size of the population is too large from an economic point of view. In contrast, if the amount of money received from selling the additional harvest of one year is invested in some other way (for example, in a bank account), a positive rate of interest will be obtained. This means that it is profitable to reduce the level of population from X_{msy} as long as the contribution of the marginal population unit is lower than the appropriate interest received from selling the catch and investing the money in the most profitable way. Thus the fact that the owner of a capital asset can receive interest in a market economy implies that, for the owner of a fish population, it is profitable to maintain the stock below the level of X_{msy}.

However, there are two other things to be taken into account. The cost of harvesting the fish population tends to rise as the stock size is reduced. The reason is that the smaller the population, the fewer fish the fishermen can harvest given fixed working hours and fishing capacity. This has a positive effect on the optimal size of the population. Another reason for keeping up a larger population size is that the stock may be valuable *in situ*. For example, in the case of sea mammals, many people share the view that these animals have existence value (or, for example, observational and photographic value) and that the correct size of the population cannot be determined by taking into account only the value of the raw material received. This implies another positive effect on the economically optimal population size.

The requirement that a fish population as a capital asset must yield a rate of interest implies that the optimal stock size may be smaller than X_{msy}, while the dependence of harvesting costs on the stock size and the *in situ* value of the animals implies a larger optimal stock size. The economically optimal population size and harvesting level depends in each case on the relative strengths of these different effects.

It is important to note that if the property rights of a fish population are well defined (for example, if there is one owner of the population), then profit maximization is usually in line with harvesting the resource on a sustainable basis. However, it is important to ask whether economic rationality and carefully defined property rights guarantee that the stock is not driven to extinction. This important question was first studied by Clark (1973).

Let us assume that the cost of harvesting the resource is independent of the size of the stock and that only the raw material value of the population matters. If the rate of interest in the economy is high compared with the growth rate of marginal population units, then the owner of the population may always think it profitable to reduce the size of the population and invest the returns in a more profitable way in the capital market.[8] This shows that, especially if *in situ* or existence value is not taken into account, there is nothing to guarantee that sustainable resource harvesting yields the highest profits to the resource-owner. However, in reality, it being profitable to harvest the entire stock is the exception rather than the rule, because harvesting costs in the case of a small population may be too high compared to the market price of the resource. This usually guarantees the optimality of harvesting the stock on a sustainable basis. It is likely that renewable populations are overexploited only in an open-access harvesting situation.

4.2 Dynamics of Open-access Fisheries

Established fisheries in different parts of the world are sometimes characterized by a situation in which fishing industry profits are low and the harvest level is only a small proportion of its level in the past. The economic model of open-access fisheries explains the dynamic economic forces that can create this kind of resource outcome. It is useful to consider the underlying economic forces of open-access resource utilization because without this understanding it is difficult to design a regulation policy which effectively and equitably corrects the problem of overexploitation.

The cost of harvesting a fish population consists of two distinct components. First, there are wage expenses and the costs of fishing gear, fuel and so on. These are the private costs for each fisherman. The other cost component cannot be directly observed. It is an implication of the limited size and limited reproductive capacity of a fish stock. Because of the limited size of the fish stock additional harvesting always means lower harvesting possibilities in the future. In other words, an uncaught fish left in the sea is valuable because it guarantees the future harvest and profits for the fishermen. The value of uncaught fish[9] depends on many different factors, such as the rate of interest, future markets for fish, technological development of fishing gear and so on. If the fish population has a private owner whose harvesting policy is in line with the principles described above, then he will approximate 'the value of the fish in the sea' by using all his knowledge of fish markets, cost of fishing, the rate of reproduction of the stock and so on to maximize his stream of profits. The value of uncaught fish prevents a rational fisherman from overfishing his stock. In this way, rational profit maximization means that part of the resource is conserved to be used in the future. In contrast, when the fish stock is harvested under an open-access regime, no fisherman can be sure of who will benefit from the value of an uncaught fish. Thus fishermen have no incentive whatsoever to take the price of the fish in the sea into account when they make decisions about their individual harvesting levels. In a free-access situation, no individual fisherman can effectively conserve the resource by refraining from harvesting. Doing so will only enhance the harvesting opportunities for his competitors, which is the tragedy of free-access harvesting.

According to the model of Smith (1968), evolution of a free-access fishery may typically proceed as follows: in the initial stage, the fishing industry may earn very high profits because it is exploiting the natural resource at an excessively high rate by neglecting the value of the unharvested resource. It is thus earning present and future profits at the same time. In addition, the industry's profits include resource rent, that is, the economic surplus associated with the natural resource and which belongs to the owner of the resource as a compensation for having a valuable capital asset. However, because of free access there is no owner of the resource. This means that the short-term profit level in this industry exceeds the normal profit level in the economy. Because there are no property rights, the high profit level for the fishermen makes the fishing industry attractive to new fishermen, who will enter the industry. As a consequence, supply increases and the price of fish in the market will fall. This will reduce earnings in the fishing industry to the level where the profit for the fishermen is nearly zero. In addition, the higher level of fishing means that the size of the fish population may decrease, which means that the profit of a typical fisherman will eventually become negative. Some of the fishermen may be forced to leave the business and sell their boats at a low price. If private harvesting costs are insensitive to the size of the fish population, extinction may occur. In many cases the costs of overfishing a small fish population are formidable. This prevents the industry from destroying its own resource basis by harvesting the population to extinction. According to pioneering work by Gordon (1954), the evolution of the fishery may stabilize to a situation called 'bionomic equilibrium'. At this equilibrium, the population size, harvesting levels and the number of fishermen are approximately stable. The situation is, however, economically inefficient. The fishing industry is overcapitalized. In other words, there are an excessive number of fishing vessels compared with the low levels of harvest and fish population. As a consequence, the whole economic rent, that is, the amount of net economic benefit which can be derived from the renewable resource, is wasted. Compared to this situation it is theoretically possible to have fewer vessels harvesting a larger fish stock and thus yielding a positive level of profits, a portion of which may be used to compensate those fishermen who leave the industry.

Perhaps the most serious open-access situation is when different countries exploit the same fish stocks. An interesting example of the dynamics of a free-access fishery is described in a study by Björndal and Conrad (1987). They analysed the open-access exploitation of North Sea herring during the period 1963–77. The stock was harvested by Norway, Denmark, The Netherlands, Germany and the United Kingdom. The evolution of the fishery closely resembles the theoretical model described above. Figure 21.6 shows that in 1963 the size of the fish population was about 2.4 million tons, and that there were about 120 fishing vessels. Over the next ten years the size of the population declined to one million, but the number of fishing vessels increased six-fold. The low level of the population caused harvesting costs to increase, and after 1972 the number of fishing vessels started to decline. In 1977 the authorities realized that the stock was seriously overharvested and Norway and the European Union agreed to cease fishing. The model of Björndal and Conrad predicted that, without banning, extinction might have occurred in 1983. Under the moratorium, which lasted until 1981, the stock recovered and it was estimated that in 1983 the stock level was 0.6 million tons.

It is important to realize that in an open-access situation there are no 'automatic' economic forces that can solve the problem of overexploitation. Fishery economists agree that public intervention is necessary to achieve economic efficiency. However, there are numerous examples of public

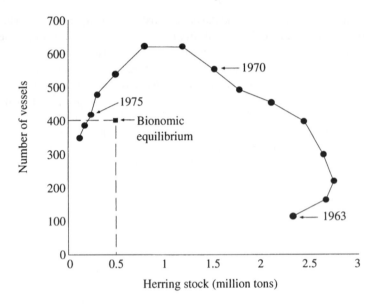

Source: Björndal and Conrad (1987).

Figure 21.6   Dynamics of an open-access fishery of North Sea herring

authorities having made the situation even worse by taking inappropriate
regulatory measures. Let us consider these problems.

4.3   Regulation of the Fishery

Public authorities have taken various control measures to reduce the problem
of overcapitalization and to save populations from extinction. At a practical
level, regulation of fisheries is in many cases an unsolved problem (Munro and
Scott, 1985). The authorities seem to neglect the economic forces behind overexploitation. This has led to regulatory measures which may temporarily reduce
the level of overharvesting, but which still include the market signals that cause
overexploitation. The other problem is that fishery regulation faces the
conflicting interests of different groups. A particular regulation may be effective
and beneficial to some subgroup but may yield economic losses to others.

Most public regulation alternatives can be classified as follows:

1. *Closed seasons* are used to limit harvesting during crucial periods when
   the fish population is reproducing.
2. *Gear restrictions* limit the use of 'too-effective' catching devices or try to
   preserve the habitat of the harvested population.

3. By *limited entry* the authorities restrict the number of fishing vessels. The authorities may first require a vessel to have a licence to operate and then proceed to limit the number of licences.
4. *Aggregate catch quotas* try to shorten the fishing period. The authorities may have a monitoring system for ceasing fishing when the cumulative harvest level equals the aggregate quota.
5. *Taxes* can be imposed on the catch or on some harvesting input.
6. *Individual transferable quotas* limit the level of harvest for each individual fisherman per fishing period.

The aim of closed seasons and gear restrictions is to reduce the effectiveness of harvesting or increase the real cost of fishing. The reason for these policy measures seems to be a biological one. The aim is to reduce the level of harvest to the maximum sustainable yield or below, in order to protect the stock from overharvesting. Even if these goals are met, they may still cause economic inefficiency and waste of resources, that is, excessive working hours for fishermen and large expenditures on capital and fishing equipment to achieve the desired level of harvest. Economic efficiency requires the level of the annual harvest to reflect the true value of the fish in the sea and to harvest at the lowest possible cost. By increasing the cost of harvesting, the regulatory policy reduces the income level of fishermen and increases the price of fish for the consumer.

Limiting the number of vessels in a particular fishing area may first reduce the level of harvest, but in the long run this policy will easily lead to a phenomenon called 'capital stuffing'. This means that, while the number of vessels is restricted, the harvesting capacity of existing vessels is increased by increasing the size of engines, using larger nets or by adding more electronic devices to find the schools of fish more efficiently. Thus this form of regulation causes economic losses without necessarily solving the problem of overharvesting.

The Baltic Sea salmon fishery serves as an example in which the Finnish authorities monitor the cumulative harvest during the fishing season and ban fishing when the aggregate catch quota is reached. The implications of this kind of regulation are quite straightforward. The regulation may increase the economic inefficiency of free-access harvesting. The fishing period starts in early summer when the catch will remain fresh for only a few days. However, fishermen have a strong incentive to start harvesting at full capacity because being too slow at the beginning of the season may imply that their annual share of the total quota will be small. Fishermen must invest in strong engines and use their time as effectively as possible to be able to compete successfully with other vessels. This implies that there is an oversupply of salmon during the summer and that the price of fish is at its minimum. The season is closed during the autumn. At Christmas the demand for salmon is at its maximum, but there is no supply and salmon are imported from Norway. In general there is no guarantee that this kind of regulation will increase the welfare of the fishermen or consumers (Mickwitz and Pruuki, 1992).

On the face of it, a tax on catches or landings appears very appealing. The fundamental problem of the open-access fishery is that fishermen have no incentive to take into account the value of fish left in the sea. Public authorities can impose a tax on a unit of catch, which will represent these neglected costs. The aim of profit maximization forces the fishermen to reduce the level of harvest and, if the authorities have calculated the tax level accurately, an optimal harvesting policy will follow. The problem is, however, that this regulation measure may be politically unfeasible. The reason is simply that the tax transfers the economic rent from the fishing industry to the public authority. In other words, the tax policy may imply an economically optimal harvesting policy, but it redistributes income between the government and the fishing industry. As a consequence, fishermen will use all their political strength to prevent this kind of policy from coming into force (Munro and Scott, 1985).[10]

Under the system of individual transferable quotas (ITQ) the authorities determine the optimal seasonal aggregate catch and subdivide it among the fishermen. In this way the government links property rights to the harvested population. The individual quotas allow the holder to harvest a given amount of a specified type of fish. In addition, it is possible to sell the quotas to other fishermen. Consequently, the fishermen have no incentive to overcapitalize. They can freely decide on the fishing equipment they want to use and on the length of the fishing season. Moreover, it is possible to sell part of the individual quotas in a particular year or to leave the business completely. The ITQ system has the same effect as a tax on catches, but it leaves the net economic welfare (that is, the economic rent) to the fishing industry. The main difficulty of this system is the initial allocation of quotas to the vessels. One possibility is that the authorities allocate quotas in proportion to historical catches. The ITQ system has been applied in New Zealand from 1983 onwards and to some extent also in the USA and Canada.

4.4 An Example of Renewable Resource Management Catastrophe: Canada's Atlantic Fisheries

Fisheries have always been a highly important economic industry in Atlantic Canada and Newfoundland. Historically the most important stock has been the cod stock, extending from southern Labrador to south-eastern Newfoundland, often referred to as 'Northern cod'. Before 1977, Canada's jurisdiction over the fishery resources did not extend beyond 12 miles and the stock was harvested by several nations, including Russia and Spain. During 1970s the annual total harvest of Northern cod was normally in the range of 250–300 thousand tons annually. According to marine biologists, the annual maximum sustainable harvest of the resource was about 559 thousand tons. The prevailing fishery management strategy was to stabilize the stock to the maximum sustainable level.

In 1977 the property rights arrangements of the fish stocks were changed and among other nations Canada was given jurisdiction over fishery resources out to 200 nautical miles from shore. After 1977 the aim of Canada's fishery authorities was to rebuild the stocks since it was believed that before 1977 the stocks were overharvested under a free-access regime. The total allowable harvest was set at 140 thousand tons. It was anticipated that after some years the stock would increase, after which the total allowable harvest would increased to 400 thousand tons. What actually happened during the 1990s was quite different. The total harvest reached 270 thousand tons in 1988, but after that the fishing authorities were forced to reduce the allowable harvest and in 1992 the Northern cod fishery was totally closed due to a dramatic collapse of the fish stocks. As a consequence many thousand fishers and processing workers lost their jobs.

Researchers do not have a single explanation for the tragedy. Among the hypotheses is excessive exploitation and overcapitalization of the fleet and processing sector, and fishing authorities' failure to oppose the continuous political demand to increase the level of total allowable catch. Another argument notes the rapid growth of harp seal stocks (which eat an important prey of cod), following the successful European campaign to destroy the market for seal pelts. The third explanation emphasizes that the level of uncertainty in fisheries management may be a much more serious problem than previously realized. For example, the methods available for estimating the level of existing fish stocks may not yield reliable results. As a consequence some researchers have urged governments to adopt more risk-averse management policies to prevent similar collapses in the future (Gordon and Munro, 1996).

Economic analysis of fisheries provides an interesting perspective on the utilization of natural resources. In many respects this analysis may also be extended to other biological resources such as game. Natural resource economists share the view that renewable stocks should be considered capital assets with a biological reproduction mechanism. Here we have described the growth of biological resources using the simple growth model shown in Figure 21.5. It is important to keep in mind that empirically more accurate models may include the age classes of the population, male/female structure, interaction between different species and spatial distribution of the stock (see, for example, Clark, 1990). In addition to biological features, attention must be paid to the definition of property rights. Without combining economic and biological perspectives and without appropriate property rights or correctly designed regulation policy, the economic benefits from these resources, including the value *in situ*, are easily wasted.

5. ECONOMICS OF FORESTRY

Forests cover 35 per cent of the total land area in Europe and the average for the world is 32 per cent. They provide a wide variety of materials and services to the economies of the world. These include raw material for housing, wood products, and pulp and paper products. However, this is by no means all; forest economists have until recently tended to overlook services other than wood production when considering the optimal management of forests. This may be partly due to the common property or even free-access nature of most of the other services. However, the increasing importance of environmental problems has also directed attention to the non-timber services. Forests provide habitats for wildlife and recreation possibilities for humans, absorb carbon dioxide, and produce oxygen. Forests also help to preserve water resources, and they prevent land erosion.

The traditional problem for forest economics has been the optimal management of forests with respect to timber production. In view of what has been said above, this is clearly a very narrow perspective. Instead, society should find an optimal mix of all the different services provided by forests. It is obvious that in different regions the optimal use of forest resources can vary considerably. In some cases, for example, in managed second-growth boreal forests, even intensive use for timber production may not seriously conflict with the other uses or distort the ecological balance of the environment. In contrast, some forests should be used very little, if at all, for timber production. For example, the boreal forests near the forest borders in the northern parts of the European, Asian and American continents, and the rainforests where the ecosystems are especially vulnerable, should be managed with great caution.

The present situation indicates an unfortunate polarized development in the utilization of the world's forest resources. In Europe, where timber production mainly occurs in managed and plantation forests, the resource is increasing. The same holds for most managed boreal forests, although in the USA and Canada, felling old-growth timber still supplies a part of the raw material for the wood processing industry. By contrast, in the tropical regions deforestation is continuing at an alarming rate (World Resources Institute, 1990). Deforestation results not only in diminishing wood resources but also in intensifying global warming and erosion, and reducing agricultural production and biodiversity.

5.1 Approaches to the Forest Rotation Period: at What Age Should a Tree be Cut?

In the Nordic countries and in many other parts of Europe a major part of the forest land is owned by households (or non-industrial private forest owners). For example, in Finland these own approximately 60 per cent of the forest land area and supply about 80 per cent of the timber. Thus their timber harvesting decisions determine both the economic welfare from forestry and the state of nature preservation for large geographic areas, and so it is important to understand their forest harvesting decisions.

Historically, there has been an interest in promoting households' timber harvesting activity. A more recent aim in forest policy is to change households' forest management practices in order to promote nature preservation or bio-diversity goals. In either case it is possible to cause serious problems if forest-owners' decision-making is inadequately understood. This problem is underlined by the fact that, in the case of forestry, markets may not give eco-nomically correct signals. This follows because non-timber or *in situ* values may not have market prices, and because time horizons in forestry are very long compared to the life cycle of an average forest-owner.

We focus on models that determine the rotation period for even-aged stands,[11] since in the Nordic countries forestry is based on even-aged management with the typical cutting area being about 1–2 hectares. The analysis focuses on the economic aspects; the biological details are highly stylized. With the rotation model, it is possible to make the biological aspect as detailed as needed without making major changes in the economic aspects of the problem (see, for example, Valsta, 1993). Within even-aged forestry management, the length of the rotation period determines the age-class structure in a given forest (a forest is defined as a collection of stands) and the age of the oldest trees. Thus the length of the rotation period determines the living conditions of various species living in the forest environment.

Timber-harvesting is a solution to a decision-making problem. We study how such a problem can be formulated and what aspects may determine the length of the rotation period. Interesting issues include how different values can be included in the decision-making model and how they change the harvesting decision and, for example, the quantities of timber supplied and the price of timber. From the point of view of nature preservation an important question is how much should forest-owners be compensated if the aim is to maintain their welfare level when their forests are included in nature conservation programmes.

Maximum sustainable yield in forestry

Perhaps the most traditional approach in forestry practices is the concept of maximum sustainable yield (MSY). Recall that a similar view has been dominant in the case of fisheries (Clark, 1990). In forestry the intuition behind this approach is that the growth rate of trees is low in cubic metres, both when the trees are young and old (see Figure 21.7, before and after the ages s_1 and s_2). Thus applying a very short or long rotation period does not utilize the most efficient biological growing capacity. This leads to the idea that a stand should be harvested in order to maximize the annual average yield, that is, $q(s)/s$, where $q(s)$ gives the stand biomass q as a function of its age s (see Figure 21.7). Maximization of $q(s)/s$ implies that the stand is to be cut when

$$q(s)/s = q'(s), \qquad (21.1)$$

which means that at the optimal cutting moment the average annual growth equals the growth rate of the biomass or the 'growth during the last growing season'. If the MSY concept is applied to the maximization of biomass production, the rotation period can be surprisingly short. According to a recent study, it may lead to rotation periods that vary between 40 and 60 years in the cases of *Picea abies*, *Pinus sylvestris* and *Betula sp.* (Valsta, 1997). These rotations are surprisingly short compared to actual rotations, which vary between 70 and 110 years.

In the normative sense, the MSY approach takes a very restrictive view of human objectives since it suggests that forest-owners should maximize the production of biomass. No other economic activity aims to maximize physical

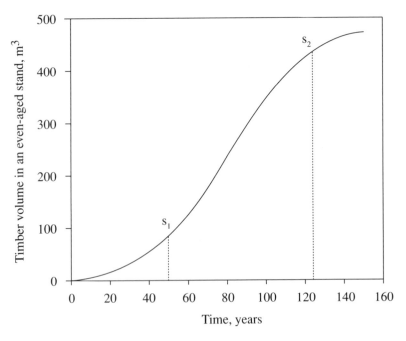

Figure 21.7   Typical growth function for an even-aged stand of one hectare

output. Biomass maximization also neglects that the market price of timber from old trees may be much higher than the price of timber from young trees.

From the point of view of economics, the assumption that decision-making is rational implies that a normative model should obtain support from empirical testing. The MSY rule is highly problematic as an empirical description of how household forest-owners behave. The model hypothesizes that biological factors alone determine the forest-harvesting decision. However, numerous empirical studies show that timber supply decisions are related, for example, to the price of timber (Binkley, 1981; Dennis, 1990; Kuuluvainen and Tahvonen, 1999). Moreover, the MSY approach does not generate predictions of the price of forest land.

Forest rent

A model called 'forest rent' or net sustainable yield takes into account timber prices and the costs of planting a new stand. The aim is to maximize over the rotation period the annual economic net yield, that is, $[px(s) - w]/s$, where p is timber price, w is planting costs and $x(s)$ gives the commercial cubic metres of timber as a function of stand age. Maximization requires that

$$px'(s) - [px(s) - w]/s = 0. \qquad (21.2)$$

Thus, according to this rule, a stand is cut when the increase in stand value equals the average annual growth in stand net value. The rotation period defined by (21.2) may be considerably different from MSY rotation. This follows because of the economic parameters and especially because biomass growth is replaced by commercial cubic metres of timber.

Although this approach uses some economic parameters, the aim of maximizing the average annual net economic yield reflects a zero rate of interest. Thus, as a normative rule, the model is valid only if forest-owners can borrow and lend money at zero interest. This is possible only in highly exceptional circumstances. Another problem with this model is that, like the concept of maximum sustainable yield, it does not generate a sensible hypothesis for the value of forest land. If we sum the net benefits over an infinite horizon rotation programme, the model suggests that the value of forest land is infinite, which is in contradiction with the empirical data on land markets.

Faustmann rotation model

The traditional economic approach to forestry decisions is the Faustmann (1849) rotation model. This simply adds the rate of interest to the model of forest rent. The Faustmann model is usually specified by assuming that initially the forest-owner has bare forest land just after clear-cutting. However, it is quite possible to take any stand age as the starting-point without altering the results of the analysis. The profits of the owner of bare forest land can be written as

$$V = \sum_{i=1}^{\infty} \left[px(s)e^{-rs} - w \right] e^{-rsi}, \tag{21.3}$$

where r is the rate of interest, s the stand age and V the value of forest land. Note that $px(t)e^{-rs} - w$ is the net present value benefit from one rotation. Each subsequent benefit is then discounted by one more rotation period. Using the theorem for an infinite geometric series, we can write the value of forest land as $V = [px(s)^{-rs} - w]/(1 - e^{-rs})$. Differentiating this with respect to the rotation length gives the Faustmann optimal rotation equation:

$$px'(s) - rpx(s) - r[px(s)e^{-rs} - w]/(1 - e^{-rs}) = 0 \tag{21.4}$$

According to this view the stand is cut when the value of letting the stand grow an additional year, $px'(t)$, equals the combined interest costs on the first harvest, $rpx(s)$, and on the value of bare forest land, $r[px(s)e^{-rs} - w]/(1 - e^{-rs})$. It is possible to show that the Faustmann rotation period is the longer, the higher the planting costs and the lower the timber price and rate of interest (Johansson and Löfgren, 1985, p. 82). For example, in southern Finland, the Faustmann rotation period is very sensitive to variations in the rate of discount but typically varies between 50 and 90 years.

The Faustmann model has a history of 150 years (see Johansson and Löfgren, 1985; Samuelson, 1976). The model was long unknown in economics and many famous economists have specified the rotation problem incorrectly. The most usual mistake has perhaps been to take into account only the first harvest instead of the infinite chain of rotations. This shortsighted view implies an excessively long rotation period and reflects the assumption that land is not a scarce factor of production in forestry.

The Faustmann model specifies the value of bare forest land when the rotation period in (21.3) equals its optimal length as determined implicitly by (21.4). Note that a forest-owner has only a finite lifetime. The infinite horizon reflects either the possibility that forest-owners have bequest motives or that they can sell the forest land in perfectly functioning land markets. The chain of transactions implies that each forest-owner has economic incentives to apply an infinite horizon in his harvesing decisions. Differentiating the value of bare forest land and taking into account that $\partial V/\partial s = 0$, since the land value is maximized, yields the results that the value of forest land depends positively on timber price but negatively on planting costs and the rate of interest.

Figure 21.8 shows a numerical example of how the value of bare land depends on the rate of interest. When $r > 0.036$, the land value is negative.

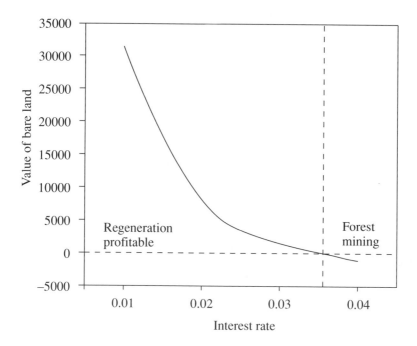

Figure 21.8   The value of bare forest land and forest mining

This simply means that even the maximized land value or profit is negative and the replanting costs exceed the present value gross timber income, that is, $px(s_f)e^{-rs_f} - w < 0$, where s_f is the Faustmann rotation. Besides the rate of discount, the cause of negative land value can be a low timber price, high planting costs, or low growing capacity of the forest land. With negative values for bare land, a profit-maximizing land-owner does not replant a new stand after the harvesting. If natural regeneration is absent, this leads to the outcome called 'forest mining'.

The possibility that the model may 'recommend' forest mining has caused much discussion and confusion. It can be hypothesized that in Finland the value of bare land is negative in large forest areas. There have been two different types of response to this. First, Finnish forest law requires that replanting be done within five years after the harvest. Second, since the Faustmann model is widely used in determining the rotation period and land value, the model is 'modified' by lowering the rate of discount below the levels suggested by the market rate of interest. In fact forestry experts apply different rates of interest in different parts of the country in order to prevent negative land values and to obtain the 'correct' rotation period. This approach is clearly implausible; any other model parameter could also be 'modified' from the correct values to obtain a certain desired result.

As a reaction to the undesired implication of discounting, the ecology textbook by Begon et al. (1996, p. 666) suggests that a 'new economics' is needed that is able to treat values in a broader sense than merely prices of things that are bought and sold. This statement is understandable in the sense that, for example, the Faustmann model and similar models in fishery economics are often too restrictive. However, in a broader context the statement may be unwarranted since it is based on a very limited view of the existing economics, which is not at all restricted to values directly realized in markets.

5.2 Some Recent Developments in Modelling Timber Supply from Household Forest-owners

According to several empirical studies, timber-harvesting decisions depend on forest-owner-specific parameters like non-forest income, which are absent from the Faustmann model (for example Dennis, 1990). Moreover, some recent studies suggest that the price paid for forest land may depend on certain buyer- and seller-specific characteristics, such as their wealth and income levels, that do not enter into the Faustmann land value formula (Aronsson and Carlén, 1997). Thus the Faustmann model is problematic as an empirical description of how forest-owners behave. As a normative rule, the Faustmann model is problematic since it is restricted to profit maximization. In the context of individuals or households, economic decision-making is usually explained by applying some form of the theory of rational choice. In our context this leads to maximization of lifetime welfare. Compared to this, the aim of profit maximization is highly restrictive since it does not taken into account any other aspects of the forest-owner's economy. The Faustmann model also assumes that forests are valuable only because of timber, and all values related to bio-diversity, recreation, scenery and so on are neglected.

As a response to these difficulties, forest economic research now has two different traditions (see Amager, 1997). One tradition follows the Faustmann model and continues to rely on the profit maximization hypothesis. Within this tradition, for example, Hartmann (1976), Strang (1983) and Clark (1990) have extended the model to cover non-market or *in situ* values. The problem that remains is that these specifications are still based on profit maximization and cannot explain why forest-harvesting decisions depend on forest-owner-specific factors like non-forest income.

The second tradition is the two-period approach in which the profit maximization assumption is generalized to utility maximization. This includes many studies that try to explain why forest-harvesting decisions empirically depend on parameters not included in the Faustmann model. However, as noted, for example by Johansson and Löfgren (1985, p. 8), the two period specification does not describe the forest-harvesting decision as a rotation problem. Instead, the forest is described as a homogeneous biomass which is harvested continuously as in the homogeneous biomass fishery models (recall section 4 and Figure 21.5, Clark, 1990 or Begon et al., 1996, p. 652). This simplification of forest biology greatly simplifies the mathematics of economic optimization, but the approach neglects the fact that the growth of a forest depends on its age composition. Thus these models cannot describe some of the most essential features of forestry, like the optimal rotation period.

A third alternative for extending the classical Faustmann approach is to include both utility maximization and *in situ* values directly in the Faustmann model. Such an approach would combine the biologically relevant description of forest growth in the Faustmann model and the richer description of the forest-owner's economy studied within the two-period tradition. These types of models show how, in the presence of *in situ* value of forests, the forest-owner's harvesting decisions and optimal rotation period become dependent on forest-owner-specific factors like his preferences, wealth level and age. One basic outcome of the model is that *in situ* valuation of forests may lengthen the economically optimal rotation period. The model also predicts that if a forest-owner is rich enough and has *in situ* preferences, it may be optimal to leave the forest totally uncut. A more complex version of the model predicts that *in situ* valuation of forests may work in favour of small clear-cut areas or perhaps (when biologically possible) uneven-aged management (see Tahvonen, 1998 and Tahvonen and Salo, 1999).

5.3   Forest Resources Utilization in Europe

According to Sedjo and Lyon (1992), the conventional wisdom among most foresters is that the forest resource is becoming increasingly scarce. The available statistics on sawn timber prices (USDA, 1988) indicate a rising long-term trend (see also Ruttan and Callahan, 1962), which seems to support the conventional wisdom. An explanation of this secular trend may be the mining (that is, clear-cutting without planting new trees) of old-growth forests.

However, Sedjo and Lyon (1992) also mention that not all timber prices have followed a rising trend. In particular, there does not seem to be a long-term rising trend in the price of pulpwood. Even the rising trend in sawn timber prices seems to have levelled off since 1950. The fairly stable pulpwood prices and levelling off of the other price trends may be partly explained by the transition from harvesting old-growth timber to harvesting managed forests. For example, in Finland timber prices have increased on average less than 0.5 per cent per year during the past 50 years. Still the total amount of raw material wood used in Finland after the Second World War is larger than the present standing stock.

The results of an inquiry conducted by the FAO's Economic Commission for Europe (ECE) actually indicate that the harvest rate in Europe is much below the annual increment of European forests (Pajuoja, 1995). In Figure 21.9(a) the expected development of the growing stock of European forests, annual increment and total fellings (harvest) is projected to the year 2040. Thus the maximum sustainable harvest rate, that is, the rate of harvest that would keep the timber stock constant, is higher than the present harvest rate. This, together with the observation that timber prices have not increased or have increased only modestly in Europe during the past 40 years, indicates that the demand for wood is below the present growth of European forests. This partly reflects the imports of wood raw material from other parts of the world (FAO, 1997).

That the present large growing stock has a net annual increment (NAI) larger than fellings (Figure 21.9(b)) may reflect the fact that European forestry has traditionally had goals other than purely economic ones (for example, the *in situ* value of growing stock). Alternatively, demand may not have reached expected levels, or it may be that the interest rates used in forestry are considerably lower than those expected in other parts of the economy. Recently other explanations for the substantial increases in European forest resources have also been proposed. For example, Kauppi et al. (1992) suggest that the explanation may rest partly with the fertilization effects of pollution (acid rain), which are offsetting the adverse effects of pollutants, at least for the time being.

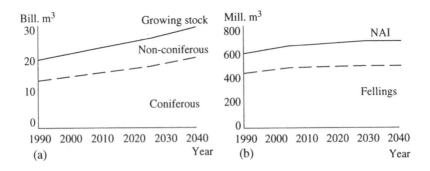

Figure 21.9   Future development of European forests

ACKNOWLEDGEMENT

Jari Kuuluvainen gratefully acknowledges financial support from Maj and Tor Nessling Foundation.

NOTES

1. In Finland, Norway and Sweden 'everyman rights' allow one to walk, camp and pick berries and mushrooms in forests owned by others.
2. Bromley (1991) argues that free-access and common property regimes must be carefully separated and that with well-defined rights and duties common property regimes may well lead to rational resource use.
3. Pastures in many places are of poor quality and the amount of lichen, vital to reindeer, has declined considerably.
4. That is, increasing the consumption of the resource for a year increases benefits, but the higher the level of consumption, the lower the increase in benefits if an additional resource unit is used.
5. Note that discounting makes commensurable economic benefits and costs that occur at different times.
6. The analysis is completed when the initial level of the royalty is defined so that the utilization programme exhausts the resource over a specified time horizon, which may be infinite.
7. A third source of non-optimality arises if two or more oil companies are drilling the same oilwell. This leads to the common-pool or free-access situation.
8. This is mathematically true if the slope of the growth function of the population is always below the highest rate of interest the owner may receive from some other investment.
9. This value can be compared with the concept of royalty in the case of non-renewable resources.
10. There is a close connection between the problems of implementing pollution charges and implementing tax policy in fishery regulation.
11. A stand consists of a number of even-aged trees that are managed as one unit. A forest is a collection of stands.

REFERENCES

Amager, G. (1997), 'The design of forest taxation: a synthesis with new directions', *Silva Fennica*, **31**, 101–19.

Aronsson, T. and O. Carlén (1997), 'The determinants of forest land prices: an empirical analysis', Department of Forest Economics, Report 242, Swedish University of Agricultural Sciences, Umeå, Sweden.

Barnett, H. and C. Morse, (1963), *Scarcity and Growth*, Washington, DC: Resources for the Future.

Begon, M., C. Harper and C. Townsend (1996) *Ecology: Individuals, Populations and Communities*, Oxford: Blackwell Science.

Berck, P. (1976), 'Natural resources in a competitive economy', dissertation, Department of Economics, MIT, Massachusetts.

Binkley, C. (1981), 'Timber supply from private nonindustrial forests', Yale School of Forestry and Environmental Studies, Bulletin no. 92.

Binkley, C. (1987), 'Economic models of timber supply', in M. Kallio, D. Dykstra and C. Binkley (eds), *The Global Forest Sector: An Analytical Perspective*, New York: John Wiley & Sons, pp. 109–36.

Björndal, T. and J. Conrad (1987), 'The dynamics of open access fishery', *Canadian Journal of Economics*, **20**, 74–85.

Bromley, D. (1991), *Environment and Economy: Property Rights and Public Policy*, Oxford: Basil Blackwell.

Clark, C.W. (1973), 'Profit maximization and the extinction of species', *Journal of Political Economy*, **81**, 950–61.

Clark, C. (1990), *Mathematical Bioeconomics: The Optimal Management of Renewable Resources*, New York: John Wiley & Sons.

Dennis, D. (1990), 'A probit analysis of harvesting decisions using pooled time-series and cross-sectional data', *Journal of Environmental Economics and Management*, **18**, 176–87.

FAO (1997), 'Provisional outlook for global forest products consumption, production and trade to 2010', Food and Agricultural Organization of the United Nations, Rome.

Faustmann, M. (1849), 'Berechnung des Wertes welchen Waldboden sowie noch nicht haubare Holzbestände für die Waldwirtschaft besitzen', *Allgemeine Forst- und Jagd-Zeitung*, **15**, 441.

Gordon, D. and G. Munro (eds) (1996), *Fisheries Under Uncertainty; A Precautionary Approach to the Resource Management*, Calgary: University of Calgary Press.

Gordon, H.S. (1954), 'The economic theory of a common property resource: the fishery', *Journal of Political Economy*, **62**, 124–42.

Hartman, R. (1976), 'The harvesting decision when a standing forest has value', *Economic Inquiry*, **4**, 52–8.

Hotelling, H. (1931), 'The economics of exhaustible resources', *Journal of Political Economy*, **39**, 137–75.

Johansson, P.-O. and K.-G. Löfgren (1985), *The Economics of Forestry and Natural Resources*, Oxford: Basil Blackwell.

Kauppi, R., K. Kuusela and K. Mielikäinen (1992), 'Biomass and carbon budget of European forests, 1971 to 1990', *Science*, **256**, 70–74.

Kuuluvainen, J. and O. Tahvonen (1999), 'Testing the forest rotation model: evidence from panel data', *Forest Science*, **45**, 539–51.

Leontief, W. (1977), *The Future of the World Economy*, New York: Oxford University Press.

Ligon, E. and U. Narain (1999), 'Government management of village commons: comparing two forest policies', *Journal of Environmental Economics and Management*, **37**, 272–89.

Malthus, T. (1798), *An Essay on the Principle of Population as it Affects the Future Improvement of Society*, London: Ward Lock.

Meadows, D.H., D.L. Meadows, J. Randers and W. Behrens (1972), *The Limits to Growth: A Report for the Club of Rome's Project on the Predicament of Mankind*, New York: Signet.

Meadows, D.H., D.L. Meadows and J. Randers (1992), *Beyond the Limits: Global Collapse or a Sustainable Future*, London: Earthscan.

Mickwitz, P. and V. Pruuki (1992), 'Individual transferable quotas in the Finnish salmon fishery – prospects for the future', manuscript, Finnish Game and Fisheries Research Institute, Helsinki.

Mill, J.S. (1862), *Principles of Political Economy*, New York: Appleton.

Munro, G. and A. Scott (1985), 'The economics of fisheries management', in A.V. Kneese and J.L. Sweeney (eds), *Handbook of Natural Resource and Energy Economics*, Vol. 11, Amsterdam: North-Holland.

Nordhaus, W. (1992), Lethal models 2: 'The limits to growth revisited', *Brookings Papers on Economic Activity*, **2**.

Pajuoja, H. (1995), 'The outlook for the European forest resources and roundwood supply', ETTS V Working Paper, Geneva: United Nations Economic Commission for Europe.

Ruttan, V.W. and J.C. Callahan (1962), 'Resource inputs and output growth: comparisons between agriculture and forestry', *Forest Science*, **8**, 68–82.

Salo, S. and O. Tahvonen (2000), 'Oligopoly equilibria in nonrenewable markets', *Journal of Economic Dynamics and Control*, forthcoming.

Samuelson, P. (1976), 'Economics of forestry in an evolving society', *Economic Inquiry* **XIV**, 466–93.

Sedjo, R.A. and K.S. Lyon (1992), *The Long-Term Adequacy of World Timber Supply*, Washington, DC: Resources for the Future.

Slade, M. (1982), 'Trends in natural resource commodity prices: an analysis of the time domain', *Journal of Environmental Economics and Management*, **9**, 122–37.

Smith, V. (1968), 'Economics of production of natural resources', *American Economic Review*, **58**, 409–31.

Strang, W. (1983), 'On the optimal forest harvesting decisions', *Economic Inquiry*, **4**, 567–83.

Sweeney, J. (1993), 'Economic theory of depletable resources: an introduction', in A.V. Kneese and J.L. Sweeney (eds), *Handbook of Natural Resource and Energy Economics*, Vol. 11, Amsterdam: North-Holland.

Tahvonen, O. (1997), 'Fossil fuels, stock externalities, and backstop technology', *The Canadian Journal of Economics*, **XXX**, 855–74.

Tahvonen, O. (1998), 'Bequest, credit rationing and *in situ* values in the Faustmann–Pressler–Ohlin forestry model', *Scandinavian Journal of Economics*, **100**, 781–800.

Tahvonen, O. and S. Salo (1999), 'Optimal forest rotation with *in situ* preferences', *Journal of Environmental Economics and Management*, **37**, 106–28.

Tahvonen, O. and S. Salo (2000), 'Economic growth and transitions between renewable and nonrenewable energy resources', *European Economic Review*, forthcoming.

US Department of Agriculture (USDA), Forest Service (1988), 'US timber production, trade, consumption, and price statistics 1950–1986', Miscellaneous Publications no. 1453, Washington, DC: USDA.

Valsta, L. (1993), 'Stand management optimization based on growth simulators', Finnish Forest Research Institute, *Research Reports* 453.

Valsta, L. (1997), 'Uudistushakkuiden ajoitus', in K. Mielikäinen and M. Riikita (eds), *Kannatlava puuntuotanto*, Helsinki: Metsälehtikustannus. (In Finnish)

World Resources Institute (1992), *World Resources 1992–1993*, Oxford: Oxford University Press.

22.   Waste management

R. Kerry Turner

1.   INTRODUCTION

The increasing scale of economic activity (industrialization, urbanization, rising standards of living and, in many developing countries, population growth) has inevitably led to huge increases in waste in the form of materials and energy flows. Municipal solid waste (MSW) in the OECD countries grouping, for example, has been growing by 2.6 per cent per annum since 1980 (see Table 22.1). This large and increasing mass of redundant goods, by-products and a variety of other organic and inorganic residues must be disposed of somehow and at a cost. The environment has a large waste assimilation capacity, but this is not infinite. Too much waste entering the environment rather than being recycled or reused will put too much stress on the assimilative capacity of the environment to handle such waste safely. The result will be a range of pollution and resource degradation impacts, and consequent economic damage cost.

The economic growth process has delivered enormous increases in economic welfare. Material wealth per capita has increased significantly and the range of choices for consumers has been widened. Because of the laws of thermodynamics, economic production and consumption activities always generate some pollution and waste that requires proper disposal. Further, it is not possible to have 100 per cent recycling systems. Nevertheless, society does have a choice over the total amount of waste that its economic system produces. In a general sense policy-makers could weigh up the social benefits of various productive activities and compare them with the social costs (including disposal) imposed by these activities. Policy-makers may then decide to intervene in the economic process in order to change/modify production processes, products or packaging and distribution methods.

What the policy-makers should be searching for is the socially acceptable balance between waste minimization (also known as source reduction), recycling and final disposal of waste. Policy-makers will have a set of consequential decisions to make about the recycling or disposal of the waste that continues to arise, since all waste management options carry both costs and benefits. A cost–benefit balance has to be found between recycling schemes and

Table 22.1 Municipal solid waste: total and composition (1990s)

	Total MSW (000 tonnes)	MSW (kg/person/year)	Composition (%)							
			Paper/board	Plastic	Glass	Metal	Organics	Textiles	Other
Austria	2 644	430	22	10	8	5	30	2	23
Belgium	4 781	470	30	4	8	4	45	–	9
Canada	11 000	630	28	11	7	8	34	13	4
Denmark	2 788	520	29	5	4	13	28	–	38
France	25 000	560	31	10	12	6	25	4	12
Germany (W)	121 892	360 (W + E)	18	5	9	3	44	–	20
Greece	–	310	22	11	4	4	49	1	11
Italy	27 000	470	23	7	6	3	47	–	14
Japan [a]	58 431	410	46	9	7	8	26	8	–
Netherlands	8 354	540	25	8	5	4	52	2	5
Poland	11 352	290	10	10	12	8	38	–	22
Portugal	3 600	350	23	4	3	4	60	–	6
Spain	22 000	370	20	7	8	4	49	–	10
Turkey	–	390	37	19	9	7	19	–	18
UK	29 000	350	35	11	9	7	20	2	16
USA	34 692	730	38	9	7	8	23	15	–
India (Delhi)	–	140	6.0	0.9	0.6	1.0	47.0	0.6	44.5
China (Wuhan)	–	200	2.0	0.5	0.6	0.5	17.8	0.6	78.0
S. Africa (Soweto)	–	150	9.0	3.0	12.0	3.0	9.0	1.0	63.0
Peru (Lima)	–	300	14.0	4.0	3.0	4.0	56.0	4.0	2.0
Mexico (Mexico City)	–	550	17.0	6.0	4.0	6.0	56.0	6.0	5.0

[a] errors in reported percentages for composition.

Sources: OECD (1993, 1997), Blight (1996).

a range of disposal options (see Table 22.2). Recycling is not necessarily a costless and environmentally benign activity, and different disposal options – for example, landfill, incineration and composting – all entail different financial costs and environmental impacts.

Table 22.2   Municipal solid waste: treatment options (%), 1990s

	Recycling	Composting	Incineration	Landfill
Austria	23	15	14	48
Belgium	21	2	38	39
Denmark	9	–	79	12
France	–	7	46	47
Germany	23	5	17	51
Greece	7	–	–	93
Italy	–	–	6	94
Netherlands	28	18	31	23
Spain	1	11	5	83
Sweden	16	3	42	39
UK	6	1	6	88
USA (1986)	27	–	7	66
Japan (1980s)	2.8	0.1	64	33

Source: *Warmer Bulletin*, **61** (1998); OECD *Environmental Data* (various years).

In developed countries, there has been a move towards determining the best predictable environmental option (BPEO) for waste. This takes a cross-media and long-term perspective. In order to assess the diverse range of environmental costs and benefits associated with the various options, so-called life-cycle assessment (LCA) can be adopted (Powell et al., 1996; Powell et al., 1997). Any such assessment procedure inevitably highlights the difficulty of balancing financial and non-financial impact costs and benefits. The economic damage approach applies a common scale of monetary values to as many costs and benefits as is feasible in order to minimize the trade-off complexity. Economic damage values are available for a number of environmental and social impacts including gaseous emissions, road congestion and casualties from road traffic accidents. A complementary approach, multi-criteria evaluation, can also be used to appraise waste management options (Powell, 1996). A scoring system is used to obtain weightings that are then applied to each impact before the weighted impact scores are aggregated. Sensitivity analysis is usually included in the procedure in order to determine the effort of varying the weighting schema.

Contemporary policy debates about waste management have tended to focus on the 'second-stage' questions outlined above, rather than on the more fundamental questions about how much waste and what types of waste are socially acceptable. The second stage of the policy-making process is essentially a search for the least-cost configuration of recycling and disposal options. The search for a more socially acceptable waste management strategy has, however, been inhibited by a paucity of reliable data.

While there are a variety of sources of data on waste, no single database exists that is comprehensive, extensive and up to date. Many countries lack acceptable forecasts for the amount and composition of waste streams which are essential for the planning of an effective and economically efficient waste management scheme. Tables 22.1 and 22.2 contain the data that are available, but they are far from up to date and are of questionable accuracy below the aggregate tonnage level. An effective system will have to integrate waste minimization, recycling/reusing and processing, transport and final disposal activities. An economically efficient system will have to be composed of the least-cost (in social cost terms) combination of management options (Turner and Powell, 1993).

There have been signs during the 1990s that clean technology, economic incentives, business sustainability strategies and community participation in waste minimization futures are beginning to coalesce around local Agenda 21 and urban sustainability initiatives in general. The strictures of the Kyoto Agreement should also provide a boost to methane reduction via options such as energy from waste plants. Agenda 21 objectives include waste minimization, reuse and recycling maximization, the promotion of sound waste disposal and treatment techniques and the extension of waste services provision. This requires a more integrated and holistic approach to waste management than has been apparent so far.

A 'strong' interpretation of the sustainable economic development concept would prescribe that persistent (potentially hazardous) wastes should not be allowed to accumulate and thereby disrupt nutrient and material cycles in the environment. It also recommends that waste discharges are limited to rates that are significantly less than natural, or human-augmented, assimilative capacity (Turner, 1993). This recommendation is therefore based on the so-called 'precautionary principle' (see Chapter 5) and on a risk-averse attitude.

The available evidence suggests that the industrial countries are finding it increasingly difficult (and costly) to dispose of waste. For some countries, such as the USA, The Netherlands and Germany, there is a growing physical shortage, either regionally or nationally, of environmentally acceptable landfill disposal sites. For other countries the 'shortage' of disposal sites (for landfill or incineration) has more to do with social constraints and the NIMBY (not in my back yard) syndrome. National policy-makers in the European Union (EU) face the added complexity that the European Commission and Council has laid down that 'the proximate principle' should be an accepted part of all member states' waste management policy. Under the proximity principle, individual countries are encouraged to aim at self-sufficiency in waste disposal. This principle seems to be based on political reasoning linked to the risk that some people would be exposed to a disproportionate share of the waste disposal cost impacts if the traded waste were concentrated in particular countries or even certain sites. But a simplistic and uniform application of the waste disposal principle across the EU would produce market distortions and inefficiency. This is because for some waste materials (secondary materials) there is already a functioning international market which facilitates recycling activities (collection, processing and utilization as production inputs). From an economic perspective, the proximity principle should only apply to those materials for which there are very limited or zero market opportunities.

The full social costs of waste disposal have traditionally been disguised or underestimated. Thus in the UK, for example, the financial costs of landfill disposal continue to be relatively low (£5 ($9)/tonne to £20 ($35)/tonne for municipal solid waste (MSW)), representing an underpricing of the waste-assimilating service of the environment. The full economic price for landfill should include all relevant costs – for example, for pre-treatment and proper pollution containment measures plus any remaining environmental impact costs – and is much higher than the lower-bound financial cost. Thus households do not typically pay the proper cost of disposal for their waste. They tend to be charged only for the financial operating costs of the collection and disposal system, rather than for the full costs, including costs of environmental safe-guarding of the site and facilities. Further, many households do not pay the marginal cost (that is, for each bag or bin of waste) but only some notional average cost not tied to the amount of waste they generate.

The externalities connected with waste disposal include air emissions that contribute to global warming, conventional air pollutants (SO_x, No_x and particulates) airborne toxic substances from incinerators, leachate from landfill sites and pollution and accidents associated with road transport. Displaced pollution is treated as an external benefit in any economic calculation. This occurs when the energy recovered from waste displaces energy generated by coal (the least efficient type of electricity-generating power station in the UK) and thus also displaces the associated gaseous emissions. Some of the negative externality effects, for example, landfill or incinerator site disamenity costs, are difficult to value in monetary terms. A calculation undertaken in the mid-1990s in the UK estimated air pollution and transport-related disamenity effects for several waste disposal options (Department of Environment, 1993). The results were as follows: landfill with energy recovery £1 to £2 per tonne extra cost over financial costs, landfill without energy recovery £3.50 to £4.20 per tonne, and incineration with energy recovery £2 to £4 (benefit) per tonne.

Producers also fail to minimize and/or recycle as much waste as they would if they were faced with a fuller, more efficient set of cost-price incentives. Depending on the kind of waste to be minimized, economic incentives in the form of, say, charges, could be imposed on producers or consumers. Consumers would internalize the increased cost of disposal by reconsidering their purchasing decisions, and by reusing or recycling some of their product purchases. Producers would normally not be able to pass on all their increased disposal costs to consumers (because of the risk of losing some of their share of the market) and would therefore have to think seriously about recycling, process modifications and product redesign.

The rest of this chapter is organized as follows. We start in section 2 with a brief overview of the price mechanism and how it can be restructured so as better to incorporate environmental resource usage efficiency. In section 3 we investigate the full social costs (private and external) imposed on society by the waste disposal process. In section 4 we examine the various components of an overall waste management system which is designed to mitigate the waste disposal problem. A more detailed analysis of the economics of waste recycling and disposal from the individual firm's perspective is presented in section 5; and a range of potential policy instruments for more efficient and effective waste management is assessed in section 6.

2. THE PRICE MECHANISM AND THE ENVIRONMENT

The primary virtue of the price mechanism (the market) is that it signals to consumers what the cost of producing a particular product is, and to producers what consumers' relative valuations are, based on their willingness to pay (see Chapter 3). But an unfettered price mechanism will 'use too much' of the environment's goods and services. These environmental resources, waste assimilation capacities, landscape and amenity services, raw materials and the overall life support system, are, by and large, non-market goods and services with zero or very small price tags. The problem caused by the absence of prices is compounded by the 'public' characteristics of many environmental resources. Many of the environmental resources are open-access or virtually open-access resources (see Chapter 21). The end result is that unfettered markets fail to allocate environmental resources efficiently (Turner et al., 1993).

All this is not to argue, however, that freely functioning 'unfettered' markets cannot achieve improvements in environmental quality. If consumers change their tastes in favour of less polluting products (as indicated, at least in principle, through eco-labelling), market forces will lead to a change in the 'pollution content' of final products and services. Green consumerism may do little to alter production processes since the consumer is generally not well informed about the precise nature of such processes, and is in any case less able to affect the choice of processes in any direct way. But process changes will occur if industry also becomes environmentally conscious, and/or the cost signals to industry alter.

There are two ways in which markets can be restructured so as to ensure that environmental services enter into the market systems more effectively. First, we could create markets for previously free services. This would require restriction of access to such resource services by charging entrance fees and/or changing property rights (see Chapter 1).

Second, we could 'modify' markets by deciding centrally the value of environmental services and ensuring that these values are incorporated into the prices of goods and services via charges or taxes on emissions. Thus in the case of MSW a user fee (that is, a fee based on the volume or weight of waste discarded) could be levied on householders or small traders. Alternatively, a charge could be imposed on a producer or a product relating to a particular 'problem' component of the waste stream, for example, a packaging levy, charge or tax. This type of regulatory approach is known as the market-based incentives approach. It is to be contrasted with a direct (command and control) regulatory approach which involves the setting of mandatory environmental standards and targets without the aid of market-based incentives (see Chapter 6).

3. ENVIRONMENTAL STATE: EXTERNAL COSTS OF WASTE DISPOSAL

The physical and thermal properties of the various types of waste (usually categorized as MSW, that is, waste from households and small traders, agricultural waste, industrial waste, mining and quarrying waste, demolition and building waste and sewage sludge), such as calorific value, ash, moisture and bulk density, provide a reasonable indication of the likely environmental response to processes such as collection, transport and incineration. Much more uncertainty surrounds the biodegradation processes in landfill sites and the transfer of pollution (leachate) plumes into surface water and groundwater around such sites.

All the available disposal options (landfill, incineration with and without energy recovery, sea dumping, composting and physical or chemical treatment) carry with them 'externalities'. These are costs and benefits that are borne by, or accrue to, society in general and which are not accounted for in private agents' decisions about waste. The external cost effects include social cost such as disamenity (noise, smell, unsightliness) because of the presence of a disposal site or facility in or near a neighbourhood, as well as air and water pollution, health impacts and congestion costs.

But the recovery of energy that occurs if methane is captured at a landfill site or from an incineration process is an example of an external benefit. The value of the energy produced is not itself an external benefit because it is already accounted for in the costs and revenues of the site-owner, but the energy recovered will displace energy produced elsewhere in the economic system, for example, by displacing power generated at an older and less efficient coal-fired power station. This pollution avoided is then an external benefit of the methane capture or energy recovery at the landfill site or incinerator facility, respectively.

A number of factors contribute to the generation of external costs during the waste disposal process:

- the composition of the waste stream;
- the size of the disposal site or facility;
- the physical characteristics of the disposal site;
- the age of the disposal site or facility;
- the spatial location of the site or facility;
- the degree of engineering (that is, containment and abatement measures) adopted or planned for new sites.

The net externalities from waste disposal (assuming energy recovery is practised) can be calculated in monetary terms as follows:

Waste disposal externality = site/fixed externality + variable externality

The site externality is 'fixed'; that is, it is not directly related to the amount of waste going through the site. There is a cost whatever the scale of the site. The variable externality is related to the amount of waste going through the site and therefore increases as the tonnage of waste increases (Department of the Environment, 1993).

The fixed element of the externality impact relates to the overall site or facility disamenity. The variable externality is made up of:

- global pollution costs, related to greenhouse gas emissions such as carbon dioxide and methane;
- conventional air pollution costs related to sulphur dioxide, NO_x and particulates;
- costs related to 'air toxics' (such as dioxins);
- water pollution costs;

- transport costs (air pollution, congestion and accidental costs);
- displaced pollution damage (because of energy recovery systems).

A UK Department of the Environment report (1993) concluded that the external cost of landfill sites with energy recovery was £1–2 per tonne and without energy recovery £3.50–4.20 per tonne, and that new incinerators have net external benefits of £2–4 per tonne. This gives a difference of £3–8 per tonne, which is broadly consistent with the landfill tax of £5–8 per tonne which was actually introduced on a weight basis in November 1994.

As society demands more definitive risk management knowledge, a difficult balance will have to be maintained between attempts formally to model and forecast hazardous waste-related risks and the concealment of inevitable uncertainties behind a mass of jargon and statistics. It is now a well-established psychological research finding that expert and lay opinion of the riskiness of things often differ considerably. Opinion polls show that chemical waste disposal is at the top of public concerns. Yet risks from such sites (active and inactive) only rank 8 and 13 on the US Environmental Protection Agency's list of 31 cancer risks.

Waste disposal facilities in particular have suffered from the NIMBY syndrome, with health risk perception usually at the centre of people's concern. But why is it that people perceive the health risks to be unacceptable when formal analysis does not confirm these perceptions? Experts tend to use the 'relative risk' approach, that is, the risk posed by toxic chemical exposure from a waste site versus risks posed by, for example, smoking, alcohol, poor diet and traffic accidents. On this basis the chemical hazard may be considered a relatively low risk. Individuals, however, continue to see risks as absolutes and do so often involuntarily, possible because of misinformation and misperception. On the other hand there is a psychosocial basis for the NIMBY syndrome. Waste facilities defined as hazardous are inherently stigmatized and therefore classed as undesirable. Deeper and wider social concerns may also underlie local opposition, including invasion of people's privacy and territory, loss of personal control, stress and lifestyle infringement, loss of trust in public agencies and lack of accountability of the 'system'. Here the waste site is merely the catalyst to unlock concerns about trends in society in general.

4. WASTE MANAGEMENT SYSTEMS

Environmentalists have long advocated what they call the 'waste management hierarchy'. In 1996 the European Commission adopted a waste management strategy which confirmed the 'hierarchy' but also contained a caveat that stressed flexibility and the need to establish the 'best practicable environmental option'. According to this doctrine waste prevention/minimization options should take priority over recycling/reuse options, and the latter should, in turn, take priority over final disposal activities (see Table 22.3). Reuse activities include, for example, returnable bottle systems, while recycling requires some reprocessing of the material that has been collected. Interpreted as a general guide, this hierarchical approach seems to make economic and environmental sense. However, the notion should not be pressed too hard; to do so would be overly simplistic and environmentally risky. Rather, we should adopt the economic cost–benefit approach and attempt to quantify the social benefits and social costs of all options regardless of their assumed place in the 'hierarchy'.

Table 22.3   EC waste management hierarchy

•	Prevention:	including adoption of clean technologies and products; reduction of hazardous wastes; and the establishment of best practice standards and waste reduction targets.
•	Recovery:	both reuse and recycling schemes, with a preference for materials over energy recovery systems.
•	Final disposal:	in cases where disposal is the only feasible option, incineration with energy recovery and controlled containment landfill operations and sites are to be used.

The three ways in which the flow of material waste to the environment could be reduced are:

- waste minimization (source reduction);
- reuse;
- recycling.

These options can be assessed in terms of financial cost-effectiveness. Recycling schemes and waste minimization measures can be evaluated according to their financial profitability and payback, and disposal options according to their net financial cost per tonne of waste. Schemes generating the highest net profitability and shortest payback period, and the least costly disposal options, would have high priority in the management strategy.

Alternatively, waste management options could be subjected to an economic evaluation via the medium of cost–benefit analysis. The adoption of such a risk–benefit/cost–benefit decision framework would also help to clarify a persistent misunderstanding about the distinction between financial profitability and economic efficiency that has remained prevalent in regulatory circles. From the economic efficiency perspective the requirement should not be that options must be financially profitable, but rather that they should yield a net social benefit. The introduction of a recycling or waste minimization scheme should therefore be preceded by an economic cost–benefit appraisal underpinned by a life-cycle assessment. Such a procedure would examine the impacts of a product or service from the mining of the resources, manufacture, distribution, use, reuse, recycling or disposal, in terms of raw materials and energy use, emissions to air and water and solid waste. Given some evaluation method, the total environmental costs and benefits of a given option could be determined (Powell et al., 1997). The introduction of such a scheme or measure should only be sanctioned, on efficiency grounds, if the measure or scheme contributes to a reduction in overall net social costs (private financial costs plus externalities) of the management system. A recycling scheme, for example, should be compared with the currently available least-cost disposal option. A recycling scheme will generate overall net social benefits, as long as the net social costs of the least-cost disposal option are higher than the net social costs associated with the combined recycling and disposal option.

5.   THE FIRM AND WASTE MANAGEMENT

5.1   In-plant and Inter-plant Recycling Flows

It is possible to distinguish between the so-called primary industries and their secondary counterparts. This distinction is made on the grounds of raw material input, with the primary category comprising firms which utilize virgin natural resources, and the secondary category made up of firms utilizing recycled material inputs (secondary materials). In practice, plants in many industries make use of a mixture of virgin (primary) and secondary material inputs. Thus, for example, the very evolution in the chemical and allied industries as an inter-related set of activities designed to take advantage of the by-product streams generated at various points in the chemical transformation process guaranteed a high level of in-plant recycling.

Nevertheless, it is possible to discern what can be labelled a secondary chemicals sector in which used chemicals are collected from their generation points by external firms specializing in the reprocessing and/or disposal of chemical (often hazardous) wastes. The reprocessed chemicals are usually sent back to the original waste-generating plant or sold to other plants capable of utilizing the recovered and often degraded chemical.

All industrialized economies therefore contain private reclamation industries which concentrate their efforts on the recycling of only certain types of waste flows (see Table 22.4). The physical characteristics of these types of waste stream, that is, high mass, relatively low contamination, good homogeneity and concentrated location, combine to offer financially profitable opportunities

Table 22.4   Comparative recycling rates: components of municipal solid waste

	Paper			Glass			Steel cans	Aluminium cans	
	1984	1990	1995	1984	1990	1995	1989	1989	1997
Netherlands	46.0	49.0	77.0	53.0	66.0	80.0	48.0	n.a.	30.0
Luxembourg	32.9	35.2	n.a.	42.0	60.0	n.a.	28.0	n.a.	n.a.
Germany	38.1	43.0	67.0	39.0	54.0	75.0	58.0	n.a.	86.0
Austria	n.a.	n.a.	66.0	n.a.	n.a.	76.0	n.a.	18.0	50.0
Italy	26.1	25.7	29.0	25.0	50.0	53.0	n.a.	n.a.	41.0
France	34.1	34.4	39.0	26.0	45.0	42.0	26.0	n.a.	17.0
Denmark	29.3	33.2	44.0	19.0	40.0	68.0	n.a.	n.a.	n.a.
Switzerland	44.0	61.0[c]	61.0	45.0	56.0[d]	86.0	n.a.	38.0[e]	88.0
Portugal	45.0	39.1	37.0	10.0	30.0	42.0	n.a.	n.a.	17.0
Spain	41.0	38.7	52.0	13.0	27.0	32.0	n.a.	n.a.	20.0
UK	28.6	30.4	37.0	10.0	21.0	26.0	n.a.	5.3[e]	34.0
Eire	n.a.	n.a.	20.0	7.0	18.0	39.0	n.a.	16.0[g]	20.0
Greece	15.1	n.a.	31.0	n.a.	16.0	29.0[f]	n.a.	20.0	33.0
USA	27.3	30.00[c]	n.a.	10.0[b]	n.a.	n.a.	30.0	n.a.	n.a.
Japan	50.1	48.2[d]	n.a.	42.1	47.6[c]	n.a.	43.6[d]	42.5	n.a.
Australia	22.0	30.0[c]	n.a.	17.0[a]	n.a.	n.a.	n.a.	61.0	n.a.

Notes:
n.a. = not available.
[a]   1980
[b]   1985
[c]   1988
[d]   1989
[e]   1990
[f]   1994
[g]   All cans

Source: Turner et al. (1993); European Environment Agency website (1998):
www.eea.dk/frdb.htm

for the would-be reclaimer and/or in-plant recovery unit. These characteristics also underpin an international trade in secondary materials (Grace et al., 1978). In fact the reclamation business is dominated by the 'grade structure–end use' relationship. The lower the grade of the potentially recyclable material (that is, because of unfavourable physical characteristics such as high levels of contamination or small mass), the more expensive is the collection and processing system and the more limited are the end uses available. Financial costs are therefore more likely to outweigh financial revenues in such lower-grade recycling activities. The recycling of MSW is a good example of this problem.

But as we mentioned earlier, industrial waste generators, whether they dispose of their own waste or pay for waste contract services, typically pay less than the full social cost of waste disposal. Theoretically, in the absence of government intervention in the form of an environmental quality protection/management policy, materials or energy recovery will take place up to the level where the marginal cost of an additional unit of recycled material or energy just equals its market value in a reclaimed condition. Both the recovery costs (collection plus processing costs) and the value of the recovered item will be subject to change over time.

The condition for optimal recycling is:

$$MB_R = MC_R$$

or

$$(P_R) + (C_{DW}) + (C_{RC}) + (C_{CR})$$

where:

P_R = price of recycled material;
C_{DW} = marginal cost of disposal (financial plus external costs);
C_{RC} = marginal environmental cost of recycling;
C_{CR} = marginal cost of separate collection and processing for recycled material.

The left-hand side of the equation is the marginal benefit of recycling and the right-hand side is the marginal cost of recycling.

Thus lower-grade recyclable materials arising in small amounts in scattered locations and with only limited end uses are problematic from both a financial profitability and economic efficiency perspective. Such recycling activities will often involve a financial loss because of the low market prices paid for inferior grade materials and the high collection system costs. This financial loss may not be offset by the environmental gains that are claimed for recycling, that is, reduced overall resource extraction and processing social costs when secondary materials are substituted for primary materials; and reduced overall waste disposal social costs.

5.2   Recycled versus Virgin Material Inputs

The previous sections were concerned with the issue of how a firm or waste disposal authority should appraise recycling given that an amount of waste, Q, had to be dealt with in some fashion or other. We now consider the choice for the firm of using virgin materials or recycled materials as inputs to the production of the good that generates the waste. Clearly, this choice dictates the market possibilities for the use of recycled waste if the material is being reused within the same industry.

Consider the following situation of a firm with an output X and just two inputs, recycled material (R) and virgin material (V). In order to maximize profits, price should be set equal to marginal cost, but that marginal cost is now composed of two elements; MC_V and MC_R. Figure 22.1 illustrates how the quantities of R and V are determined. From the equivalence of marginal revenue and (combined) marginal cost, one can determine the output of X and the price of X (P_X). The curve MC_J shows the combined marginal cost curve. The amounts of V and R used can be 'read off' the diagram by tracing the horizontal from the $MR = MC_J$ back to the vertical axis. This horizontal line, FG, cuts the two marginal cost curves and these intersections then determine the amount of the inputs used. In the case of Figure 22.1 we see that the output of X produced with virgin materials is X_V and the output produced with recycled products is X_R. To find the inputs required we then simply need to know the relationship between X and the inputs R and V; that is, we need to know the production function.

For illustration, two quite arbitrary production functions are shown in the lower half of Figure 22.1. One function shows how much can be secured with virgin materials and the other shows how much can be secured with recycled materials. If these production functions apply, we can trace the values of X_V and X_R through the functions to the input levels V_0 and R_0. (The bottom half of the diagram is best viewed sideways with X as the vertical axis; it then becomes a familiar production function diagram.)

Thus we have 'solved' the issue of how much of each of the two inputs to use. Effectively, we require knowledge of the production function and the prices of the materials. We now need to consider whether the picture will change if we introduce external costs and benefits, so that instead of securing the private optima shown in Figure 22.1 we aim for the social optima.

In those cases where it can be shown that recycling itself generates external net benefits (that is, zero or minimal environmental costs of its own and avoidance of the financial and environmental cost of disposal), then in terms of Figure 22.1 we need to subtract these from the marginal cost curve relating to the use of recycled inputs. Figure 22.2 shows how this might be done. The original MC_V and MC_R curves are shown, as is the combined marginal cost curve (MC_{V+R}). These dictate output levels of X_V and X_R for the respective uses of virgin and recycled materials accordingly. Now, if we subtract external benefits from MC_R we secure $MC_{R'}$ and a new joint marginal cost curve $MC_{V+R'}$. The former intersection of marginal revenue and marginal cost was at M and

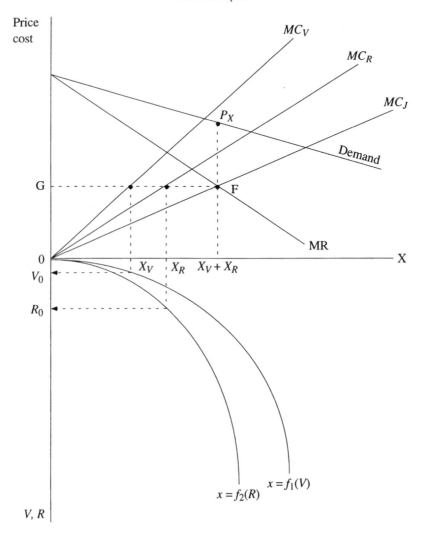

Figure 22.1   Optimal recycling/virgin material input levels

it is now at *K*. This dictates the use of virgin and recycled materials to produce outputs of X_V nd X_R, respectively. The important finding is that the amount of virgin material being used is now less than before and the amount of recycled material is more. Reflection shows that this is exactly what we would expect, since we have effectively lowered the 'price' of *R*.

Clearly, to secure this shift requires an actual act of policy, that is, government intervention. The recycled input could be subsidized by an amount equal to

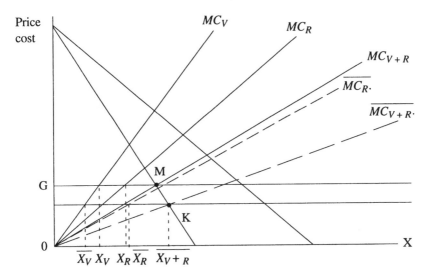

Figure 22.2   Effect of allowing for external benefits of recycling

the marginal external benefits at the optimal output level. The virgin material could be taxed by an amount equal to these marginal external benefits. Either policy will, other things being equal, secure the correct 'mix' of recycled and virgin material inputs. We investigate these policy instruments in section 6.

To sum up: the extent to which materials and energy recycling is practised (in-plant and/or via external recovery firms) will be a function of the cost of recovered residuals as a raw material input into production, relative to primary raw material inputs. But these relative costs will be determined by a complex flux of factors including:

- technological innovation in primary and secondary process industries;
- technical advances in primary material extraction;
- secondary and primary material market conditions and structure;
- end-product output specifications;
- government policy on environmental quality protection and, in particular, on final disposal of wastes.

5.3   Process Modifications, Product Redesign and Recycling

At some point in the waste reduction process, as environmental quality and waste disposal standards become increasingly stringent, firms may be faced with a basic trade-off between process and/or product redesign in order to reduce waste generation, and investments in materials energy recovery systems.

Industrial waste generators have been encouraged to reorient their residuals management policy away from end-of-pipe control towards the elimination or reduction of waste at source. One of the principal tenets of this 'cleaner technology' movement has been that environmental protection and profitability goals can be jointly pursued. While there are many opportunities for firms to meet such twin objectives, fundamental waste reduction measures will often prove to be financially unprofitable. It may, however, be the case that promoting a more 'environmentally friendly' image may still bring long-term increases in market share and profits for firms adopting 'cleaner technology'. Moreover, as waste disposal costs rise in the long run, some source reduction measures will prove more and more economically viable, others may even become financially profitable.

There are at least three overlapping phases in the development of waste reduction programmes (see Chapter 11; Loehr, 1985; Turner and Powell, 1993):

Initial waste reduction phase

In this situation waste generators have probably adopted a number of end-of-pipe abatement measures, sufficient to meet prevailing ambient quality regulations, but have not proposed more stringent ones. It is likely that a range of low-cost waste reduction opportunities remains unexploited, either by default or ignorance. Waste streams can be further reduced by the adoption of relatively cheap and simple means, for example, good housekeeping, separation of waste streams and so on. Policy instruments that can be deployed in order to provide incentives to facilitate and stimulate the take-up of such measures can be limited to, for example, better information dissemination, government-assisted waste exchanges, levies on disposal sufficient to cover the full (that is, financial plus external) costs of landfill or incineration, or the provision of recycling credits. No substantive change in established production processes will occur.

A recent waste minimization project in the UK, the Aire and Calder Project, has provided some good evidence of these Phase 1-type opportunities. Eleven plants in Yorkshire which discharge liquid effluent, directly or indirectly, into the Rivers Aire and Calder were studied. The identified waste reduction opportunities were composed of reductions in water usage (18.8 per cent), liquid effluent (32.3 per cent), raw materials (21 per cent), energy (12.5 per cent), and 'other' (14.5 per cent). Over 500 opportunities to improve environmental and/or cost performance were assessed, 41.5 per cent of which involved good housekeeping measures and 41 per cent technology modifications. On-site reuse provided a further 12.5 per cent of the opportunities, followed by input substitutions (4.5 per cent) and product modifications 0.5 per cent. Payback periods of less than one year were common (69 per cent) and the majority of opportunities (89 per cent) had payback periods of less than two years. If all the planned waste reduction measures were implemented, then the settleable solids loading on the rivers would be reduced by some 155 tonnes and the chemical oxygen demand would be reduced by 5090 tonnes.

Second phase: technological development phase

In this phase, the least financially costly waste reduction methods have been exploited and there is a need for waste generators to review and implement more comprehensive 'clean techniques', some of which may involve significant capital investment. The basic production processes, however, are retained, perhaps in a modified form. In this phase public policies can be oriented, for example, towards research and development support and incentive charges and marketable permits which provide a dynamic incentive mechanism.

Third phase: technological maturity phase

Waste generators in this situation begin to confront the political, economic and technical limits of waste reduction activities. Major changes in production processes, 'clean processes', leading to the establishment of integrated low-emission production technologies, or product redesign or substitutions, are required. Technological innovation is required, but also a more sophisticated environmental assessment procedure. Socially acceptable limits of waste reduction will have to be agreed, with the aid of risk assessment, life-cycle analysis and cost–benefit decision frameworks.

5.4 Eco-efficiency and the 'Porter Hypothesis' Debate

A key concept in any response to the waste reduction challenge is 'resource efficiency/productivity' or 'eco-efficiency' (Von Weizsaker et al., 1997). The idea is that resource efficiency can be increased by reducing materials and energy wastage at all stages in the production–consumption cycle. Existing and new technologies, if properly deployed and encouraged, can achieve such savings. So society gets more economic benefit (goods and services) while at the same time using up fewer resources, including waste assimilation and other services provided by the environment. Resource productivity gains by a factor of four and even ten may be achievable (Von Weizsäker et al., 1997). Thus capitalism and technological innovation can in the future be directed to produce significant resource productivity gains, just as in the past when economic growth was stimulated by labour productivity improvements (see Table 22.5).

Critics of the eco-efficiency strategy warn that it is not a panacea, even if it did prove feasible to get resource productivity gains of a factor of four or more. There may be 'rebound effects' such as reduced pressure on resources, price falls and increased overall consumption. A 10 per cent fuel efficiency increase

Table 22.5   Eco-efficiency: definition and measurement

Definition
  Eco-efficiency is achieved via the delivery by business of competitively
  priced goods and services that satisfy human needs and enhance the quality
  of life, while progressively reducing ecological impacts and resource intensity
  throughout a product's life cycle (production–consumption–recycle/disposal),
  to a level at least in line with the earth's estimated carrying capacity, including
  the ability to assimilate wastes.

'Factor four' thesis
  The argument is that, given suitable incentives in the form of environmental regulation reform, such as a phased shift of taxation from labour to natural
  resources, huge improvements in resource efficiency (air conditioning
  systems efficiency, vehicle engine fuel efficiency, materials inputs efficiency
  and so on) by a factor of four, and in some cases up to ten are achievable and
  may be necessary if sustainable development is to be realized.

'Ecological rucksacks'
  This is a measure of the total tonnage of materials represented by the use of
  one tonne of finished product; for example, one tonne of copper displaces 800
  tonnes of other materials; one newspaper carries a rucksack of 10 kilograms
  of other materials. At the national level it is possible to calculate an indicator
  called total material requirement (TMR). On this basis, per capita resource
  consumption in terms of TMR is levelling off at 75–85 tonnes per year in The
  Netherlands, Germany and USA, but it is only 45 tonnes in Japan.

Source: Von Weizsäker et al. (1997); World Resources Institute (1997).

in cars, for example, could stimulate a 1 per cent to 4 per cent increase in
driving and would not necessarily reduce the total number of cars on the roads.
Congestion costs and possible extra road-building costs would still be incurred.

   Other policies will also be required to complement eco-efficiency measures.
Reform of the subsidies that exist in all countries on, among others, energy,
electricity and transport activities would reduce consumption and related
pollution. A recent study in the UK has estimated that environmentally
damaging subsidies currently exceed £20 billion, with the largest single subsidy
going to users of transport infrastructure (Maddison et al., 1997).

   Eco-efficiency theory suggests that environmental policy should be reoriented
away from direct regulations and towards voluntary, market-based incentive
measures such as pollution taxes or product charges (Russell and Powell, 1996).
But the sheer scale of economic change implied by Factor Four, an eco-

efficiency revolution (Von Weizsäker et al., 1997), and the consequent social effects mean that the need for government intervention and indicative planning will not diminish if the goal of sustainability is to be achieved.

The role that technology and innovation might play in any future sustainable development strategy is clearly a big question. It underlies the eco-efficiency viewpoint which seeks to challenge the conventional wisdom that improved environmental quality comes at the expense of industrial competitiveness, as firms are forced to carry increasing pollution abatement and related costs. According to the 'Porter hypothesis', properly designed environmental regulations can trigger innovation that may partially or more than fully offset the costs of complying with them (Porter and van der Linde, 1995). This hypothesis has spawned a debate in the literature (Oates et al., 1994; Schmalensee, 1993; Jaffe et al., 1995).

It is possible to demonstrate that in the context of a static model of the theory of the firm, more stringent environmental regulations imposed on firms that have already made their cost-minimizing choices will lead to increased cost and reduced industrial competitiveness on world markets (see Figure 22.3).

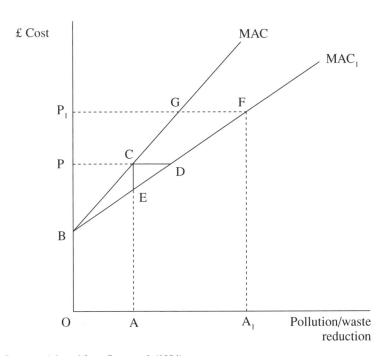

Source: Adapted from Oates et al. (1994).

Figure 22.3   Pollution control costs escalation

Assume that a polluting firm, with given technology and costs, can, if it chooses to, reduce its marginal pollution abatement costs (*MAC*) from *MAC* to MAC_1; this firm is currently faced with environmental regulation in the form of a pollution charge (*P*). The profit-maximizing level of pollution reduction for the firm is (*A*), corresponding to point (*C*), where *MAC* = the pollution charge (*P*). So the research and development costs incurred by the firm, if it did switch from *MAC* to MAC_1, must be greater than the gains to the firm from the switch. Profits (Π) at C must be greater than profits (Π) at D. Since the firm has chosen point C and not point D, the costs of switching must be greater than BEDC.

Now environmental regulations are tightened and the pollution charge is increased from *P* to P_1. Assume the firm does not respond by investing in new research and development. This implies that profits at F, Π, (F) are greater than profits at G, (G), or that *R* < BEDFGC; and the new level of pollution reduction is A_1.

But it is now possible to show that profits Π (C) (with the pollution change at *P* and no research and development innovation investment) are greater than profits (F) (with the increased large P_1 and innovation investment costs being incurred). Following the Porter hypothesis, assume $Π_1$ (F) > Π (C). But for a given technology, profit will be lower when the pollution charge is at P_1 than at *P*, so Π, (D) > Π, (F); and Π, (F) > Π, (C) implying that *R* > BECD. If it was the case that the firm earns a higher profit at F than at C, then it must also earn a higher profit at D than at C. However, if this were true, the firm would have adopted the new technology (*I*) at the old pollution charge level of *P*, and moved from C to D. But the firm did not originally make this switch; therefore it must be the case that profits at F, Π, (F) must be less than profits at C, Π (C). So the firm is worse off under more stringent environmental regulation and, if it has to compete with foreign firms not constrained by such regulation, it will lose competitive advantage.

The simple analysis detailed in the figure can, however, be made more complex and realistic by assuming strategic behaviour among polluting firms and the regulatory agency. Such behavioural assumptions, however, need not always lead to results which support the Porter hypothesis. For example, a polluting firm might suspect that the regulator has a long-run strategy to ratchet up environmental standards. The firm might then respond by delaying its investment in innovation technology, or it may engage in the development of new techniques which permit existing environmental requirements to be achieved at lower and lower cost, without providing much scope for significant improvements in environmental standards (Heyes and Liston-Heyes, 1997).

Firms might also threaten to relocate abroad if domestic environmental standards are made too stringent. But one recent study has not found any empirical evidence that such movements have occurred since 1970 (Janicke et al., 1997). The data that exist suggest that there has not been a significant relocation of 'dirty' basic industries (paper and paperboard, petroleum products, primary metals, glass and chemicals and so on) to developing countries. Further, the high-income market economies have remained net exporters of fertilizers, paper and pulp, crude steel and lead and zinc.

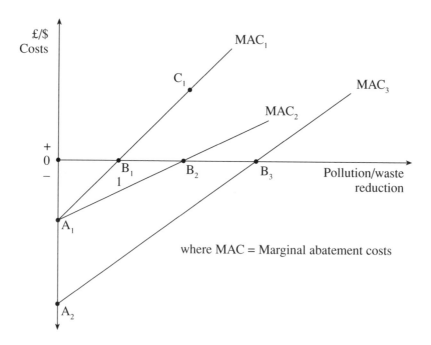

Notes:
The figure illustrates a situation facing the polluting firm in which unexploited cost-saving opportunities are present, section A, to B, on the marginal pollution abatement cost curve MAC_1. More investment in innovation technologies might result in abatement cost curve MAC_2 or even a shift in the curve to MAC_3 and a range of innovation offset opportunities.
Two basic categories of offsets, product and process have been defined:

- Product offsets occur when environmental regulations produce not just less pollution but also create better-performing, or higher-quality products, safer products, reduced product costs (because of less or substitute materials or packaging), products with higher resale or scrap value.
- Process offsets result in higher resource productivity such as higher process yields, less shutdown time, material savings on production inputs, better utilization of by-products etc.

Table 22.6 gives some examples of such innovation offsets.

Figure 22.4   Product and process offsets

Supporters of the Porter hypothesis have deployed two further arguments in support of their case. They argue that tougher environmental regulation is likely to promote an expansion of the pollution control technology industry (external to, but seeking to service the needs of polluting firms). The export potential of this industry is also highlighted, given 'early-mover' advantages in international markets; that is, countries that adopt stricter environmental standards, it is argued, will stimulate firms to provide the necessary technology to reduce pollution; when other countries catch up and want to improve their environmental standards, they provide an export market for firms from the country that first improved its ambient environment.

Second, in the real world firms are not always able or willing to function as the textbooks assume and as a result unexploited opportunities for cost savings and improvements in product quality are often present (known as the existence of 'slack' or 'x-inefficiency' in the economy, Leibenstein, 1966). The Aire and Calder Project mentioned in section 5.3 provides good evidence that such 'slack' is present in real-world operational conditions. The firms surveyed in the project included companies of international repute. If 'slack' is present and properly designed environmental regulations are introduced, then the firms' capacity for innovation and improvement in productivity terms can be harnessed. Many innovations can partially or more than fully offset the costs incurred. According to Porter and van der Linde (1995) such 'innovation offsets' will be common because reducing pollution is often coincident with improving the productivity with which resources are used (see Figure 22.4 and Table 22.6). Relatively lax environmental regulations have stimulated 'end-of-pipe' or secondary waste treatment investment responses. More stringent regulations could force firms to take a fresh look at their processes and products and adapt accordingly.

6. WASTE MANAGEMENT AND POLITICAL ECONOMY[1]

6.1 Regulatory Approach

Waste management policy has traditionally been secured through the use of a regulatory standards approach. Under this approach the regulatory authority sets an environmental standard (target) and the polluter is required to honour this standard, under the threat of some penalty system.

Menell (1990) has concluded that although policies such as mandatory separation of household waste and product bans respond to some of the symptoms of the MSW problem, they fail systematically to address the causes

Table 22.6 Examples of innovation offsets

Pollutant	Input/source	Industry	Source of heterogeneity	Improved technology
Salts/minerals	Residue of irrigation	Agriculture	Water-holding capacity of soil	Drip or sprinkler irrigation instead of furrow irrigation
Nitrates	Residue of chemical fertilizers	Agriculture	Plant health, soil quality	More accurate timing and application; pre-plant and spring nitrate tests
Chemicals or pesticides	Residue of pesticide	Agriculture	Weather, wind and land quality	IPM; ground application instead of aerial spray
Carbon dioxide	Coal combustion	Electricity generation; cement; steel	Vintage and age of capital; quality of management	Washed coal; natural gas or coal gas. Dry process and high-efficiency air classifiers for cement; high-quality coal or electric furnaces for steel
Carbon dioxide	Electricity/heat from fossil fuel combustion	Households	Education, income, age of buildings	Energy-efficient appliances, improved ceiling and wall insulation
Sulphur dioxide	Coal combustion	Electricity	Vintage of capital; quality of management	Washed coal; low-sulphur coal; natural gas
Acetylene	Calcium carbide	Ductile iron	Design of equipment and operating practices	Calcium carbide with finer particles
Volatile organic compounds	Solvent-based paints	Wood furniture; fabricated metal products	Operating and maintenance practices	Use of high-volume low-pressure spraying of paint; powder-coating and electrodeposition, water-based solvent
Hydrocarbon halogens, acetic acid, phosphates	Dyes	Textiles	Operating and maintenance practices	Alternative chemicals (Remazol or Procion); alternative dyeing processes (spraying, pad–batch dyeing, application through foam media)
Chromium III	Chromium sulphate	Leather tanning	Operating and maintenance practices	Synektan Tal, a non–chrome tanning agent; Baychrome high-exhaust/intake process
Carbon monoxide, VOC	Gasoline	Automobiles	Age, maintenance practices	Ultra-light fuel-efficient vehicles

Source: Adapted from Porter and van der Linde (1995); and Khanna and Zilberman (1997)

of the problem. They do not remedy the distorted incentives that underlie consumer and producer behaviour. Product choice, as well as the disposal decision, determine the social costs of MSW. Focusing solely on the separation decision (for example, via mandatory separation) can lead to perverse results.

Households pay for waste collection and disposal through a local property-based tax system that is unrelated to the quantity of refuse discarded or to the full costs actually imposed on society. The result is that households face a marginal cost of refuse disposal equal to zero. As a consequence the likelihood is that the demand for the solid waste service will be too high (there is an under-valuation of the waste disposal service of the environment); see Figure 22.5 for a landfill disposal situation.

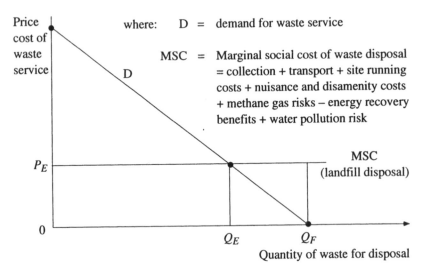

Figure 22.5   Household demand for waste disposal service

For the quantity of waste not only to decline but also to be at an economically efficient level, the price charged for waste collection/disposal should reflect the full social cost of such services. In Figure 22.5 this price is equivalent to P_E, which has the effect of reducing the amount of waste requiring disposal from Q_F to Q_E.

Industrial waste generators are controlled in terms of technology-based standards (best available control technology) which lay down often quite rigid process/technique requirements and emission/discharge limits. In the EU certain waste generators have to adopt a BATNEEC approach (best available technology not entailing excessive cost) (see Chapter 5). The NEEC portion of BATNEEC means that the presumption in favour of BAT can be modified by two sorts of consideration, that is, whether the costs of applying BAT would be excessive in relation to the environmental protection achieved, and whether they would be excessive in relation to the nature of the industry (for example, its age and competitive position). The cost implications are usually interpreted (with no great consistency) as financial concepts, rather than as economic ones, in which the wider social costs of pollution and waste disposal are included.

The inefficient nature of such regulatory control is compounded by the information requirements (that is, types of process in use, likely future state-of-the-art processes about to come on-stream, types of effluent discharged and treatments available and so on) that such a system imposes on the regulatory agency (paid for by taxpayers); and by the fact that often the standards are imposed on a uniform basis, regardless of the actual pollution control cost situation that individual plants face. A good example of the uniform regulatory target-based approach to waste and pollution control is provided by the policies on packaging waste that are facilitated by the 1994 EC Packaging and Packaging Waste Directive, and have been adopted by a number of countries. It has rapidly become clear that the cost implications of these measures are very significant.

Two further target-based EC directives are under consideration: The Directive on End of Life Vehicles and the Directive on the Landfilling of Waste. The former draft regulation contains a target 85 per cent recycling rate for ELVs and a minimum recycling rate of 80 per cent by 2005, rising to 95 per cent and 85 per cent respectively by 2015. The latter draft directive contains an allowable disposal target of 75 per cent of total biodegradable waste produced in 1995, to be achieved by 2006 (or 2010 for countries with more than 85 per cent of municipal waste flowing to landfill). The disposal component is then set to fall to 50 per cent by 2009 (or 2017) and down to 35 per cent by 2016 (or 2020).

6.2 Economic Instruments Approach

Economic instruments have special attractions in the field of solid waste management. Since there are various options for waste disposal (landfill, incineration and recycling being the main ones) and for the reduction of waste at source, changes in the cost of one disposal route should encourage the diversion of waste to other routes. There is also the possibility that illegal disposal methods such as 'fly tipping' (dumping) will be stimulated.

In principle, the full range of instruments – unit pricing, deposit–refunds, product charges, recycling subsidies, and taxes on primary product inputs – have possible applications (see Table 22.7). Getting the appropriate mix of instruments which foster cost-effectiveness in environmental regulation is, however, not a straightforward matter. In the USA, for example, the authorities have been considering both regulatory and economic instruments approaches in order to reduce solid waste disposal and increase recycling/reuse. The policies reviewed include subsidies for recycling, taxes on primary inputs to production, deposit–refunds for beverage containers, lead-acid batteries and other products, minimum recycled content standards for newsprint and other products, investment tax credits for the purchase of recycled equipment, bans on certain packaging containers and mandatory kerbside waste, collection systems (Pearce and Turner, 1993; Palmer and Wallis, 1996).

Table 22.7   Examples of economic instruments

Country	Type of instrument	Charge/rate: ECU unit
	Taxes on non–recovered products:	
Belgium	Disposable razors	0.25/unit
	Disposable cameras	7.5/unit
	Batteries	0.5/unit
	Beverage packaging	0.4/unit
Denmark	Papers and plastic bags	0.05/bag
	Beverage packaging	0.01–0.08/unit
	Virgin construction material	varies across material
Germany	Disposable plates and cutlery	variable
Finland	Beverage packaging	0.68 (0.17 if recycled)
Netherlands	Scrap vehicles	65/vehicle
	Batteries	0.01–1.30/unit
	Plastic window and door frames	2.1/window or 0.01/dg plastic
Sweden	Batteries	5.3/t– 7.5/kg
	Cars	tax/return 100
	Disposal charges	ECU/tonne
Belgium	Incineration	–20
	Landfilling	3–100
Denmark	Incineration	28–35
	Landfilling	45
France	Landfilling	MSW 6 hazardous 12
Italy	Landfilling	MSW 10 commercial 5
Netherlands	Landfilling	28
Sweden	Landfilling	30
UK	Landfilling	active waste 10 inert 4

Source: *Warmer Bulletin*, **61** (1998).

The comparative economic case for market instruments is one of achieving some predetermined standard/target at least social cost, that is, cost-effectively. Market instruments, it is argued, will achieve a more efficient allocation of pollution reduction across polluters with varying clean-up costs than will a policy based solely on regulations ('static cost minimization' benefit). In addition, market instruments may also provide a 'dynamic incentive' benefit by encouraging further cost-effective pollution reductions beyond the minimum necessary regulatory compliance level.

Russell and Powell (1996) argue, however, that the efficiency (static and dynamic) case for an across-the-board application of market incentive instruments is not as robust in practice as it might seem. They point out that achieving static efficiency under ambient environment conditions which vary from location to location will impose impracticable information and computing burdens on control agencies (under charges) or polluters (under marketable permits). The case for a blanket introduction of market instruments if further weakened by the lack of a general rule that charges linked to uniform marginal costs across polluters beat an arbitrary assignment of discharge reduction responsibilities. Incentive instruments are not necessarily second-best options. Once the setting is made, dynamic matters become even more complicated. A growing body of analysis adopts the evolutionary perspective in which the direction of technical change and economic activity is not seen as an autonomous phenomenon, but as an endogenous process conditioned by the structure of economic incentives, technological opportunities and prevailing institutions (Dosi, 1988). Future outcomes are relatively unpredictable because of the complex interaction taking place between different actors who are endogenous to the process of change. Technical innovations are the outcome of learning processes inside firms but progress is hindered by inertia in the firms' organizational routines and by path dependency, with the attendant risk of technological 'lock-in' effects. Public investment or grants/credits may have a role to play in overcoming such impediments (Lockhart, 1998). Mendelsohn (1984), for example, found that under endogenous technical change regulatory standards were relatively more desirable than they were in its absence.

The deployment and evaluation of the chosen economic instrument in society are conditioned by various cross-currents reflecting different political and social pressures (Goulder, 1995; Turner et al., 1998). At least six 'principles' can be identified and all of them form the political-economy context into which green taxes have to fit (see Table 22.8). Clearly, compliance with all six principles simultaneously (and therefore getting the appropriate mix of policies, both regulatory and economic instruments) is a formidable requirement, especially since in some circumstances the principles are conflicting and trade-offs will be necessary. The politics of taxation and public spending will reflect a wide range of pressures exerted by different stakeholders and this will undoubtedly

Table 22.8   Political economy and green taxes

Economic efficiency principle
    The instrument should interfere as little as possible with well-informed private
    resource allocation decisions in competitive markets, and should provide a
    continuous incentive for seeking least-cost solutions.
Environmental effectiveness principle
    The instrument should be appropriately linked to the pollution and resource
    usage impacts problem so that effective mitigation results (in particular the
    minimization of health impacts and risks).
Fairness principle
    The instrument should not be significantly regressive, that is, should not
    impose a disproportionate cost burden on the least well-off in society.
Administration cost-effectiveness principle
    The instrument should involve low administrative and compliance costs.
Institutional concordance principle
    The   instrument   should   be   compatible   with   existing   national
    regulations/legislation, and with European Union Directives; the industries
    affected should also be present in a majority of member countries so that the
    rules of the single market are not seriously compromised.
Revenue-raising principle
    The instrument should be able to raise appropriate amounts of finance for
    given expenditures.

Source: See Russell and Powell (1996) for a more detailed and comprehensive taxonomy.

exert a considerable influence over the choice, combination, specification and
overall evaluation of economic and regulatory instruments.

The environmental economics literature has analysed the relative merits, in
economic efficiency terms, of a number of economic instruments and regulatory
approaches to the solid waste disposal and recycling balance issue (Dinan,
1993; Fullerton and Kinnaman, 1995). The general finding was that policies
focusing only on input use or on waste outputs cannot generate the optimal
(economically efficient) balance between recycling, disposal and production
output. Thus recycling subsidies directed at input use cannot generate the
efficient amount of waste disposal unless coupled with a tax or subsidy on
consumption. Primary product taxes need to be coupled with both an output tax
and a tax on other production inputs to be economically efficient. A regulatory
measure such as a recycling content standard also cannot generate the efficient
level of output and waste disposal unless it is augmented by taxes on other
inputs to production, together with either a tax or a subsidy on the final product.

Acquiring the detailed firm-specific information necessary in order to set the efficient levels of taxes and standards is clearly not a practicable proposition for public-policy-makers.

This same body of analysis finds that the deposit–refund instrument (in which the product tax and the refund are equal to the marginal social cost of waste disposal) is an efficient mechanism and is equivalent to taxing disposal (for non-returners) but without the attendant illegal disposal problems. The efficiency advantage of the deposit–refund instrument will in practice be reduced the higher the administration and consumer inconvenience costs involved (Porter, 1978; Pearce and Turner, 1992). The deposit–refund instrument has a range of possible applications, including hazardous wastes.

The pollution problems themselves also vary considerably in their complexity, and this will affect the type and design of the economic instrument chosen. If the concentration of pollution, either in particular localities or over certain time periods, is important, more complex forms of tax instrument will be needed, for example zoned taxes to account for spatial variations. A particularly difficult problem is posed by hazardous waste which has accumulated over time from past disposal practices, and which is causing damage to humans and the environment (or is considered a potential damage risk) in the current time period. The retrospective tracking of polluters and/or beneficiaries of past disposal practices in order to assign liability and target new taxes has proved to be a formidably difficult task with some unfortunate consequences. The message in this context is that the 'right' package of mitigation measures will not be easy to determine.

In the USA a hybrid approach, based on legal liability and environmental taxes, called 'Superfund', has been used as the cornerstone of hazardous waste policy. The Superfund programme imposes retroactive, strict and often joint and several liability standards on disposers of hazardous waste. Disposers would be liable for both the clean-up costs at a hazardous waste disposal site thought to pose an actual or potential risk, and the transaction costs involved, that is, the legal, consulting and other expenses that are incurred as a result of litigation under Superfund.

The concept of joint and several liability has proven to be problematic. It lays down that any one individual or agent who can be identified as having contributory responsibility is then held responsible for all the costs of cleaning up the site or the pollution. That 'responsible' party must then go to court to seek compensation from other contributors. The enforcement of this principle has led to conflicting criticisms of unfairness (especially for small polluters lacking funds to pay the clean-up costs, or to go to court to contest the ruling or sue other parties) and also inefficiencies: given that any one polluter may face the prospect of paying for the whole site clean-up or avoiding all the costs. Large polluting firms (with deep corporate financial pockets) are obvious targets for the enforcement agency and may therefore take more than the efficient level of precautionary action, including going to litigation. Small polluting firms, on the other hand, may reason that they will be ignored by the enforcement agency and have no incentive to take action at all.

Three Superfund taxes have also been created to help provide revenue for the Superfund trust fund. They were not market-based incentive instruments since they are not related to environmental damage costs caused by waste disposal. The taxes were excise taxes on chemicals and petroleum, and a corporate environmental income tax. The first two taxes are levied on intermediate goods (thought to contain hazardous substances) for use in producing final chemical and petroleum products. The environmental income tax was levied on industry in general on the assumption that hazardous substances are present in a broad range of goods used by industry.

A recent review of Superfund concluded that the clean-up of the 1134 non-federal sites in EPA's National Priorities List in 1994 would not, with the exception of the mining industry and parts of the insurance industry, impose an overwhelmingly large financial burden on many industries (Probst et al., 1995). The three Superfund taxes have a very small effect on the overall US economy and on product prices. Nevertheless, the administration and compliance costs involved with these special taxes have been unnecessarily high and the revenues collected relatively small. Probst et al. (1995) remark that large cost savings would have been enjoyed if one simple tax (especially a pre-existing tax) had been used, instead of the three new taxes. The taxes' final incidence has been on consumers (via higher prices) rather than on the firm managers or share-holders who were responsible for past pollution. Many of these consumers would also not have benefited from the past low product prices that did not cover the full social cost of previous waste disposal practices. Thus these taxes do not conform with either the polluter pays principle or the beneficiary pays principle.

In 1996, the EPA announced four new policy measures. The aim is to accelerate the clean-up of Superfund sites and protect small waste contributions from costly litigation. The four actions announced were:

- appointment of an ombudsman in all ten EPA regions to make sure the programme is significantly more responsive to the needs of local communities;
- creation of a $50 million fund ('orphans' share compensation' fund) to be spent in 1996 to speed up site clean-ups by targeting financially insolvent polluters who pose obstacles to settlement agreements;
- establishment of interest-bearing accounts to facilitate faster clean-up cost settlement agreements;

- widening the scope of clean-up cost exemptions for small firms and municipalities.

All of this confirms that this regulatory and liability-based scheme continues to become more complex, cumbersome and administratively costly.

6.3 Landfill Disposal Levies

In principle, a levy on landfill sites should reflect the *external costs* associated with landfill. An external cost is any loss of human well-being associated with the process of landfilling waste which is not already allowed for in the price charged to those who dispose of waste on landfill sites. Strictly speaking, and to use economists' language, the levy should be equal to the *marginal external* cost of landfill net of any marginal external benefit. 'Marginal' here simply means 'extra', so the levy should be equal to the loss of well-being associated with disposing of an extra tonne or extra cubic metre of waste.

Figure 22.6 shows the relationship between the market for recycled products, the recycling credit and the externalities from landfill/incineration (Brisson, 1993). The downward-sloping line is the marginal profit from recycling, that is, the extra profit secured by recycling an extra tonne of waste. If recycling were left entirely to market forces, then the amount of waste that would be recycled is W_{II}, that is, the amount corresponding to the point where marginal profits are

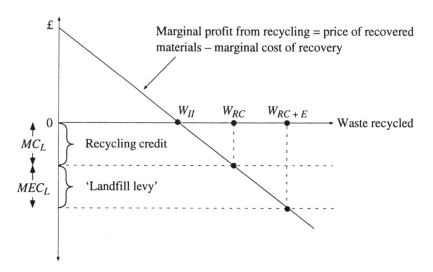

Figure 22.6   Recycling credit and landfill levy

zero and hence total profits are maximized. This amount is not optimal because the structure of the waste disposal industry is such that waste disposers do not bargain with recyclers to avoid the cost of disposal. Hence government intervenes through the medium of recycling credits which equal the marginal *private* cost of disposing of waste (MC_L). The effect of the credits is then to expand recycling beyond its privately profitable level to W_{RC}. But even this level of recycling is still not socially optimal because recycling credits do not account for the environmental costs of landfill (and incineration). The effect of placing a levy equal to MEC_L on landfill/incineration (or of making payments to the recycling industry equal to this amount) is shown in Figure 22.6 as the shift from W_{RC} to W_{RC+E}. This is then the socially optimal level of recycling.

If there are external costs associated with recycling, then W_{RC+E} will be too high and MEC_L should be reduced.

Strictly speaking, however, each waste disposal route should attract a levy or charge equal to the net marginal external costs of the specific disposal route. There would then be a landfill levy and an incineration levy. Since recycling tends to generate external benefits, it should attract a negative levy or subsidy. However, great care has to be taken in formulating a complete set of such levies and subsidies. It would not be correct, for example, to put a levy on landfill and incineration and a subsidy on recycling if the recycling subsidy already reflected the externalities from landfill and incineration. This would amount to correcting for the same externality twice, and that would be inefficient. Additionally, the external benefits from waste disposal through incineration are quite significant.

In the UK a decision to introduce a weight-based tax commencing in October 1996 was announced in the November 1995 Budget. The *ad valorem* tax was dropped in favour of a weight-based tax because the latter was deemed to be preferable in both economic and environmental terms. The tax was set at a standard rate of £7 per tonne, and a lower rate for 'inactive' waste (that which does not biodegrade) of £2 per tonne. The objectives of the tax were to ensure proper pricing of landfill disposal, to apply the polluter pays principle and to promote a more sustainable approach to waste management. As the tax was not intended to increase overall business costs, it was partially offset by a reduction of 0.2 per cent in employers' National Insurance contributions (to be applied to all businesses). Therefore the landfill tax represents one of the first moves by the UK government to transfer taxation away from labour towards pollution and resource use, thus exemplifying the double dividend effect. A second consultation phase in 1996 resulted in the exemption of contaminated soil from the tax, expansion of the lower rate category and tax credits for waste removed from landfills for incineration or recycling.

In designating the levy on landfill disposal a 'tax', the government ensured that it could not be earmarked or 'hypothecated' for a purpose directly associated with landfill. However, there was pressure to use the revenue to finance environmental protection, and in the event it was decided to use the revenue to finance environmental protection through the Environmental Body Tax Credit Scheme. Landfill operators can make a donation to an environmental body, for which they can receive a rebate from Customs and Excise of 90 per cent of their contribution, up to a maximum of 20 per cent of their total landfill tax payments. The environmental bodies are non-profit-making organizations either already in existence or established specifically for this purpose, and are supervised by ENTRUST, an independent private sector body. The donations must be used for various 'approved purposes' (see Table 22.9).

Table 22.9 Environmental-body-approved objectives

1. Reclamation, remediation or restoration, or any other operation intended to facilitate the use of land whose use has been prevented or restricted by an activity which has now ceased;
2. Operations to prevent or reduce actual or potential pollution, or to remedy the effects of any actual pollution, from land, which has been caused by an activity which has now ceased;
3. R&D, education or the collection and dissemination of information for the purpose of encouraging the use of more sustainable waste management practices;
4. Provision, maintenance or improvement of a public park or other public amenity in the vicinity of a landfill;
5. Maintenance, repair or restoration of a building or other structure which is a place of religious worship or of historic or architectural interest which is open to the public and in the vicinity of a landfill site.

Source: HM Customs and Excise (1996).

Many companies began or stepped up waste minimization activities as a result of the tax, or have been encouraged to consider alternative waste disposal methods (Coopers and Lybrand, 1997). Nevertheless, research also indicates that some businesses are failing to reduce their waste (Hogg, 1997). There is an emerging sense of partnership between some waste disposal companies and their customers, with the larger operators acquiring materials recycling facilities or installing them at their landfill sites.

On the negative side, some evidence is emerging in the UK which points to the link between increasing costs of waste disposal and the incidence of illegal disposal or fly-tipping. A survey has uncovered some data from which a trend might be emerging. Before the introduction of the UK's landfill tax in 1996, some 48 per cent of local authorities deemed fly-tipping to be a 'significant' or 'major' problem. This percentage had risen to 54 per cent in 1996/97. The number of local authorities dealing with fewer than 40 cases of fly-tipping a year fell from around 22 per cent in 1994/95 to only 8 per cent in 1998. Local authorities and landowners were also asked to rank the various types of waste contributing to the illegal disposal problem. Household waste followed by building and garden waste was the most common type of illegally dumped waste, but there were less frequent, although more dangerous, examples of clinical and hazardous waste dumping (Tidy Britain Group, 1997). Firm figures are difficult to come by, but anecdotal evidence (Bliss, 1998) suggests that at least 60 000 tonnes of waste is dumped illegally in England and Wales. This is undoubtedly an underestimate and the relevant bodies have come together to form a monitoring forum to better assess the scale and severity of the problem.

One of the tax's most significant effects has been to divert large quantities of inert waste away from landfill to tax-exempt uses such as landscaping, golf courses and foundations of buildings. An estimated 18–21 million tonnes of inert waste (almost 50 per cent) was diverted from landfill sites within the first year (Hogg, 1997). As a result, landfill operators who previously used inert material for site engineering or ran inert landfill sites have had difficulty obtaining the materials, and in some cases operators have had to purchase virgin aggregates instead. This has led to calls for removing the tax from inert waste. The tax has been successful in generating much needed data on waste generation in the UK although the focus has been more on costs within individual companies than on detailed amounts of waste generated.

The tax does not directly reward those who are in a position to lessen the environmental impact because the costs are borne by waste producers, but the benefits are more dispersed via the reduced National Insurance contributions. Financially, the impact of the tax on individual firms will vary with the number of employees and the level of waste production. Research has found that although the landfill tax typically comprises just 0.01–0.08 per cent of most businesses' turnover (Hogg, 1997), many companies have seen their waste disposal costs rise by over 10 per cent (Coopers and Lybrand, 1997). Companies have been better able to absorb additional costs than local authorities, which in some cases have been forced to reduce other council services. There is also some indication that the tax has caused a greater reaction in regions with a previously low landfill charge, suggesting that it has been the relative rather than the absolute increase that has made the most impact.

Despite an initial slow start, about 600 environmental bodies had enrolled by the end of January 1998, undertaking over 2000 projects with a cumulative value of £200 million (Sills, 1997). The government initially estimated that £20 million would be donated within the first year, but with a last-minute flurry of donations, £26 million had been invested by 30 September 1997 and £49 million by the beginning of December, exceeding all expectations (Sills, 1997). Nevertheless, it appears to be the larger landfill companies that are taking part in the scheme. Whilst those bodies that have been established are operating successfully, a feeling of reticence and confusion remains, with many companies, particularly the smaller ones, calling for more advice (Read et al., 1997). Overall, the environmental body scheme has taken off successfully and represents a very useful source of environmental funding for the future.

In the summer of 1997 a review of the landfill tax was launched, with announcements to follow in the spring Budget of 1998. The 450 or so respondents to the review commented on a range of issues including the tax rates, the tax bands, the provision of lead-in times, the issues of engineering waste, exemptions and the operation of ENTRUST. There were also calls for a stricter definition of inert waste and possibly the exemption of inert waste used for site engineering. In March 1998, the Chancellor announced that the standard tax rate would be increased from £7 to £10 per tonne from 1 April 1999. The tax rate for inert waste was to remain at £2 per tonne but from October 1999, inert waste used in the 'restoration of sites' should be exempt from the tax.

There remains scope for increasing the rate of the tax, as the rate reflects some of the external costs of landfill disposal but excludes disamenity values. The UK still has one of the lowest landfill costs in Europe, and elsewhere there have been much more dramatic increases in landfill taxes. For example, Denmark and Belgium have each experienced a 600–700 per cent increase within less than a decade, which would suggest that the UK landfill tax might become £25–30 by the year 2000 and £50–60 by the year 2002 (Read et al., 1997).

7. PACKAGING WASTE

Packaging waste, one component of the solid waste stream, has become a focus of attention for policy-makers in a number of countries. This concern is revealed in measures implemented or being considered by Germany and the European Commission to secure: (1) source reduction of packaging; and (2) increased recycling of packaging waste. Table 22.10 shows broad estimates of packaging waste arising in the EU. There is, however, uncertainty about the true magnitudes.

Brisson (1993) has concluded that command and control approaches, such as recycling and source reduction targets, are most likely to be cost-ineffective and dynamically inefficient, as firms will have little or no incentive to develop new technologies which facilitate high recycling rates or light-weighting. As opposed to this, market-based instruments are found to be both cost-effective and dynamically efficient. By internalizing the external effects associated with the disposal of packaging, firms will include them in their decision-making and thus are provided with an economic incentive to develop technologies which to a greater extent facilitate recycling and light-weighting. However,

Selected topics

Tables 22.10   Existing recycling rates for selected packaging

Material	Country	%	Year
Aluminium	Sweden	83	1990
Aluminium	Norway	80	1990
Glass	Switzeeland	61	1990
Glass	Netherlands	66	1990
Glass	Austria	60	1990
Beverage cartons	Germany	6	1996
	Germany	69	1997
	Norway	25	1996
	Norway	35	1997
	Sweden	30	1996
	Sweden	30	1997
	Austria	27	1996
	Austria	29	1997
	Belgium	19.5	1996
	Belgium	29	1997
	Finland	8	1996
	Finland	11	1997
	UK	0.2	1996
	UK	0	1997
All plastics waste	W. Europe	1.11	1994
(excluding exports	W. Europe	1.32	1995
for recycling)	W. Europe	1.57	1996
	W. Europe	1.81	1997
PET bottles	W. Europe	7.3	1997
	W. Europe	18.7	1998
	UK	1.7	1997
	UK	2.25	1998

Sources: House of Lords, Select Committee on the European Communities (1993); ENDS report, 1999.

with respect to social incidence, the effects of market-based instruments will typically be regressive, with the possible exception of kerbside waste collection charges, which have been found to be less regressive than traditional flat-rate charges.

Three command and control approaches aimed at packaging waste have been taken by Germany, the EU and The Netherlands. They all carry with them significant cost implications for producers and consumers, as exemplified by recent experiences in Germany with the so-called 'green dot' or Duales scheme.

The EU Commission's proposal for a directive on packaging and packaging waste was passed to the Council in September 1992, and after a consultation process an amended proposal was submitted in September 1993 and passed into law in 1994.

It contains the following targets:

1. Recover 50 per cent and recycle 25 per cent of packaging by 2001.
2. A minimum recycling rate of 15 per cent for glass paper/board, plastics, aluminium and steel.

The lack of reprocessing capacity and markets for reprocessed materials continues to inhibit attempts to reach these targets.

Various member states have adopted their own national schemes designed to mitigate the packaging waste problem (for example, the German packaging law and collection systems; the French law and collection system (eco-emballages); and Dutch non-statutory 'packaging covenant'). What is of concern in this context is not so much the market interventionist nature of these policies, but the apparent lack of any financial/economic cost–benefit analysis which would have shed some light on the true impacts, costs and benefits to society of such interventionism.

An example of the regulatory method of waste control is the German 'green dot' system which was developed in an attempt to make the 'polluter pay'. The Duales System Deutschland (DSD) was developed by manufacturers and distributors to meet the requirements of the Ordinance on Avoidance of Packaging Waste passed in 1993, which requires minimum levels of collection and recycling of packaging waste. The members pay for a licence to mark their packaging with a green dot. In return DSD guarantees recovery of sales packaging from the consumer for recycling or reuse.

The system has been heavily criticized within both Germany and the EU. It has proved to be extremely expensive to operate, with the result that the DSD had to be rescued with a large cash injection from the state and industry. This has occurred for various reasons: (1) the lack of a mandatory government-imposed charge on packaging producers; (2) the unexpectedly high levels of waste recovered (an anticipated 450 000 tonnes of plastics in 1993); (3) the high price for collection and sorting demanded by the waste contractors; and (4) the shortage of facilities to process the recovered materials (276 000 tonnes per year). The high cost of storage facilities and the lack of markets for the recycled products have also resulted in an oversupply and consequential drop in value of the materials. Recovered paper and plastics have been exported at highly subsidized prices, which has affected the secondary materials markets in many countries, particularly the UK and France. It has been suggested that in some cases the recovered materials are not always recycled but incinerated or landfilled.

The DSD has also proved to be difficult to control: consumers often place non-recyclables in the container for 'green dot' packaging; waste contractors are thought to claim for greater quantities of recyclables than they actually collect; and some companies are openly not paying the DSD for a licence although the 'green dot' is still used on their packaging.

There has been a call in Germany either to end the DSD system or to change it radically. One option would be to impose mandatory deposits on sales packaging materials. Another option would be to ban plastic packaging, which is seen as the main problem, or to allow it to be incinerated for energy recovery. The German plastics industry has been criticized for its lack of progress in expanding its processing capacity.

The DSD and the German aversion to landfill and incineration as disposal options have resulted in significant market distortions. The virtual dumping of surplus German-recovered paper and plastics onto the international market is putting at risk the viability (that is, downward pressure on secondary material prices) of existing recycling efforts and activities. There is a need for a more sophisticated interpretation of the so-called 'proximity principle', under which member states are encouraged to aim at self-sufficiency in waste disposal. Given that an extensive international market in selected recycled materials has existed for many decades, the proximity principle should apply to those materials for which there is no, or only a very limited, secondary market and therefore those which have no, or a very low, positive market price. A related canon of EU waste policy, 'the waste management hierarchy', also needs to be interpreted with some caution. Interpreted as a rigid rule, it is both inefficient and environmentally unsound. It must be subject to a cost–benefit analysis for all possible options and should not, *a priori*, discriminate against any course of action, including incineration with energy recovery.

The EU has signalled that too much packaging and packaging waste is being produced, but the best way to protect the environment in this context is to encourage the minimization of waste in the first place. Economic instruments offer an efficient mechanism for sending direct signals to producers to produce less packaging. The policy package includes the following instruments: packaging waste tax, landfill disposal levy/tax, tax concessions for increased use of recycled materials in the product, deposit–refunds, tax on virgin raw materials, household waste charges, recycling credits and the 'non-fossil-fuel obligation', which can be used to encourage energy recovery from waste schemes. Some combination of economic incentives operating within regulatory guidelines is likely to provide both a more economic and environmentally sound waste management policy.

Under the economic instruments approach, a packaging charge reflecting disposal costs associated with packaging waste could be introduced. On the basis of a life-cycle analysis, it can be argued that external effects occurring earlier in the life cycle of packaging (such as external costs associated with energy use in the production of packaging) are more efficiently dealt with at the point of generation, rather than by attempting to bundle all such external costs together in one all-encompassing packaging charge. In fact, since some externalities are already dealt with through regulatory policies, including them in a packaging charge would merely result in double taxation, which would be economically inefficient. It can be argued, then, that a packaging charge should only include marginal collection costs (*MCC*), marginal external waste costs (waste disposal (*MDC*) and litter costs (*MLC*)) and marginal landfill user costs (*MLUC*). Consideration should be given to the amount of recycling taking place and source reduction, as both result in less waste being landfilled.

Taking the example of beverage containers, a formula for a packaging charge measured in currency per 100 litres of beverage is (Pearce and Turner, 1992; Brisson, 1993):

$$t_i = (1000W_i/L_i) \times (1 - r_i) \times (MCC + MDC + MLUC)$$

where:

t_i = the charge on the container of type i in currency per 100 litres;
W_i = the weight of container of type i;
L_i = litres per container of type i, so W/L is weight per litre of beverage;
r_i = the recycling rate for containers of type i.

This formula assumes that external costs are related to the weight of the waste, but it may be that the volume of waste is a better indication of some external cost effects. If this is the case the formula can be converted into a volume-based calculation (Brisson, 1993). On the basis of a simplified weight-related formula (ignoring *MCC* and *MLUC*), the charge on a PET plastic bottle in the UK can be calculated as:

$$t_i = 100 \frac{W_i}{L_i} (1 - r_i) \times (MDC + MLC),$$

and we get:

$$\frac{W_i}{L_i} = 3\text{kg}/100 \text{ litres};$$

$$r_i = 5\%$$
$$MDC = \text{£}20/\text{tonne};$$
$$MLC = \text{£}6/\text{tonne};$$

Hence:

$$t_i = 100\left(\frac{3}{100}[1 - 0.05]\frac{20 + 6}{1000}\right)$$
$$= \text{£}0.07 / 100 \text{ litres}$$

8. CONCLUSIONS

The polluter pays principle (Chapter 5) lays down that both producers and consumers should pay the full social costs of their actions. It has been argued in this chapter that the full (financial plus environmental) costs of disposal are not currently reflected in the charges made for waste-related services or in the prices of products. The result is too much waste and too little waste minimization, reuse and recycling. But simplistic policy responses, such as mandatory recycling targets, rigid acceptance of the 'proximity principle' for waste disposal and the 'waste management hierarchy', will impose significant and unnecessary cost burdens on society. Two related questions need to be better addressed: first, how much waste should there be (that is, what is the correct balance between waste minimization, recycling and final disposal)? Second, what is the least-cost combination of options available to best manage the waste that does arise?

Overall, economies require, but currently lack, an integrated, effective and efficient waste management system. The foundations of such a system must be buttressed by a combination of enabling regulatory and market-based (economic) instruments. It has been argued in this chapter that so far regulatory measures have dominated waste management policy and thereby have imposed a significant cost burden on society. Market-based economic incentive instruments can play an important role in delivering a more efficient management system. Increased efficiency will be vital if society continues to expect/demand ever more stringent standards for pollution and waste disposal.

A variety of factors lies behind the recent upsurge of interest in economic instruments, including some disenchantment with the efficiency and effectiveness of the direct regulation approach to environmental policy. Nevertheless, some of the pressure for change has been generated by wider public finance, employment and social concerns. The political economy of public finance and fiscal regimes is complex and mirrors the various stakeholder and political interests present in contemporary industrial/post-industrial societies. In principle, market-based economic instruments offer efficiency gains over direct regulation measures, but the magnitude of the efficiency advantage is conditioned by the real-world context and application. Moreover, economic efficiency is only one of at least six principles that are thought to be relevant in any policy instrument choice situation. These principles are not necessarily complementary and serve to highlight difficult 'political' trade-offs. Thus, while economic instruments are inherently efficient and effective, the social gains they offer are currently limited by a policy process driven by multiple conflicting objectives.

The waste management policy arena is one in which the use of economic instruments could prove effective, and the combination of landfill tax and recycling credits is a first tentative step in this direction. Instruments such as charges, permits and subsidies score well on efficiency grounds but they are more problematic in terms of their institutional requirements and their political feasibility. On the other hand, instruments such as product prohibitions, technology specification and information provision, for example, face relatively little political resistance and have low institutional demands, but are relatively inefficient (high aggregate costs of meeting a given ambient standard). Other instruments such as liability law present intermediate cases.

FURTHER READING

For a good general survey of a number of waste management issues, see:

Bradshaw, A.D., R. Southwood and F. Warner (eds) (1992), *The Treatment and Handling of Wastes*, London: Chapman and Hall.
Alter, H. (1991), 'The future course of solid waste management in the US', *Waste Management and Research*, **9**, 3–20.
Powell, J.C. (1996) 'The evaluation of waste management options', *Waste Management and Research*, **14**, 515–26.

For more technical information on packaging waste, see:

Alter, H. (1989), 'The origins of municipal solid waste: the relations between residues from packaging materials and food', *Waste Management Resources*, **7**, 103–14.
Porter, R.R. (1983), 'Michigan's experience with mandatory deposits on beverage containers', *Land Economics*, **59**, 177–94.
Bohm, P. (1981), *Deposit-Refund Systems*, Baltimore: Johns Hopkins University Press.
White, P.R., M. Franke and P. Hindle (1995), *Integrated Solid Waste Management: A Lifecycle Inventory*, London: Blackie Academic and Professional.

NOTE

1. See Chapter 6 for details on policy instruments in general.

REFERENCES

Bliss, D. (1998), 'The regulator's approach to construction waste', paper presented at the Construction Industry Environmental Forum, 'Construction waste: Effects on the Landfill Tax', 29 January 1998, London.

Brisson, I. (1993), 'Packaging waste and the environment: economics and policy', *Resource, Conservation and Recycling*, **8**, 183–292.

Coopers and Lybrand (1997), *Landfill Tax – is it Working?* London: Coopers and Lybrand.

Department of the Environment (1992), *The UK Environment*, London: HMSO.

Department of the Environment (1993), *Externalities from Landfill and Incineration: A Study by CSERGE, Warren Spring Laboratory and EFTEC*, London: HMSO.

Dinan, T.M. (1993), 'Economic efficiency effects of alternative policies for reducing waste disposal', *Journal of Environmental Economics and Management*, **25**, 242–56.

Dosi, G. (1988), 'The nature of the innovative process', in G. Dosi, C. Freeman, R. Nelson, G. Silverberg and L. Soete (eds), *Technical Change and Economic Theory*, London: Pinter, pp. 221–38.

Environmental Data Services (1999), *ENDS REPORTS* (monthly), Finsbury, London.

European Commission (1990), 'Draft proposal for a Council Directive on packaging and waste', December, Brussels.

Fullerton, D. and T. Kinnaman (1995), 'Garbage, recycling and illicit burning or dumping', *Journal of Environment Economics and Management*, **29**, 78–91.

Goulder, L.H. (1995), 'Environmental taxation and the double dividend: a reader's guide', *International Tax and Public Finance*, **2**, 157–83.

Grace, R., R.K. Turner and I. Walter (1978), 'Secondary materials and international trade', *Journal of Environmental Economics and Management*, **5**, 172–86.

Heyes, A. and C. Liston-Heyes (1997), 'Regulatory "balancing" and the efficiency of green research and development', *Environmental and Resource Economics*, **9**, 493–507.

HM Customs and Excise (1996), 'Environmental bodies', Landfill tax Information Note 8/96. London: HMSO.

Hogg, D. (1997), 'The effectiveness of the UK landfill tax – early indications', paper presented at the IBC Conference on Environmental Economic Instruments, London.

House of Lords, Select Committee on the European Communities (1993), 26th Report, *Packaging and Packaging Waste*, London: HMSO.

Jaffe, A.B., S.R. Peterson, P.R. Portney and R.N. Stavins (1995), 'Environmental regulation and the competitiveness of US manufacturing; what does the evidence tell us?', *Journal of Economic Literature*, **XXXIII**, 132–63.

Jänicke, M., M. Binder and H. Mönch (1997), '"Dirty industries": patterns of change in industrial countries', *Environmental and Resource Economics*, **9**, 467–91.

Khanna, M. and D. Zilberman (1997), 'Incentives, precision technology and environmental protection', *Ecological Economics*, **23**, 25–44.

Leibenstein, H. (1966), 'Allocative efficiency vs. x-efficiency', *American Economic Review*, **56**, 392–415.

Lockhart, J. (1998), 'Environmental tax subsidies in the US: examples of water quality and conservation programmes', *Environmental Taxation and Accounting*, **2**, 43–54.

Loehr, R.C. (ed.) (1985), *Reducing Hazardous Waste Generation*, Washington, DC: National Academy Press.

Maddison, D., D. Pearce, N. Adger and H. Mcleod (1997), 'Environmentally damaging subsidies in the United Kingdom', *European Environment*, **7**, 110–17.

Mendelsohn, R. (1984), 'Endogenous technical change and environmental regulation', *Journal of Environmental Economics and Management*, **11**, 202–7.

Menell, P.S. (1990), 'Beyond the throwaway society: an incentive approach to regulating MSW', *Ecology Law Quarterly*, **17**, 655–739.

Oates, W.E., K. Palmer and P.R. Portney (1994), 'Environmental regulation and international competitiveness: thinking about the Porter hypothesis', Resources for the Future Working Paper 94–02, Washington, DC.

OECD (1991), *Environmental Data Compendium*, Paris: OECD.

OECD (1993), *Environmental Data, Compendium 1993*, Paris: OECD.

OECD (1997), *Environmental Data, Compendium 1997*, Paris: OECD.

Palmer, K. and M. Wallis (1996), 'Optimal policies for solid waste disposal: taxes subsidies and standards', GSBGM Working Paper 5196, Wellington, New Zealand: Victoria University.

Pearce, D.W. and R.K. Turner (1992), 'Packaging waste and the polluter pays principle', *Journal of Environmental Planning and Management*, **35**, 5–15.

Porter, M. and C. van der Linde (1995), 'Towards a new conception of the environment –competitiveness relationship', *Journal of Economic Perspectives*, **9**, 97–118.

Porter, R.C. (1978), 'A social benefit–cost analysis of mandatory deposits on beverage containers', *Journal of Environmental Economics and Management*, **5**, 351–75.

Powell, J.C. (1996), 'The evaluation of waste management options', *Waste Management and Research*, **14**, 515–26.

Powell, J.C., A.L. Craighill, J. Parfitt and R.K. Turner (1996), 'A lifecycle assessment and economic valuation of recycling', *Journal of Environmental Planning and Management*, **39**, 97–112.

Powell, J.C., D.W. Pearce and A. Craighill (1997), 'Approaches to valuation in LCA impact assessment', *International Journal of Lifecycle Assessment*, **1**, 11–13.

Probst, K.N., D. Fullerton, R.E. Litan and P.R. Portney (1995), *Footing the Bill for Superfund Cleanup*, Washington, DC: The Brookings Institution and Resources for the Future.

Read, A.D., P.S. Phillips and A. Murphy (1997), 'Environmental bodies and landfill tax funds: an assessment of landfill operators in two English counties', *Resources, Conservation and Recycling*, **20**, 153–82.

Royal Commission on Environmental Pollution (1993), *Seventeenth Report: Incineration of Waste*, London: HMSO.

Russell, C.S. and P.T. Powell (1996), *Practical Guidelines and Comparisons of Instruments of Environmental Policy*, Nashville: Vanderbilt Institute for Public Policy Studies.

Schmalensee, R. (1993), 'The costs of environmental regulation', Massachusetts Institute of Technology, Centre for Energy and Environmental Policy Research Working Paper 93–015, Cambridge, MA.

Sills, R. (1997), 'The status of ENTRUST', paper presented at the IBC Conference 'Environmental Economic Instruments', 1–2 December 1997, London.

Tidy Britain Group (1997), 'Effects of the landfill tax on fly-tipping', The Pier, Wigan.

Turner, R.K. (1993), 'Sustainability: principles and practice', in R.K. Turner (ed.), *Sustainable Environmental Economics Management*, London: Belhaven.

Turner, R.K. and J.C. Powell (1993), 'Case study: economics – the challenge of integrated pollution control', in R.J. Berry (ed.), *Environmental Dilemmas, Ethics and Decisions*, London: Chapman and Hall.

Turner, R.K., D.W. Pearce and I. Bateman (1993), *Environmental Economics: An Elementary Introduction*, Hemel Hempstead: Harvester Wheatsheaf.

Turner, R.K., R. Salmons, J. Powell and A. Craighill (1998), 'Green taxes, waste management and political economy', *Journal of Environmental Management*, **53**, 121–36.

UNECE (1987), *Environment Statistics in Europe and North America*, New York: UN.

USEPA (1990), Report EPA/530-SW-90–042A, Washington, DC.

Warren Spring Laboratory UK (1991), personal communication.

Weizsaker, E. von, A.B. Lovins and L.H. Lovins (1997), *Factor Four: Doubling Wealth, Halving Resource Use*, London: Earthscan.

World Resources Institute (1997), *Resource Flows: The Material Basis of Industrial Economics*, Washington, DC.

Index